FROMMER'S

BELGIUM, HOLLAND & LUXEMBOURG

SUSAN POOLE

1990–1991

Published by Prentice Hall Trade Division
A Division of Simon & Schuster Inc.
15 Columbus Circle
New York, NY 10023

ISBN 0-13-217803-6
ISSN 1044-2413

Manufactured in the United States of America

Although every effort was made to ensure the accuracy of price information appearing in this book, it should be kept in mind that prices can and do fluctuate in the course of time.

CONTENTS

Part Two

HOLLAND

MAPS

Dedication

To Marilyn, whose enthusiasm for the Benelux countries first inspired my own itchy feet to turn in that direction.

ACKNOWLEDGMENTS

The names of all the warm, welcoming people in Belgium, Holland, and Luxembourg who made researching this book such a joy would double the size of this volume. They greeted me in airports, taxis, buses, trains, hotels, restaurants, shops, from adjoining sidewalk café tables, and on street corners where my befuddled expression brought instant, smiling directions even before I asked. They forgave my ignorance of their respective languages and time after time shared very personal knowledge of the Benelux countries to pass along to you through these pages. They have my eternal gratitude.

To these tourism professionals whose help and enthusiasm went all the way to friendship, a special vote of thanks: Frederique Raemaekers of the Belgium Tourist Office in New York; Cecile Pierard, Monique 't Kint, Elisabeth Puttaert, and Peter Esterhazy in Brussels; Barbara Veldkamp of the Netherlands Board of Tourism in New York; Willem Schouten, Els Wamsteeker, and the scores of other VVV personnel in Holland; Anne Bastian of the Luxembourg National Tourist Office in New York; and George Hausemer and Jean-Claude Contor in Luxembourg.

INFLATION ALERT

Like the rest of Europe—indeed, the world—Belgium, Holland, and Luxembourg are not immune to the ravages of inflation. In addition, currency exchanges continue to fluctuate in response to international monetary trends.

While I have made every effort to quote the most reliable prices and price forecasts, conditions change so rapidly in today's world that during the second year of this edition—1991—the wise traveler will *add about 15%* to prices quoted and will carefully *check the exchange rate* at the time of travel.

DISCLAIMER

I have personally checked the recommendations contained in the main body of this book. You should note, however, that those establishments described under the title "Readers' Suggestions" have *not* in many cases been inspected by the author and are the opinions of individual readers only. They do not in any way represent the opinions of the publisher or author of this book.

INTRODUCING BELGIUM, HOLLAND, AND LUXEMBOURG

Perhaps nowhere else in all of Europe are so many compelling reasons to visit compressed into so tiny an area as in the three small countries of Belgium, Holland, and Luxembourg. Topping the list are such purely aesthetic attractions as lyrically beautiful landscapes, artistic masterpieces, cultural events, and intriguing relics of a long and colorful history. At the other end of the scale are the more mundane (but essential) advantages of convenience, economy, and friendly populations. And somewhere in between lie a host of travel delights—the exquisite food and drink of Brussels, the exuberant sociability of Amsterdam, Luxembourg's sidewalk cafés and awesome casements—unique to each country, yet all within a stone's throw (or a couple of hours) of each other. The advantages of a stay in the Benelux countries (the name comes from a Customs Union agreement signed in 1944 by all three governments while in exile) are virtually endless.

As a gateway to Europe, all three countries offer easy access via outstanding airlines and excellent ongoing transportation to other continental destinations. But the visitor who scurries across their borders will miss a treasure house of travel gems. So, let me say right up front that one of the primary purposes of this book is to entice you to *loiter*, rather than scurry, through Belgium, Holland, and Luxembourg. If you follow that advice, when you finally do cross their borders you'll leave with a wealth of background information and firsthand experience that will serve as the best possible foundation for the best possible appreciation of the rest of Europe.

There's hardly a thread in the rich tapestry of European history and cultural development that cannot be traced across the faces of Belgium, Holland, and Luxembourg. Here you'll find remnants of prehistory, feudalism, tugs-of-war between medieval monarchs and those who fancied themselves monarchs, heroic resistance to oppression and pragmatic compromise, the ups and downs of commerce and trade on a worldwide scale, and incomparable artistic accomplishment. Each of the three countries has its own history to relate, and we'll listen to each in chapters to come—but to set the stage for those more detailed stories, herewith a quick, albeit sketchy, look at the region as a whole.

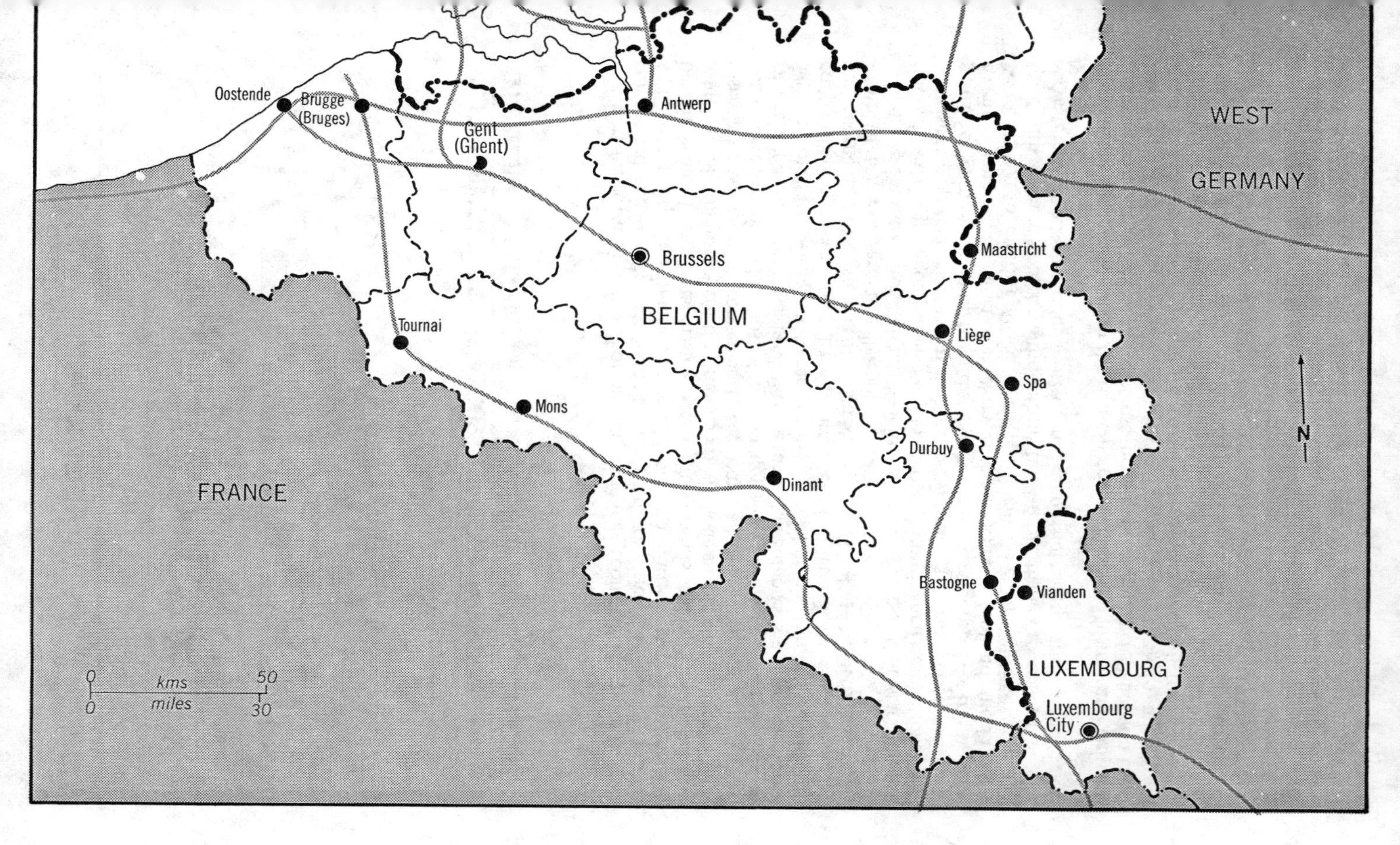
WEST GERMANY
Oostende
Brugge (Bruges)
Antwerp
Gent (Ghent)
Maastricht
Brussels
BELGIUM
Tournai
Liège
Spa
Mons
Durbuy
N
Dinant
FRANCE
Bastogne
Vianden
LUXEMBOURG
0 kms 50
0 miles 30
Luxembourg City

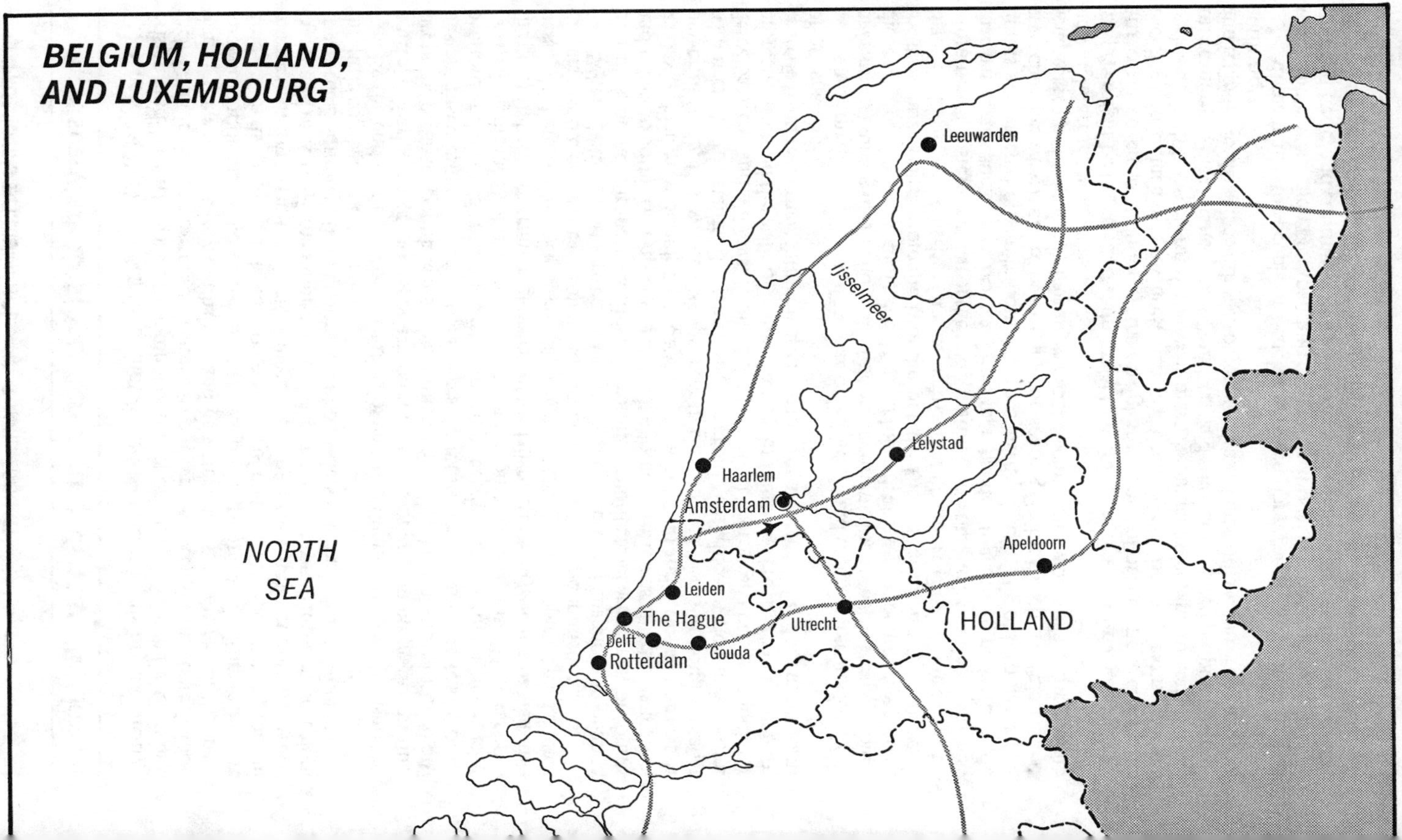
BELGIUM, HOLLAND, AND LUXEMBOURG
NORTH SEA
Leeuwarden
Ijsselmeer
Lelystad
Haarlem
Amsterdam
Apeldoorn
Leiden
The Hague
Utrecht
HOLLAND
Delft
Rotterdam
Gouda

1. History's Footsteps Across the Benelux Region

Ghosts of the fierce Belgae (acknowledged by Caesar as his bravest enemy), Frisian, and Trier tribes haunt the mists of prehistoric Benelux, with the Celts and their Druidic rituals close on their heels. And had it not been for the strategic location of their marshy, lowland habitat and its watery access to the rest of the then-known world, they might never have attracted the attention of a Roman Empire dead set on dispatching its legions on missions of conquest to open the way for still more expansion. As it was, Rome managed to bring all but the feisty Frisians to their knees, and by A.D. 47 the Empire stretched its tentacles through most of the region. It was the beginning of a long, long list of outsiders who bickered and fought over this little corner of the continent.

By the end of the 5th century the Romans had themselves been banished by hordes of barbarians, who swept across Europe in a mighty rampage that in turn swept the ordinary populace into the waiting arms of local lords whose fortified castles promised protection from the savages. In return, peasants swore fealty to the overlord and pledged their unquestioning service, whether it be toiling in the fields or swelling the ranks of the military—or both, should the need arise. Thus was born the decentralized governmental system of feudalism, based on *feodalite,* or "faithfulness." And out of feudalism grew ceaseless power struggles that pitted feudal lords one against the other as each sought to expand his territory and influence.

When the year 800 arrived, it was the great King Charlemagne who reigned over most of the European continent, creating a middle-level aristocracy of counts and dukes to administer his large realm on a local basis. It was Charlemagne, too, who was chiefly responsible for the spread of Catholicism and the establishment of powerful bishoprics, whose bishops were in time to lock horns in deadly combat with upstart Protestants. But feudalism was greatly enfeebled by new invasions of fierce Saracens and Vikings. Around the year 1000, Europeans began to look for protection behind the walls of fortified towns and cities, where they banded together to demand from their former masters written guarantees of freedom in the form of city charters.

These medieval centers (they were called *bourgs* and their inhabitants *burghers,* or *bourgeois*) sprang up and flourished along important waterways and seaports, and those territories we now know as Belgium, Holland, and Luxembourg were among the most prized sites. From the 12th through the 15th centuries, Brugge, Antwerp, Brussels, Liège, Amstelledam (Amsterdam), and Lützelburg (Luxembourg) rose to prominence, fostering much of the trade, cultural, artistic, and educational progress that has left us such a rich heritage. Free men banded together in powerful trade guilds and erected ornate buildings as their headquarters. The old Romanesque-style churches were replaced by magnificent, soaring Gothic structures. Painters and sculptors came into their own in answer to the demand for works of art to adorn the new architectural wonders.

As might be expected, it didn't take long for these centers of the good life to attract the covetous attention of their neighbors. Control of such prize cities (and the city-states, duchies, provinces, etc., that defined their boundaries) ricocheted back and forth between royal houses as marriage, inheritance, and military adventure came into play. France, Spain, England, and Austria all played the power game, and religious leaders vied with each other as well as counts, dukes, and even kings for authority.

All the while, the people of Benelux endured oppression, fought it when that was feasible, went right on expanding their international ventures through exploration and trade, and continued to nurture the soul-nourishing arts that were so important to their culture. Always fragmented into geographical divisions that dated back to those feudal lords, they also nurtured the dream of independent national identity.

Finally, the long centuries of foreign domination ended for most of the region when Napoleon was defeated at Waterloo in 1815. Holland came out on top in the concluding treaty, with control over Belgium vested in the Dutch. But not for long. In 1830 King Leopold I was declared leader of an independent Belgium and, shortly thereafter, almost half of the Duchy of Luxembourg. A proud—and very firm—declaration that "The Grand Duchy of Luxembourg forms a free state, independent and indivisible" in 1868 appeared to put an end for all time to the odious presence of outside rule in the Benelux region.

The 20th century, however, held cruel disillusionment. With the eruption of World War I in 1914, Belgium, Holland, and Luxembourg were overrun, occupied, and ravaged by German troops, a nightmare that was to recur in 1940 when Hitler's forces blitzkrieged across all three. Before the end of World War II, there would be years of heroic struggle, terrible sacrifice, and devastating military battles that left the Benelux region one of the most blood-soaked in Europe.

Since the coming of peace once again, the Benelux story has been one of steady progress in every area, both domestically and internationally. Ironically, other nations have seen fit to look to these small nations to house their institutionalized hopes for lasting world peace. And, somehow, that seems very fitting—if history is to take a turn away from war, where better to place its steps than along the path already strewn with footprints left in its long march down the centuries.

2. Belgium, Holland, and Luxembourg in Today's Europe

The road to recovery from World War II devastation was a rocky one for all three Benelux countries. Yet it has been traversed with surprising speed. All are crisscrossed by superb highway networks; all have erased virtually all scars of physical destruction; and perhaps because they have always been keen practitioners of commerce, they have all steadily climbed to prominence in the ranks of international trade, industry, and finance. In the political arena, the Benelux countries have become the very center of joint European political and economic planning.

Despite fluctuations in its economy marked by a period of international recession during the late 1970s, Belgium has built Antwerp into the world's fifth-largest port, as well as perhaps its most important diamond center. It has enticed scores of international firms to establish headquarters and/or subsidiaries within its borders. As the host country of NATO and the European Economic Community (known as the Common Market), it boasts of being the "Capital of Europe."

The Dutch take equal pride in their development of high-technology industries to offset meager raw materials for manufacturing hard goods. Fifteen jurists from as many nations convene in the impressive Peace Palace for sessions of the International Court of Justice. And Amsterdam regularly disputes Antwerp's claim to "most important" diamond center.

Tiny Luxembourg attracts such a large number of international financiers that it has been chosen as headquarters of the European Investment Bank, and its active stock exchange executes trades in currencies of all nations. From a prominent site overlooking the city of Luxembourg, its European Center houses the Secretariat of the European Parliament and facilities in which the Council of Ministers of the European Community meet for three months of each year. In addition, the Court of Justice of the European Community holds its meetings in Luxembourg.

1

A BENELUX OVERVIEW

When it comes to planning any trip, the bottom line is always detail. It's the specifics of travel that can spell the difference between a smashing success and a howling disaster, and this book is designed to point the way to a Benelux visit that nets happy experiences and golden memories based on exactly that kind of information.

1. Using This Guide

In the final analysis, it's money that will set the style in which you travel. If you're going top-drawer, you'll want to know where to find luxury hotels and restaurants. If you're like the majority of travelers, it's moderate prices you'll be looking for. Budgeteers need to know just where to find a good place to stay that won't cost an arm and a leg, and where to eat well but inexpensively. In addition, if you're a wise traveler you'll look for those places that come up with the *best value for the dollar*—no matter what your budget. And that's what this book is all about. I've looked for those accommodations, restaurants, casual bars and cafés, sightseeing attractions, shops, and after-dark spots where your money will be well spent.

Bear in mind that my inspections have come from a purely personal, very subjective, point of view—there's no set formula in my notebook to be checked off point by point. Nor do the owners or managers of recommended places always know what I'm about during a drop-in inspection. All of which means that there can be a certain lack of uniformity in just what constitutes "value for the dollar." And for that I make no apology.

AN EXPLANATION

If my years of travel have made one single thing clear, it's that "bargain" has many shades of meaning. For example, a "bargain-priced" hotel room that is dirty and furnished with a lumpy bed is no bargain. On the other hand, a bargain—at whatever price—can be the deluxe hotel that comes up with personal comforts and pampering at just the time in my travels they're sorely needed and is located within walking distance of the places I want to go. The same holds true for restaurants: discovering that very special little eatery with near-gourmet meals at less-than-gourmet prices is a real thrill, yet when one of the world's finest restaurants is available to me at prices I'd never pay at home, the memorable dining experience becomes a travel bargain regardless of the tab.

In other words, "value" becomes a very personal matter. With that in mind, I have tried to give you in this book an accurate description of just what you'll find, where you'll find it, and what it will cost. The result is a guide to help you decide just how "value for the dollar" translates *for you.*

Of one thing you may be sure: each recommendation comes from personal observation, and my standards are high!

A FEW WORDS OF CAUTION

In the first few pages of this book, there's an "Inflation Alert," which deals with wavering price levels. Well, there's one other variable to consider—the changing nature of the travel scene itself. For instance, the lovely moderately priced restaurant you'll read raves about in this guidebook may have proved so successful that it's moved upmarket and doubled its prices by the time you arrive. Conversely, a terrific eatery or exceptional hotel may have changed ownership or management and gone right down the tubes since my visit. About the best any guidebook can do is to try to stay abreast of that kind of change—and that's where our readers come in.

A REQUEST FOR YOUR VIEWS

Frommer's Belgium, Holland, & Luxembourg is meticulously updated and revised every other year. As with all Frommer publications, we rely heavily on our readers to help make those revisions as helpful as possible. So when you come across an especially delightful hotel or restaurant or overlooked sightseeing attraction or shopping bargain, I'd like to hear from you. Perhaps even more important, I want to know if you find conditions changed at any of my recommended places—recommendations are certainly not cast in stone in this book, and your comments can help eliminate those that have slipped in standards of quality, service, price, or whatever.

Please do write me: Susan Poole, c/o Frommer Books, Prentice Hall Travel, 15th Floor, 15 Columbus Circle, New York, NY 10023. While I can't promise to answer each letter personally, you have my word that I will read every one and *pay attention.* My thanks in advance.

2. Where to Stay

The range of accommodations throughout the Benelux countries and their universally high standards are sure signs that you're a very welcome guest. In fact, to make absolutely certain you won't be disappointed, Belgium, Holland, and Luxembourg set up the Benelux Hotel Classification System back in 1978, then updated standards in 1984. Each establishment that accepts guests must publicly display a sign indicating its classification (from "1" for those with minimum amenities to "5" for deluxe, full-service hotels).

National tourist boards do an excellent job of providing full accommodations listings and booking ahead for their visitors. Addresses for each country will be found in the appropriate chapters, but here's a look at the Benelux accommodations scene in general.

HOTELS

In all three countries, you can choose between posh (and expensive) hotels in city or rural locations, smaller urban hotels with moderate rates and somewhat limited facilities, and charming, family-run country inns. All will be spotlessly clean, and whatever your choice, you can count on a staff dedicated to personal attention and excellent service, from one end of the price scale to the other. Also, the rates quoted vill always include service charge (usually 15%) and tax, and, in most cases, breakfast.

As for prices, for double occupancy, expect them to begin at $95 or up at deluxe hotels; $75 and up for those in the next category down; $35 to $50 and up in the moderate range; and anywhere from $20 to $35 for the least expensive. Rates for singles will be slightly lower. You should know, however, that many hotels have a variety of room rates, regardless of classification, and it's sometimes possible to pay less if you'll settle for a shower instead of full bath facilities. Also, weekend or mid-week rates are often available. Be sure to inquire about any special rates in effect when you book.

BED-AND-BREAKFAST

In Holland, it's possible to stay with private families in virtually every region. Because there's no national listing of such homes, however, you'll have to check with local tourist offices as you go for names, addresses, and prices (very inexpensive in most cases). In Belgium and Luxembourg, B&B translates to a small hotel or pension.

HOSTELS

The Benelux countries are literally filled with high-grade hostels, both in urban settings and in some of the most scenic spots in Europe. Prices for a dormitory bed run around $6; with breakfast, about $8.

CAMPING

Recreational vehicles are increasingly popular with touring families, and there are outstanding camping grounds throughout Belgium, Holland, and Luxembourg. Prices run between $8 and $15 per night, depending on location and facilities. Each country can furnish a directory of its campgrounds.

3. Where and What to Eat

If I were asked to give one unconditional guarantee for your Benelux visit, it would be this: you will eat well, and you'll never be far from a good place to eat. Standards of ingredients, preparation, presentation, and service are extraordinarily high throughout Belgium, Holland, and Luxembourg—and the number and diversity of restaurants is nothing short of staggering. This is perhaps the one single area in which you'll get the most value for your dollar, in every price range from budget to deluxe.

WHERE TO EAT

In Belgium, Brussels proudly proclaims itself the "Restaurant Capital of the World"—and views that same claim by Paris or Hong Kong as puny stuff indeed by comparison. Comparisons are, of course, odious, and I'd be quite willing to see the culinary title shared by all three (with New Orleans thrown in for good measure).

The thing is, even with Brussels' nearly 2,000 restaurants, it can stand alone in quality as well as quantity. From the smallest, most modest café or bistro on the most obscure side street, right up to the most elegant and expensive of its several restaurants that have won international acclaim, Brussels insists on meals that make it to table only if made of the finest ingredients, well prepared, and attractively presented.

As for getting your money's worth, you'll certainly do that in terms of portions —they're more than ample. In other respects you can follow the dictates of your budget—and perhaps your mood—to set a price that can range from $5 or less all the way to $75. In fact, regardless of budget considerations, after a few days of superlative restaurant dining in Brussels, you may well opt for the delightful change of taking a day off, as I once did, and quelling hunger pangs as they occur by simply stopping at a street vendor for those marvelous *frites* (french fries), waffles, and other assorted goodies that are so delicious and filling they have absolutely nothing to do with "fast food" as known elsewhere in the world.

Outside Brussels, the caliber of eateries upholds the standards of the "Capital," many times at lower prices and in the most unexpected places. Some of my finest Belgian meals have been in country inns tucked away in Ardennes villages, and even roadside cafés seem to come up with memorable lunches.

Luxembourg's restaurants—in town or country—follow the lead of their Belgian neighbors in standards, cuisine, and the variety of ambience, but within a more modest price range.

In Holland eating standards are no less stringent, and the restaurants of Amsterdam are as richly textured as a canvas by one of the Dutch masters. There are coffeehouses everywhere for drop-in casual meals or snacks, modest little restaurants with modest little prices, posh dining rooms in posh high-rise hotels, and elegant restaurants in atmospheric, centuries-old buildings. And if you happen to be there for the beginning of the herring season, it's an absolute obligation—at least once—to interrupt your sidewalk strolls for a "green" herring from a pushcart. Prices run the gamut from dirt-cheap to astronomical.

Out of the long Dutch tradition of trade with countries around the globe has come a love of international cuisine that makes Holland a loving host to the foods of Indonesia, China, Italy, France, Greece, Yugoslavia, Hungary, and—well, the list is simply endless.

In all three Benelux countries sidewalk cafés are as numerous as blooms in a Dutch tulip field—and it's a safe bet you'll quickly become as fond of them as are the locals. What may come as a surprise is the fact that these charming oases lining city streets and village squares adhere to the same high standards as more upscale restaurants. Your fare may be modest, but it will be fresh and well prepared—and if there's a more perfect presentation than in the shade of an umbrella on a sun-filled street, I have yet to encounter it.

There's a very good reason for those unfailingly high standards. People who live in the Benelux countries like to eat—and they like to eat well. I'm convinced that in this corner of Europe a restaurant that didn't measure up simply would never survive. Also, a high percentage of the places in which you'll dine are family owned and operated, with family pride very much at stake every time a meal is served.

Benelux diners add another ingredient to the restaurant scene: as much as they value good food, they also savor the ambience of a restaurant—its personality. To some degree, dining out takes on the aspect of entertainment. Indeed, whereas most Americans view dinner as a prelude to an evening, for people here, dinner *is* the evening. They would no more tolerate rudeness or being rushed through their meal than they would bad food poorly prepared. And therein lies a caution—be sure you allow enough time for each meal. That impeccable service may not be indifferent, but to Americans it can sometimes seem slow. My best advice is to do as the natives do and give yourself over to the occasion. Relax, enjoy your surroundings and your companions, and you may even find that the wait between courses adds a fuller appreciation for each new dish.

You'll find my personal recommendations in the appropriate chapters, but it's a virtual certainty that after browsing through the rich buffet of Benelux restaurants, you'll go home with a list of your own—a very long list!

WHAT TO EAT

For the most part, the food you eat in Belgium will be based on French cuisine, but to that base Belgian chefs add their own special touches, incorporating native specialties like *jambon d'Ardennes,* ham from the hills and valleys of the Ardennes, or savory *boudin de Liège,* a succulent sausage mixed with herbs. Almost every menu lists *tomates aux crevettes,* tomatoes stuffed with tiny, delicately sweet North Sea shrimp and light, homemade mayonnaise—filling enough for a light lunch and delicious as an appetizer. A very special treat awaits visitors in May and June in the form of Belgian asparagus, and from October to March there's endive, which is known in Belgium as *witloof,* or "white leaf."

If you're basically a steak-and-potatoes person, you're in good company, for Belgians dote on their *biftec et frites,* which is available at virtually every restaurant, even when not listed on the menu. Lest you think that *frites* in Belgium are the same as french fries at home, let me hasten to enlighten you. These are twice-fried potatoes, as light as the proverbial feather. They're sold in paper cones on almost every street corner and (in my opinion) are best when topped with homemade mayonnaise, though you may prefer curry or even your usual catsup. Frites will also accompany almost anything you order in a restaurant.

Seafood anywhere in Belgium is fresh and delicious. *Moules* (mussels) are absolutely addictive and are a specialty in Brussels, where you'll find a concentration of restaurants along the Petite rue des Bouchers that feature them in just about every guise that can be imagined. *Homard* (lobster) also comes in a range of dishes, and a heavenly Belgian creation is *écrevisses à la liègeoise,* crayfish in a rich butter, cream, and white wine sauce.

Dutch national dishes tend to be of the ungarnished, hearty, wholesome variety. Solid, stick-to-your-ribs stuff. A perfect example is *erwtensoep,* a thick pea soup cooked with ham or sausage that provides inner warmth against cold Dutch winters and is filling enough to be a meal by itself. Similarly, *hutspot,* a potato-based "hotchpotch," or stew, is no-nonsense nourishment that becomes even more so with the addition of *klapstuk* (lean beef). Hutspot also has an interesting intangible ingredient—a story behind its name that is based on historical fact (see Chapter XIII).

Seafood, as you might imagine in this traditionally seafaring country, is always fresh and simply—but very well—prepared. Fried sole, oysters from Zeeland, mussels, and herring (fresh in May, pickled other months) are most common. The Dutch are uncommonly fond of eel, a taste I've personally never acquired. I am, however, assured by my Dutch friends that once past a "typically American" squeamishness, I'd surely become as addicted as they are themselves. So, if you're adventurous or nonsqueamish, you'll want to sample this Dutch favorite.

At lunchtime, you're likely to find yourself munching on *broodjes,* small buttered rolls usually filled with ham and cheese or beef. Not to be missed are the delicious, crêpe-like pancakes called *pannekoeken* or *poffertjes,* which are especially good topped with apples, jam, or syrup. Desserts at any meal lean toward fruit with lots of fresh cream, ice cream, or *appel gebak,* a lovely and light apple pastry.

So much for native dishes. Holland, however, has imported so many international dishes that one—the Indonesian *rijsttafel,* a feast that brings small portions of usually at least 17, up to as many as 30 different dishes to table to eat on a base of plain rice—has become such a favorite it can almost be considered "national." Be assured that should you develop a yearning for some other national cuisine while in Holland, it will probably be available somewhere close by.

Luxembourg, like Belgium, leans toward the cooking of France, but appropriates bits and pieces from next-door Germany. Smoked pork and sauerkraut (*jud mat gardebo'nen*) is a favorite. A Luxembourg specialty is roast thrush (*grives*), and if you're there during the game season, try wild boar. The pastries are outstanding, and the ubiquitous pastry shops are a constant temptation to stop for a sweet.

WHAT TO DRINK

In a word, *beer*. It's Belgium's national drink; it's practically an institution at any Dutch lunch and after work; and Luxembourg pits its breweries against any in the world. Imported beers are freely available, but you won't want to miss sampling at least a few of the more than 300 brews produced in Belgium alone. Most are lagers, but local breweries have been extremely inventive in adding such unexpected ingredients as cherries.

Wine lovers will find the best vintages from France widely available, and there are some remarkably good table wines at quite low prices. Luxembourg's Moselle Valley wineries produce outstanding riesling, rivaner, auxerrois, and several sparkling wines that rival champagne and come at lower prices.

Holland's native *jenever*, a deceptively smooth, mild-tasting gin, rivals beer in the affections of the Dutch. It comes in a colorless *jonge* (young) form or the amber-colored *oude* (old) version—either can be lethal if not sipped slowly, or if sipped in extravagant quantities.

4. Shopping Tips

While the Benelux countries are not known for their bargain prices, they do constitute one of the best marketplaces in the world when it comes to variety of goods for sale. After all, it has been trade that has built and sustained these nations from earliest times. Consequently, there is within their boundaries a vast supermarket of items produced at home and others from around the world.

BELGIUM

Shopping is one of Belgium's oldest and most honored traditions, and shoppers will find exquisite examples in shops around the country. Look especially for antique lace—a bit pricey, but good value. European antiques may be found in Brussels shops and street markets. Excellent galleries in Brussels offer paintings by recognized masters of the past as well as budding masters of the future. As the diamond-cutting center of Europe, Antwerp offers excellent shopping for these precious stones. "Chocoholics" will be in pig-out heaven here. Other gustatory delights to take home include thin, spicy biscuits known as *speculoos*.

HOLLAND

Serious shoppers in Holland will be drawn to delftware from Delft and Makkum, the antique shops of Amsterdam and The Hague, and diamonds from master cutters in Amsterdam. Others will look for charming, old-fashioned clocks, crystal, and pewter. Farther down the "serious" (and also "expensive") list, come chocolates, cheeses, liqueurs, flower bulbs, and wooden shoes.

LUXEMBOURG

Paintings by artists from the Grand Duchy, as well as the rest of Europe, are featured at many fine galleries in the city of Luxembourg. Porcelain plates decorated with painted landscapes of the duchy, and cast-iron wall plaques produced by Fonderie de Mersch depicting castles, coats-of-arms, and local scenes are excellent souvenirs of a Luxembourg visit.

5. A Sightseeing Overview

What will you, as a tourist, find in today's Benelux countries? The pages of this book will point you to each country's riches, but here's an advance overview.

BELGIUM

To begin with, there's Brussels. And what a beginning! Its great enclosed plaza, the Grand' Place, is surrounded by ornate houses of the guilds, which have survived from the Middle Ages. The Butchers' Guild, known as the House of the Swan, sports a giant swan on its front; hops climb the columns of the House of the Brewers; and six connected houses once held guilds of masons, cabinetmakers, millers, tanners, wine and vegetable merchants, sculptors, stone cutters, roofers, and masons. Also in the Grand' Place, the 15th-century Town Hall is a sumptuous Gothic structure topped by an airy tower whose spire holds a huge gilded statue of St. Michael, Brussels' patron saint. Inside, Le Musée Communal is a city museum filled with paintings, maps, sculpture, and tapestries. And that's just for starters in Brussels' buffet of sightseeing attractions.

Museums devoted to everything from exquisite antique Belgian lace to art to the peaceful uses of atomic energy dot the city, and on the lighter side there's the amusing and much loved *Mannekin Pis,* a bronze statue of a small boy urinating into the air—with a dozen different local legends to explain just what it commemorates. Dining in the restaurants of Brussels becomes an evening's entertainment, whether in posh restaurants of international fame or in simple bistros. Then there are the lively open-air markets. After dark, there's theater, ballet, and concerts ranging from operatic to jazz. Around the countryside are important sightseeing destinations like the plains of Waterloo (which your imagination will people with the likes of England's Duke of Wellington leading his troops to defeat Napoleon); Brugge, a perfectly preserved medieval city where every street, house, shop, and square is a museum unto itself, frozen in time; Gent, another survivor from medieval times, now abustle with 20th-century commerce; Antwerp and its fascinating diamond dealers and harbor; Liège, whose independent spirit is almost visible in its streets, and whose Sunday street market is the oldest in Europe; the mountains and forests of the Ardennes (and Bastogne, a name with particular significance to Americans); and for art lovers, the homes and masterpieces of such master painters as Rubens, Brueghel, Magritte, and Van Eyck.

HOLLAND

Holland is all the things you've ever imagined it to be—windmills, acres and acres of tulips and other flowering bulbs—plus picturesque and historic towns, canal boats loaded with blossoms, and a sophisticated, swinging nightlife in its largest city.

Amsterdam is a wonderfully lively mix of quaint old houses and public buildings, magnificent art museums, a network of canals, and a cultural scene that happily features one of the world's best symphony orchestras, ballet, opera, jazz, and disco. Sightseeing begins with a canal-boat ride that floats you past gabled houses that turn their best faces to the water, under graceful bridges, past the official residence of the burgomaster (mayor), and into the large, busy harbor. In the very heart of the city, Dam Square is where you'll find the Royal Palace, the Nieuwe Kerk (New Church), and a busy complex of shops, restaurants, and hotels.

Among the art museums you won't want to miss is the Rijksmuseum, a repository for such works as Rembrandt's *The Night Watch* and masterpieces by Vermeer,

Frans Hals, Rubens, van Dyck, and Ter Borch; the Amsterdam Historical Museum, which holds another fascinating collection of paintings by Dutch masters; and the Vincent van Gogh Museum, a three-story building crammed with more than 200 of the master's works.

If you've been touched by Anne Frank's moving diary of her two years in hiding in Amsterdam, you'll want to visit the house whose attic sheltered her until Nazi forces discovered the eight Jewish people under its roof during World War II. And Holland's famous Aalsmeer flower auction lies only about three miles from Amsterdam's Schipol Airport.

After dark, Amsterdam really shines: literally during the summer months, when many of her famous buildings and most colorful homes are floodlit; figuratively year round, when entertainments range from concerts to ballet to opera to theater to canal-boat dinner cruises to discos and nightclubs.

Use Amsterdam as a base from which to explore many of Holland's outstanding regions on day trips. Roam north to the town of Broek, where you can watch cheeses being made; and Marken, where natives dress in traditional costume; and Edam, for a delightful look at Dutch life in the 18th century. Farther along, Hoorn is the birthplace of the seaman who first rounded the southern end of South America and named it Cape Horn for his hometown.

A day's drive south of Amsterdam will take you through Holland's bulb fields, which stretch from just north of Leiden to Haarlem. At Lisse, look for the famous Keukenhof Gardens, 70 acres of floral beauty, with a windmill and sculpture gardens on the grounds, and not far from Haarlem, the Franz Roozen nursery at Vogelenzang. In Haarlem, visit the Frans Hals Museum to view many of the artist's works displayed alongside other 16th- and 17th-century Dutch masters.

Then there's Leiden, where the Pilgrim Fathers lived for some 12 years before they set sail for the New World. And you'll want to visit The Hague, home of the Dutch government, and the Peace Palace. Rotterdam is a modern city of steel, concrete, and glass that rose from the ashes of World War II bombings; Delft is famous for its blue-and-white earthenware and its native son, the painter Vermeer; Gouda, of course, is known for its cheeses; and nearby Oudewater still maintains scales that were used in the 16th-century to certify that women accused of being witches were much too heavy to fly about on broomsticks.

LUXEMBOURG

The tiny Grand Duchy—only 1,000 square miles—is a treasure house of historic castles and scenic landscapes. Its thousand-year-old capital city is dominated by the massive Luxembourg Castle on the Bock rocks, and has no fewer than 110 bridges. Not to be missed are the casemates, a network of underground passages hewn from solid rock to connect the town's fortresses; or the Grand Ducal Palace, dating from the 16th century; or the Cathedral of Notre Dame with its magnificent sculptures. On every hand are marvelous old homes of the nobility. Just three miles away from the city is a military cemetery that is the final resting place for more than 5,000 American soldiers slain in World War II, and Gen. George Patton, Jr.

Public concerts and folklore performances entertain throughout the summer, while winter months bring an outstanding theatrical and musical season.

From the city of Luxembourg, venture forth to such enchanting spots as Vianden, a small 9th-century town that was once home to Victor Hugo, where a chair lift takes you aloft for splendid panoramic views of the countryside. In Wellenstein, visit wine cellars famous for their Moselle wines. For riesling wines, head for Wormaidange. In Wiltz, there's the Museum of the Battle of the Bulge. For pure tranquility in an idyllic setting, it would be hard to beat the three small farming villages of Dahl, Goesdorf, and Nocher, situated on one of the most beautiful plateaux of the Ardennes.

6. About Languages

This short—but sweet—section is added here because of my own trepidations when I first set out to visit the Benelux countries. Like most Americans, I am less than expert in the tongues of other nations, even those with which I struggled during the course of my formal education. When I learned that within this relatively small geographical area fluency in French, Flemish, Dutch, Luxembourgish, and German is common, I admit to having had palpitations—how on earth would I get on?

If you should suffer from the same insecurities, herewith my empathetic reassurance. I got on very well, thank you. And so will you. English is also widely spoken (plus, I might add, a generous splattering of "Americaneze"), not only well, but happily. Even those occasional non-English-speakers I encountered went about finding someone with whom I could communicate in the friendliest of manners.

Perhaps it's their long history of commerce with the rest of the world that explains Beneluxers' willingness to forgive and forget my own linguistic awkwardness. But whatever the reason, after my first few days I relaxed, made laughable attempts (which were not once ridiculed) to use the local words I picked up, and forgot about the whole thing. My only regret since then has been that my lack of expertise in this area cuts down drastically on effective eavesdropping as I travel about—an activity I consider one of the prime pleasures of any trip.

So if you are reluctant to spend time in Belgium, Holland, and Luxembourg because of perceived language differences, I have just one bit of advice: *not to worry.* Go! Trust the natives to look after you—in English—and enjoy.

7. Frommer's Dollarwise® Travel Club—How to Save Money on All Your Travels

In this book we'll be looking at how to discover your value-for-money in Benelux, but there is a "device" for saving money and determining value on *all* your trips. It's the popular, international Frommer's Dollarwise Travel Club, now in its 28th successful year of operation. The club was formed at the urging of numerous readers of the Frommer and $-a-Day Guides, who felt that such an organization could provide continuing travel information and a sense of community to value-minded travelers in all parts of the world. And so it does!

In keeping with the budget concept, the annual membership fee is low and is immediately exceeded by the value of your benefits. Upon receipt of $18 (U.S. residents), or $20 U.S. by check drawn on a U.S. bank or via international postal money order in U.S. funds (Canadian, Mexican, and other foreign residents) to cover one year's membership, we will send all new members the following items.

(1) Any *two* of the following books

Please designate in your letter which two you wish to receive:

Frommer Guides

Australia
Austria and Hungary
Belgium, Holland & Luxembourg
Bermuda and The Bahamas
Brazil

Canada
Caribbean
Egypt
England and Scotland
France
Germany
Italy
Japan and Hong Kong
Portugal, Madeira & the Azores
Southeast Asia
South Pacific
Switzerland and Liechtenstein
Alaska
California and Las Vegas
Florida
Mid-Atlantic States
New England
New York State
Northwest
Skiing USA—East
Skiing USA—West
Southern Atlantic States
Southwest
Texas
USA

(Frommer Guides discuss accommodations and facilities in all price ranges, with emphasis on the medium-priced.)

Frommer $-a-Day® Guides

Europe on $40 a Day
Australia on $30 a Day
Eastern Europe on $25 a Day
England on $50 a Day
Greece on $30 a Day
Hawaii on $60 a Day
India on $25 a Day
Ireland on $35 a Day
Israel on $40 a Day
Mexico (plus Belize and Guatemala) on $30 a Day
New York on $50 a Day
New Zealand on $40 a Day
Scandinavia on $60 a Day
Scotland and Wales on $40 a Day
South America on $35 a Day
Spain and Morocco (plus the Canary Is.) on $40 a Day
Turkey on $30 a Day
Washington, D.C., & Historic Virginia on $40 a Day

($-a-Day Guides document hundreds of budget accommodations and facilities, helping you get the most for your travel dollars.)

Frommer Touring Guides

Australia
Egypt
Florence
London

Paris
Scotland
Thailand
Venice

(These new, color illustrated guides include walking tours, cultural and historic sites, and other vital travel information.)

Gault Millau

Chicago
France
Italy
London
Los Angeles
New England
New York
San Francisco
Washington, D.C.

(Irreverent, savvy, and comprehensive, each of these renowned guides candidly reviews over 1,000 restaurants, hotels, shops, nightspots, museums, and sights.)

Serious Shopper's Guides

Italy
London
Los Angeles
Paris

(Practical and comprehensive, each of these handsomely illustrated guides lists hundreds of stores, selling everything from antiques to wine, conveniently organized alphabetically by category.)

A Shopper's Guide to the Caribbean

(Two experienced Caribbean hands guide you through this shopper's paradise, offering witty insights and helpful tips on the wares and emporia of more than 25 islands.)

Beat the High Cost of Travel

(This practical guide details how to save money on absolutely all travel items—accommodations, transportation, dining, sightseeing, shopping, taxes, and more. Includes special budget information for seniors, students, singles, and families.)

Bed & Breakfast—North America

(This guide contains a directory of over 150 organizations that offer bed-and-breakfast referrals and reservations throughout North America. The scenic attractions, and major schools and universities near the homes of each are also listed.)

Frommer's Belgium

(Arthur Frommer unlocks the treasures of a country overlooked by most travelers to Europe. Discover the medieval charm, modern sophistication, and natural beauty of this quintessentially European country.)

California with Kids

(A must for parents traveling in California, providing key information on selecting the best accommodations, restaurants, and sightseeing attractions for the particular needs of the family, whether the kids are toddlers, school-age, preteens, or teens.)

Frommer's Cruises
(This complete guide covers all the basics of cruising—ports of call, costs, fly-cruise package bargains, cabin selection booking, embarkation, and debarkation, and describes in detail over 60 or so ships cruising the waters of Alaska, the Caribbean, Mexico, Hawaii, Panama, Canada, and the United States.)

Frommer's Skiing Europe
(Describes top ski resorts in Austria, France, Italy, and Switzerland. Illustrated with maps of each resort area. Includes supplement on Argentinian resorts.)

Guide to Honeymoon Destinations
(A special guide for that most romantic trip of your life, with full details on planning and choosing the destination that will be just right in the U.S. [California, New England, Hawaii, Florida, New York, South Carolina, etc.], Canada, Mexico, and the Caribbean.)

Marilyn Wood's Wonderful Weekends
(This very selective guide covers the best mini-vacation destinations within a 200-mile radius of New York City. It describes special country inns and other accommodations, restaurants, picnic spots, sights, and activities—all the information needed for a two- or three-day stay.)

Manhattan's Outdoor Sculpture
(A total guide, fully illustrated with black-and-white photos, to more than 300 sculptures and monuments that grace Manhattan's plazas, parks, and other public spaces.)

Motorist's Phrase Book
(A practical phrase book in French, German, and Spanish designed specifically for the English-speaking motorist touring abroad.)

Paris Rendez-Vous
(An amusing and *au courant* guide to the best meeting places in Paris, organized for hour-to-hour use: from power breakfasts and fun brunches, through tea at four or cocktails at five, to romantic dinners and dancing 'til dawn.)

Swap and Go—Home Exchanging Made Easy
(Two veteran home exchangers explain in detail all the money-saving benefits of a home exchange, and then describe precisely how to do it. Also includes information on home rentals and many tips on low-cost travel.)

The Candy Apple: New York for Kids
(A spirited guide to the wonders of the Big Apple by a savvy New York grandmother with a kid's-eye view to fun. Indispensable for visitors and residents alike.)

The New World of Travel
(From America's #1 travel expert, Arthur Frommer, an annual sourcebook with the hottest news and latest trends that's guaranteed to change the way you travel—and save you hundreds of dollars. Jam-packed with alternative new modes of travel that will lead you to vacations that cater to the mind, the spirit, and a sense of thrift.)

Travel Diary and Record Book
(A 96-page diary for personal travel notes plus a section for such vital data as passport and traveler's check numbers, itinerary, postcard list, special people and places

to visit, and a reference section with temperature and conversion charts, and world maps with distance zones.)

Where to Stay USA
(By the Council on International Educational Exchange, this extraordinary guide is the first to list accommodations in all 50 states that cost anywhere from $3 to $30 per night.)

(2) Any one of the Frommer City Guides

Amsterdam and Holland
Athens
Atlantic City and Cape May
Boston
Cancún, Cozumel, and the Yucatán
Chicago
Dublin and Ireland
Hawaii
Las Vegas
Lisbon, Madrid, and Costa del Sol
London
Los Angeles
Mexico City and Acapulco
Minneapolis and St. Paul
Montréal and Québec City
New Orleans
New York
Orlando, Disney World, and EPCOT
Paris
Philadelphia
Rio
Rome
San Francisco
Santa Fe, Taos, and Alberquerque
Sydney
Washington, D.C.

(Pocket-size guides to hotels, restaurants, nightspots, and sightseeing attractions covering all price ranges.)

(3) A one-year subscription to *The Dollarwise Traveler*

This quarterly eight-page tabloid newspaper keeps you up-to-date on fast-breaking developments in low-cost travel in all parts of the world bringing you the latest money-saving information—the kind of information you'd have to pay $35 a year to obtain elsewhere. This consumer-conscious publication also features columns of special interest to readers: **Hospitality Exchange** (members all over the world who are willing to provide hospitality to other members as they pass through their home cities); **Share-a-Trip** (offers and requests from members for travel companions who can share costs and help avoid the burdensome single supplement); and **Readers Ask . . . Readers Reply** (travel questions from members to which other members reply with authentic firsthand information).

(4) Your personal membership card

Membership entitles you to purchase through the club all Frommer publications for a third to a half off their regular retail prices during the term of your membership.

So why not join this hardy band of international budgeteers and participate in its exchange of travel information and hospitality? Simply send your name and address, together with your annual membership fee of $18 (U.S. residents) or $20 U.S. (Canadian, Mexican, and other foreign residents), by check drawn on a U.S. bank or via international postal money order in U.S. funds to: Frommer's Dollarwise Travel Club, Inc., 15 Columbus Circle, New York, NY 10023. And please remember to specify which *two* of the books in section (1) and which *one* in section (2) you wish to receive in your initial package of members' benefits. Or, if you prefer, use the order form at the end of the book and enclose $18 or $20 in U.S. currency.

Once you are a member, there is no obligation to buy additional books. No books will be mailed to you without your specific order.

II

THE PRACTICALITIES

While not exactly exciting, this chapter may turn out to be one of this book's most important contributions to the success of your Benelux trip. It is, essentially, a general look at some of the things you should know about the Benelux region *as a whole* before you leave home. Specific, detailed information for each country is included in the appropriate chapters, and those chapters should be studied meticulously once you've decided from which country you'll enter the region and just how you'll travel around.

To help you make informed decisions, here are some solid facts, plus comments and suggestions that pertain to the entire Benelux region.

1. Preparing for Your Trip

Decisions, of course, can be made about those aspects of your travel that are optional. Your very first order of business, however, must be to take care of those matters in which you have no choice. In the Benelux countries, they are few, but at the top of the list are—

TRAVEL DOCUMENTS

If you're a citizen of the U.S., the U.K., Canada, and most European countries, the only document you'll need to enter Belgium, Holland, or Luxembourg is a valid passport. If your homeland doesn't fall into these general categories, be sure to check on your country's status before you leave. None of the three Benelux countries requires a visa unless you plan to stay longer than three months within its borders. Nor are health or vaccination certificates required. Drivers need only produce a valid driver's license from their home country. When crossing the border from one country to another, you'll need only your passport.

TOURIST INFORMATION

The official tourist agency for each country maintains overseas branches from which you can obtain excellent, in-depth information on a vast array of subjects, among which you are quite likely to find any special interests, hobbies, or other matters that will influence how you spend your time in a particular country. You'll find national tourist office addresses within each country in the appropriate chapters; useful overseas addresses for all three are listed below:

Belgian Tourist Office

745 Fifth Ave.
New York, NY 10151
(tel. 212/758-8130)

For mail and telephone inquiries only:
c/o JRL
187 Place d'Youville
Montréal, PQH24–2B2
(tel. 514/845-7500)

38 Dover St.
London W1X 3R3
(tel. 01/499-5379)

Netherlands Board of Tourism

355 Lexington Ave.
New York, NY 10017
(tel. 212/370-7367)

255 N. Michigan Ave., Suite 326
Chicago, IL 60601
(tel. 312/819-0300)

605 Market St., Suite 401
San Francisco, CA 94105
(tel. 415/543-6772)

25 Adelaide St. East, Suite 710
Toronto, ON M5C 1Y2
(tel. 416/363-1577)

25-28 Buckingham Gate
London SW1E 6LD
(tel. 01/630-0451)

Luxembourg National Tourist Office

801 Second Ave.
New York, NY 10017
(tel. 212/370-9850)

36 Piccadilly
London W1Z 9P8
(tel. 01/434-2800)

MONEY MATTERS

For safety's sake, you'll want to carry most of your money in traveler's checks instead of cash. Arm yourself with about $100 worth of the currency of your entry country for those first few days' expenses; then cash traveler's checks as you need them—you'll usually get a better exchange rate with these than with cash. Try to avoid having to cash them on weekends or holidays when banks are closed: exchange rates in hotels or shops are never as favorable. Needless to say, you should keep your traveler's checks separate from the record of their numbers so that if you should be so unlucky as to lose them, replacement is a simple matter.

Major credit cards are widely accepted throughout the Benelux countries and can be a real convenience when you're traveling. Be aware, however, that you may be billed at an exchange rate different from the one in effect when you made the charge, and that can sometimes add dollars to (or sometimes subtract dollars from) your costs.

One of the most useful items that goes into my purse when I head overseas is the calculator/currency converter sold by Deak International, one of the leading currency-exchange companies on the international scene. It's credit-card size, and you set the exchange rate just once—it will remain constant even when you push the "Off" button. As rates change, or as you cross borders and deal with different currencies, it's a simple matter to set in the new rate. The International Currency Converter is available at most Deak offices, or by mail or telephone from Deak International, 630 Fifth Ave., New York, NY 10019 (tel. 212/757-6915).

WHAT TO PACK

When you go, what you plan to do, and how you intend to get around are the three determining factors in your packing. The Benelux climate features, in general, moderate temperatures with few days of extremes in the direction of either hot or cold. Winters in Holland tend to be the coldest in the region, and along Holland's coast it can get pretty cold and blustery even in summer. In all three countries, it's a good idea to have a shawl or sweater along for cool evenings in summer. Layering of blouses or shirts, sweaters, and jackets during fall, winter, and early spring months allows easy adjustment to temperature changes during the day. In all seasons you're likely to encounter a good bit of rainfall, so there is one item that's an absolute *must,* no matter what time of year you come or what you plan on doing. You guessed it, it's a raincoat. I find that a lightweight raincoat comes in handy not only to keep dry, but as a wrap on chilly evenings as well.

As for the rest of your packing, keep in mind that these are basically rather casual countries when it comes to sightseeing and most daytime activities. When night falls, your choice of where to dine or the evening's entertainment will dictate the kind of clothes you'll need. In all probability you won't want to miss at least a taste of theater, nightclubbing, concerts, or whatever in the sophisticated cities of Brussels and Amsterdam, and Luxembourg is no less rigorous in its dress codes for top restaurants and theaters. There's also the matter of that unexpected invitation to a more formal function from someone you've met in your travels. Personally, I like to take along a long skirt that has seen long and faithful service for just such an occasion. It's drip-dry, wrinkle-proof, doesn't take up much room, and fills the bill admirably with a dressy top. If long skirts aren't your cup of tea, a simple skirt and dressy top will usually do just as well. For men, a sports jacket and a tie will serve for most "dressy" occasions in the city, and in most good restaurants they'll be required.

If you plan to do more than just sample the sparkling nightlife of the Benelux countries, women will want to have along a cocktail dress and appropriate shoes, and their male escorts will be more comfortable with a dark suit for those nights on the town.

For most of your traveling around, stick to every veteran traveler's tried-and-true formula of packing sensibly and *light.* If your plans call for a rental car with loads of trunk space, maybe that extra suitcase won't be a burden. But believe me, it's a very different story when you're juggling luggage around railway platforms or airports!

So no matter how much you'd love to take along that smashing pure-silk dress or linen jacket, if it won't drip dry or must be ironed every time you unpack, *leave it at home.* Interchangeable tops and bottoms (pants or skirts, depending on your personal preference) will see you through and lighten your load. The mix-and-match principle applies to shoes as well. I'm not suggesting that your stout walking shoes will go waltzing out to dinner or the theater, but sandals or pumps that match a dressy top as well as a sports outfit do double duty easily. One more word about shoes: Stick in one pair more than you think you'll need. That's not a violation of the "pack light" principle, it's just a bit of practical advice. Unexpected showers can leave your feet pretty soggy, and a spare pair of shoes can be a godsend (an inexpensive can of waterproofing spray to treat your shoes before leaving home is also a good investment). Also, cobblestones abound and can wreak havoc on your shoes and leave your feet and legs aching—a change of walking shoes will work wonders.

One of the most awkward items to pack is my toiletries case, and I've learned to carry along only an initial supply of such things as toothpaste, shampoos, etc., and then buy replacements as I go along. Benelux pharmacies and department stores are well stocked with many of the brands you use at home. As for medications, it's a good idea to bring along prescriptions (for eyeglasses, as well) from your local doctor just in case you need refills.

Far be it from me to set down a strict "how to pack" formula, but I do have some suggestions for a method that I've evolved over the years and that works pretty well. First of all, the "pack light" theme begins with my suitcase. A sturdy dufflebag or one of the wide variety of lightweight, flexible nylon bags now on the market adds almost no weight and seems to have endless space in which to fit one more item. Zippers are all-important with this kind of luggage, so be sure you conduct a careful inspection before leaving home.

Bulky items like shoes or hairdryers or the toiletries case go in first and provide a firm bottom layer. Underwear and T-shirts go in next, followed by layers of blouses, shirts, trousers, and skirts. A commodious shoulder bag carries the items I'll need en route and traveling around the country (and I find it handy to stick in a traveling toothbrush and small tube of toothpaste for those times it's inconvenient to go scrounging around the suitcase).

There's one more thing I never leave home without—an extra nylon bag that folds into a tiny envelope cover. That's for all the things that I inevitably pick up along the way and for those things that just won't go back into their original place in the bag I brought over. I pack that at home simply because I happen to have one, but if you don't own one, you can easily pick up an inexpensive nylon dufflebag or folding bag in department stores almost anywhere in the Benelux countries.

2. When to Come

"In-season" in the Benelux countries means mid-April through mid-October. The peak of the tourist season is July and August, and in all honesty, that's when the weather is at its finest. Weather, however, is never really extreme at any time of year, and if you're one of the growing numbers who favor shoulder- or off-season travel, you'll find Belgium, Holland, and Luxembourg every bit as attractive during those months. Not only are airlines, hotels, and restaurants cheaper and less crowded during this time (with more relaxed service that means you get more personal attention), but there are also some very appealing things going on in all three of the Benelux countries.

In Belgium, for example, Brussels swings into its rich music season in April, and Tournai turns out for the colorful thousand-year-old Plague Procession the first Sunday of September. Holland's bulb fields are bursting with color from mid-April to mid-May, its concert and theater season blossoms in January, and on the third Tuesday in September, Queen Beatrix boards a golden coach drawn by eight magnificent horses to ride to the Knights' Hall in The Hague to formally open Parliament amid a burst of old-world pageantry. Theater is most active during winter months in Luxembourg, and outside the city, on the second weekend in September, Grevenmacher celebrates its Wine and Grape Festival with a splendid folklore procession.

3. How Long to Stay

The sheer diversity of historical, cultural, and entertainment attractions in Belgium, Holland, and Luxembourg is a strong argument for spending your entire holiday in the Benelux region, no matter how much or how little time you have available. Let me say right up front that I would personally go beyond a mere recommendation to *urge* that you do just that—you'll come back with a smattering of virtually everything European with a minimum of miles covered. You'll find suggestions for detailed itineraries in each country in the appropriate chapters of this book.

Because this is one of Europe's most convenient gateways, however, you may simply want to sample Benelux itself before moving into other parts of the continent. So let's look at the possibilities of dividing your time among the three countries if your plans call for stays of one, two, and three weeks.

As you'll see, planning is simplified because distances are short and one-day excursions simple. My recommendation that you base yourself in the capital of each country is made in light of two basic considerations: you just won't be ready to leave any one of the three after just one or two days, and additional evenings will permit you to explore them further as well as feel the pulse of these fascinating cities. And—of prime importance to me, personally—you won't have to pack and juggle the luggage every day.

ONE WEEK

This time span allows only a brief introduction to the Benelux countries, so plan on two days in each capital city, with one day for travel. Distances are so short between Brussels, Amsterdam, and Luxembourg, and train schedules so convenient, that your one full day of travel will be split into no more than a few hours in a single day. Also, it's a simple matter to book ongoing European travel by air or by train from any of the three cities.

TWO WEEKS

This amount of time will allow you to experience the Benelux countries in surprising depth by allotting five days each to Belgium and Holland and three to Luxembourg, with a total of one full day for travel from one capital to another. You'll have to make some hard choices from the possibilities in each country that are listed below.

Belgium

Most of your sightseeing is possible in easy day trips from a Brussels base. After devoting your first two days to the city's sightseeing attractions, reserve the remaining three for day trips by excellent excursion coaches or by car to your choice of the following sightseeing destinations: medieval Brugge; historic Gent; Oostend, Knokke, and other resorts along a 40-mile-long stretch of Belgian coast; Tournai, with its historic churches and museums; Mons and its nearby ruined castles and abbeys; Waterloo battlefield and the picturesque ruins of Villers-la-Ville abbey; Antwerp and its diamond cutters (via Mechelen, with its famous bell ringers); and Liège (home of Europe's oldest street market, held every Sunday).

Holland

No fewer than two full days should be given over to the attractions and charms of Amsterdam. During the next three days, take your pick of day trips to: Allsmeer,

The Hague, Rotterdam, and Delft; the bulb fields and famous Keukenhof gardens; the fishing villages of Volendam and Marken, with their traditionally garbed populace; the medieval town of Edam and the nearby concentration of windmills; a fascinating (eight-hour) tour of the enclosing dike and the Zuiderzee.

Luxembourg

Spend your first day exploring Luxembourg city, with its unique network of cliffside casements, impressive cathedral, Grand Ducal Palace, fortress remains, and European Center (a very good half-day coach excursion will give you a quick look at all these plus the nearby countryside). On one of the remaining days, take a day-long coach tour of the Ardennes region, to see Wiltz (site of the Battle of the Bulge in the winter of 1944–1945), and the feudal castles at Eschsursure, Clervaux, Vianden, and the Sure Valley. On your second day, a half-day tour will take you to the Moselle Valley and the famous Bernard Massard Wine Cellars at Grevenmacher.

THREE WEEKS

Lucky you! With three weeks at your disposal, you can add two more days to your stay in both Belgium and Holland, and one more in Luxembourg. You can then add to the above these overnight destinations for each country, with ample time to travel between points.

Belgium

Explore the lovely Belgian Ardennes from a base in Spa (which gave its name to a whole new concept of resort) and include a pilgrimage to Bastogne to tip your hat to Brigadier General MacAuliffe and his 101st Airborne Division troops who made such a valiant stand here in 1944. Stop in at tiny Durbuy ("the world's smallest town"), then ramble through wooded hills and charming villages set on the banks of rushing rivers. Move on to the Meuse Valley (a good base is Dinant, where its ancient citadel sits on a rocky perch high above the town) to visit historic Namur and some of the many castles and abbeys that dot the countryside hereabouts.

Luxembourg

From your day-trip overview of the Grand Duchy's lovely countryside, select a favorite rural town or village and hie yourself off for a serene overnight in one of the many quaint, comfortable inns that abound outside the city—it's the perfect end to your Benelux holiday, and an even better beginning if you arrive suffering from the stresses and strains of modern-day civilization.

4. Getting There

BY AIR

Brussels, Amsterdam, and Luxembourg city are European gateways for major airlines, and all three offer good connections to most other continental capitals. Your Benelux itinerary, as well as fares available, will play a big part in your choice of airline, but you may well want to consider one other factor—a very important one for me, personally—the *personality* of an airline.

When you fly Sabena into Brussels, for example, or KLM into Amsterdam, your Benelux experience begins the very moment you settle into your seat. The Sabena crew will be Belgian; the KLM crew will be your first encounter with the Dutch; and while Luxembourg's leading airline, Icelandair, cannot be considered to have a national character, it has from the beginning used Luxembourg as its European base, and its personnel is well versed in the ways and manners of the Grand Duchy. A nice beginning.

You'll find detailed information on each of these three airlines in the appropriate chapters, but all share more or less the same fare structures. Although in recent years air fares have seen about as many ups and downs as a yo-yo, the basics of fare shopping have remained just about the same.

The least expensive fares in all categories are offered during the off-season, November through March (excluding the Christmas and New Year's holidays). Of the three airlines, Icelandair has long been a leader in the very cheapest fares from the U.S. to Luxembourg via Iceland, with restrictions attached to some (see Chapter XXI).

The least expensive fare category for all airlines is usually the APEX (Advance Purchase Excursion) rate, which carries quite a few restrictions: 21-day advance booking and purchase of your ticket, minimum and maximum stays, substantial penalties for a change in flying date in either direction, and forfeiture of the entire purchase price if you cancel or miss your flight. Excursion fares cost more than APEX, but there's no advance-purchase requirement (although most do require a stated minimum stay); regular economy fares are higher than excursion; and business and first class vie for most expensive, but come with no restrictions and many comforts and luxuries to make them worth the difference.

The above are standard rate categories, and the wise traveler will want to look at several options that can stretch those precious dollars. Charter flights, booked through a reliable travel agent, often offer the best value for the dollar. Many now come with discount car rentals and accommodations that let you freewheel around the Benelux countries on your own. Also, the airlines themselves regularly come up with seasonal promotional fares that are real moneysavers if your travel plans are flexible enough to take advantage of them. Airlines frequently offer attractive fly-drive package fares. And if you'd really rather leave the driving to someone else, a good travel agent can tell you about the many excellent conducted coach tours offered in the Benelux region, with all-inclusive rates well below any you could manage on your own.

Bearing all the above in mind, your first value-for-the-dollar step will be to study the various fares available, be alert for any package deals or promotional fares, and work closely with a reputable travel agent.

BY SEA

In my book, there's just no more romantic and relaxing way to travel to or from Europe than by sea. And, of course, Cunard's *Queen Elizabeth 2* adds the ultimate in luxury. It is currently the only liner offering regular transatlantic service between New York and Europe, and since it docks in Southampton, you reach the Benelux countries by way of excellent car-ferry or air schedules from London. The transatlantic crossing takes five days, and Cunard offers terrific package fares that let you travel one way by air, the other by ship at moneysaving prices (starting at $1,330 and climbing to $8,415 in 1989).

Those five days are likely to remain in your memory as a glorious beginning or ending for your Benelux holiday, and "luxury" hardly begins to describe your surroundings (a moneysaving tip—some of the B-grade staterooms are even more spacious than the A-grade line, which were built on after a later date, so it pays to request one of these older, wood-paneled cabins). There are four outstanding restaurants (which serve a full 20% of the world's consumption of caviar!), a midnight buffet, morning and afternoon tea service, and 24-hour room service. If five days of leisure sound like a drag, consider just some of the activity options: deck sports, a Golden Door Spa with daily fitness classes, a jogging track, four swimming pools, a Youth Center with disco and video games, an Adult Center with games, children's playroom, and a 530-seat theater showing first-run films. For those of a more studious nature, drawing cards will be celebrity lecturers, the library, or the computer learning center.

For current schedules and fares (including a variety of package fares that include land tours, hotel discounts, etc.), contact travel agents or Cunard Line Limited, 555 Fifth Ave., New York, NY 10017. If you'll be arriving from the United Kingdom, there are good sea connections to Holland via car, bus, train, and ferry. (Details are outlined in Chapter XIII.)

5. Getting Around

Without question, there's no better way to get around Belgium, Holland, and Luxembourg than by car. No other transportation gives you so much freedom to ramble at your own pace, either on or off the beaten path. Road conditions are excellent throughout all three Benelux countries, service stations are plentiful, and highways are plainly signposted. Traffic congestion in both Brussels and Amsterdam, however, can cause monumental tieups—in these two cities, it is best to garage the car at your hotel and walk or use local transportation (the best way, incidentally, to see either city).

Nondrivers will find one of the best railway and bus systems in the world operating in these small countries. There is virtually no spot so remote that it cannot be easily and inexpensively reached by trains that are fast and clean and are always on time. As a frequent user of both trains and buses, I can tell you that this is a marvelous way to meet the people who live here, because the people of the Benelux countries spend as much time riding public transportation as they do behind the wheel of an automobile. My one caution also stems from personal experience: schedules are *exact*—if departure is set for 12:01 p.m., that means 12:01 p.m. precisely, not 12:03 p.m.—and station stops are sometimes as short as three or four minutes, which means you must be fleet of foot in getting on and off. There have been times when I fully expected to see half my luggage go chugging off to my next destination, leaving the other half and me on the station platform because I didn't get aboard fast enough!

The five-day Benelux Tourrail Ticket, is good for unlimited travel in all three countries (for any 5 days in a 17-day period). It is a good buy at BF 4,150 ($133.75) for first class, and BF 2,800 ($90.25) for second class. And if you also plan to travel around the whole of Europe, the Eurailpass permits unlimited travel on the rail systems of 15 countries at a cost of $298 for 15 days, $370 for 21 days, $470 for one month, $650 for two months, and $798 for three months. The Eurailpass must be purchased before leaving the United States, and is available from travel agents. The Eurail Youth Pass is available to those under 26 years of age at a cost of $320 for one month and $420 for two months.

Both Belgium and Holland have discount rail and bus passes for travel within their borders, and Luxembourg has good connections with both countries as well as discounted weekend and public-holiday passes. All three provide good service to other European countries. Bicycles are permitted on trains throughout the region, and in Belgium they can be rented at discount rates at many railway stations. You'll find details in the appropriate chapters.

Perhaps the most luxurious way of all to see the highlights of Belgium and Holland is via Horizon Cruises Ltd.'s deluxe 18-passenger cruiser, M.S. *Rembrandt,* which cruises between Amsterdam and Brugge. The six-night "Charms of Holland and Belgium" cruise features stops to see the Pilgrim Fathers' House in Leiden, the pottery centers in Delft, Rotterdam, Gouda, The Hague, the windmills of Kinderdijk, Schoonhoven's silversmith's workshops, and medieval Gent (Ghent) before reaching the storybook medieval city of Brugge (Bruges). Regular season is from May 24 to November 1. Prices in 1989 began at $1,140 per person for double occupancy; special tulip season departures (April 5 to May 17) begin at $1,350.

There is also a six-night "Heart of Holland" round-trip cruise from Amsterdam that highlights The Hague, the Frans Hals Museum in Haarlem, the cheese town of Alkmaar, the ancient market town of Purmerend, and the Ijsselmeer (formerly the Zuiderzee), with prices beginning at $1,100 during the regular season. For details and booking, contact travel agents or Horizon Cruises, 16000 Ventura Blvd., Suite 200, Encino, CA 91436 (tel. 818/906-8086, or toll free 800/421-0454).

PART ONE

BELGIUM

III

INTRODUCING BELGIUM

Across the centuries, all the great powers of Europe have fought for, won, lost, and won again domination over the territory that now goes by the name of Belgium and the adjoining lands once known collectively as "The Low Countries." The attraction? A network of splendid waterways—the Scheldt and Meuse Rivers among the most prominent—connecting far-flung inland points to strategic North Sea ports.

The story of those great struggles across the landscapes of fragmented holdings of the counts ("counties") and dukes ("duchies") of Flanders, Liège, Brabant, and Hainaut is a fascinating one. Played out sometimes on the fields of battle, again in the marriage bed, and occasionally around the treaty table, its convoluted plot touches every phase of European history. As the tale unfolds, the stage is set for the entrance of today's Belgium, an independent nation at last, with a population vividly reflecting its heritage from a host of alien conquerors.

1. A Brief History

Julius Caesar marched his Roman legions against the ancient Belgae tribes in 58 B.C., and for nearly five centuries thereafter great roads were built to carry a procession of goods from all over the continent to these all-important ports. Thus it was that this corner of Europe early on began its tradition of commerce and trade.

From the beginning of the 5th century Roman rule gave way to the Franks, who held sway for nearly 200 years. In the year 800 the great Charlemagne was named Emperor of the West and instituted an era of agricultural reform, setting up underling local rulers known as counts. In 814 Charlemagne's death resulted in the bold usurping of absolute power by the very counts on whom he had relied for allegiance to his Carolingian throne. By 843 his son had acceded to the Treaty of Verdun that split French-allied (but Dutch-speaking) Flanders in the north from the southern (French-speaking) Walloon provinces.

Then came Viking invaders, who attacked the northern provinces, and a Flemish defender known as Baldwin Iron-Arm became the first count of Flanders in 862, whose royal house eventually ruled over a domain that included the Netherlands and lands as far south as the Scheldt in France. Meanwhile, to the south powerful prince-bishops controlled most of Wallonia from their seat in Liège.

As Flanders grew larger and stronger, its cities thrived and their citizens wrested more and more self-governing powers. Brugge (Bruges) emerged as the leading center of European trade as its monopoly on English cloth attracted bankers and financiers from Germany and Lombardy, with nary an inkling that its fine link to the sea, the River Zwinn, would eventually choke with silt and leave it high and dry, forever landlocked. Gent (Ghent) and Ieper (Ypres) locked into the wool trade and prospered. Powerful trade and manufacturing guilds emerged and erected splendid edifices as their headquarters. In Liège, great fortunes were made from iron founderies and the manufacture of arms.

The era from the 12th through the 15th centuries was one of immense wealth, much of which was poured into fine public buildings and soaring Gothic cathedrals that survive to this day. During the 14th century, wealthy patrons made possible the brilliant works of such Flemish artists as Van Eyck, Bosch, van der Weyden, and Memling.

As cities took on city-state status, the mighty count of Flanders, with close ties to France, grew less and less mighty, and in 1302, France's Philip the Fair made a bid to annex Flanders to his country officially. In his bold grab for such a rich prize, however, he reckoned without the stubborn resistance of Flemish common folk. Led by the likes of Jan Breydel, a lowly weaver, and Pieter de Coninck, a butcher, and armed with little more than spiked iron balls attached to chains that could be twirled overhead and aimed at the enemy with deadly accuracy, they rallied to face a heavily armored French military. Confrontation came on July 11, 1302, in the fields surrounding Kortrijk, and when it was over, victorious artisans and craftsmen scoured the bloody battlefield, triumphantly gathering hundreds of golden spurs from slain French knights. Their victory at the "Battle of the Golden Spurs" is celebrated to this day by the Flemish.

Sadly, that valiant resistance had been crushed by 1328 and Flanders suffered under both the French and the English during the course of the ensuing Hundred Years' War, eventually building strong ties with England. When Philip the Good, Duke of Burgundy in the mid-1400s and ally of England's King Henry V, gained control of virtually all of the Low Countries, he was able to quell political troubles in Ghent and Bruges, but unable to prevent extensive looting in Dinant or the almost total destruction of Liège. His progeny, through a series of advantageous marriages, managed to consolidate their holdings into a single Burgundian "Netherlands." Brussels, Antwerp, Mechelen, and Louvain attained new prominence as centers of trade, commerce, and the arts.

By the end of the 1400s, however, Charles the Bold, last of the dukes of Burgundy, had lost the Duchy of Burgundy to the French king on the field of battle, and once more French royalty turned a covetous eye on the Netherlands. Marriage to Mary of Burgundy, the duke's heir, appeared a sure route to bring the Netherlands under French rule, and a proposal (in reality an ultimatum) was issued to Mary to accept the hand of the French king's eldest son. To his consternation, that lady promptly wrote Maximilian of Austria proposing a marriage that would save the provinces from the French. His acceptance made them, instead, a part of the extensive Austrian Habsburg empire.

It was a grandson of that union, Charles V, born in Ghent and reared in Mechelen, who for 40 years presided over most of Europe, including Spain and her New World possessions, and who was beset by the troublesome Protestant Reformation, which was playing hob with a formerly solidly Catholic populace. It all proved too much for the great monarch, and he opted in favor of abdication, giving way to his son, Philip II of Spain.

Philip took control in an impressive ceremony in the Palace of the Coudenberg in Brussels in 1555. An ardent Catholic who spoke neither Dutch nor French, he brought the infamous instruments of the Inquisition to bear on an increasingly Protestant (and increasingly rebellious) Netherlands population. The response from his Protestant subjects was violent—they went on a rampage of destruction that in a single month of 1556 saw churches pillaged, religious statues smashed, and religious works of art burned.

An angry Philip commissioned the zealous duke of Alba, his most able general, to lead some 10,000 Spanish troops in a wave of retaliatory strikes that should have brought the rebels to their knees. The atrocities committed by order of the duke of Alba as he swept through the "Spanish Netherlands" constitute a tale of horror virtually unparalleled in the annals of European history. He was merciless, and when the Catholic counts of Egmont and Hornes tried to intercede with Philip, he put them under arrest for six months, then had them publicly decapitated in the Grand' Place in Brussels as an example meant to intimidate other "softies."

Instead of submission, however, this sort of intimidation led to open warfare, a brutal conflict that lasted from 1568 to 1648. Led by William the Silent and other nobles who raised private armies, Protestants fought doggedly on until at last independence was won for the seven undefeated provinces to the north, which became the fledgling country of Holland. Those in the south remained under the thumb of Spain and gradually returned to the Catholic church. As an act of revenge, Holland closed the River Scheldt to all shipping, and Antwerp, along with other Flemish cities, withered away to a shadow of their former prosperity.

And so it went for Flanders until the beginning of the 18th century, when the grandson of Louis XIV mounted the Spanish throne and brought French domination to Spain's possessions in the Low Countries. That domination was short-lived, however, and in 1713 the Spanish Netherlands was handed back to the Habsburgs of Austria. A series of revolts against reforms instituted by Joseph II, Emperor of Austria, served to give birth to a unifying sense of nationalism among the Low Country natives, who—for the first time—began to call themselves Belgians. Austrian-Belgian conflicts raged fiercely until 1789, when all of Europe was caught up in the French Revolution.

In 1795 Belgium wound up once more under the rule of France, and it wasn't until Napoleon Bonaparte's crushing defeat at Waterloo, just miles from Brussels, that Belgians began to think of national independence as a real possibility. Its time had not yet come, however, for the Congress of Vienna decreed that Belgium become once more united with the Netherland provinces of Holland. It didn't take long for the Dutch to learn that governing the unruly Belgians was more than they had bargained for, and by 1830 rioting in Brussels was the last straw. A provisional Belgian government was formed, with an elected National Congress. On July 21, 1831, Belgium officially became a constitutional monarchy when Queen Victoria's uncle, Prince Leopold of Saxe-Coburg-Saalfeld, became king, swearing allegiance to the constitution.

The new nation set about its own version of the industrial revolution with a vengeance, developing its natural resources of coal and iron and rebuilding its textile, manufacturing, and shipbuilding industries. The country was hardly unified by this process, however, for most of the natural resources were to be found in the French-speaking Walloon regions in the south, where prosperity returned much more rapidly than in Flanders.

The Flemish, many of whom felt more closely allied to the Dutch nation across their border, saw themselves as shunted into a secondary position and bitterly resented the greater influence of their French-speaking compatriates. The acquisition of a French-speaking Belgian colony in the African Congo region was viewed by many as further evidence of domination by an oppressive enclave, and there were increasing signs of trouble within the boundaries of their own country.

It took yet another invasion to bring a semblance of unity, and when German forces swept over the country in 1914, Belgians mounted a defense that made them heroes of World War I, even though parts of the Flemish population openly collaborated with the Germans, hailing them as "liberators" from Walloon dominance. Still, tattered remnants of their national army, led by their "soldier-king," Albert I, held a tiny strip of land between De Panne and France for the entire four years of the war.

With the coming of peace, Belgium found its southern coal, iron, and manufacturing industries reeling, while the northern Flemish regions were moving steadily ahead developing light industry, especially around Antwerp. Advances in agricultural methods brought more productivity and higher profits to Flemish farmlands. And by the end of the 1930s the Flemish population outnumbered Walloons by a large enough majority to install their beloved language as the official voice of education, justice, and civil administration in Flanders.

With the outbreak of World War II, Belgium was once more in the forefront of German army advances. In the face of overwhelming military superiority, King Leopold III elected to surrender to the invaders, remain in his country, and try to soften the harsh effects of occupation. By the war's end he was imprisoned in Germany, and a regent was appointed as head of state. His controversial decision to surrender led to bitter debate when he returned to the throne in 1950, and in 1951 he stepped down in favor of his son, Baudouin.

The years following Baudouin's accession have seen the emergence of a new Belgian spirit. Flemish and Walloon regions are more inclined to work together in sharing power and influence than to fight for dominance by either. That same spirit has inspired Belgian political leadership in the development of a European community in which nations work together for common goals.

2. Belgium Today

Against its background of almost continual occupation by foreign troops, Belgium has emerged as a natural location for the coming together of European nations in their efforts to work for continental unity of purpose. Its long centuries of accommodation make it a sympathetic host to the European Economic Community headquarters, and its strategic location has been a vital consideration in the siting of North Atlantic Treaty Organization headquarters in Brussels.

Belgium's long history as a center of trade continues unabated, and it is a leading exporter among industrial countries, with more than 50% of its industrial production destined for shipment outside its borders. Along with high-technology industry, traditional crafts like lacemaking and tapestry weaving continue to flourish. Scores of international organizations are headquartered within the country, and Brussels is home base for perhaps the world's largest concentration of international diplomats.

What the traveler will find in Belgium today is a rich repository of splendidly preserved architecture, masterful works of art, and historic medieval cities little changed over the centuries. Best of all, the Belgian people—whether Flemish or Walloon—have a warm welcome for foreigners who come in search of inner riches rather than conquest.

3. The People

There is probably no more ambiguous word in any lexicon than the designation "Belgian." True, it's the nametag of all those who live within the confines of the country known as Belgium, yet that nametag takes on two very different hues when applied to the two very different regions of the country. Nor is this surprising in light of a history that has finally drawn arbitrary borders around people of two such different cultures. All those invaders across the centuries have left in their wake differences as basic as the very language of the land.

In the northern provinces, some 5½ million inhabitants speak a derivation of German that evolved into Dutch and its Flemish variation, a legacy of the Franks. To the south, about 4½ million Walloons speak the language of France. In Brussels the two languages mingle. So strong is the feeling for each language in its own region, however, that along the geographic line where they meet it's not unusual for French to be the daily language on one side of a street while neighbors on the opposite side chatter away in Flemish. And throughout the country, road signs acknowledge both languages by giving two versions of the same place name—Brussel/Brussels/Bruxelles or Brugge/Bruges, for example. There is even one small area in eastern Belgium where German is the spoken tongue! Belgium, then, is left with not one, but three, official languages: Dutch, French, and German.

History has left its stamp on more than just language, and in both Flanders and Wallonia people cling as tightly to their traditions and customs as they do to their speech. Religious lines are sharply drawn as well, with little mingling of Catholics, Protestants, and anticlerics. In the area of public life that will most affect you as a visitor, you will find three separate national tourism agencies offering assistance: one for Flanders, another for Wallonia, and yet another for that special case, Brussels. If that sounds complicated, it's not, for there's little overlapping and they work together with a smoothness that seldom lets on to the visitor just which agency is helping you along.

In short, far from being a homogeneous, harmonious people with one strong national identity, Belgians take considerable pride in their strongly individualistic attributes. Do they get along with one another? Well, in a manner of speaking. After all, for hundreds of years both the Flemish and the Walloons were forced to adopt an outward appearance of compatibility with all sorts of alien rulers, yet time and again events brought to the surface their strong inner devotion to independence. Thus the thoroughly independent Flemish go along with a Brussels located in *their* geographic territory that conducts the country's business in French, and Walloons head for the beaches of Flanders without a second thought. Virtually every Belgian is bilingual, with English thrown in for good measure. So they not only get on fairly well with each other, but they make it easy for the visitor as well. With centuries of practice behind them, they are quite willing to fit the language to the occasion, all the while fiercely protecting and preserving the heritage that is uniquely their own.

Courtesy based on mutual accommodation of differences is the prevailing rule among Belgians, and it is the thing you'll notice most on your first encounters, whether with salespeople in the shops, restaurant personnel, taxi drivers, or railway station porters. It is, however, a courtesy dispensed with a healthy dollop of reserve. Now, that sort of cautious courtesy can sometimes come across as a cool aloofness that is rather off-putting. But don't be misled. If there is one characteristic all Belgians have in common, it's the passion with which they pursue any special interest, be it art, music, sports, or that greatest of all Belgian passions, food. Show your own interest in the subject at hand, and coolness evaporates as you're welcomed into an affectionate fraternity.

It is no doubt from that passionate nature that the Belgian's appreciation for the good things of life springs. Indeed, appreciation is at the bottom of a national insistence on only the best. Standards are high in every facet of daily life, and woe betide the chef who tries to hoodwink patrons with less-than-fresh ingredients, the shopkeeper who stocks shoddy merchandise, or any service person who deals in rudeness—their days are surely numbered. Belgians—Flemish or Walloon—are practical almost to a fault, and none is even about to spend hard-earned cash for anything that doesn't measure up.

Ah, but when standards are met, to watch Belgian eyes light up with intense enthusiasm is nothing less than sheer joy. Appreciation then moves very close to reverence, and it can be generated by perfection (or near perfection) in just about anything, from a great artistic masterpiece to a homemade mayonnaise of just the right lightness to one of Belgium's 300 or more native beers. Having shared that experience with a Belgian companion, chances are you'll find your own sense of appreciation taking on a finer edge.

The Belgians? There simply is no way to capture their personality in a single word or phrase. There are some ten million of them, and they're a complex lot—some say schizophrenic—but one thing they're definitely *not* is boring. And they're fun to visit!

4. The Lay of the Land

It's a small, compact country—11,800 square miles (about the size of Maryland) and only 150 miles across from the sea to the Ardennes—yet Belgium holds within its borders astounding scenic diversity. Its landscape drapes itself around water. Rivers that run from south to north carve out the great Meuse and Scheldt basins, then hurry to empty into the North Sea in estuaries that serve as the natural harbors that have, from the beginning, attracted the covetous attention of the great European powers. Major highways trace river routes. In the Ardennes, heavy rain swells rushing mountain streams most years. Annual rainfall in Belgium, in fact, is almost double that in Holland.

For a graphic picture of the two ethnic regions, Flanders and Wallonia, draw an imaginary line almost exactly halfway across the country and through the middle of the province of Brabant. The northern provinces of East and West Flanders, Antwerp, Limburg, and that part of Brabant north of a line drawn just south of Brussels are Flemish. This is where you'll find the medieval cities of Ghent, Mechelen, Ypres, and Bruges, the port and diamond industry of Antwerp (home of the great Flemish painter, Rubens), and some 40 miles of gorgeous beaches along the coast of West Flanders. It is also home to approximately one million more inhabitants than Wallonia.

South of that imaginary line, Wallonia consists of the provinces of southern Brabant, Hainaut, Namur, Liège, and Luxembourg. The art cities of Tournai and Mons, historic castles by the score, and scenic resort towns of the Ardennes are the tourist attractions of this beautiful region.

IV

BELGIAN PRACTICALTIES

Planning a visit to Belgium is easy. Good transportation by almost any means is plentiful; getting around is a simple matter, whether you prefer to drive or use the excellent public transport system; accommodations to suit every taste and pocketbook are always at hand; sightseeing and nightlife provide an exciting combination of the old and the new; and you can look forward to some of the best dining you're likely to experience in a lifetime.

1. Getting to Belgium

If you're coming from the United States or Canada, most international airlines will get you to Brussels. From the U.K. you can arrive by air, train, boat, or car; and from anywhere in Europe, there are good air and rail connections as well as an excellent network of highways.

BY AIR

No fewer then 35 international airlines fly into Brussels' Zaventem Airport, making Belgium easily accessible from almost any point around the globe. Zaventem is a free port, with very good duty-free shopping.

Your Choice of Airline

Your choice of airline will, of course, be based on price and convenience. To those, I always add the advantages of flying any country's national airline, and chief among those is the fact that your experience of the country actually begins when you board the plane. In some cases price considerations and airline standards make that out of the question, but when it comes to Belgium, Sabena makes it easy.

Sabena has been flying since 1923, when it began with a small fleet of just 14 aircraft. Those planes were, however, in perfect flying condition and spotless inside, manned by cabin crews adept in seeing to passengers' comfort. Those high standards have not only been steadfastly maintained in the years since, they've actually been improved.

Today, in each of the planes of the large fleet flying to 76 cities in 42 countries (every continent except South America!), there's a very special, intangible cargo on every flight—Sabena calls it *savoir faire,* and its most visible form is in the warm graciousness of cabin crews. Service, from economy to first class, is not only superbly polished and professional, it is first and foremost friendly without ever being intrusive. Each passenger is in effect given a very personal welcome to Belgium, delivered with the pride in perfection that is so characteristic of the Belgian people.

First-class passengers enjoy, in addition to the usual amenities that come with the fare, wide, easily converted sleeper-seats and an upper-deck lounge and bar (except in some 747s in which the upper deck accommodates business class). In major airports there's a special lounge for first- and business-class passengers, as well as priority unloading of luggage. Economy-class passengers find themselves pampered and cared for with the same personal attention as those up front. As for food, all classes enjoy an advance taste of the world-famous treats that await them in Belgium.

For schedules and reservations, contact your travel agent or Sabena International Airlines. In the U.S. and Canada, contact them at 720 Fifth Ave., New York, NY 10022 (tel. 212/936-7800), 303 E. Wacker Dr., Chicago, IL 60601 (tel. 312/236-5591), or 3 Place Ville-Marie, Montréal, PQ H3B 2E3 (tel. 514/861-9641).

About Fares

What you pay will depend on several factors: the season you travel, what class seat you select, and the airline you choose. For Belgium, lowest fares are in effect from November to March; the highest, from June 1 to October 1.

The least expensive way to fly to Belgium is by **charter** or **organized tours** that include air fare. Travel agents are your best source of information on what's available when you plan to travel, and a leading agency in the U.S. that has proved reliable for many years and which includes Belgium in many of its reasonably priced European tours is Cosmos Tours, 69-15 Austin St. (P.O. Box 862), Forest Hills, NY 11375 (tel. 718/268-7000, or toll free 800/228-0090).

Most airlines also feature **promotional fares** each year that are real money-savers. Whenever you plan to fly, and by whatever airline, it will pay to ask about any special prices in effect.

APEX (Advance Purchase Excursion) represents the best value for the dollar if you can meet the restrictions. These are always sold on a round-trip basis, and advance purchase time varies by airline, from 7 to 30 days. APEX fares apply to weekdays only (Monday through Thursday), require a minimum stay of 7 days and allow a maximum stay of 21 days, and impose penalties for changing travel dates or for cancellation. In 1989 Sabena's APEX fare from New York to Brussels was $619 during the high season, $479 during the two shoulder seasons, and $421 during the November to March season.

Economy, or excursion, fares are next up the price scale, and they may carry no advance-purchase requirement, no penalty for changes or cancellations, and are good for one year. Round-trip economy fares from New York to Brussels on Sabena ranged from $789 to $952 in 1989.

Business class, in a forward cabin, with wider seats, free drinks, and other extras, has no booking restrictions and cost $1,964 year round from New York to Brussels on Sabena in 1989.

BY SEA FROM THE U.K.

There's excellent ship and jetfoil service for foot passengers as well as cars and drivers between Dover/Folkstone in England and Oostende on the Belgian coast,

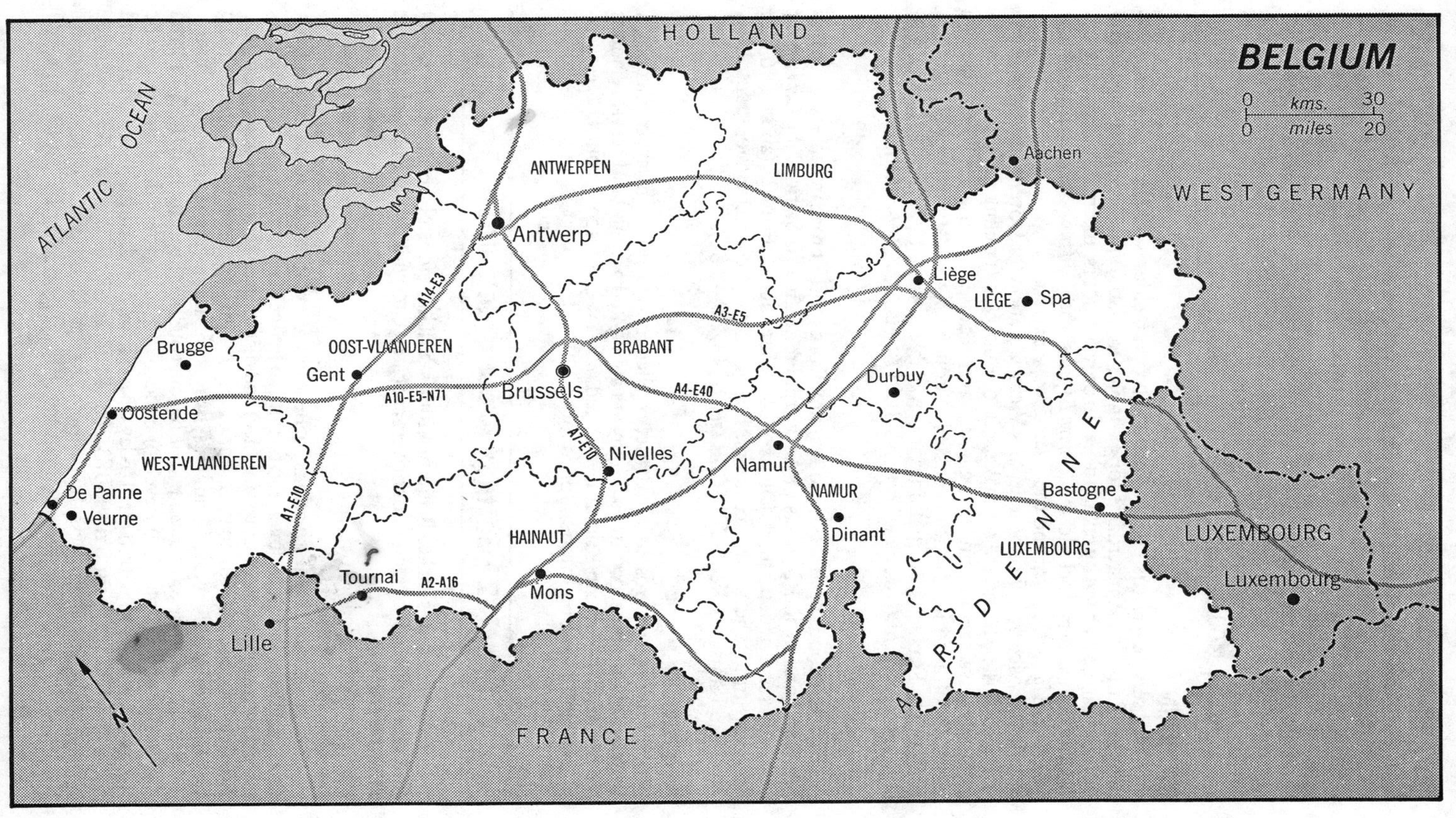
BELGIUM
0 kms. 30
0 miles 20
HOLLAND
WEST GERMANY
FRANCE
LUXEMBOURG
ATLANTIC OCEAN
ARDENNES
N
ANTWERPEN
LIMBURG
OOST-VLAANDEREN
WEST-VLAANDEREN
BRABANT
LIÈGE
HAINAUT
NAMUR
LUXEMBOURG
Antwerp
Brussels
Brugge
Gent
Oostende
De Panne
Veurne
Nivelles
Namur
Liège
Spa
Aachen
Durbuy
Dinant
Bastogne
Luxembourg
Tournai
Mons
Lille
A14-E3
A10-E5-N71
A3-E5
A4-E40
A7-E10
A1-E10
A2-A16

with a minimum of eight sailings daily and sometimes as many as 18 per day during the peak tourist season. Channel crossings take about 3½ hours by boat, and just under 2 hours by jetfoil. Expect to pay between £85 ($146.25) and £100 ($172) each way for a car and two adults, depending on season, but it will pay you to inquire about any midweek or weekend specials offered when you plan to travel. Schedules and exact fare information are available from any Belgian Tourist Office, or contact: **Carferries,** Administration de la Marine, rue Belliard 30, 1040 Brussels, or Natienhaai 5, 8400 Oostende (tel. 059/70-76-01).

BY TRAIN

Rail service to Brussels from major European cities is frequent, fast, and inexpensive. Paris and Amsterdam, for example, are both only three hours away, and London can be reached by rail (and sea) in only 6½ hours. International trains from points farther away include the *North Express,* the *Oostende-Vienna Express,* the *Oostende-Moscow Express,* and the *Trans-Europe Express.*

Rail service from London departs Victoria Station for Dover, with a transfer to jetfoil to Oostende and rail on to Brussels or Antwerp. Traveling time from London to Brussels averages just under five hours, and because this service is so popular, it's best to book as far in advance as possible through railway stations in either London or Brussels. Detailed information is also available from Brit Rail Travel International, Inc., 630 Third Ave., New York, NY 10017 (tel. 212/599-5400).

BY BUS

There's good coach service to Belgium from most European centers, as well as between London and Brussels or Antwerp. From Victoria Station, the *City Sprint* service has several departures daily at one-way fares of less than £25 (about $46.50). Traveling time is just over six hours. For full details, contact **Hoverspeed Ltd.,** Freepost, Ramsgate, Kent CT12 2BR (tel. 0843/59-48-81).

BY CAR

Belgium is crisscrossed by a dense, excellent network of highways connecting it with other European countries. Highways are lighted at night and service stations are frequent. To drive in Belgium, you need only a valid passport, your U.S. driver's license, and a valid registration for your car.

2. Getting Around Belgium

Its compactness makes Belgium a tourist's delight for sightseeing. Drivers will find excellent roadways, and nondrivers are catered to with one of Europe's densest railway systems.

BY TRAIN

All major tourist destinations in Belgium are within easy reach by rail from Brussels. What's more, trains are so fast and so frequent (every half hour during peak travel hours, about every hour at midday) and distances so short that day trips from a Brussels base are easily managed. For example, Antwerp is only 29 minutes away; Gent, 32 minutes; Namur, 40 minutes; Brugge, 55 minutes; and Liège, 75 minutes.

If all or most of your travel will be by rail, your best investment is the **B-Tourrail Ticket** that covers unlimited travel for either 5 or 8 days (travel does not have to be on consecutive days) within any 16-day period from March through September and costs BF2,450 ($79) for 5 days, BF3,200 ($103.25) for 8 days for first-class travel. Second class costs slightly less. If you intend to travel more than 8 days, then there's the "Abonnement réseau" unlimited-travel ticket good for 16 days at BF4,380 ($141.25), first class.

Even if you make only one or two day trips by rail, be sure to inquire about Belgian Railways' "Un beau jour à . . ." ("a beautiful day at . . .") **one-day excursion** tickets to major sightseeing destinations at discount prices.

For those traveling in all three Benelux countries, the five-day **Benelux Tourrail Ticket** is a good buy, and for rail travel throughout Europe, the best value is the Eurailpass (see Chapter II).

BY CAR

Driving conditions are excellent in Belgium, with lighted highways at night, roadside telephones connected to the 900 emergency number, and **"TS"** (Touring Secours) yellow cars that patrol major motorways to render emergency service at minimal cost. If you have car trouble, simply pull off the road and lift the hood and wait for the TS.

To drive in Belgium, U.S. citizens need only a valid passport, a U.S. driver's license, and a valid auto registration. Minimum age for drivers is 18. On motorways, speed limits are 70 km/h (43 mph) minimum, 120 km/h (74 mph) maximum; in all cities and urban areas, the maximum speed limit is 60 km/h (37 mph). One important driving rule is the "priorité à droite" (priority of the right), which makes it perfectly legal to pull out from a side road if it's to the right of the flow of traffic. That means, of course, that you must keep a sharp eye on the side roads to *your* right.

Distance is measured in kilometers (1 kilometer = 0.62 miles), and a quick way to make an approximate conversion into miles is to multiply kilometers by 6 and round off the last digit. The accompanying chart is more exact:

Kilometers	Miles
5	3.1
10	6.2
30	18.6
50	31.0
60	37.3
80	49.7
100	62.1

Rental cars with U.S. specifications are available from **Hertz,** with offices at blvd. Maurice Lemonnier 8 in Brussels and at Brussels Airport, and **Avis,** at the airport and rue Américaine 145 in Brussels (tel. 537-1280). Rates begin at about BF1,025 ($33) per day for a small car, and there's a small charge for each kilometer traveled. If you plan to arrive by train, you can book a rental car through Belgian Railways to meet you at most major stations.

3. The ABCs of Belgium

The information below is a quick, convenient reference for some of the more important practicalities.

AMERICAN EMBASSY The American Embassy is located at boulevard du Régent 27, 1000 Brussels (tel. 02/513-38-30), and there are consular offices at boulevard du Régent 25 (tel. 02/513-38-30), and Nationalestraat 5, 2000 Antwerp (tel. 03/225-00-71).

AMERICAN EXPRESS You'll find American Express International, Inc., at place Louise 2, 1000 Brussels (tel. 02/512-17-40).

BANKING HOURS Banks are usually open Monday through Friday from 9:15 a.m. to 3:30 p.m., and some branches also open on Saturday morning.

CLIMATE Belgium's climate is moderate, with few extremes in temperature in summer or winter. It does, however, rain a *lot,* although there are more drizzles than downpours. Temperatures are lowest in December and January, when they average around 42°F, and highest in July and August, when 73°F is the average temperature.

CLOTHING First and foremost, bring along a raincoat. Showers are frequent and often unexpected. Otherwise, casual clothes for daytime activities, comfortable walking shoes (cobblestones abound and can be murder on shoes), and at least one semi-dress outfit for after-dark Brussels. Needless to say, lighten your luggage as much as possible via the mix-and-match dress method (see Chapter II).

CRIME Whenever you're traveling in an unfamiliar city or country, stay alert. Be aware of your immediate surroundings. Wear a moneybelt and don't sling your camera or purse over your shoulder; wear the strap diagonally across your body. This will minimize the possibility of your becoming a victim of crime. Every society has its criminals. It's your responsibility to be aware and be alert even in the most heavily touristed areas.

CURRENCY The **Belgian franc (BF)** is made up of 100 centimes, and notes are issued in 50-, 100-, 500-, 1,000-, and 5,000-franc denominations. Coins come in 1, 5, 10, and 20 francs, and it's a good idea to keep a small supply of these on hand for tips, telephone calls, and the like. As we go to press the exchange rate is hovering around $1 U.S. = BF31, which is the figure used in conversions throughout this book (prices have been rounded off). The table below is a useful guide for conversions at this rate, but in light of currency fluctuations in past months, you should *be sure to check the current rate when you travel.*

BF	US$
1	.03
5	.16
10	.32
20	.64
50	1.61
75	2.42
100	3.23
200	6.45
300	9.68
400	12.90
500	16.13
1,000	32.26
5,000	161.29

CUSTOMS Before leaving home, be sure to register with Customs (at the airport) any camera, typewriter, etc., you plan to carry with you that could have been purchased abroad. Otherwise you may very well have to pay duty on these items when you return home if you cannot prove they were not brought on your trip.

Upon your arrival in Belgium by either air or sea, you may leave luggage containing dutiable items with Customs officials for safekeeping while you travel around the country.

When reentering the U.S., citizens (regardless of age) are allowed up to $400 exemption for goods bought overseas if they have been away for more than two days and have not had the same duty exemption within one month. Within that amount, those over 21 are allowed one liter of alcohol, 100 cigars (no Cuban cigars, however), 200 cigarettes, and one bottle of perfume with a U.S. trademark. Works of art and antiques more than 100 years old may be brought in duty free (be sure to have verification of age to present to Customs). No agricultural products or meats from overseas may be brought into the U.S.—these will be confiscated if they're in your luggage. With the exception of alcohol, tobacco, and perfumes valued at more than $5, purchases worth up to $50 may be mailed to the U.S. as gifts, but only one per day to the same addressee.

ELECTRIC CURRENT If you plan to bring a hairdryer, radio (other than battery-operated), travel iron, or any other small appliance with you, pack a current transformer and European-style adapter plug, since electric current in Belgium is almost always 220 or 130 volts AC, 50 cycles.

EMERGENCIES In case of **accident,** dial 900. For emergency **medical service** in the Greater Brussels area (around the clock), dial 479-18-18 or 648-80-00. Emergency **dental service** is available by phoning 426-10-26 or 428-58-88 in Brussels. Should you need **police** assistance, the number to call is 101.

GOVERNMENT Belgium is a constitutional monarchy headed by King Baudouine and Queen Fabiola, and the royal title is hereditary. Executive power is vested in the Cabinet of about 20 ministers and a prime minister, but its actions are subject to a majority vote in Parliament, which consists of the Senate and House of Representatives. In recent years, recognition of regional differences has resulted in a good deal of government administration being passed on to local governmental bodies in Flanders and Wallonia.

HOLIDAYS Legal holidays are: January 1 (New Year's Day), Easter Monday, May 1 (Labor Day), Ascension Day, Whit Monday, July 21 (Independence Day), August 15 (Assumption Day), November 1 (All Saints Day), November 11 (Armistice Day), November 15 (Dynasty Day), and December 25 (Christmas).

INFORMATION In the U.S., advance information for your trip is available through the **Belgian Tourist Office,** 745 Fifth Ave., New York, NY 10151 (tel. 212/758-8130). In Belgium, the main office is at rue du Marché-aux-Herbes 61, Brussels (tel. 02/513-90-90). There are more than 40 local tourist offices throughout Belgium, and a complete list of addresses and telephone numbers is available from the main office in Brussels.

PASSPORTS AND VISAS U.S. and Canadian citizens who plan to be in the country 90 days or less need bring only a valid passport—no visa is required. Citizens of other countries should consult the nearest Belgian consulate.

PETS Pets entering the country must have a veterinarian's certificate attesting to good general health and rabies vaccination in the prior 12 months. The certificate must be dated no less than 30 days or more than one year from the date of entry.

POSTAGE Airmail postage to the U.S. and Canada is BF12.50 (40¢) for the first 5 grams plus BF2.50 (8¢) for each additional 5 grams. The local letter rate is BF6.50 (20¢).

SHOPPING HOURS Shops generally stay open from 10 a.m. to 6 p.m. Monday through Saturday, although more and more are also open on Sunday. Most department stores have late hours on Friday, remaining open until 8 or 9 p.m.

TAXIS The minimum rate for taxis is BF80 ($2.50), and charges per kilometer vary from BF31 ($1) to BF62 ($2), depending on location. *Tip and taxes are included in the meter price, and you need not add another tip unless there has been exceptional service* (help with heavy luggage, etc.).

TELEPHONE Direct dialing to other European countries as well as overseas (including the U.S. and Canada) is available in most hotel rooms in Brussels. Coin telephone boxes that display stickers showing flags of different countries can be used to make international calls with operator assistance. Holders of AT&T credit cards may obtain details of the moneysaving USA Direct Service by calling toll free 800/242-1013, ext. 6191, in the U.S.

Coin telephones accept BF5 (15¢) and BF20 (65¢) coins, and it's advisable to have a good supply of these coins when you place a call. Most local calls cost BF10 (30¢).

TIME Belgium is six hours ahead of Eastern Standard Time in the U.S. (9 a.m. in New York is 3 p.m. in Belgium). Daylight savings time begins in April and ends in October.

TIPPING Restaurants and hotels will almost always include a 16% service charge and the 19% value-added tax (VAT)! No more quick math in your head—unless, that is, you've had really exceptional service and want to add a little more. Taxis, as noted above, include the tip in the meter reading.

As a general guide, these are the usual tips for other services: in theaters, BF10 (30¢) to the usher or usherette; hairdresser, 20% of the bill (leave it with the cashier when you pay up); porters, BF20 (65¢) per piece of luggage, except after dark at Brussels railway stations when you should tip BF25 (80¢) per piece.

4. Where to Stay

Belgium is well prepared for guests, with a wide range of city hotels from deluxe to budget, charming country inns, youth hostels, and camping facilities. What's more, the Belgian Tourist office will reserve accommodations for you at no charge before you leave home—contact them at the addresses given in Chapter II ("Tourist Information" in Section 1) for the form you must complete, and *be sure to contact them well in advance of your travel date.*

HOTELS

Brussels, often called "The Capital of Europe," has some of the most sophisticated luxury hotels in the world, and although prices are also in the deluxe category, they still represent good value for the dollar. In style and décor, they range from Old

World to art nouveau to streamlined modern. Amenities may include such extras as swimming pools, tennis courts, health-club facilities, and/or a fine dining room. In most cases there will be a concierge to provide almost any service you might require, from theater tickets to restaurant reservations to travel arrangements. Outside the city there are several outstanding hotels housed in elegant old mansions set in magnificent lawns and gardens which also rate the "deluxe" classification. Nearly all of these top-grade establishments include a continental breakfast in their rates.

In the moderate price range, Brussels boasts outstanding values in clean, comfortable and well-run hostelries, with counterparts around the country. Most have rooms both with and without private bath, and the rate nearly always includes a continental breakfast. Motels are not as common as in the U.S., but the list is growing, and most offer standard, modern rooms and conveniences. Budget travelers will have to search a bit to find accommodations below the moderate range, but with a little effort (and help from local tourist board staffs) they will unearth a few in most regions of the country.

Contact the **Belgian Tourist Office** at the addresses given in Chapter II for their "Official Hotel Guide," which lists hotels and motels by province, showing facilities and prices, as well as their "Benelux classification," based on degree of comfort. When booking, if at all possible you should confirm it in writing to the hotel, stating the number of rooms desired, single- or double-bed preference, private bath or shower requirements, any room-location preferences (with view of garden, river, etc.), length of time you expect to stay, and the exact date and approximate time of your arrival.

FARM HOLIDAYS

Although it's a fairly new trend in Belgium, more and more farm families are offering home stays to tourists. This is a marvelous way to experience firsthand life inside those farm complexes that still retain their medieval, farmyard-centered architecture and/or Belgium's more modern farmhouses. Breakfast will always be provided, and it's possible in some cases to arrange for a home-cooked evening meal. Arrangements (including prices) must be made directly with farm families, and for detailed information, contact the **Belgian Tourist Office** for their "Budget Holidays" brochure.

YOUTH HOSTELS

The first thing to be said about hostels is that, although they're called "Youth Hostels," you'll be welcomed if you're 6 or 60. The second thing to be said is that in order to use them you must have an International Youth Hostel Card, which *must be purchased before you leave home.* It's available from **American Youth Hostels, Inc.,** P.O. Box 37613, Washington, DC 20013, and costs $10 for those under 18 or over 54, and $20 for those ages 18 to 54. For another $10.95 ($8.95 plus $2 for postage and handling) you can purchase their *International Youth Hostel Handbook* (Vol. I, Europe and the Mediterranean) in which you'll find Belgian hostels listed.

If you'd like a list of only the hostels in Belgium, write directly to **Infor-Jeunes,** rue du Marché-aux-Herbes 27, 1000 Brussels; or **Info-Jeugd,** Gretrystraat 28, 1000 Brussels.

CAMPING

The **Belgian Tourist Office** can supply a brochure listing camping facilities, or you may write for a directory and other information to: **Royal Camping and Caravanning de Belgique,** rue de la Madeleine 31, 1000 Brussels (tel. 02/513-12-87).

5. Where and What to Eat

With more than 1,500 restaurants in Brussels alone, and thousands more scattered across the country, you'll never be in danger of going hungry. Nor will you ever have to worry about either quality or quantity—both are extravagant.

WHERE

One of the best things about all those restaurants is that they come in all styles, sizes, cuisines, and price ranges. French cuisine overshadows every other, but there are some exquisite Belgian specialties you shouldn't miss. If budgetary considerations determine your choice of restaurant, this is the one place on earth you can dine well with a slim purse. However, it's my firm conviction that even the poorest purse should have a secret pouch in which to put aside the wherewithal for at least one big splurge in one of Brussels' fine restaurants—expensive, but food for the soul as well as the stomach!

All your Belgian meals will not, however, be taken in city restaurants. I'll venture an educated guess that you'll fall quite happily into the very Belgian habit of lunching at sidewalk cafés or simply munching on waffles or frites (french fries with a Belgian difference) from street vendors. Tiny village bistros and roadside cafés set out light or hearty meals with as much pride and professionalism as their city cousins.

No matter where you eat, you should know that service will be professional, but is guaranteed to be slower than you're accustomed to. Belgians don't just dine, they savor each course—if you're in a hurry, you're better off heading for a street vendor or one of the imported Yankee fast-food joints. Just thought I'd warn you.

Note: Most Belgian restaurants are open seven days a week from noon to 2:30 p.m. for lunch and from 7 to 10 p.m. for dinner. These hours may be flexible, however.

WHAT

Aside from virtually any of your own favorite French dishes, you'll find Belgian specialties on every menu. Seafood is always fresh, the Belgians swear they have the best beef in the world, any vegetable becomes a delicacy, pastries and sweets are an art form, and each course is presented with a flourish worthy of its ingredients. The following are especially worth looking for:

biftek—steak, which comes in many forms: sautéed, served with butter or béarnaise sauce; with marrow (entrecôte à la moelle); with cracked black pepper (steak au poivre)

moules—mussels, a Belgian national dish

frites—twice-fried french fries, lighter than any you've ever encountered, served with biftek or moules or in paper cones and topped with homemade mayonnaise or catsup

lapin à bière—rabbit cooked in beer; inexpensive, hearty, and delicious

jambon d'Ardenne—smoked ham from the Ardennes: positively addictive

crevettes—tiny shrimp from the cold waters of the North Sea, served in a variety of ways: look for *tomato aux crevettes* (tomato stuffed with shrimp and mayonnaise) and *croquettes de crevettes* (crusty, deep-fried cakes)

oie à l'instar de vise—goose that has been boiled, then sautéed

marcassin—wild boar from the Ardennes, usually served roasted

asperges à la flamande—lovely local white asparagus served with sliced or crumbled egg and melted butter for dipping

chicorée-witloof—Belgian endive, wonderful when served wrapped in thin slices of ham with a topping of cheese sauce

gaufres—those wonderful Belgian waffles; try them with sugar, fruit, and/or whipped cream

gaufres de Liège—a heavy waffle topped with caramelized sugar

gaufres aux fruits—small, thin waffles filled with a prune or apricot mixture

What to drink with all those tasty dishes? Why, **beer**—of course! Belgium is justly famous for its brewing tradition, and there are more than 300 brands produced within its borders (some say it's more nearly 1,000). Needless to say, with such a choice it may take quite a bit of sampling to find a favorite (my own turned out to be Chimay, a dark, rich brew), and among names to look for that you won't find anywhere outside Belgium are those still brewed by Trappist monks, Orval and Westmalle; Faro, Krieklambiek, and Lambiek from the area around Brussels; and Leuven.

If, by chance, you're not a beer drinker, or eventually reach a must-have-a-change point, the finest wines from France, Italy, Spain, Portugal, Luxembourg, and Germany are always at hand at prices much below what you'd pay at home.

6. Where to Go and What to Do

Belgium is so crammed full of places to go and things to see and do that you'll be hard-pressed to decide just how to spend your time. Not to worry. The country is so compact that you'll be able to pack an amazing amount of sightseeing and other activities into whatever time you have. The itineraries below are merely suggestions for a stay of one week or two—they may be juggled to suit your personal interests and style of travel.

SUGGESTED ITINERARIES

With only one week in Belgium, my strong recommendation is to base yourself in Brussels and make day-long forays to historic cities that are at most a little more than an hour away by train. In that way you'll have time to get a real feel for the heartbeat of this intriguing capital as well as the highlights of the great centers of art and history nearby. If you're driving, you may choose to overnight in, say, Brugge, Antwerp, or Liège rather than return to Brussels. Drivers can pick up an excellent and very detailed "Itineraries for Motorists" booklet from the Belgian Tourist Office that sets out driving routes in every region.

First Week

Days 1 and 2: Don't budge from Brussels without a minimum of two days to explore the most outstanding of its sightseeing splendors.

Day 3: Travel to Antwerp via Mechelen (with a stop to visit its medieval town square and carillon museum). In Antwerp, visit the house that was home to Rubens and St. James Church to see examples of works by Rubens and other master painters. Return to Brussels for dinner and evening entertainment.

Day 4: Spend the day in Gent, ancient seat of the Counts of Flanders. Visit St. Bavo's Cathedral and view *The Adoration of the Mystical Lamb,* masterpiece of the Van Eyck brothers. Take time for a boat trip on the canals or the River Leie. Return to Brussels.

Day 5: Get an early start to allow a full day in Brugge, a fairy-tale medieval city that has been called the most romantic in the world. Start with a boat ride through the canals, then go shank's mare to see Michelangelo's *Madonna and Child* in marble at the Church of Our Lady, the Memling Museum, and the busy, colorful Markt at the city's center. Return to Brussels.

Day 6: Another early start for the long drive or 75-minute train ride to Liège, one of Belgium's oldest and liveliest cities. Take a look at the 11th-century Palace of the Prince-Bishops, the Cathedral of St. Paul, the fascinating Museum of Walloon Life, and the Museum of Walloon Art. If this is a Sunday, don't miss the colorful street market that is Europe's oldest. Return to Brussels.

Day 7: Unless you decide to devote this last day to further exploration of Brussels, travel to Tournai, where you'll want to visit the awe-inspiring Cathedral of Notre-Dame that dates from the 11th century, the Museum of Fine Arts that houses masterpieces by the likes of Van der Weyden (a native son of Tournai), Rubens, van Gogh, Brueghel, and a host of others. Return to Brussels.

This itinerary, perforce, limits you to sightseeing highlights, but if you have two weeks in Belgium, add the following to the above. While a car is not absolutely essential for this part of your visit, it will have the distinct advantage of giving you total freedom to ramble through scenery that invites more loitering than quick travel by public transport. The suggested order may be reversed to suit your travel plans—save the coastal resorts for last if you're flying out of Brussels, the Ardennes if you're traveling on in Europe.

Second Week

Days 1 to 3: Travel the 75 miles from Brussels to Oostende on Belgium's 40-mile coastline. Choose an accommodations base from Knokke (with its casino and golf course), Oostende (busy, good shopping center), or the quieter resorts of Blankenberge, Den Haan, and De Panne. Primary attraction is the wide white-sand beach that stretches the entire length without interruption.

Day 4: Travel leisurely across country to the Ardennes, Belgium's hilly, heavily wooded beauty spot, and settle into a sightseeing base at Durbuy (a charming old castle town that is known as the smallest town in Europe), Dinant, La Roche, Malmedy, Saint-Hubert, or Bouillon.

Days 5 to 7: You're within easy driving distance of Spa (which gave its name to a whole resort concept) and Bastogne, as well as magnificent scenery and some of the best dining in the country (this is the region famed for its smoked ham—and not nearly famed enough for its freshwater trout).

SIGHTSEEING

Such is Belgium's sightseeing wealth that it's quite impossible to summarize it in this limited space. You'll find detailed information in the upcoming chapters, but the following very brief listing by category will help in planning an itinerary to suit your personal interests. Needless to say, some categories overlap (many historic cities are also great art cities), which is a travel bonus of the first order.

Historic Cities

Brussels, which can trace its beginnings all the way back to a trading settlement in the 300s, preserves its history in its beautiful Grand' Place, with buildings dating back to the late 1600s, as well as scores of other historic buildings and museums.

Antwerp's long history stems from its strategic port facilities, and it's a sightseeing mecca for both history and art buffs because of the many well-preserved churches and public buildings dating from the 1600s on, the home of master painter Rubens, a centuries-old, still-thriving diamond-cutting industry, and its many fine museums.

Brugge (Bruges) is a lovely old city of the Middle Ages whose ancient cobblestone streets and canal houses have changed not one whit since this was one of Europe's leading ports before the River Zwinn silted up and cut it off from the sea. A visit is truly a walk back in time.

Gent was the center of power for the Counts of Flanders, and while it has always had an industrial flavor, much remains of its medieval heritage. Visit an ancient castle, three aged abbeys, canal houses in much their original state, and the magnificent St. Bavo's Cathedral, which houses the equally magnificent *The Adoration of the Mystical Lamb* by the Van Eyck brothers.

Huy sits on the banks of the Meuse and dates from the Middle Ages, when merchants of wine, tin, and copper made it an important commercial center. Its ancient castle, atop a high precipice overlooking the city, is gone, but you can ascend by cable car to visit the 1818 Citadel that replaced it.

Ieper (Ypres), sister city to Brugge and Gent, suffered almost total destruction during World War I, but its historic buildings have been rebuilt to their original plans and specifications, an object lesson in preserving history in spite of mankind's warring nature!

Liège is a city of living history, where a two-mile walk in the city center will bring you face to face with impressive old buildings, many housing modern administrative offices, and more museums than you can possibly visit. Go on a Sunday and wander through La Batte, the street market that has been conducted here for centuries.

Mechelen's claim to fame rests in its history as Belgium's ancient center of religion. Its Grote Markt (main square) is surrounded by buildings right out of the Middle Ages, and its carillon school is considered the best in the world. Visit the Carillon Museum in its gothic Busleyden Manor setting and enjoy periodic carillon concerts. The ancient art of tapestry weaving is alive and well here.

Tournai, a Frankish royal seat, is Belgium's second-oldest town (Tongeren is older), and the oldest private houses still surviving in all of Europe are here (rue Barre Saint-Brice 10 and 12), dating from 1175. Its impressive Cathedral of Notre-Dame holds treasures that include a reliquary cross that dates back to the 6th century.

Art Cities

Entire books could be—and have been—written about the art of Belgium, and these cities should top art lovers' lists of where to find some of the country's artistic highlights: Antwerp, for Rubens' lovers; Brugge for the Memling Museum; Brussels for its Museum of Classic Art (Flemish primitives, Rubens, Brueghel, etc.) and Museum of Modern Art (Ensor, Permeke, Delvaux, Magritte, etc.); Gent for the Van Eyck masterpiece; Liège for both old and new works of Walloon artists; Mons and Tournai for their beaux arts museums; Namur for its fine museum holding sculptures, paintings, and copperworks from the Middle Ages and Renaissance periods.

Battlefields

Ieper (Ypres) is surrounded by more than 40 cemeteries in which lay victims of some of World War I's fiercest fighting. At Bastogne, the "Nuts" museum honors American General MacAuliffe's no-surrender message to German forces in World War II, and the Mardasson Memorial honors American soldiers slain in the Battle of the Bulge. World War II battlefields also surround Antwerp and Bruges.

Resorts

Chief among health resorts is Spa, whose waters are therapeutic for arthritis and gout, and where carbonized water baths, mud baths, and turf baths are center attractions. Mineral waters and thermal baths are also to be found in Oostende.

Beach lovers will gravitate to the coastal resorts of Oostende (with its racetrack and many other entertainments), Knokke-Heist (more sophisticated and with an exciting casino), Zeebrugge (artistic enclave), or the family-oriented towns of Den Haan, Wenduine, Westende, Nieuwpoort, Oostduinkerke, and De Panne.

In the mountains, resort centers (all small, peaceful, and quiet) are Dinant, Durbuy, La Roche, Bouillon, Malmedy, and Saint-Hubert.

SPORTS

The sports-minded will find a wide variety of facilities available in Belgium. There are bowling alleys in most major cities, riding stables around the country (including many in the immediate vicinity of Brussels), race courses in Oostende and Waregem, ice skating rinks in Brussels, public swimming pools galore, tennis courts in every major location, canoeing clubs in several cities, a host of golf courses open to visitors, and around Liège, there's good skiing in winter months.

For names and addresses of sports federations that can furnish details of what's on when you're in Belgium and how you can participate, contact the **Belgian Tourist Office** in New York or at rue du Marché-aux-Herbes 61, 1000 Brussels (tel. 02/512-30-30), or the **Brussels Tourist Information (T.I.B.)** office in Town Hall, Grand' Place, 1000 Brussels (tel. 02/513-89-40). Local tourist offices will also have this kind of information as you travel around.

There's also excellent fishing around the country. You'll need a license, which is available at any post office, and its cost will depend on the number of days you plan to fish and the number of lines to be used. Any Belgian Tourist Office can furnish more detailed information on where to fish for what, seasons, etc.

AFTER DARK

Nighttime in Brussels can be just about anything you want it to be. Cocktail bars vary from the old, established, almost "clubby" type to the avant garde to the bizarre, and there are café theaters, a traditional puppet theater, café cabarets, dinner shows, nightclubs, concerts, ballet and opera and legitimate theater in season (September to May), jazz clubs, and discothèques. Elsewhere, major cities have good theater, concerts, and musical variety houses, but few sophisticated dinner shows or nightclubs, except for Antwerp, Liège, and resort areas along the coast and in some Ardennes locations.

Gambling casinos featuring roulette and baccarat are in Oostende, Blankenberge, Chaudfontaine, Knokke-Heist, Middelkerke, Namur, and Spa. To gain admittance, you must be over 21, present your passport and driver's license, and pay a small admission fee. Minimum bets are quite low, and you'll pay a 6% tax on your winnings. Never mind that croupiers speak French—they're all expert linguists and will be quite happy to take your money in English.

For current information on after-dark entertainment during your visit, pick up a copy of "BBB Agenda" for a small charge at the Tourist Information Brussels office in the Town Hall, Grand' Place, Brussels (tel. 02/513-89-40).

V

BRUSSELS

1. BY WAY OF BACKGROUND
2. ORIENTATION
3. THE ABCs OF BRUSSELS
4. WHERE TO STAY
5. WHERE TO EAT
6. THINGS TO SEE AND DO
7. BRUSSELS AFTER DARK
8. SHOPPING
9. AROUND THE BRUSSELS AREA

"Brussels is the Paris of the Belgians," a 19th-century visitor wrote. These days, Belgians will tell you—with at least a modicum of justification—that Brussels has outstripped Paris by a long shot. After all, isn't this the city that's known universally as the "capital of Europe"? And isn't it true that Parisians many times come by train for the sole purpose of a night at the opera and a fine meal in restaurants even better than those at home?

Of course, comparisons, at best, are to be avoided, and Brussels has no need of Paris as a measuring stick—she stands quite firmly on her own as a leading city of Europe and the world, a wonderful old-world metropolis that has skipped merrily into the 20th century wearing her treasured traditions as a glittering wrap while she assesses and adds to her private horde the treasures of today.

Nor is she a novice at the business of holding onto the old while adapting to the new: centuries of practice in taking for her own the best from each new conqueror lie behind the Brussels of today. It is her *history* that has uniquely equipped this European belle to welcome European Economic Community diplomats with the same open arms that embrace North Atlantic Treaty Organization military leaders, spruce up her heritage from the colorful past, and set out a bountiful table overflowing with gourmet goodies for all comers.

1. By Way of Background

No one knows for certain just when trading first began at this point on the River Senne. Archeologists tell us that neolithic man was here, and Romans once built their opulent villas in the vicinity. It's fairly certain that the bishop of Cambrai found a Merovingian farm haven here in 695. By 966 there surely was a village in existence, for it was mentioned by the name "Bruocsells" ("brook dwelling") in a document from the hand of Emperor Otto I the Great.

BRUSSELS BECOMES A TOWN

It wasn't until 977, however, that it began to take on the form of a proper town. That's when Charles of Lorraine, Duke of Lower Lotharingai (the beginning of the dukes of Brabant line), built a castle on the island of Saint Géry in the Senne that became a gathering point for traders and craftspeople. Two years later he took up residence, thus giving Brussels a firm date (979) on which to hang her 1,000 years, celebrated with much ceremony in 1979.

By the year 1100 fortifications surrounded the settlement, by then expanded to include some 5,000 inhabitants and the new Coudenberg castle to which the duke had repaired. In 1379 a second line of fortified ramparts enclosed what is now the heart of Brussels—today a modern boulevard traces their course (changing names several times along the way, but nearly always called *petite ceinture*—"small belt"—by residents).

FOREIGN RULERS COME AND GO

Those fortifications, however, failed to prevent the tugs of war, political intrigues, and marriages that saw Brussels first under one foreign banner, then another, through the next few centuries. Civil unrest, usually led by members of the crafts guilds, waxed and waned, as citizens chaffed under yokes that were sometimes harsh, sometimes benign.

Flemish, Austrian, Burgundian, and Spanish rulers came and went, leaving behind Belgian heroes still revered today, among them Everard 't Serclaes, who led a mere 100 men against Flemish troops in the 1300s, and the beloved counts of Egmont and Hornes, who paid with their heads in 1568 for leading the opposition to Inquisition horrors imported from Spain. The latter were publicly decapitated on the Grand' Place, where in 1402 the Luxembourg Duchess Jeanne and Wenceslas, her husband, had seen to the beginning of construction on the Town Hall, which became the centerpiece of a magnificent array of buildings housing the different trade and craft guilds.

The Habsburgs of Spain held Brussels in thrall through most of the 17th century, but when Charles II of Spain died leaving no heir, Louis XIV of France sent his armies, with maréchal de Villeroy at their head, to wrest control. In two of the most destructive days in its long history, the city sustained a bombardment from August 13 to 15, 1695, that demolished nearly 4,000 buildings, damaged half a thousand more, and reduced the Grand' Place to utter ruin, with only the Town Hall left standing among the rubble. In an amazing show of determination and building skill, carpenters, stonemasons, and other artisans set to work to rebuild the vanished Guild Houses, and by 1698 the gloriously ornate conglomerate of baroque buildings you'll see today was complete in all its splendor.

In 1716 Brussels fell into the hands of the Habsburgs of Austria, and once more the crafts guilds rumbled with discontent. In 1719 yet another hero entered Brussels folklore when François Anneessens, a respected craftsman and outspoken advocate of municipal rights, was decapitated. He lies buried in Notre-Dame de la Chapelle, on rue des Ursulines.

THE STIRRING OF INDEPENDENCE

The city was in a state of shock from which it did not begin to recover until the arrival of Charles of Lorraine in 1744, but by 1789—despite factional riots in the streets—Brussels followed the example of revolutionary France and joined the people of Brabant in proclaiming (in January of 1790) the United Belgian States. Divisions between factions continued to deepen, however, and after one or two Austrian attempts to take over, the revolutionary French government moved in to put Brussels once more under a French heel.

There it remained until Napoleon went down to inglorious defeat on the Waterloo battlefield not far from the city. Independence eluded Belgium once more, however, and under terms promulgated by the Congress of Vienna in 1815, control of Belgium was awarded to the Dutch. Brussels became a second capital of the Kingdom of the Low Countries, owing allegiance to Holland's William I of Orange.

INDEPENDENCE AT LAST

William's rule was destined to be another in the line of very short reigns, for the cantankerous citizens of Brussels became more and more vocal in their aspirations to bring self-rule to their country. Finally, on a warm night in August 1830, it was an audience attending the opera *La Muette de Portici* in the Théâtre de la Monnaie not far from the Grand' Place who responded enthusiastically to an aria that spoke of "Sacred Love of Country" and lit the fuse that was to kindle a strong, steady flame to burn away forever the yoke of foreign rule.

Their applause and lusty shouts of patriotism were picked up by passing pedestrians outside, who took up the cry and carried it throughout the city. Before long a Belgian national flag appeared on the scene and crowds were singing a new national anthem. The fervor grew until the end of September, when the Dutch ruler sent 14,000 troops to quell this annoying disturbance. Patriots from Liège rushed to join the ranks of Brussels soldier-citizens, and when open battle broke out in the Park of Brussels, it took just four days to rout the Dutch. On September 27, 1830, the Kingdom of Belgium came into being, and Brussels, with its 100,000 inhabitants, was declared its capital. Belgium was, at long last, its own ruler.

AFTER INDEPENDENCE

In the years since independence Brussels has stepped out with spirit and verve to take its proper place on the world stage. By 1834 a university was founded; in 1835 Europe's first railway line ran from Brussels to Mechelen; another European "first," the covered pedestrian thoroughfare, Galeries Saint-Hubert, appeared in 1846, a mecca for fashionable gatherings and shopping; in 1871 the unsightly River Senne was covered by one of the beautiful wide boulevards constructed along the line of the city's ancient fortifications; great public buildings were erected; Brussels hosted three World Expositions (in 1880, 1888, and 1897), for which it constructed the Park of the Cinquentenaire; Brussels architect Victor Horta inaugurated the ornate "art nouveau" era; a 20th-century Brussels hero emerged when Burgomaster Adolphe Max led defiance of German invaders in 1914, and his example inspired Van der Meulebroeck to do the same in 1940; the 1958 International Exposition left a soaring model of the atom as a permanent reminder of peaceful uses for atomic power; the European Economic Community chose Brussels as headquarters in 1959; NATO followed suit in 1967; and a multitude of international corporations flocked into Brussels as it gained more and more prominence and world stature, and its population has mushroomed to one million, of whom more than one-fourth are of foreign origin.

It's small wonder that Brussels is now widely recognized as "The Capital of Europe"!

2. Orientation

Although the heart-shaped inner city of Brussels, roughly 1½ miles in diameter, holds enough sightseeing treasures to keep any visitor busy for more days than are likely to be available, none of the 19 separate, self-governing municipalities that fill the 62½ square miles of Greater Brussels is without attractions of its own. And in this densely populated city, nearly 14% of Saint-Josse-ten-Noode, Saint-Gilles, Koekelberg, Etterbeek, Schaerbeek, Molenbeek-Saint-Jean, Ixelles, Genshoren, Forest, Jette, Woluwé-Saint-Lambert, Berchem-Sainte-Agathe, Evere, Anderlecht, Wolowé-Saint-Pierre, Bruxelles, Auderghem, Uccle, and Watermael-Boitsfort consists of parks, woods, and forests, making this one of the greenest urban centers in Europe.

The center city lies within a slightly flattened-out heart shape once ringed by fortified ramparts and now encircled by broad boulevards known collectively as the Petite Ceinture. Flat in its center and western areas, to the east it climbs the hills that make up upper Brussels and are crowned by the Royal Palace and some of the city's most affluent residential areas and prestigous office buildings. The Grand' Place (Grote Markt) is at the very heart of the heart and serves as a handy point of reference for most visitors. Brussels' excellent railway system runs almost directly through the middle, with the Gare du Nord (Noord Station) just across the northern rim of the Petite Ceinture, the Gare Centrale (Central Station) in the center city not far from the Grand' Place, and Gare du Midi (Zuidstation) near the southern rim.

Streets are signposted in both French and Dutch, and you'll hear both languages on television and radio. Shops, restaurants, and hotels, however, are usually staffed by at least one or two fluent English-speakers.

3. The ABCs of Brussels

The following are practical details that will be useful as you move around the city.

AMERICAN EMBASSY The American Embassy is located at boulevard du Régent 27, 1000 Brussels (tel. 02/513-38-30), and the consulate is at boulevard du Régent 25, 1000 Brussels (tel. 02/513-38-30).

AMERICAN EXPRESS American Express International, Inc., is located at place Louise 2, 1000 Brussels (tel. 02/512-17-40).

BANKING HOURS Banks are open Monday through Friday from 9:15 a.m. to 3:30 p.m., and some branches are also open on Saturday morning.

CLIMATE The average temperature in Brussels during the summer is 60°F (16°C); in winter, 37°F (3°C). Remember to pack a raincoat—you're sure to need it.

EMERGENCIES In case of **accident,** dial 900. For day or night emergency **medical service,** call 479-18-18 or 648-80-00. For emergency **dental service,** phone 426-10-26 or 428-58-88, and for **police** assistance, 906 or 101.

INFORMATION There's an Information Service at the Reception Office at **Brussels Airport** (tel. 722-30-00 or 722-30-01), and multilingual hostesses are available in the luggage hall to assist tourists.

In Brussels, the **Belgian Tourist Office** is located at rue du Marché-aux-Herbes 61 (tel. 02/512-30-30), and the **Tourist Information Brussels (T.I.B.)** office is in the Town Hall, Grand' Place (tel. 02/513-89-40). In addition to tourist information, the T.I.B. also operates a money-exchange service; sells 24-hour tourist tickets for the métro, trams, and buses; makes hotel reservations; and has well-trained, multilingual tourist guides who may be engaged by the hour or day.

Hours at the Brussels offices are: October through April, 9 a.m. to 6 p.m. Monday through Saturday, 1 to 5 p.m. on Sunday; May through September, 9 a.m. to 8 p.m. weekdays, to 7 p.m. on Saturday and Sunday.

POSTAL SERVICES The post office at Gare du Midi, Avenue Fonsny 48A, is open 24 hours every day; all others are open from 9 a.m. to 5 p.m. weekdays, and are closed weekends and public holidays. Conveniently located post offices are at Centre Monnaie, Gare Centrale, Gare du Nord, rue du Progrès 80, the Bourse, and the Palais de Justice.

Airmail postage to the U.S. and Canada is BF12.50 (40¢) for the first five grams plus BF2.50 (8¢) for each additional five grams. The local letter rate is BF6.50 (20¢).

RELIGIOUS SERVICES For information on hours of religious services—including Catholic, Protestant, Jewish, Eastern Orthodox, and Anglican—contact: **Bruxelles-Accueil-Ponte Ouvente ASBL,** rue de Tabora 6, 1000 Brussels (tel. 511-27-15 or 511-81-78), between 10 a.m. and 6 p.m. Monday through Saturday. They also serve as a social information center for foreigners.

SHOPPING HOURS Shops generally stay open from 10 a.m. to 6 p.m. Monday through Saturday, and many are also open on Sunday for shorter hours. Most department stores have late hours on Friday, remaining open until 8 or 9 p.m.

TAXIS The minimum rate for taxis is BF75 ($2.40), and charges per kilometer vary from BF31 ($1) to BF62 ($2), depending on location. *Tip and taxes are included in the meter price, and you need not add another tip unless there has been exceptional service* (help with heavy luggage, etc.).

TELEPHONE Direct dialing to other European countries as well as overseas (including the U.S. and Canada) is available in most hotel rooms in Brussels. You can use coin telephone boxes that display stickers showing flags of different countries to make international calls with operator assistance. If you have an AT&T charge card, get details on the moneysaving USADirect service by calling toll free 800/242-1013, ext. 6191. Coin telephones accept BF5 (16¢) and BF20 (65¢) coins; it's advisable to have a supply of these coins when you place a call.

TIME Belgium is six hours ahead of U.S. Eastern Standard Time (9 a.m. in New York is 3 p.m. in Belgium). Daylight savings time begins the last Sunday in September and ends the last Sunday in March.

TIPPING Restaurants and hotels will almost always include a 16% service charge and the 19% value-added tax (VAT). If you've had really exceptional service, you may want to add a little more, but it isn't necessary. Taxis, as noted above, include the tip in the meter reading.

The usual tips for other services are: in theaters, BF10 (30¢) to the usher or usherette; hairdresser, 20% of the bill (leave it with the cashier when you pay up); porters, BF20 (65¢) per piece of luggage, except after dark at Brussels railway stations, when you should tip BF25 (80¢) per piece.

TRANSPORTATION Brussels has an excellent network of **métro** (subway) lines that cover 17 miles running east and west through the city. Métro entrances are clearly marked by signs bearing a white "M" on a blue background. Lest you dread the thought of descending below ground to get around the city, let me hasten to say that, in this city, every such descent takes you into a center of art, with paintings especially commissioned by contemporary Belgian artists. All are excellent, and some are quite innovative, having been planned to complement the curve of a wall or sweep of a ceiling.

Above ground, yellow **trams and buses** run from 6 a.m. to midnight, and timetables are posted at stops. Tram and bus stops are marked by red-and-white or

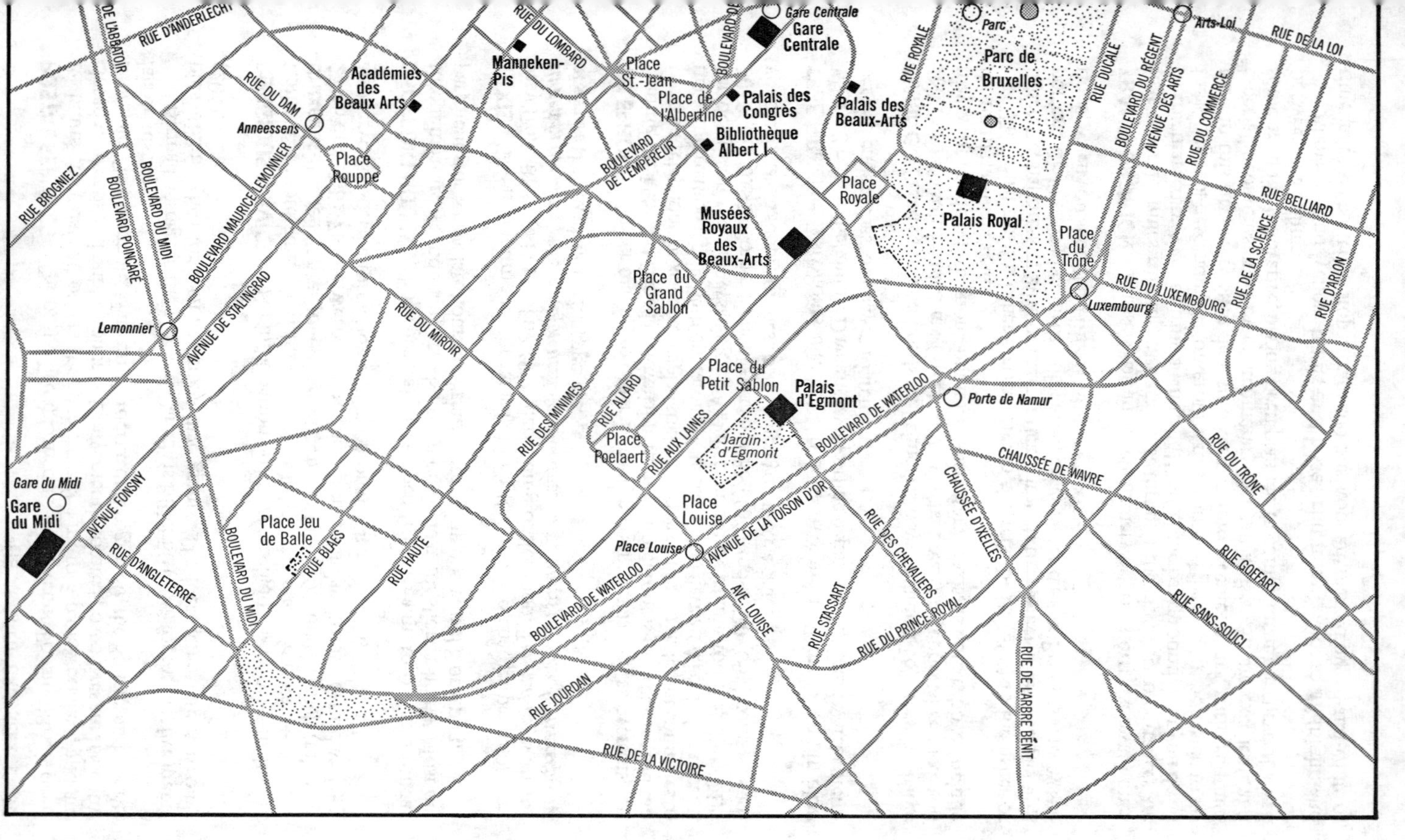

RUE D'ANDERLECHT
DE L'ABBATOIR
RUE DU LOMBARD
Gare Centrale
Gare Centrale
Parc
Arts-Loi
RUE DE LA LOI
Manneken-Pis
Place St.-Jean
BOULEVARD DE
RUE ROYALE
Parc de Bruxelles
RUE DUCALE
BOULEVARD DU RÉGENT
AVENUE DES ARTS
RUE DU COMMERCE
Académies des Beaux Arts
RUE DU DAM
Anneessens
Place de l'Albertine
Palais des Congrès
Palais des Beaux-Arts
Bibliothèque Albert I
BOULEVARD DE L'EMPEREUR
Place Rouppe
RUE BROGNIEZ
BOULEVARD POINCARE
BOULEVARD DU MIDI
BOULEVARD MAURICE LEMONNIER
Place Royale
Palais Royal
RUE BELLIARD
Musées Royaux des Beaux-Arts
Place du Trône
RUE DU LUXEMBOURG
RUE DE LA SCIENCE
RUE D'ARLON
Luxembourg
Place du Grand Sablon
Lemonnier
AVENUE DE STALINGRAD
RUE DU MIROIR
Place du Petit Sablon
Palais d'Egmont
Porte de Namur
RUE DES MINIMES
RUE ALLARD
RUE AUX LAINES
Jardin d'Egmont
BOULEVARD DE WATERLOO
Place Poelaert
CHAUSSÉE DE WAVRE
RUE DU TRÔNE
Gare du Midi
Gare du Midi
AVENUE FONSNY
Place Jeu de Balle
Place Louise
CHAUSSÉE D'IXELLES
RUE DES CHEVALIERS
RUE D'ANGLETERRE
RUE BLAES
RUE HAUTE
Place Louise
AVENUE DE LA TOISON D'OR
RUE GOFFART
BOULEVARD DU MIDI
BOULEVARD DE WATERLOO
AVE. LOUISE
RUE STASSART
RUE DU PRINCE ROYAL
RUE SANS-SOUCI
RUE JOURDAN
RUE DE L'ARBRE BÉNIT
RUE DE LA VICTOIRE

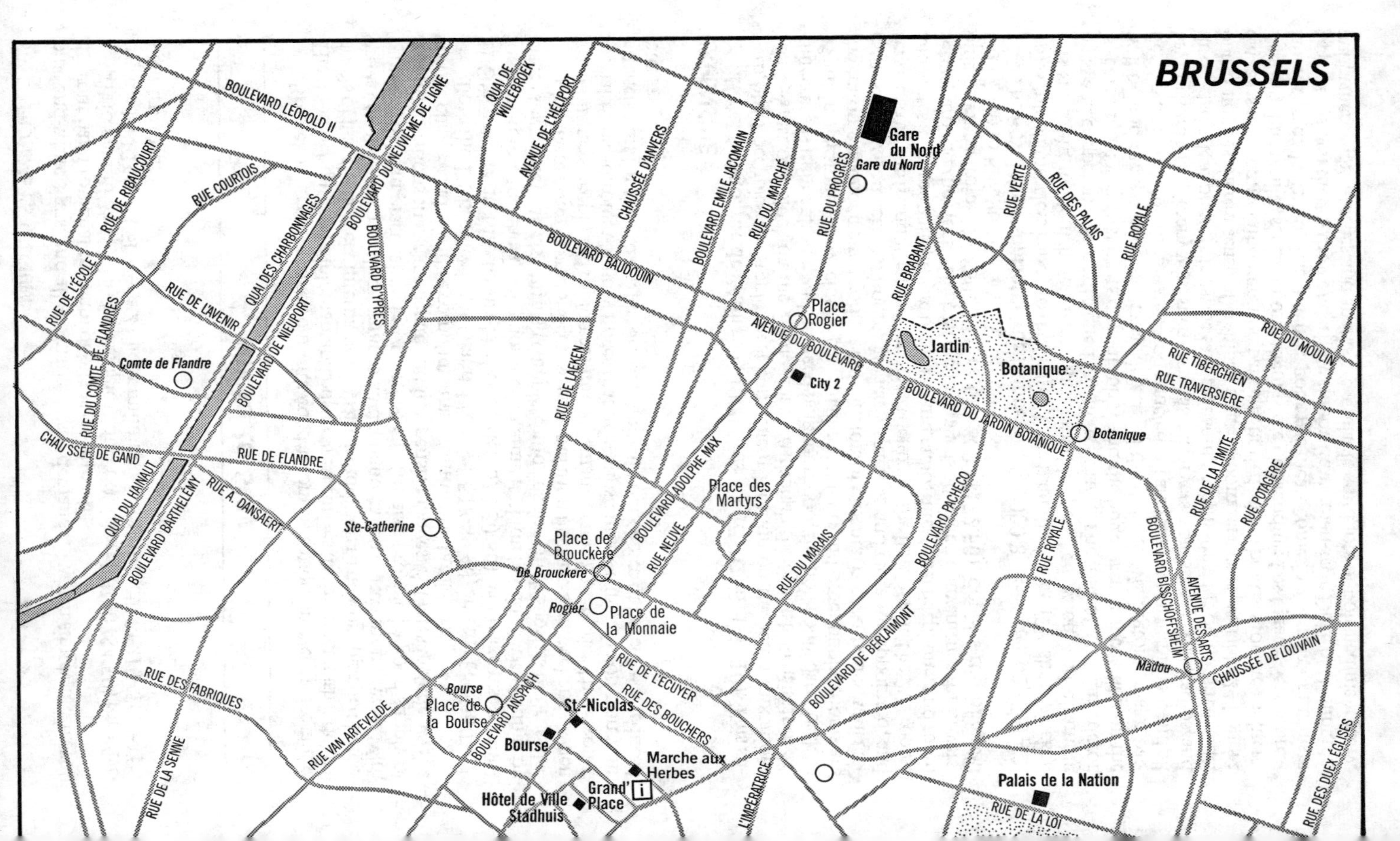

BRUSSELS
BOULEVARD LÉOPOLD II
BOULEVARD DU NEUVIÈME DE LIGNE
QUAI DE WILLEBROEK
AVENUE DE L'HÉLIPORT
CHAUSSÉE D'ANVERS
BOULEVARD EMILE JACQMAIN
RUE DU MARCHÉ
RUE DU PROGRÈS
Gare du Nord
Gare du Nord
RUE VERTE
RUE DES PALAIS
RUE ROYALE
RUE DE RIBAUCOURT
RUE COURTOIS
QUAI DES CHARBONNAGES
BOULEVARD D'YPRES
BOULEVARD BAUDOUIN
RUE BRABANT
RUE DE L'ÉCOLE
RUE DE L'AVENIR
BOULEVARD DE NIEUPORT
Place Rogier
AVENUE DU BOULEVARD
Jardin Botanique
RUE DU MOULIN
RUE TIBERGHIEN
RUE TRAVERSIERE
RUE DU COMTE DE FLANDRES
Comte de Flandre
RUE DE LAEKEN
City 2
BOULEVARD DU JARDIN BOTANIQUE
Botanique
CHAUSSÉE DE GAND
RUE DE FLANDRE
BOULEVARD ADOLPHE MAX
Place des Martyrs
RUE DE LA LIMITE
RUE POTAGÈRE
QUAI DU HAINAUT
RUE A. DANSAERT
Ste-Catherine
Place de Brouckère
De Brouckere
RUE NEUVE
RUE DU MARAIS
BOULEVARD PACHECO
RUE ROYALE
BOULEVARD BISSCHOFFSHEIM
BOULEVARD BARTHELÉMY
Rogier
Place de la Monnaie
AVENUE DES ARTS
Madou
CHAUSSÉE DE LOUVAIN
RUE DE L'ECUYER
BOULEVARD DE BERLAIMONT
RUE DES FABRIQUES
Bourse
Place de la Bourse
BOULEVARD ANSPACH
St.-Nicolas
RUE DES BOUCHERS
Bourse
RUE VAN ARTEVELDE
Marche aux Herbes
RUE DE LA SENNE
Grand' Place
Hôtel de Ville Stadhuis
L'IMPÉRATRICE
Palais de la Nation
RUE DE LA LOI
RUE DES DUEX ÉGLISES

blue-and-white signs, and all are marked "sur demande," which simply means you lift your hand to signal the tram or bus as it approaches.

Prices are BF35 ($1.15) for a single ("direct") ticket; BF140 ($4.50) for a five-trip card; BF140 ($4.50) for a 24-hour unlimited-rides card; and BF210 ($6.75) for a ten-trip card.

4. Where to Stay

Brussels is literally broken out with good accommodations in every price range. The flood of high-level diplomats and business executives has brought with it deluxe hotels of just about every international chain, in addition to new or upgraded home-grown establishments, all catering to affluent and expense-account budgets. With typically Belgian practicality, however, the city has also provided a good supply of accommodations in the moderate and inexpensive ranges. All rates include VAT, a service charge, and usually a complimentary continental breakfast.

Both the T.I.B. office in the Grand' Place (tel. 513-89-40) and the Belgian Tourist Office at rue du Marché-aux-Herbes 61 (tel. 512-30-30) will make reservations for a small fee, and the T.I.B. publishes an annual "Hotel Guide" with listings by price range. They can also furnish complete information on the hostels of Brussels.

One more note on prices: Because its population fluctuates on weekends, when many business people and diplomats are away, many of the higher-priced hotels offer special Friday-through-Sunday prices that offer substantial savings. If you plan your Brussels visit for those days, be sure to inquire if your choice of hotel has a reduced rate.

EXPENSIVE

Hôtel Amigo, rue de l'Amigo 1, 1000 Brussels (tel. 02/511-59-10). This superb hotel occupies the single most convenient location on the accommodations scene—just one block off the Grand' Place. Although the Spanish Renaissance architecture is right at home with its aged neighborhood, the hotel only dates back to 1958. Its flagstone lobby, clubby bar, small restaurant, and other public rooms are the epitome of understated good taste, with lots of Oriental rugs, antiques, wall tapestries, and wood accents. Rooms are fairly spacious and elegantly appointed, and service from the friendly, efficient staff is as deluxe as the hotel itself. The 200 rooms and suites all come with private bath, TV and radio, direct-dial telephone, and room service around the clock. The basement garage is an added convenience for drivers. Singles range from BF2,850 ($92) to BF5,350 ($172.50); doubles run BF3,650 ($117.75) to BF5,900 ($190.25).

The **Royal Windsor Hotel,** rue Duquesnoy 5, 1000 Brussels (tel. 02/511-42-15). Only slightly less handy to the Grand' Place than the Amigo (2½ short blocks), this sparkling modern hotel incorporates marble, polished wood, and gleaming brass and copper in a décor designed to suit its setting. The tone of its elegant décor is set from the very first by its elegant lobby and the huge circular medallion on the wall behind the reception desk that depicts all the duke of Wellington's major battles. Some of the 300 rooms are wood paneled, all are luxuriously furnished, and all have private baths (many with such extras as hairdryers, scales, etc.), TVs, radios, and direct-dial telephones. It must be said that some rooms are a bit on the small side, but in none is there a sense of cramped space. Room service is available 24 hours a day, as is on-premises underground parking, both decided bonuses for late-nighters. As for public facilities, star among them is the outstanding Les Quatre Seasons restaurant (see "Where to Eat"), where gourmet meals come in a setting of intimate elegance. Then there's the wonderfully clubby Edwardian-style Duke of Wellington pub, where light lunches and snacks are available amid lots of polished mahogany, etched glass, and leather upholstery. The exotic nightclub, the Crocodile Club, provides dancing into the wee hours for nightbirds. Rates are BF7,500 ($242) single, BF8,800 ($284) double, with lower weekend rates of BF4,200 ($135.50) single and BF5,000 ($161.25) double available; all include complimentary breakfast.

Hilton International Brussels, boulevard de Waterloo 38, 1000 Brussels (tel. 02/513-88-77). Located away from the city center in ultra-smart "upper Brussels," this 27-story, 365-room ode to modernity offers rooms that are the epitome of Hilton standards. They're large and beautifully furnished, with a plush, modern décor and every amenity you can think of. For those to whom money is truly no object, the Hilton offers four floors of executive rooms and suites. Some of the city's best shopping is just steps away, and both its rooftop En Plein Ciel restaurant and the elegant dining room, Maison du Boeuf, have won local acclaim. Singles are in the BF6,000 ($193.50) to BF7,500 ($242) range, with doubles priced from BF7,200 ($232.25) to BF8,700 ($280.75).

Hôtel Metropole, place de Brouckere 31, 1000 Brussels (tel. 02/217-23-00). This classic Old-World hotel dates from the late 1800s, and its splendidly ornate interior is a turn-of-the-century showcase of marble, gilt, soaring ceilings, potted palms, and lavishly decorated public rooms. What's more, it's right in the middle of the city center, with excellent shopping just out the backdoor and the Grand' Place only a few blocks away. The 410 rooms and the corridors leading to them also hark back to former days, with a spaciousness seldom encountered these days. Room furnishings are also classic, and amenities include private baths and showers, TVs, radios, and direct-dial telephones. The very elegant L'Alban Chambon restaurant, named after the original in-house architect-decorator, will delight even the most sophisticated gourmet (see "Where to Eat"), and the richly victorian Café Metropole, with its unique gas lamps and heated sidewalk terrace, is utterly charming. Both are worth a visit even if you don't elect to stay here. A recent addition is the relaxation center, which offers fitness junkies a sauna, Turkish bath, Jacuzzi, solarium, and a flotation tank. Drivers will find three public car parks in the immediate vicinity.

Rates for singles run BF3,600 ($116.25) to BF5,000 ($161.25); doubles range from BF4,200 ($135.50) to BF5,500 ($177.50); and lovely suites are available from BF7,700 ($248.50) up. All rates include service charges and complimentary breakfast.

Hyatt Regency Brussels, 250 rue Royale, 1210 Brussels (tel. 02/217-12-34). This fine luxury hotel is an ideal location for exploring both the "old Brussels" of the city center and the newer "upper city," and is adjacent to the Botanical Gardens. Décor in the public rooms is in the manner of elegant modern, featuring lots of mirrors, marble, and crystal chandeliers. The 315 guest rooms are somewhat smaller than in some other hotels of this category, but all are attractively and comfortably furnished, and all come with private baths, TVs, in-house movies, and direct-dial telephones. Hugo's, its gourmet restaurant, features French cuisine; there's Chee Nang for Chinese specialties; and Hugo's Cocktail Lounge takes care of the libations department. Indoor parking is available. Rates, excluding breakfast, are BF6,000 ($193.50) to BF6,300 ($203.25), single or double.

Hotel President, boulevard Emile-Jacqumain 180, 1210 Brussels (tel. 02/217-20-20). Adjacent to the World Trade Center and within walking distance of the northern train and bus station, the President is a recent addition to the Brussels hotel scene, and although it's a bit out from the city center, there is a convenient shuttle service (also to the airport), and the location offers a welcome quietness that can be a relief from usual city noises. Its lobby and public rooms fairly glitter with marble, mirrors, and elegant chandeliers, and there's a quite nice, moderately priced grill room, the more expensive La Maison Blanche restaurant (much favored by business people for its business lunch), and the popular President Club piano bar. All 289 guest rooms are nicely furnished in a modern décor and come with private baths (with such niceties as heated towel rails and hairdryers), TVs, in-house movies, radios, mini-bars, and direct-dial telephones. Suites are especially spacious, and the star of the place is the Presidential Suite, with its kitchen, large sitting room and dining area, two bedrooms, and a magnificent Jacuzzi in the shape of an oversize seashell. Other facilities include a fitness club with Jacuzzi, sun bed, sauna, and Ping-Pong, as well as billiards and snooker for less athletic types. Rates, which include breakfast, are BF5,600 ($180.75) single, BF6,700 ($216.25) double, BF9,100 ($293.50) to BF10,600 ($342) for suites, and BF40,000 ($1,290) for that sumptuous Presidential Suite. Lower weekend rates in the BF2,850 ($92) to BF3,600 ($116.25) range are available, and drivers will welcome the ample parking.

Arcade Stephanie, avenue Louise 91-93, 1050 Brussels (tel. 02/539-02-40). Décor at this rather small hotel (140 units) is so sleekly modern it looks for all the world as if it were designed for the 21st century. Every feature, from lobby design and fittings to furnishings in the kitchenette suites, is streamlined, functional, and representative of the very best in avant-garde planning. It's located in a pretty section of avenue Louise, one of the city's most select shopping streets. Rates, which include breakfast despite the do-it-yourself facilities, are BF4,530 ($146.25) single, BF5,490 ($177) double.

Brussels Europa Hotel, rue de la Loi 107, 1040 Brussels (tel. 02/230-13-33). Out near the European Economic Community complex, the Europa projects an English image in the décor of its rooms (not *old* English, however, but very contemporary design) and its highly respected Les Continents Restaurant. Clientele includes many European Economic Community dignitaries and visitors. Rates are BF5,300 ($171) for singles, BF6,300 ($203.25) for doubles.

The **Jolly Hotel Atlanta,** boulevard Adolphe-Max 7, 1000 Brussels (tel. 02/217-01-20). The prestigious Jolly hotel chain based in Italy has transformed this Brussels landmark into a model of modern comfort and sophisticated décor they dub "Italian modern." Its location couldn't be better for shopping, and the Grand' Place is only a few minutes' walk away. Rooms feature such extras as a mini-bar, remote-control TV, an extra telephone in the bathroom, and hairdryers. An outstanding breakfast (included in the rate) is served in the window-walled rooftop dining room overlooking the city, and the cozy lounge just off the lobby features piano music as well as light snacks. Rates for singles are BF4,900 ($158); for doubles, BF6,000 ($193.50). Children under 12 stay free in same room with their parents, and there are some very attractive reduced weekend rates.

The **Hotel Mayfair,** avenue Louise 381, 1050 Brussels (tel. 02/649-98-00). This small hotel south of the city center is tastefully decorated, and its 100 rooms are comfortable and pleasantly furnished. There's a nice bar, but no restaurant. Rates for singles or doubles begin at BF5,660 ($182.50).

MODERATE

Hôtel Arlequin, rue de la Fourché 17-19, 1000 Brussels (tel. 02/514-16-15). Among moderately priced hotels, the Arlequin takes first place on several counts. First of all, its location is in the very heart of the city, just steps away from the Grand' Place, with the restaurant-lined Petite rue des Bouchers right outside its back entrance. That entrance, incidentally, is inside a shopping arcade, but there's easy access from both the rue de la Fourché and Petite rue des Bouchers. Then there are the terrific views, many of the towering Town Hall spire (spectacular when lit at night), others overlooking rooftops and narrow medieval streets, with taller landmarks in the distance. On a personal note, I must add my compliments to the obliging staff, from whom I enjoyed nothing but friendly courtesy during my stay. Décor in the 60 guest rooms is on the plain side, with color schemes of light gray and beige; furnishings are modern and comfortable; and all rooms have private showers, color TVs, and telephones. Rates are another plus, since at this writing they are extremely moderate for such a standard and location—BF1,400 ($45.25) single, BF1,600 ($51.50) to BF2,000 ($64.25) double, and BF2,500 ($80.75) triple—although it is uncertain whether or not they will rise appreciably during the life of this edition. All rates include breakfast, service charges, and taxes. Highly recommended.

Hôtel Bedford, rue du Midi 135, 1000 Brussels (tel. 02/512-78-40). This modern hotel is an easy walk from the Grand' Place. Its public areas, which include a bar and a restaurant, are tastefully decorated, and each of the attractive 275 guest rooms has modern, comfortable furnishings. Each comes with private bath, TV, and telephone. Convenient garage parking is available. Rates are BF3,020 ($97.50) to BF3,350 ($108) for singles, BF3,760 ($121.25) to BF4,200 ($135.50) double, and include a buffet breakfast.

Hôtel Pullman Astoria, 103 rue Royale, 1000 Brussels (tel. 02/217-62-90). A reader wrote to tell me about this grand old hotel that dates from 1909, with all the belle époque and art nouveau panache of that era. My own inspection bears out that reader's raves, and I found the Corinthian columns, antique furnishings, and textured marble of its lobby quite charming, as was the ornately decorated Pullman Bar just off the lobby. Guest rooms are attractive and nicely furnished, and some are equipped for the physically handicapped. Singles go for BF3,920 ($126.50) and doubles run BF5,840 ($188.50). Rates are exclusive of breakfast.

Alfa Sablon Hôtel, rue de la Paille 2-4, 1000 Brussels (tel. 02/513-60-40). An easy walk from the place du Grand-Sablon, this hotel is ultramodern in décor and furnishings, with much use of gray and black in the color scheme. Guest rooms are quite adequate in size, with private baths, TVs, and telephones, and there's a bar. Rates, which include breakfast, range from BF4,200 ($135.50) single to BF5,500 ($177.50) double. Lower weekend rates are available.

Hôtel Albert-I, place Rogier 20, 1210 Brussels (tel. 02/217-21-25). Rooms here are rather basic, but comfortable and attractive. Each has a full bath, mini-bar, and color TV. There's a restaurant on the premises, and a buffet breakfast is included in the rates of BF1,950 ($63) to BF2,250 ($72.50) for singles, BF2,350 ($75.75) to BF2,550 ($82.25).

Hôtel Vendôme, boulevard Adolphe-Max 98, 1000 Brussels (tel. 02/218-00-70). This small hotel is one of Brussels' most conveniently located moderately priced hotels, a short walk from good shopping, slightly farther to the Grand' Place. Rooms are rather plain, but comfortably furnished, and all come with private bath, TV, and telephone. Some have mini-bars as well. A very good continental breakfast —included in the rates—is served in the cheerful, greenery-filled winter garden, with a skylight to shed natural light. Rates range from BF1,930 ($62.25) to BF2,395 ($77.50) and BF2,660 ($85.75) for doubles. Newer and larger "Business Club" rooms are available at only slightly higher rates.

Hôtel Chambord, rue de Namur 82, 1000 Brussels (tel. 02/513-41-19). Located in a posh shopping area, this 69-room hotel is under the same ownership and management as the Vendôme and offers modern comfort at moderate rates in this expensive neighborhood. Rooms are nicely appointed, and there's an attractive bar that also serves as a breakfast room. Rates, which include breakfast, start at BF2,450 ($79) for singles, BF2,850 ($92) for doubles.

Hôtel l'Agenda, rue de Florence 6-8, 1050 Brussels (tel. 02/539-00-31). This exquisite little hotel (only 38 rooms) is just steps away from avenue Louise, and its very modern rooms come with mini-bar and complete kitchen (try for the room that overlooks the inner courtyard). Breakfast is not included in the very reasonable rates of BF2,400 ($77.50) single, BF2,800 ($90.25) double.

Hôtel Alfa-Louise, rue Blanche 4, 1050 Brussels (tel. 02/537-92-10). In the "upper Brussels" district, not far from the fashionable avenue Louise, this small gem has 85 rooms, all with bright modern furnishings and some with kitchenettes. A breakfast buffet, included in the rate, is served in a pleasant and intimate dining room. Singles pay BF2,850 ($92); doubles, BF3,250 ($104.75).

La Cascade, rue de la Source 14, 1060 Brussels (tel. 02/538-88-30). Only 42 rooms in this comfortable hotel in "upper Brussels." Breakfast is included in the rates of BF2,345 ($75.75) for singles, BF2,915 ($94) for doubles.

City Garden, rue Joseph-II 59, 1040 Brussels (tel. 02/230-09-45). Situated in the business district near the European Economic Community headquarters, only four minutes by subway from the city center, this very modern hotel offers all flats, varying in size from studio to one or two bedrooms. All have complete kitchen units, and there's a coffeeshop serving breakfast, as well as a restaurant and winter garden. Rates are BF2,390 ($77) single, BF3,200 ($103.25) to BF4,500 ($145.25) double.

Hôtel Delta, chaussée de Charleroi, 1060 Brussels (tel. 02/539-01-60). A hearty English or American breakfast is included in rates at this large (253 rooms), modern hotel in "upper Brussels." Rooms are comfortably furnished and décor throughout is quite attractive. The reasonable rates are in the BF2,700 ($87) to BF3,000 ($96.75) range for singles, BF3,200 ($103.25) to BF3,500 ($113) for doubles.

Hôtel Ascot, place Loix 1, 1060 Brussels (tel. 02/538-88-35). This pleasant, 58-room hotel is located in an old quarter of the city, with comfortable, plainly furnished rooms. Rates, which include breakfast, are BF1,850 ($59.75) to BF2,000 ($64.50) single, BF2,250 ($72.50) to BF2,600 ($83.75) double.

BUDGET

La Madeleine, rue de la Montagne 22, 1000 Brussels (tel. 02/513-29-73). Situated in an area of gabled houses, the charming La Madeleine sits almost at the very edge of the Grand' Place, in the midst of art galleries and interesting small shops. Each of its 52 rooms is nicely furnished and has a private bath or shower. Seasonal rates for singles run from BF1,345 ($45) to BF1,700 ($54.75); for doubles, BF1,900 ($61.25) to BF2,400 ($77.50).

Aux Arcades, rue des Bouchers 36, 1000 Brussels (tel. 02/511-28-76 or 513-53-27). There's a bar, but no restaurant, in this 17-room hotel, which is quite understandable, since it sits on one of Brussels' most noted restaurant streets, just off the Grand' Place. The plainly furnished rooms are quite comfortable, and all have showers. Rates, which include breakfast, start at BF1,000 ($32.25) for singles, BF1,300 ($42) for doubles.

Élysée, rue de la Montagne 4, 1000 Brussels (tel. 02/511-96-82 or 512-32-46). Also very near the Grand' Place, the Élysée's 18 rooms are reached by stairs only—no elevator. Those rooms are comfortable enough, however, and you may choose between those with or without private bath. Breakfast is included in the budget rates of BF850 ($27.50) to BF1,175 ($38) for singles, BF1,060 ($34.25) to BF1,800 ($58) for doubles.

Arcade Sainte-Catherine, rue Joseph-Plateau 2, 1000 Brussels (tel. 02/513-76-20). Located in the fascinating (and central) "fish market" district, this is a large, modern member of one of Europe's leading budget-priced hotel chains. Rooms are brightly furnished, bathrooms have stall showers, and there's a children's play area. Rates, which do not include breakfast, start at BF1,750 ($56.50) for singles, BF2,000 ($64.50) for doubles.

Hôtel Résidence Sabina, rue du Nord 78, 1000 Brussels (tel. 02/218-26-37 or 218-05-54). As its name implies, this small hostelry is very like a private residence, presided over by the friendly and hospitable Renée and Jean Boulvin. A warm, homey atmosphere is reflected in the gracious living room, and although rooms vary in size, all are quite comfortable and nicely furnished. For bare-bones budgeteers, there's a small room with no shower that goes for only BF750 ($24.25), while singles and doubles with private facilities range from BF790 ($25.50) to BF1,300 ($42).

PRIVATE HOMES

Brussels has an excellent bed-and-breakfast organization, which will send you a complete list of host families, charming and very personal profiles of the families, and rates charged. They can make bookings and assist in all sorts of other arrangements. There's a small, one-time booking fee. For details, contact **The Windrose,** avenue des Quatre-Vents 9, 1810 Wemmel, Brussels (tel. 02/460-34-59).

5. Where to Eat

Brussels spreads a buffet of no fewer than 1,500 top-quality restaurants for your dining pleasure. Spend as much as $70 for dinner in one of the culinary giants or as little as $10 for one prepared with as much loving care—and often with as much expertise—in an intimate, informal "little giant." Turn to Brussels residents for advice and you'll get as many passionate raves on "the best kitchen in Brussels" as the people you ask.

Quite simply, the people of this city regard dining as a fine art and their own favorite chef as a grand master. They demand near perfection from the kitchen—and quite often they get it. In recognition of the levels within "near perfection," they grade restaurants in the city by awarding irises, the flower of Brussels, instead of traditional stars, and each year the Tourist Office issues a comprehensive dining directory entitled "Gourmet" that includes each establishment's rating. It's a very good idea to pick up a copy at the beginning of your stay in the city. A warning, however: You're very likely to discover your own "best kitchen" early on and find yourself returning to the same eatery time after time.

Whatever your choice, your meal will be cooked to order and served with aplomb, *but never with speed.* To savor the food as do the people of Brussels, be prepared for a minimum of two hours at dinner. And do make a reservation in most restaurants—that booking makes the table yours for the evening if you so choose, and you'll never be hustled out in favor of late arrivals who show up unannounced.

One more tip regarding price: With few exceptions, restaurants will include a fixed-price selection, which can save you money over à la carte prices. Beverages, however, will not be covered by the special price, so adjust your calculations according to wine, beer, or coffee additions.

The Brussels restaurant scene literally covers the entire city, but there are one or two culinary pockets you should know about. For example, it has been said that you cannot have truly visited this city if you have not dined at least once along either the **rue des Bouchers** or its offshoot, **Petite rue des Bouchers.** Huddled very near the Grand' Place, both are lined with an extraordinary array of small, ethnic (everything from French to Spanish, Italian, Greek, etc.) restaurants, most with a proudly proclaimed specialty, and all with prices that are unbelievably modest (under $10). Reservations are not usually necessary in these colorful, and often crowded, restaurants—if you cannot be seated at one, you simply stroll on to the next one that offers the cuisine your palate calls for. Food preparation in virtually every one will meet those high Brussels standards.

Then there is the **Marché aux Poissons** ("fish market") section with its cluster of small restaurants boasting truly excellent kitchens. Only a short walk from the Grand' Place, in the Sainte-Catherine area, this is where fishermen once unloaded their daily catches from a now-covered canal onto the quai au Bois-à-Bruler on one side or the quai aux Briques on the other. Seafood, as you'd expect, is the star in this particular part of Brussels' culinary firmament (to my knowledge, there is only one place that features steak), and here, too, it would be hard to find disappointment in any one of the many dining choices. Here, however, you must book ahead—a delightful afternoon's occupation is a stroll through the area to examine the bills of fare exhibited in windows and make your reservation for the evening meal (the marvelous, everyday, fruit and vegetable outdoor market in the place Ste-Catherine is also a sightseeing attraction in itself).

Warning: Many restaurants close on Sunday, so it pays to plan ahead for weekend meals.

Departing from this book's usual format, I am beginning the following restaurant listing with a few that, in my opinion (no, I'm *not* from Brussels, but it's hard to resist a "favorites" list), are very special, and their places in my affections have nothing whatsoever to do with price. They represent a wide range of location, cuisine, ambience, and price, and all have given me priceless dining experiences.

VERY SPECIAL IN ALL PRICE RANGES

Of the several expensive, internationally recognized restaurants in Brussels, **La Maison du Cygne,** rue Charles-Buls 2 (tel. 511-82-44), is perhaps the grande dame. Overlooking the Grand' Place from the second floor of one of the few private residences among those splendid guildhalls, the "House of the Swan" provides a setting that is the epitome of luxury. Polished walnut walls, bronze wall sconces, and lots of green velvet accent the stylish interior, and the caring, stylish service is as elegant as the décor. Just as this setting is a Brussels classic, so the menu sticks faithfully to haute-cuisine French classics, with never a glance at culinary trends that come and go. Mouthwatering examples are the waterzooi de homard, veal sautéed with fresh cèpes, and excellent tournedos with green peppercorns. There are also fine chicken and fish dishes, and specialties such as huftnes au champagne, goujonnette de sole mousseline, and dos d'agneau façon du Cygne. Because of its location, the Swan is usually crowded at lunchtime, and dinner reservations are somewhat more available (but book as far in advance as possible). Prices on the à la carte menu can add up to BF1,500 ($48.50) to BF2,500 ($80.75) without wine, but in my book, every dollar buys double value. Open for lunch every day but Saturday and Sunday; for dinner, every day except Sunday. Closed between Christmas and New Year's and the week of August 15.

With a setting and ambience as different from the above as it could possibly be, my highest recommendation also goes to the small, casual **Le Prevot,** rue Victor-Greyson 95 (tel. 649-14-65 or 649-94-97). A Brussels friend insisted that "in the mouth, meals here are better than the best"—and he was right. The gourmet kitchen of Marie-Gisele and Pierre Cambier has made this tile-walled former butcher shop in the Ixelles section of the city a mighty rival of even the most formidable of Brussels' world-famous restaurants. For the past 13 years they've been turning out exquisite dishes that have made regulars of diplomats, royalty (the sister of the Grand Duke of Luxembourg is an enthusiastic booster), and top business executives, who mingle happily with neighborhood residents who consider it their very own. It's a small place (just a short taxi ride from the Grand' Place), and reservations are absolutely essential. Décor is whimsical (take a trip to the unisex rest room, even if only on the pretext of washing your hands—I won't spoil the surprise, but don't miss it), but the Cambier approach to food is deadly serious. Sauces are float-away light, ingredients are the very best, and seasonings are applied with deft expertise. Try the escalope de saumon frais au basilic or the ris de veau aux champignons des bois for special taste treats, but you won't be disappointed with any selection on the surprisingly extensive menu. Prices are amazingly low: a five-course meal from the à la carte menu runs BF1,500 ($48.50) to BF2,000 ($64.50), *including wine!* Open for lunch every day except Saturday and Sunday; for dinner, every day but Sunday.

In the fish market area, Robert Van Duüren's small, casually elegant **La Sirène d'Or,** place Sainte-Catherine 1A (tel. 513-51-98), is another gem that has won my heart. Small wonder, since this outstanding chef once cooked for a very demanding Prince Albert of Liège! I love the setting here: wood-stained walls, overhead beams, velvet-seated chairs, and Belgian lace curtains at the windows. But it's the cuisine that sets this place apart. There's a lovely grilled turbot with ginger, and an absolutely magnificent bouillabaisse Grand Marius (a luscious fish concoction properly redolent of garlic). À la carte prices run BF1,200 ($38.75) to BF1,800 ($58) without wine, but there's always a special "le menu du chef" for less (around BF750, or $24.25, at lunch). Here again you must book ahead, and don't come on Sunday or Monday, when it's closed. Open for lunch and dinner other days except for the first three weeks of July, Christmas, and New Year's.

Kriekenboom Taverne-Restaurant, avenue Dolez 364 (tel. 374-30-00), is a delight, and a complete change of pace. Located in the Uccle area, it's the best example I've found of a real Brussels neighborhood center of conviviality and good eating. "Rustic" is the word for décor inside, and outside an ancient cherry tree (from which the place takes its name) presides over a garden (more properly, a lawn) with rather ordinary metal chairs and tables set about for good-weather dining. You just won't find a more cordial welcome than at this family-run establishment, and the short, inexpensive menu is little indication of the high food quality. The specialty here is steak and french fries—and what steak it is! Marvelous beef, tender and cooked exactly to your order, it comes with the potatoes and a salad at prices that start at BF450 ($14.50) and climb no higher than BF1,000 ($32.25) for a chateaubriand for two! At even lower prices, the menu also lists pork chops, fish sandwiches, and omelets, but it's the steak and the genial place itself for which you'll come. Closed on Monday; evening reservations recommended.

Despite the plethora of good restaurants around the Grand' Place, if hunger pangs attack when I'm in that area, I take myself to the rustic downstairs **'t Kelderke** ("The Cellar"), Grand' Place 15 (tel. 513-73-44). Here's where you'll find the classic *hearty* dishes of Belgian cuisine, and you'll eat in the company of Brussels' natives, who often bring the family. The friendly staff are marvelous at helping you choose from such dishes as côtes de mouton provençale (mutton chops), lapin à la bière (rabbit cooked in beer), hoche-pot (a tasty beef stew), moules (mussels) in season in eight different versions, and a large menu of other selections. Since I discovered the rabbit cooked in beer, I haven't had that problem, but eventually I hope to get through a number of other appealing dishes. Prices? Most dishes are in the BF225 ($7.25) to BF450 ($14.50) range on the à la carte menu, and even with wine or beer, your bill won't top $20. It's open every day from noon till 2 a.m., with continuous service.

Those are my personal picks—yours may be among the following.

THE TOP RESTAURANTS

Comme Chez Soi, place Rouppe 23 (tel. 512-29-21 or 512-36-74). Tiny in size (it seats only 45), this elegant restaurant is in an old town house just a short six blocks from the Grand' Place. Oil paintings and beveled mirrors set in mahogany wall panels are grace notes, and owner Pierre Wynants—one of the most revered chefs in Europe—masterminds meals that can only be called perfection. Two specialties for which he is known are chicken of Provence with a crayfish sauce ("le poussin des marchés de Provence et sa béarnaise d'écrivisses") and a luscious concoction of veal sweetbreads and kidneys in a cream sauce flavored with Ghent mustard ("la cassolette de ris de rognon de veau à la moutarde gantoise"). Prices from the à la carte menu run from BF2,500 ($80.75) up, but there's a set four-course menu for around BF1,750 ($56.50). Needless to say, you must reserve *way* in advance, and lunch, when it's often not so booked, is a good alternative to dinner. Closed Sunday and Monday and the month of July.

Barbizon, Welniekendedneef 95 (tel. 657-04-62 or 657-40-66). Gourmet seafood delights are specialties at this timbered farmhouse a short drive or taxi ride to the southeast of the city. The décor is rustic of course, and there's a small outside garden for good-weather dining. La fantaisie de coquilles Saint-Jacques poelées, salmon steamed with chervil, a lobster-based waterzooi (thick, creamy soup), and shrimp mousse are just a few of the outstanding creations on the menu. Prices are in the BF2,000 ($64.50) to BF3,000 ($96.75) range if ordered à la carte, BF1,675 ($54) to BF2,700 ($87) on the fixed-price menu. Closed Tuesday and Wednesday and one week in February. It's small, so reserve as far in advance as possible.

Villa Lorraine, avenue du Vivier-d'Oie 75 (tel. 374-31-63). Classic French dishes issue forth from one of the city's top kitchens in this renovated château on the fringes of the lovely forest park, Bois de la Cambre. Dining rooms are spacious, with wicker furnishings, flower arrangements everywhere, and a skylight to enhance the garden-like setting. In good weather you may elect to have drinks outside under the trees. Among the superb menu offerings are saddle of lamb in a delicate red wine and herb sauce, cold salmon with a herb sauce, partridge cooked with apples, and baked lobster with butter rosé. You'll pay somewhere around BF2,700 ($87) for five courses ordered à la carte, less from the set menu, and even less for both at lunch. It's closed on Sunday and for three weeks in July. Despite its size, Villa Lorraine is so popular you should book ahead.

Romeyer, chaussée de Groenendaal 109, Hoeilaart (tel. 657-10-16 or 657-17-77). Well worth the trip to this lovely old country house in the Forêt de Soignes in the suburbs, the cuisine here focuses on the marvelous, innovative creations of talented owner/chef Pierre Romeyer. Try trout fresh from streams right on the estate, or chicken sautéed with mushrooms from the forest, or oysters in champagne, or excellent game dishes in season. Best of all, choose the chef's special of the day—it's guaranteed to be outstanding. Prices will run between BF2,200 ($71) and BF2,700 ($87), and it's best to reserve. Closed Sunday evening, February, and August.

EXPENSIVE

Chez Christopher, place de la Chapelle 5 (tel. 512-68-91). Christopher Luff, son of a British NATO diplomat, and his attractive Belgian-born wife have created a real gem in this old house near the place Royale in the Sablon section of Brussels. The décor is an eclectic collection of oil paintings, mirrors, antique furnishings, and touches of whimsey that pop up unexpectedly in the semi-elegant, dark-green-walled dining room. André Gorissem is the perfect maître d': cordial, friendly, and very happy to share his extensive knowledge of food and wine. The menu is more or less French classic, with selections such as turbot and salmon in a purée of parsley and butter, duck, and Aberdeen Angus beef. Lunch costs about BF1,450 ($46.75); at dinner, four courses will run BF2,350 ($75.75) to BF2,700 ($87).

L'Ecailler du Palais Royal, rue Bodenbroek 18-20, Grand Sablon (tel. 512-87-51 or 511-99-50). Without doubt, one of Brussels' finest seafood restaurants (with the same ownership and management as the Villa Lorraine), L'Ecailler du Palais Royal *looks* like a fish house—but one with more than a touch of classic elegance. Sea-green wall tiles are quite comfortable with burnished dark-wood walls and marble-topped bar, and brass wall sconces add a finishing touch. Fish specialties range from the simplicity of traditional croquettes de crevettes (Belgian shrimp croquettes) to the subtle sophistication of raviolis de homard au curry léger (lobster with delicate curry seasonings). Dinner from the à la carte menu can run BF1,600 ($51.50) to BF2,500 ($80.75) without wine, but there's a plat du jour offering for under BF1,000 ($32.25). Closed Sunday, public holidays, and the month of August. Reservations are a must.

Bernard, rue de Namur 93 (tel. 512-88-21 or 512-68-05). This is another very good seafood restaurant, and also a local after-theater favorite. The traditional menu presents a continental cuisine, and classy late-night "snacks" might include caviar or foie gras. Dinner prices from the à la carte menu average between BF1,700 ($54.75) and BF2,200 ($71), but plat du jour prices are under BF650 ($21). Closed Monday evening and the month of July.

Bruneau, avenue Broustin 73-75 (tel. 427-69-78 or 427-47-44). This small, elegant restaurant in the Uccle area serves classic dishes built around choice ingredients available each day. Specialties include mousseline of loup de mer (sea bass served with caviar), or grilled trout with endive and pine nuts. Prices run BF2,000 ($64.50) to BF2,500 ($80.75). Closed Tuesday evening, Wednesday and Thursday, and public holidays. Reservations are essential.

Les Quatre Saisons (The Four Seasons), in the Royal Windsor Hotel, rue Duquesnoy 5 (tel. 511-42-15). This quietly elegant restaurant is done up in soft shades of pink and cream and has an air of romantic intimacy. Named the best hotel restaurant in Brussels in 1987 by a leading Belgian restaurant guide, it specializes in French cuisine under the guidance of head chef Jan Raven, who has won several prestigeous awards for his culinary expertise. Seasonal menus change four times each year, with different specialties each month. Among favorites in this popular restaurant are crépinette de pigeon (pigeon in spinach leaves), rosé de saumon au femet de seiches (salmon with squid sauce), and terrine de lotte marinée a sel marin (terrine of monkfish). At lunch, there's a menu du jour at BF900 ($29), as well as a three-course business lunch at BF1,150 ($37); dinner prices are in the BF1,600 ($51.50) to BF2,300 ($74.25) range; and there's an excellent and comprehensive wine list. Reservations are advisable. Highly recommended.

MODERATE

L'Alban Chambon Restaurant, in the Hotel Metropole, place de Brouckère 31 (tel. 217-23-00). In this wonderfully romantic Old-World dining room, you dine by candlelight, surrounded by the elegance of a world long vanished. Cuisine is chiefly French and definitely falls into the gourmet category, and service is of the pampering style. Not surprisingly, there's a very good wine list, and the venerable Mr. Wery has been voted the best sommelier in Belgium. Prices average about BF1,200 ($38.75) à la carte, and at lunch there's a plat du jour for under BF500 ($16.25). Reservations are advised for dinner. Highly recommended.

Ravenstein, rue Ravenstein 1 (tel. 512-77-68). Dining at the Ravenstein is an esthetic as well as culinary experience. This was the home of a Brussels nobleman back in the 16th century, and you'll step into an elegant cocoon that retains its Flemish character by means of copper-hooded fireplaces and lots of polished wood paneling. Just a short walk from the Grand' Place, the restaurant offers seafood and continental specialties, at prices of BF1,500 ($48.50) to BF2,000 ($64.50), with a three-course lunch for BF725 ($23.50). Open weekdays only, and closed during August.

L'Épaule de Mouton, rue des Harengs 16 (tel. 511-05-94). Just steps off the Grand' Place, this charming little restaurant is everything a Brussels bistro should be: intimate, stained-glass windows high above the entrance, oil paintings, starched white table linen, and a warm, friendly staff who take a personal interest in everyone who walks through the door. Maybe all that comes from long experience—back in 1660 a restaurant known as "The Sturgeon" opened its doors in this location, and it has never been anything other than an eatery in all the years since! Francis Mercier, the present owner, has known it all his life and now runs L'Épaule de Mouton with real dedication to traditional French cooking of the highest standards. Try such delicacies as the asperges Dominique (asparagus with a herb sauce and fresh salmon), or the delicious coquille Saint-Jacques Moitreyée (scallops cooked in court-bouillon with traces of curry and orange), or sole with spinach in a delicate white wine sauce, or any one of the marvelous lamb dishes. Among desserts, the brochette de fruits Lucifer (grilled fresh fruits, ice cream, vanilla, orange, and liquor) is outstanding, and there's a good selection of moderately priced wines available, as well as an unusual and interesting selection of Belgian cheeses. An average à la carte meal with wine will run BF1,500 ($48.50); the special menu (with wine), about BF1,300 ($42); lunch with wine, BF850 ($27.50). Reservations are essential, and it's closed Sunday and Monday.

Aux Armes de Bruxelles, rue des Bouchers 13 (tel. 511-55-98 or 511-55-94). This one is a Brussels tradition, with gracious, rather formal service, but a casual, relaxed ambience. It's an excellent place for your introduction to Belgian/French cooking, since it offers just about every regional specialty you can think of (including mussels in every conceivable guise) from a menu that will let you sample anything from their excellent beef stewed in beer to a delicious waterzooi to a steak with pepper-and-cream sauce, all at quite reasonable prices. Expect to pay between BF900 ($29) and BF1,700 ($54.75). It's closed Monday and all of June.

Chez Léon, rue des Bouchers 18 (tel. 511-14-15). This bistro on Brussels' "street of restaurants" stays busy and can be noisy, but is worth seeking out among its 80 or so neighboring eateries. Belgian specialties are featured, and prices run BF1,000 ($32.25) or so. It's open daily from noon to 10:45 p.m.

Taverne du Passage, galerie de la Reine 30 (tel. 512-37-31). Located in a glass-roofed shopping "passage," or arcade, this art deco bistro (with a side entrance on rue des Bouchers) specializes in Brussels favorites, and you'll find locals dropping in for the grilled beef or Ardennes ham (and frites, of course) until the wee hours. Top price is about BF1,250 ($40.25).

Falstaff, rue Henri-Maus (tel. 511-98-77, 511-87-89, or 511-87-88). This colorful art nouveau–style tavern and restaurant across from the Bourse in what were originally private mansions of the late 1800s is a tribute to the Shakespearean hero of *The Merry Wives of Windsor.* Huge stained-glass scenes in the style of Pieter Brueghel the Elder memorialize the Falstaff legend, and the Brueghelian style is carried out in table settings and in the period dress of waiters and waitresses. There's even a Brueghelian Menu, featuring Belgian specialties like melle Beulemans (chicken with chicory) or rabbit casserole in Gueuze. The à la carte menu is an extensive one, and if there's a Brussels dish not included, I couldn't spot it. Prices are so reasonable that this can be considered either moderate or inexpensive, depending on your appetite when you stop in. An average dinner will run between BF700 ($22.50) and BF900 ($29), but it's possible to eat for much less. Service is continuous and there's no need to reserve.

Jacques, quai aux Briques 44 (tel. 513-27-62). This small, rather plain brasserie is a favorite of at least nine out of ten Brussels residents who eat regularly in the fish market district. That's easy to understand from the minute you enter the place and savor the delicious smells from the kitchen. Seafood is the thing to order here, although three versions of steak appear on the menu. It's seafood in all its forms that draws loyal customers back time and again. The long menu lists just about every version of shellfish and fish you can imagine, and when your choice arrives at table, you can rest assured it will be at its best. Crevettes, the tiny gray shrimp of the North Sea, are excellent here, whether in croquettes or served cold with lighter-than-light mayonnaise in a ruby-red tomato, and make an excellent starter—anything that follows will live up to the same high standards. Prices run about BF830 ($26.75) for an average dinner, and there's a good list of reasonably priced wines.

Space is too limited to list *all* the good restaurants in the Marché aux Poissons, but in addition to Jacques and the superb La Sirène d'Or (see the "Very Special" listings at the beginning of this section), you can eat very well at any of the following for under BF1,250 ($40.25): **La Belle Maraichère,** place Sainte-Catherine 11A (tel. 512-97-59); **La Villette,** rue du Vieux-Marché-aux-Grains 3 (tel. 512-75-50), a real charmer and the only one in the area (as far as I could ascertain) that specializes in steak—especially in Aberdeen Angus beef—as well as seafood; **Aux Vieux Port,** quai aux Bois à Bruler 21 (tel. 218-01-02), where the owner is also a fish wholesaler; **Le Quai,** quai aux Briques 14 (tel. 512-37-36), which specializes in lobster; and **Cochon d'Or,** quai aux Bois à Bruler 15 (tel. 218-07-71).

Les Jardins de la Galerie, place du Grand-Sablon 36 (tel. 512-55-37). Located in an enclosed shopping gallery, this pretty restaurant is centered around an inner courtyard, complete with flower-bordered fountain. The food emphasis is on seafood and nouvelle cuisine dishes, and prices are quite reasonable. Lunch, including wine, will run about BF800 ($25.75); dinner (four courses and wine), BF1,250 ($40.25). A good place to begin or end a ramble through the Grand Sablon antiques flea market on Sunday.

Trente rue de la Paille, rue de la Paille 30 (tel. 512-07-15). Owner/chef André Martiny has created a lovely country look in this small, cozy restaurant right around the corner from place du Grand-Sablon. Lots of plants and flowers, and candlelight in the evening. The menu includes innovative seafood dishes as well as traditional favorites, and prices average around BF800 ($25.75) for lunch, BF1,900 ($61.25) for dinner. Closed Saturday for lunch, all day Sunday, public holidays, and the month of July. A real charmer.

Au Duc d'Arenberg, place Petit-Sablon 9 (tel. 511-14-75). This popular tavern/restaurant serves well-prepared traditional dishes that range from BF1,750 ($56.50) to BF2,250 ($72.50) in a rustic setting.

Al Piccolo Mondo, rue Jourdan 19 (tel. 538-87-94). In the trendy section of Brussels that includes posh shopping along avenue Louise, Al Piccolo Mondo dishes up Italian specialties like saltimbocca alla romana, veal cutlets milanaise, and spaghetti with a variety of sauces at prices that average BF1,000 ($32.25) for four courses and wine. It's a pretty place, with fireplaces, arches, brick walls, and oil paintings—and it's open until after midnight every night of the week.

Le Mozart, chaussée d'Alsemberg (tel. 344-08-09). There's more than a little bit of whimsey in the décor of this café and restaurant, with its kleig lights, big-band musician puppets suspended from the ceiling (along with a vintage Chevy adorned with steer's horns!), and photos of jazz greats on the ceiling. Not surprising, perhaps, since the proprietors of this lively place are Remo and Linda Gozzi, who also own the Brussels Jazz Club. Specialties in the food department are excellent steaks, chops, and seafood dishes, with prices that run about BF1,000 ($32.25) for a full meal, less for lighter fare such as salads, sandwiches, etc. As you might expect, this place attracts professional musicians, which may be the reason it's open until 3 or 4 a.m. weekdays, 5 or 6 a.m. on Friday and Saturday. Closed Sunday and Monday.

Au Stekerlapatte, rue des Prêtres (tel. 512-86-81). For hearty food in a convivial atmosphere, you can't do much better than this old brasserie in the old working-class district of Les Marolles. The rambling old building has the comfortable feel of an establishment that has picked up its bits and pieces of furnishings, mirrors, and wall paneling over the years and left them as they fell. Oilcloth-covered tables are packed virtually one against the other, and there's the rise and fall of conversation between regulars who come here for the ample servings of waterzooi, eels cooked with herbs, smoked ribs, sausages, and duck. An average dinner will run about BF775 ($25), and hours are 7 p.m. to 1 a.m. every day except Monday.

INEXPENSIVE

Le Paon, Grand' Place 35 (tel. 513-35-82). You'll dine by candlelight in this 17th-century house, where the menu features regional specialties like waterzooi, rabbit cooked in beer, and other traditional dishes. Prices are under BF700 ($22.50). Open every day.

La Maison du Cerf, Grand' Place 20 (tel. 511-47-91). This beautiful old town house that dates from the early 18th century now is home to one of the most beautiful bars in Brussels, a quiet refuge from all that colorful activity outside in the Grand' Place. Upstairs, where light meals of gourmet quality come at budget prices, an impressive fireplace, works of art, and tapestries continue a tradition of elegance. The downstairs bar is a luxurious mixture of varnished leather walls and wood paneling, paintings, and fine cordovan leather-covered chairs. Sophisticated barmen Jean Marie, Michel, and Maurice mix more than 60 cocktails, and the list of fine wines, cognacs, and rare whiskies is impressive. Open well after midnight every day.

El Greco, Grand' Place 36 (tel. 511-89-82). This happy home of singing waiters turns inexpensive dining into real fun. Moussaka and other traditional Greek dishes come at prices well below BF600 ($19.25).

Le Roy d'Espagne, on the Grand' Place, is one of the many "drop-in" inexpensive drinking establishments serving food that line the square. It's a large, rustic-style place, with wooden puppets hanging from the ceiling, puppets serving as newel posts for the center stairs, and a full-size stuffed horse right in the center of things (I never did get the story on how or why it's here—you might ask!). There's a menu consisting primarily of sandwiches (including one of smoked ham of the Ardennes), cheese, and other snacks, all priced below BF200 ($6.50). A good place for a light lunch accompanied by Belgian beer.

Le Paon Royal Taverne-Restaurant, rue du Vieux-Marché-aux-Grains 6 (tel. 513-08-68). In the fish market district, this is one of my favorite small, inexpensive cafés. Not only is the rustic wood-and-exposed-brick interior with its beamed ceiling a relaxing place to stop for one of the 65 brands of beer behind the tiny bar and a snack, but at lunchtime there's a hearty plat du jour consisting of a traditional Belgian dish that carries an amazing BF210 ($6.75) price tag. And in the little park just across the street Le Paon Royal has set out chairs under the trees, just the place to enjoy a sunny day and one of those beers. Closed Sunday and Monday.

Chopin, boulevard Adolphe-Max 70 (tel. 219-04-68). Chopin is an unexpected treat along this busy, sometimes scruffy section of a major boulevard. It's a delightful combination of pub, tea room, and restaurant that owner/manager William Van Ieghem has managed to imbue with a casual, yet semi-sophisticated ambience. Inside, lots of light wood, a marble fireplace, brass wall sconces, and flowers create an air of soothing relaxation. The small bar mixes a nice selection of classic cocktails, as well as a few house creations named for—what else?—composers like Chopin, Bach, Beethoven, Mozart, and Mendelssohn. Wines, beers, champagnes, cognacs, liqueurs, soft drinks, and fruit juices complete the beverage list, and a total of 29 blends of teas are on hand for non-alcoholic occasions. From the kitchen, you can order light meals of salads, crêpes, soups, croquettes, and full meals priced from BF250 ($8) to BF600 ($19.25). Periodically, there's live music in the classical vein. Chopin opens its doors at 9:30 a.m. and stays open until midnight or later, making this a perfect drop-in spot almost any hour of the day.

Cava Krassas, rue de la Fourché (tel. 513-71-18). The proprietor of this delightful Greek restaurant on a small street one block over from petite rue des Bouchers, is especially proud of his seafood recipes, many of which he brought with him from Greece nearly 30 years ago. Specialties like stuffed squid with fish sautéed in champagne and lobster Athenian style are very popular with his loyal local clientele, but I must confess a personal weakness for ecxochiro, a Greek country-style lamb dish made of lamb, feta cheese, and vegetables in papalette, and the lovely fricassee of lamb (or veal, if you prefer) with artichoke hearts. You can dine well for BF500 ($16.25), with lobster and a few other entrees climbing to BF1,000 ($32.25). The plat du jour is a real bargain at BF280 ($9), as is the fixed-price menu of three courses at BF395 ($12.75).

Auberge des Chapeliers, rue des Chapeliers 1-3 (tel. 513-73-38). Just steps off the Grand' Place, this 150-year-old building has been serving up bistro food for more than a quarter of a century in a setting of dark wood, exposed beams, and checkered tablecloths. Popular with locals who live and work in the area, as well as with tourists who are fortunate enough to find it, it can be chock-a-block at the height of lunch hour, so it's a good idea to come just after noon or just after 2 p.m. The menu features traditional Belgian pork, chicken, beef, and seafood dishes, and an excellent waterzooi. Servings are more than ample, and as for prices, it would be difficult to spend much more than BF500 ($16.25) for a substantial meal (although you can easily eat well for much less).

Orac Restaurant, rue des Teinturiers 17 (tel. 512-14-65). You certainly won't go away hungry from this rather plainly decorated Yugoslavian eatery within walking distance of the Grand' Place. Here huge servings of hearty home-cooked meals come in a setting of whitewashed walls adorned only with colorful woven panels from the proprietress's homeland. This venerable lady does her cooking in full view of her patrons and is many times both chef and waitress, offering helpful suggestions about the menu's offerings and the Yugoslavian wines and liqueurs on the wine list (do try the Kruskovac liqueur—luscious!). Among my favorites here are the saucisson paprika, brochettes de mouton, and Yugoslavian cheeses. Best of all, you'll seldom spend as much as BF400 ($13); there's a plat du jour for only BF200

($6.50); and as I said, you won't go away hungry. Hours are 11 a.m. to 10:30 p.m., with continuous service.

6. Things to See and Do

Brussels is a sightseer's paradise, with such an incredible variety of things to see and do that it can sometimes be overwhelming. History is encountered around every corner, there are no fewer than 74 museums dedicated to just about every special interest under the sun, impressive public buildings beckon for inspection, leafy parks and interesting squares lined with sidewalk cafés offer respite for weary feet, and there's good public transport to those attractions beyond walking distance of the compact, heart-shaped city center. That city center could, in fact, quite easily consume your entire sightseeing time, for this is where you'll find a hefty concentration of Brussels' most popular attractions.

SIGHTSEEING INFORMATION

Your very *first* stop should be at the **Tourist Information Brussels (T.I.B.)** office in the Town Hall in the Grand' Place to pick up their comprehensive guidebook and city map. The helpful guide does not confine itself to sightseeing, but is a gold mine of information on the practicalities of your stay in the city. If your stay is a short one, you may want to engage one of their multilingual guides (a full dozen languages are spoken), available at very reasonable rates, to make the best use of your time. They also publish a series of five brochures outlining special-interest walks throughout the city: footpaths in Uccle, in search of the cherubs, in search of art nouveau, typical bistros, and the European quarter. There's a small charge for each, as well as for an excellent map showing the main monuments and sightseeing attractions.

SIGHTSEEING TOURS

Coach tours, approximately three hours in duration, are available from the following: **Panorama Tours,** rue du Marché-aux-Herbes 105 (tel. 513-61-54), charges BF550 ($17.75) for its extensive coach tour; **De Boeck Sightseeing Tours,** rue de la Colline 8 (tel. 513-77-44), charges BF600 ($19.25); and the **ARAU (Workshop for Urban Research and Action),** rue Henri-Maus 37 (tel. 513-47-61 or 512-56-90), conducts Saturday-morning tours at BF400 ($13) based on original examples of art nouveau architecture, art deco architecture of the 1930s, and the squares, parks, and gardens of the city (offered on a rotating basis, with only one of the three offered each Saturday). Bookings for the first two may be made through most hotels, and arrangements can be made for hotel pickup; reservations for the last named must be made through their office, and pickup is at designated points in the city center. Tours operate from March to November, but private tours may be arranged all year.

IMPORTANT PUBLIC SPACES

These are the major physical landmarks of the city's landscape, orientation points for much of your sightseeing.

Grand' Place

The Grand' Place (the Grote Markt in Flemish) is today, as it has been since the 12th century, the very heart of Brussels. This large cobblestone square has been the stage on which Belgium's great pageant of history made joyous entrances and tragic exits. Monarchs came and went, traipsing through en route to victory or defeat. Patriots shouted rebellion, then lost their heads, in front of the Town Hall (Hôtel de Ville). From the lofty spire of that 15th-century civic building, the patron saint of Brussels, Saint Michael, keeps watch over it all as he perches above the city permanently frozen in the act of crushing the devil beneath his feet.

Your first sight of the Grand' Place will be a memorable one. In fact, I hereby challenge you to enter the square from any one of the narrow streets that converge there without an audible gasp at the pure splendor of it all. Impressive as it is by day, it's most beautiful in the golden glow of floodlights after dark. Completely enclosed by tall, gabled buildings literally dripping with ornamentation and statuary, the huge space is alive with the hubbub of daily commerce exactly as it has been from the beginning—only the nature of the commerce and the costumes of those so busily engaged have changed. Daily, there's a colorful flower market; Sunday mornings are given over to a bird market; and on weekend evenings in summer, there are frequently band concerts.

The remarkable thing is that back in 1695 only the venerable **Town Hall** (begun in 1404 and completed in 1480) was left standing after a savage 48-hour bombardment from forces of the French king, Louis XIV. Resilient Belgian cabinetmakers and carpenters, masons and stonemasons, painters and sculptors set to with a tremendous will, and in a little under four years had erected the magnificent gaggle of edifices you see today. Built to house the craft guilds that sponsored their construction, their curvy, baroque façades are very similar, yet each is distinctively individual.

Look for the neo-Gothic and misnamed **King's House** (it has been used for any number of civic purposes, but never has housed a monarch!), the repository of the municipal museum since the late 1800s. Victor Hugo spent part of his anguished exile at no. 26 ("The Pigeon"). The six connected houses at the upper end of the square are known collectively as the **House of the Dukes of Brabant,** and those noteworthies are represented by 19 busts prominently displayed at the top of the ground floor—see if you can identify by the emblems on display higher up the guilds that set up residence here (cabinetmakers, millers, masons, wine and vegetable merchants, tanners, and the "Four Crowned Crafts," a quartet consisting of stone cutters, roofers, masons, and sculptors). Be sure to save time for a visit to both the Town Hall and the Municipal Museum in the King's House (see the section below).

Place du Grand-Sablon

The place du Grand-Sablon, just off rue de la Régence, is also lined with houses of master craftsmen, and the square sports a lovely statue of the goddess Minerva, given to the city in 1751 by one Lord Bruce, Count of Ailesbury, as a token of appreciation for his hospitable reception. At the top of the square sits the flamboyantly Gothic **Notre-Dame-du-Sablon,** built by the crossbowmen of the city in the 15th century to replace an earlier chapel that was destroyed. Antiquing is especially good in this neighborhood, and on Saturday and Sunday mornings a marvelous **antique flea market** sets up shop, providing entertainment for half of Brussels' residents and a good part of her visitors.

Place du Petit-Sablon

Just across rue de la Régence, the place du Petit-Sablon is virtually a statuary garden, with figures of great 16th-century humanists at one end, some 48 bronze statuettes adorning the surrounding wrought-iron fence (symbolizing the Brussels Corporations), and statues of two of Brussels' favorite heroes, the patriotic counts of Egmont and Hornes, who were beheaded in the Grand' Place during the 16th century for actively resisting Spanish oppression.

Place Royale

The place Royale is the dividing point between rue de la Régence (which leads to the Palais de Justice) and rue Royale, and is just opposite the Royal Palace. Of interest here is **St-Jacques-sur-Coudenberg,** where there's a notable collection of sculptures.

Parc de Bruxelles

Brussels Park is bordered on one side by rue Royale, on the other by rue Ducale. At one end, across rue de la Loi, is the massive Palais de la Nation, and across the place des Palais at the other end is the Palais Royal. This beautiful park was once the private domain of the Dukes of Brabant, and in 1830 it was where Belgian patriots confronted Dutch troops in a conflict that ended in independence for their country.

The Bois de la Cambre and Forest of Soignes

Known affectionately as simply "the Bois," the Bois de la Cambre lies at the top of avenue Louise. Its centerpiece is a small lake centered by a small café. Back in the 1800s, beech trees of the huge adjoining Forêt de Soignes covered a full 30,000 acres, dwarfing its present size, even though it's still monumental by modern standards.

IMPORTANT BUILDINGS, CHURCHES, AND MONUMENTS

It's almost impossible to walk more than a block or two without bumping into a monument or building of historic importance. The following are those you won't want to miss.

Manneken Pis

At the top of almost every visitor's "must see" list is an irreverent little bronze statuette known as *Manneken Pis.* A small boy caught in an act of nature, he stands atop a fountain on rue de l'Etuve, not far from the Grand' Place. Among the speculations on his origins: that he was the son of a Brussels nobleman who became lost and was found while answering nature's call; and that sprinkling in this fashion a hated Spanish sentry who passed beneath his window was the little boy's form of rebellion.

The true story of "Little Julian" is lost in the mists of history, but there's been an effigy in his form at least since the time of Philip the Good, when it was formed of sugar. In the 17th century an ancient stone figure was replaced by a bronze replica, which suffered more than its share of tribulations, including kidnappings by both the English (in 1745) and the French (in 1747), and a theft (in 1817) that left it shattered. The pieces were carefully fitted to make the mold from which the present figure was cast.

It was Louis XV of France who began the tradition of presenting colorful costumes to Little Julian (the king was outraged by the French kidnapping and took this way to make amends). Since then, he has acquired a vast 341 wardrobe changes, now housed in the Communal Museum in the Grand' Place.

Palais du Roi

Overlooking the Parc de Bruxelles, the King's Palace was begun in 1820 and had a facelift in 1904 in the grandiose Louis XVI fashion. The older side wings date from the 18th century and are flanked by two pavilions, one of which (the one on the right) sheltered numerous notables during the 1800s as the Hôtel de Bellevue, and later became a part of the Belgian royal family residence. The mansion is now a repository for treasures of Belgian royalty and open to the public as a museum (see below).

Palais de Justice

At the foot of rue de la Régence, the Palace of Justice sits rather ironically on the spot where the city's criminals once swung from the gibbet. The massive building, built in the 1800s, holds 245 offices and consulting rooms, plus 27 courtrooms. There's no charge to visit between 9 a.m. and 3 p.m., and on Saturday and Sunday there are guided tours by request (tel. 513-28-00).

Palais de la Nation

At the rue de la Loi end of the Parc de Bruxelles, with an entrance at rue de Louvain 13, the Palace of the Nation is the seat of the Senate and Chamber of Representatives. When Parliament is in session, visitors are not allowed, but you can request a guided tour, for which there is no charge (tel. 513-38-40).

Notre-Dame-du-Sablon

At rue de la Régence 3B, this magnificent 15th- and 16th-century marvel sits at one end of place du Grand-Sablon and holds a celebrated statue of St. Hubert that was seized in Antwerp and returned to Brussels in 1348.

Notre-Dame de la Chapelle

This marvelous Romanesque-Gothic church at rue des Ursulines 4 (tel. 02/572-03-70), is interesting both historically and architecturally. François Anneessens, a Brussels hero who lost his head for civil rights, is buried here (you'll find a commemorative plaque in the Chapel of the Holy Sacrament), and the epitaph to Pieter Brueghel the Elder and his wife is also in one of the chapels. Open to visitors during July, August, and September from 10 a.m. to noon and 2 to 4 p.m. every day except Sunday, when hours are 9 a.m. to noon.

Le Cathédrale de Saint-Michel

Dating from the 13th century, this magnificent church in place Sainte-Gudule only acquired the "cathedral" title in this century (1961). Its impressive towers and stained-glass windows are worth a visit, and the historically minded will note that its crypt holds several members of royalty. It's open to visitors at no charge from 9 a.m. to 6 p.m. every day except Sunday, when you may visit from 1:30 to 5 p.m. From May to September, guided tours of the carillon are available (with a BF30, or 95¢, donation) on request Monday through Saturday (tel. 513-83-20). However, the cathedral will be undergoing reconstruction during the next few years, so at present very little of the cathedral can be seen.

La Bourse

Brussels' stock exchange (Bourse), a massive building at rue Henri-Maus 2, stands on the site that once held the Convent of the Recollets. Built in 1873, it's open to the public from 10:30 a.m. until 2:30 p.m. every weekday except public holidays. You may request a guided tour by calling 512-51-10.

Church of St. Nicholas

At the back of the Bourse, on rue au Beurre, this lovely little church is almost hidden by the fine old houses surrounding it. Traditionally the spiritual home of hopeful dancers, it holds a small painting by Rubens *(Virgin and Child)* and the beautiful *Milkmaid* by Marc Devos.

MUSEUMS

Although technically not a museum, the **Hôtel de Ville (Town Hall),** in the Grand' Place (tel. 02/512-75-54), should top any sightseer's list, not only for a fascinating glimpse into Brussels' tempestuous past, but for a firsthand look at offices of functioning aldermen and impressive chambers in which the City Council convenes. Walls are hung with marvelous tapestries that date from the 16th, 17th, and 18th centuries, and huge paintings depict many of the strong foreign leaders who have so mightily influenced the city's past. One look, for example, at the Duke of Alba's cruel features brings instant insight into the brutal oppression he imposed on Belgium. You may visit the Town Hall Tuesday through Friday from 9:30 a.m. to 5 p.m. except when there's an official reception or when the council is in session.

Musée Communal

Exhibitions in this Museum of the City of Brussels, located in the Maison du Roi (King's House) in the Grand' Place, trace the city's development both in historical and archeological relics. Porcelain and ceramic collections are especially noteworthy, as are two 15th- and 16th-century altar screens and a Pieter Brueghel the Elder painting. This is also where you'll find the fine wardrobe of the *Mannekin Pis*. Hours are 10 a.m. to 12:30 p.m. and 1:30 to 5 p.m. Monday through Friday, 10 a.m. to 1 p.m. on Saturday and Sunday.

L'Arbre d'Or (Brewery Museum)

In the beautiful Guild House of the Brewers at Grand' Place 10 (tel. 511-49-87) you'll find numerous paintings, stained-glass windows, and collections of pitchers, pint pots, and old china beer pumps. The lovely old house, with its arched cellars, is a veritable beer museum, where you can admire an authentic 18th-century brewery with its wooden fermentation and brewing vats and all the tools of the time. April through October it's open weekdays from 10 a.m. to noon and 2 to 5 p.m., and on Saturday from 10 a.m. to noon; closed Sunday. There's an admission charge of BF50 ($1.50).

Musée Royale d'Art et d'Histoire

Famed throughout the world, the Royal Museum of Art and History, Parc du Cinquantenaire 10, Etterbeek (tel. 733-96-10), holds fabulous artifact collections from the ancient Egyptian, Near Eastern, Greek, Roman, and South American civilizations. Other sections include lace, tapestry, Far Eastern furniture, toys, stained glass, ceramics, jewels, folklore, and old vehicles that include lovely 18th-century coupés, sedan chairs, sleighs, and royal coaches. There's also a very good Exhibition for the Blind set up by the Education Department. Hours are 9:30 a.m. to noon and 1:30 to 5 p.m. Tuesday through Friday, and 10 a.m. to 5 p.m. on Saturday, Sunday, and public holidays; closed Monday.

Musée de l'Hôtel de Belle-Vue

In this former royal residence at place des Palais 7 (tel. 511-44-25), salons have been restored with 18th- and 19th-century furnishings to frame memorabilia collections of lace, costumes, silver, china, hunting guns, jewelry, fans, and earthenware birds. Open from 10 a.m. to 4:45 p.m., except Friday and public holidays when it's closed. Guided tours are available for a small charge.

Musée Horta

Brussels owes its rich collection of art nouveau to Victor Horta, a resident architect who led development of the style. His home and adjoining studio at rue Américaine 25, Saint-Gilles (tel. 537-16-92), are now open as a museum and are a delight to visit. Restored to their original condition, the large, airy rooms hold prime examples of Horta's genius, and there's a marvelous stained-glass skylight. Open from 2 to 5:30 p.m. every day except Monday and public holidays for a small admission charge.

Musée d'Art Ancien

Masterpieces from the 14th to the 17th century are featured at the Museum of Ancient Art, rue de la Régence 3 (tel. 513-96-30). The Flemish Primitive section includes works by van der Weyden, Bouts, and Memling; Renaissance masters represented include Brueghel and Bosch; and Rubens and Van Dyck are prominent in the baroque collection. Open daily except Monday from 10 a.m. to noon and 1 to 5 p.m. with no admission charge, and guided tours are available by request.

Bibliothèque Royale Albert I

The Royal Albert I Library, at boulevard de l'Empereur 4 (public entrance on Mont des Arts; tel. 519-53-11), is an astounding tribute to the written word down through the centuries, with manuscripts and ancient books in the Book Museum and typographical, binding, and lithographical exhibits in the Printing Museum. Admission is free, and hours are 9 a.m. to noon and 2 to 5 p.m. every day except Sunday and public holidays. Closed the last week in August.

Royal Museum of Central Africa

At Leuvensesteenweg 13, Tervuren (tel. 767-54-01), this museum has excellent exhibits dealing with both human and natural sciences in Africa. It's free, and hours are 10 a.m. to 4:30 p.m. daily.

Musée des Enfants

This excellent children's museum at rue du Bourgmestre 15, Ixelles (tel. 640-01-07), offers hands-on experience with a wide range of everyday-life objects. Open on Wednesday, Saturday, and Sunday from 2:30 to 5 p.m.

Atomium

From the moment you arrive in Brussels, you'll be aware of this striking replica of a molecule of iron at Heysel, Laeken (tel. 478-48-66 or 478-44-38)—it's visible against the skyline from any vantage point in the city. Built for the 1958 World's Fair, it has now become a museum, with permanent exhibitions on the peaceful uses of atomic energy. Well worth a visit both for the exhibits and the panoramic views of the city (and there's also an inexpensive restaurant on the premises). Open from 9:30 a.m. to 6 p.m. every day.

Brupark

Adjacent to the Atomium, at Heysel, Laeken, this 12-acre leisure park features a **"Mini-Europe" exhibit,** with some 400 models of buildings, landscapes, roads, and railways. Admission is BF210 ($6.75), and for BF65 ($2), you can visit a re-creation of Brussels as it was in its youth as a medieval village. If water sports appeal, head for the **Oceadium Water Leisure Center,** where admission to the pools is BF250 ($8).

7. Brussels After Dark

Nightlife in Brussels runs the gamut from opera and ballet to cabaret to traditional puppet theater to jazz to discothèques to late-night bistros to an officially recognized red-light district—as highbrow or as avant garde as you choose. That is not to say, however, that it's always easy to find just what you have in mind when the sun goes down—as is true in most cosmopolitan cities, nightspots in Brussels come and go with amazing swiftness.

The listings herewith are accurate at the time of writing, but there's really no way to project just what will be on when you visit. The only sure way to know before you go in the evening is to pick up a copy of the Tourist Board's weekly publication "B.B.B. Agenda" or check the daily newspapers, and even then a telephone call before you leave your hotel will head off disappointment.

IN THE CLASSIC VEIN

Brussels' historic **Théâtre Royal de la Monnaie,** place de la Monnaie 1000 (tel. 218-12-02), founded back in the 17th century, is the home of the Opéra National and the venue of periodic performances of the Ballet Béjart. If you come in June, check to see if there are operettas scheduled.

The **Palais des Beaux-Arts,** rue Ravenstein 23 (tel. 512-50-45), is home to the Belgium National Orchestra, and concerts are also often performed at the **Cirque Royal,** rue de l'Enseignement 81 (tel. 218-20-15).

THEATER

There's usually a bit of theater activity in Brussels, with most plays performed in French (a few in Flemish). Check current schedules at the following: **Théâtre Royal du Parc,** rue de la Loi 3 (tel. 511-41-47), for contemporary drama and comedies; **Théâtre Royal des Galeries,** galeria du Roi 32 (tel. 512-04-07), the "out-of-town" opening for many plays slated for Paris theaters; **Théâtre National de Belgique,** Centre Rogier (tel. 217-03-03 or 218-58-22), in a modern high-rise; **Raffinerie du Plan K,** rue de Manchester 21 (tel. 523-18-34), for avant-garde productions in a renovated sugar factory in the industrial district; and the **Nouveau Théâtre de Quat'Sous,** rue de la Violette 28B (tel. 512-10-22), where the mood is also avant garde.

Puppet Theaters

A special word is in order about a rather special sort of theater—the wooden marionettes that have entertained Belgians for centuries. In times past, puppet theaters numbered in the hundreds around the country (Brussels alone had 15), and plays were much like our modern-day soap operas, with story lines that went on and on, sometimes for generations. Working-class audiences returned night after night to keep up with the "Dallas" of the times. Performances centered around folklore, legends, or political satire.

Specific marionette characters came to personify their home cities: in Brussels, it was a cheeky ragamuffin named Woltje (Little Walloon); Antwerp had the cross-eyed, earthy ne'er-do-well, Schele; in Ghent, Pierke was modelled on the traditional Italian clown; and Liège's Tchantchès stood only 16 inches high, and always appeared with patched trousers, a tasseled floppy hat, and his constant companion, the sharp-tongued Nanesse (Agnes).

Today a few Belgian puppet theaters still survive, and their popularity has increased in recent years after a decline following World War II, when bombing raids severely damaged many theaters and destroyed a lot of marionettes. Brussels is fortunate to have the **Théâtre Toone VII,** in the tiny alleyway, impasse Schuddeveld, just off Petite rue des Bouchers 21 (tel. 511-71-37)—look for the small wooden sign at the alley entrance. It's the last in the Toone line that began in the early 1800s, the title being passed on from one puppet master to the next (talent, not heredity, determines the line of succession). The present Toone VII is José Géal, a genius whose amazing vocal virtuosity is demonstrated nightly as he mouths an ancient Brussels dialect for every character in every performance. In 1987 the schedule included *Hamlet, Faust,* and *Carmen,* as well as many folk tales.

Toone really should not be missed—you may never have an opportunity to witness its like again, and it beats TV hands down! Don't let the dialect put you off, for the colorful and lifelike action tells the story even when you don't understand one word of dialogue (a bit like grand opera). The theater is small, an upstairs room above the rustic pub by the same name, so it's a good idea to stop in for a drink early on in your visit to see when tickets are available. The cost is only BF300 ($9.75), which also covers admission to an interesting marionette museum during the intermission. This one's highly recommended for all ages.

DINNER SHOWS AND DANCING

Musical variety takes center stage Tuesday through Saturday at **Adagio,** rue de l'Épée 26 (tel. 511-79-03).

In a risqué mood, at the dinner show in **Chez Flo,** rue au Beurre 25 (tel. 513-31-52), costumes are all feathered.

A gypsy orchestra plays Russian music at **Le Slave,** rue Scailquin 22 (tel. 217-66-56).

And there's dinner and dancing every night but Sunday at **En Plein Ciel** in the Hilton Hotel, boulevard de Waterloo 38 (tel. 513-88-77), and **Hugo's Restaurant** in the Hyatt Regency, rue Royale 250 (tel. 215-46-40).

There's marvelous Hungarian and gypsy music into the wee hours at **Le Huchier,** place du Grand-Sablon (tel. 512-27-11), where you can also order light snacks along with your libations.

JAZZ

The **Brussels Jazz Club,** Grand' Place 13 (tel. 512-40-93), is a long-standing mecca for outstanding jazz performers, and you'll find a headliner scheduled most nights. Call early for reservations and be prepared to pay a cover charge and high prices for drinks.

In addition there are a dozen or so small taverns and bistros where jazz is played in a much more intimate fashion (and unless you're nightclub oriented, it's lots more fun!). Just such a neighborhood spot is **Pops Hall,** rue Lincoln 53 (tel. 345-95-81) in the Uccle district. The small corner bistro is owned by a jazz musician who often takes the stand himself. Since music is not scheduled every night, best call ahead to see if it's on—although this place is so much fun I'd recommend an evening there even without the music. Prices are as small as Pops Hall itself, and they cover an enormous amount of nighttime entertainment, whether it be music or just lively conversation.

At last count, no fewer than 26 cafés and restaurants were advertising periodic jazz sessions, so it will pay you to check with the Tourist Board and local newspapers during your visit.

DISCOTHÈQUES

Unless things have changed since my visit to research this book, these discothèques are in full swing, but best check "B.B.B. Agenda" or the daily newspapers before you go: **Scrupules,** Grand' Place 16 (tel. 513-72-76); **Golden Gate,** galerie Louise 98 (tel. 511-20-48), which is closed on Tuesday; and the splendid **Crocodile Club** in the Royal Windsor Hotel, rue Duquesnoy 7 (tel. 511-42-15), which is closed Sunday.

BISTROS

A favorite Brussels night out is one spent in one of the small bistros where drinking and conversation fill the entertainment bill. A few that are typical are: **'t Spinnekopke,** place du Jardin-aux-Fleurs 1 (tel. 511-86-95), in an 18th-century house; **À l'Image de Notre-Dame,** Impasse, rue du Marché-aux-Herbes 6 (tel. 218-19-74); **Cirio,** rue de la Bourse 18 (tel. 512-13-95), worth a visit for the décor; and **Toone VII,** Impasse Schuddeveld, Petite rue des Bouchers 21 (tel. 511-71-37), home of the puppet theater and an artistic hangout.

A bistro of rather special character, much loved by locals, is **À la Mort Subite** (which translates to "sudden death"), rue Montagne-aux-Herbes-Potagères 7 (tel. 513-13-18). That strange name stems from an ancient "double or nothing" game once played here. The place is now in its third generation of ownership by the same family, and it is famous for its wide variety of Belgian beers: gueuze (which takes some getting used to), faro, kriek (cherry), framboise (raspberry), cassis (black currant), and on and on. They also offer a great tartine beurre, a long slice of homemade bread slathered with butter—goes down well with the beer. Always crowded, À la Mort Subite is a friendly place to meet and mingle with Belgians of all ages and stations in life.

In a different vein, **La Fleur en Pâpier Doré,** rue des Alexiens 55 (tel. 511-16-59), located in a 16th-century house, has been a bistro and pub since 1846, and from the beginning it has been a mecca for poets and writers. Even now, about once a month young Brussels poets gather there informally for poetry readings—the date varies, but you might inquire by phone, or better yet, just drop by and ask in person. This is a wonderfully atmospheric old pub, much like a social club, where patrons gather for good conversation and welcome any and all newcomers. They also serve what is possibly the best onion soup in Brussels, a great late-night snack.

OTHER BITS AND PIECES

The Tourist Board can furnish a list of gay and lesbian bars, cabaret shows featuring nudism or female impersonators, and red-light districts.

8. Shopping

Brussels is not the place to come in search of bargains—on the whole it's rather expensive—but it is the place to look for those Belgian specialties that are either unavailable or even more expensive elsewhere. What to look for? Lace, of both antique and recent manufacture; leather goods; and edibles like chocolates (some of the world's best), pralines, and the thin, spicy biscuits called speculoos.

Shopping hours are generally 10 a.m. to 6 p.m. Monday through Saturday, and you'll find many stores observing the same hours on Sunday. Department stores stay open later on Friday, until 8 or 9 p.m.

Note: An excellent magazine devoted almost entirely to Belgian shopping, *Belgian Promenade,* is published by the Chamber of Commerce for Art, Quality Goods, and Services. You may find a free copy in your hotel room—if not, look for it at newsstands.

MAIN SHOPPING CENTERS

Primary shopping streets are: **avenue Louise,** for luxury boutiques; **galeries Saint-Hubert,** for quality goods; **rue Neuve,** a pedestrian shopping mall, with department stores and a wide variety of shops; **boulevard Adolphe-Max,** with many quality shops; **galeries de la Monnai; Anspach Center;** and the **galerie du Sablon** and surrounding area, for antiques.

STREET MARKETS

The colorful street markets that are a Brussels tradition can many times yield up bargain buys, and always provide good people-watching. For a complete list of times and places, consult the Tourist Office. Here are a few that are worthy of special note: for antiques and secondhand goods, the **place du Grand-Sablon,** every Saturday and Sunday; the **flower market** every day in the Grand' Place and the Sunday-morning **bird market** (for sightseeing mostly—impractical, of course, for travelers); for a fabulous array of clothing, exotic foods, and a little bit of everything from around the world, the daily **flea market** around the Gare du Midi; the Friday-morning **horse market** at the place de la Duchesse de Brabant, Molenbeek, is the place to see some first-class street trading.

A FEW SPECIAL RECOMMENDATIONS

Here's a short list of very personal, subjective recommendations that don't even come close to being a complete list of Brussels' best shopping. From past experience, however, they provide a little something extra in the way of shopping ambience, as well as value for the dollar.

Books

For the best and most comprehensive selection of English-language books, go to **W. H. Smith & Son,** boulevard Adolf-Max 71-75 (tel. 219-50-34 or 219-27-08).

Food and Wines

In the food and drink department, my first "don't miss" is a small shop in the fish market area, **De Boe,** rue de Flandre 36 (tel. 511-13-73). It's a place of heavenly smells (they roast and blend coffee beans), a fantastic selection of wines that cover the price range from $5 to $500 (an excellent place to pick up wines for hotel-room consumption or to carry home), and a marvelous array of specialty crackers, nuts, spices, teas, and gourmet snacks, many of which come in tins that make them suitable to bring back home. Best of all, Mr. and Mrs. De Boe and their daughter are in attendance, graciously tending the business begun more than 90 years ago by Mr. De Boe's grandfather.

For candies to take home or mouthwatering rolls, breads, pastries, and cakes for on-the-spot consumption, go by **Wittamer,** place du Grand-Sablon 12-13 (tel. 512-37-42). They've been turning out sinfully indulgent goodies since 1910, and I absolutely defy you to walk out empty-handed.

Dandoy, rue au Beurre 31, is a tiny little shop where buying crisp butter cookies, molded gingerbread cakes, or cinnamon cookies becomes a very special Brussels shopping treat, and whether you carry them home or yield to the temptation of instant munching, they're an extraordinary taste treat.

Lace

Among the many lace shops in Brussels, I especially like the **Maison Antoine Old Brussels Lace Shop,** Grand' Place 26, and **Rose's Lace boutique,** rue des Brasseurs 1 (a tiny street just off the Grand' Place). Both offer wide selections and a good price range.

Leather Goods

Some of the most beautiful handmade leather items to be found in all of Europe come from **Delvaux,** rue de l'Empereur 7. The quality and beauty of each piece make it a good buy, even if expensive.

Sculpture

Gallery Dieleman, Sablon Shopping Gardens, place du Grand-Sablon 36, is a wonderland of exquisite bronze sculptures that range in size from pieces small enough to carry in a handbag to massive works of art that would demand a special setting. They carry only signed originals, and each comes with a folder that has information on its creator and a photo and description of the piece. Any one of the large selection would make a lasting travel souvenir that could only appreciate in value.

9. Around the Brussels Area

The lovely Brabant countryside around Brussels is one of scenic beauty, as well as one dotted with sightseeing attractions well worth the short trip.

THE CASTLE OF BEERSEL

Only 5½ miles to the south of the city, a little off the Mons road (watch for the signpost), the only example of a fortified medieval castle still intact is at Beersel. Set in a wooded domain and surrounded by a moat, the three-towered 13th-century, castle is reached by way of a drawbridge, and its interior sends the imagination spinning back to those long-ago turbulent years when narrow arrow slits were the only windows. Pick up the excellent English-language guidebook at the entrance for a detailed history of the castle and its inhabitants, then wander through its rooms for a trip back through time. End your visit with a stop at the magnificent mausoleum that holds the recumbent alabaster effigies of Henry II of Witthem and his wife, Jacqueline de Glimes, who lived here during the early 1400s. Visiting hours can vary, so it would be best to check with the T.T.B., Grand' Place, when you're on the spot.

Leafy pathways through the grounds invite leisurely walks, and this is a favorite rural retreat for Brussels residents, especially during the summer months. At the entrance to the park, you'll find the charming **Auberge Kasteel Beersel,** Lotstraat 65, 1650 Beersel (tel. 376-26-47), a rustic restaurant with décor of dark wood, exposed brick, and accents of copper and brass. In good weather there's service on the shaded outside terrace. Light meals (omelets, salads, soups, sandwiches, etc.) are available, as well as complete hot meals for both lunch and dinner, and prices are in the moderate range. Booking is not usually necessary, and you're very welcome to stop in just for a relaxing draft of Belgian beer, but it's closed on Thursday.

GAASBEEK

The ancestral château of the counts of Egmont is at Gaasbeek, some eight miles from Brussels out the Mons highway. Its furnishings are nothing less than magnificent, as is the castle itself. All the rooms are splendid, and far from presenting a dead "museum" appearance, they create an eerie impression that the counts and their families may still be in residence and will come walking through the door any moment. Before each guided tour, there's a slide show that will increase your appreciation for the countless works of art, silver items, religious artifacts, and priceless tapestries.

WATERLOO

European history—indeed, the history of the entire world—was changed by the fierce conflict that took place on the battlefield at Waterloo in 1815 when Napoleon Bonaparte met defeat at the hands of England's duke of Wellington. Today it has reverted to a landscape of peaceful, rolling farmland broken by the high memorial mound La Butte du Lion (Lion's Mount). Anyone with a sense of history and an average imagination, however, will people the fields with charging armies and fill the air with the cries of battle. The 100-yard-high mound, with a bronze lion at the summit, was built through the efforts of Belgian housewives, who brought earth by the bucketful to place on the spot where Holland's prince of Orange was wounded in the battle. Some 226 steps lead to its top, where there's an observation platform. A building at the foot of the mount houses *Panorama,* a 360° painting of the battle. Nearby is an old inn, now the **Wellington Museum** (open every day year round except Christmas and New Year's Days from 10 a.m. to noon and 2 to 7 p.m.), in which the duke of Wellington headquartered the night before the battle was joined. Napoleon's headquarters, on the Charleroi road, is named the Musée du Caillou and is open every day except Monday from 10:30 a.m. to 8 p.m. April through October, 3:30 to 7 p.m. in other months.

Plan your Waterloo pilgrimage around lunch or dinner and book at **La Maison du Seigneur,** chaussée de Tervuren, 1410 Waterloo (tel. 02/354-07-50). It's a 17th-century Brabantine farm serving gourmet French cuisine. Expect to pay BF1,300 ($42) and up.

MECHELEN

Situated on the De Dije River and the Leuven Canal, Mechelen is just ten miles from Brussels and the same distance from Antwerp—a perfect stop when traveling between those two cities on the E10 motorway. It's a city that wears its long history well (the Gauls and Romans were here as early as 500 B.C.), and its medieval town square evokes the late 1400s and 1500s, when this was a religious, cultural, and artistic center of Europe.

The **Tourist Office,** located in the Town Hall, offers four conducted tours, including one to **St. Rombold's Cathedral** and a climb to see its famous carillon—at noon, you can hear a brief recital of the bells ringing out over the city. The **Royal**

Carillon School here is the most famous in Europe and possibly in the world, attracting students from around the globe. Visit the **City Museum,** which includes a carillon section, as well as classic and modern paintings and sculpture. In **Tivoli Park** there's a Children's Farm, as well as a Bee-Keeping Museum inside the castle. Children (of all ages) will love the fairytale **Toy Museum,** at Nekkerspoelstraat 21. The **Grote Markt** reverts to its original purpose on Saturday mornings, when a street market is held just as in medieval times.

Mechelen has been an important center of tapestry weaving since medieval times, and Belgium's magnificent tapestry presented to the United Nations headquarters in New York was woven here. There's a **Tapestry Museum,** and two tapestry "factories" are still in operation. It's sometimes possible to visit one or the other; inquire at the Tourist Office for arrangements.

For an excellent lunch or dinner in Mechelen, book into the **Julden Anker,** Brusselsesteenweg 2 (tel. 42-25-35), in the hotel of the same name. The expensive **Pekton,** Van Beethovenstraat 1 (tel. 41-35-35), also serves a gourmet menu—in the home of Beethoven's grandparents. For a casual, inexpensive meal, try **Taverne Keizershof,** Grote Markt 28, where there's sidewalk café service as well as a glassed-in dining room overlooking the square.

VI

ANTWERP

Antwerp owes its life to the River Scheldt, its soul to the artist Rubens, and its name to a giant of ancient days called Druon Antigon. Legend says that Druon levied exorbitant tolls on every Scheldt boatman who passed his castle, and if anyone would not or could not pay up, the big man gleefully cut off his hand and threw it into the river. Druon's comeuppance, however, came in the form of a Roman centurion named Silvius Brabo, who slew the cruel giant and promptly cut off *his* hand and threw it into the river, thus avenging the poor, wronged boatmen. The Flemish "hand-werpen" ("throwing of the hand") eventually became Antwerpen, the city's Flemish name.

Of course, historians who deal only in dry, dull facts tell a different story. They hold that seamen on ships sailing up that broad pathway to the sea bringing the commerce of the world to the city's wharves described its location as "aan-de-werpen" ("on the wharves"). But, then, what do historians know? To the people who live here, the severed, bleeding "Red Hand of Antwerp" is the very symbol of their city. Today you'll find two statues in the town commemorating the brave Roman's act of revenge, and replicas of the giant's hand appear in everything from chocolate to brass.

But when you come right down to it, if there were no River Scheldt, there would be no Antwerp by any name. It is the natural, deep-water harbor that first made it a Gallo-Roman port in the 2nd century B.C. and over the centuries attracted a bevy of covetous invaders.

As for Rubens, that great master is only one of the several artists who left their baroque mark on the face of this city and a great love of beauty in the hearts of its inhabitants. You'll see that love expressed in their buildings and in works of art publicly displayed and in the contents of some 20 museums. It is, in fact, in one of the world's most beautiful objects—the diamond—that Antwerp has found its most prestigious industry. It is acknowledged internationally as the "Diamond Center of the World," leading all others as a market for cut diamonds and lagging behind only London as an outlet for raw and industrial diamonds.

1. By Way of Background

From the beginning of Antwerp's recorded history in the 7th century until the 14th century, the city and its port suffered invasion by the Norse, followed by a parade of rulers that included the Salic Franks of Germany, the dukes of Brabant, the counts of Flanders, the dukes of Burgundy, and in the 1500s, the Habsburgs, whose Charles V brought welcome prosperity. Antwerp outstripped its rival, Bruges, an important port on the River Zwinn; set up a commercial exchange that was a model for the Royal Exchange in London; and attracted a slew of banking princes who brought their counting houses with them.

By the late 1500s it was thoroughly Protestant and the headquarters of William the Silent. That religious persuasion brought down upon its head the wrath of the duke of Alba during his sweep through the Low Countries to quell the revolt against Philip II of Spain. In November of 1576 his soldiers slaughtered some 8,000 Antwerp citizens and destroyed 1,000 buildings in a single night.

Thus conquered and occupied by Catholic Spain, Antwerp was fair game for the victorious Protestant Dutch to the north, whose territory held the Scheldt's estuary. In a cruel act of retribution against Catholic rule in Antwerp, they closed the river in 1648, cutting off Antwerp from the sea and ushering in a full two centuries of economic decline, although it continued to be a commercial center and a rising cultural force as Peter Paul Rubens and Anthony van Dyck came to the fore. It wasn't until the French Revolutionary Convention reopened the Scheldt in 1795 and Napoleon built a naval depot in 1800 as a base for operations against the English that Antwerp's port again came into its own. Then, in 1815, it came under Dutch rule once more when Belgium was ceded to the Netherlands by treaty.

With the coming of Belgian independence in 1830, the Dutch held onto Antwerp until 1832, and from then until the 1860s they continued to exact a toll on ships sailing through the Dutch stretch of the Scheldt to reach Antwerp. Free navigation on the river brought with it a rapid expansion of the port, and since then Antwerp has never looked back, although it suffered in both World Wars I and II and was even the target of German V-1 and V-2 rocket attacks long after the city had been liberated by Allied troops in World War II.

Today it's one of the major European gateways, with its port relocated some eight miles downstream from the city proper. Its thriving diamond-cutting industry includes 4 of the world's 18 diamond exchanges, growing petrochemical and banking industries add new luster to its commercial enterprise, and with it all, Antwerp protects and cherishes its cultural heritage.

2. Orientation

Antwerp is a good walking city, with its major sightseeing attractions easily reached from one major street that changes its name as it goes along.

The Central Rail Station serves as a focal point. When you're standing in front of the station, the large square opposite you is Koningin Astridplein; to the east is the 25-acre Dierentuin zoological gardens, and to your left is Pelikaanstraat, a major diamond center street. De Keyserlei runs toward the river and joins the Meir, Antwerp's main shopping street that leads into the Schoenmarkt, a short street that curves around the 24-story Torengebouw to reach a large square known as the Groenplaats, where there's a statue of Rubens and the Cathedral of Our Lady. One short block beyond the Groenplaats (toward the river) puts you right into the large Grote Markt (Market Square), bordered by its Renaissance Town Hall and 16th-century Guild Houses. This is also where you'll find one of those statues of the Roman soldier Brabo. Follow the quaint little street named Suikerrui (it means "sugar quay") right down to the river, where you'll see the medieval fortified castle, Steen, that now houses the Maritime Museum.

3. Useful Information

The **Tourist Office,** Grote Markt 15 (tel. 03/232-01-03), is open from 8:30 a.m. to 6 p.m. weekdays and 9 a.m. to 5 p.m. on Saturday, Sunday, and holidays. A smaller **Inquiry Office** is at Koningin Astridplein facing the Central Station (tel. 03/233-05-70), open from 8:30 a.m. to 8 p.m. weekdays, 9 a.m. to 7 p.m. on Saturday, and 9 a.m. to 5 p.m. on Sunday and holidays.

Trams are the best way to get around the city, and at the Central Station you can buy a one-day toeristenkaart for BF100 ($3.25) that allows unlimited rides on both trams and buses. The most useful tourist line is the one that runs all the way from the cathedral to the Central Station. There's also a long-distance bus from the Sabena Airline office in De Keyserlei to Brussels airport. The number to call for **taxis** is 232-79-00.

4. Where to Stay

There are good hotels right in the city, and rates are a little lower than those in Brussels. However, many of the top hotels are on the city's outskirts in pleasing settings of greenery and peace and quiet. *A word of warning* to budget travelers: The "Tourist Rooms" that usually mean accommodation bargains in private homes are something rather different in Antwerp—it's a discreet way of advertising very personal services that have nothing to do with a room for the night.

The Tourist Office has a free, same-day reservation service—you make a BF200 ($6.50) deposit, which is then deducted from your hotel bill. They also publish a booklet listing all Antwerp accommodations and rates.

The rates quoted below include a continental breakfast and **VAT.**

EXPENSIVE

The **Pullman-Park Hotel,** Desguinlei 94, 2018 Antwerp (tel. 03/216-48-00). This ultramodern luxury hotel gives you the best of Antwerp's two worlds—the scenic beauty of the park in which it is set, with the city's attractions about five minutes away. Each of the 218 rooms is superbly furnished and equipped with TV and video, radio, mini-bar, and direct-dial telephone. In addition to a gourmet restaurant, there's a lovely outdoor terrace on which meals are served. Other amenities include a fitness club and sauna, a piano bar, and a disco. Rates are BF2,900 ($93.50) single, BF5,400 ($174.25) double, unless you take advantage of special weekend packages with huge rate reductions. Children 12 years and under stay free in the same room with their parents.

De Keyser Hotel, De Keyserlei 66-70, 2018 Antwerp (tel. 03/234-01-35). Just one block from the Central Station, this seven-story, modern hotel boasts a striking marble lobby and rooms that are nicely furnished, and each has TV and video, radio, and direct-dial telephone. There's good parking nearby, important for drivers who want to stay in the city. Also, one-day laundry and dry cleaning are available. A good restaurant and popular bar complete the amenities. Rates run BF4,180 ($134.75) single and BF5,340 ($172.25) double, and special weekend rates are available.

Quality Inn, Luitenant Lippenslaan 66, 2220 Antwerp (tel. 03/235-91-91), is located on the outskirts of town, just off the ring express motorway. Rooms are modern and functional, meeting the usual standards of this chain. Rates are in the BF3,300 ($106.50) to BF4,100 ($132.25) range.

MODERATE

Novotel, Luithagen-haven 6, 2030 Antwerp (tel. 03/542-03-20). Also a little out from the city, this modern hotel is set in garden-like landscaped grounds, and has bright, well-furnished rooms, good parking, a garden terrace, restaurant, a golf practice range, three tennis courts, and a heated swimming pool. Rates range from BF2,450 ($79) to BF3,600 ($116.25), with discounts for U.S. Army personnel and IAPA members. Special weekend rates are also offered.

Empire Hotel, Appelmansstraat 31, 2018 Antwerp (tel. 03/231-47-55). In the heart of the diamond quarter, not far from the Central Station, this modern hotel equips each room with a kitchenette, as well as TV, radio, and direct-dial telephone. There's garage parking nearby, as well as good shopping, theaters, and restaurants. Singles cost BF2,900 ($93.50); doubles, BF4,500 ($145.25). Ask about lower weekend rates.

Theater Hotel, Arenbergstraat 30, 2000 Antwerp (tel. 03/231-17-20). Kitchenettes also come with the rooms here, and the location is convenient to the Rubens House and the theater district. Furnishings are modern and attractive, and include TV, radio, and direct-dial telephone. No restaurant, but there are several nearby, and there's parking at the hotel. Rates are in the BF2,900 ($93.50) to BF4,120 ($133) range. Weekend package rates are available.

Congress Hotel, Plantin en Moretuslei 136, 2018 Antwerp (tel. 03/235-30-00). This modern hotel, with a good restaurant and attractive bar, is a bit out from the city center, not far from a major express motorway. Furnishings are quite nice, and include TV, video, radio, mini-bar, and direct-dial telephone in each room. Parking is free at the hotel. Rates run BF2,480 ($80) to BF2,860 ($92.25), and include a buffet breakfast. Weekends come cheaper if you ask for the special rate.

INEXPENSIVE

Antwerp Docks, Noorderlaan 100, 2030 Antwerp (tel. 03/541-18-50). This comfortable, 83-room hotel is in the dock area, as you'd expect, but standards are quite satisfactory, and it has long been patronized by officers of ships coming into the port of Antwerp. Rooms with private bath are BF2,500 ($80.75); those without cost BF1,000 ($32.25).

The **Rubenshof,** Amerikalei 115, Antwerp (tel. 03/237-07-89). Near the Royal Fine Arts Museum, this small hotel has only 13 rooms, 7 of which have private baths. Plain, comfortable rooms here will run BF1,000 ($32.25) to BF1,500 ($48.50).

Tourist Hotel, Pelikaanstraat 22, 2018 Antwerp (tel. 03/232-58-70). Train travelers will find this reliable hotel's location just beside the Central Station quite convenient. Rooms are not fancy, but quite adequate and comfortable, and most have private bath or shower. Rates are in the BF1,400-($45.25)-and-under range.

Hostel-type accommodations (no hostel membership card required) are available for BF395 ($12.75) to BF750 ($24.25) at the **Boomerang,** Volkstraat 58, Antwerp (tel. 03/238-47-82); the **Square Sleep-Inn,** Bolivarplaats 1, 2000 Antwerp (tel. 03/237-37-48); and the **New International Youth Pension** (no age limit), Provinciestraat 256, 2018 Antwerp (tel. 03/230-05-22).

5. Where to Eat

With something like 300 restaurants scattered around the city, you can opt for a casual, inexpensive lunch and elegant, gourmet—and costly—dining at night; pubby eating for pennies all the way; moderate prices for all meals; or any mixture of the choices that appeals. The Tourist Office has a handy restaurant booklet that lists most eateries in town, shows prices, and has an ethnic-foods breakdown.

What follows is, it goes without saying, the merest of mere sampling of Antwerp's restaurant offerings. Rest assured that wherever you find yourself when assailed by hunger pangs, there will be good food at hand, and best of all, your waiter or waitress will serve it with a smile and the traditional Flemish "Smakelijk!" ("Enjoy your food!"). And it's a safe bet that you will.

EXPENSIVE

Sir Anthony van Dijck, Oude Koornmarkt Vlaeykensgang 16 (tel. 231-61-70). In a charming Renaissance setting (practically beneath the cathedral tower) that reflects the best of Antwerp's "good living" flair, the Sir Anthony van Dijck provides exquisite, lightly sauced meals in complete harmony with the tapestries, oil paintings, and overhead beams with which they are surrounded. Seafoods are outstanding, and the goose liver is not to be missed. Prices are high—BF1,800 ($58) and up for a full dinner without wine—but you can eat for less from the à la carte menu if you choose with care. My best advice here, however, is to "go for broke"—it's an experience that doesn't come along every day! Open for lunch and dinner, and advance booking is a must.

La Pérouse, Ponton Steen, Steenplein (tel. 232-35-28). Moored at the foot of the Suikkerui, this is a floating restaurant that from June to September abandons its fine cuisine to take on full-time sightseeing voyages. If you get here any other month, however, try not to miss a marvelous, authentically Belgian lunch or dinner on the Scheldt. The waterzooi de poussin is a prime example of how this thick, creamy stew should be prepared. A full dinner without wine will cost about BF1,900 ($61.25). Closed Sunday and Monday.

't Vermoeid Model, Lijnwaadmarkt 2 (tel. 233-52-61). This rustic Flemish restaurant is a delight, both esthetically and gastronomically. Built right into the walls of the cathedral, it specializes in seafoods, with smoked trout a local favorite. Dinner here will run around BF1,800 ($58) and up, and well worth it! It's open seven days a week.

MODERATE

De Peerdestal, Wijngaardstraat 8 (tel. 231-95-03). In this large, rustic restaurant near the cathedral, you can enjoy a light meal of omelets, salads, stuffed tomato, and the like, or indulge in heartier fare such as fish or steak. Despite its size, there's something almost cozy about the place, and patrons are so much "at home" that you frequently see them reading newspapers as they eat at the long bar. The extensive à la carte menu carries prices in the BF200 ($6.50) to BF500 ($16.25) range, with a few fish selections rising as high as BF700 ($22.50). Open every day except Sunday from noon to 11 p.m.

Au Gourmet sans Chiqué, Vestingstraat 3 (tel. 232-90-02). This charming little bistro is just a stone's throw from the diamond district, and its kitchen has made a specialty of whole small roast chicken on the spit. To go with it, however, you can choose from such starters as trout or Ardennes pâté, have apple sauce and salad with the charcoal-browned chicken, and end with one of their luscious desserts. For all this on a set menu (without wine), you'll pay BF850 ($27.50) à la carte, a meal can run between BF650 ($21) and BF1,000 ($32.25). Trout and scampi are also available, but not specialties. Closed Saturday at lunch and all day Friday.

De Manie, H. Conscienceplein 3 (tel. 232-64-38). This bright, modern restaurant comes up with such originals as an appetizer of quail salad with goat cheese and artichoke, and baked goose liver with bilberries and honey, as well as innovative main dishes—filet of salmon with saffron sauce and grilled wood pigeon with gratinéed Brussels sprouts are typical of menu specialties, which change every six months. The food is excellent, and the setting is exceptionally relaxing. There's a set four-course lunch at BF900 ($29) including wine, and à la carte dinner selections will run around BF1,100 ($35.50) without wine.

Rooden Hoed, Oude Koornmarkt 25 (tel. 233-28-44). Another of the good eateries near the cathedral, this pleasant, rather old-fashioned restaurant with a rustic décor serves good, hearty food at very moderate prices. Mussels, sausages (which come with sauerkraut and mashed potatoes in a delicious "choucroute d'Alsace"), waterzooi, and fish star on the menu, and prices run about BF800 ($25.75) for a full meal. Closed Wednesday and Thursday, and from mid-June to mid-July.

V.I.P. Diners, Lange Nieuwstraat 95 (tel. 233-13-17). Seafood, lamb, and traditional dishes are featured in this old quarter restaurant. Coquille St-Jacques at BF450 ($14.50), and saddle of lamb at BF700 ($22.50), are typical of the à la carte prices. A full meal will cost BF995 ($32) to BF1,200 ($38.75).

Pottenbrug, Minderbroedersrui 38 (tel. 231-51-47). There's a casual, relaxed atmosphere in this place that goes with the sand on the floor and the stove in full view. The menu is mainly traditional Flemish dishes, with French additions. Typical prices are BF480 ($15.50) for steak, BF450 ($14.50) for leg of lamb, and BF500 ($16.25) for fish.

In de Schaduw van de Kathedraal, Handschoenmarkt 17-21 (tel. 232-40-14). Traditional Belgian cuisine gussied up a bit is featured in this attractive restaurant. Mussels and eel are featured in several guises, and pork, chicken, and beef are well represented on the menu, with prices in the BF475 ($15.25) to BF635 ($20.50) range.

Panaché, Statiestraat 17 (tel. 232-69-05). You pass through a sandwich, snack, delicatessan ("charcuterie") section to reach the large, busy restaurant here. The menu is as large as the place itself, so you can let your appetite of the moment steer you through such widely diversified choices as spaghetti, chicken croquettes, veal, chicken, steaks . . . well, if your appetite calls for it, you're sure to find it! Your bill can run as low as BF400 ($13). It's open until late seven days a week, except August.

INEXPENSIVE

't Hofke, Oude Koornmarkt Vlanikensgang 16 (tel. 233-88-30). For inexpensive, but tasty, food in a heart-winning setting, my vote goes to this cozy little eatery. To reach it, go down the very same small alleyway that leads to the pricey Sir Anthony van Dijck—'t Hofke is just across the way from that elegant restaurant. Inside, to the strains of classical music, you can order a complete breakfast (eggs, bacon, toast, and coffee) for BF145 ($4.75), plus sandwiches, omelets, spaghetti, or whatever owners Lester and Ingrid Benoit are featuring for the day. Top price on their menu is BF300 ($9.75), and there's no charge at all for the charm of the place.

For the most control over your food costs, go to Panaché (see above) and make your selections from the long counter that includes sandwiches, herring, cheese, pastries, and a host of other goodies, all with low price tags, that can be combined to make up a satisfying, inexpensive meal.

For rock-bottom eating, consult the long lists of snackbars, pizza parlors, waffle and pancake houses, and tea rooms in all sections of Antwerp that appear in the restaurant guide published by the Tourist Office.

6. Things to See and Do

Antwerp's sightseeing treasures are best seen at a leisurely pace—after all, who would want to gallop through Rubens' home at a fast clip? But if time is a factor or if you'd like a good overview before striking out on your own, the city makes it easy by providing guides for walking tours, regularly scheduled coach tours, and a series of boat trips to view Antwerp from the water, as so many of her visitors have first seen her down through the centuries.

If, on the other hand, you're a dedicated do-it-yourselfer, the Tourist Office has maps and sightseeing booklets to guide you through this rich treasure house. Walking trails have been marked within the city that will lead you through typical streets and squares to find the main points of interest. There's even a free ferryboat ride across the Scheldt if you decide against one of the boat excursions.

SIGHTSEEING TOURS

The Tourist Office can arrange for a highly qualified guide to accompany you on **walking tours** around the city at a set rate of BF800 ($25.75) for the first two hours, BF400 ($13) for each additional hour.

The Flandria boat line offers two **cruise** options. There's a 50-minute excursion on the river, with half-hourly departures during summer months, at a cost of BF300 ($9.75), and an extensive trip around the harbor that lasts 2½ hours and costs BF400 ($13). For departure points (most leave from the Steen) and exact sailing schedules, contact Flandria Boat Excursions, Steenplein (tel. 233-74-22).

ADMISSION FEES

Many of Antwerp's museums and churches are open to the public at no charge, and where there is an entrance fee, it's minimal.

THE MAIN SIGHTS

One of the nicest things about Antwerp is that you'll bump into many of its most interesting sightseeing attractions in the course of moving about the city—and a good many of them are still in daily use by the people who live here. In sightseeing as in so much else, Antwerp has such an overabundance of attractions that it's possible to list only highlights in our limited space. Best hie yourself off to the Tourist Office and peruse their excellent brochures before making judicious judgments on how to compose your own list of "must sees."

The Grote Markt

This large square, while not nearly so glittering as Brussels' Grand' Place, is no less the center of much everyday activity. In its center is a huge fountain showing Brabo in the act of throwing Druon's severed hand into the Scheldt, a tribute to the triumph of right over might. The Renaissance **Stadhuis (Town Hall)** was built in the mid-1500s, burned out by the Spanish in 1576, and rebuilt as you see it now. Look for the frescoes by Leys, an important 19th-century painter, some interesting murals, and in the burgomaster's room, an impressive 16th-century fireplace. Except during official receptions, it's open from 9 a.m. to noon on Monday, 9 a.m. to 3 p.m. Tuesday through Thursday, and noon to 3 p.m. on Friday and Saturday. Admission, which includes a guided tour, is BF20 (65¢).

Around the square and in the surrounding streets you'll see excellent examples of 16th-century Guild Houses. One worth a visit is the **Vleeshuis (Butcher's Hall),** Vleeshouwersstraat 38-40, a short walk from the Stadhuis. A magnificent Gothic structure, it now functions as a museum of archeology, ceramics, arms, religious art, sculpture, musical instruments, coins, and medieval furnishings. The collections give a good general idea of the daily life in Antwerp during the 16th century, as do the historical paintings (look for the striking *The Spanish Fury,* picturing Antwerp's darkest hour). There's also an Egyptian section. Open from 10 a.m. to 5 p.m.; closed Monday and major holidays. Admission is BF50 ($1.50) for adults; BF20 (65¢) for children 12 to 18, unemployed persons, students, and pensioners; and free for children under 12, soldiers, and inhabitants of Antwerp.

Steen Castle

Always referred to simply as "The Steen," Steenplein 1 (tel. 232-08-50), this medieval fortress dates from the 10th century and is Antwerp's oldest building. Built on the banks of the River Scheldt (at Steenplein), it has served a number of purposes over the centuries, and today it houses the **National Maritime Museum.** There's an extensive library on river navigation and almost every nautical subject, as well as interesting exhibits about the development of the port and maritime history in general. The most eye-catching of all are models of oldtime sailing ships, in particular, East India Company clippers. Hours are 10 a.m. to 5 p.m. daily except major holidays.

Next to the museum there's an interesting industrial archeological division with the remains of the old Antwerp port. Open Easter to November 1.

Cathedral of Our Lady

You'll want to see this towering Gothic edifice at Handschorn Markt for several reasons. Its architecture is simply stunning—there are seven naves and 125 pillars! —and it's the largest church in both Belgium and Holland. Begun in 1352, the cathedral's original design included five towers, but only one was completed. Its history includes devastation by religious iconoclasts, deconsecration in 1794 that resulted in the removal of its Rubens masterpieces, and slow rebirth beginning after Napoleon's defeat in 1815. Today, three Rubens masterpieces to be viewed with awe in this reverent setting are *Elevation of the Cross,* his *Deposition,* and *Assumption.* Rombouts' *Last Supper,* an impressive stained-glass window dating from 1503, is also outstanding. The cathedral is open from noon to 5 p.m. weekdays, noon to 4 p.m. on Saturday, and 1 to 4 p.m. on Sunday and holidays from April to mid-October, with shorter hours in other months. Admission is BF30 ($1).

St. James's Church (St. Jacobskerk)

This flamboyant Gothic church at Lange Nieuwstraat 73 with its baroque interior is the final resting place of Peter Paul Rubens, Antwerp's most illustrious resident from the world of art. Several of his works are here, as well as some by van Dyck and other prominent artists. There's also a glittering collection of gold and silver and religious objects. It's open from 2 to 5 p.m. from Easter through October every day except Sunday and bank holidays, and admission is BF30 ($1).

Rubens House

Peter Paul Rubens, whose father was an Antwerp attorney who went into exile in Germany and died there, was brought back to this city at an early age by his mother. By the time he was 32 his place as a star in Europe's artistic firmament was firmly established, and his effect on the city was profound. In 1610, when he was only 33, his great wealth enabled him to build this impressive home and studio at Wapper 9-11 along what was once a canal, the Wapper (it's about midway down the Meir). Today you can wander through its rooms, with the décor and furnishings of Rubens' time, and come away with a pretty good idea of the lifestyle of patrician Flemish gentlemen of that era. More than that, there are examples of his work scattered throughout, as well as others by master painters who were his contemporaries. In the dining room, look for his self-portrait, painted when he was 47 years old. Rubens was a lover and collector of Roman sculpture, and some of the pieces in his sculpture gallery appear, reproduced in amazing detail, in his paintings. The house is open every day from 10 a.m. to 5 p.m., and a visit is pretty much essential if you are to fully appreciate most of what you'll see elsewhere in Antwerp.

Royal Museum of Fine Arts

Housed in this impressive neoclassic building on Leopold de Waelplaats is a collection of paintings by Flemish masters that is second to none in the world. To see them, pass through the ground-floor exhibitions of more modern artists' canvases and ascend to the second floor, where you'll find more Rubens masterpieces in one place than in any other one place. They're in good company—Jan van Eyck, Rogier van der Weyden, Dirck Bouts, Hans Memling, Pieter Brueghel the Elder and his sons, Rembrandt, and Hals are all represented. All told, these walls hold paintings that span five centuries. To view them is a moving experience, and one that Antwerp presents to visitors as a gift—there's no admission charge. Hours are 10 a.m. to 5 p.m. every day except Monday and major holidays.

Plantin-Moretus Museum

From this stately patrician mansion at Vrijdagmarkt 22, Christoffle Plantin established a printing workshop in the late 1500s whose output set print and publishing standards that have had widespread influence on the world at large. Here, for example, was published the world's first atlas and the first newspaper. An astonishing multilanguage (Hebrew, Greek, Syrian, Latin, and Aramaic) edition of the Bible and translations of great works of literature came from these presses. Plantin's name survives in today's publishing world as a widely used typeface. His grandson, Balthasar Moretus, was a contemporary and close friend of Rubens, who painted the family portraits you'll see displayed here and illustrated many of the books published by the Plantin-Moretus workshop. Open from 10 a.m. to 5 p.m. daily except major holidays.

Antwerp Port

Although it has now been shifted to Zandvliet some eight miles downstream from the city proper, Antwerp's port is the very reason for its existence, and is well worth a visit if only to appreciate its vast size. There are no less than 95 km—60 miles!—of quays, and the entire harbor/dock complex covers 40 square miles. The Flandria boat cruises and coach tours (see above) offer the best view for tourists, but the Tourist Office can furnish detailed information for those who wish to drive the plainly marked "Havenroute" (if this includes you, keep a sharp eye out for hazards of this busy workplace—open bridges, rail tracks, moving cranes, etc.).

Antwerp Zoo

This amazing 25-acre zoo is just east of Antwerp's Central Station at Koningin Astridplein 26. Its large collection of animals from around the world roam freely through spaces that are restricted for the most part by artificial reproductions of natural barriers; for example, bright lights instead of closed cage doors keep the aviary bird population at home. There's also an aquarium, winter garden, Egyptian temple, anthropoid house, museum of natural history, and a planetarium. For nature lovers, this is truly a standout among Antwerp's treasures! Admission is BF260 ($8.50), and daily hours are 8:30 a.m. to 6:30 p.m. during summer months, until 5 p.m. during the winter.

ABOUT DIAMONDS

If anyone knows for certain exactly when Antwerp began to develop as an important facet of the diamond industry, he isn't talking. It probably began so gradually that no one at the time took note of what was happening. That's a state of affairs that has not, however, existed for a long, long time, and today the city is acknowledged to be the world's leading diamond center. Some 70% of the world's diamonds are traded here annually—valued at more than $6 billion!

More than 12,000 expert cutters and polishers are at work here, and it's fascinating to watch as undistinguished stones are transformed into gems of glittering beauty. To take a firsthand look at the whole process, you have only to go by **Diamondland,** Appelmanstraat 33A (tel. 234-36-12), between the hours of 9 a.m. and 6 p.m. Monday through Saturday. Located just a few steps from the Central Station, this luxurious showplace provides a guided tour of its workrooms, and if you should fall under the sparkling spell of the finished product, you'll be able to take home a souvenir of lasting value for a price tag considerably lower than you'd pay elsewhere.

Of course, diamonds have always held mere mortals in thrall with their ageless beauty, and the **Provincial Diamond Museum,** Lange Herentalsestraat 31-33, is the place to view exhibits that trace their history, as well as their journey from mine to m'lady's finger or throat or crown. Hours are 10 a.m. to 5 p.m. every day except Monday and major holidays; no admission fee.

7. After Dark

Culture in this culture-rich city does not end at museum doorsteps, nor is it confined to "culture" in a stuffy sense—Antwerp is as lively after dark as it is busy during daylight hours. Be your tastes purely classical or more attuned to lighter amusements of more recent vintage, you'll find entertainment aplenty. To check on what's doing while you're in the city, pick up a copy of *Antwerpen,* a monthly publication available at the Tourist Office.

Main entertainment areas are around the Grote Markt and along De Keyserlei, both of which contain concentrations of bars, cafés, and theaters.

NIGHTLIFE, HIGH- AND LOWBROW

Antwerp's **KVO (Royal Flemish Opera)** company is a segment of the Opera of Flanders; there are frequent performances by the **Flanders Ballet;** symphony concerts are held at **Queen Elisabeth Concert Hall** at Koningin Astridplein, and two theater companies **(Jeugdtheater** and **KNS, the Royal Flemish Theater)** stage periodic productions. There are ten theaters to accommodate all this activity, and you should be aware that plays will be presented in Dutch or the Flemish dialect. The same is true of puppet performances in **Vancampens Puppet Theater,** Lange Nieuwstraat (call 651-99-11 for schedules). More often than not, however, you'll be able to follow the plot line, regardless of language difficulties, and the quality of the shows merits attendance.

In a lighter vein, Antwerp may well lead all of Belgium in the number of **movie theaters** and foreign films shown. All movies are shown in their original languages, with Dutch and French subtitles, and you'll find most of the theaters along De Keyserlei and its side streets. As for the films, they might be anything from the latest award winner to porn—Antwerp is sophisticated enough to take each at face value.

In this same area there's a conglomeration of **disco** and strip bars, some very high class, others (obvious at a glance) frankly low class or vulgar. If you're looking for a respectable disco, check the area between the Groenplaats and the Grote Markt.

ANTWERP'S FAVORITE AFTER-DARK ACTIVITY

When the sun goes down, the people who live here head for their favorite café or bar for an evening of Belgian beer and good conversation—and you'll be very welcome to join their circle, in whichever locale suits your fancy. All are relaxed and friendly, and if you miss an evening so occupied, it's safe to say that you haven't really seen Antwerp! These are just a few among the hundreds of pubs you might enjoy: **Groote Witte Arend** (Great White Eagle), on Reyndersstraat; **Pelgrom,** on Pelgrinsstraat; **Engel,** in the Grote Markt; and **Elfde Gebod,** on Torfbrug.

Then there's the sumptuous **Kulminator,** Vleminckveld 32 (tel. 232-45-38), which displays a huge selection of beers behind glass. Virtually every Belgian beer made is on hand, and it's a mecca for beer lovers. Open only 5 p.m. to 1 a.m. on Saturday and Monday, 11 a.m. to 1 a.m. weekdays; closed Sunday.

IN FLANDERS' FIELDS

1. BRUGGE (BRUGES)
2. GENT (GHENT)
3. IEPER (YPRES)

Everyday life in medieval Europe is as vivid as the images on today's television screen when you walk the streets of Brugge or Gent—not medieval Europe *restored,* but medieval Europe *preserved.* Ieper (pronounce it "Ee-per") has another story to tell: having suffered centuries of intermittent warfare and almost total destruction during World War I, it has picked itself up in the years since and restored its legacies from a colorful past. In these three towns of Flanders the spirit of the Flemish people becomes a tangible substance, walking by your side, looking over your shoulder, whispering in your ear, "This is how it was; this is how we lived; this is what has made us what we are today."

Outside the towns, the famous fields of Flanders, immortalized in the famed World War I poem, along the alluvial plains of the River Scheldt are actually polders, much like those in Holland, which consist of land reclaimed after disastrous floods that began a few centuries before the birth of Christ and occurred time and time again right up to the 10th century A.D. Extending some six to ten miles inland from the sea, the polders create a landscape of rich farmland crisscrossed by canals and ditches lined with poplars and fields dotted with solitary farmhouses surrounded by their outbuildings. In medieval times these were the large land holdings of feudal lords and wealthy abbeys, and few have been broken into smaller plots in the intervening years—farm boundaries today remain much as they were then.

It is the enduring Flemish spirit that farms those fields of Flanders and walks the streets of this region's towns and villages and that inspired Flemish poet Emile Verhaeren to write:

> I am a son of this race
> With their heads
> More solid
> More passionate,
> More voracious
> Than their teeth.

It is a spirit that has prevailed through centuries of armed conflict, commercial strife, and religious controversy.

Always a buffer between warring political factions, the region nevertheless went about the business of providing a ready market for England's wool, which its weavers transformed into the Flemish cloth so highly prized in Europe and much of the medieval world—it's the cloth you see draping the figures depicted in the great paintings of the Middle Ages. In the process Brugge's River Zwinn's access to the sea made it the busiest port in northern Europe, and the cloth mills of Gent set an industrial pattern still obvious today.

When the Zwinn inexplicably dried up, its disappearing waters took with them a prosperity that had seemed destined to last forever. But it was to Brugge that Catholic priests and nuns fled for safety during the religious persecutions of the late 1500s. Their housing quarters and places of refuge are there to this day, and when Brugge's perfectly preserved medieval beauty was brought to the attention of the rest of the world in this century, it became a mecca for tourists anxious to touch the past.

Gent fought one ruler after another, with mixed results, always holding onto a fierce sense of the working man's independence that has brought it into modern-day industrial importance in a setting that quite happily blends reminders of the past with commercial requirements of today. And Ieper suffered through sieges and open warfare that left it impoverished, but with its indomitable spirit intact, a spirit that shines in the perseverance underlying its incredible 20th-century rebuilding of 13th-century buildings.

Each of these three towns is easily visited on day trips from Brussels, and for drivers it's a compact circular travel route. Despite their proximity to the capital city, however, it's highly probable you'll lose your heart to either Brugge or Gent and hanker for a longer visit (Ieper is an ideal half-day visit from either). For that reason, accommodation recommendations are included in the sections of this chapter, as well as those for some of Belgium's finest restaurants.

1. Brugge (Bruges)

Surely one of the most romantic towns in Europe, Brugge is a fairytale mixture of gabled houses, meandering canals, narrow cobblestone streets, a busy market square, and a populace intent on providing a gracious and warm welcome to its visitors. It's a place that would melt a heart of even the hardest stone, and a visit—no matter how brief—is guaranteed to generate a glow you'll carry away as an impenetrable shield against the slings and arrows of our own outrageous "civilization."

ORIENTATION

The heart of Brugge is encircled by a broad ring canal that opens at its southern end to become the **Lac d'Amour** (Lake of Love). In your mind's eye, see the lake as the busy port of the Middle Ages, before the demise of the Zwinn, and save time for at least one walk through the green park along its shores. To one side of the lake is the **railway station,** and very near is the largest of several underground car parks at 't Zand (if you're driving, stash your car here and forget it—not only is this walking territory, but driving the narrow streets can be murder!). If you arrive by train, taxis are available to get you to your hotel if you plan an overnight stay; otherwise, it's a short walk into the heart of the old city.

The **Grote Markt** (Market Square) is, as it was in the beginning, the heart of the heart and the focal point of your sightseeing. Major points of interest are no more than five or ten minutes' walk away, and the very efficient **Tourist Office** is at Burg 11 (tel. 050/33-07-11).

WHERE TO STAY

If a high-rise, luxury hotel is your cup of tea, then my best advice is that you stay in Brussels and commute to Brugge. But if the idea of a small, atmospheric hostelry (perhaps right on the banks of a picturesque canal) that has modern (if not luxurious) facilities, appeals, then you'll find that accommodations here will actually

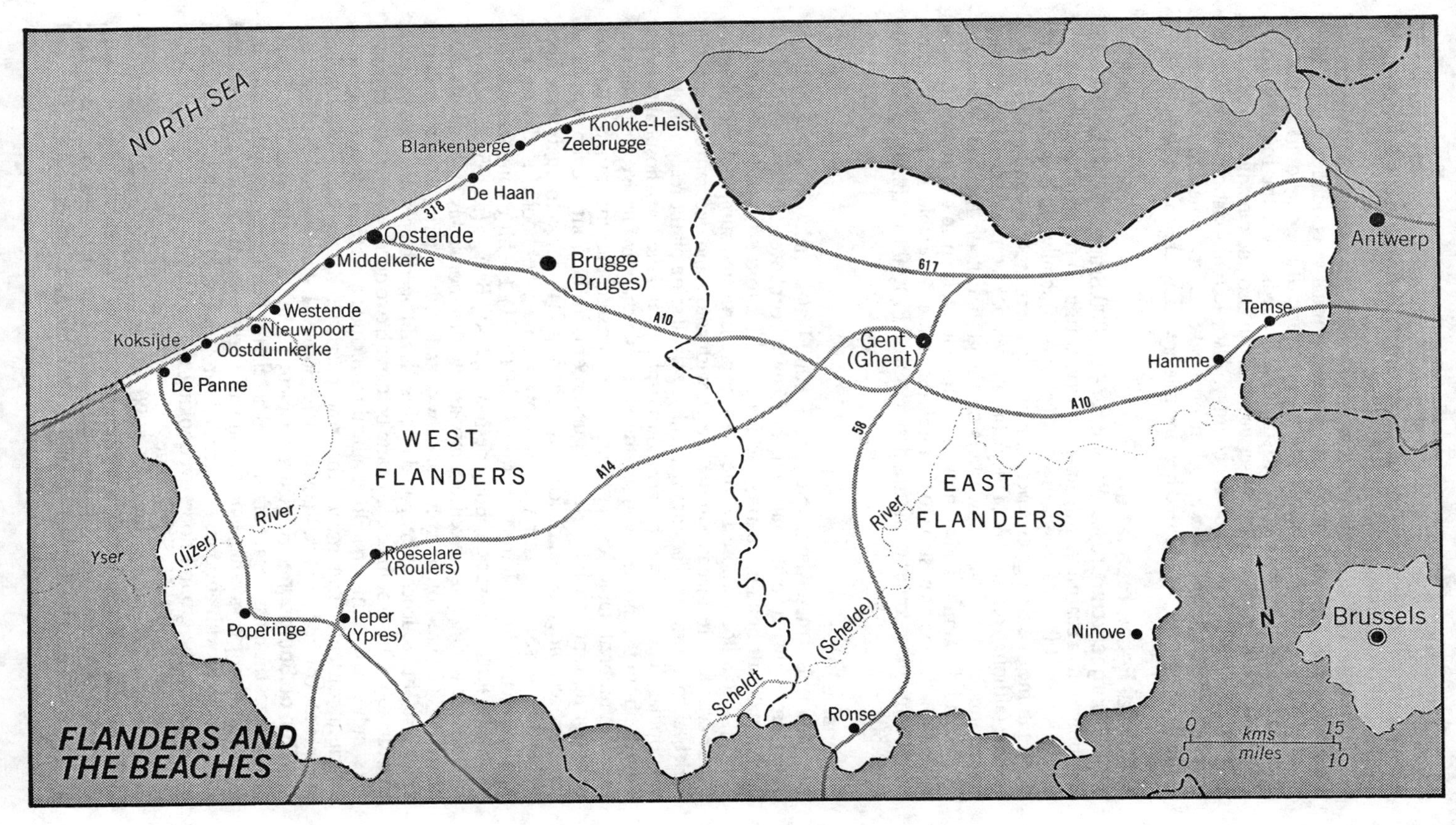
FLANDERS AND THE BEACHES
NORTH SEA
Knokke-Heist
Zeebrugge
Blankenberge
De Haan
318
Oostende
Middelkerke
Brugge
(Bruges)
Westende
Nieuwpoort
Koksijde
Oostduinkerke
De Panne
A10
617
Antwerp
Temse
Hamme
Gent
(Ghent)
A10
58
A14
WEST
FLANDERS
EAST
FLANDERS
River
(Ijzer)
Yser
River
(Schelde)
Scheldt
Roeselare
(Roulers)
Poperinge
Ieper
(Ypres)
Ronse
Ninove
Brussels
N
0
kms
15
0
miles
10

enhance your visit by giving you an opportunity to sink into the timelessness of Brugge rather than taking only a surface look.

Having said that, let me add that you *should not arrive without a reservation!* Brugge is one of Belgium's premier tourist cities, and it's a good idea to make reservations at least two weeks before you plan to come. If by some quirk of fate you come into town and have no place to stay, head immediately to the Tourist Office—they have a very good reservation service, and can also book in advance for you, as can tourist offices throughout the country. Also, accommodations are much less heavily booked during the week than on weekends, so come Monday through Thursday if you can. Rates listed here include breakfast, service, and VAT.

A Special Recommendation

't Bourgoensche Cruyce, Wollestraat 41, 8000 Brugge (tel. 050/33-79-26). Opening onto a charming little inner courtyard right in the middle of things (the Belfry is just 100 yards away), this tiny (six rooms) family-run hotel provides the very epitome of a Brugge experience. Not only are the rooms comfortable and attractive (although certainly not fancy), but all overlook a canal. Also, one of the best restaurants in town is just downstairs on the ground floor. Mr. and Mrs. Roger Traen head the family, and along with their children keep an expert eye on everything from the rooms upstairs to the meals that come to the table. It's hard to believe that rooms here come at the modest rates of BF1,400 ($45.25) to BF2,000 ($64.50).

Expensive

Oud Huis Amsterdam, Spiegeirei 3, 8000 Brugge (tel. 050/34-18-10). The Traen family, owners of 't Bourgoensche Cruyce (see above), have transformed this large canalfront building, parts of which date back to the 1300s (most from the 1500s), into a hotel whose 17 guest rooms are large and sumptuously furnished (some even feature a Jacuzzi in the bath!), with colors and decorative accents that hark back to its origins. The entrance hall, the small salon off the reception area, and the popular "The Meeting" bar are all atmospheric, and the Traen hospitality reigns supreme from the moment you register. There's a charming little courtyard at the rear with umbrella tables and a garden just to one side, the setting for Sunday concerts during June and July. Elegant guest rooms in the front overlook the canal; those in back, the garden and picturesque rooftops. From May through September, an 1800s horse-drawn carriage transports those who book for dinner at 't Bourgoensche Cruyce. Rates start at BF3,750 ($121). Highly recommended.

Hotel Pullman Brugge, Boeveriestraat 2, 8000 Brugge (tel. 050/34-09-71). In a unique setting (a 17th-century monastery) this thoroughly up-to-date hotel is located at 't Zand, not far from the railway station. Its interior is pretty standard "modern," but touches like exposed brick walls and open fireplaces soften the effect considerably. Guest rooms are large and light, with two queen-size beds, telephones, TVs, radios, and mini-bars. Other amenities include a heated indoor pool, sauna, solarium, garden, restaurant, and the atmospheric Jan Breydel bar. Drivers will appreciate the covered car park. Rates run BF3,500 ($113) to BF4,500 ($145.25).

Duc de Bourgogne, Huidenvettersplein 12, 8000 Brugge (tel. 050/33-20-38). Perhaps the most elegant of the small hotels, the Duc de Bourgogne is in a 15th-century building on a canal. Guest rooms are fairly large and luxuriously furnished and decorated, with antiques scattered all through the hotel. There's a very good restaurant on the ground floor, overlooking the canal. Rates are in the BF2,750 ($88.75) to BF4,500 ($145.25) range.

De Snippe, Nieuwe Gentweg 53, 8000 Brugges (tel. 050/33-70-70). Set in an early-18th-century building and long known as one of Brugges' leading restaurants, De Snippe also offers seven truly luxurious rooms. Many of the spacious rooms have fireplaces, and all have furnishings of restrained elegance. Rates begin at BF3,500 ($113).

Moderate

Pandhotel, Pandreitje 16, 8000 Brugge (tel. 050/34-10-64). This lovely old town house is right in the center of town, and its exquisite, old-fashioned furnishings (but modern conveniences) lend a special grace to the comfortable rooms. Rates range from BF2,400 ($77.50) to BF3,200 ($103.25).

Die Swaene, Steenhouwersdijk 1, 8000 Brugge (tel. 050/34-27-98). There's a homey atmosphere in this small hotel overlooking a canal. Rooms are nicely furnished and very comfortable, and rates run BF3,000 ($96.75) and up.

Navara, St. Jakobsstraat 41, 8000 Brugge (tel. 050/34-05-61). In a very central location not far from the Belfry, this was the home of the Prince of Navara during the 16th century. Its guest rooms are simply furnished but comfortable, and rates begin at BF3,000 ($96.75).

Hotel Erasmus, Wollestraat 35, 8000 Brugge (tel. 050/33-57-81). Just steps away from the Belfry, this modern hotel is set in a picturesque little square alongside a canal. Rooms all have private baths, telephones, TVs, radios, mini-bars, writing desks, and attractive, modern furnishings. There's a safe available to guests, and each guest receives one free drink in the bar. Rates are in the BF2,250 ($72.50) to BF3,500 ($113) range.

Alfa Dante Hotel, Coupure 29, 8000 Brugge (tel. 050/34-01-94). This ultramodern brick hotel is set alongside a lovely canal, not far from the center of Brugge. There are 22 nicely furnished guest rooms with private baths, TVs, radios, telephones, and mini-bars. Also, a good restaurant, bar, and private parking. Seasonal rates range from BF2,500 ($80.75) to BF3,750 ($121).

Inexpensive

There are several very good budget hotels in Brugge, most with rooms above restaurants on the ground floor. Some come with baths, but a moneysaving device is to share a bath down the hall, no real hardship in these establishments. Among those concentrated along the east side of 't Zand are the **Graaf van Vlaanderen,** 't Zand 19, 8000 Brugge (tel. 050/33-18-80), with rates of BF1,000 ($32.25) to BF1,550 ($50), and the **Leopold,** 't Zand 26, 8000 Brugge (tel. 050/33-51-29). More centrally located, not far from the Grote Markt, you'll find the **Fevery,** Collaert Mansionstraat 3, 8000 Brugge (tel. 050/33-12-69), with rates in the BF1,450 ($46.75) to BF1,650 ($53.25) range. Right on the market square is the gabled **Central,** Markt 30, 8000 Brugge (tel. 050/33-18-05), which charges BF1,000 ($32.25) to BF1,500 ($48.50).

Recommended hostels, with rates that average BF300 ($9.75) or under, are: **Bruno's Youth Hotel,** Dweersstraat 26, 8000 Brugge (tel. 050/34-02-32); **Bauhaus International Youth Hotel,** Langestraat 135-137, 8000 Brugge (tel. 050/34-10-93); and **Europa Jeugdherburg** Baron Ruzettelaan 143 (tel. 050/35-26-79).

READERS' HOTEL SELECTIONS: "The **Coppens-Lefevere,** Westmeers 132, 8000 Brugge (tel. 050/33-78-99), is excellent, close to the train station, and inexpensive. Also, the proprietor's son spoke English very well, a great help" (Schundler, Califon, N.J.). . . . "At the **De Butler Hotel,** Restaurant, Taverne, Noordzandstraat 8, 8000 Brugge (tel. 050/34-28-15), Mr. Williams treated us like family. Our room was warm, cozy, romantic. The food was excellent, the service superb, the prices moderate. We could walk to the square and enjoy the lights and the people" (B. Rothbeind, MacVista, Calif.). . . . "My wife, year-old baby, and I stayed at the **Hotel St. Christophe,** Nieuwe Gentweg 76, 8000 Brugge (tel. 050/33-11-76), and found it very nice. The hotel is operated by Mr. and Mrs. Fernand Vermeersch, who are quite kind and hospitable. The room we had overlooked a beautiful garden. Moreover, it is near the central train station and most of Brugge's main attractions" (C. Eilers, Sunnyside, N.Y.).

WHERE TO EAT

't Bourgoensche Cruyce, Wollestraat 41 (tel. 33-79-26). The rustic charm of this small dining room overlooking a canal is just one intimation of the culinary delights in store. From the kitchen, chef Philip Traen sends forth regional specialties that are just simply perfection itself. The menu reflects the very best ingredients that are available in any season, and there's a six-course "gastronomic sampling menu" if you just can't make a decision. Also, regardless of season, a dish not to be missed is the marvelous mosaïque de poissons or any of the other superb seafood dishes. Lunch, without wine, will cost about BF1,200 ($38.75); dinner, about BF1,500 ($48.50). Best to reserve far in advance at this popular place.

De Snippe, Nieuwe Gentweg 53 (tel. 33-70-70). Set in a gabled private house that dates back to the 16th century, De Snippe enjoys a reputation as one of Brugge's finest restaurants. It's a reputation well earned, especially for its native dishes. Try the crayfish creations or the scampi. Prices will run BF1,500 ($48.50) to BF1,950 ($63) without wine. Reservations are a must, and the doors are closed Sunday evening and all day Monday.

't Pandreitje, Pandreitje 6 (tel. 33-11-90). The interior of this Renaissance-era private home has been turned into an elegant Louis XVI setting for a menu of classic French and Belgian dishes. A superb four courses will cost about BF2,500 ($80.75) from the à la carte listing, but there's a "menu" of preselected choices that are excellent and cost no more than BF1,850 ($59.75). Closed Sunday and Wednesday (for lunch), the last two weeks of December, and three weeks in March.

Duc de Bourgogne, Huidenvettersplein 12 (tel. 33-20-38). This large dining room overlooking a canal (it's illuminated at night) is elegant and just this side of "formal" in décor, although in summer there's no rigid dress code enforced. The classic menu is a lengthy one, and four courses will average about BF1,850 ($59.75). Closed Monday for lunch and three weeks in January.

't Dreveken, Huidenvettersplein 10-11 (tel. 33-95-06). This charmer, right on a canal, is a stone house with flowers blooming at diamond-paned windows. There's a cozy, intimate room downstairs, and a pleasant, larger one upstairs. Seafood and regional dishes are the specialties here, and prices are moderate: dinner without wine runs about BF600 ($19.25), and you can lunch for no more than BF300 ($9.75).

De Visscherie, Vismarkt 8 (tel. 33-02-12). As you might expect in this attractive restaurant facing the old fish market, "fruits of the sea" have top billing on the menu. A full dinner, without wine, will run about BF1,200 ($38.75).

Den Gouden Cop, Steenstraat 1 (tel. 33-41-84). This is my personal favorite of the many small brasseries, tea rooms, and cafés that line the Grote Markt. There's outdoor dining or a glassed-in room that also overlooks the square, and prices run from as low as BF70 ($2.25) for a bowl of delicious homemade soup to BF900 ($29) for a full meal featuring Flemish dishes made with fresh local ingredients. Sandwiches, snacks, and crêpes (a large variety, and all good) are available, and service is continuous, making it a convenient stop any time the feet and appetite call for it.

Grand Café du Théâtre, Kuipersstraat 14 (tel. 33-45-36). Just 50 yards from Pthe Grote Markt and directly across from the back corner of the Théâtre, this is a large, rather plain restaurant and bar that serves terrific omelets, salads, croquettes, spaghetti, and a few other hot meals that cost anywhere from BF200 ($6.50) to BF500 ($16.25). It's open until midnight or later every day except Wednesday, when it closes at 2 p.m.

The **Ristorante le Due Venezie,** Sint Amandstraat, is a drop-in sort of eatery facing a pleasant little square. Menu choices are likely to be Italian—lasagne, veal cutlet milanese, spaghetti with seafood sauce, etc.—and prices for a three-course meal will seldom exceed BF300 ($9.75).

Perhaps the least expensive place to eat in Brugge is the Sarma Department Store's cafeteria, on Steenstraat near the cathedral, where daily specials are under BF150 ($4.75). It's open during normal shopping hours, and a great favorite with locals on a budget.

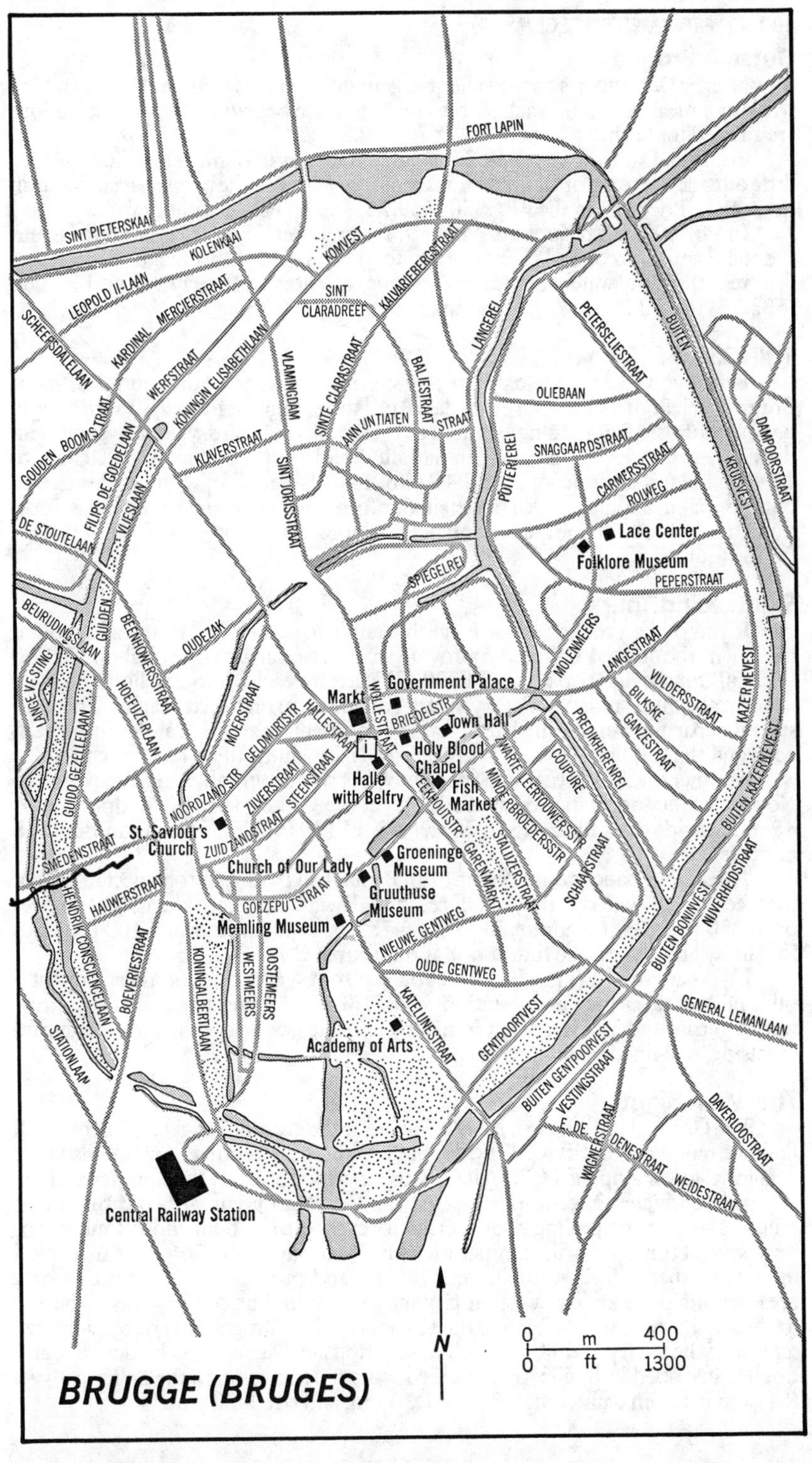
FORT LAPIN
SINT PIETERSKAAI
KOLENKAAI
KOMVEST
LEOPOLD II-LAAN
KARDINAL MERCIERSTRAAT
SCHEEPSDALELAAN
SINT CLARADREEF
KALVARIEBERGSTRAAT
KONINGIN ELISABETHLAAN
WERFSTRAAT
VLAMINGDAM
SINTE CLARASTRAAT
BALIESTRAAT
LANGEREI
PETERSELIESTRAAT
BUITEN
KRUISVEST
DAMPOORTSTRAAT
OLIEBAAN
ANN UNTIATEN STRAAT
SNAGGAARDSTRAAT
CARMERSSTRAAT
ROLWEG
POTTERIEREI
GOUDEN BOOMSTRAAT
FILIPS DE GOEDELAAN
VLIESLAAN
KLAVERSTRAAT
SINT JORISSTRAAT
DE STOUTELAAN
Lace Center
Folklore Museum
PEPERSTRAAT
SPIEGELREI
GULDEN
BEURUDINGSLAAN
OUDEZAK
BEENHOUWERSSTRAAT
MOLENMEERS
LANGESTRAAT
KAZERNEVEST
VULDERSSTRAAT
BILKSKE
GANZESTRAAT
LANGE VESTING
HOEFIJZERLAAN
MOERSTRAAT
Government Palace
Markt
WOLLESTRAAT
BRIEDELSTR
Town Hall
Holy Blood Chapel
HALLESTRAAT
GELDMUNTSTR
ZWARTE LEERTOUWERSSTR
COUPURE
PREDIKHERENREI
BUITEN KAZERNEVEST
GUIDO GEZELLELAAN
NOORDZANDSTR
ZILVERSTRAAT
STEENSTRAAT
Halle with Belfry
Fish Market
EEKHOUTSTR
MINDERBROEDERSSTR
St. Saviour's Church
ZUIDZANDSTRAAT
Groeninge Museum
Church of Our Lady
GARENMARKT
STALIJZERSTRAAT
SCHAARSTRAAT
SMEDENSTRAAT
HAUWERSTRAAT
GOEZEPUTSTRAAT
Gruuthuse Museum
Memling Museum
NIEUWE GENTWEG
OUDE GENTWEG
BUITEN BONINVEST
NIJVERHEIDSTRAAT
HENDRIK CONSCIENCELAAN
BOEVERIESTRAAT
KONINGALBERTLAAN
WESTMEERS
OOSTEMEERS
KATELIJNESTRAAT
GENTPOORTVEST
GENERAL LEMANLAAN
STATIONLAAN
Academy of Arts
BUITEN GENTPOORTVEST
VESTINGSTRAAT
DAVERLOOSTRAAT
F. DE. DENESTRAAT
WAGNERSTRAAT
WEIDESTRAAT
Central Railway Station
N
0 m 400
0 ft 1300
BRUGGE (BRUGES)

Outside Brugge

Nearby **Damme** has two excellent restaurants that are worth the short drive (or work in a meal between canal-boat excursions—see below). Advance reservations are advised for both.

Breugel, Damse Vaart Zuid 26, Damme Oostkerke-Damme (tel. 50-03-46), a little outside the town of Damme in a farmhouse, is one of the best fish restaurants in the region. Prices are in the BF1,850 ($59.75) and up range, without wine.

Die Drie Zilveren Kannen, Markt 9, Damme (tel. 35-56-77), provides an authentic Flemish décor and extraordinary food to match, with a menu that features fish fresh from the waters off nearby Zeebrugge. Prices will average about BF1,050 ($33.75) to BF2,200 ($71), including wine.

THINGS TO SEE AND DO

Before you take even one sightseeing step in Brugge, go by the **Tourist Office** at Burg 11 (tel. 33-07-11), open every day: April to September, from 9:30 a.m. to 6:30 p.m. weekdays, 10 a.m. to noon and 2 to 6:30 p.m. on Saturday, Sunday, and holidays; other months, it closes on Sunday and holidays and is open from 10 a.m. to 12:45 p.m. and again from 2 to 5:45 p.m. It's a large office, with brochures that outline walking tours, as well as detailed information on many sightseeing attractions, a helpful and friendly staff, and practical information on every facet of Brugge for the tourist.

Sightseeing Tours

If you'd like a trained, knowledgeable guide to accompany your walks around the town, the **Tourist Office** can provide that service at a charge of about BF700 ($22.50) for the first two hours, BF350 ($11.25) for each additional hour.

An absolute "must" for every visitor is a **boat trip** on the city canals. There are several departure points (all plainly marked on city maps available at the Tourist Office), and the half-hour cruise costs BF125 ($4) for adults, BF60 ($2) for children.

Another lovely way to tour Brugge is by **horse-drawn cab,** and from March to November they are stationed at the Burg (in the Grote Markt on Wednesday). A 35-minute ride costs BF450 ($14.50) *per cab,* BF100 ($3.25) for each additional 15 minutes.

Three-hour **coach tours** depart from Beursplein twice a day on selected days of the week (check with the Tourist Office, since days are subject to change), with fares of BF350 ($11.25) for adults, BF175 ($5.75) for children, and BF1,100 ($35.50) for family groups of up to four. Book at the Tourist Office.

If you arrive in Brugge by train, you can **rent a bicycle** (you must present a valid rail ticket) at the railway station for BF150 ($4.75) per day, and it's a terrific way to get around, or even to get to nearby Damme (see below) by way of beautiful canalside, tree-lined roads.

The Main Sights

The Grote Markt, the vast Market Square at the heart of Brugge, is where you'll find the renowned **Belfry of Brugge,** built in the 13th century. An awe-inspiring octagonal tower atop the Halles (the "Halls" in which much of the commerce of the city was conducted in centuries past), it holds a magnificent 47-bell carillon that sends its silver notes pealing out over the city every quarter hour and in longer concerts several times a day in summer months. If you climb the 366 steps that spiral upward to the Belfry's summit, your huffing and puffing will be rewarded by a breathtaking panoramic view of the city and its surrounding countryside all the way to the sea. Just outside the Halles, the Kiwanis Club of Brugge has erected a bronze replica of the Belfry and Halles with descriptions in Dutch, French, German, and English inscribed in Braille for unsighted visitors. Admission to the Belfry is BF30 ($1) and it's open daily from 9:30 to 11:30 a.m. and 4 to 5:30 p.m.

That **statue** in the center of the Grote Markt depicts two Belgian heroes, butcher Jan Breydel and weaver Pieter de Coninck, who led the 1302 uprising against wealthy merchants and nobles who dominated the Guilds and went on to victory against French knights later that same year in the Battle of the Golden Spurs. On the corner of Sint Amandstraat at the Grote Markt, the small, castle-like building—the **Cranenburg**—was used to imprison Maximilian of Austria, an act for which he later exacted a penalty from the citizens of Brugge that added a note of pure beauty to the city: they were obliged to keep swans in the canals forever. The large neo-Gothic **Government Palace** dates from the 1800s and houses the administrative offices of West Flanders.

Several points of interest are located in the **Burg,** a public square just steps away from the Grote Markt where Baldwin of the Iron Arm once built a fortified castle, around which a village (or "burg") developed. The **Town Hall** is here, a beautiful Gothic structure that is the oldest town hall in Belgium (built in the late 1300s). Be sure to see the upstairs Gothic Room ("Gotische Zaal") with its ornate décor and wall murals depicting highlights of Brugge's history. There's a BF30 ($1) admission charge, and it's open to the public from 9:30 a.m. to noon and 2 to 6 p.m. every day except Friday.

Also on the Burg is the **Basilica of the Holy Blood,** repository since 1149 of a fragment of cloth believed to be soaked with the blood of Christ, which was brought to Brugge during the Second Crusade by the count of Flanders. The public gets to see it every Friday from 8:30 to 11:45 a.m. and 3 to 4 p.m. Every Ascension Day a wonderfully colorful Procession of the Holy Blood displays the relic (carried by a bishop of the church) through Brugge's streets, accompanied by beautifully costumed residents acting out biblical episodes. The 12th-century basilica is worth a visit for the richness of its design and the other treasures it holds, even if you have no interest in the relic. Admission is BF20 (65¢), and hours are 9:30 a.m. to noon and 2 to 4 p.m.

It took two centuries (13th to 15th) to build the **Church of Our Lady,** on Mariastraat, and its soaring 360-foot-high spire is a Brugge point of reference. Among its many art treasures to look for are the marble *Madonna and Child* by Michelangelo, paintings by Anthony van Dyck, and the impressive bronze figures of Mary of Burgundy and Charles the Bold on their 13th-century tombs. Admission is BF30 ($1), from 10 to 11:30 a.m. and 3 to 5 p.m. Monday through Saturday, from 3 to 5 p.m. only on Sunday.

The **Gruuthuse Museum,** Dijver 17 (an integral part of the Groeninge Museum), is the gloriously ornate mansion that Flemish nobleman Louis de Gruuthuse called "home" in the 1400s. Among the astonishing 2,500 numbered antiquities in the house are paintings, sculptures, tapestries, laces, weapons, glassware, and richly carved furniture. Admission is BF80 ($2.50) with hours from 9:30 a.m. to noon and 2 to 6 p.m. Closed Tuesday from October through March.

The **Hospital of St. John,** or **Memling Museum,** on Mariastraat, dates from the Middle Ages. To see how the vast wards looked when this was a functioning hospital, take a look at the old painting near the entrance that shows small, efficient bed units set into cubicles around the walls. The old Apothecary Room is furnished exactly as it was when this building's main function was the care of the sick. Nowadays visitors come to see the typical medieval hospital buildings filled with furniture and other objects that illustrate their history, as well as the magnificent collection of paintings by Hans Memling. The artist came to Brugge after the death of Rogier van der Weyden, and became one of the city's most prominent residents. Rogier van der Weyden actually had his workshop in Brussels, but died in Brugge, and Memling worked in his atelier in Brussels. Here you'll find such masterpieces as *The Mystic Marriage of St. Catherine,* the *Ursula Shrine,* and *Virgin with Child and Apple.* Hours are 10 a.m. to noon and 2 to 5 p.m. every day except Wednesday,

October through March; and 9 a.m. to 12:30 p.m. and 2 to 6 p.m. daily, April through September.

The **Groeninge Museum,** Jijver 12, ranks among the leading traditional museums of fine arts, and the collection contains a survey of painting in the southern Netherlands and Belgium from the 15th to the 20th century. The famed Gallery of Flemish Primitives holds some 30 works of painters such as Jan van Eyck, Rogier van der Weyden, Hieronymus Bosch, Hans Memling, etc. Works of Magritte and Delvaux are also on display. Hours are Wednesday through Monday from 9:30 a.m. to 6 p.m., April through September; 9:30 a.m. to noon and 2 to 5 p.m., October through March; closed Tuesday. Admission is BF80 ($2.50).

The **Lace Center,** Balstraat 14 (tel. 33-00-72), is a fascinating place—the lace of Brugge is, after all, famous the world over, and you'll be hard-put to resist taking some away as your most lasting memento of Brugge. This is where the ancient art of lacemaking is passed on to the next generation, and you get a firsthand look at the ladies who will be making many of the items for future sale in all those lace shops. Incidentally, the most famous laces to look for are "bloemenwerk," "rozenkant," and "toveressesteek." Hours are 2 to 6 p.m. (to 4 p.m. on Wednesday and Saturday).

After Dark

Brugge is one of the best places in Belgium to see the fascinating puppet theater that has been a favorite entertainment in the country for centuries. There's a marvelous collection of puppets and plays at the **Marionettentheater Brugge,** St. Jakobsstraat 36 (tel. 33-47-60). Call for performance schedules and prices. Highly recommended.

Outside Brugge

Just four miles away is the tiny town of **Damme,** once the outer harbor of Brugge. The marriage of Charles the Bold and Margaret of York was celebrated here in 1468, an indication of the importance of Damme during that era. Today visitors come to see the picturesque Marktplein, which holds a statue of native Jacob van Maerlant, the "father of Flemish poetry," and for the breathtakingly beautiful scenery lining every one of the four miles en route from Brugge.

One of the nicest ways to get from Brugge to Damme is by **canal boat.** In summer, departures in Brugge are from the Noorweegse Kaai several times a day, and the half-hour ride is a delight to the senses as you glide through a landscape straight out of the Flemish paintings you've seen in museums. One-way fare is BF150 ($4.75), the round-trip fare runs BF200 ($6.50), and sailings are frequent enough in both directions to make possible a day trip to Damme, with lunch at one of the many restaurants lining its Marktplein and plenty of time for a sightseeing stroll. The **Damme Tourist Office** is at Jacob van Maerlantstraat 3 (tel. 050/35-33-19).

2. Gent (Ghent)

If you were to draw an oval from Brussels to Antwerp to Brugge to Ieper and back to Brussels, Gent would be almost exactly in the center, and that's rather fitting, because this magnificent old city has always been a sort of pivot point for this part of Flanders. Standing at the confluence of the Rivers Leie and Scheldt, Gent was the seat of the counts of Flanders, and its importance long before they came to power is underscored by the fact that the great castle those counts built in 1180 was actually raised on foundations of even earlier fortifications, some dating to the 900s. Hands-on rule began very early on here, and the plain people—skilled weavers and craftsmen—never learned to like it enough to stifle their rebellious natures and live with it.

During the Middle Ages Gent became as great a manufacturing center as Brugge was a trading center, and the working class rebelled not only against an exploitive nobility, but even among themselves, guild against guild. Over the centuries the people of Gent fought the counts of Flanders, the counts of Burgundy, the king of France, the king of Spain, their rivals in Brugge, and . . . well, whenever *anyone* turned up with plans to implement absolute rule, they took up arms. The fact that they so seldom prevailed for any length of time did not deter them in the least—with each new conquest, they'd settle down for a spell, begin to seethe with indignation, finally reach a boiling point, then take to the warpath all over again. Small wonder, then, that in 1815 it was Maurice de Broglie, a bishop of Gent, who stirred the pot of religion and lit a fire under the rule of Dutch Protestants, a fire that in 1830 would finally burst into the flame of national independence for Belgium.

With a long history of economic ups and downs that has kept Gent on a seesaw of growth and decline, the city today has emerged once more as a major industrial center. Her medieval treasures are preserved, not as dry, showcase relics, but as living parts of her present every bit as much as they have been in her past. And to lighten what could be the overpowering grayness of an industrial city, there are the flowers—flowers everywhere create oases of color as a constant reminder that this is also the center of a prosperous horticultural center. In short, Gent is a busy, lively city, whose reminders of the past are as comfortable as a pair of well-broken-in shoes.

WHERE TO STAY

The **Tourist Office,** located in the crypt of the Town Hall, Botermarkt, 9000 Gent (tel. 091/24-15-55), provides an up-to-date "Hotels and Restaurants" booklet at no cost and will also make hotel reservations at no charge. In summer, its hours are 9 a.m. to 8 p.m. Sunday through Thursday, until 9 p.m. on Friday and Saturday.

Because of its proximity to both Brussels and Brugge, Gent is often regarded by tourists as a day-trip destination, but recent years have seen the erection of several very good hotels, both in the city center and on its perimeter, making it a convenient sightseeing base.

Two Real Gems

Hotel Gravensteen, Jan Breydelstraat 35, 9000 Gent (tel. 091/25-11-50). This lovely mansion was built in 1865 as the home of a Gent textile baron. You enter through the old carriageway—and that carriageway, a wonder of ornamented pillars and an impressive wall niche occupied by a marble statue, sets the tone for what you'll find inside. The elegant, high-ceilinged parlor is a sophisticated blend of pastels, gracious modern furnishings, and antiques, with a small bar tucked into one corner. The 30 rooms are furnished to provide every comfort (private bath, telephone, color TV, and radio), with attractive décor. Those in front look out on the moated castle of the counts, a sightseeing bonus indeed, while those to the back have city views. There's a top-floor "Belvedere" with windows all around to give magnificent views of the city. Afternoon tea is also available. Rates at this very special place are BF2,400 ($77.50) to BF2,890 ($93.25) single, BF3,600 ($116.25) to BF3,950 ($127.50) double, with special weekend rates available.

Hôtel Cour Saint-Georges ("St. Jorishof"), Botermarkt 2, 9000 Gent (tel. 091/25-47-33). Directly opposite the Town Hall, the Cour Saint-Georges is a historical treasure—it dates back to 1228! It has been an inn of quality from the very beginning, and it counts among its patrons of the past such notables as Mary of Burgundy, Charles V, and Napoleon Bonaparte. You'll dine in the large Gothic Hall with its mammoth fireplace at one end, and even the "modern" annex that houses most guest rooms has foundations that date back to the 9th century. Décor is traditional in the 66 pleasant and comfortable rooms, all with bathrooms, and rates are amazingly low for such a prime location and all that atmosphere: BF1,825 ($58.75) to BF3,400 ($109.75) single, BF2,350 ($75.75) to BF3,500 ($113) for doubles. Needless to say, you should reserve as far in advance as possible.

Expensive

Novotel, Goudenieeuwplein 5, 9000 Gent (tel. 091/24-22-30). The location of this modern hotel couldn't be more convenient for sightseeing—it's very near the Town Hall, within easy walking distance to all major sights. To this chain's credit, the modern edifice has been designed to fit into its ancient surroundings with scarcely a bump between the centuries. Inside, facilities are all you'd expect from a top hotel, with light, airy public rooms (the attractive bar has become a meeting place for local businessmen) and there's a garden terrace. Guest rooms are nicely furnished and fitted out with private bath, direct-dial telephone, color TV, and individual heating controls. Rates are BF3,100 ($100) for singles, BF3,675 ($118.50) for doubles. All rates include breakfast.

Holiday Inn, Ottergemsesteenweg 600, 9000 Gent (tel. 091/22-58-85). Drivers who don't wish to drive into the city center will find this a convenient stopping point at a major highway intersection on the outskirts of town. In addition to the modern guest rooms typical of this chain (two double beds, private bath, color TV, direct-dial telephone), there are a swimming pool, tennis court, children's garden, and sauna. Rates are BF3,400 ($109.75) single, BF4,400 ($142) double.

Moderate

Carlton, Koningin Astridlaan 138, 9000 Gent (tel. 091/11-88-36 or 11-88-38). In the same area as the railway station, this modern-style hotel features rooms with pretty standard décor and furnishings, all with private bath, TV, and mini-bar. No restaurant or bar, but several are in the neighborhood. There's convenient parking in a next-door garage. Rates here are BF1,100 ($35.50) to BF1,500 ($48.50) for singles, BF1,375 ($44.25) to BF1,775 ($57.25) for doubles. Ask about weekend and midweek package rates at substantial reductions.

Hotel Barloria, Baarleveldestraat 3, 9810 Gent (tel. 091/26-74-32 and 27-15-32). This modern hotel has a good restaurant and bar, and guest rooms are attractive, with comfortable furnishings. Each comes with a bath or shower, color TV, and telephone. Rates for singles run BF1,200 ($38.75) to BF1,375 ($44.25); doubles cost BF1,575 ($50.75) to BF1,750 ($56.50).

The **Arcade Hotel** Nederkouter 24 (tel. 091/25-07-07), is a modern hotel with bright, comfortably furnished rooms, but little in the way of extras. Breakfast, for instance, is not included in the rate, and you pay to have TV in your room. Good accommodations at moderate rates: BF1,540 ($49.75) for singles, BF1,810 ($58.50) for doubles.

Europahotel, Gordunakaai 59, 9000 Gent (tel. 091/22-60-71). This is a modern hotel set in the greenery of the Blaarmeersen suburb on Gent's outskirts. Rooms are large, with bright, attractive furnishings, and come with private bath, TV, direct-dial telephone, etc. There's a bar, restaurant, and good parking. Rates are BF1,750 ($56.50) for singles, BF2,100 ($67.75) for doubles.

Inexpensive

The most inexpensive accommodations in Gent are those upstairs rooms (perfectly respectable and comfortable, but without bath or "extras") above the cafés and restaurants along the Kornmarkt, near St. Nicholas Church. Two good examples, both with rates in the BF750 ($24.25) to BF1,000 ($32.25) range, are **De Progrès,** Korenmarkt 10, 9000 Gent (tel. 091/25-17-16), and **'t Vosken,** Baafsplein 19, 9000 Gent (tel. 091/25-73-61).

Dormitory bunk-bed accommodations cost about BF250 ($8) at the **Jugendherberg "De Draecke" hostel,** 12 St. Pietersplein (tel. 091/22-50-67). Also, inquire at the Tourist Office about availability of rooms in the University of Gent residence halls from mid-July to mid-September at very low rates.

WHERE TO EAT

One of the nicest things about Gent's restaurants is that almost all serve generous portions of traditional Flemish dishes, dishes like the thick, creamy waterzooi (a soup that borders on being a stew, it's so thick), and lapin à la flamande (rabbit with beer, vinegar, and currant juice), or if it's the right season, the delicate asparagus that comes from the Mechelen area. What's more, even the most expensive restaurant sports prices well below those in the gourmet establishments in Brussels. The helpful "Hotels and Restaurants" booklet published by the Tourist Board (free) lists eateries by cuisine as well as by price.

Expensive

Apicius, Maurice Maeterlinckstraat 8 (tel. 22-46-00). This elegant restaurant serves gourmet French dishes interspersed with Flemish delicacies. They take their food and its service very seriously here, and you should allow a minimum of 2½ hours for an evening meal, in the sure knowledge that you'll be rewarded with a memorable procession of courses. If you're there during asparagus season, don't miss their lovely preparation of asparagus with lobster; otherwise, you're very safe in ordering from their set menu, which will run about BF1,500 ($48.50) to BF2,500 ($80.75), without wine. Closed for Saturday lunch, Sunday, and major holidays.

Auberge du Pêcheur, Ponstraat 41, Latem/Deurle (tel. 82-31-44). Although it's about a 25-minute drive or taxi ride from the city, no listing of Gent restaurants would be complete without mention of this excellent restaurant in a country inn (you'll see signs for Deurle on the A14, the motorway that leads to Deinze). The six-course set dinner menu features seafood, lamb, and the freshest local specialties available each day. Dinner will run about BF1,950 ($63) without wine, but the daily "business lunch" is in the BF950 ($30.75) neighborhood, an excellent buy and a fine way to combine good eating with a sightseeing foray into the countryside. If you'd like to linger overnight, there are 17 very comfortable hotel rooms, with TVs, mini-bars, and radios.

Waterzooi, Sint Veerleplein 2, 9000 Gent (tel. 25-05-63). Some 250 years ago, this house was built as a restaurant on the ruins of a church on the square facing the Castle of the Counts, and since then has retained the same name. The eatery itself, however, has undergone several changes, chiefly from the cozy, family style of many years' standing to the luxurious gourmet restaurant it has become under the guidance of Mr. and Mrs. Gerrit Daluwein. Lucie Daluwein is the chef, and she presents superb, creative dishes based on fresh, seasonal products. Lunch will run about BF900 ($29); dinner, BF1,500 ($48.50) to BF2,000 ($64.50). There's also a set dinner menu that includes wine for BF2,750 ($88.75).

Moderate

Jan Breydel, Jan Breydelstraat 10 (tel. 25-62-87). Top honors go to this exquisite restaurant on a quaint street near the Castle of the Counts. Its interior is a garden-like delight of greenery, white napery, and light woods. Proprietors Louis and Pat Hellebaut see to it that dishes issuing from their kitchen are as light and airy as their setting, with delicate sauces and seasonings to make the most of incredibly fresh ingredients. Seafoods or regional specialties are all superb. Prices are in the BF1,037 ($33.50) and under range for dinner without wine. Highly recommended.

Cour St-Georges (St. Jorishof), Botermarkt 2 (tel. 24-24-24). The Gothic Hall in this ancient inn (see "Where to Stay," above) is a marvel of dark woodwork, massive fireplace, and stained glass, surrounded by an upstairs balcony. One of the Flemish dishes in which it specializes is eel with green sauce, and the chicken waterzooi enjoys a good local reputation. The special menu ("menu Charles Quint") is BF900 ($29), and the restaurant is closed Sunday and public holidays.

Graaf van Egmond, St. Michielsplein 21 (tel. 25-07-27). In a marvelous old

Gent town house of the 1200s on the River Leie, the Graaf van Egmond serves Flemish specialties like carbonnade flamande (beef stew) and asparagus à la flamande, along with French creations. If you can get a window seat, there's a spectacular view of the towers of Gent. A four-course dinner without wine will run about BF700 ($22.50). Upstairs, there's a grill (with the same view) for simpler meals at about BF375 ($12).

Oranjerie, Corduwaniersstraat 8, Patershof (tel. 24-10-08). Patershof (which means "cave" or "hole" in which monks lived a hermit's existence) is an ancient enclave not far from the Castle of the Counts that is fast becoming a gastronic center as more and more small restaurants move into renovated old buildings. Oranjerie is one of the most delightful of these, and as you might guess from its name, has the bright, cheerful aspect of a garden. The dining rooms are light and airy, there's a skylight, a fountain, a lovely small garden, and lots of lush greenery. The menu here focuses on fish and vegetarian dishes, beautifully prepared and presented. You can dine nicely for around BF600 ($19.25), and there's a good set menu for BF1,100 ($35.50). Hours are 7 to 10 p.m. every day except Wednesday, and advance reservations are advised.

As a part of the restoration of **Het Panj,** Onderbergen 1 (tel. 25-01-80), a Dominican monastery near St. Michael's which was in continual use from A.D. 1128 to the 1860s, a very good, moderate price restaurant and attractive bar have been installed. Fish and fresh local produce are featured in the restaurant, and the bar is a clubby affair, with marble bar, arched ceilings, and leather chairs. Call for lunch and dinner hours and prices.

Special Note: While in this area, look for the small doorway marked "Katrien" at Sint-Michielsplein 1. This is the home of Katrienspekken, special bonbons that have been made with brown sugar for three generations by the same family. They're a Gent tradition, cost a pittance, and are a real treat.

Het Cooremetershuys, Graslei 12 (tel. 23-49-71). To reach this special little restaurant, mount the stairs in one of the gorgeous old gabled houses lining the canal that date from the 14th century. The strains of taped classical music greet your entrance into a rather plain room whose walls are hung with musical instruments. The menu is French nouvelle, and lunch will run BF650 ($21) to BF840 ($27); a five-course dinner, BF1,200 ($38.75). Hours are noon to 2 p.m. and 7 to 9 p.m.

Inexpensive

Raadskelder, Sint-Baafsplein (tel. 25-43-34). If for nothing more than a coffee or beer, every visitor to Gent should stop by this large restaurant/tavern deep in the vaulted crypt of a building adjoining the Belfry in front of the cathedral. Seating is in church pews, and the à la carte menu is chock full of Flemish dishes: waterzooi, of course; pork cutlets cooked in beer; rabbit cooked with prunes. Certainly not gourmet cooking—this is a massive operation, with seating for 300—but good, hearty fare at prices that will provide a full meal for around BF300 ($9.75). There's also a "tourist menu" of four courses at BF520 ($16.75). It's open every day from 9:30 a.m. to 10 p.m.

For more inexpensive eating, all more or less the same and costing about BF250 ($8), stop at any of the small restaurants around Saint Bavo's Square. Most have sidewalk tables, which is pleasant in good weather, and all offer very adequate renderings of Flemish dishes.

THINGS TO SEE AND DO

Gent is a city to be seen afoot. Indeed, it's only by walking her streets, gazing at her gabled guild houses and private mansions, looking up at her massive and forbidding Castle of the Counts, and stopping on one of her bridges to ponder the canal beneath, that you can begin to get a sense of the extraordinary vigor of the people who have lived here over the centuries. But before setting off, stop in at the Tourist

Office and arm yourself with literature that will bring to life the ghosts of this city's past as you explore its streets.

Tourist Information

The **Tourist Office** is located in the crypt of the Town Hall, Botermarkt (tel. 24-15-55), with hours from 9 a.m. to 8 p.m. Sunday through Thursday, until 9 p.m. on Friday and Saturday from April to November; in other months, 9 a.m. to noon and 2 to 5 p.m.

Sightseeing Tours

The Tourist Office can arrange qualified guides for private **walking tours** at a charge of BF700 ($22.50) for the first two hours, BF350 ($11.25) for each additional hour. You should inquire at the Tourist Office about organized group walking tours sometimes conducted during summer months at a fee of BF60 ($2) for adults, half that for children.

Ask at the Tourist Office about **horse-drawn carriages** that sometimes depart from Sint-Baafsplein and Korenlei for half-hour rides at a cost of BF520 ($16.75).

A tour that should be a part of every visitor's itinerary is a **boat ride along the canals.** Covered boats depart from the Graslei during summer months, leaving every 30 minutes from 10:30 a.m. to 7 p.m., with an interesting narrative given in several languages. The trip lasts about 30 minutes, with fares of BF90 ($3) for adults, BF60 ($2) for children. Open boats leave from the Korenlei (Grasbrug) every ten minutes, with the same fares, but no narrative.

On specified days during the summer (ask at the Tourist Office) you can also take a **boat trip from Gent to Brugge** and back, at an adult fare of BF350 ($11.25), BF250 ($8) for children.

Orientation

The Korenmarkt Square is known as the "Centrum" (if you arrive by rail, take tram no. 1, which will take you directly to the Centrum), which is a little misleading when you consider that it's not at all "central" to the Town Hall, cathedral, etc., as is true in most Belgian towns with a central Grote Markt. However, most of the sights you'll want to see lie within a half mile or less of the Korenmarkt. The River Leie twists through the city to meet the Scheldt, with major watery offshoots at the Lieve and Ketelvest Canals, as well as several minor waterways. The Citadel Park, location of the Museum of Fine Arts, is near St. Pieter's Railway Station, which lies about a mile and three-quarters south of the Korenmarkt.

THE MAIN SIGHTS

First of all, just so you'll know: the "Three Towers of Gent" you'll hear referred to often are those of St. Bavo's Cathedral, the Belfry, and St. Nicholas Church, which form a virtually straight line in the direction of St. Michael's Bridge.

St. Bavo's Cathedral

If you see nothing else in Gent, you shouldn't miss a visit to this massive cathedral on Sint-Baafsplein. Don't be put off by its rather unimpressive exterior, an uncertain mixture of Romanesque, Gothic, and baroque architecture. Although it was built in the 14th and 15th centuries, its crypt contains traces of the Church of St. John, which stood on this site in the 12th century. Inside, its vastness, filled with priceless paintings, sculptures, screens, memorials, and carved tombs, will literally make you catch your breath in awe. About midway the length of the vaulted nave is one of the most striking pulpits you're ever likely to see. Of white marble entwined with oak, its base is covered with remarkable carvings.

The showpiece of St. Bavo's, however, is the 24-panel *The Adoration of the Mystic Lamb.* A stunning work rich in color and detail, it was a commission to the artist

Hubert van Eyck in 1420 from a wealthy alderman for this very chapel, where it has remained since its completion in 1432 (possibly by the artist's brother, Jan van Eyck, after his brother's death in 1426).

There are other art treasures in the cathedral, one of which is the *Conversion of St. Bavo* by Rubens, painted in 1624. It's in the Rubens Chapel, one of the many that form a semicircular ambulatory behind the high altar, and to walk through them is much like visiting an exquisite art gallery.

The BF50 ($1.50) admission charge to enter the Vijd chapel (there's no charge for the cathedral itself) also admits you to the Romanesque Crypt, which holds a wealth of religious antiquities, vestments, sculptures, and paintings. Do look for the faint, primitive frescoes still to be seen on some of the arches (if, that is, they have not been cleaned away—several have disappeared in the wake of restorative "progress").

The Belfry

Just across the square from the cathedral is the 14th-century Belfry and the Cloth Hall over which it towers. From the Belfry bells sounded the call to arms down through the centuries (a rather frequent occurrence in this rebellious city). The most beloved of the bells was a 1315 giant known as "Roeland," and one of the harshest punishments ever suffered by Gent citizenry was its destruction at the hands of a vindictive Charles V in 1540. Some 37 of the 51 small bells that now make up the huge carillon are made from the remains of "Roeland," and the massive "Triomphante" that was cast in 1660 to replace the favorite now rests in a small park at the foot of the Belfry, still bearing the crack it sustained in 1914. A great iron chest was kept in the Belfry's "Secret" to hold the all-important charters that spelled out privileges wrested from the counts of Flanders by the guilds and the burghers of medieval Gent. If the elevator up to the Belfry's 215-foot-high upper gallery is in operation when you visit, you can see the bells as well as a fantastic panoramic view of the city.

The Cloth Hall

Adjoining the Belfry, this 1425 building was the gathering place of wool and cloth merchants during the Middle Ages. Today its main attraction is a marvelous audio-visual production called *Gent and Charles V* that is presented every day of the week except Monday. The remarkable 20-minute light-and-sound show utilizes a miniature model of 16th-century Gent, with relevant sections illuminated as the story of the city's stormy relationship with its famous—or infamous—native son. Presentations are given in four alternating languages, which means you may have to wait until English rolls around. It's worth the wait, however, for it sends you out into the streets of Gent with a much deeper understanding of much you will encounter. Admission is only BF50 ($1.50), and it's shown every day except Monday from 9 a.m. to noon and 1:30 to 5 p.m.

The Town Hall (Stadhuis)

At the corner of Botermarkt and Hoogpoort, this two-faced giant of a building turns a rather plain Renaissance profile to the Botermarkt, and an almost garishly ornamented Gothic face to the Hoogpoort. The explanation of its schizophrenic appearance probably lies in the fact that Charles V interrupted its construction, begun in 1518, and work did not begin again until the end of that century and the early 1600s, with final completion delayed until the 18th century. Along those years, both public tastes and available monies went through changes reflected in the building's style. In its Pacificatiezaal (Pacification Room) the historically significant Pacification of Ghent was signed in 1567, a document that declared to the world the Low Country provinces' repudiation of rule by the Spanish Habsburgs and their intention to permit freedom of religion within their boundaries. Although it held for a relatively short period, it was a remarkable foreshadow of declarations of independence to come. Open to the public when accompanied by a guide. There are guided visits in several languages from the beginning of May till the end of October every Monday, Tuesday, Wednesday, and Thursday afternoon.

Castle of the Counts (Gravensteen)

"Grim" is the word that comes instantly to mind at one's first view of the fortress stronghold maintained by the counts of Flanders, and it is safe to say that its very appearance did much to instill the awe and fear necessary to keep the people of Gent in line. Surrounded by the waters of the Leie, it was built by Philip of Alsace, a count of Flanders fresh from the Crusades in 1180 with images of a similar crusaders' castle in Syria fixed firmly in his mind. According to local legend, supported to some degree by Gallo-Roman artifacts uncovered in recent excavations, the count built on foundations originally laid down by Baldwin of the Iron Arm back in the 800s. If its six-foot-thick walls, battlements, and turrets failed to intimidate attackers, the counts could always turn to a well-equipped torture chamber inside, from which tales of incredibly cruel and painful death were spread to cause second thoughts on the part of any who contemplated storming the castle. Relics of that inhuman chamber—a small guillotine, spiked iron collars, racks, branding irons, thumb screws, and a special kind of pitchfork designed to make certain that those poor souls being burned at the stake stayed in the flames—can be viewed in a small museum in the castle. On a happier note, if you climb to the ramparts of the high building in the center, the donjon, you'll be rewarded by a great view of the rooftops and towers of Gent. The Gravensteen is open from 9 a.m. to 5:15 p.m. during the summer, 9 a.m. to 3:15 p.m. in winter. Admission is BF50 ($1.50).

Graslei

Not one historic building, but a solid row of towering, gabled Guild Houses were built along this quay between the 1200s and 1600s, when the waterway formed the harbor of Gent. To fully appreciate their majesty, walk across the bridge over the Leie to the Korenlei on the opposite bank and view them as a whole, then return to saunter past each, conjuring up in your imagination the craftsmen, tradespeople, and merchants for whom these buildings were the very core of their commercial (and civil liberties) existence. To identify them briefly: no. 1 was the House of the Free Boatmen, dating from the 1500s; no. 2, the Annex House of the Grain Measurers, from the 1600s; no. 3, the House of the Receiver of the Staple (Customs), from the 1600s; no. 4, the Staple Warehouse, from the 1200s; no. 5, the Main House of the Grain Measurers, from the 1500s; no. 6, the House of the Free Masons, from the 1500s; and no. 7, the House of the Un-Free Boatmen. Within the walls of each, enough drama was acted out to fill a library of books based on Gent's independence of spirit. This is *not* a street to pass by quickly!

The Vrijdagmarkt (Friday Market Square)

During the city's long history, when trouble erupted in Gent, as it so often did, this huge square was nearly always the rallying point. The statue of Jacob van Arteveld that stands in the square is a loving tribute to a leader of revolt in the 1300s, and its base is adorned by the shields of some 52 guilds. The square also houses the building in which Belgium's Socialist Party was born under the direction of Gent's native son, Edward Anseele. Today this is a major shopping area and the scene of lively and colorful street markets every Friday morning and Saturday afternoon. A short distance away, the smaller Kanonplein square is guarded by a gigantic cannon affectionately known as Mad Meg (Dulle Griet), which thundered away in the 1400s in the service of Burgundian armies.

Museums

The **Museum of Fine Arts,** Nicolaas de Liemaeckereplein 3. Located in the Citadel Park not far from the railway station, this fine museum houses both ancient and modern art masterpieces, highlights of which are works by Rubens, Anthony van Dyck, and Bosch, along with such moderns as James Ensor and Yves de Smet. The museum is open every day except Monday from 9 a.m. to 12:30 p.m. and 1:30 to 5:30 p.m., with a BF50 ($1.50) admission for those over the age of 12 (free for those younger).

The **Bijioke Museum,** Godshuizenlaan 2. Incorporated in an ancient abbey that dates from the 14th century is an outstanding collection of weapons, uniforms, clothing, and household items from the everyday life of years past. An authentic Gent home has been reconstructed inside the house of the abbess. Hours are the same as for the Museum of Fine Arts, with the same admission fee.

The **Museum of Folklore,** Kraanlei 65. This fascinating museum is set in almshouses dating from the 1300s and later, and instead of glass-case exhibits there are authentic replicas of actual rooms in which crafts and skills were practiced. There's also a marionette theater which presents performances on specified days of the week (check with the Tourist Office for current schedules). Hours November through March are 10 a.m. to noon and 1:30 to 5 p.m., closed Monday; hours, April through October, are 9 a.m. to 12:30 p.m. and 1:30 to 5:30 p.m. every day. Admission is BF50 ($1.50).

Flowers

Gent's flower growers are centered around nearby Lochristi, and if you're here the last weekend of August, you'll enjoy the colorful Begonia Festival.

Festivals of Flanders

You'd have to be here in August and September for this to be a legitimate thing "to see and do," but if that's when you'll be coming you should plan extra days in Gent, since international concerts are presented in about 20 settings of medieval splendor. For full details before you come, contact Festivals of Flanders Secretariat, B.R.T.-Omroepcentrum, Eugeen Flageyplein 18, 1050 Brussels (tel. 02/648-14-84).

AFTER DARK

From October through mid-June, international opera is performed in the 19th-century **Royal Opera,** Schouwburgstraat 3 (tel. 25-33-77 or 25-24-25).

Puppet theaters are: the **Museum of Folklore,** Kraanlei 65 (tel. 23-13-36); the **Nele,** Vlaanderenstraat 37 (tel. 23-11-93); and **Magie,** Haspelstraat 39 (tel. 26-42-18).

In typical Flemish fashion, the favorite after-dark entertainment in Gent is frequenting its atmospheric **bars and taverns,** of which it has perhaps more than its share. You'll have a memorable evening in any one you choose, but **Oud Middelhus,** Graslei 6, provides a 17th-century setting plus more than 300 varieties of beer—well worth searching out.

3. Ieper (Ypres)

Ieper, set in the flat polder plains of Flanders, owed its early prosperity to a flourishing textile industry, which reached its pinnacle in the 13th century. Sadly, over the centuries the town has been victimized by one war after another and has become a mere ghost of what it was in its heyday.

By far the most devastating of all her wars was World War I, when hardly a brick was left standing after fierce fighting between German and British forces. Many visitors, in fact, come to pay homage to those who fell on the surrounding battlefields and who lie buried in the massive military cemeteries here. Ieper pays its respects at 8 p.m. every day of the year, when traffic beneath the Menen Gate is halted and members of the local fire brigade sound the Last Post on silver bugles that were gifts of the British Legion. But perhaps the most poignant tribute of all came from the poet John McRae, whose lament began "In Flanders' fields the poppies blow, between the crosses, row on row. . . ."

Homage could well be paid also to the determined citizens of Ieper who have rebuilt, brick by brick, the most important of its medieval buildings exactly as they were, carefully following original plans still in existence. It's impossible to walk or ride through Ieper without a mental tip of the hat to those who managed this incredible feat.

The drive from Brugge or Gent is well worthwhile for its scenic beauty, and either is easily accomplished in a half day or less. There is also rail and bus service from Brussels, Gent, Brugge, and the Belgian coast.

WHERE TO EAT

There are a number of quite adequate, moderately priced restaurants for lunch or dinner. For dining a cut above adequate, look to either of these: **Yperley,** St. Jacobsstraat 1 (tel. 20-54-70), an elegant restaurant specializing in seafood, where dinner without wine will run BF1,350 ($43.50) to BF1,550 ($50); or **Dikkebus,** Vijverdreef 31 (tel. 20-00-85), about three miles southwest of town on Lake Dikkebus, where you'll pay BF700 ($22.50) to BF1,200 ($38.75).

TOURIST INFORMATION

The **Ieper Tourist Office** is in the Town Hall, Grote Markt 1 (tel. 057/20-26-26 or 20-26-23), with hours of 9 a.m. to 6 p.m. weekdays, till 5 p.m. on Saturday, Sunday, and holidays; shorter hours October through March.

SIGHTSEEING TOURS

The Tourist Office can furnish details on tours in an open London bus, usually reserved for groups, which will sometimes let you go along.

THE MAIN SIGHTS

In your walks around Ieper you'll want to look for one or two special sights. One of the few fortifications not demolished during World War I are the **ramparts** that once surrounded the town. You can reach them via stairs at the Menen Gate, and if you walk around to the Rijselpoort (Lille Gate), there's one of the most beautiful of the **British war cemeteries** dozing beneath a grass coverlet many local people will tell you is greener than any other in Europe. Notice, too, the many streets lined with reconstructed **17th-century façades**—these are the homes of a valiant populace who have reached back to their past for surroundings of their present.

Cloth Hall

Ieper's medieval glory is reflected in this beautiful Gothic building, the original of which stood from 1260 to 1304. From its center rises a 210-foot-square **Belfry tower,** and also in the hall is the moving **Ieper Salient Museum,** filled with mementoes of the horrendous 1914–1918 fighting.

The Menen Gate ("Menenpoort")

On panels set in this 130-foot memorial arch you'll find the names of some 54,896 British soldiers who fell in the World War I fighting around Ieper and who have no known grave—a memorial famed throughout Britain and the continent as the "Missing Memorial."

St. Martin's Cathedral

Its graceful spire is a landmark in the town, and St. Martin's holds the tomb of a bishop of Ieper named Jansen, whose heretical theories played such havoc in the 17th century.

Museums

The **Merghelynck Museum,** Merghelyuckstraat 2 (tel. 057/20-20-42 or 20-06-05), is a wonderfully lavish manor house furnished with Louis XV and XVI antiques. It's closed on Sunday and holidays and the last two weeks in July; open other days from 10 a.m. to noon and 2 to 5 p.m., with an admission fee of BF50 ($1.50).

The **Bellegodshuis Museum,** 38 Grotemarkt, counts among its treasures the *Virgin and Child* painting of Ieper's own artist, Melchior Broederlam. Open from 10 a.m. to 1 p.m. and 3 to 6 p.m. every day except Monday during the months of July and August; shorter hours other months.

Festival of the Cats

Lucky you, if you can get to Ieper on the second Sunday in May 1990–every other year (the even-numbered ones), Ieper celebrates one of Europe's most colorful pageants, the Festival of the Cats ("Kattenwoensdog"). That's when hundreds of velvet cats are thrown by the town jester from the Belfry to crowds below. The custom originated centuries ago when the great Cloth Hall, filled with cloth stored there until it could be sold, attracted thousands of mice, and cats by the hundred were imported to eliminate them. Once the cloth was sold, however, the cats themselves became a problem, and eventually the solution agreed upon to rid the town of the felines was to fling them from the Belfry. How it got from that practical (albeit, gory) practice to today's lively carnival I have no idea, but that seems to matter little when you're caught up in the general revelry that begins with the Procession of the Cats!

VIII

BELGIUM'S BEACHES

1. KNOKKE-HEIST/HET ZOUTE
2. OOSTENDE
3. OOSTDUINKERKE
4. DE PANNE

Belgium's beaches are without doubt some of the best in northern Europe. Strung along a 41-mile North Sea coastline, the beaches are one continuous vista of fine white sand backed by countless dunes and dotted with lovely seaside resorts. There are, in fact, 13 resort towns, each as individual as shells that wash in from the sea.

For the visitor, the Belgian coastline presents a happy dilemma—whether to opt for an au naturel holiday of sea and sand and sun, or one of high-flying casino and nightclub action, or a "bust-out" of sheer gustatory gluttony, or a seaside sightseeing expedition. They're all here awaiting your choice, and with judicious planning it's quite possible to get around to them all in an incredibly short amount of time.

The dedicated beach bum will find wonderfully wide beaches that stretch back as much as 500 yards at low tide, and a gently sloping decline into the sea that makes for some of the safest swimming in Europe (although authorities constantly warn against swimming along isolated stretches of beach, a warning I hasten to echo). You can skim along the sand on wind-blown sail carts, pedal neat little beach buggies, or join the sun worshippers stretched full length in search of the perfect tan.

When the sun goes down, there are nightclubs that attract top performers during the summer months and four casinos (at Knokke-Heist, Oostende, Blankenberge, and Middelkerke) to tempt the gambler in your soul year round. Without a lot of time to spare, the gourmand will surely leave frustrated at not being able to gorge at every single one of the excellent restaurants in this small area. Sightseers will be kept busy discovering a unique fishing museum, one dedicated solely to surrealistic paintings, another that houses an important post-impressionist-era art collection, and tramping through nature reserves tinged with the hue of sea lavender and alive with the whir of bird wings in a protected environment.

How to plan the holiday that will exactly suit *you?* First you must take a close look at the personality of the individual resorts and choose the one with the most personal appeal. The four major points of reference are discussed in this chapter, with comments on the smaller communities that should help you decide which location is best for you.

Not to worry about accommodations: hotels, holiday flats, even boarding houses, are plentiful, and with few exceptions rates are considerably below what you'd expect to pay in such popular vacation spots. Which is not to say, however, that you should just drop in—Europeans come here in droves, and the English think nothing of hopping across the Channel for annual outings. The smart thing to do is book directly or through one of the local tourist offices before you arrive, and it's absolutely essential to book ahead if you're coming on a weekend, since that's when Belgians flock to the sea from inner cities for brief work breaks.

As for planning your time along the coast, it's an easy matter to dabble in a little bit of every option, and you won't even need a car! There's a marvelous "Tram de la Côte" (Tourist Tram) that runs the entire length of the coast, with 15-minute departures during summer months. Charges vary from point to point, but if you decide to go the distance—from Knokke-Heist to De Panne (a two-hour ride)—you'll pay only BF150 ($4.75).

1. Knokke-Heist/Het Zoute

Snuggled up close to the Dutch border, this is the classiest of the Belgian beach areas. Of course, "class" comes in levels, and there are several in the Knokke-Heist/Het Zoute neighborhood. Sometimes called "the garden of the North Sea coast," this area actually consists of five beaches: Heist, Duinbergen, Albertstrand, Knokke, and Het Zoute. Heist attracts average-income (classy average-income) families; Duinbergen is chiefly residential and caters to families; Albertstrand is more sporty; and then things begin to reach the upper levels of "class."

Knokke is fashionable—not as exclusive as it once was, but very, very fashionable. Het Zoute is ultra-fashionable. You can tell by the very look of it, with its main shopping street, the Kustlaan, sporting shops adorned with designer names of international fame (some designer collections have actually been shown here before Paris!), jewelers, and art galleries. The winding residential streets of Het Zoute fairly shriek "money," and it's big money—this is the nesting place of Europe's jet set, and the lovely villas proclaim owners of both wealth and exquisite taste. Whether or not you fit easily into this monied environment, a drive, cycle, or walk through Het Zoute provides an interesting glimpse of the wealthy, gracious lifestyle of its inhabitants.

WHERE TO STAY

Some of the most luxurious (and expensive) coastal hotels are located in this area, but there are also many accommodation choices in a wide price range. As in resort areas the world over, rates fluctuate according to the season and there are periodic midweek reductions, so be sure to ask. Rates listed below include breakfast, service, and VAT.

Expensive

Sofitel La Reserve, Elisabethlaan 160, 8300 Knokke-Heist (tel. 050/61-06-06), is so large it's virtually a small town unto itself, but La Reserve nevertheless has a comfortable, almost country, air about it. It's directly across from the casino, a short walk from the beachfront, and is the home of Knokke's important health spa, the Thalassa Center. Guest rooms, all with balconies, are spacious and come with such extras as mini-bars and color TVs that receive a full dozen channels—in addition, of course, to the usual private bath, modern furnishings, and the comforts of a luxury hotel. There's a good restaurant, a lounge, and acres of tennis courts. Seasonal rates range from BF1,570 ($50.75) to BF4,100 ($132.25) for singles, BF2,550 ($82.25) to BF4,850 ($156.50) for doubles.

Pauwels, Kustlaan 353, 8300 Knokke-Heist (tel. 050/61-16-17). This elegant small hotel rubs elbows with upper-stratosphere shops in Het Zoute, and its guest rooms are exceptionally well furnished, all with private bath. There's a restaurant, a bar, and garage parking. One block from the beach. Rates are in the BF2,200 ($71) to BF2,400 ($77.50) range for singles, BF3,000 ($96.75) to BF3,200 ($103) range for doubles.

Moderate

Shakespeare, Zeedijk 795, 8300 Knokke-Heist (tel. 050/60-11-77). Guest rooms in this small, attractive hotel come with private bath, color TV, and direct-dial telephone. There's a bar and restaurant, as well as private parking. Rates are BF1,350 ($43.50) to BF2,000 ($64.50) for singles, BF2,000 ($64.50) to BF2,800 ($90.25) for doubles.

Parkhotel, Elisabethlaan 204, 8300 Knokke-Heist (tel. 050/60-09-01). Only 12 rooms in this nice little hotel some two blocks from the beach. Its nicely appointed rooms all have private bath, color TV, radio, and telephone. There's an excellent restaurant, a cozy bar, and private parking. Rates run BF2,500 ($80.75) to BF3,000 ($96.75), single or double.

Lido, Zwaluwenlaan 18, 8200 Knokke-Heist (tel. 050/60-19-25). Modern to the *n*th degree in both décor and furnishings, the Lido has well-done-up, bright guest rooms that come with private bath, color TV, radio, and telephone. There's a bar on the premises and private parking. Rates are in the BF1,500 ($48.50) to BF1,800 ($58) range for singles, BF2,000 ($64.50) to BF2,500 ($80.75) for doubles.

Inexpensive

The Corner House, Hazegrasstraat 1, 8300 Knokke-Heist (tel. 050/60-76-19). Located not far from the Zwinn nature reserve, and quite a distance from the beach, the Corner House offers nice accommodations at BF650 ($21) for singles and BF900 ($29) for doubles without private bath, BF1,250 ($40.25) for doubles with private bath.

You'll also find several good budget hotels located along the Lippenslaan in Knokke that offer no-frills double rooms without private bath for under BF1,500 ($48.50).

WHERE TO EAT

Limited space permits a listing of only the highlights of good restaurants along this part of the Belgian coast—you'll find dozens of fine eateries to supplement the ones below.

Aquilon, Bayauxlaan 70 (tel. 60-12-74). This ground-floor restaurant just in front of the casino is by far the most outstanding in the area. It's also the most elegant, and dinner here is more than just a treat for the taste buds. Allow plenty of time to savor such specialties as veal with mushrooms and truffles or lobster Marguerite. Reservations are absolutely essential, especially on weekends, and expect to pay between BF1,500 ($48.50) and BF2,500 ($80.75), without wine. It's closed Tuesday for dinner and all day Wednesday.

Panier d'Or, Zeedijk 659 (tel. 60-31-89). Seafood, especially their renowned fish soup, stars at this seaside restaurant. It's a medium-sized place with traditional décor, and prices are in the BF950 ($30.50) to BF1,350 ($43.50) range for four courses without wine. Closed Tuesday; reserve ahead.

Casa Borghèse, Bayauxlaan 27 (tel. 60-37-39). Seafood and Italian specialties come in an attractive setting and at prices of BF700 ($22.50) and under. Closed Thursday.

TOURIST INFORMATION

The **Tourist Office** is at Zeedijk Knokke 660, Lichttorenplein (tel. 050/60-15-16 or 60-16-16).

THINGS TO SEE AND DO

Top on the list of attractions, it goes without saying, are the five fine **beaches,** where all manner of seaside sports are available. From time to time there are half-hour **sea trips** in an amphibious vessel launched right from the beach; sand castle competitions flourish; and kite flying is a favorite pastime.

In town, take a 30-minute ride through the streets in the **miniature train** that departs from Van Bunnenplein at the promenade. On foot, follow the "Bloemen Walk" signposts. Bikers and/or drivers will enjoy the 30-mile "Riante Polderroute" that begins in Knokke and guides you through wooded parks, gardens, past the Zwinn reserve, into polder farm country, past canals and ditches, and on to Damme and Oosterkerke.

Het Zwinn Nature Reserve

It was along this stretch of coast that the River Zwinn estuary met the sea and gave Brugge its greatness as a leading European port. Since fickle fate silted up the river and Brugge has settled into a landlocked prominence of quite another sort, the old riverbed of the Zwinn (just east of Het Zoute) has turned into a salty, sandy marshland. The spongy soil nurtures an amazingly rich vegetation, and it's a lovely sight in summer to see it covered with sea lavender. Hundreds of nesting birds—geese, plovers, white storks among them—find a refuge here, and you see them both in the interesting aviary near the entrance and flying free as you tramp through a landscape that has been returned to nature. There's also a nice restaurant, Chalet du Zwinn, as you come in, as well as a well-stocked bookshop. Entrance to the refuge is BF60 ($2), and there's a two-hour guided tour every Sunday and Thursday morning (Sunday only during winter months) starting at 10 a.m.

Casino of Knokke

Located across from the Albertstrand beach at Zeedijk 509, this great 1920s casino is the epitome of elegance, with plush gaming rooms, nostalgic bits of art deco, and glittering chandeliers illuminating a glittering, dressed-to-the-nines clientele. There are two nightclubs, in addition to a ballroom that features leading European entertainers. Its magnificent Salle Magritte dining room is a tribute to the surrealist painter René Magritte, whose paintings have been transformed into gigantic murals that adorn the walls. Despite all the glitter—or more accurately, *because* of it—there's a cosmopolitan relaxation about the casino that makes it fun, and it's well worth taking along dressy attire to have a night here. You'll also need to bring your passport, and you'll pay a BF500 ($16.25) entrance fee, after which I can only wish for you the smiles of Lady Luck.

Thalassa Zeecentrum

A cure for all your ills may just be waiting for you at this combination spa, fitness center, and gymnasium. In the "thermal institute," indulge in hot sea-mud baths and a number of other seawater treatments, work out on a wide variety of exercise equipment, or simply swim in the seawater pool or laze in the sauna. You'll find the Zeecentrum in the Sofitel La Reserve Hotel, Elisabethlaan 158 (tel. 050/60-06-12), and if you're a guest there, admission to the fitness club comes with your room rate—others pay BF300 ($9.75) plus charges based on any additional treatments chosen.

2. Oostende

Oostende's place as "Queen of the Coast" is quite secure—she has, after all, been in residence here since the 10th century, seen Crusaders embark for the Holy Land, been hostess to pirates who found her a convenient base, resisted Spanish rule from the end of the 16th century into the 17th, been the terminal for sea service to England since 1846, seen her harbor blocked to thwart German submarines in World War I, been bombed during World War II—and emerged from that long, eventful history as a busy port and lively recreational haven that sports Belgium's largest casino, a racetrack, an outstanding art museum, a spa, and no fewer than five excellent sandy beaches.

Though "queenly" Oostende most certainly is, she is also very much a "queen of the people," welcoming all income levels, with very little of the posh exterior so much a part of Knokke-Heist and Het Zoute. Located at almost the exact midpoint of the Belgian coastline, Oostende divides the Oostkust (to the northeast) from the Westkust (to the southwest), and is the ideal touring base for coastal exploration. That fact, coupled with a mass of entertainment facilities that operate around the calendar, draws visitors by the thousands, and Oostende welcomes every one, with more than 100 hotels and over 250 restaurants to cater to their comfort.

The elevated Albert I Promenade that runs the entire length of Oostende's 3½-mile beachfront was, before World War II, lined with elegant private seaside villas, many the holiday homes of European royalty. From the debris of bombings during that war that demolished so many of those fine old homes have sprung hotels and apartment buildings of a purely modern form. There is also a very good shopping district and an Olympic-size indoor swimming pool at the seafront. Outdoor pools are filled with heated sea water.

WHERE TO STAY

Oostende doesn't lack for accommodations, and they're available in every price range, from luxurious hotels right on the beachfront to budget rooms several blocks away from the water. You should *not,* however, leave your reservations until the last minute—book several weeks ahead during the summer, either directly with your choice of hotel or through any Belgian Tourist Office.

The rates shown below are for the summer months (high season), and you should know that they are lower other times of the year. Also, most hotels have special package rates available: summer midweek stays, winter weekends, etc.

Expensive

Andromeda Hotel, Albert I Promenade 60, 8400 Oostende (tel. 059/80-66-11). The undisputed queen of luxury hotels in Oostende, this modern hotel also has the best possible location—right on the beachfront and just next door to the casino. The marble lobby is an indication of the quality rooms upstairs, its Gloria restaurant provides excellent meals in an attractive room, and its Byblos cocktail bar opens to the sea, with terrace tables for sunny days. Guest rooms are the latest word in comfort and décor, with armchairs in which to relax and view the sea through glass sliding doors that open to balconies. All have private bath, color TV, and direct-dial telephone. You'll pay more for ocean-front rooms—BF4,000 ($129) single, BF4,500 ($145.25) double—less for those facing south looking inland—BF2,000 ($64.50) single, BF2,500 ($80.75) double.

Oostende Compagnie, Koningstraat 79, 8400 Oostende (tel. 059/70-96-08 or 80-10-86). This luxurious small hotel began life as a royal villa, and it retains the same "home" atmosphere, although it's home on a grand scale. Its setting is a quiet seaside location beyond the busy town center, about 100 yards from the casino. A pretty terrace and garden face the sea, floor-length windows with the same view line the drawing room, and the dining room is known for its kitchen (see below). The guest rooms, too, are much like those in a private home, and the two lovely suites that can sleep up to four people—at BF8,500 ($274)—provide such perfect comfort and beauty that they'll tempt you to settle in for a long spell. Six large rooms, beautifully furnished, cost BF3,250 ($104.75), and two smaller ones are BF2,100 ($67.75). All have private bath, telephone, radio, and television. Rates are *per room,* single or double occupancy (or more, in the case of the suites). Breakfast is BF250 ($8). There's private parking on the grounds. This is a rather special place and highly recommended. It's also very popular, so book as far in advance as possible. Closed the month of October.

Hotel Thermae-Palace, Koningin Astridiaan 7, 8400 Oostende (tel. 059/50-09-79). An integral part of the sprawling thermal baths complex, this slightly old-fashioned, 49-room hotel (built in the '30s) has comfortable, attractive, fairly standard guest rooms, each with private bath, telephone, and TV. Its Promenade restaurant serves high-standard meals with moderate prices beginning at BF600 ($19.50). Rates range from BF2,500 ($80.75) to BF3,000 ($96.75).

Moderate

Hostellerie Old Shakespeare, St. Petrus and Paulusplein 18, 8400 Oostende (tel. 059/70-51-57). Just across from the railway station, overlooking the yacht harbor, and near the car-ferry terminal, the Old Shakespeare has a dozen pretty rooms, each with private bath, telephone, radio, and TV. Its restaurant is outstanding (see below), and there are special "gastronomic weekend" rates available during some seasons. Rates are in the BF1,500 ($48.50) to BF2,000 ($64.50) range.

Strandhotel, Visserskaai 1, 8400 Oostende (tel. 059/70-33-83 or 70-76-31). This pleasant 20-room hotel is situated near the railway station, yacht harbor, and car-ferry terminal. Its comfortable rooms have private bath, telephone, and TV, and rates run from BF2,000 ($64.50) to BF2,500 ($80.75). Closed December and January.

Hotel Bero, Hofstraat 1a, 8400 Oostende (tel. 059/70-23-35). A short distance back from the beachfront, this 60-room modern hotel has been owned and operated by the same family for three generations. There's a swimming pool, fitness sauna, solarium, and whirlpool. The nicely appointed rooms all have bath, telephone, radio, and TV, and rates are in the BF1,500 ($48.50) to BF1,800 ($58) range.

Hotel Danielle, Ijzerstraat 5, 8400 Oostende (tel. 059/70-63-49). Close to both the beach and the casino, this is a modern hotel with attractive rooms that come with private bath, color TV, and telephone, and there's a good restaurant with moderate prices. Rates range from BF1,200 ($38.71) to BF2,350 ($75.81).

Hotel Prado, Leopole II laan 22, 8400 Oostende (tel. 059/70-53-06). Located on a major midtown street, this modern hotel has 32 comfortable rooms with private bath, telephone, and color TV at rates of BF1,600 ($51.50) to BF2,300 ($74.25).

Inexpensive

Hôtel du Parc, Marie-Joséplein 3, 8400 Oostende (tel. 059/70-16-80 or 70-65-80). Conveniently located to the casino, the beach, and shopping, this pleasant 47-room hotel has rooms both with and without private facilities. For a room without bath, rates are BF900 ($29) to BF1,100 ($35.50); those with, BF1,500 ($48.50).

Hotel Royal Astor, Hertstraat 15, 8400 Oostende (tel. 059/50-49-70). This is a nice, centrally located hotel that has single rooms without bath for BF900 ($29) to BF1,100 ($35.50), and doubles with bath for BF1,400 ($45.25) to BF1,600 ($51.50).

Note: The Tourist Office can also book you into inexpensive boarding houses.

READER'S HOTEL SELECTION: "A ship passenger from Dover to Oostende recommended a small hotel, the **Burlingston,** Kapellestraat 90, 8400 Oostende (tel. 059/70-15-52 or 80-21-18), which was only four blocks from the steamer terminal in Oostende. The hotel faces the yacht harbor and is alongside a pedestrian shopping street that had a shopping fair in progress. We had a very nice room with complete bath, and the moderate rate included breakfast. We liked the hotel so much that we made a reservation for our return stop" (C. Cooper, Orinda, Calif.).

WHERE TO EAT

Most Oostende restaurants, not surprisingly, specialize in seafood. Not surprising, either, is the freshness of the seafood and the expertise with which these seacoast chefs prepare it—fishing boats deliver daily catches to the Visserskaai (fisherman's quay), and these cooks are backed by a tradition of treating the fruits of the sea with respect. With some 250 restaurants at hand, you'll seldom be disappointed in any, and Oostende is the ideal place for "window shopping" each day for the setting and menu that has the most momentary appeal. Those listed below are a very personal, subjective list and meant only as an indication of what you'll find on your own. Most serve both a specialty of the day, based on the freshest ingredients available, and a three-course tourist menu, at a set price. And if you're attacked by hunger pangs late at night, look for a nearby snackbar—almost all are open until the wee hours.

Expensive

If you plan on just one "big splurge" meal at the seaside, I highly recommend that you consider either of these superb restaurants, where both cuisine and ambience will give the spirit a lift.

Villa Maritza, Albert I Promenade 76 (tel. 50-88-08). This exquisite restaurant is housed in a seaside villa that was once the holiday home of a Hungarian baroness. Built in 1526, it's one of the few ornate old buildings that once lined the shore, most of which were destroyed by World War II bombings. Inside, Oostende native Jacques Ghaye has created a sophisticated, elegant restaurant, with cuisine every bit as elegant as the décor. Seafood specialties vary with the season, but a superb typical dish is blanc de turbot à la mousse de crevettes grises, a lovely combination of turbot, white wine, and the tiny gray shrimp of the North Sea. A four-course dinner, without wine, will run about BF1,350 ($43.50), and there's a set menu de dégustation for BF1,950 ($63). Best to book ahead, especially in the evening. Closed Monday.

Au Vigneron, Koningstraat 79 (tel. 70-96-08 or 80-10-86). This restaurant in the Oostende Compagnie hotel (see above), one of the finest along the entire coast, features classic French haute cuisine. The menu changes according to the best available ingredients, but you can always depend on their menu de dégustation for a memorable meal at a set price of BF2,000 ($64.50), without wine. Closed Monday and every Sunday evening.

Moderate

The Bacchianal, Casino-Kursaal (tel. 70-51-11). Even if you don't plan to play the tables at the casino, you can enjoy a meal in its upstairs restaurant. Seafood and filet steak prepared with duck livers and Périgord sauce are specialties, and a four-course dinner without wine will run about BF1,350 ($43.50).

Old Shakespeare, St. Petrus en Paulusplein 18 (tel. 70-51-57). This intimate restaurant in a small hotel near the railway station (see above) serves near-gourmet meals at less-than-gourmet prices. Choose from their nightly specials, or select the menu du dégustation, and expect to pay between BF850 ($27.50) and BF1,000 ($32.25), without wine. They are, incidentally, well known for their wine cellar. Closed Wednesday.

Prince Charles, Visserskaai 19 (tel. 70-50-66), is one of the nicer restaurants along the quay, where an exceptionally good seafood dinner will cost between BF750 ($24.25) and BF1,000 ($32.25), without wine.

Adelientje, Bonenstraat 9 (tel. 70-13-67), has very good seafood, with a three-course dinner costing in the BF600 ($19.25) to BF900 ($29) range.

Villa Borghese, Van Iseghemlaan 65B (tel. 80-08-76), offers Italian cuisine at prices of BF400 ($13) to BF750 ($24.25). Best reserve on Saturday and Sunday.

Inexpensive

Le Basque, Albert I Promenade 62 (tel. 70-54-44). Oostende sole and seafood kebabs are featured in this seaside restaurant, at prices of BF300 ($9.75) to BF500 ($16.25).

Belgica, Visserskaai 42 (tel. 70-09-91), has excellent seafood in a setting overlooking the fishing quay. Prices are in the BF300 ($8) to BF500 ($12) range.

Note: There are several attractive restaurants along the Albert I Promenade where it's possible to enjoy a good meal for BF300 ($9.75) and under—the place to window-shop for your budget eatery.

TOURIST INFORMATION

The main **Tourist Office** is at Stedelijk Feest-en Kultuurpaleis, bus 5, Wapenplein, 8400 Oostende (tel. 059/70-11-99 and 70-60-17). During July and August, there's also a suboffice at the railway station, Natienkaai 2 (tel. 059/50-62-84).

THINGS TO SEE AND DO

While Oostende is the best base from which to explore the entire coast, there's plenty to keep you occupied at this one resort location.

The James Ensor House

The post-impressionist painter James Ensor (1860–1949) lived most of his life in Oostende, and his home, at Vlaanderenstraat 27 (tel. 80-53-35), has been restored as it was when his aunt and uncle kept a ground-floor shells and souvenir shop. Ensor's studio and lounge are on the second floor, and if you're familiar with his paintings you'll recognize some of the furnishings and views from the windows. Open daily except Tuesday from 10 a.m. to noon and 2 to 5 p.m., with an admission charge of BF40 ($1.25).

Fine Arts Museum

On Wapenplein, Stedelijk Feest-en Kultuurpaleis (tel. 70-61-31), the paintings of native sons James Ensor, Jan De Clenck, Constant Permeke, and Leon Spilliaert are featured in this second-floor museum (the Folklore Museum occupies the first floor; see below), along with Belgian impressionists. The museum is open every day except Tuesday from 10 a.m. to noon and 2 to 5 p.m. Admission is BF40 ($1.25).

P.M.M.K. Museum of Modern Art

Set in a former department store building at Romestraat 11 (tel. 059/50-81-18), the Museum of Modern Art houses over 1,500 items, including paintings, sculpture, graphics, video, and film that together comprise a rather complete picture of modern art in Belgium from its very beginnings up to the present. There are also a specialized library with reading room and a coffee bar. Hours are 10 a.m. to 12:30 p.m. and 1:30 to 6 p.m. in April, May, September, and October; 10 a.m. to 1:30 p.m. and 5 to 8:30 p.m. in June, July, and August; and 10 a.m. to 12:30 p.m. and 1:30 to 5 p.m. November through March. Closed Monday year round. Admission is free for children under 14, BF40 ($1.25) for adults, BF20 (65¢) for students and old-age pensioners.

Folklore Museum "De Plate"

Also on Wapenplein, Stedelijk Feest-en Kultuurpaleis (tel. 80-53-35), in addition to exhibits depicting the native dress, folklore, and history of Oostende, has interesting displays of neolithic and Roman artifacts that have been excavated in the vicinity. There's a re-created fisherman's pub, a fisherman's home, and an old tobacco shop, and the Marine section deals with shipbuilding, fishing boats, and the Oostende–Dover ferry line. Hours are 10 a.m. to noon and 2 to 5 p.m.; closed Tuesday and Sunday. Admission is BF40 ($1.25).

North Sea Aquarium

In the town center, along the Visserskaai (the old fishing harbor), a marvelous display of many of the North Sea fish, mollusca, and crustacea, as well as interesting shell collections, make this a good sightseeing stop. Open from 9 a.m. to noon and 2 to 5 p.m. every day; admission is BF40 ($1.25).

Casino (Kursaal)

There's been a casino at this spot on Monacoplein (tel. 70-51-11) since 1852, but the one you find there today was built after World War II, when bombings left the beachfront in ruins. The present Kursaal is one of the largest in Europe, with a concert hall, restaurant, nightclub, disco, and—of course—gaming rooms. The gaming rooms open at 3 p.m. every day, and you pay a BF500 ($16.25) "membership fee" to be admitted (bring along your passport).

Wellington Racecourse

You'll find the only racetrack on the coast here, just across from the seafront at the end of the Royal Arcades. There's a grass track for flat and hurdle racing and a lava track for the trotters. Admission to the field opposite the grandstand is free; you pay BF200 ($6.50) for grandstand seats Monday through Friday, BF250 ($8) on Saturday and Sunday, and BF350 ($11.25) on public holidays. The Tourist Office can furnish a detailed schedule of races.

Music

Carillon concerts ring from the Festival Hall tower periodically through the summer, and there are **bandstand concerts** on the Market Square from June to September.

AFTER DARK

Nighttime activity is at its most frenetic at the casino nightclub, and on Friday, Saturday, and Sunday in its disco. There are also symphonic concerts, operettas, and ballet performances in the casino concert hall.

For late-night dance clubs, cabarets, and bars, hie yourself off to the Langestraat, near the eastern end of the beach.

3. Oostduinkerke

Oostduinkerke is one of the coast's small, family-oriented resort towns, yet it holds much of interest to art and nature lovers, whether based here or in Oostende or De Panne, both within easy reach by auto, bike, or tram. Its five miles of beachfront encompasses the neighboring small towns of Koksijde and Sint-Idesbald.

WHERE TO STAY

Hotel accommodations are rather limited, but those listed below can be recommended. The Tourist Office can also furnish names of agents for holiday cottages or flats, most of which are available on a weekly basis.

Hotel Artan, Ijslandplein 5, Zeedijk, 8458 Oostduinkerke Koksijde (tel. 058/51-59-08). Units at this modern hotel that sits right on the beach feature kitchenettes and sleeping space for as many as four. Other facilities include a coffeeshop, cafeteria, nice bar, exercise room with sauna, and an indoor swimming pool. Rates are in the BF2,600 ($83.75) to BF3,700 ($119.25) range.

Hotel Westland, Zeedijk 9, 8458 Oostduinkerke Koksijde (tel. 058/51-31-97), is a modern hotel on the beach. The Westland's rooms are comfortable, attractive, and functional at rates of BF1,100 ($35.50) to BF1,600 ($51.50).

Hotel Gauquié, Leopold II laan 251, 8458 Oostduinkerke Koksijde (tel. 058/51-10-88). This large, whitewashed old hotel is a block from the beach, with nicely furnished rooms (all with private bath) that carry rates of BF950 ($30.75) to BF1,100 ($35.50).

Pension M. Vanneuville, Albert I laan, 8458 Oostduinkerke (tel. 058/51-26-20). Comfortable rooms without private baths are available at rates in the BF850 ($27.50) and below range.

There's also a 100-bed hostel, **Huis Duinenrand,** Koksijdesteenweg, 8458 Oostduinkerke Koksijde (tel. 058/51-10-54).

WHERE TO EAT

Fresh-caught shrimp are the center of many culinary specialties here, and although neither of the moderately priced restaurants listed here can lay claim to being posh or gourmet, their kitchens—like most of those you'll find in the immediate area—turn out seafood creations that come very close to that gourmet label, with price tags that are unbelievably affordable.

Christophe, Albert I laan 43 (tel. 51-38-08). Right on the coastal tram route, the Christophe offers set menus utilizing the best available ingredients of each day at prices of BF550 ($17.75) to BF900 ($29), without wine.

Edelweis, Leopold II laan 276 (tel. 51-23-78). Three- or four-course meals in this attractive restaurant are in the BF500 ($16.25) to BF700 ($22.50) range.

TOURIST INFORMATION

The **Tourist Office** is in the Town Hall, Leopold II laan 2, 8458 Oostduinkerke (tel. 058/51-11-89), with hours of 8 a.m. to noon and 1:30 to 5 p.m. mid-June through mid-September, weekdays only; and there's also a Tourist Office in Astridplein (tel. 058/51-13-89) which stays open both weekdays and weekends during summer months from 10 a.m. to noon and 2 to 6 p.m.

THINGS TO SEE AND DO

Oostduinkerke's chief attraction is its beautiful, wide **beach,** the site of a very special activity you'll find nowhere else along the coast and one that may well be on its way to disappearing altogether. It is here that seven stalwart (and aging), yellow-slickered, and oilskin-clad gentlemen each day mount sturdy horses and wade into the surf at low tide to drag large nets behind them, ensnaring large quantities of the delicious crevettes—those tiny, gray shrimp that thrive in the waters of the North Sea. They are carrying on a tradition that dates back several centuries, and it's very uncertain if there will be anyone to follow in their footsteps (hoofprints?). A good part of the catch will go into the kitchens of cafés owned by those same horseback fishermen, but if you take yourself to the National Fishing Museum's next-door neighbor, the De Peerdevisser pub, soon after the fishermen return, you can purchase the just-caught, just-boiled delicacies by the sackful.

Sand-yachting is a popular sport at Oostduinkerke, and there are several places on the beach where you can rent the colorful vehicles and participate in the fun. Other beach activities include various festivals throughout the summer (ask the Tourist Office for a complete list to see what's on during your visit), sand castle competitions, and **horseback riding** on the strand. Horses can be hired from Hacienda, Weststraat 3 (tel. 51-69-50) and Pylyserlaan 50 (tel. 51-20-00).

Free guided **walking tours** are conducted from mid-June to mid-September, with a 9 a.m. departure at the foot of the Hoge Blekker and another at 2:30 p.m. from the Hôtel La Péniche.

Oostduinkerke's beach is backed by impressive **sand dunes,** one of which, De Hoge Blekker, rises over 100 feet, the highest in the country. Dune hiking and climbing is fascinating, and very popular with visitors.

There are two interesting museums you won't want to miss in this locality, as well as interesting ruins of a 12th-century Cistercian abbey and a remarkable agricultural school conducted in an ancient abbey farmstead.

The National Fishery Museum

This marvelous museum, located at the rear of the Town Hall in a small park at Pastoor Schmitzstraat 5 (tel. 51-24-68), traces on maps the sea routes followed by local fishing fleets, and exhibits the implements they have used through the centuries, sea paintings, a fishing harbor model, North Sea aquarium, and a wonderful collection of fishing-boat models that depict those used from as far back as 800 right up to the present. The interior of a typical fishermen's tavern is another highlight. Hours are 10 a.m. to noon and 2 to 6 p.m. daily, with admission of BF50 ($1.50) for adults, BF20 (65¢) for children.

Paul Delvauxmuseum

At Kabouterweg 42 (tel. 51-29-71) in the adjoining town of St. Idesbald, the nephew of internationally famous surrealist artist Paul Delvaux has turned a Flemish farmhouse into a modernized museum for outstanding works of his uncle. Delvaux's adulation of the female form is conveyed in many of the paintings, as is his love of trains and train stations. Hours are 10:30 a.m. to 6:30 p.m. daily except Monday, with an admission charge of BF90 ($3).

Dunenabdij (The Abbey of the Dunes)

During much of the 12th century, the Cistercian abbey here at Koninklijke Prinslaan 8 (tel. 51-19-33) was a center of culture for the region. It lay in peaceful ruins for several centuries, but in 1949 excavations were begun that have revealed archeological artifacts that shed considerable light on coastal history and the development of this settlement. A small museum on the site presents interesting exhibits, and the exposed foundations of the abbey church and the cloister clearly show their large dimensions. Open from 10 a.m. to 6 p.m. during the Easter holidays, July, and August; shorter hours other times; closed January. Admission is BF60 ($2).

Ten Bogaerde

Near the Abbey of the Dunes, this large abbey farmstead that includes a 12th-century barn is now an agricultural school. It's typical of the large farm holdings of ancient abbeys.

4. De Panne

De Panne is Belgium's closest coastal point to France and England. Its sandy beaches have been the scene of several significant historical high points: in 1830 Leopold I set foot on newly independent Belgian soil to become the first of the country's own kings (though, Lord knows, it had seen its share of foreign royalty!); during World War I it was here that King Albert I and his queen clung to Belgian resistance against German occupying forces; and in 1940 there was the evacuation of ill-fated troops of the British Expeditionary Forces.

From the wide beach at De Panne you can see the tall port cranes of Dunkirk, scene of England's heroic rescue mission that brought some 338,000 beleaguered troops to safety in a makeshift armada of small craft gathered from boat owners around the country in late May and early June of 1940 while under almost continuous bombing attacks from German planes. When it was over, the 7½-mile stretch of beach between Dunkirk and De Panne was a mass of military equipment litter. It's a little-recognized fact that the British commander, Lord Gort, headquartered not in Dunkirk, but here in De Panne.

But it's the wide beach (500 yards at low tide) and spectacular dunes (about one-third of all unspoiled duneland along the Belgian coast) that today bring hordes of tourists to De Panne each year, especially in July and August, when accommodations can be hard to come by despite the presence of thousands of holiday homes and flats. Those dunes are made all the more spectacular by vast wooded areas that turn them into a wonderland of greenery banding the creamy sands of the beach and azure sea beyond.

WHERE TO STAY

Holiday homes, some built as replicas of traditional fishermen's cottages, are the most popular form of accommodation in this largely family-oriented resort. The Tourist Office can furnish a complete list of rental agents, but you should know that most places are booked months in advance and for periods of no less than a week. One of the largest of the so-called holiday villages is **Duinhoek,** Duinhoekstraat 127, 8470 De Panne (tel. 058/41-38-98 or 23-49-10). The Tourist Office can also direct you to private homes, where a double room and breakfast runs about BF1,000 ($27.78).

The following recommended hotels include breakfast, service, and VAT in the rates quoted.

Moderate

Seahorse, Toeristenlaan 7, 8470 De Panne (tel. 058/41-27-47). It's small—only 19 rooms—but the Seahorse is by far the most outstanding hotel in De Panne, the standards of décor and furnishings much more modern than most. Rooms come with private bath, telephone, TV, and radio, and rates are BF1,100 ($35.50) single, BF1,700 ($54.75) double.

Des Princes, Nieuwpoortlaan 46, 8470 De Panne (tel. 058/41-10-91). Guest rooms are spacious and nicely appointed in this comfortable hotel, and rates run BF1,300 ($42) to BF1,650 ($53.25).

Le Gai Séjour, Nieuwpoortlaan 42, 8470 De Panne (tel. 058/41-13-03), considered by many to outrank all other De Panne hotels, features comfortable and attractive rooms above a ground-floor restaurant only one block from the beachfront. Rates are BF1,400 ($45.25) to BF2,500 ($80.75), depending on season and location of room.

Hotel Terlinck, Zeelaan 175, 8470 De Panne (tel. 058/41-26-21), is a modern hotel just a block from the sea. The Terlinck's guest rooms come both with and without private bath, and there's a good restaurant. Those with begin at BF1,700 ($54.75); those without, BF1,500 ($48.50).

Strand Motel, Nieuwpoortlaan 153, 8470 De Panne (tel. 058/41-11-96). Units at this beachfront motel have kitchenettes, as well as such standard fixtures as telephones and TVs. Rates are in the BF1,000 ($32.25) to BF2,000 ($64.50) range, depending on season and location.

Inexpensive

Hôtel Français, Kasteelstraat 31, 8470 De Panne (tel. 058/41-17-39). These are pleasant and comfortable rooms above a good restaurant. Those with private bath run BF1,250 ($40.25) and up; those without, BF1,000 ($32.25) and up.

Hôtel du Sablon, Duinkerkelaan 19, 8470 De Panne (tel. 058/41-11-03). Comfortable and well-kept rooms here are in the budget price range of BF850 ($27.50) to BF1,000 ($32.25).

WHERE TO EAT

Restaurant L'Avenue, Nieuwpoortlaan 56 (tel. 41-13-70). This restaurant is famed for its fine meals, yet prices are in the modest range of BF650 ($21) for three courses, BF1,100 ($35.50) for a five-course chef's special set menu without wine.

Le Fox, Walckierstraat 1 (tel. 41-28-55). Exceptional seafood dinners at this leading restaurant cost BF800 ($25.75) to BF1,200 ($38.75), without wine.

There are nearly 100 restaurants in De Panne, covering a wide range of specialties and prices, with a heavy emphasis on seafood, especially shrimp from local waters, and none in the really high-price range. For the least expensive, look to those along the Zeedijk, the beachfront promenade—it's half-tiled, with café terraces right on the sand. On the Nieuwpoortlaan there's a row of chip shops selling mussels and frites for next to nothing.

TOURIST INFORMATION

You'll find the **Tourist Office** in the Town Hall, Zeelaan 21, 8470 De Panne (tel. 058/41-13-02 or 41-13-04). During summer months there's also an **Information Desk** on the Zeedijk promenade (tel. 41-29-63).

THINGS TO SEE AND DO

Outdoor recreation is what people come to De Panne for, and with all those dunes to explore and the beach for sunning, swimming, and sand-yachting, time will never hang heavy. Herewith, a few suggestions.

In Town

A walk through De Panne's tree-lined residential streets, with rows of villas left over from another era, is a delight. Old fishermen's cottages still in use are on Veurnestraat.

Nature Walks

The Tourist Office can furnish a series of beautifully illustrated informative brochures on the dune areas, and they organize special guided tours periodically during summer months.

The 850-acre **Westhoek Nature Reserve** encloses a fascinating dune landscape, with vegetation that varies from full-grown trees to scrubby shrubs. It's a unique opportunity to observe the formation of sand dunes, since you'll see some in their beginning stages, and others that, although formed years ago, are constantly, but almost imperceptibly, changing. Signposted footpaths guide you all the way.

Straddling the Belgian/French border, the 230-acre **Domein Cabour** is another area that provides interesting walks, and there are frequent guided walks during summer months (ask at the Tourist Office about schedules).

Calmeynbos (Calmeyn Wood) covers only 110 acres, but is the loving legacy of one man, Maurice Calmeyn, who in 1903 began to plant trees in this area in order to preserve the dunes. Some 25 varieties of his plantings are thriving today.

For the Young

It's instant enchantment for children (of all ages?) at **Meli-Park,** Adinkerke (tel. 058/41-25-55), the famous honeybee-theme and leisure park. A multitude of delightful attractions will appeal to virtually every member of the family. There's Apirama (exploring the bees' kingdom by boat); Elfira (a fairytale wonderland), the animal park, jungle fantasy parrot show, water symphony, Carioca (all sorts of playground activities), and Phantom Guild, with three different fun fairs filled with rides. Open April through September, Meli-Park is a real treat, and the admission ticket of BF330 ($10.75) covers all attractions, while children less than one meter (3¼ feet) tall go in free.

ART OF THE WALLOONS

1. TOURNAI
2. MONS

Hainaut, the large Wallonian province that stretches across most of the Belgian/French border, has been the setting for countless conflicts between French nobility who coveted the rich Low Countries and fractious Flemish who were just as determined to resist French domination. Each called on the resources of allies, confiscated vast regions by way of political marriages, periodically engaged in pitched battles, and struggled to keep the local populations properly subdued.

Later, as coal mining grew in importance, yet another struggle between strong opposing forces developed when growing industrialization threatened to overrun the traditional rural, agricultural way of life. Charleroi, largest city in the province, sits in the central coal basin, and even today, though there is no longer any coal mining in Belgium, great slagheaps dot the Borinage countryside around Mons. Industrialization now, however, exists in the form of engineering and manufacturing rather than slagheaps and coal mines, and peaceful farmlands still exist as they have for centuries. As you drive through a lush, verdant landscape, it's difficult to picture the days, not so many years ago as Belgium counts time, when this was dubbed Belgium's "black country."

The province has a rich, colorful history and is the repository of great art treasures from the past. Charleroi is of little interest to visitors outside the engineering field. It is Tournai, undisputed art center of Hainaut, and Mons, its administrative center and site of many antiquities and museums, that draw us like powerful magnets.

1. Tournai

When you talk about Tournai, you must speak of survival. This second-oldest city in Belgium (Tongeren is the oldest) has, since the century before the birth of Christ, survived a multitude of political, military, and economic disasters that would have swamped many another. For centuries it maintained a position of prominence in Europe as an ecclesiastical center. Its importance for even more ancient centuries was not revealed, however, until an accidental discovery brought to light the fact that the early Roman settlement known as Tornacum at this point on the

River Scheldt, a major trade route crossroad, was also the first capital of the Frankish empire.

When a workman, quite by chance, opened the tomb of Childeric, King of the Franks, whose son, Clovis, founded the Merovingian Dynasty that ruled for nearly three centuries, it was firmly established that in A.D. 482 Tournai had indeed been the seat of royalty. The tomb also yielded breathtaking royal treasures that the city proudly displays.

In the years since Childeric and Clovis, Tournai has endured a veritable yo-yo existence of foreign rule, with successive domination by the French, the English (it was the only Belgian city King Henry VIII managed to conquer, in 1513), the Spanish, the Dutch, the French again, the Austrians, French Empire revolutionary forces, and for a time before Belgium became a kingdom in its own right in 1830, the Dutch once more.

Throughout it all Tournai retained its magnificent works of art and architecture that were the legacy of its platoons of painters, sculptors, goldsmiths, tapestry weavers, and porcelain craftsmen who persistently kept at their labors during all those eventful years. And then came the devastation of World War II, when a full 60% of its buildings were destroyed. It can only be deemed a miracle that the great cathedral emerged with little damage; but if that fact was due to the intervention of Divine Providence, it is surely to the very human perseverance and richness of spirit that we must attribute the fact that Tournai today greets us with its glorious monuments once more intact and its past recaptured so completely that the scars of conflict are scarcely visible.

Talk about survival!

WHERE TO STAY

If you elect to stay in the Tournai/Mons area rather than making easy day trips from Brussels, you'll find the hotel supply in Tournai rather limited. A wider selection is available at Kortrijk, about 18 miles away, and in Mons. There's also a real gem of a hostelry between the two cities that carries my highest recommendation.

Special Recommendation in the Area

Hostellerie le Vert Gazon, 7980 Stambruges-Grandglise (tel. 069/57-59-84). Just off Hwy. A16 that runs from Tournai to Mons, out from a charming little village, this turreted château is set in green, flower-bordered lawns. Its six rooms are beautifully furnished, as are the reception rooms and dining room, where excellent meals are served for about BF1,600 ($51.50), without wine. This restful place is an ideal base for sightseeing forays into both Mons and Tournai, and rates run BF2,000 ($64.50) and up. Be sure to reserve as far in advance as possible.

In Tournai

Aux Armes de Tournai, place de Lille 24, 7500 Tournai (tel. 069/22-67-23 or 22-57-89). In the center of town, this small (20 rooms) hotel offers comfortable rooms with private bath for BF1,600 ($51.50) and up.

L'Europe, Grand-Place 36, 7500 Tournai (tel. 069/22-40-67). The eight guest rooms are above a pleasant, moderately priced restaurant in this hotel right on the central square. Rooms with private bath run BF900 ($29) to BF1,400 ($45.25).

Tour St-Georges, place de Nédonchel 2, 7500 Tournai (tel. 069/22-53-00 or 22-50-35). There are ten comfortable and attractive guest rooms in this quiet, conveniently located hotel, with a good restaurant and rates of BF1,250 ($40.25) to BF1,600 ($51.50).

Centre le Panoramique, place de la Trinité 2, 7542 Mont-St-Aubert (tel. 069/23-31-11). Located about three miles from the city center, this is a modern recreational complex set atop a hill. Its 29 guest rooms have sleek, functional furnishings and come with private bath, radio, TV, and refrigerator. All have terraces affording panoramic views, and there are some especially furnished for the handicapped. On the premises are a bar and a pretty restaurant with moderate prices, and an indoor swimming pool. Rates start at BF2,500 ($80.75) for doubles, BF1,500 ($48.50) for singles.

WHERE TO EAT

Almost any of the sidewalk cafés lining the Grand-Place will provide excellent meals at moderate prices. Listed below are those exceptional eateries worth seeking out.

Expensive

Top recommendation goes to the elegant **Le Pressoir,** Marché aux Poteries 2 (tel. 22-35-13), just across from the cathedral entrance. In a setting of subdued sophistication are mouthwatering specialties of duck, with turbot featured among the fish specialties. There's a marvelous six-course set menu for BF1,100 ($35.50), and dinner from the à la carte menu can range from BF900 ($29) to BF1,500 ($48.50), all without wine, of course. It's important to reserve for lunch, and advisable to do so for dinner.

Charles Quint, Grand-Place 3 (tel. 22-14-41). This popular, elegant restaurant is nearly always crowded at lunch, and deservedly so. Its kitchen produces excellent fish, fowl, and meat dishes at prices of BF800 ($42). Hours are noon to 2:30 p.m. and 6:30 to 10 p.m. Closed Wednesday evening and all day Thursday.

Moderate

L'Europe, Grand-Place 36 (tel. 22-40-67), a pleasant restaurant looking out to the square, turns out good meals in the BF650 ($21) to BF850 ($27.50) range, and its sidewalk café is an ideal stopping place for one of those good Belgian beers or coffee and a snack to break up a sightseeing tour.

Flambée, rue Dame-Odile 4 (tel. 23-31-86). Grilled steaks, as well as a nice selection of fish choices, are featured in this rustic restaurant, where prices are in the BF800 ($25.75) and under range.

Inexpensive

Taverne-Restaurant Aux Trois Pommes d'Orange, rue de la Wallonie 28 (tel. 23-59-82). Not far from the cathedral, this restaurant specializes in moderately priced Belgian dishes (rabbit cooked in beer, etc.) at prices of under BF600 ($19.25). It's also a popular tavern and a good stop-in spot.

For inexpensive meals that will average under BF400 ($13), try the restaurants in the **Place Crombez** near the railway station.

TOURIST INFORMATION

The large **Tourist Office (Centre de Tourisme),** with its friendly and efficient staff, is located at Vieux Marché aux Poteries, 7500 Tournai (tel. 069/22-20-45). They can furnish excellent brochures outlining self-guided tours in and around the town, as well as a host of other information, including a beautifully photographed "Guide to Tournai" that details major religious and artistic attractions, as well as public monuments and museums.

THINGS TO SEE AND DO

For some idea of how Tournai looked back in medieval times, take a stroll through **rue Barre-Saintbrice** on the opposite side of the Scheldt from the city center. There, nos. 10 and 12 date from the late 1100s and are the oldest private houses in all of Europe. In the same neighborhood, **rue des Jésuites** holds 13th-century houses built in the Gothic style.

Notre-Dame Cathedral (Cathedral of Our Lady of Tournai)

The magnificent five-towered cathedral on place P-E-Janson was completed in the late 1100s, but it's not the first place of worship to stand on this spot. As early as A.D. 761 there was a church here, and it's thought the site had once held a pagan temple before that. The 8th-century church was replaced by an 850 structure, which was burned to the ground in 881 by invading Norsemen, only to be quickly replaced. When fire once again destroyed the church in 1060, it was rebuilt by 1089 and became a place of refuge for a plague-stricken population. It was on September 14, 1090, with the dread disease finally lifted, that a grateful bishop led a great procession through the cathedral to honor Our Lady, who was credited with several miraculous cures after hordes of the stricken had poured into the cathedral to pray before her statue. In the years since, only once—in 1559 when Calvinists broke into the cathedral in a destructive orgy and were not subdued until after the traditional procession date—has the **Procession of Tournai** failed to take place. Anyone planning a September visit to Europe should reserve the second Sunday of that month for Tournai in order to view its splendid pageantry.

Historians disagree about the exact date the present cathedral—one of the most striking examples of **Romanesque architecture** in Europe—was completed, but concur that it was sometime between 1140 and 1171. The thickness of its walls and its tiny windows were classical Romanesque, which, in the eyes of a 13th-century bishop, made it hopelessly old-fashioned compared to Gothic buildings that were then appearing all over Europe. He promptly had the Romanesque choir replaced by one in the Gothic style, ordered stained-glass windows, and before the money ran out entirely, had managed to create a soaring, graceful choir adjoining the long, low Romanesque nave, which never did get its Gothic facelift. Amazingly, when you visit this schizophrenic building today, there is no sense of disharmony, but rather a strange sort of compatible marriage of the two styles.

The cathedral itself holds such treasures as paintings by Rubens and Jordaens, 700-year-old murals, a marvelous baroque pulpit, and a "rose window" (so called because of its shape) of stained glass. But even these wonders pale before those to be seen in the cathedral's **Treasury.** Centerpiece of a vast collection of priceless religious relics and antiquities is the reliquary casque known as *The Shrine of Our Lady,* with its astonishingly beautiful gold-sculpted covering created by Nicholas of Verdun in 1205, which always takes the place of honor in the annual Procession of Tournai each September. Other treasures include 14th-century tapestries (one is a full 72 feet long!), a jewel-encrusted Byzantine cross of the 6th century, and a 14th-century ivory statue of the Virgin.

The Cathedral and Treasury are open from 10 a.m. to noon and 2 to 6 p.m. daily, with an admission of BF30 ($1).

The Belfry

Rising from the Grand-Place, the Belfry of Tournai dates from the late 1100s, making it the oldest in Belgium. The 44-bell carillon plays Saturday-morning concerts, and if you're fit for it, you can climb the 265 steps to its top for a glorious view of the town and surrounding countryside. Admission is BF30 ($1), and it's open every day except Tuesday.

Museums

All museums in Tournai are open daily except Tuesday from 10 a.m. to noon and 2 to 5:30 p.m. during summer months, shorter hours in fall and winter. There is never an admission charge—a lovely gift from the city to its residents and visitors.

Located in a 17th-century pawnshop on rue des Carmes, the **Museum of History and Archeology** is a collection of Tournai relics that covers virtually every period, beginning with the Gallo-Roman period of the 1st through 4th centuries. Art takes center stage in the form of paintings, sculptures, tapestries, and exquisite 18th-century porcelain and china.

It's hard to say of the **Museum of Fine Arts,** rue Saint-Martin, which is the more impressive, its 700 works of art or the building that houses them. It's a marvelous white stone building designed by the noted architect Victor Horta, and its interior illumination is that of natural light. The art collection contains such outstanding works as *Virgin and Child* by native son Roger de la Pasture, the 15th-century artist known to us as Rogier van der Weyden. Manet is represented, as is Brueghel the Younger, James Ensor, Henri de Braekeleer, and Sir Anthony van Dyck.

Tower of Henry VIII (Musée d'Armes), place Verte. The English king held Tournai for five years, from 1512 to 1518, and left in his wake this 80-foot tower that now houses an impressive museum of weaponry and a fascinating exhibit centered around World War II Belgian underground resistance.

Museum of Folklore, Réduit des Sions. Two rather marvelous buildings of the 17th century, complete with gables and mullioned windows, provide just the right setting for a series of authentically re-created rooms that might have been found in an ancient farmhouse, tavern, weaver's workroom, blacksmith's forge, and many more. Wax figures enhance the reality of life as it once was in and around Tournai.

Behind the Horse and on the Water

From April to September, **hansom cabs** are available to take you through the cobblestone streets and perhaps cause a faint stirring of the heart as you see the city as its citizens did in years gone by. The Tourist Office can give details on places of departure, and charges will be around BF80 ($2.50) for a one-hour ride.

The "Tournai Seen from the River" **boat cruise** on the Scheldt lasts about an hour, departing from the landing stage at the quay Taille-Pierre every day except Monday from May to September, at a BF80 ($2.50) fare. Check with the Tourist Office for exact sailing times.

2. Mons

Mons, the administrative capital of the Province of Hainaut, began life as a fortified Roman camp, and today it's home to the Supreme Headquarters Allied Powers Europe (SHAPE). Between those military bookends of history, it has lived a history that would rival many a novel.

The Roman camp became a town, set in this landscape of rolling hills (Mons, in fact, means "mount" in Latin), when St. Waudru, daughter of one of the counts of Hainaut, founded a convent here in the 600s. It was fortified by Baldwin of Mons in the 12th century, and again by the Dutch in the early 1800s. But its modern character was formed during the period when it was the center of Belgian coal mining, a development that saw it become an industrial city and cast a grimy pall over its collection of ancient buildings. Today its Grand' Place (Main Square) remains little changed, surrounded by fine buildings of the past, while its outskirts hold suburbs much like those of any modern city.

WHERE TO STAY

The best hotels lie outside the city center, but within easy driving distance. Those in the city are small, with moderate prices.

Expensive

Casteau Moat House, chaussée de Bruxelles 38, 7460 Casteau (Soignies) (tel. 065/72-87-41). This large hotel is some four miles northeast of Mons, very close to

SHAPE. Rooms are well furnished and attractive, with private baths, telephones, and color TVs, and there's a good restaurant with moderate prices. Doubles cost BF3,360 ($108.50); singles, BF2,400 ($77.50)—breakfast is included in these rates.

Hôtel Amigo, chaussée Brunehault 3, 7000 Mons (tel. 065/72-36-85), is one of the city's larger hotels (52 rooms), a little out of town in quiet, rural surroundings. The nicely appointed guest rooms come with bath, telephone, and color TV, and there's a good restaurant on the premises. Rates are in the BF2,650 ($85.50) to BF3,650 ($117.75) range.

Moderate

Hostellerie Le Prieuré Saint-Géry, rue Lambot 9, 6574 Sorle-Saint-Géry (tel. 071/58-85-71). This lovely old stone inn in the center of a quiet little village is worth the 13-mile drive from Mons (take the road for Beaumont), and if your next destination happens to be the Ardennes, it's just a little off your probable route. It's a small place, with only six atmospheric rooms, with an exceptional restaurant. Rates are BF 1,000 ($32.25) single, BF1,500 ($48.50) double.

Hôtel Résidence, rue André-Masquelier 4, 7000 Mons (tel. 065/31-14-03). This small, in-town hotel has six comfortable rooms with bath that cost BF850 ($27.50) single, BF1,300 ($42) double.

Hôtel Saint-Georges, rue des Clercs 15, 7000 Mons (tel. 065/31-16-29), is a small hotel, with rather plain but comfortable rooms, at a rate of BF1,300 ($42).

WHERE TO EAT

One of Mons's best restaurants is **Devos,** rue Coupe 7 (tel. 33-13-35), where prices start at BF1,600 ($51.50). Seafood dishes are a specialty.

In the moderate price range—BF600 ($19.50) to BF900 ($29), the **Pâtisserie Saey,** Grand' Place 12 (tel. 33-54-48), has buffet service.

Moderately priced meals at BF900 ($29) are also good at **Robert,** boulevard Albert-Elizabeth 12 (tel. 33-59-08), open noon to 3 p.m. and 6 to 9 p.m.; closed all day Tuesday and Sunday evening.

TOURIST INFORMATION

The **Tourist Office** is at Grand' Place 20, 7000 Mons (tel. 065/33-55-80).

THINGS TO SEE AND DO

Mons is a sightseer's dream: almost everything you'll want to see is no more than a short walk from the Grand' Place.

The Belfry Tower

The first thing you're likely to notice about Mons is its Belfry Tower. It sits at the highest point in the town, and don't worry if you feel an irresistible urge to giggle at your first sight of it—its appearance *is* a bit comical, and as Victor Hugo remarked, it does look a bit like "an enormous coffee pot, flanked below the belly-level by four medium-sized teapots." And don't be perplexed if you hear it referred to as "le château"—it sits near the site of an old castle of the counts of Hainaut, and even though the castle was demolished in 1866, people hereabouts have never broken the habit of using the old designation. Actually, the 285-foot-high tower is of 17th-century baroque design, the only one in Belgium, and the view from its top gives you a perfect orientation, with the inner city of Mons below, its industrial suburbs a little farther out, and the countryside beyond. There's nothing left of the castle, but you can see interesting subterranean passages.

Chapel of Saint Calixt

Just a short distance from the Belfry Tower, the Chapel of Saint Calixt (tel. 34-95-55) is the oldest structure in Mons (1051), and although it's closed for repairs as we go to press, check to see if it has reopened. It is primarily interesting because of three sleeping tomb figures that go back to the 9th century.

Collegiate Church of St. Waudru

This remarkable Gothic church built in 1450 honors that daughter of the count of Hainaut whose 7th-century convent marked the beginning of Mons. It stands below the Belfry Tower Hill, a little to the west. Inside its vast, vaulted room are sculptures and wall carvings of Mons-born Jacques du Broeck that date from the 16th century. Around the choir, a series of 16th-century stained-glass windows depict biblical scenes. At the entrance of the church, the "Car d'Or" (Golden Chariot) waits for its annual spring outing (see below).

The Grand' Place

This is where you'll find the interesting 15th-century Gothic **Town Hall,** which dates from 1458. As you go through its main entrance, look to the left and perhaps stop to rub the head of "the monkey of the Grand-Garde," an iron monkey that's been here since the 15th century granting good luck to all those who make that gesture. Needless to say, by this time he has a very shiny pate! Inside the Town Hall are interesting tapestries and paintings.

Museums

The main quadrangle of the Town Hall leads to the Jardin du Mayeur ("The Mayor's Garden"), a courtyard that leads to a cluster of four museums, collectively known as the **Centenaire Museum,** all occupying the 1625 Mont-de-piété (municipal pawnshop). Outside, there's a prehistoric standing stone and an American tank from World War II, both indicative of what's inside.

Inside **Le Musée de Guerre** are a very complete and sobering World Wars I and II collection, as well as exhibits to illustrate Mons's position of importance in both wars. Then there are the **Ceramics Museum;** with more than 3,000 pieces from the 17th through the 19th centuries, the **Museum of Medals and Coins** (more than 13,000); and the **Museum of Prehistory,** based on local prehistory of the Gallo-Roman and Frankish periods. Open from 10 a.m. to 12:30 p.m. and 2 to 6 p.m. every day except Monday, with a BF30 ($1) admission.

To one side of the Jardin du Mayeur, with its entrance on rue Neuve, you'll find the **Musée des Beaux-Arts** (the Museum of Fine Arts), with an emphasis on 19th- and 20th-century paintings and sculpture. It's open from 10 a.m. to noon and 2 to 6 p.m. daily except Monday, and there's a BF30 ($1) admission charge.

An interesting collection of furnishings, and folk, and craft objects is located in the **Maison Jean Lescarts, Musée du Folklore,** on rue Neuve (tel. 31-43-57). Housed in a 17th-century home, the collections make interesting viewing. No admission charge, and hours are 10 a.m. to 12:30 p.m. and 2 to 6 p.m. every day except Monday during summer months, with 5 p.m. closings on Friday and Sunday during winter.

Canon Puissant Museum, rue Notre-Dame-Debonnaire 22 (a 16th-century lodging house), holds a rich collection of Gothic and Renaissance furnishings, and nearby is the restored 13th-century **Chapel of St. Margaret,** with its beautiful examples of religious art. Open 10 a.m. to noon and 2 to 6 p.m. daily except Monday. Admission is BF30 ($1).

Ducasse de la Trinité Festival

Each spring on Trinity Sunday (the first Sunday after Whitsun) Mons erupts in a burst of pageantry filled with vivid color, mock drama, and general revelry. It begins with the Procession of the Golden Chariot, when that gorgeous vehicle (see above) is drawn through the streets by a team of white horses, followed by richly dressed girls and clerics bearing the silver reliquary that holds the skull of St. Waudru. When the procession has returned to the church, there follows a mock battle between St. George and the Dragon (known here as the "Lumecon"), hilariously enjoyed by the throngs who continue to celebrate until the evening performance by some 2,000 musicians, singers, and actors of the *Pageant of Mons* brings the day to a close.

Castles

If you're a romantic, the Province of Hainaut has castles to suit your every fancy, three of them within easy reach of Mons. The one you really shouldn't miss is Beloeil.

Beloeil Castle, 7970 Beloeil (tel. 069/68-96-55 or 68-94-26), some 13½ miles from Mons, has been called the "Versailles of Belgium," and I, for one, would never dispute that title. It is, quite simply, magnificent. The ancestral home of the Prince de Ligne, it sits in its own park, on the shores of a huge ornamental lake amid French-style gardens. For more than a thousand years the de Ligne family has been intimately involved with virtually every significant historical happening in Europe. They have lived in grand style, a style that pervades the vast rooms filled with priceless antiques, paintings by the masters, historical mementos (there's a lock of Marie Antoinette's hair!), and more than 20,000 books, many of them quite rare.

It's an enchanting place to visit, and if you can get together a party of 20 or more, it's possible to arrange a private candlelight dinner in the palatial dining room, attended by liveried servants. A once-in-a-lifetime experience for most of us!

The castle itself is reason enough to visit, but a bonus is the exquisite Minibel, a ten-acre site that holds reproductions on a 1/25th scale of some of Belgium's most beautiful and interesting structures. There's the Brussels Town Hall and Grand' Place, the Belfry in Bruges, and many others you'll recognize from your travels. A mini-train takes you to the site from the castle. There's a self-service restaurant for full meals at prices under BF500 ($16.25) or light snacks, and hours are 10 a.m. to 6 p.m. daily from April through September and weekends in October. An all-inclusive admission for castle, grounds, and Minibel is BF300 ($9.75) for adults, BF220 ($7) for students and seniors, with a family ticket for parents and two or more children at BF900 ($29).

Le Roeuix Castle, home of the Princes of Croy, is 17½ miles from Mons, 4½ miles northwest of La Louvière. Surrounded by a lovely park and a French garden that holds over 100,000 roses, it's luxuriously furnished with antiques and works of art. Open every day except Wednesday from 10 a.m. to noon and 1:30 to 6 p.m. during summer months, with an entrance fee of BF50 ($1.50).

Mariemont Castle, 16 miles from Mons, is primarily of interest because of its superb park grounds and its museum of antiques, jade, and porcelain.

LIÈGE AND THE MEUSE VALLEY

One of Belgium's most important waterways, the River Meuse rises in France, crosses Belgium, and empties into the sea in Holland. Along its Belgian banks are some of the country's most striking scenery, historic towns and cities, and industrial plants whose commercial livelihood is linked closely to the river.

With so much to see in such a small area, you can base yourself in Liège or Namur and return to comfortable lodgings after day-long rambles. Also, both cities are gateways to the lovely Ardennes region, and if you have only limited time for that beautiful countryside, it's quite possible to pop over for a quick look from either base along the Meuse.

1. Liège

First and foremost, Liège is a city of rebels. It has, in fact, well earned its nickname, "La Cité Ardente" (the hot-blooded city). Its most beloved symbol is Tchantchès, a puppet dressed in blue smock, patched trousers, tasseled floppy hat, and red scarf who has since the 1850s been the spokesman of the streets, grumbling at just about everything in sight while espousing every noble cause in sight—the very personification of your average, everyday Liègeois.

The powerful prince-bishop of Liège, who held sway over both secular and religious matters, rebelled against every foreign would-be ruler (so angering Charles the Bold of Burgundy that in 1468 he ordered the complete destruction of the city, a task that continued for several weeks and became one of history's most awesome feats of utter devastation, leaving only the churches intact), and the citizens rebelled against the prince-bishops. Not really surprising, since those citizens had been granted the guarantee that "pauvre homme en sa maison est roi" (the poor man in his home is king) in a 12th-century charter, and they were not about to forget it—an attitude that is vividly alive in 20th-century Liège.

Not surprising, either, that the French Revolution found ardent supporters in the fiery, rebellious Liègeois. When it ended, so was the rule of the prince-bishops. Then, when Napoleon was defeated, it was the Dutch who moved in, but not for long—volunteers left Liège in droves to become a vital part of the Brussels uprising in 1830 that kicked out the Dutch and firmly established Belgium as a nation in its own right. Invading German troops, upon reaching Liège in 1914, met a resurgence of that same fiercely independent spirit from its heroic defenders.

Through it all the city nurtured an impressive list of musicians whose names are legendary: César Franck was a native son, and violinists Ysaye, Bériot, and Vieuxtemps studied here.

Today Liège is one of Belgium's most important crossroads, with a railroad network, a busy airport, and three major motorways linking it to the rest of Europe, and—as it has been for centuries—the watery Meuse serving as a principal commercial trade route.

ORIENTATION

Liège straddles the Meuse, with a backdrop of Ardennes foothills. Using the Meuse as a focal point, you'll find the **Old City** on its west bank, the **Outremeuse** (really a large island) on the other. You'll do your major sightseeing in the Old City, while you'll cross one of several bridges to Outremeuse for lively bars, discothèques, and cabarets at night—unless, it must be added, you decide there's enough nighttime entertainment in the small **"carré district"** of the Old City, circled by rue de la Régence, boulevard de la Sauvenière, and rue Pont-d'Avroy. Several small streets off place St-Lambert are good shopping streets that are reserved for pedestrians only. Tree-lined walks follow the river's banks. For the best views of the city, take to one of the three hills on the periphery.

WHERE TO STAY

What may surprise you about Liège is that its two leading hotels bear the names of American chains. There is, however, an exceptional country inn just 18 miles away, one that offers a much more regional experience yet is within easy driving distance of the city. Unless otherwise noted, all rates quoted here include breakfast, service, and VAT.

A Nearby Gem

Hostellerie Saint-Roch, rue du Parc 1, Vallée de l'Ourthe, 4171 Comblain-au-Pont (tel. 041/69-13-33). Although it entails an 18-mile drive to and from the city, this exquisite country inn is so loaded with charm that it merits my personal top recommendation. It also makes an ideal base for Ardennes day trips. Its gourmet restaurant makes the drive worthwhile for a meal, even if you elect to stay elsewhere (see below). The inn itself is a lovely mix of rural scenery and luxury accommodations. The elegant dining room looks out onto well-tended lawns and gardens dotted with comfortable seating, and there's a relaxing riverside terrace for drinks of a summer evening. Each of the 12 guest rooms has a private bath and is done up in refined country style. Owners Frances and Nicole Dernouchamps are gracious hosts, and I suspect it is their warm friendliness that prompts so many Americans to extend a planned overnight stay into several days. Although usually fully booked out for summer weekends, weekdays are often pretty quiet, but advance reservations are strongly recommended. Rates are BF2,200 ($71) single, BF2,900 ($93.50) to BF4,600 ($148.50) double. Highest recommendation.

Expensive

The **Post House,** rue Hurbise, 4400 Herstal (tel. 041/64-64-00). This deluxe, 100-room modern hotel is just outside Liège, off the E40 motorway. If it's comfortable accommodations you're after, this is *the* place to make your base while in the area. Guest rooms are all nicely furnished and decorated, and come with private bathrooms with showers, telephones, TVs, and radios, and the restaurant is highly recommended (see below). Rates are in the BF2,850 ($92) to BF3,500 ($113) range.

The **Ramada Liège,** boulevard de la Sauvenière 100, 4000 Liège (tel. 041/22-49-10). In a top location, on the edge of the Old City, the Ramada is thoroughly modern, with 105 rooms that are comfortable and attractive. Its restaurant, too, can be highly recommended. Rates run BF2,800 ($90.25) to BF3,700 ($119.25).

The **Holiday Inn Liège,** esplanade de l'Europe 2, 4000 Liège (tel. 041/42-60-20). On the Outremeuse side of the Meuse, this giant (224 rooms) of a modern hotel offers all you'd expect of this chain, with exceptionally large, nicely decorated rooms that have queen-size beds in addition to all the usual amenities. No restaurant, but plenty nearby. Rates are in the BF2,600 ($83.75) to BF3,700 ($119.25) range.

Moderate

Le Cygne d'Argent, rue Beeckman 49, 4000 Liège (tel. 041/23-70-01). This small hotel has 22 quite nice rooms, all with private bath, in the BF1,600 ($51.50) to BF2,000 ($64.50) price range.

Hôtel de la Couronne, place des Guillemins 11, 4000 Liège (tel. 041/52-21-68). Guest rooms in this 79-room hotel near the railway station come in a variety of styles, all with private bath or shower. All are comfortable, with modern furnishings, but rather plain in décor. Rates run BF1,600 ($51.50) to BF2,600 ($83.75).

Hôtel de l'Univers, rue des Guillemins 116, 4000 Liège (tel. 041/52-26-50). The 53 guest rooms here are also quite comfortable, all have private bath facilities, and range from BF1,600 ($51.50) to BF2,000 ($64.50).

Inexpensive

Le Duc d'Anjou, rue des Guillemins 127, 4000 Liège (tel. 041/52-28-58). Only seven rooms here, but all are comfortable and quite acceptable, but without private bath. There's a good restaurant on the ground floor, and rates are in the BF600 ($19.25) to BF1,000 ($32.25) price range.

Pension Darchis, rue Darchis 18, 4000 Liège (tel. 041/23-42-18). Comfortable rooms with private bath or shower cost BF1,400 ($45.25).

WHERE TO EAT

The Liègeois are especially proud of their local white sausage, boudin blanc de Liège, and are also fond of thrushes (grives) and goose.

Out of Town

Hostellerie Saint-Roch, rue Parc 1, Comblain-au-Pont (tel. 041/69-13-33). Meals in this delightful inn just 18 miles from Liège (see above) are worthy of the "gourmet" designation. The setting alone is worth the trip out from town, but when pike or trout fresh from the river outside arrives at table accompanied by vegetables from the inn's own garden, well, all else fades into insignificance. In season, venison from the Ardennes region also makes an appearance. There are set-menu meals of BF1,200 ($38.75) and BF1,700 ($54.75), without wine, and a good à la carte selection. Hours are noon to 2:20 p.m. and 6 to 9 p.m., and it's closed Monday and Tuesday except during July and August. Best to call and book before driving out.

Expensive

Au Vieux Liège, quai de la Goffe 41 (tel. 23-77-48). This marvelous restaurant is located in a four-story, 16th-century town house furnished in antiques of that era, creating an instant time warp as you climb the narrow stairs to dine in rooms where only the clothing of the diners hint that this is a 20th-century establishment. Dinner is by candlelight, waiters are in formal attire, and the food outshines even the setting. Try almost any fish dish (canneloni de poisson au fenouil is a good choice), and expect to pay BF1,600 ($51.50) and up for dinner without wine. Closed Sunday and from mid-July to mid-August.

La Diligence, in the Post House, rue Hurbise, Herstal (tel. 64-64-00). Just on the outskirts of Liège in the large modern hotel listed above, this fine restaurant is worth the drive. Set-menu prices run about BF700 ($22.50) at lunch and BF1,500 ($48.50) at dinner, without wine.

Moderate

Brasserie As Ouhès, place du Marché 21 (tel. 23-32-25). Liège specialties are served with a flair in this tastefully decorated, rather large restaurant set on a narrow oblong public plaza that also holds a number of quite adequate, moderately priced eateries. As Ouhès, however, is acknowledged by all to be the best in its price range, and its menu is large enough to suit everyone's taste. Duck appears in more than one guise, and I am partial to the homard grillé, sauce béarnaise. Prices on the à la carte menu allow a three-course meal as low as BF800 ($25.75) or as high as BF1,300 ($42). It's extremely popular with local business people at lunch, so go early or late: noon to 2:30 p.m. are serving hours at lunch; dinner is from 6 p.m. and open until midnight. Closed Saturday for lunch and all day Sunday.

Rôtisserie de la Sauvenière, Hotel Ramada Liège, boulevard de la Sauvenière 100 (tel. 22-49-10). Nouvelle cuisine adaptations of classic French cuisine are featured at this elegant hotel restaurant. Prices for both set-menu and à la carte selections will keep a three-course dinner in the BF1,300 ($42)-and-under price range, without wine of course.

Rôtisserie l'Empereur, place du 20-Août 15 (tel. 23-53-73), close by the university in the Old City, is the place to go for grills and seafood. A good stop on your sightseeing itinerary. Prices for three courses from the à la carte menu will run between BF800 ($25.75) and BF1,500 ($48.50).

Aux Vieux Remparts, rue de la Montagne 4 (tel. 23-17-17). Shrimp flambéed in Calvados is just one specialty of the chef in this cozy restaurant, with other fish dishes high on the list of local favorites. Dinner prices without wine range from BF850 ($27.50) to BF1,350 ($43.50). Closed Monday and Tuesday.

Le Jardin des Bégards, rue des Bégards 2 (tel. 23-54-02). In the center of the city, French cuisine stars in this intimate, 16th-century setting with its magnificent garden. Dinner prices (without wine) are in the BF1,100 ($35.50) to BF1,400 ($45.25) range.

Inexpensive

A concentration of quite good, inexpensive restaurants (along with a few costlier eateries that have moved across the river) can be found along **rue Roture** in Outremeuse (there's a convenient footbridge to reach it from the Old City). Meals in most can be selected from à la carte menus with main courses at about BF300 ($9.75). Don't be guided by outward appearance, for many of these present a near-shabby face to the street, yet along with the plain exteriors (and interiors, as well) come very good food, with pleasant service and the company of locals who know good value when they see it.

Not far away on the riverfront, **Café Lequet,** 17 quai sur Meuse (tel. 22-21-34), is a tavern with similar prices that can be recommended for its regional specialties. The **Restaurant Flo,** quai sur Meuse 16 (tel. 23-55-04), presents French cuisine in a traditional setting for prices starting at BF300 ($9.75).

TOURIST INFORMATION

Tourist offices are located at En Féronstrée 92 (tel. 041/22-24-56) and Gare des Guillemins, 4000 Liège (tel. 041/52-44-19). Hours are 9 a.m. to 6 p.m. weekdays, 10 a.m. to 4 p.m. on Saturday, and 10 a.m. to 2 p.m. on Sunday. There's an office of tourism for the Province of Liège (Fédération Provinciale du Tourisme) at boulevard de la Sauvenière 77, 4000 Liège (tel. 041/22-42-10).

THINGS TO SEE AND DO

The Tourist Office can furnish brochures outlining self-guided walking tours and during summer months furnish a qualified guide to accompany you at very modest fees. Most of the places you'll want to see lie along a two-mile route, easily covered on foot, and from May to September there are boat cruises on the Meuse (sailing schedules and points of departure are available from the Tourist Office).

Main Sights

St. Lambert Square and neighboring **Market Square** are the hub of Liège's throbbing daily life. This is where you will find the Perron fountain that dates from 1698 and is the symbol of freedom to these freedom-loving people. The 18th-century Town Hall, with its lobby sculptures by Delcour, is also here.

At the **Palace of the Prince-Bishops,** place St-Lambert, it's easy to feel the immense power of Liège's longtime rulers as you approach this massive Gothic structure, which took the form you see today from a 16th-century reconstruction. Of primary interest are the two inner courtyards, one lined with 60 carved columns depicting the follies of human nature, the other a quiet, beautiful space that held the gardens of the prince-bishops when they were in residence. The council chambers of the palace are hung with gorgeous Brussels tapestries, and it's sometimes possible to arrange a guided tour through the Tourist Office. Now the Palace of Justice, this historic building houses courtrooms and administrative offices.

The **Church of St. Bartholomew,** place Paul-Janson, is a twin-towered Romanesque church dating back to 1108, and its baptismal font is the creation of master metalsmith Renier de Huy. Cast in copper and brass in the early 1100s, it is counted among "Belgium's Magnificent Seven." The huge font rests on the backs of ten small oxen and is surrounded by five sculpted biblical scenes. Truly magnificent —and you may view it any day from 8 a.m. to 6:15 p.m. at no charge.

The **Museum of Walloon Life,** cour des Mineurs. From treasures of the church to treasures of the people! And in this 17th-century convent setting have been gathered an incredible array of exhibits that bring to vivid life the days of 19th-century Liègeois and the rich Walloon traditions and customs that colored those days. It is very moving to view in one place examples of popular art, crafts, recreation, and even the workings of a coal mine reproduced in the building's basement. Here, too, is a marvelous puppet collection, including the beloved Tchantchès. Open every day except Monday from 10 a.m. to 12:30 p.m. and 2 to 5 p.m., with an admission of BF50 ($1.50).

Museum Tchantchès, rue Surlet 56. If you've fallen under the spell of Liège's favorite puppet, this is where you'll find a marvelous collection of his cohorts and their costumes. Open on Wednesday and Thursday from 2 to 4 p.m., on Sunday morning. From mid-September to Easter there are frequent marionnette performances. Closed in July.

The Curtius Museum, quai de Maestricht. One of Liège's most beautiful houses and Belgium's most important museums, this brick mansion was built in the early 1600s by a local industrialist. Its archeological and crafts collections trace the history of the Meuse region from Gallo-Roman and Frankish eras through the medieval period and on into the 18th century. Coins, jewelry, swords, and hundreds of other artifacts tell the continuing story. One room holds relics of the brilliant Bishop Notger of the 900s, whose "Evangeliary" (prayer book) is covered with exquisitely carved ivory. There are portraits of the prince-bishops, and even some of their richly embroidered vestments. Furniture and works of art from homes of wealthy Liègeois are also on display. Housed here as well is the Glass Museum, with fine examples of Venetian, Phoenician, Roman, Chinese, and—of course!—Belgian glassware. The museum presents a remarkable glimpse of the breathtaking riches of this city's past. Open daily except Tuesday from 10 a.m. to 12:30 p.m. and 2 to 5 p.m. Admission is BF50 ($1.50).

The **Cathedral of St. Paul,** rue St-Paul. Except during church services, you may apply to the sacristan at rue St-Paul 2a to see the cathedral's priceless treasures (not to worry, you'll be expected). It's a sight not to be missed, if only because of the exquisite gold reliquary that was Charles the Bold's gift of penance after wiping out the city and every able-bodied man in it. The work of Charles's personal court jeweler, the small masterpiece shows a repentant Charles kneeling as St. George looks on. Nearby, a bas-relief depicting the Crucifixion is believed to contain a piece of the True Cross.

The **Church of St. Jacques,** place St-Jacques 8. A happy mixture of architectural styles that are the result of some 400 years of reconstruction and renovation gives this church a Gothic Flamboyant exterior, Romanesque narthex, and Renaissance porch. But it is its intricately designed vaulted ceiling inside that makes it one of the most beautiful interiors in Liège. Open from 8 a.m. to noon on weekdays; to 5 p.m. on weekends, Easter holidays, and during July, August, and September. For guided tour information, call 041/22-35-36.

Museum of Arms, quai de Maestricht 8. The manufacture of weapons for sale around the world has been a major industry in Liège for centuries, and this impressive collection of prime examples (more than 12,000) from the past (as far back as the prehistoric stone axe and muzzle-loaded firearms of the 15th century) is exhibited in a private mansion that housed Napoleon when he visited in 1803. Open Tuesday through Saturday from 10 a.m. to noon and 2 to 5 p.m., on Sunday and holidays from 10 a.m. to 2 p.m. Admission is BF50 ($1.50).

The **Museum of Walloon Art,** Féronstrée 86. A good collection of local artists and sculptors, both modern and ancient. Hours are 10 a.m. to noon and 2 to 5 p.m. every day except Monday.

La Batte Market

On Sunday the oldest street market in Europe—and surely still one of the most colorful—is strung out along the quai de la Batte on the city side of the Meuse. If there is anything not sold in this mile-long bazaar of stalls, it doesn't come to mind as you stroll past items of brass, clothes, flowers, foodstuffs, jewelry, birds, animals, books, radios, and . . . the list is simply endless. Shoppers from as far away as Holland and Germany join sightseers like you and me, as well as what seems to be at least half the population of Liège. If you're anywhere near Liège on a Sunday, do plan to pop in on this marvelous shopping hodgepodge, even if only for the people-watching.

Other Shopping

Liège makes shopping a joy by the simple expedient of closing principal streets to all but pedestrian traffic. Those to seek out, all lined with shops and boutiques carrying merchandise of every description and price range, are: rue du Pont-d'Avroy, Vinave d'Ile, rue des Dominicaines, rue Saint-Paul, boulevard d'Avroy, boulevard de la Sauvenière, rue de la Cathédrale, rue Charles-Magnette, rue de la Régence, rue de l'Université, place du Marché, Neuvice et Féronstrée, rue Puits-en-Sock, and rue Jean-d'Outremeuse. If you can't find *something* to carry home as a souvenir of your Liège visit in the more than 5,000 shops on those streets, then you're simply hopeless as a shopper!

Walking Highlights

For a feel of Old Liège, stroll through the narrow, twisting streets and stairways on **Mont St-Martin,** all lined with fine old houses.

For superb views of the city and the broad, curving Meuse, climb the 353 steps of **de Beuren staircase** off rue Hors-Château. They lead to the hill of Sainte Walburge, which has been the setting of more than its share of the bloodier side of Liège's history. It was here, in 1468, that 600 citizens made a heroic attempt to assassinate Charles the Bold, who was encamped there with his Burgundian troops. They failed and were massacred to the man. In 1830 a decisive battle in Belgium's fight for independence took place here, in 1914 locals held German forces at bay here long enough for the French to regroup and go on to the vitally important Battle of the Marne, and in 1940 invading German troops met with that same stubborn resistance from the city's defenders.

On the hill of Cointe, the wooded **Park of Birds** is a pleasant, relaxing vantage point for panoramic views of the city. The third hill overlooking Liège is Robermont, where 50 local patriots were executed en masse in 1914.

In the Area

Within easy day-tripping is **Tongeren,** Belgium's oldest town. Founded in the 1st century A.D., it has the imposing **Basilica of Our Lady,** a Gothic church with Brabantine tower and Romanesque cloister. Its rich treasury has rare religious objects d'art from the Merovingian era up to the 18th century, and it's open from 9 a.m. to 5 p.m. daily, with admission of BF30 ($1). Also worth a visit is the **Provincial Gallo-Roman Museum,** with some 18,000 artifacts that date from the mists of prehistory through the Roman and Merovingian periods. The Roman period is very important because of the huge collection from Atuatuca Tungrurum, the capital of the Civitas Tungrorum, its cemetery, and the surrounding countryside. Indeed, from the entire province of Limburg, there are collections of pottery, glassware, bronze articles, terracotta, and sculptures. They're organized by theme to illustrate everyday life in the countryside and the city, religious practices, etc. Adjacent to the museum is a library and the Provincial Cabinet of Coins. Open from 9 a.m. to noon and 2 to 5 p.m., except on Sunday morning and all day Monday. Admission is BF30 ($1).

An interesting Ardennes day trip is to nearby **Spa,** the town whose name has come to mean any health and fitness center. See Chapter XI for details on Spa.

Both **Huy** and **Namur** (see below) are close enough for comfortable day trips.

AFTER DARK

When the sun goes down (and even when it's *up*), the native Liègeois head for their pick of the city's hundreds of cafés and taverns to quaff Belgium's famous beers and engage in their favorite entertainment, good conversation. If a quiet evening of the same appeals to you, you'll have no problem finding a locale. Two that can be recommended are the **British Pub,** rue Tête-de-Boeuf 14, and **Tchantchès,** En Grande-Beche 35 in Outremeuse.

For livelier nighttime fun, there are numerous nightspots in the Old City's **"carré"** (bounded by rue du Pot-d'Or, rue St-Jean, rue Tête-de-Boeuf) and along **rue Roture** in Outremeuse.

The **Théâtre Royal de Liège,** near the Church of St. Jacques, presents concerts by the city's excellent Philharmonic Orchestra, as well as operas, operettas, and ballets. Concerts are also performed at the **Conservatory of Music.**

Theaters staging puppet shows performed by the **Théâtre des Marionnettes** (in dialect, but easy to follow) are in the Museum of Walloon Life, the Tchantchès Museum, and the Al Botroule Museum. Liègeois wit is especially visible as the puppets appear, each sized according to his historical importance—for example, a huge Charles the Bold is attended by midget archers (although just how important Charles would have been without those archers may be debatable!).

2. Along the Meuse to Huy and Namur

The drive from Liège to Namur traces the River Meuse, and once beyond the industrial outskirts of Liège, the scenery along the river evolves into small towns every few miles, with one of the many castles of the Meuse Valley never far away. To visit one of the most beautiful of these, take a short detour off the Liège–Huy road

(N17) to the small village of Jehay-Bodeegnée (look for the turnoff to Amay, then turn left at Amay toward Tongres).

THE CASTLE OF JEHAY

This wondrous moated castle is now presided over by the talented and charming Comte Guy van den Steen de Jehay, whose personal history is as fascinating as that of his home. Artist, sculptor, and ironwright, with a keen interest in archeology, he is often on hand as visitors roam through the castle that has belonged to his family since the late 1600s. Moats reflect the castle's striking construction of light and dark stone arranged in checkerboard fashion, with round towers at each end of a central rectangular block. Inside, rooms are filled with a rich bounty that would require an entire book to detail: paintings, tapestries, lace from the private collections of the prince-bishops of Liège, silver and gold pieces, jewels, porcelain and glass, antique furniture, and family heirlooms.

Not the least of the castle's treasures, however, are the works of the present count. Although the pieces on view change due to exhibitions elsewhere, be sure to look especially for the bronze *Pythagoras* and a stunning *Marsyas Tortured by the Nymphe,* a three-dimensional progressive relief in an innovative technique pioneered by the count. The magnificent ironwork you see in the form of gates and railings is also his work.

Before leaving the castle for the grounds (in which the count has restored and redesigned lawns and gardens beautified with many sculptures and Italian fountains), anyone with even a smidgin of historical curiosity will want to inspect the Celtic foundations that have been unearthed by the present owner. His archeological findings on the estate have revealed clear evidence that this site was inhabited more than 30,000 years ago, and there's a fascinating museum in the vaulted cellars where you can view the leavings of the mesolithic age, Romans, Gauls, Carolingian Franks, and their successors into the Middle Ages. No visitor should leave without seeing this remarkable private collection of man's past in the Meuse Valley. Nor should you miss the castle's chapel on a small islet, which has always served as the parish church, as it does today.

The castle is open from May through mid-September on Saturday, Sunday, and public holidays from 2 to 6 p.m. Visits can sometimes be arranged at other times by telephone request (tel. 085/31-17-16 or 51-28-49). Admission is BF150 ($4.75).

HUY

This charming little town on the Meuse began as a thriving center for tin, copper, and wine merchants (its charter was granted in 1066), and has a long tradition of local metalwork. Its most famous native son, Renier de Huy, was the 12th-century goldsmith who designed the baptismal font in Liège's Church of St. Bartholomew. Today pewter holds center stage and Huy shops are filled with lovely pewter bowls, goblets, pitchers, and other items. The **Town Museum (Musée Communal),** on rue Van-Keerberghen, displays local metalwork, as well as glass objects.

In the Grand' Place, that beautiful copper fountain dates back to the 1400s and is known locally as **Li Bassania.** Also in the Grand' Place—not a work of art perhaps, but certainly a haven for the weary sightseer—the Whitbread Pub makes a good stop to refresh body and soul as you contemplate the daily life of this little medieval town. Better yet if you're there when the carillon in the elegant 18th-century Town Hall rings out "Brave Liègeois," as it does every hour.

Huy is an enchanting place in which to stroll through quaint little streets that contrast so dramatically with today's busy thoroughfares. From the Grand' Place, walk down rue des Rôtisseurs, rue des Augustins, and rue Vierset-Godin.

The 14th-century Gothic **Notre-Dame Collegiate Church** is famed for its mammoth *Li Rondia,* a beautiful ten-yard rose window, as well as stained-glass windows in the choir. In its treasury, the star is an impressive Romanesque shrine of St.

Mengold and many items in chiselled copper. Take notice, too, of the stone bas-reliefs along tiny arcaded rue des Cloîtres that runs along the side of the church.

High atop a hill overlooking the town, the **Citadel** is almost modern as Belgium measures time—it was built in 1818. It sits where a castle rose in ancient times, and it affords a marvelous view of the town and river below. Take the cable car over, May 1 to mid-September from 9 a.m. to 6:30 p.m., for a BF70 ($2.25) fare.

For lunch or dinner, look for the medieval **Hôtel de la Clothe** that dates from the 1400s and whose atmospheric dining room serves good meals at moderate prices. For sheer elegance and gourmet dining, it's **l'Aigle Noir,** quai Dautrebande 8 (tel. 085/21-23-41), on the right bank of the Meuse, downstream from the bridge, with dinner prices in the BF1,500 ($48.50) neighborhood. Some eight miles to the east, **La Commanderie,** rue Joseph-Peirco 28 (tel. 51-17-01), is a lovely old manor house in Villers-le-Temple where exceptional food comes at moderate prices.

NAMUR

It is at Namur that the Meuse is joined by the River Sabre, and it is dominated by the awesome Citadel atop a cliff above the town, which hugs the riverbanks. It's considered by many to be the true "Gateway to the Ardennes," and many choose to make this their touring base. Hotel accommodations are limited, however, and you may want to look a little farther into the Ardennes, where several rather special hostelries await.

Where to Stay

Château de Namur, avenue Ermitage 1, 5000 Namur (tel. 081/22-25-46). A bit out from town, near the Citadel, this 30-room hotel in a scenic setting has a good restaurant, tennis courts, and a swimming pool. Guest rooms are attractive and comfortable, with private baths, telephones, and TVs. Rates are in the BF2,700 ($87) to BF3,000 ($96.75) range.

Queen Victoria, avenue de la Gare 11, 5000 Namur (tel. 081/22-29-71 or 23-08-59), although small (only 21 rooms), is one of the best of the in-town hotels. There's a bar and restaurant, and guest rooms come with private baths, telephones, TVs, and radios. Rates are BF1,000 ($32.25) to BF1,600 ($51.50).

Porte de Fer, avenue de la Gare 4-5 (tel. 081/23-13-45). The 14 guest rooms in this small hotel have private baths, TVs, and telephones, at rates of BF1,900 ($61.25) to BF2,500 ($80.75).

Not quite three miles from Namur, there's the excellent 110-room **Novotel Namur,** chaussée de Dinant 1149, 5150 Wépion (tel. 081/46-08-11), where rooms with private facilities, buffet breakfast, and many amenities run BF2,500 ($80.75) to BF3,725 ($120.25).

Where to Eat

The best meals in Namur are in the restaurants of the hotels listed above, with prices in the moderate range. For inexpensive meals, look to the cluster of restaurants near the Citadel. A good fish restaurant with moderate prices is the **Rive Gauche,** boulevard Baron-Huart 28 (tel. 22-04-70), and the modern **Restaurant le Belvedere,** avenue Milieu-du-Monde 1 (tel. 22-38-24), serves moderately priced meals with a panoramic view.

A little farther afield (about 15 miles), but more than worth the drive, is **Le Vivier d'Oies,** rue de l'État 7, Dorinne (tel. 083/69-95-71). Set in an old stone residence, with a charming enclosed courtyard shaded by ancient trees, this restaurant is of such a high standard that patrons often make the one-hour drive from Brussels for a meal. Specialties depend on the season, as everything is prepared from the freshest possible ingredients, but count yourself lucky if turbot au champagne or saumon à la coriandre are available. There's an excellent menu dégustation for only BF700 ($22.50), without wine, and an average meal with wine runs about BF2,500 ($80.75). Because of its widespread reputation and popularity, you *must* book ahead. Closed Tuesday and Wednesday evenings, in February, and June 25 to July 15. Highly recommended.

Closer to Namur (about 2½ miles), the **Relais du Roy,** chaussée de Charleroi 18 (tel. 081/44-48-47), also serves superb meals in the same price range. Closed Sunday evening and Monday.

Tourist Information

The **Tourist Office** is in the Square Léopold near the railway station (tel. 081/22-28-59), open from 9 a.m. to 12:30 p.m. and 1:30 to 6 p.m. weekdays, to 3 p.m. on Saturday and Sunday. Also, a Tourist Office for the Province of Namur is at rue Notre-Dame 3 (tel. 081/22-29-98).

Things to See and Do in Town

The presence of that great, brooding Citadel is evidence of the strategic importance attached to Namur in centuries past. Today, however, you will find it a quiet, peaceful town with interesting churches and rows of brick homes that date back to the 17th century. Although hardly a center of swinging nightlife, Namur has a lively casino that is open year round, with a bar and restaurant.

The **Citadel** is a sightseeing "must." There has been a fortification atop this bluff since Celtic times, after which came the Earls of Namur, and then the Dutch, who are responsible for its present shape. Visitors are shown a film on the history of the Citadel, and there is access (by torchlight) to intriguing underground caverns as well as a tour of the fortifications themselves. There's an interesting Weapons Museum, as well as the International Museum of the Second World War, the Underground Army, and the Concentration Camps, and a Museum of the Forest. A small excursion train runs through the extensive grounds. Hours are 11 a.m. to 7 p.m. daily, and admission is BF100 ($3.25). The excursion train is another BF60 ($2), but you can buy a combination ticket for BF130 ($4.25). It's possible to reach the Citadel by car via a narrow, winding road, but I strongly advise using the comfortable cable car that leaves from the Pied-du-Château Square from 9 a.m. to 7 p.m., Easter to October—the view during the trip is breathtaking.

The **Cathedral of St. Aubain,** rue de l'Évêché. This 18th-century Renaissance Italian cathedral is rather somber inside, but holds several paintings of note, including a Jordaens and several paintings from the studio of Rubens. The nearby Diocesan Museum has an impressive collection of gold plate and sculptures. Open 10 a.m. to 6 p.m. except on Monday and holidays.

The **Convent of the Sisters of Notre-Dame,** rue Julie-Billiart 17, holds Namur's richest prize, the treasures of Oignies Priory that feature the work of the 13th-century master goldsmith Brother Hugo of Oignies. The jewel-studded crosses and reliquaries are decorated with forest motifs and hunting scenes. Look for the reliquary showing men jousting on stilts, a popular pastime of the day that is said to stem from an incident during a siege of the city by Count Jehay, ruler of the Province of Namur. When a delegation sought an audience with the count to seek relief, he retorted that he would receive no one who arrived "on foot, horse, carriage, or boat," whereupon the resourceful Namur delegation promptly appeared on stilts and so amused the count that the siege was lifted. Open from 10 a.m. to noon and 2 to 5 p.m., with an admission of BF30 ($1). Closed Sunday morning and Tuesday.

The **Museum of Old Namur Arts and Crafts,** place St-Aubain 2. An interesting collection of paintings, copper works of art, and sculptures from the Middle Ages and the Renaissance occupy this 18th-century mansion, and in the courtyard, the work of native son Félicien Rops, a 19th-century engraver and painter, are on display in a separate museum. Hours are 10 a.m. to noon and 2 to 5 p.m. daily, except Sunday; admission is BF50 ($1.50).

Two other museums in Namur worth a visit are the **Archeological Museum** in the old Meat Hall on rue du Pont, with artifacts from the Roman, Frankish, and Merovingian eras, and the **Hôtel de la Croix Museum,** on rue Saintraint, an 18th-century mansion filled with 17th- and 18th-century works of local painters, sculptors, glassmakers, goldsmiths, and cabinetmakers. Both have the same hours and admission fees as the Arts and Crafts Museum.

Out of Town Attractions

Les Jardins d'Annevoie, 5181 Annevoie (tel. 082/61-15-55). If there is one single beauty spot that should top every sightseeing list for this part of Belgium, it is the gardens and manor house at Annevoie, ten miles south of Namur. Their present owner, Jean de Montpellier, lives here with his family and presides over what is sometimes called the "Versailles of Belgium."

While there are indeed similarities to such French classics, those at Annevoie are also reminiscent of Italian and English gardens, yet they possess a unique quality that gives them special character not found elsewhere—the fountains, waterfalls, lagoons, and peaceful canals that are their centerpiece are all engineered without the use of any artificial power. No throbbing pump or other machinery intrudes on their sylvan tranquility. By an ingenious use of canals to channel natural streams through an uneven terrain, the designer created an entirely *natural* landscape of exquisite beauty. Originally laid out in the mid-1700s by a member of the de Montpellier family, these splendid grounds have been carefully tended and added to by successive generations (the present owner has added new flower gardens). The result is a marvelous mix of formality and relaxed, natural greenery—a refreshing uplift for the spirit!

The **château** reflects that same kind of ongoing affection from this caring family. The 18th-century home and its outbuildings are laid out in a harmonious design reflected in the lagoon alongside, and inside there are fine architectural details in the woodwork, stuccos, fireplaces, and family chapel.

The Annevoie gardens are open every day, April 3 to November 1, from 9 a.m. to 7 p.m.; the château, from 9:30 a.m. to 6:30 p.m. in July and August, on weekends and holidays only from mid-April through June and the month of September. Visits are limited to one-hour guided tours at a cost of BF170 ($5.50) for both, BF140 ($4.50) for the gardens only, BF90 ($3) for the château only. In addition to a gift shop, there's a rustic pub, decorated with ancient farming implements, that serves snacks, and a full restaurant for heartier meals.

THE ARDENNES

The Ardennes are Belgium's wildest, most heavily forested region—and its least heavily populated. The country's landscape slides easily from Flanders' flatness into rolling countryside along the Meuse Valley, then almost abruptly begins to climb into the dense greenery of this mountain range, an extension of the Eifel Massif that stretches from Germany across Luxembourg and this part of Belgium and on into France.

Villages become farther apart and take on a more uniformly medieval look. To the northeast, German is the language most often heard, a residue from the years before 1919 when the entire eastern Ardennes was a part of Germany. To the south and west, it is French that almost universally greets the visitor, reflecting a long and close relationship with France.

For Belgians, the Ardennes vie with the coast as a vacationland par excellence: for the tourist, they are a scenic treat, a gastronomic delight, and a welcome respite from sightseeing centered around ceaseless museum hopping. That is not to say that the Ardennes are without worthwhile museums—only that with the change in landscape comes a shift of emphasis, from treasures hoarded indoors to outdoor treasures of bracing air, scenic winding mountain roads, sparkling streams, and tranquil lakes. Add a sprinkling of pretty resort towns and the sheer joy of nights lodged in quaint old country inns that provide the ultimate in comfort without losing one ounce of their unique character, and you pretty much have the essence of a tour through the Ardennes.

For the sports lover, the Ardennes is a cornucopia of possibilities: canoeing, fishing, hunting, golf, tennis, horseback riding, and swimming. Tourist offices can point the way to any necessary rental equipment, and always there will be contingents of local enthusiasts to share the fun.

It's fair to say that the best way to explore the Ardennes is by car, yet it would be unfair to say it's the only way. A good railway and bus network reaches most points, and in many places it's possible to rent a bicycle at one train station and return it at another—and biking is a marvelous way to get around in this corner of Belgium. Camping is very popular with the young of Europe, and hundreds of them flock here during summer months, hiking or biking to the exclusion of any other mode of transportation.

This is the home of that delicately smoked Ardennes ham so proudly served all over Belgium, and other regional specialties are trout and pike fresh from mountain streams and the game that is so plentiful in this hunter's paradise.

It is difficult to recommend an itinerary for the Ardennes: this is *rambling* country, yet so compact an area that it's equally suited to returning to the same "home away from home" each night or to booking into a different superb country hostelry each night as you move through the region. My personal preference is a night or two in the Dinant-Bouillon district followed by the same in the vicinity of Durbuy-Spa.

1. Dinant, Bouillon, and Orval

Dinant has never escaped any of the conflicts that raged in the Meuse Valley over the centuries, and it has gone head-on with the Liègeois, the Burgundians, the French, and the Germans. It was the Duke of Burgundy who demolished the town completely in the 1400s and drowned more than 800 of its residents in the Meuse. In World War I the Germans—in a chilling replay of that 15th-century tragedy—executed nearly 700 citizens in reprisal for their stubborn resistance. A reminder of its military background is never out of sight in Dinant, for the 1530 Citadel that crowns a 100-yard bluff completely dominates the skyline.

Despite all the wars, the town developed such skill in working hammered copper that its engravings were sought after as early as the 13th century. Charles the Bold put a stop to such artistry when he razed the town, but in recent years it is once more coming to life, and you will see fine examples in town shops.

Some 38½ miles southeast of Dinant, the little town of **Bouillon** sits at a strategic bend of the Semois River. For centuries it guarded the major route from Eifel to Champagne, and the awesome 10th-century feudal castle of Godefroy de Bouillon, leader of the First Crusade to the Holy Land, still stands guard over the town today, looking for all the world like something straight from the pages of a fairy tale. It is a stirring sight to see it floodlit, as it is every evening during the summer months.

From Bouillon it's only 17 miles to the Abbey of **Orval.** In its setting of green forests, the impressive complex of religious buildings is administered by a handful of monks, who carefully tend reminders of its history from the coming of the first Cistercians in 1110. The ruins of French destruction in 1793 are cared for and cherished as tenderly as the present church, its gardens, and the brewery that produces one of Belgium's finest beers.

WHERE TO STAY

In this pocket of the Ardennes, there are outstanding inns that provide much, much more than just accommodations. Scattered around the three main sightseeing points, they should be considered if for no other reason than their unique ambience and, in virtually every case, their fine kitchens.

Very Special in the Area

Auberge du Moulin Hideux, route de Dohan 1, 6831 Noirfontaine (tel. 061/46-70-15), is 2½ miles from Bouillon. One of Belgium's prettiest country inns, this elegant pink inn sits beside an old water mill, with wooded hills almost at its doorstep. Inside there's a sort of warm, subdued sophistication to the décor, and a focal point is the crackling log fire, with luxurious leather furniture and touches of brass to complete the lounge scene. Greenery outside is complemented by plants in the glassed-in bar, and the dining room gets top rating (see below). The ten pretty guest rooms, all with private bath, are done with the same sense of style and have rates of BF4,960 ($160), while the three super-suites go for BF6,510 ($210). If you plan to treat yourself to only one "big splurge" accommodation in the Ardennes, let it be this one!

Auberge les Falizes, rue de France 70, 5430 Rochefort (tel. 084/21-12-82), 20 miles from Dinant, 30 miles from Bouillon. If there is such a style as "rustic formal," it best describes this lovely little inn that sets velvet-covered chairs in a beamed-ceilinged dining room whose plain white walls are as comfortable with gilt-framed paintings as with shelves of country china. That dining room enjoys the highest of reputations around the country, and the six guest rooms combine comfort with country charm. One of the best of the small Ardennes inns. Rates are BF1,000 ($32.25) to BF1,600 ($51.50), and advance reservations are advised.

Hostellerie du Pieuré des Conques, route de Florenville 179, 6803 Herbeumont (tel. 061/41-14-17), 48 miles from Dinant, 14 miles from Bouillon. Set in what was a 7th-century convent (although the oldest surviving remains only go back as far as the 12th century), a dependency of the great abbey at nearby Orval, this 11-room hotel overlooks green lawns, rose gardens, and the Semois River. Charming guest rooms all have individual shapes and character, some with alcoves, some peeking from under eaves, and their comfort rates just as high as their charm (seating arrangements include easy chairs). The vaulted main dining room is warmed by an open fire, and any overflow of diners spills into a bevy of smaller rooms, also vaulted. Rates for such perfect tranquility on the edge of an Ardennes forest are BF2,600 ($83.75) to BF3,000 ($96.75).

Hostellerie de la Poste, avenue de Criel, 5370 Havelange (tel. 083/63-30-90), 18 miles from Dinant. This 200-year-old roadside stone hostelry began life as a coach stop, and its nine charming guest rooms are still in the business of taking care of travelers. The restaurant is of gourmet quality (see below), there's a slightly sophisticated look to the décor, rather than the rustic ambience you might expect, and rooms are especially attractive and comfortable. Rates are in the BF1,650 ($52.25) to BF1,725 ($55.75) range, depending on whether or not you wish to have breakfast included (and you really should!).

L'Augerge de Bouvignes, rue Fétis 112, route de Namur, 5500 Dinant (tel. 082/61-16-00), two miles from Dinant. This lovely soft-rose brick inn on the banks of the Meuse has one of the best kitchens around (see below), and its six charming guest rooms are perfect retreats after a day of busy sightseeing. Those with private bath are BF1,500 ($48.50); those without, BF1,200 ($38.75).

In the Towns

Hôtel de la Couronne, rue Adolphe-Sax 1, 5500 Dinant (tel. 082/22-24-41 or 22-27-31). In the center of town, this pleasant hotel, which has a good, moderately priced restaurant and tavern, has comfortable and attractive rooms both with and without private bath. Those with full facilities run BF1,200 ($38.75) to BF1,950 ($63); those without, BF800 ($25.75) to BF1,400 ($45.25). All rates include breakfast.

Hôtel de la Citadelle, place Reine-Astrid 5, 5500 Dinant (tel. 082/22-35-43). There's no restaurant in this centrally located hotel, but its 20 rooms are well kept and comfortable at rates of BF1,000 ($32.25) to BF1,400 ($45.25) for rooms with private bath.

Aux Armes de Bouillon, rue de la Station 9-13, 6830 Bouillon (tel. 061/46-60-79). This large (68 rooms) hotel has a nice restaurant, a bar, and nicely appointed rooms that come with private bath. Rates are in the BF1,600 ($51.50) to BF3,000 ($96.75) range.

Hostellerie du Cerf, route de Florenville, 6830 Bouillon (tel. 061/46-70-11). With a pleasant restaurant and bar, this small hotel (13 rooms) has rooms with private facilities, but few amenities (no telephone in rooms), in the BF800 ($25.75) to BF1,000 ($32.25) range.

WHERE TO EAT

The Ardennes is famed for its wealth of gourmet restaurants, and most are part and parcel of the country inns in which the innkeeper is very often a fine chef.

This particular area of the Ardennes has more than its share of these gastronomic gems.

Special in the Area

Auberge du Moulin Hideux, route de Dohan 1, Noirefontaine (tel. 46-70-15), 1½ miles from Bouillon, 36 miles from Dinant. In this beautiful setting (see above), one of Belgium's top restaurants serves gourmet meals featuring baby lamb, saddles of pork, game, and fish delicacies such as the baby lobsters kept in a tank out in the garden until retrieved for each order. Everything is cooked to order, so be prepared to give the fine dinner that will arrive at your table the time it deserves. If you order from the set menu, prices will be in the BF1,850 ($59.75) to BF2,200 ($71) range: à la carte orders are likely to total about BF2,500 ($80.75), without wine. The wine list here is excellent and a good selection really should be indulged in to do justice to the food it will accompany.

Les Ramiers, rue Basse 32, 5332 Crupet (tel. 083/69-90-70), ten miles from Dinant. This country-style restaurant in a romantic little village is known for its gourmet creations. Try, for instance, the excellent salade tiède de saumon et langoustine au Noilly (salmon and shrimp) or grilled herbed lamb. In cool weather, eat in the simple beamed dining room; have dinner outside on the terrace when it's warm. Set-menu prices are in the BF1,300 ($42) to BF2,100 ($67.75) range, and it's best to book ahead.

Hostellerie du Pieuré des Conques, route de Florenville 179 (tel. 061/41-14-17), 48 miles from Dinant, 14 miles from Bouillon. Plan at least one meal in this atmospheric inn on the banks of the Semois, where fresh produce, fish, and meats are presented in simple but elegant combinations. Rack of lamb comes to table in the company of pommes dauphinoises and a fluffy turnip purée and is a favorite with patrons. Set-menu prices run BF1,200 ($38.75) to BF2,000 ($64.50), with à la carte totals a little higher. There's a very good wine list at moderate prices. Book ahead if possible.

Hostellerie de la Poste, avenue de Criel 26, Havelange (tel. 083/63-30-90), 18 miles from Dinant. Alain Courmont, the outstanding Belgian-born chef here, worked in leading French and New York restaurants before coming back to take over the gleaming kitchen here. It has been said of him that "his kitchen is his wife and his mistress at the same time," and you won't doubt that double dedication for a moment after one of his gourmet meals. You might try, for example, his bisquit de truite et saumon fumé, or for that matter any one of the other specials. There's an excellent set menu for BF1,100 ($35.50) to BF1,800 ($58), and à la carte meals average between BF1,200 ($38.75) and BF2,000 ($64.50). More than worth the drive.

L'Auberge de Bouvignes, rue Fétis 112, route de Namur (tel. 082/61-16-00), two miles from Dinant. In a rural setting on the banks of the Meuse, this lovely rustic inn (see above) is a delightful place for lunch or dinner. Its kitchen turns out such specialties as les aiguillettes de canard au porto (a lovely duck with port creation) and le poêlée de queues de langoustine aux sauternes (fried scampi tails with wine). The excellent menu dégustation is BF1,800 ($58); selections from the à la carte menu will run a little more. There are also five attractive rustic guest rooms at BF1,100 ($35.50).

In the Towns

Hostellerie Thermidor, rue de la Station 3, Dinant (tel. 22-31-35). Crayfish dinantaise is a specialty of the owner/chef in this pleasant dining room, and your check will run BF1,600 ($51.50) and up.

Good, inexpensive meals—under BF800 ($25.75)—in pleasant surroundings can be found at both the **Plateau,** at the Citadel (tel. 22-28-34) in Dinant, and the **Central,** Grand' Place 7, Dinant (tel. 22-22-29).

TOURIST INFORMATION

Tourist offices are at: rue Grande 37, Dinant (tel. 082/22-28-70), open weekdays from 8:30 a.m. to 5 p.m.; and in the Castle, Bouillon (tel. 061/46-62-57), open only from March through November.

THINGS TO SEE AND DO

The countryside itself constitutes the Ardennes' primary tourist attraction, but monuments from the past beckon for their fair share of your attention.

In Dinant

The **Citadel,** built in 1530 and perched high above the town and river, can be reached by car or cable car (my personal recommendation; fare is BF80, $2.50, and well worth it)—of course, if you're feeling particularly energetic or can't turn down a challenge, there are 400 steep steps leading to the bluff top. The weapons museum and war museum at the Citadel are interesting, but it's the view that takes your breath away. Open from 9 a.m. to 7 p.m. in summer, from 10 a.m. to 5 p.m. other months.

The **Adolphe Sax Museum** is in the home of this native son who invented the saxophone.

In Bouillon

Bouillon stretches along the banks of the Semois looking for all the world like a fairytale book illustration, with the massive, sprawling fortified **castle** that was home to Godefroy de Bouillon, leader of the First Crusade to the Holy Land. That worthy gentleman actually put the castle in hock in order to raise funds for his venture, and sadly, he died in that foreign land, far from this pile of stone. That was back in 1096, and the mortgaged castle passed by default into the hands of the prince-bishops of Liège, who continued to hold it for half a century. Since that time it has been conquered and reconquered as rulers and invading rulers fought over this strategic spot. Life within its thick walls during those turbulent years will come to vivid life as you walk through the ruins and see the old prisons and gallows and so-called Hall of Justice. Open every day, March to November, from 9 a.m. to 5 or 6 p.m. (times change); admission is BF100 ($3.25). The interesting **Godfrey of Bouillon Museum,** on the grounds, holds souvenirs of the Crusades; admission is BF80 ($2.50), which includes admission to the Ducal Museum.

The **Ducal Museum,** rue du Petit 1, located in a house from the 18th century, holds exhibits on the region's archeology and folklore. Open daily (changing hours, but usually closed from noon to 2 p.m.).

In Orval

A visit to **Orval Abbey,** in its setting of hushed green forests, is an exercise in serenity these days, with little to suggest the enormous power its Cistercian monks wielded in past centuries. Ruins of the old abbey are fascinating, and legend has it that somewhere in the web of underground passages that connected it to seven nearby lakes, a vast treasure lies hidden. It is a tribute to the caretaking monks of this order that ruins are not all there is to be seen today, for it wasn't until 1926 that they began to rebuild after the devastating pillage of the Napoleonic period.

---

2. Bastogne

For most Americans, Bastogne is a place of pilgrimage. It is also the town that did more during World War II to familiarize the world with the Ardennes than had any other single occurrence in history. It was here, during the fierce and near-fatal

Battle of the Bulge in the bitter winter of 1944, that American troops under the command of Brig. Gen. Anthony MacAuliffe held overpowering numbers of German troops at bay until weather conditions improved and Allied reinforcements could be flown in. It was a near thing—but for that valiant 101st Airborne Division and their heroic leader, Hitler could have turned the tide and perhaps come out the winner in World War II. Outnumbered and seemingly cut off from any support, the American commander answered German demands for surrender with a single word that has come to stand for raw courage: "Nuts!"

Since the end of the war Bastogne has been the appointed keeper of memorials to that near disaster and the men who prevented it.

WHERE TO STAY

Bastogne is a nice day trip from almost any point in the Ardennes and a little out of the way to use as a base for exploring. The following are recommended just in case you decide to overnight here.

The **Hôtel Lebrun,** rue du Marché 8, 6650 Bastogne (tel. 062/21-54-21). With 24 comfortable, but a little plain, rooms, this pleasant hotel is the largest in town. Rooms with private bath and telephone are in the BF1,650 ($53.25) to BF2,200 ($71) range; those without, BF1,400 ($45.25).

Hôtel du Sud, rue du Marché 39, 6650 Bastogne (tel. 062/21-11-14). Double rooms are available with private bath at this small, 13-room hotel for BF900 ($29).

Hôtel La Claire Fontaine, route de Hotton 64, 6980 La Roche en Ardenne (tel. 084/41-12-96). About 15 miles from Bastogne in this pretty little town, the attractive La Claire Fontaine sits beside the River Ourthe and has an excellent restaurant. Its 24 attractive rooms have rates of BF1,800 ($58) and up.

WHERE TO EAT

The **Hôtel Lebrun** (see above) has a very good dining room, where you can expect to pay as little as BF700 ($22.50) or as much as BF1,700 ($54.75) for three or four courses. Specialties here include trout and locally made pâtés.

Aux Luxembourg, place Mac-Auliffe 25 (tel. 21-12-26). Ardennes ham and other local specialties are featured here at prices of BF850 ($27.50) and up.

THINGS TO SEE

Mardasson Hill is a well-signposted mile outside the town, and this is where you'll find both the **American Memorial** and the **"Nuts" Museum.** A visit to the museum first will lay the groundwork for a better appreciation of films of the actual battle you'll see in the gigantic star-shaped gallery that is the memorial. Those interested in retracing the course of the battle will find battlefields clearly posted to identify key points.

3. Durbuy and Spa

Either of these resort towns makes an ideal touring base for the Ardennes. Completely different in character, they each have strong individual appeal. Which one you choose depends on your taste.

Durbuy is every image that the word "quaint" evokes. It is a tiny medieval town on a bend of a picturesque river, with narrow, twisting streets lined with pretty, flower-trimmed stone houses, and with an 11th-century castle to complete the scene.

Spa, on the other hand, has from the start been a busy, bustling resort that owes its existence to the curative powers of its mineral waters. Since a medieval blacksmith from other parts bought up the land holding these wondrous springs, the town that grew up around them has catered to the likes of Charles II of England, Montaigne, the Queen of Sweden, and Czar Peter the Great of Russia (probably its most illustrious visitor). So universally was its name equated with the miracles of thermal springs and mineral waters that "spa" nowadays is applied to health and fitness centers of every description.

Celebrities are seldom seen in Spa these days, and those that come are of the lesser sort. But Belgians and tourists alike continue to gather both for the healing treatments and for its lively casino action.

WHERE TO STAY

Your decision to stay in Durbuy or in Spa will be based largely on whether you prefer to stay in a quiet, quaint little village or in a livelier resort with a casino and other nighttime entertainment at hand.

In Durbuy

Hôtel Cardinal, rue des Récollectines 66, 5480 Durbuy (tel. 086/21-10-88). This little gem is just the sort to make you want to settle in and stay forever! Raves come naturally after one look at the seven pretty apartments that owner Maurice Caerdinael (the award-winning chef of Le Sanglier des Ardennes) has created in a stone building that once was part of an ancient convent. Set at the end of a street in the old town, behind walls that enclose a small and peaceful garden shaded by fine old trees, the house has a square tower at one side. Inside, the flats are beautifully furnished and come with private baths in which even the towels and soap have been selected with care to provide the very best. Each flat's refrigerator holds a supply of gourmet goodies—pâté, cheese, beverages, etc.—that reinforces the notion that this is truly your "home away from home." Top recommendation could go to the Cardinal for either its accommodations or its setting—the combination is irresistible! The cost for such pampering runs BF3,200 ($103.25) to BF4,200 ($135.50), value for the dollar in anyone's book.

Le Vieux Durbuy, rue Jean-de-Bohème, 5480 Durbuy (tel. 086/21-10-88). Owned by the same Maurice Caerdinael, this is another fine old building, once a private home, on a narrow street in the heart of the old town. Its 12 rooms are fitted out with period pieces quite in keeping with their setting, and the same loving care has been taken in supplying baths with luxury supplies. Breakfast is taken in the superb restaurant Le Sanglier des Ardennes, just a short walk away. The rate here is BF2,500 ($80.75) and up, including breakfast. Highly recommended.

Hôtel des Roches Fleuries, Grand' Place 96, 5480 Durbuy (tel. 086/21-28-82). This large stone hotel faces the town's large and busy central square. Its rooms are comfortably furnished, and there's a good restaurant as well as a popular bar downstairs. Rates range from BF1,800 ($58) to BF2,600 ($83.75).

Hostellerie Le Sanglier des Ardennes, Grand' Rue 99, 5480 Durbuy (tel. 086/21-10-88). There are 25 comfortable rooms replete with old-fashioned charm above the internationally known restaurant downstairs. Those on the back overlook the River Ourthe, while those on the front face the old town with mountains in the background. For rooms with private bath, rates are BF1,500 ($48.50) to BF2,200 ($71).

Hôtel La Falize, rue A-Eloi 59, 5480 Durbuy (tel. 086/21-26-66). Old-fashioned, comfortable, cozy—all apply to this small hotel, its doorway flanked by colorful potted plants, on a quiet, narrow street in the old town. Its parlor, with a cast-iron stove in one corner, is reminiscent of those homey living rooms several generations back, as is the warm friendliness of the owners. Rooms are simply furnished, but come with mini-bar. Those without private bath cost BF1,250 ($40.25); those with, BF1,900 ($61.25).

Le Clos des Recollets, rue de la Prévoté, 5480 Durbuy (tel. 086/21-29-64). The ten comfortable rooms in this small hotel have rates of BF1,000 ($32.25) with private bath, BF850 ($27.50) without.

In Spa

Manoir de Lébioles, 4880 Spa-Creppe (tel. 087/77-10-20). For the ultimate fantasy come true, book into this turreted 18th-century castle only two miles from Spa. It sits on a high plateau, with unbroken 20-mile views from the terraced formal gardens. Inside, there's a baronial entrance hall, a pretty sitting room where one takes afternoon tea before the open fire, and a formal restaurant (see below). As for the guest rooms, they could more properly be called suites because of their immense size. They, too, have fireplaces, and—wonder of wonders—a fire is actually *lit* when you arrive! Needless to say, those heartstopping views are just outside every window. Furnishings and décor are luxurious throughout, as befits a true castle, and the BF4,000 ($129) to BF6,000 ($193.50) rates are genuine "value for the dollar."

Hôtel La Heid des Pairs, avenue Professor-Henrijean 143, 4880 Spa (tel. 087/87-73-46). Out from the center of town, surrounded by lawns dotted with ancient trees, this villa was built for Baron Nagelmackers, whose family founded the *Orient Express.* And the ambience is still that of a private home, with a comfortable drawing room and homey rooms comfortably furnished with a mixture of period and functional pieces. The "at home" touch begins with the fruit and sweets in your room on arrival. Three of the rooms have private balconies, and you may elect to have your breakfast served there or on the terrace downstairs. All rooms have private baths, direct-dial telephones, TVs, and radios. Rates, including breakfast, range from BF2,700 ($87) to BF4,200 ($135.50).

Dorint Hôtel Ardennes, route de Balmoral 33, 4880 Spa (tel. 087/77-25-81). Also on the outskirts of town, this 97-room hotel is a study in modernity, with its gleaming glass front a somehow surprising accent among the pines that surround it. All the guest rooms are spacious and sunny, and all have balconies as well as all the luxury touches you'd expect in a hotel of this quality (private baths, telephones, TVs, radios, etc.). Other amenities include an indoor swimming pool and sauna, bars, and a restaurant. Rates are in the BF2,650 ($85.50) to BF3,500 ($113) range.

L'Auberge Spa, place du Monument, 4880 Spa (tel. 087/77-36-66). In the town center, this attractive hotel opens from a small square, and its ground floor houses a good restaurant. Older rooms are comfortable and homey, have private baths, and look out through casement windows to the town outside. Rates, which include breakfast, are in the BF1,800 ($58) to BF2,100 ($67.75) range. More modern bedrooms are available at BF2,900 ($93.50), excluding breakfast. There are also 12 luxury suites, with bedroom, large living room, fully equipped kitchen, and bath. Tastefully furnished, each suite can accommodate up to four people, and the price for the suite is BF4,900 ($158) for one to four.

WHERE TO EAT

Some of your best meals will be taken in the hotels recommended above. There are also a number of good restaurants in or near Spa and Durbuy.

In Durbuy

Le Sanglier de Ardennes, Grand' Rue 99 (tel. 086/21-10-88). In a nest of cozy dining rooms and a covered terrace overlooking the River Ourthe, master chef Maurice Caerdinael creates classic dishes touched with his personal genius that continually win international acclaim. Fish straight from the river outside come to table full-flavored, with subtle sauces or seasonings that only add to their delicacy. Game from the Ardennes, the famed smoked jambon (ham), and other regional specialties take on extra dimension after passing through this talented kitchen. The extraordinary wine cellar also reflects the chef's expertise in selecting more than 500 bottles stored with care and sold for surprisingly moderate prices. The price range for this superb restaurant is, in fact, much more moderate than you would expect: the average dinner without wine ranges from BF1,200 ($38.75) to BF1,600 ($51.50).

Relais du Vieux Pont, Grand' Rue 85 (tel. 086/21-21-67). Good, inexpensive meals are served in this rustic setting, at à la carte prices of BF300 ($9.75) to BF600 ($19.25).

Prévoté, rue Prévoté 64 (tel. 086/21-23-00). This pleasant, restful restaurant serves good fish from local streams and nice grills at prices below BF800 ($25.75).

In Spa

Le Manoir de Lébioles, Creppe (tel. 087/77-10-20). Well worth the two-mile drive from Spa, dinner in this lovely place (see above) is served in an elegant dining room beneath antique chandeliers, with service as sparkling as the crystal at every place setting. The menu is strictly traditional haute cuisine, and an excellent selection is their Menu Gastronomique, a seven-course feast that features whichever main-course specialty is in season. At BF2,500 ($80.75) it's expensive, but it is also *memorable!* A four-course Menu Traditional is just as memorable at BF1,500 ($40.50). Both prices are without wine, of course.

La Retraite de L'Empereur, Theux (tel. 087/37-62-15). In a long stone building set right on the main street of a tiny village near Spa, this beautifully rustic (not a contradiction in terms in this case) restaurant has distinguished itself by winning several prestigious awards for its classical French cuisine. Specialties include game (in season) and lobster, as well as local fish. Set menus offer excellent selections at BF850 ($27.50) to BF1,350 ($43.50), and house wines are as low as BF450 ($14.50). The drive out through tranquil, rolling countryside is a delight, a fitting prelude to a superb meal. Closed Wednesday and the month of August.

Hôtel des Bains, Lac de Robertville (tel. 080/67-95-71). A short drive from Spa out the E5 highway (exit A27, signposted Malmedy-Waimes), this beautiful hotel sits on the shores of an idyllic lake in the Hautes Fagnes Eifel nature reserve. The basically classic French cuisine is served with a light, delicate touch, and often pike from the lake comes to table poached and served on lettuce with a white butter sauce —*the* choice when it's available. Set-menu prices run BF900 ($29) to BF1,300 ($42), while à la carte meals can reach BF2,300 ($74.25) or more.

Le Grand Maur, rue Xhrouet 41 (tel. 087/77-36-16). Classic French/Belgian cuisine is served in this elegant restaurant, where dinner is in the BF1,400 ($45.25) and up range. It's closed Sunday night and all day Monday, and advance reservations are suggested whenever you plan to come.

Les Jardins du Casino, rue Royale 4 (tel. 087/77-39-29). Always packed, and for good reason—at least one meal in the casino's restaurant is virtually obligatory! Each day's menu is centered on the best available fresh ingredients, and the price for three very good courses will not exceed BF1,000 ($32.25). Outstanding value, and fun.

TOURIST INFORMATION

The Durbuy Tourist Office is in the Grand' Place; in Spa, you'll find it in the Pavillon des Petits Jeux on the place Royale.

THINGS TO SEE AND DO

Tourist offices in both towns can furnish maps for scenic woodland walks, a pastime that should not be overlooked even if you're not an avid walker.

In Durbuy

Wandering the streets of the little town itself is a walk back in time, and if you're armed with the "Walk Through the Past of Durbuy" booklet available from the Tourist Office, virtually every building will reveal its past as you stroll by.

In Spa

If you come for the "cures," head for the ornate **Établissement Thèrmal** on the place Royale. There, they can tell you everything you'll need to know about thermal cures, walking cures, drinking cures (*not* the alcoholic kind!), and probably a few other categories. If casino action is what you're after, the turn-of-the-century **Grand Casino** is at rue Royale 4, in the center of town.

PART TWO

HOLLAND

INTRODUCING HOLLAND

First of all there is the matter of its name—Holland, or The Netherlands? Actually, it's both, and before either of those it was called Batavia. Why all the changes? Listen to one Thomas Coryate, writing in 1611: "The name of Batavia was commonly in use til the yeare of our Lord 860, at what time there hapend such an exceeding inundation as overflowed a great part of the country, and did so scowre and wash the very bowels of the earth that it hath bene ever since . . . hollow and spungie. For which cause the old name of Batavia was afterward changed to Holland, . . . or Hol-land . . . for hol in the Flemish tongue doth signifie as much as our word hole."

Technically in modern times that name applies only to the two western provinces of North and South Holland, and the country itself bears the label The Netherlands, meaning "low lands," a designation that from medieval times until 1830 included Belgium—collectively, they were known far and wide as the Low Countries. That title, however, is seldom used outside officialdom, and for both its citizens and its visitors all of this amazing little country is now referred to simply as "Holland."

1. A Brief History

Every schoolchild knows that Holland would be a good deal more "hollow and spungie" were it not for the dikes (and, of course, for that legendary boy-hero of the dikes who plugged a leak with his finger and saved the country from more flooding). Those all-important barriers that hold back the sea came into being in an evolutionary process that began as far back as the 1st century A.D., when the country's earliest inhabitants settled on unprotected marshlands in the northern regions of Friesland and Groningen. Their first attempts at protection were hugh earthen mounds (*terpen*) on which they built their homes as safe ground during recurring floods. Along about the 8th and 9th centuries they were building proper dikes, and by the end of the 13th century entire coastal regions were enclosed by dikes that held at bay the unruly rivers as well as the sea.

Incidentally, if your image of a dike is that of a high wall, you will be surprised to see that they are actually still great mounds of earth and stone that extend for miles much like a huge rope, rather than forming a circular terpen. Indeed many of the roads you travel are built along the tops of dikes.

Historians believe Holland's first settlers were members of German tribes, the Frisians in the north, the Saxons in the east, and the Franks in the south. The Frisians appear to have arrived before the Christian era, and the others came in with barbarian invasions about the 4th century A.D. That the Frisians were traders has been pretty well established with discovery of Roman artifacts in excavation of ancient terpen.

Romans came as invaders in 12 B.C. and stayed around until about A.D. 300, when the Saxons and the Franks poured in. Through it all those hardy terpen dwellers, the Frisians in the north, refused to be conquered, even by religion—although the Franks in the south embraced Christianity in the late 15th century, it would be another 200 years before the Frisians abandoned their pagan gods, and then only at the swordpoint of Charlemagne, Emperor of the Franks.

It was after Charlemagne's death in 814, when his vast empire was divided among his sons, that the colorful threads of Dutch history began forming the intricate patterns of alliances, marriages, feuds, and outright warfare that characterize Europe's complex past. Suffice it to say that by the 13th and 14th centuries the nobility—chief among them the counts of Holland, the counts of Flanders, and the dukes of Brabant—were busy building most of the castles and fortified manor houses that are now sightseeing staples throughout Holland. The Catholic hierarchy had also grown both powerful and wealthy—the bishoprics of Maastricht and Utrecht were forces to be reckoned with in the political antics of the era as they erected splendid cathedrals, abbeys, and monasteries.

Eventually, as the 16th century began, political maneuvering landed Holland squarely under the rule of Charles V and thus Spain. This turn of events coincided with a wholesale Dutch revolt against Catholicism as they rushed to embrace the Protestant church following the conversion of Count William of Orange (known as William the Silent for his skill in tactfully keeping his mouth shut at critical points of diplomacy). Charles, of course, had grappled with that same problem in Spain, and his solution was the cruel Inquisition, spearheaded by his son, Phillip II. When he handed over the Spanish throne to Phillip in 1555, things took a nasty turn for the Dutch colonies as the new king dispatched the infamous duke of Alva to the Low Countries to carry out the Inquisition's "death to heretics" edict. William of Orange, more prophetic of Dutch policy in centuries to come than he could have dreamed, declared: "I cannot approve of princes attempting to use the conscience of their subjects and wanting to rob them of the liberty of faith." Nor, as history has proved time and again in the years since, could his subjects!

Rallying behind William the Silent, the Dutch mounted fierce resistance and doggedly persisted even as siege after siege ended with city after city falling into Spanish hands. The turning point came at Leiden. In a desperate and brilliantly successful move, William of Orange flooded the province and sailed his ships to the very walls of the city, catching Spanish troops at their dinner. The result was a rout—and a new national dish for the Dutch! The stewpot left bubbling by the fleeing enemy became a cherished symbol of the triumph of freedom, and you'll eat a duplication of the stew it held every time you order *hutspot* from a menu in Holland.

It wasn't until the Union of Utrecht, signed in 1579, that the seven provinces that make up Holland agreed to turn a united face to their covetous neighbors, the French, Spanish, and English. And even then the struggle with Spain was to go on until 1648, a conflict history would call the Eighty Years' War. By the early 1600s, however, William's son, Prince Maurice, headed a States-General governing body for the seven Dutch provinces, and a new era was in the offing.

Sometimes called Holland's "Golden Age," the next century saw Dutch ships all over the globe. The newly organized Dutch East India and Dutch West India companies engaged in spice trade that would become a legend—Dutch explorers were everywhere, trading with the Indians for "Manhattes" Island and establishing the infant Nieuw Amsterdam; Abel Tasman was sailing around the South Pacific discovering New Zealand, the Fiji Islands, Tonga, and Tasmania; Indonesian colonies were established to underpin the spice trade. At home, merchants financing all those voyages grew richer, built grand gabled houses, dug canal after canal, and applauded as the young William III married into the English royal family and wound up sharing the English throne with his wife.

During that busy century the arts thrived as sculptors and stonemasons created lasting monuments to their genius and artists won wealthy patrons whose support allowed them to give free reign to talents that so enrich our 20th-century museums. Even the lowly common citizen was not, it seems, immune to the general passion for art. According to one Peter Mundy, writing of his 1640 travels in Europe and Asia, "yea many tymes blacksmithes, coblers, etts, will have some picture or other by their forge and in their stalle. Such is the general notion, enclination and delight that these countrie natives have to paintings."

Holland was also fast becoming the world's greatest refuge for the displaced of Europe. The Pilgrims stopped here for a dozen years before heading off to America; Jews fled the oppressive Spanish and settled into the tolerance of the Dutch; refugees straggled in from France and Portugal. William of Orange had set Holland firmly in the path of benign tolerance, and it was proving to be the pathway for a multitude of talented newcomers, all with something to contribute to the expanding economic, social, artistic, and intellectual climate of the country.

Things were heating up, however, between Holland and England, in part because of their lively competition on the seas of the world, and a whole series of misadventures began to cast a very bad tarnish on Holland's Golden Age. Needless to say, strong Dutch support of the new United States of America (they were the first to recognize the new struggling nation and they extended three substantial loans to the new government) did little to heal the breach with the British. By the time William V, with his mixed Dutch-Anglo background, arrived on the Dutch throne anti-British sentiment was so strong that the ruler was banished to exile in England and a new Batavian Republic was set up, aligning itself with France.

And then came Napoleon. Never satisfied with one conquest, he moved into Holland from France, declared his brother, Louis Bonaparte, king, and installed him in a palace that had been Amsterdam's Town Hall. Four years later Napoleon was back, drawn by the threat of a British landing in Zeeland.

And then came Waterloo in 1815. With Napoleon finally defeated once and for all, the Dutch recalled the House of Orange and installed yet another William as king, this time as head of a constitutional monarchy. To mark the beginning of their new republic, the Dutch decided that *this* Willem (their native spelling) should discard his inherited House of Orange number in the succession of Williams and become Willem I. It was the beginning of the House of Orange-Nassau that has occupied the throne ever since.

In this century Holland escaped the ravages of World War I by managing to maintain a staunch neutrality. It was a different story in 1940, when World War II spilled over its borders in the form of hordes of Nazi troops. The occupation was complete and devastating: Rotterdam in particular sustained heavy bombings and the remainder of the country suffered terribly at the hands of its invaders. From centuries past, however, the admonition that a ruler must not be allowed to "use the conscience of his subjects" rose in Dutch minds and they organized and operated for the duration of the war one of the most effective underground movements in Europe. The Dutch underground, in fact, was a decisive factor in the liberation of Holland in 1945. Their queen, Wilhelmina, who had inherited the crown when only 10 years old, ruled in exile and such was this tiny woman's strong character that Winston Churchill declared her "the only man in the Dutch government."

World War II also saw the capture of Dutch colonies in the East by the Japanese, and at war's end the natives of those colonies took up a determined fight for their independence, finally achieving that goal in 1949.

The beloved Queen Wilhelmina, having occupied the throne for half a century, chose to abdicate in 1948 in favor of her daughter, Juliana. The precedent was set, and Queen Juliana stepped aside in 1980 for the present queen, Beatrix, her daughter.

2. Holland Today

Since the close of World War II Holland has largely prospered, although it did not escape the economic recession of the 1970s.

There have been continuing increases in the reclamation of land from the sea, as a large part of the new "polder," Flevoland, fell dry in 1957, followed by another in 1968. Thus some 100,000 Dutch citizens now live and work on land that was covered by the Zuiderzee before 1938, when the great Enclosing Dike was closed in and that salty arm of the North Sea began the long process of becoming a freshwater lake known as Ijsselmeer.

Work goes on to create yet more polders as Holland's population continues the growth that has seen a threefold increase since this century began. With a projected 15 million population by the turn of the century, due in part to immigration from her former Indonesian colonies, Holland faces problems inherent in its status as one of the most densely populated countries in the world.

Faced with an economy short on raw materials, and feeling the economic loss of Indonesia, the country is making a concerted—and thus far very successful—effort to develop high-technology industries. Many multinational conglomerates now have headquarters, branch operations, or plants here. With this influx of new industry and the EEC as a market for over 70% of her exports, Holland manages to keep her unemployment down to 5%, an enviable record.

For the visitor, Holland today presents much the same face she has over the centuries—a serenely scenic landscape peopled with an industrious, contented population who treasure their age-old tradition of tolerance and are happy to open their doors to all comers.

3. The Lay of the Land

While visiting Holland in 1859, Matthew Arnold was so incredulous at what he saw that he wrote home, "the country has no business to be there at all." Well, maybe so—50% of its land is, after all, below sea level and surely meant by the Almighty to stay that way. But the Dutch have a ready answer: "God made the earth," they'll tell you, "and the Dutch made Holland." That they did, and they made a fine job of it. Of the nearly 16,000 square miles that make up Holland today, almost 1,000 square miles was under water just 100 years ago! And they're still at it, working away at Zeeland's huge Delta Project (see Chapters XVIII and XIX) to wrest even more land from the sea with the same dogged determination and patience that over the centuries have created this land where land had no business to be at all.

Of course there are still 1,100 square miles of water within the country, but even those, because of Dutch industry and ingenuity, are mostly channeled water—canals and rerouted rivers and lakes that once were open sea. Indeed it is the rivers that have given Holland her historically strategic position in world shipping and trading, for this is where three of Europe's important waterways empty into the sea. From earliest recorded history the Rhine, the Maas (it's the Meuse until it crosses Holland's border from Belgium), and the Waal have brought the products of the rest of the continent to this point on the North Sea for shipment to markets around the world.

The rivers also serve to draw natural divisions across the terrain of the country. To the north, above the rivers, the land is lowest; below the rivers, in the south, lie the closest thing to "highlands" in Holland—if, that is, you can call its highest mountain, at 1,093 feet, really "high." That modest peak is in the southeast province of Limburg, and except for the forests in the central provinces of Gelderland and Utrecht, most of Holland's countryside is a landscape of the same flat green fields dotted with orange-roofed farmhouses under wide, luminous skies that turn up time and time again on the canvases of the Dutch masters.

Those natural geographical divisions also mark religious boundaries. To their north the population is, almost to a man, Calvinist, while below the rivers the southern population is traditionally Catholic.

4. The People

The people who inhabit this improbable country are every bit as improbable themselves. They are, without doubt, the most contradictory people on the face of the earth! Serious-minded almost to a fault, yet when they put serious matters aside no one under the sun enjoys a beer, a good meal, and the lighter side of life—most of all, a good laugh—more than the Dutch. Fanatics about personal privacy, they turn right around and go to great pains to display their living quarters through windows at which drapes are never drawn. Home lovers to the *n*th degree, they would absolutely perish without their "brown cafés." Adhering to strict moral and ethical codes themselves, they are the most tolerant people on the face of the earth of the beliefs of others. Lovers of rules and regulations, they are quite willing to fight to the death to preserve their independence.

With all that, there is one dominant characteristic of the Dutch that impresses me more with every visit. This is their absolute refusal to recognize anything as impossible. There is, I am told by a Dutch friend, the word *onmogelijk* in their language that carries the "impossible" connotation. Yet ask of them what you will, and although they may chide you (like a Dutch uncle?) for making such a foolish request, in the end they'll come right back with "no problem." Those two words, I suspect, have replaced *onmogelijk* entirely in the average Dutch vocabulary! Given all the impossibilities they have turned into accomplishments—who else, after all, takes for granted thriving towns and farmlands on what was once the bottom of the sea—it's little wonder that this is so, but the abundant good humor with which "no problem" solves a travel problem (be it major or trifling) always comes as a wonderfully pleasant shock when I'm in Holland.

A good many of those character contradictions, in fact, stem from their history, as well as from the physical aspects of their environment. For example, they must embrace the rules and regulations that enforce order, else their elbow-to-elbow existence in one of the most densely populated areas of the world would dissolve into utter chaos. But their history amply demonstrates the lengths to which they will go to oppose rules and regulations not of their own choosing.

A product of history, too, is the astounding linguistic ability of the Dutch. Acutely conscious of their strategic location and the international trade it engenders, they consider it a natural consequence that they must be able to converse easily with anyone with whom they do business. For the English-speaking tourist that's a tremendous bonus—English is spoken fluently and willingly throughout the country, as are almost all major European languages.

Above all, the Dutch are sticklers for organization and detail, again qualities that are essential for the smooth operation of their little corner of the world. You'll see it in such things as their rail schedules—if your train is scheduled to leave at 12:01 p.m., it will leave precisely then, not one second sooner or later. You may expect it, too, in such seemingly casual matters as an invitation to "do come by for a drink": don't say that to the Dutch unless you mean it; they mean precisely what they say and expect the same of you. If you should happen to give your word in something more substantial than a drink or two, be prepared to live up to it; in Holland your word is your bond, and even in the most complex business dealings it's considered binding.

They are lovers, too, of the rules of good behavior—common courtesy, if you will. *Dank u wel* comes naturally and often to Dutch lips; it means "thank you very much," and it closes every sale or restaurant order or any other transaction. And what could be more courteous than the *Eet smakelijk* that comes with every single meal you'll be served while in Holland. The thoughtful, courteous gesture—flowers when you come to call—while not obligatory, is given more than its proper share of appreciation and is automatic on their part.

How to sum up the Dutch as a people? I'm not sure it can be done. One thing of which I am certain, however, is that you'll find them intriguing, gracious hosts who will move heaven and earth to make your stay a pleasant one.

THE PRACTICALITIES OF HOLLAND

Holland is one of the more important gateways to Europe. From the United States and Canada, there are frequent flights on major airlines, and from Great Britain, good sea, air, and bus schedules. Rail and bus connections to other European destinations are excellent, as they are within the country itself. And whether you choose to drive or use the excellent Dutch public transport system, getting around is a simple matter.

This chapter concerns itself with the practicalities of a visit to Holland—and above all else, Holland is a practical country. Long accustomed to welcoming and caring for her visitors, she provides accommodations to suit every taste and pocketbook. You'll dine well in inexpensive cafés, moderately priced family restaurants, and—when the budget permits—in posh restaurants with equally posh prices. As for sightseeing, this country is an exciting combination of lifestyles and artistic treasures from the past and imaginative projections into the future.

1. Getting to Holland

From the United States or Canada several international airlines fly regular schedules to Amsterdam. From the U.K. you have a choice of air, train, boat, or rental-car transportation; and from anywhere in continental Europe, there are good air and rail connections as well as an excellent network of highways.

BY AIR

Amsterdam's **Schiphol Airport** is served by airlines from around the globe and is the home base of KLM, Holland's national airline.

Opened in 1968, Schiphol is consistently rated the best in the world when international travelers are polled (it certainly gets my vote as the most efficient!). As modern as tomorrow, the terminal itself is a wonder of good organization, with signs in English guiding you every step of the way and an automated baggage system that actually manages, nine times out often, to have your luggage patiently waiting by the time you've deplaned and made your way through a streamlined Customs desk and a well-planned escalator/moving-sidewalk network. There are even free luggage trolleys to eliminate the hassle of trying to find a porter (although they seem to be in abundant supply). There's also good bus service and a fast rail link into Amsterdam, as well as a taxi rank just outside the terminal. When it comes to duty-free shops, again Schiphol outdoes almost every other, and when departure time rolls around, every traveler should allow ample time to browse through the more than 50 shops filled with more than 40,000 different items—that's a lot of bargains.

Your Choice of Airline

As stated earlier in this book, there is much to be said for arriving at any foreign destination via its national airline, always bearing in mind, of course, price and convenience. Foremost among the advantages of such a choice is the fact that your experience of the country actually begins en route rather than after deplaning. Rarely is that advantage so enhanced as in the case of Holland's KLM. Maybe that's because the Dutch have always been travelers themselves, sending out the likes of Abel Tasman to explore new horizons, search out new trade routes, and make new connections with other nationalities.

When travel moved away from the sea and into the skies, the Dutch were right there with **KLM.** It was in 1920 that KLM (Koninklijke Luchtvaart Maatschappij) established the first regularly scheduled air service anywhere in the world with an Amsterdam–London run. Not content with just one record, the airline looked farther afield and in 1929 began service between Amsterdam and Jakarta, the longest scheduled passenger service in the world until World War II erupted. That war left Schiphol Airport in shambles, yet in 1946 KLM marked up still another "first" when it became the first European airline to inaugurate transatlantic passenger service after the war's end. Today the airline flies to 129 cities in 79 countries on six continents. From North America, KLM flies to Holland from New York, Atlanta, Chicago, Houston, Los Angeles, Anchorage, Calgary, Vancouver, Montréal, and Toronto.

On that first 1920 flight, passengers in the open-cockpit plane were fitted out with leather jackets, flying helmets, gloves, goggles, ear plugs, and hot-water bottles. The need for that sort of survival gear has long since vanished, but not so KLM's concern for passenger safety and comfort. So outstanding is their service operation at Schiphol that 40 *other airlines* send their staffs to KLM for training and their planes to KLM for servicing. Very reassuring, that! When it comes to comfort, cabin crews are among the best anywhere. Endowed with the natural Dutch penchant for hospitality, they are trained to assist passengers in all the usual ways, as well as to meet any emergency situations that might arise. Creature comforts include soft pillows and blankets, amusements for children, and current newspapers and magazines.

Cliché of clichés—flying KLM is a *real* Dutch treat!

About Fares

What you pay is determined by the season you travel, the class of seat you select, and the airline you choose. For Holland, lowest fares are in effect from November to March, the highest from June to mid-September.

The least expensive way to fly to Holland is by **charter** or **organized tours** that include air fare. Travel agents are your best source of information on what's available when you plan to travel, and a leading agency in the U.S. that has proved reliable for many years and which includes Holland and the other Benelux countries in many of its reasonably priced European tours is **Globus-Gateway,** 95-25 Queens Blvd., Rego Park, NY 11374 (tel. toll free 800/221-0090 in the eastern U.S.), or 150 S. Robles Ave., Pasadena, CA 91101 (tel. toll free 800/556-5454 in the western U.S.).

Many airlines also feature **promotional fares** each year that are real moneysavers. For example, during the winter of 1987–1988, KLM reduced round-trip fares between New York and Amsterdam by nearly one-third, with comparable reductions from the other U.S. gateway cities. They also offered package deals at attractive prices. Whenever you plan to fly, and by whatever airline, it will pay to ask about any special prices in effect.

APEX (Advance Purchase Excursion) represents the best value for the dollar if you can meet the restrictions. These are always sold on a round-trip basis, and advance purchase time varies by airline. Advance-purchase requirements may vary from 7 to 21 days, and tickets may be booked with an open return, good for a maximum of one year, with penalties for changing travel dates or for cancellation.

Economy, or excursion, fares are next up the price scale, and they may carry no advance-purchase requirement and/or no penalty for changes or cancellations, and are good for six months.

Business class, in a forward cabin with wider seats, free drinks, and other extras, has no booking restrictions.

First class (KLM calls it "Royal Class") is the absolute tops, in luxury as well as price. Every airline has its own brand of extras that justify the price—KLM, for example, offers a choice of five main dinner courses, including the Indonesian rijsttafel, after-dinner liqueurs, and deluxe airport lounges at several destination airports.

BY SEA FROM THE U.K.

There's excellent **Sealink car-ferry service** for foot passengers as well as cars between London (via train to Harwich) and the Hook of Holland, where trains carry you on to Rotterdam, The Hague, or Amsterdam, with both day and night crossings. North Sea Ferries also operates a rail/sea service between Hull and Rotterdam (Europoort). The crossing by ferry or jetfoil from Dover to Oostende, in Belgium, is slightly shorter (see Chapter IV), but entails more changes between rail and ship (rail to Brussels, change for Amsterdam, etc.). Details on schedules and prices may be obtained from British railway stations; in the U.S. detailed information is available from Brit Rail Travel International, Inc., 630 Third Ave., New York, NY 10020 (tel. 212/599-5400).

BY TRAIN

Rail service from major European cities is frequent, fast, and inexpensive. International trains include the *Amsterdam/Brussels/Paris Express,* and connections in Brussels with the *North Express,* the *Oostende–Vienna Express,* the *Oostende–Moscow Express,* and the *Trans-Europe Express.*

BY BUS

There's good coach service to Holland from most European centers, as well as between London and Amsterdam (via Hovercraft), with two departures daily in the summer. Travel time is just over ten hours. For full details, contact Hoverspeed Ltd., Freepost, Maybrook House, Queens Gardens, Dover, CT17 9UQ (tel. 0304/24-02-02).

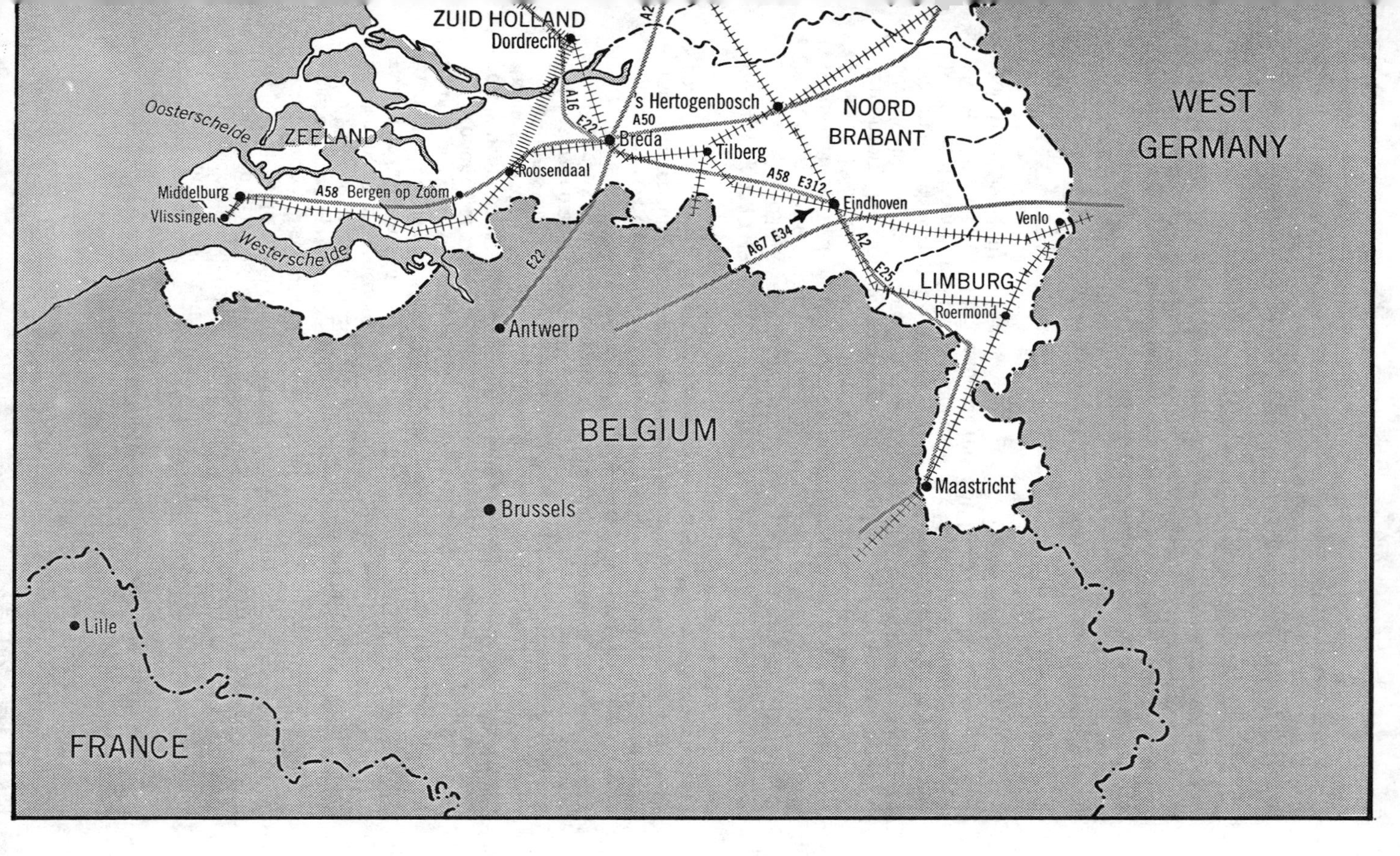
ZUID HOLLAND
Dordrecht
Oosterschelde
ZEELAND
A16
E22
A2
's Hertogenbosch
A50
Breda
Tilberg
NOORD
BRABANT
WEST
GERMANY
Roosendaal
Middelburg
A58
Bergen op Zoom
Vlissingen
Westerschelde
E22
A58
E312
Eindhoven
A67
E34
Venlo
A2
E25
LIMBURG
Roermond
Antwerp
BELGIUM
Maastricht
Brussels
Lille
FRANCE

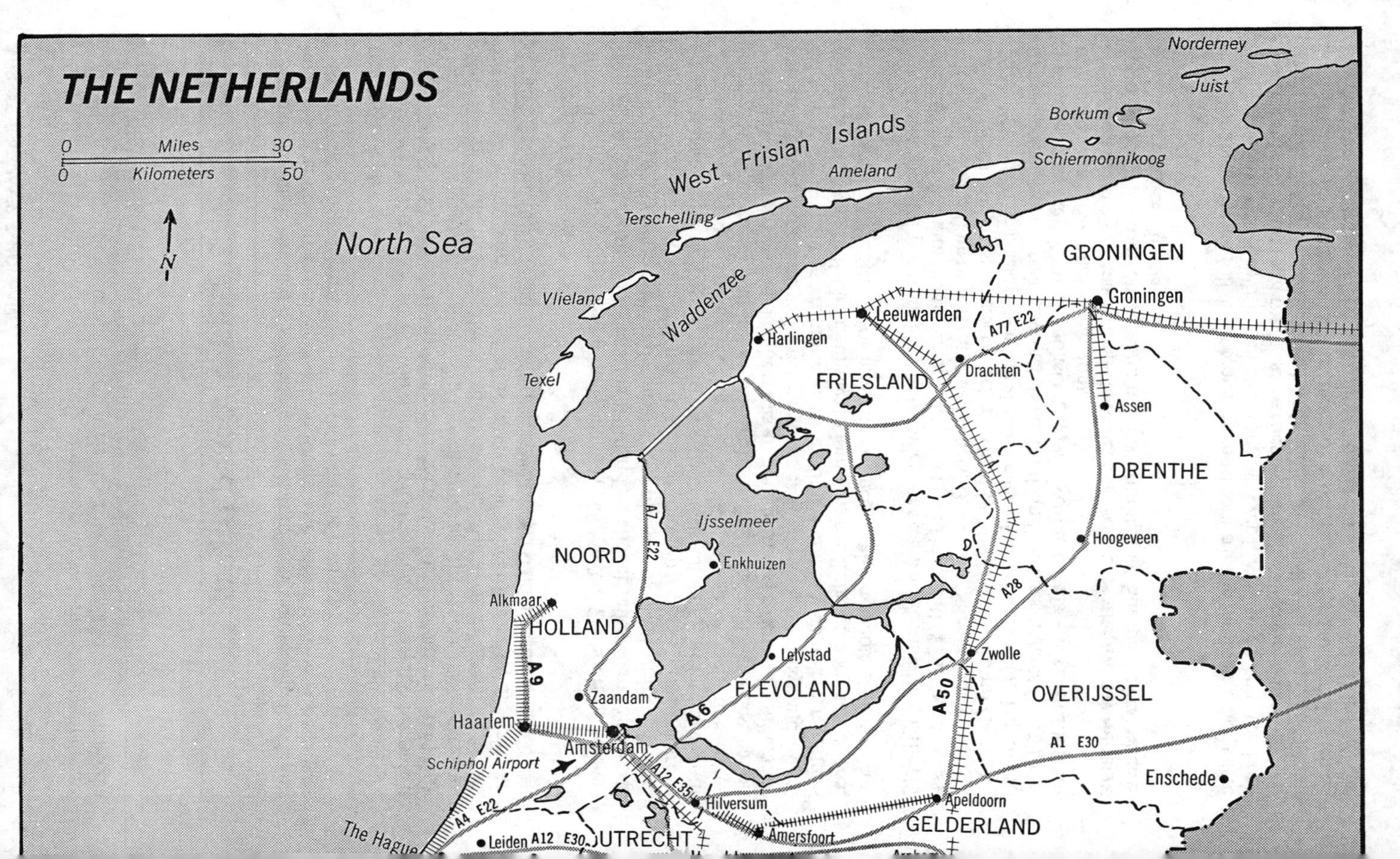
THE NETHERLANDS
0 Miles 30
0 Kilometers 50
N
North Sea
West Frisian Islands
Norderney
Juist
Borkum
Schiermonnikoog
Ameland
Terschelling
Vlieland
Texel
Waddenzee
GRONINGEN
Groningen
Leeuwarden
Harlingen
A7 E22
Drachten
FRIESLAND
Assen
DRENTHE
Ijsselmeer
Enkhuizen
NOORD
HOLLAND
A7 E22
Hoogeveen
A28
Alkmaar
A9
Lelystad
Zwolle
Zaandam
FLEVOLAND
A50
OVERIJSSEL
A6
Haarlem
Amsterdam
A1 E30
Schiphol Airport
A12 E35
Enschede
Hilversum
Apeldoorn
A4 E22
GELDERLAND
The Hague
Leiden A12 E30
UTRECHT
Amersfoort

BY CAR

Holland is crisscrossed by an excellent network of well-maintained highways connecting it with other European countries. To drive in Holland, you will need a valid passport, your U.S. driver's license, and a valid registration for the car you drive.

2. Getting Around Holland

Like Belgium, Holland is so compact it makes for easy sightseeing. Roads and express motorways are excellent, and nondrivers have one of Europe's best railway systems to take them to virtually any point within the country.

BY AIR

Because Holland is so small, you'll need to fly from one city to another only if you're very short of time. If that's the case, then the KLM subsidiary, **NLM City Hopper,** can fly you to Rotterdam, Eindhoven, and Maastricht. They also fly to London, Birmingham, Belfast, the Channel Islands, Antwerp, Brussels, Stuttgart, Bremen, Hamburg, and Düsseldorf. If you're only going for the day, they offer attractive discounts on one-day round trips, as well as weekend discounts.

BY TRAIN

All major tourist destinations in Holland are within 2 to 2½ hours of Amsterdam via **Nederlandse Spoorwagen,** Holland's national rail system. Spotlessly clean and always on time, the trains are a delightful way to travel with the Dutch, who use them even for short journeys to the next town up the line. Schedules are so frequent that you can almost just go to the station and wait for the next train to your destination, in the sure knowledge that your wait will be a short one—to even the smallest stations, there is half-hour service in both directions, and major destination points have between four and eight trains an hour *in both directions,* so you'll never get stuck out in the country. Service begins as early as 5 a.m. weekdays and 7 a.m. on Sunday and holidays, running until around 1 a.m. A complete rail timetable *(Spoorboekje)* is available at railway stations for a small charge, and there's a free intercity timetable (sufficient for most tourist needs) also available at railway stations.

If all or most of your travel will be by rail, your best investment is one of the **NS special fares** for unlimited travel: one-day tickets are Dfl. 52.50 ($23) second class, Dfl. 78.75 ($34.50) first class; three-day tickets, Dfl. 79.50 ($35) second class, Dfl. 118.50 ($52) first class; seven-day tickets, Dfl. 115.50 ($50.75) second class, Dfl. 167.75 ($73.50) first class. There are also several very attractive bargain day fares to specific destinations, a train-and-bicycle fare, and family excursion fares. The "Touring Holland by Rail" booklet published by NS gives full details—it's available from tourist offices or major railway stations.

If you're going to travel in all three Benelux countries, the five-day **Benelux Tourrail Ticket** is a good buy, and for rail travel throughout Europe the best value is the Eurailpass (see Chapter II).

BY CAR

Driving is easy in Holland except, as in most countries, in the larger cities where traffic congestion can be positively ulcer-causing. Outside the cities, however, both major motorways and local roads are excellent—they're well planned (as you'd expect from the efficient Dutch), well maintained, and well signposted, and many are lighted at night. If you're a member of a national automobile club such as the American Automobile Association, you are automatically entitled to the services of ANWB Royal Dutch Touring Club. They sponsor the fleet of yellow *wegenwacht,* a sort of repair shop on wheels that you'll see patroling the highways, and there are special yellow call boxes on all major roads to bring them to your assistance. Emergency call boxes marked "Politie" will bring the police on the double.

To drive in Holland, U.S. citizens need only a valid passport, a U.S. driver's license, and a registration for the car you drive. Minimum age for drivers is 18. On motorways, the speed limit is 100 km/h (60 mph); in all cities and urban areas, 50 km/h (30 mph); and in the outskirts of towns and cities, 80 km/h (48 mph). Traffic approaching from the right has the right of way, and pedestrians on the wide stripes at crossings *always* have the right of way.

Distance is measured in kilometers (1 kilometer = 0.62 miles), and a quick way to make an approximate conversion into miles is to multiply kilometers by 6 and round off the last digit. For a chart showing more exact conversions, see Chapter IV.

See the accompanying table (in kilometers) for distances between Amsterdam and major sightseeing points.

Rental cars with U.S. specifications are available from rental desks at Schiphol Airport and the following Amsterdam addresses (airport pickup and drop-off is also available in most cases): **Hertz,** 333 Overtoom (tel. 020/12-24-41); **Avis,** 380 Nassaukade (tel. 020/83-60-61); and **Europcar,** 224 Wibaul Straat (tel. 020/68-21-11). Expect to pay between Dfl. 40 ($17.50) and Dfl. 151 ($66.25) per day, depending on the type (stick shift or automatic) and model you choose. On a daily basis, you'll pay an additional per-kilometer charge, plus insurance and a 20% tax. Weekly rates, with unlimited mileage, represent a much better buy, with rates of Dfl. 539 ($235) to Dfl. 3,549 ($1,557), the latter for a luxury Mercedes.

3. The ABCs of Holland

Herewith, a quick, convenient reference for some of the things you'll want to know about Holland.

AMERICAN EMBASSY The American Consulate's address in Amsterdam is 19 Museumplein (tel. 020/64-56-61). The American Embassy to The Netherlands' address in The Hague is 102 Lange Voorhout (tel. 070/65-68-50).

AMERICAN EXPRESS You'll find American Express International, Inc., in Amsterdam at 66 Damrak (tel. 020/26-20-42) and 38 Van Baerlestraat (tel. 020/73-85-50).

BANKING HOURS Banks are open from 9 a.m. to 4 p.m. (some stay open until 5 p.m.) Monday through Friday. Some banks also open on late-hour shopping nights.

CLIMATE Holland has a maritime climate, which means that there are few extremes in temperature in summer or winter. Summer temperatures average about 67° Fahrenheit; the winter average is 35°. Do expect more than a little rain, however (it's driest from February through May). One Amsterdam hotel, in fact, has done a landoffice business with tourists from the Middle East by promising free lodging for every day it doesn't rain during any two-week stay—they don't give away many days, and their rain-parched guests go home happily drenched! The accompanying chart shows both the hours of sunshine and amount of rain for each month of the year, along with average high temperatures.

DISTANCE BETWEEN HOLLAND'S MAJOR CITIES

(Distance in Kilometers)

	Amsterdam	Alkmaar	Amersfoort	Apeldoorn	Arnhem	Breda	Delft	Dordrecht	Eindhoven	Den Haag	Groningen	Haarlem	Hoek van Holland	Leeuwarden	Maastricht	Nijmegen	Rotterdam	Utrecht	Vlissingen	Zwolle
Amsterdam	—	37	50	87	92	101	57	93	120	58	184	19	73	138	208	105	71	38	179	108
Alkmaar	37	—	84	133	129	143	89	111	164	73	166	32	91	111	250	147	93	83	107	119
Amersfoort	50	84	—	41	46	89	79	81	111	82	167	67	98	153	190	57	76	20	187	70
Apeldoorn	87	133	47	—	26	130	120	122	103	123	137	104	147	130	183	46	117	61	228	40
Arnhem	99	129	46	26	—	110	115	104	78	118	163	111	134	156	157	20	112	59	210	66
Breda	101	143	89	130	110	—	69	33	55	78	256	109	86	228	143	95	55	69	101	159
Delft	57	89	79	120	115	69	—	36	124	11	246	52	19	193	212	120	14	59	114	149
Dordrecht	93	111	81	122	104	33	36	—	88	45	248	76	53	217	176	101	22	61	105	151
Eindhoven	120	164	111	103	78	55	124	88	—	133	235	137	141	232	88	68	110	86	166	144
Den Haag	58	73	82	123	118	78	11	45	133	—	239	41	18	182	221	133	23	62	129	152
Groningen	184	166	167	137	163	256	246	248	235	239	—	198	257	57	309	183	243	187	354	97
Haarlem	19	32	67	104	111	109	52	76	137	41	198	—	59	141	225	130	61	56	175	128
Hoek van Holland	73	91	100	139	134	86	19	53	141	18	257	59	—	200	229	139	31	78	135	168
Leeuwarden	138	111	153	130	156	228	193	217	232	182	57	141	200	—	313	176	202	173	316	91
Maastricht	208	250	180	183	157	143	212	176	88	221	320	225	229	313	—	137	198	174	254	223
Nijmegen	105	147	57	46	20	95	120	101	68	133	183	120	139	176	137	—	111	76	192	86
Rotterdam	71	93	76	117	112	55	14	22	110	23	243	61	31	202	198	111	—	56	103	146
Utrecht	38	83	20	61	59	69	59	61	86	61	187	56	78	173	174	76	56	—	167	90
Vlissingen	179	207	187	228	210	111	114	105	166	129	354	175	135	316	254	192	103	167	—	257
Zwolle	108	119	70	40	66	159	149	151	154	152	97	128	168	91	223	86	146	90	257	—

	Temperature (°Fahrenheit)	Liters of Rain	Hours of Sunshine
January	40	64	46
February	41	48	66
March	47	49	112
April	53	48	160
May	61	52	205
June	66	62	210
July	69	81	190
August	69	83	185
September	65	68	142
October	57	68	102
November	48	77	53
December	42	74	40

CLOTHING As you can guess from the above, you'll certainly want to bring along a raincoat. Although the rain is not usually a heavy, splashing downpour, showers are frequent and often unexpected. A light jacket or sweater is a good idea to ward off the accompanying chill, and in winter you'll need heavy outerwear for the occasional drop in temperature that so gladdens Dutch hearts if it's severe enough for the canals to freeze over. Otherwise, bring casual clothes for daytime activities, comfortable walking shoes (sturdy enough to stand up to cobblestones), and at least one semi-dress outfit for after-dark Amsterdam. Needless to say, lighten your luggage as much as possible via the mix-and-match dress method (see Chapter II).

CRIME Whenever you're traveling in an unfamiliar city or country, stay alert. Be aware of your immediate surroundings. Wear a moneybelt and don't sling your camera or purse over your shoulder; wear the strap diagonally across your body. This will minimize the possibility of your becoming a victim of crime. Every society has its criminals. It's your responsibility to be aware and be alert even in the most heavily touristed areas.

CURRENCY Holland's basic monetary unit is the **guilder,** yet you'll see it written as Dutch florins (f., fl., or Dfl.)—it's a holdover from the past, and in ordinary commerce you simply ignore the written symbol and read all prices as guilders. There are 100 Dutch cents to a guilder, and prices are expressed in the familiar decimal system. Sounds simple, but there's a recent complication—all Dutch "cent" coins have been withdrawn from circulation, so prices are simply rounded off to the nearest multiple of 5 cents. The accompanying chart will help you sort out the various coins that are in use and the identifying colors of the bills. Those bills, incidentally, are a marvelous expression of Dutch compassion—each one has a little rough patch in one corner, which is really its worth in Braille to make things easier for the blind.

As we go to press, the exchange rate is $1 U.S. = Dfl. 2.28—you should, however, be sure to check on the *current* rate of exchange at the time you plan to travel.

There are no import and export restrictions regarding money and foreign exchange.

Dutch Coins

Dfl.	Name	Type	U.S.$
0.05	stuiver	bronze	.02
0.10	dubbeltje	small silver	.04
0.25	kwartje	silver	.11
1.00	guilder	silver	.44
2.50	rijksdaalder	silver	1.10

Dutch Bills

Dfl.	Color	U.S.$
5	green	2.19
10	blue	4.39
25	red	10.96
50	yellow	21.93
100	brown	43.86

CURRENCY EXCHANGE It's possible to change your traveler's checks or U.S. dollars outside banking hours in Holland at some 65 GWK Bureau de Change offices: 30 of them in railway stations, others at border checkpoints. They have extended evening and weekend hours and can also provide cash for holders of American Express, MasterCard, Diners Club, and VISA credit cards. Some international trains have currency exchanges, as do many tourist offices in coastal resorts.

CUSTOMS Before leaving home, be sure to register with Customs (at the airport) any camera, typewriter, etc., you plan to carry with you that could have been purchased abroad; otherwise you may very well have to pay duty on these items when you return home if you cannot prove they were not bought on your trip.

When reentering the U.S., citizens (regardless of age) are allowed up to a $400 exemption for goods bought overseas if they have been away for more than two days and have not had the same duty exemption within one month. Within that amount, those over 21 are allowed one liter of alcohol, 100 cigars (no Cuban cigars, however), 200 cigarettes, and one bottle of perfume with a U.S. trademark. Works of art and antiques more than 100 years old may be brought in duty free (be sure to have verification of age to present to Customs). No agricultural products or meats from overseas may be brought into the U.S. and will be confiscated if they're in your luggage. With the exception of alcohol, tobacco, and perfumes valued at more than $5, gifts worth up to $50 may be mailed to the U.S. as gifts, but only one per day to the same addressee.

ELECTRIC CURRENT Holland runs on 220-volt current, so if you plan to bring a hairdryer, radio (unless it's battery-operated), travel iron, or any other small appliance with you, pack a European-style adapter plug and a transformer.

EMERGENCIES In case of **accident,** dial 900. See Chapter XIV for individual medical, police, etc., emergency numbers in Amsterdam.

FLOWER BULBS One look at Amsterdam's floating flower market and something in your soul is likely to prod you to buy one of the nicest of all souvenirs. That's fine, but you must know that Dutch flower bulbs can only be exported if they have been awarded an official health certificate. The wise thing to do is *not* to stick a few in your luggage—which may well be confiscated by Customs when you return home—but place an order with one of the many authorized mail-order companies.

GOVERNMENT Holland is a constitutional monarchy headed by Queen Beatrix and her consort, Prince Claus. The popular Queen is active in affairs of state, but the final power rests with Parliament.

HOLIDAYS Public holidays are: January 1 (New Year's Day), Good Friday, Easter Sunday and Monday, Queen's Day (April 30), Ascension Day, Whit Sunday and Monday, Christmas Day, and Boxing Day (December 26). In addition, there are two "Remembrance Days" related to World War II, neither of which is an official holiday, although you may find some shops closed: May 4 honors all those who fell in that war, and May 5 celebrates Liberation Day.

HOLLAND LEISURE CARD See "Tourist Bonus," below.

LANGUAGE No problem here—almost everyone will speak English, and do so graciously. If you *do* run into someone who speaks only Dutch, you may be very sure they'll be quick to round up someone who can speak to you in your own language.

PASSPORTS AND VISAS U.S. and Canadian citizens who plan to be in the country 90 days or less need bring only a valid passport—no visa is required. Citizens of other countries should consult the nearest Netherlands consulate.

SHOPPING HOURS Shops generally stay open from 8:30 or 9 a.m. to 5 or 6 p.m. weekdays, until 4 or 5 p.m. on Saturday. Some shops close for lunch, and nearly all have one full closing day or one morning or afternoon when they are closed—signs are prominently posted announcing those closing times. Many shops, especially in Amsterdam, have late hours on Thursday and/or Friday evening.

TAXIS Taxis must either be engaged at taxi ranks at hotels, railway stations, and shopping areas or called by telephone. *Tip and taxes are included in the meter price, and you need not add another tip unless there has been exceptional service* (help with heavy luggage, etc.).

TELEPHONE Telephones in Holland are very similar to those in the United States (perhaps a little more efficient), and coin telephones accept the Dfl. 0.25 coin (kwartje). It doesn't drop until your call is answered. Direct dialing for other European countries as well as overseas (including the U.S. and Canada) is available in most hotel rooms in Amsterdam and other large cities. If your hotel is not equipped to handle international calls, they can be placed through most post offices. For the most economical international rates, dial the USA Direct operator (tel. 06/022-91-11). For directory assistance in finding a telephone number anywhere in Holland, call 008; for numbers outside the country, dial 0018.

TIME Holland is in the Central European Time zone, six hours ahead of Eastern Standard Time in the U.S. (9 a.m. in New York = 3 p.m. in Holland). Clocks are moved ahead one hour each year on March 30 and back one hour on September 28.

TIPPING Restaurants and hotels will almost always include a 15% service charge and the 19% value added tax (VAT). What a relief! Of course, the Dutch have a rather nice practice you may also want to follow: they invariably round off any bill (in a restaurant, cafe, taxi, etc.) to the nearest guilder and leave it as an extra sort of "thank you"—not really a tip, just leaving the change. Of course, if you've had exceptional service and want to add a little more, that's perfectly acceptable; it's just not obligatory. Taxis, as noted above, include the tip in the meter reading.

TOURIST INFORMATION U.S. addresses for the Netherlands Board of Tourism are given in Chapter II, Section 1, "Preparing for Your Trip."

In Holland, you'll find one of the most efficient, best-organized tourist organizations you're likely to meet up with anywhere. The **Vereniging Voor Vreemdelingenverkeer** (which means the Association for Tourist Traffic) is known by all and sundry as simply the **VVV,** and they operate more than 400 offices in cities, towns, and villages around the country. They can book accommodations for you, help with travel arrangements, tell you what's on where, and . . . well, if there's anything they *can't* do, I have yet to discover it! Look for a blue-and-white sign (many times triangular in shape) bearing the letters "VVV."

TOURIST BONUS The two best buys in Holland must be made *before you leave home.* If you're age 16 or over, don't leave home without the Holland Leisure Card and the Holland Leisure Card Plus, both available from the Netherlands Tourist Offices listed above. Believe me, you'll kick yourself all around Holland if you do! Neither of the cards is available inside Holland, and here's what each of them does for you:

The **Holland Leisure Card,** at $10, includes, among other things, discounts on shopping, car rentals, first- and second-class one-day train passes, hotels, tourist attractions, tours, and free admission to casinos. The **Holland Leisure Card Plus,** at $20, gives the same discounts as the Holland Leisure Card, plus a museum card that gives you free admission to about 350 museums in Holland.

4. Where to Stay

Holland's accommodations range from city hotels with amenities and prices at every level from budget to deluxe, to seaside resort hotels complete with casino, to simple but charming country hotels, to youth hostels and good camping facilities. Rates at all hotels, regardless of price category, generally include a continental breakfast (which in Holland means a hearty repast of lots of cheese, fresh breads, sliced meats, etc.), a 15% service charge, and VAT. The Netherlands Tourist Offices listed above can furnish a current hotel directory for the entire country that lists hotels by town, showing facilities and prices, as well as their "Benelux classification" based on degree of comfort.

If you book directly with the hotel, you should if at all possible confirm it in writing with the hotel, stating the number of rooms desired, single- or double-bed preference, private bath or shower requirements, any room location preferences (with view of garden, canal, etc.), length of time you expect to stay, and the exact date and approximate time of your arrival.

It's a good idea to book at least your first few days before you arrive, which can be done through your travel agent, directly with the hotel of your choice, or through the **Netherlands Reservation Centre,** P.O. Box 404, 2260 AK Leidschendam, Holland (tel. 070/20-25-00). If you elect to use this latter service, for which there is no fee, be *sure* to allow enough time for them to confirm the reservation to you before you leave home. They'll need to have the same information detailed above for direct bookings.

Once you're traveling around Holland, local VVV offices will gladly make hotel reservations to meet your requirements, and there is sometimes (but not always) a small charge for the service.

HOTELS

Amsterdam, as you might expect, has the widest range of hotels, some of which are very sophisticated luxury establishments, with prices to match of course, but when it comes to value received, your dollars will be well spent. In style and décor, they range from Old World to ultramodern to canalside charm. In most cases, there will be a concierge to provide almost any service you might require, from theater tickets to restaurant reservations to travel arrangements.

In the moderate price range, there are outstanding values in clean, comfortable, and well-run hostelries around the country as well as in the larger cities. Many have rooms both with and without private baths, with an appropriate price difference. Budget travelers may have to search a bit to find accommodations below the moderate range, but a little effort combined with help from local VVV offices will unearth them.

BOARDING HOUSES

Private homes around the country offer bed and board in a family style, and while there is no official listing, the VVV in each locality is usually able to supply names and addresses. One word of warning: If you plan to come in July or August and would like this kind of accommodation, you'd best make arrangements several months in advance. The Netherlands Tourist Offices in the U.S. listed above can help with addresses of local VVV offices.

YOUTH HOSTELS

As pointed out in Chapter IV, the first thing to be said about hostels is that, although they're called Youth Hostels, you'll be welcomed if you're 6 or 60. The second thing to be said is that in order to use them, you must have an International Youth Hostel Card, which *must be purchased before you leave home.* They are available from American Youth Hostels, Inc., P.O. Box 37613, Washington, DC 20013, and cost $10 for those under 18 or over 55, and $20 for those ages 18 to 59. For another $8.95 (plus $2 postage) you can purchase their *International Youth Hostel Handbook* (Vol. I-Europe and the Mediterranean) in which you'll find hostels in Holland listed.

For details on the more than 45 hostels in Holland, contact **Stichting Nederlandse Jeugdherberg Centrale (NJHC),** Prof. Tulpplein 4, 1018 GX Amsterdam (tel. 020/55-131-55).

CAMPING

The Netherlands Tourist Offices can supply a directory of all camping facilities, but all bookings must be made directly. Bikers should inquire about the special eight-day "Hospitable Bike Camping" package available during spring and summer: contact "Gastvrije Fietscampings" Foundation, P.O. Box 93200, 2509 BA Den Haag, Holland (tel. 070/14-71-47). Again, summer reservations must be made well in advance.

5. Where and What to Eat

"Simple, hearty, top-notch ingredients"—that description comes closest to describing native Dutch cuisine. "Dull" does not. Unless, that is, you personally consider beautifully fresh fish, fowl, vegetables, and fruits prepared without overembellishment dull. Add to those high-quality ingredients a wide variety of other meats, rich butter used more lavishly than you might expect, and the world's best cheeses, and you have a choice of stick-to-your-ribs meals that are interesting and always served in ample quantities.

That, briefly, is the Dutch cuisine—which is *not* to say it is the only cuisine available in Holland. Far from it! Those far-ranging Dutch explorers and traders brought back recipes and exotic spices, and by now the Dutch at home have a well-developed taste for the foods of other climes. That is especially true of Indonesian dishes, and the popular rijsttafel (rice table) has been a national favorite ever since it arrived in the 17th century. If you've never experienced this mini-feast, it should definitely be on your "must eat" list for Holland. Even if you part company with the Dutch and their love of Indonesian food, there's a good supply of other ethnic restaurants around, and you'll find the cuisines of France, China, Italy, Greece, Turkey, Yugoslavia, and several other nationalities well represented.

WHERE

Amsterdam is the home of hundreds of restaurants in all styles, sizes, cuisines, and price ranges. You will not, however, go hungry once you leave the city, since the Dutch love to eat and every locality will have several restaurants that cater to different tastes and price categories.

At the top of the restaurant scale are those posh dining rooms that are affiliated with the prestigious Alliance Gastronomique Néerlandaise or the Relais du Centre. They're likely to be elegant and sophisticated or atmospherically Old World or quaint. They will certainly be expensive, and just as certainly excel to such a degree the punch to the pocketbook won't hurt a bit.

For authentic Dutch dishes, look for the "Neerlands Dis" sign in restaurant windows. There are about 500 restaurants that specialize in the native cuisine, and tourist offices in the U.S. as well as Holland can supply a leaflet with the addresses of many.

Then there are the moderately priced restaurants that outnumber every other category except perhaps the intimate little brown cafés. Dutch families gravitate to the restaurants, while the brown cafés are an integral part of all Dutch lives as cozy social centers with simple, but tasty food often served in establishments that spread outside to sidewalk tables. Sidewalk vendors, with fresh herring and the ubiquitous *broodjes* (sandwiches) or some other light specialty, are as much a part of the national scene as the brown cafés.

A real break in the "what you'll pay" department is the Dutch Tourist Menu served in over 500 restaurants around the country, with a hefty number in Amsterdam and other large cities. They represent the single best dining value, with a three-course meal at Dfl. 19.50 ($8.50). It's a set menu, usually chosen from the restaurant's own specialties. Pick up a directory from any VVV office, or arm yourself with one from the Netherlands Tourist Office before you leave home.

Two things you should know about all restaurants: Dutch menus list *appetizers,* not main courses, under "entree"; and a 15% service charge plus VAT is included in almost all prices.

WHAT

Well, there are all those international cuisines about which you already know. The Indonesian *rijsttafel,* which may not be so familiar, is briefly described below. As for the "Neerlands Dis" menus and other traditional dishes, they consist chiefly of the following:

erwtensoep—a thick pea soup (usually available only in winter) usually served with sausage and brown bread—traditionally, it should be thick enough to hold a spoon upright!

hutspot—the thick stew of potatoes, carrots, onions, and lean meat that is said to have been left behind by Spanish soldiers as they fled the Dutch who broke the siege of Leiden in 1574.

broodjes—sandwiches made of small bread rolls filled with beef, ham, cheese, or other stuffings.

tostis—grilled cheese-and-ham sandwiches.

nieuwe haring—fresh-caught herring straight from the North Sea and eaten raw or with onion, available only in summer months; pickled herring is eaten year round.

croquetten—delicious fried croquettes with soft innards, usually of cheese or meat and served with mustard.

pannekoeken (poffertjes)—wonderfully thin, plate-size pancakes served flat, with a choice of such toppings as syrup, jam, cooked apples, hot ginger sauce, or confectioner's sugar.

saucijzenbrood—a spicy Dutch sausage wrapped in flaky pastry (looks much like a hot dog).

rijsttafel—an Indonesian "ricetable" with as many as two dozen different small dishes served, along with plenty of rice to act as a buffer when fiery spices call for a change to the blandness of steamed vegetables or fruits; best accompanied by beer, mineral water, or some similar cold drink—*not* with milk or wine.

What to drink? The Dutch favor one of their own excellent beers or the marvelous—and potent!—native gin known as **jenever.** The latter is a fiery, colorless liquid served ice cold to be drunk "neat"—it's not a mixer. *Jonge* (young) jenever is less sweet and creamy than the *oude* (old) variety, but both are known for their delayed-action effectiveness. There are also very good Dutch liqueurs, such as **Curaçao** and **Triple Sec.** Wines from all over the world are readily available.

Quite aside from alcoholic beverages, coffee lovers may agree with my personal opinion the Dutch coffee is, hands down, the best in the world.

Note: Most restaurants are open from noon to 2:30 p.m. for lunch, and from 7 to 10 p.m. for dinner seven days a week. However, these hours may be flexible.

6. Where to Go and What to Do

Holland is quite literally a country with something for everyone. Amsterdam is its best-known treasure house of great art, historic buildings, scenic canals, incredible shops, diamond markets, one of the world's leading symphony orchestras, sparkling nightspots, and a zoo that includes the largest aquarium in the country. Yet in this compact land a half-hour drive takes you into a world of wonderful little villages, whose citizens fish the sea or tend vast flower fields or shape wooden shoes or form rich cheeses—all following in the footsteps of generations of ancestors. The countryside itself brings on a spell of déjà vu, its flat, green fields, tree-lined canals, and vast, cloud-studded skies a landscape made familiar by Holland's great artists. The sea is never far away, with small resorts and a grand casino, as well as quiet little islands just off the coast.

Come for only a few days and leave with an unbelievable store of sightseeing memories: stay longer and return home with experiences that will enrich for years to come. The itineraries below are merely suggestions for a Holland vacation of one or two weeks—guidelines only, they are subject to changes to suit your own travel inclinations.

SUGGESTED ITINERARIES

If you can spend only one week in Holland, I strongly recommend that you base yourself in Amsterdam and make day trips to nearby cities and towns, none more than an hour away by train and some even closer. Or join the excellent narrated coach tours that fan out from Amsterdam each day covering important nearby destinations in only half a day. By returning each evening to Amsterdam you'll not only develop a real feeling for that intriguing and fascinating city, but you'll save a lot of the wear and tear that comes with shifting accommodations every day or so. Of course, should one of those day trips trigger an instant love affair with one special spot, *that's* the place to plant yourself—you can always let Amsterdam be the day trip.

First Week

Days 1 and 2: You'll need at least the first two days to explore Amsterdam and highlights of its outstanding cultural attractions, perhaps including the three-hour sightseeing tour that includes stops at an important museum and a diamond-cutting exhibition.

Day 3: Take a four-hour morning tour to Marken beside the Ijsselmeer, visiting a wooden-shoe workshop en route; use the afternoon to visit another of Amsterdam's museums; save this evening for the candlelight cruise of Amsterdam's canals.

Day 4: Spend this day with a city-packed, eight-hour tour that visits The Hague, Scheveningen, Rotterdam, and Delft, returning to Amsterdam for a dinner of traditional Dutch specialties at one of the Neerlands Dis restaurants.

Day 5: If your visit falls between March and May when the tulips are at their peak, spend this day visiting the famous flower auction at Aalsmeer, then drive to the beautiful Keukenhoff Gardens, passing through acres of bulb fields that lie between Haarlem and Leiden. The gardens are lovely at any time of the year, since different species bloom in different months. If flowers have no appeal, the Haarlem–Leiden drive is worthwhile solely for sightseeing. Nondrivers can take a sightseeing coach tour. Return to Amsterdam for the evening, perhaps at one of the city's prolific jazz clubs.

Day 6: If this is a Friday, be sure to visit Alkmaar and its colorful morning cheese market, where giant wheels of cheese are auctioned in the town square (there's a coach tour every week), returning to Amsterdam by a circular route for stops at Edam and Volendam through windmill-studded countryside. Nondrivers can join an afternoon tour from Amsterdam to Edam and Volendam. Evening in Amsterdam.

Day 7: Save this day for your last Amsterdam sightseeing (have you been to the Anne Frank House yet?) and last-minute preparations for departure. Or use most of the day to travel up to the great Enclosing Dike that made a freshwater lake, Ijsselmeer, from an arm of the salty Zuiderzee, returning to Amsterdam by way of a dam over the Ijsselmeer and the new town of Lelystad in the newest polder, Flevoland—it's a day that ends with great respect, and a healthy dose of awe, for all that the Dutch have accomplished in taming the sea.

Second Week

The above pretty much limits you to sightseeing highlights, but if you have two weeks to spend, add the following. A car is not essential for this part of your visit, since every destination is easily reached by train or bus. Mind you, this itinerary will keep you hopping, and you may wish to be selective and save parts of Holland for your next visit. You may also want to juggle the suggested order, but bear in mind that travel will be easier if you save Zeeland for last if you're flying out of Amsterdam, Maastricht if you're traveling on in Europe.

Days 8 to 10: Drive from Amsterdam north through Hoorn and on across the Enclosing Dike and through the picturesque harbor town of Harlingen to Leeuwarden, in the province of Friesland. With Leeuwarden as a base, explore the countryside, site of Holland's earliest earthen mounds that presaged dikes; visit nearby Groningen, the tile and ceramic factory at Makkum, the pottery town of Workum, and Hindeloopen, with its furniture painters. Nondrivers can make use of the good rail service from Amsterdam and local bus service within the Friesland region.

Day 11: Travel leisurely southward to the wooded Veluwe region of Gelderland, and overnight in Apeldoorn (it holds a royal palace and a noteworthy museum of modern art).

Day 12: Drive through Arnhem to Maastricht, historic—and surprisingly sophisticated—city in the province of Limburg. Spend the afternoon visiting the awesome Caves of St. Pietersberg, the evening dining in one of the excellent restaurants in the city, followed by a pub crawl through its interesting drinking spots. Overnight in Maastricht.

Day 13: Get an early start and drive across the country to Middleburg, in the province of Zeeland. Use the afternoon to explore this quaint city. Overnight in Middleburg.

Day 14: Make an early-morning visit to the incredibly massive Delta Project that is constructing another controlling "gate" to the sea, before driving back to Amsterdam.

SIGHTSEEING

Holland's sightseeing attractions are a curious sort of "hutspot"—a lovely blend of urban and rural destinations, of the great art of the Dutch masters and the incredibly beautiful crafts of cottage industries in tiny villages, of ancient centers and towns so newly created that the land on which they sit is barely dry from its long sojourn as sea bottom. Your itinerary will revolve around those sightseeing treats that most catch your fancy, and the following is a very brief delineation of the categories from which you can choose. You'll find more detailed information in upcoming chapters.

Towns and Cities

Amsterdam could hold you for the entire length of your stay, such are its enticements. You won't want to miss the great Rijksmuseum, whose most treasured jewel is Rembrandt's *The Night Watch,* and you shouldn't miss the van Gogh Museum, and you can top off your museum tripping with a visit to the Stedelijk Museum, with its contemporary art collection. But it's the fascinating old narrow streets, meandering canals, inviting "brown cafés" and pubs, gabled canal houses, floating flower market, and a hundred other details of this beautiful old city that will hold you enthralled.

The Hague, one of Europe's prettiest capitals, is the seat of the government, home of Queen Beatrix, and next-door neighbor of Scheveningen, beach resort par excellence.

Rotterdam has emerged from the total devastation it suffered during World War II with a totally modern face, its life centered around a tremendously efficient and busy harbor, the Europoort.

Delft, whose name has become synonymous with the unique earthenware created here, is a charming and pretty little city, the home of the painter Johannes Vermeer.

Leiden clutches a windmill to its heart, right in the middle of town, and relishes memories of the 11-year sojourn of the Pilgrims before they left to sail on to America.

Leeuwarden dates back to the 15th century, and parts of it are built on earthen mounds constructed by Holland's earliest settlers.

Apeldoorn sits in Holland's central forest, one of the most scenic locations in the country. The splendid palace that Queen Wilhelmina loved has been restored and is open to the public, as is an art museum.

Utrecht, capital of that province, is primarily an industrial city, albeit a picturesque one. It is Holland's medieval monument, with wonderful old buildings from the 16th century, when this was one of the leading religious centers of Europe—medieval churches, high-gabled houses, and winding canals.

Maastricht is Holland's oldest fortified city, tracing its history all the way back to the Romans, and filled with great medieval buildings.

The **Middleburg** town center is a wonder of Gothic and Renaissance buildings, tiny twisting streets, and a serene abbey.

Windmills

No, they haven't disappeared from Holland's landscape, but their numbers have been reduced from some 10,000 to a mere 1,000, only about 200 of which are in use these days. The VVV (or the Netherlands Tourist Office before you come) can furnish a list of those windmills officially open to the public, but you should know that the hospitable Dutch millers welcome visitors to private mills any time they hoist a flag outside to signify that they're inside and the mill is working.

Flowers

Of course you want to see Holland's famous bulb fields! And you will if you come between late March and mid-May. If you don't make it then, not to worry—there are gorgeous flowers in bloom right up to September, they just aren't tulips. What you'll see other months are hyacinths, daffodils, roses, carnations, freesias, rhododendrons, hydrangeas, and even (in nurseries) Dutch orchids. The bulb fields are concentrated in the Leiden–Haarlem–Den Helder area and around Enkhuizen. To see the most lavish display of Dutch blooms, visit the Keukenhoff garden, the world's largest flower garden, near Lisse. For cut flowers, don't miss the floating flower market on Amsterdam's Singel canal and the Aalsmeer flower auction just outside the city.

SPORTS

Water sports, as you might expect, predominate in Holland. There is hardly anything that can be done on or in the water that isn't done in this water-minded country, including sailing, yachting, windsurfing, and waterskiing. VVV offices can tell you where equipment can be rented, and you'll find the Dutch eager to assist any water sports enthusiast. Holland's beaches afford good swimming except those where currents are strong and treacherous—best to stick to resort areas where waters are safe and lifeguards present. There are also many public swimming pools, both indoor and outdoor.

Fishing is another popular sport, and the VVV can guide you to rental equipment for trying your luck in inland lakes and rivers as well as charter boats for deep-sea fishing. No license is needed for fishing out at sea or on the shore, and there are no seasonal restrictions. You must have a license for inland fishing, however, available at any post office. Consult the Tourist Board pamphlet "Fishing" for complete details on regulations and a guide to good fishing locations.

Tennis and golf facilities are fairly spotty in Holland, although local VVV offices can usually point you to tennis clubs and private golf clubs, many of which welcome visitors—only five public golf courses in the country, however, at Rotterdam, Rhoon, Oostvoorne, Velsen/Ijmuiden, and Wowse Plantage.

Equestrians will want to obtain a copy of the Tourist Board's "Horseriding" publication that gives the addresses of stables and horseriding schools, along with names of pony camps for children where they are given instruction at all levels.

AFTER DARK

Amsterdam leads all Dutch cities in the variety of after-dark entertainment available, with theaters, cabarets, nightclubs, concerts, ballet and opera, jazz clubs, and discothèques. Rotterdam's nightlife is active and more or less confined to "swinging" nightspots. There are casinos, open year round, at Scheveningen (the top casino in the country), Valkenburg, and Zandvoort. Proper dress (jacket for men) is expected, and you must present your passport. Admission fees and minimum stakes are both quite small.

The most popular after-dark activity among the Dutch centers around the "brown bars," and they're found in every province. Those in Maastricht are so atmospheric and so varied that the VVV has issued a "Pub Crawl" booklet describing some of the most interesting.

AMSTERDAM

Amsterdam has been called, among other things, "the Venice of Holland," "the City of Pleasures," "Surprising Amsterdam," and "Amazing Amsterdam." All those titles, however, fall far short of encapsulating this city's essence. Its 160 canals outnumber those of Venice, and Amsterdam's ambience has none of the static "museum city" flavor that characterizes Venice. As for pleasures, it has been written that Amsterdam is "a city of simple pleasures, sophisticated pleasures, wicked pleasures, sacred pleasures"—I certainly wouldn't quarrel with any of those; yet a "pleasure" tag ignores the thriving port and the commercial face of Amsterdam. "Surprising" it most assuredly is, no matter how many times you come, and "amazing" fits too, but both are much too vague to have real meaning.

How, then, to sum up Amsterdam? If one must tag it with a title, the only one that occurs to me is that overworked adjective "unique." Quite simply, there is just no other place *anywhere* like it!

1. By Way of Background

In the beginning it wasn't unique at all—just a camp set up by two fishermen who recognized the advantages of settling on the River Amstel where it met the IJ (it's pronounced "eye," and means "water" in ancient Dutch), the spot now occupied by Dam Square in the heart of the central city. That was nearly 1,000 years ago, and until the 12th century it remained a simple little fishing settlement. By that time a dam had been constructed across the Amstel and the village called itself Amstelledamme. For a time in the 13th century the powerful Count Floris V tried to add it to his extensive holdings, even going so far as to grant special tax and beer-brewing privileges to its citizens (even then, canny traders and advocates of civil rights!). Finally the count bowed to the inevitable and granted "Amsterdam" a city charter in 1275.

From that time on the city thrived, sending its ships farther and farther across the seas to bring back goods from around the world to stock Amsterdam warehouses. Merchants grew wealthy, a banking industry sprang up to serve them, and the port was expanded. In the 17th century the last three of the main curved canals (the Herengracht, Keizersgracht, and Prinsengracht) were added around the Singel (originally built as a moat to defend the city), which completed the watery crescents that now encircle the oldest part of the city.

Along the canals, merchants and bankers built elegant patrician homes, many times with the upper floors used as storage warehouses for goods that could be unloaded from ships sailing up the Zuiderzee, then by canal to their front doors. The distinctive hooks you see today extended from almost every gable were used to pull merchandise to those upper floors, since the narrow inside stairways would not accommodate its bulk. That was the 17th century—Holland's Golden Age.

Because Amsterdam had early on established itself as a surrogate custodian of individual rights, almost every wave of European oppressors sent a wave of the oppressed pouring into the city. And with each wave came new talents, new cultures, and yet another ingredient in the city's *hutspot.* For example, Jews fleeing Antwerp came to Amsterdam and took up the only trade not governed by a hard-to-get-into guild: diamond cutting, an important facet of the modern city's economy.

The canal system that worked so well for trade was equally effective as a defense measure, and the forces of both William II and Louis XIV were turned back when locks were opened to flood them out. Napoleon, however, arrived in the bitterly cold January of 1795, and when the same tactics were tried he sent his horse troops galloping across ice that had quickly formed on the flood waters. It was he who turned the Town Hall on Dam Square into a royal palace, installing his brother as King of Holland, a reign that was to last only five years.

With Napoleon's defeat in 1815 and the return of House of Orange rulers, Amsterdam got back to the business of meeting stiff trade competition on the high seas, primarily from the English, whose huge ships could no longer come into the city through a silting-up Zuiderzee. That competition and their narrowing access to the sea had made a big dent in Amsterdam's prosperity, but with their customary ingenuity the industrious Dutch simply cut a new canal pathway to the sea, the North Sea Canal, with depths that could accommodate the deepest keels of ocean-going vessels.

In May 1940 Nazi troops swept into the city to begin one of its darkest—and most heroic—periods. In February of the next year the conquerors had their first taste of Dutch resistance when all Amsterdam had the audacity to stage a strike protesting the wholesale exportation of Jews (I wonder if the annals of World War II chronicle any other such strike!). In the end, of course, it failed, and there were massive reprisals. The resistance worked underground all through the war years, however, maintaining constant communication with the British government and performing feats of sabotage and prisoner escape that will probably never be fully documented.

By the winter of 1944–1945 food supplies in Amsterdam were being confiscated for shipment to a Germany nearing defeat and the city's citizens were literally starving, some eating tulip bulbs just to stay alive. With no electricity, gas, or coal, centuries-old floorboards were torn up and burned. Some 5,000 premises were simply demolished for their building materials or for lack of repair materials. Known as the "hunger winter," 1944–1945 was an endless struggle for survival for the people of Amsterdam, yet its underground organization never once wavered and was in fact a key factor in Holland's liberation by Allied troops in May 1945.

Since then Amsterdam has expanded its port by once more digging a canal, the Amsterdam–Rhine Canal, this one linking it to Europe's inland industries in 1952. It has waged a highly successful campaign to attract new industries, and it has continued to welcome the oppressed, the rebellious, and just plain tourists like you and me, with an exuberant, zestful personality that makes "unique" *truly* an Amsterdam label.

2. Orientation

Right up front it must be said that it is *you* who will be unique if you don't—at least once—get lost in the maze of Amsterdam's streets. I make that unequivocable statement in the face of a city map that looks straightforward enough and streets that should be easy enough to figure out. The problem is with that "necklace" of canals around the city center, or **Centrum.** It's amazingly easy to find yourself following a curving canal in exactly the opposite direction of the one you intended. And because of that, I strongly suggest that the very first thing you do is arm yourself with a city map, either from the VVV or from your hotel (many hotels, in fact, will hand you a complimentary map along with your room key). One consolation, however: This is one place in which it's sort of fun to get lost—no matter where you wind up, it won't be dull or uninteresting, and it gives you a chance to ask passersby for directions, which often opens up a friendly, helpful conversation.

Before even scanning that map, you need to know that *gracht,* when tacked onto a name, means canal (unless, of course, it applies to a street that once was a canal and is now filled in); *kade* usually means the quay (or small street) running down the side of a canal; *straat* simply means street; *plein* is a square; *laan* is a boulevard, usually lined with trees; and *steeg* is an alley.

Map in hand, look first at the four semicircular canals that form a half moon at the heart of the city and the smaller canals that cross them much like the spokes of a wheel. Many of the places you will want to go are along these waterways. Next, look for the main focal point of Amsterdam orientation, **Dam Square.** The important street, **Damrak,** leads from Dam Square directly to the Central Station, which is built on an artificial island and is an ornate architectural wonder in itself. It's where you'll go to book railway tickets, change money, and perhaps have a good, inexpensive meal in its fine restaurant. It is also the originating point for most of the city trams and is across the canal from a main departure point for canal-boat tours. Across the square out front is the main office of the VVV, with a delightful Koffiehuis whose terrace overlooks the canal, with an inexpensive restaurant inside.

The other important squares to mark on your map are:

Muntplein (Mint Square) is reached from Dam Square by way of the **Rokin** (where there's another canal-tour dock), named for the tall, wonderfully decorated tower whose carillon rings out every half hour. Across the Singel Canal is the famous floating flower market, also a busy tram intersection crossed by a large number of tram lines.

Rembrandtsplein, another major landmark, is reached via Reguliersbreestraat from Muntplein, the home of a whole slew of restaurants, bars, sidewalk cafés, cabarets, discothèques, and cinemas. People-watching is terrific in this rather hectic square.

Leidseplein is at the end of Leidsestraat and home of the Stadsschouwburg (Municipal Theater for ballet, opera, and concert performances), the landmark American Hotel with its fanciful art nouveau restaurant/café, plus restaurants, outdoor cafés, and nightspots.

Museumplein, just beyond Leidseplein, is the very heart of Amsterdam's cultural life, holding the Rijksmuseum, the Van Gogh and Stedlijk museums, with the Concertgebouw concert hall.

The other Amsterdam areas you should know by name are: the **Jordaan,** a residential area west of the Centrum between Rozengracht and Haarlemmerdijk, settled by Jewish refugees who named area streets for flowers, and lately becoming

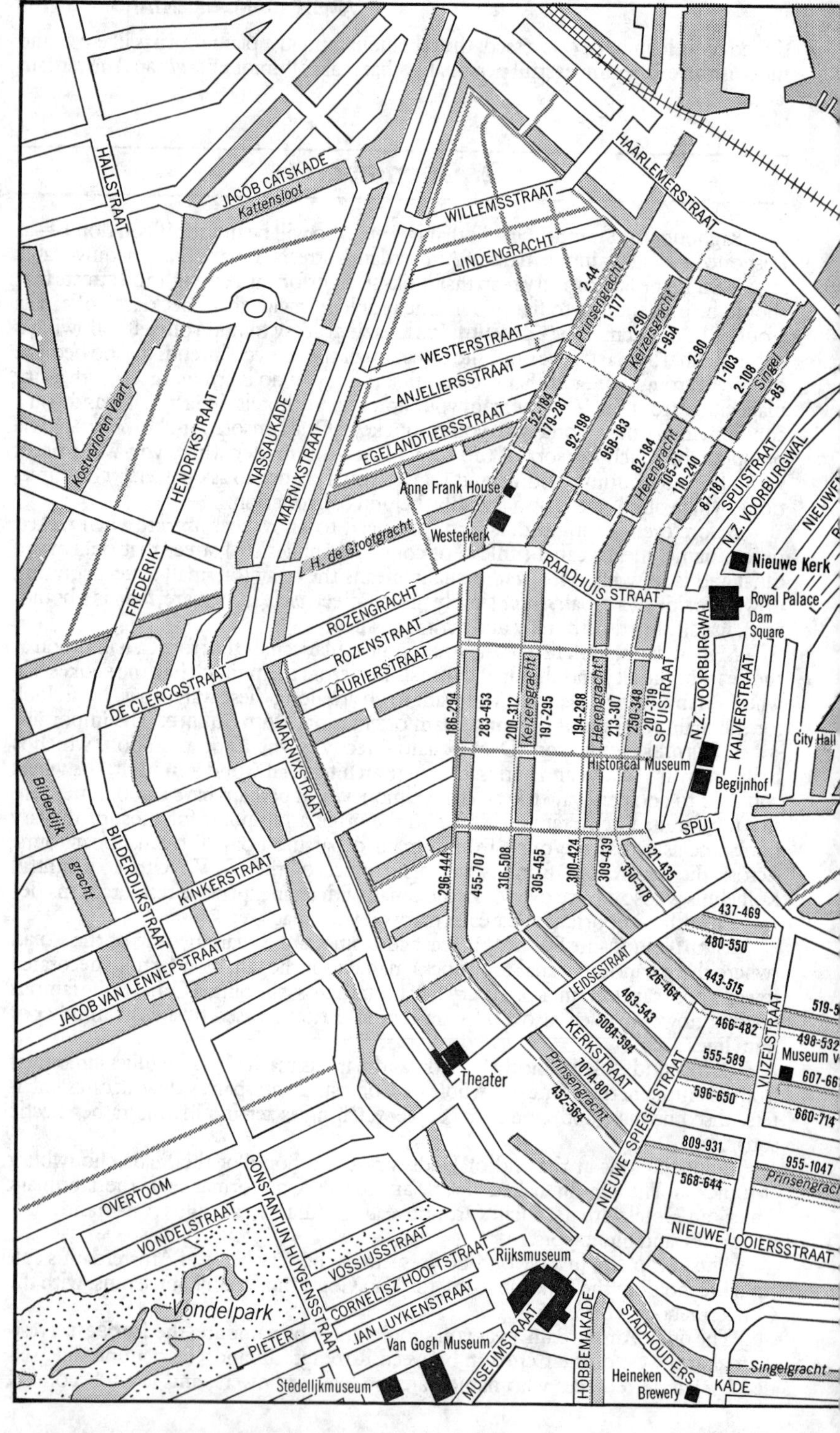

HALLSTRAAT
JACOB CATSKADE
Kattensloot
WILLEMSSTRAAT
HAARLEMERSTRAAT
LINDENGRACHT
WESTERSTRAAT
ANJELIERSSTRAAT
EGELANDTIERSSTRAAT
Prinsengracht
Keizersgracht
Singel
Herengracht
Kostverloren Vaart
HENDRIKSTRAAT
NASSAUKADE
MARNIXSTRAAT
Anne Frank House
Westerkerk
H. de Grootgracht
SPUISTRAAT
N.Z. VOORBURGWAL
Nieuwe Kerk
Royal Palace
Dam Square
RAADHUIS STRAAT
FREDERIK
ROZENGRACHT
ROZENSTRAAT
LAURIERSTRAAT
DE CLERCQSTRAAT
KALVERSTRAAT
City Hall
Historical Museum
Begijnhof
SPUI
Bilderdijkgracht
BILDERDIJKSTRAAT
KINKERSTRAAT
JACOB VAN LENNEPSTRAAT
LEIDSESTRAAT
KERKSTRAAT
VIJZELSTRAAT
Museum v
Theater
NIEUWE SPIEGELSTRAAT
OVERTOOM
VONDELSTRAAT
CONSTANTIJN HUYGENSSTRAAT
VOSSIUSSTRAAT
CORNELISZ HOOFTSTRAAT
JAN LUYKENSTRAAT
PIETER
Vondelpark
Rijksmuseum
Van Gogh Museum
Stedelijkmuseum
MUSEUMSTRAAT
HOBBEMAKADE
STADHOUDERSKADE
Heineken Brewery
Singelgracht
NIEUWE LOOIERSSTRAAT
Prinsengracht

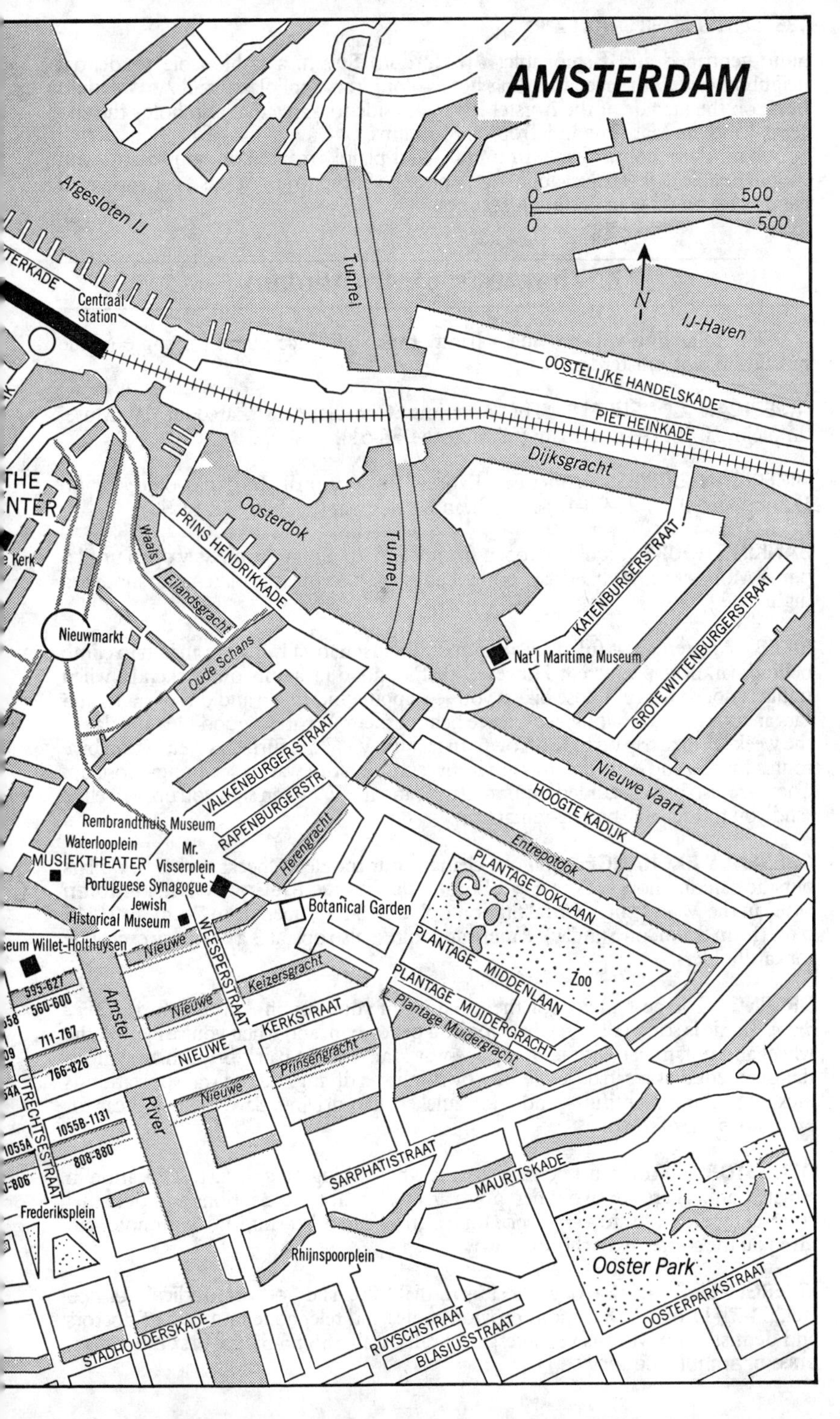
AMSTERDAM
0
500
0
500
N
IJ-Haven
Afgesloten IJ
Tunnel
Centraal
Station
OOSTELIJKE HANDELSKADE
PIET HEINKADE
Dijksgracht
Oosterdok
PRINS HENDRIKKADE
Waals
Eilandsgracht
KATENBURGERSTRAAT
GROTE WITTENBURGERSTRAAT
Nieuwmarkt
Oude Schans
Nat'l Maritime Museum
VALKENBURGERSTRAAT
RAPENBURGERSTR
Herengracht
Nieuwe Vaart
HOOGTE KADIJK
Entrepotdok
PLANTAGE DOKLAAN
Rembrandthuis Museum
Waterlooplein
MUSIEKTHEATER
Mr.
Visserplein
Portuguese Synagogue
Jewish
Historical Museum
Botanical Garden
PLANTAGE MIDDENLAAN
Zoo
PLANTAGE MUIDERGRACHT
Plantage Muidergracht
WEESPERSTRAAT
Nieuwe
Keizersgracht
Nieuwe
KERKSTRAAT
NIEUWE
Prinsengracht
Nieuwe
Amstel
River
595-627
560-600
711-767
766-826
1055B-1131
808-880
UTRECHTSESTRAAT
Frederiksplein
SARPHATISTRAAT
MAURITSKADE
Rhijnspoorplein
Ooster Park
OOSTERPARKSTRAAT
STADHOUDERSKADE
RUYSCHSTRAAT
BLASIUSSTRAAT

quite gentrified and fashionable; **Amsterdam South,** a fashionable residential neighborhood with several leading hotels along the Apollolaan; and **Amsterdam East,** on the far side of the Amstel River, a residential area that also holds the zoo (Artis) and the Maritime and Tropical Museums.

With these points firmly in mind—and plainly marked on your map—you should be able to locate just about every place you need to go. At least, perhaps it will cut down a bit on your getting-lost times.

3. The ABCs of Amsterdam

The following will provide a handy quick-reference guide for some of the practicalities of Amsterdam.

AMERICAN CONSULATE The American Consulate is located at 19 Museumplein, 1071 DJ Amsterdam (tel. 020/64-56-61).

AMERICAN EXPRESS American Express International, Inc., has offices at 66 Damrak (tel. 020/26-20-42) and 38 van Baerlestraat (tel. 020/73-85-50).

BANKING HOURS Banks are open from 9 a.m. to 4 p.m. (some stay open until 5 p.m.) Monday through Friday. Some banks are also open on late-hour shopping nights.

BIKES Amsterdam is full of cyclists, and they just naturally inspire an itch to climb behind handlebars yourself. However, that's a good idea only on weekends, when traffic is not so heavy. Those bikers you see zipping merrily in and out of trams and cars are doing so with long experience behind them. What is a good idea any day of the week is a bike trip outside of town. In fact the VVV can furnish several good bike routes for touring Amsterdam's environs, and it's a fun way to see things close up. There are also bicycle guided tours available, and the VVV can sign you up, as well as send you to a reliable bicycle-rental firm.

CURRENCY EXCHANGE You can change your traveler's checks and U.S. dollars outside banking hours at the **GWK Bureau de Change (DeGrenswisselkantoren N.V.)** in the Main Hall, Central Station (tel. 22-13-24), open from 7 a.m. to 10:45 p.m. (from 8 a.m. on Sunday). American Express also operates a currency exchange for cardholders.

DRIVING The best advice for the duration of your stay in Amsterdam is: *Don't drive.* Traffic is scary enough when you're a pedestrian, and when you're behind the wheel and unfamiliar with narrow, one-way streets just a hair's breadth away from the open edge of a canal, it can be downright terrifying. Public transportation is inexpensive and plentiful—and a lot quicker than driving. Save the rental car for excursions out of town.

DRUGSTORES You must be very specific when asking for a drugstore location in Amsterdam. There are two types: go to an *apotheek* for prescriptions and over-the-counter medications, to a *drogerijen* for toiletries and other sundries. Your hotel can give you the addresses of those close by.

EMERGENCIES In case of an **accident,** dial 900. The **Central Medical Service** (tel. 64-21-11 or 79-18-21) can provide names and telephone numbers of doctors and dentists who will answer emergency calls. Call 555-55-55 for **first aid assistance or ambulance service.**

PHOTO SERVICE All types of film are readily available in Amsterdam, as is one-day service. Shops all along Damrak and Kalverstraat have convenient drop-off points for quick developing.

POLICE The **police emergency** telephone number is 22-22-22; the main police station is at 117 Elandsgracht (tel. 555-11-11).

POSTAL AND TELEGRAPH SERVICES The new main post office is located at 250 Singel, at the corner of Raadhuisstraat and the Singel Canal, in the vicinity of the Royal Palace. It's open from 8:30 a.m. to 6 p.m. Monday through Friday (to 8:30 p.m. on Thursday) and on Saturday from 9 a.m. to noon.

RADIO IN ENGLISH There is regular English news service every day at 7 p.m. at 24/1250 AM (medium wave) and 23 (93.8 MHz) VHF, with supplementary bulletins on what's on in Amsterdam and the immediate weather forecast.

RAIL INFORMATION Call 20-22-66 Monday through Friday from 8 a.m. to 10 p.m., on Saturday and Sunday from 9 a.m. to 10 p.m., for rail information for Holland and other European destinations.

RELIGIOUS SERVICES Amsterdam is a city of churches and synagogues, and the VVV can furnish names and addresses of those holding services in English.

SHOPPING HOURS Shops generally stay open from 8:30 or 9 a.m. to 5 or 6 p.m. weekdays, until 4 or 5 p.m. on Saturday. Some shops close for lunch, and nearly all have one full closing day or one morning or afternoon when they are closed—signs are prominently posted announcing those closing times. Many shops have late hours on Thursday and/or Friday evening.

TAXIS *You cannot hail a taxi on the street,* but taxi ranks are located at major hotels, squares, and shopping areas, as well as the Central Station. Or you can call 77-77-77. Tip and taxes are included in the meter price, and you need not add another tip unless there has been exceptional service (help with heavy luggage, etc.) or unless you choose to follow the Dutch custom (not obligatory) of rounding off the charge to the next highest guilder. The basic charge when the flag falls is Dfl. 3.60 ($1.60) with an additional Dfl. 0.20 (8¢) charged for each tick of the meter or Dfl. 2.20 (95¢) per kilometer during the day, and Dfl. 2.38 ($1.05) from midnight to 6 a.m.

TELEPHONES Direct dialing to other European countries as well as overseas (including the United States and Canada) is available in most hotel rooms in Amsterdam and at the main post office (see above). For calls within Holland, coin telephones accept Dfl 0.25 (11¢), Dfl 1 (44¢), and Dfl 2.50 ($1.10) coins.

TRANSPORTATION You can't miss them, those clanging **trams** darting around the city. What's more, you really wouldn't want to miss them—they are the most efficient way to move around, and they're fun to ride. On your first ride, hop in the front door and buy a ticket from the driver (see below for fares); on all rides after that, you board at any door along the side and validate your ticket in the machines at the rear or middle of the car—it's an honor system, but periodic checks are made, and there's a fine if you don't have a ticket.

Doors in the rear of the tram *do not open automatically*—you must push the button marked "deur open," both on the outside of the car to get in and on the inside when you want to get out. Be ready to alight quickly—those doors close in seconds.

Both bus and tram routes are zoned, with different fares for each zone. Most sightseeing travel will be within Zone 1. A strip card (*strippenkaart*) good for ten

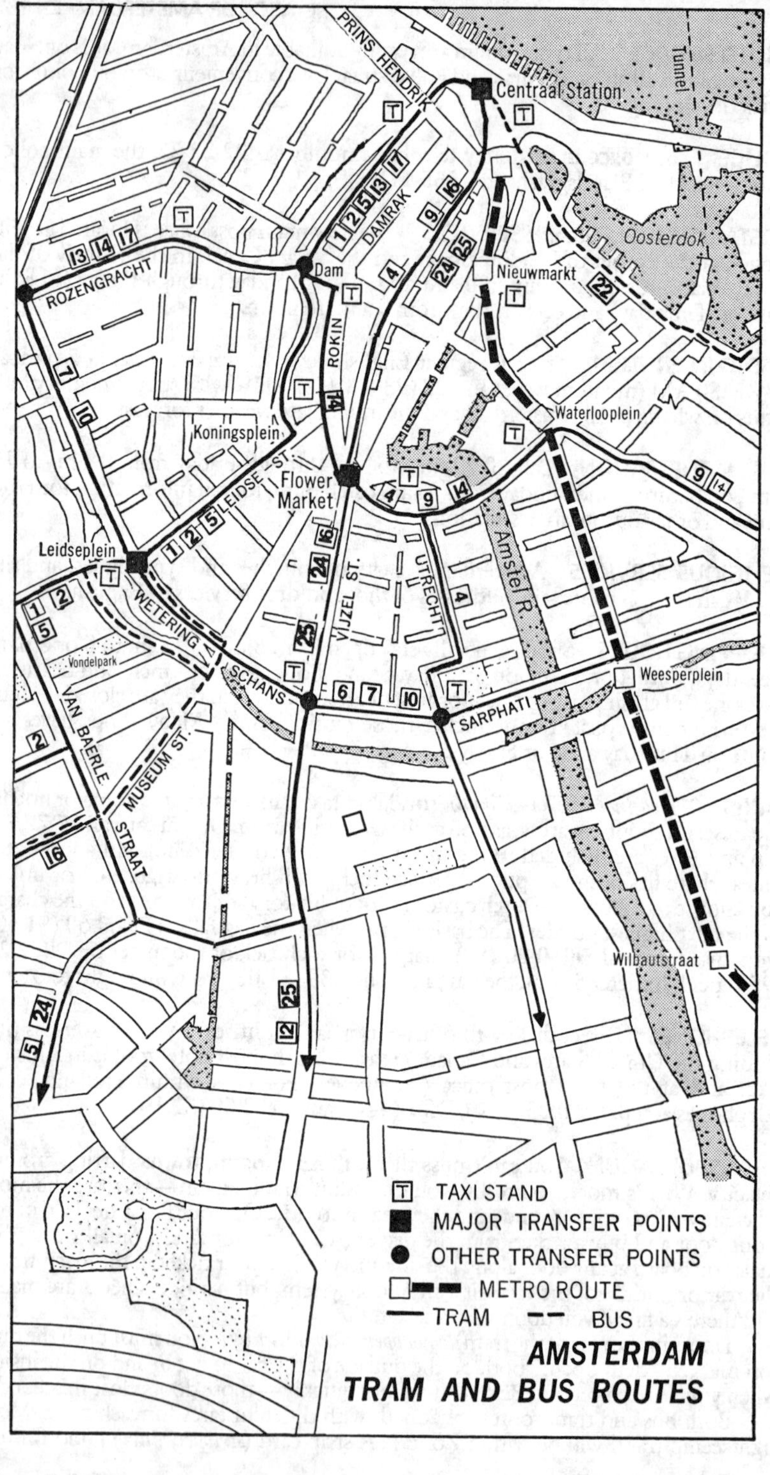

Centraal Station
Tunnel
PRINS HENDRIK
DAMRAK
ROKIN
Dam
Nieuwmarkt
Oosterdok
ROZENGRACHT
Koningsplein
LEIDSE ST.
Flower Market
Waterlooplein
Leidseplein
WETERING
SCHANS
VIJZEL ST.
UTRECHT
Amstel R.
Weesperplein
SARPHATI
Vondelpark
VAN BAERLE
STRAAT
MUSEUM ST.
Wilbautstraat
TAXI STAND
MAJOR TRANSFER POINTS
OTHER TRANSFER POINTS
METRO ROUTE
TRAM
BUS
AMSTERDAM
TRAM AND BUS ROUTES

rides costs Dfl. 8.65 ($3.75). You can also buy a day ticket (good for unlimited rides the day and night of purchase) from bus or tram drivers for Dfl. 8.65 ($3.75); tickets with longer validity must be purchased at the GVB/Amsterdam Municipal Transport ticket booths in front of the Central Station at Stationsplein, with charges of Dfl. 11.60 ($5) for two days, Dfl. 14.20 ($6.25) for three days, and Dfl. 16.30 ($7.25) for four days.

TOURIST INFORMATION The **main VVV office** is across from Central Station at 10 Stationsplein (tel. 26-64-44), open daily in summer from 9 a.m. to 11 p.m.; shorter hours other months. A subsidiary office is located at 106 Leidsestraat, with summer hours of 9 a.m. to 10 p.m.

4. Where to Stay

CHOOSING A HOTEL

Probably the most important decision to be made on any trip is where to stay at each destination. Certainly any accommodation must provide certain basic facilities, but beyond that its *personality* can mean the difference between warm, wonderful memories that color every other experience in a city and shudders every time you remember a huge, impersonal hotel when you yearned for a small, intimate place where the staff calls you by name.

Hotel Personalities

Is your preference Old-World charm combined with luxurious quarters? Glitzy international-standards modernity with every conceivable amenity? Small family-run hotels where there may not be an elevator, but you become a part of the family circle? A historic canal house that reflects the lifestyle of centuries past? A modern, medium-size hotel on the fringe of inner-city hustle and bustle? A bare-bones room in a dormitory, which frees up scarce dollars for other purposes? Amsterdam has them all, including some lovely combinations—and it has them in sufficient quantities and price ranges to make sure you won't go home with shudders.

Location

There are, at the moment, more than 25,000 beds available in Amsterdam (the majority in moderately priced hotels) with even more in the works.

Price

Because price can sometimes be *the* determining factor in choice of accommodations, the listings below are in price groupings, although—as is true in many cities—some categories overlap, as when expensive prices are reduced to moderate either by forgoing some amenities or by taking advantage of special package rates. So if a particular hotel strikes your fancy but is out of your price range, it can pay to inquire if special off-season, weekend, specific weekdays, or other restrictive packages will bring prices down to your purse level.

Prices shown below include a 15% service charge, applicable taxes (VAT), and unless noted, breakfast. These prices are those projected for the first year of this edition—*you can expect a 5% to 15% increase in the second year* (1990).

Reservations

You may, of course, make reservations directly with any of the hotels below, but be sure you do so in ample time for them to reply before you leave home. Especially during summer months and tulip season, it is advisable to go through a travel agent; through the **NRC/Netherlands Reservations Centre,** P.O. Box 404, 2360 AK

Leidschendam (tel. 070/20-25-00), which can also book apartments and theater tickets; or if you're booking from within Holland, through a VVV office.

An Off-Season Special

For the past few years certain Amsterdam hotels have offered significant rate reductions between November 1 and March 31 under a program called **The Amsterdam Way.** Amsterdam, incidentally, is as much a delight then as in the tourist-packed summer months, with a calendar full of cultural events, the full blossoming of many traditional Dutch dishes (such as the hearty, soul- and body-warming hutspot) not offered in warm weather, and streets, cafés, restaurants, and museums filled more with people who live here than with visitors.

There are participating hotels in every class and price range from deluxe to budget, and basic stays can be for one night or three, with lowered rates for each additional night you might wish to tack on. In the moderate and budget categories savings are just as dramatic, and the three days are not restricted to weekends. Along with reductions in hotel rates come discounts on several sightseeing attractions, restaurant meals, entertainments, and—something you'd *never* get in the summer—free ice skates and admission to the Leidseplein ice rink!

The Netherlands Tourist Board can provide a brochure outlining current Amsterdam Way prices and what they cover.

HOTELS BY PRICE

The following hotels come with a personal recommendation. For a complete list of hotels in Amsterdam and the rest of Holland, contact the Netherlands Tourist Board for their "Hotels" booklet.

Expensive

Hôtel de l'Europe, Nieuwe Doelenstraat 2-4, 1012 CP Amsterdam (tel. 020/23-48-36). This marvelous old 1895 hotel has a prime city-center location right on the banks of the Amstel River across from the Muntplein. You're within an easy walk of virtually everywhere you'll want to go, and its rooms are fairly dripping with traditional elegance and come with such luxury extras as terrycloth bathrobes. All have private baths, direct-dial telephones, TVs, and radios—and there's 24-hour room service. There's a small, cozy bar and two of Amsterdam's finest restaurants overlooking the river (see "Where to Eat"). Additional amenities include an indoor pool and sauna. This is a small hotel, and despite its elegance there's nothing stuffy about its friendly, obliging staff. Rates are Dfl. 325 ($142.50) to Dfl. 425 ($186.50) single, Dfl. 445 ($195.25) to Dfl. 545 ($239) double.

Hotel Amstel Inter-Continental, Professor Tulpplein 1, 1018 GX Amsterdam (tel. 020/22-60-60). It's very palace-like, this darling of royalty and visiting celebrities that opened back in 1867 on the banks of the Amstel River. All its gorgeous turn-of-the-century elegance has been retained in glittering chandeliers, lots of marble, and a concierge decked out in tails. For all that, its rooms have kept up with the times with such touches as hairdryers, mini-bars, and direct-dial telephones. All have private baths of course, and all the luxury fittings you'd expect in such a queenly establishment. Rates range from Dfl. 375 ($164.50) to Dfl. 475 ($208.25) single, Dfl. 415 ($180) to Dfl. 525 ($230.25) double.

Hotel Pulitzer, Prinsengracht 315-331, 1016 GZ Amsterdam (tel. 020/22-83-33). Inside it's as contemporary as can be, with a modern lobby and reception area and glassed-in walkways hung with changing art exhibits. But this very popular hotel's exterior has retained the façades of some 24 canal houses dating back 200 to 400 years, and those glass-walled corridors look out over a lovely and peaceful inner garden. No two of the 245 guest rooms are alike—some feature brick walls and overhead beams in a decidedly rustic décor, while others are done up in more modern dress; some overlook the canal, and others face the garden. Inner hallways take unexpected turns and have steps to change the level from one of the original houses to the next. All guest rooms are spacious and have private baths, mini-bars, direct-dial telephones, TVs with closed-circuit movies, and personal safes with a combination you set yourself. Its handsome bar is presided over by the affable Kent Page, who has made this a favorite gathering place for locals as well as guests, and its lovely restaurant (with sunny, country-style décor) serves gourmet cuisine (see "Where to Eat"). Rates at this highly recommended hotel are Dfl. 290 ($127.25) single and Dfl. 340 ($149) double.

Amsterdam Sonesta, Kattengat 1, 1012 SZ Amsterdam (tel. 020/21-22-23). As modern inside as the two above are traditional, this amazing hotel has arranged its exterior to fit into the ancient heart of Amsterdam without a ripple. It has pulled together a group of 17th-century houses and a circular church (long since deconsecrated and used for such secular purposes as a warehouse) to preserve an undisturbed streetside façade, yet its off-street entrance, public rooms, and guest rooms are as slickly luxurious as you'd find in any glass-walled international chain. Its central location couldn't be more convenient for sightseeing, shopping, and dining. As for entertainment, there are frequent open-air performances in the little square in front of its entrance, and concerts are held regularly in the old church, many utilizing the massive old pipe organ. Rooms are spacious, with private baths (and huge bathtubs), mini-bars, trouser presses, direct-dial telephones, radios, and TVs that have a feature-films channel. Rates run Dfl. 325 ($142.50) to Dfl. 395 ($173.25) single and Dfl. 395 ($173.25) to Dfl. 460 ($201.75) double, and this is one case in which breakfast is not included.

Grand Hotel Krasnapolsky, Dam 9, 1012 JS Amsterdam (tel. 020/55-49-111). Facing Dam Square, opposite the Royal Palace, for more than a century this has been simply "the Kras" to generations of Amsterdammers and guests. Over the years it has evolved into a curious mixture of Old-World elegance and streamlined modern additions. Its palm-studded Wintergarden, designed by the founder back in 1880, is stamped with the charm of yesteryear, yet guest rooms (especially in the Court Wing) are definitely of today—they come with private baths and all the extras of a deluxe hotel. The Kras has also made a special effort to make life more comfortable for women in the business world—its "Ladies' Executive Studios" add a comfortable sofa, bathrobe, hairdryer, steam iron, and a complimentary cosmetic case. The lobby coffeeshop looks out to Dam Square, and several good restaurants range in style from belle époque to Japanese. The rate range is Dfl. 275 ($120.50) to Dfl. 320 ($140.25) for singles, Dfl. 330 ($144.75) to Dfl. 390 ($171) for doubles.

American Hotel, Leidsekade 97, 1017 PN Amsterdam (tel. 020/24-53-22). This marvelous century-old hotel couldn't be more misnamed! It's as European as its name suggests it isn't, with a turreted exterior and art nouveau café so special they've been declared a national monument. Some of the guest rooms (most of which are quite spacious) have balconies overlooking a canal, and all have modern furnishings and décor, with private baths, direct-dial telephones, radios, etc. The American has become a traditional meeting place for Amsterdammers when they're in the Leidseplein area, and every tourist should take at least one look inside the splendid old building. Rates are Dfl. 255 ($111.75) to Dfl. 300 ($131.50) single, Dfl. 340 ($149) to Dfl. 399 ($175) double.

Amsterdam Marriott Hotel, Stadhouderskade 21, 1054 ES Amsterdam (tel. 020/83-51-51). Modern to the *n*th degree both inside and out, this 400-room American-style luxury hostelry faces the busy Leidseplein, a short walk from major museums, theaters, elegant shops, cafés, and the city's largest park. Guest rooms have private baths, TVs with movie channels, radios, direct-dial telephones, and a choice of regular double-bedded rooms or a bed-sitter equipped with a Murphy bed. In addition to restaurants, cafés, and live music with dancing, the Marriott also provides a health club and secretarial service (just in case you aren't on holiday). Rates are Dfl. 380 ($166.75) to Dfl. 415 ($182) for singles, Dfl. 460 ($201.75) to Dfl. 495 ($217) for doubles.

The **Amsterdam Hilton,** Apollolaan 138, 1077 BG Amsterdam (tel. 020/78-

07-80). This international chain hotel injects a lot of graciousness into its posh residential location not far from the Concertgebouw. Its tasteful lobby, for instance, has an open fire, its coffeeshop has a terrace, the bar overlooks a canal, and it sits in its own lawns. There are 11 floors of spacious guest rooms, all with private bath and in-house movies on the TV, as well as all the other trappings you'd expect from this luxury chain. Its Kei restaurant features Japanese cuisine. Rates run Dfl. 300 ($131.50) to Dfl. 390 ($171) for singles, Dfl. 340 ($149) to Dfl. 450 ($197.25) for doubles, without breakfast.

Moderate to Expensive

Jolly Hotel Carlton, Vijzelstraat 2-18, 1017 HK Amsterdam (tel. 020/22-22-66). Located just off the Singel Canal, with some rooms overlooking the floating flower market and the Mint Tower, this venerable hotel has been a fixture on the Amsterdam hotel scene for years, with a rather checkered history over the past few. Built in the days when rooms were individual in both shape and size, the Carlton had pretty much passed its heyday until the Jolly hotel firm from Italy took it over and embarked on a dedicated campaign to make the most of its spacious corridors (each floor has a small lobby space from which corridors branch off) and nonstandardized rooms. Jolly standards are high, and the Carlton (which is in the throes of renovation but should be in top form by the beginning of 1990) seems destined once more to provide accommodations befitting its fantastic central location. Some guest rooms have sitting alcoves, others are irregularly shaped, and top-floor suites are larger than many residential flats. In short, the features that give this hotel its character are being retained while the best of what was lacking is being installed (including an electric trouser press in many of the rooms and in all suites). Fortunately the Jolly people are also retaining a staff who have seen the Carlton through its ups and downs —for instance, behind the reception desk, Dino greets guests with a personal interest born of 20 years' service. For drivers, there's private garage parking. Rates are Dfl. 250 ($109.75) single, Dfl. 350 ($153.50) double. Convenience personified and very good value.

Victoria Hotel, Damrak 1-6, 1012 LG Amsterdam (tel. 020/27-11-66). This delightful old building is a marvel of old Amsterdam architecture, an ivory-colored mass with a domed turret at its entrance and an interesting carved-stone façade. Set almost directly across from the Central Station, it is convenient to canal-boat departure points, the main tram terminus, the VVV office, and railway connections to anywhere in Holland or the rest of Europe. Its public rooms have a warm sort of jazzy elegance, and one of Amsterdam's best jazz pianists, Cab Kaye, plays regularly in its Tasman Bar between sets in his own club. Here again many of the staff have been with the hotel for years, which leads to a very personalized brand of service. Guest rooms are spacious and have recently been given a facelift and all new furnishings. Besides a good restaurant, there's a sidewalk café. Rates are Dfl. 230 ($101) to Dfl. 300 ($131.50) single, Dfl. 340 ($149) to Dfl. 375 ($164.50) double.

Alexander Hotel, Prinsengracht 444, 1017 KE Amsterdam (tel. 020/26-77-21). Set on the corner of Leidsestraat and just two blocks away from the Leidseplein, this small hotel is entered through a tiny lobby adjoining the classic Dikker & Thijs restaurant, under the same ownership. Its upstairs rooms are a little on the small side, but come with telephones, TVs, radios, and contemporary furnishings. Most have full baths, but there are singles available with only a shower and toilet at lower rates. In-season rates are Dfl. 220 ($96.50) to Dfl. 240 ($105.25) single, Dfl. 270 ($118.50) to Dfl. 300 ($131.50) double, with a Dfl.-20 ($8.75) reduction in all rates from mid-November through March.

Hotel Doelen Crest, Nieuwe Doelenstraat 24, 1012 CP Amsterdam (tel. 020/22-07-22). Right next door to the elegant Hôtel de l'Europe, the Doelen is one of the city's oldest hotels and is, in fact, where Rembrandt's masterful *The Night Watch* was first hung. Its marvelous center staircase spirals up to a dome that tops the high-ceilinged lobby. Guest rooms, recently given a refurbishing, all have private bath, color TV, radio, phone, and even electric pants presses. There's a clubby, wood-paneled bar and a good restaurant. Some rooms have good views of the Amstel River, others of the Mint Tower. This is a terrific location, and good value. For singles, the rate is Dfl. 235 ($103); for doubles, Dfl. 325 ($142.50).

Hotel Jan Luyken, Jan Luykenstraat 58, 1071 CS Amsterdam (tel. 020/76-41-11). This attractive hotel occupies a corner site in a residential area near the major museums of Amsterdam and offers many of the extras usually found only in larger (and more expensive) hotels. Guest rooms, for example, have private baths with bidets. Singles are Dfl. 200 ($87.75) to Dfl. 220 ($96.50); doubles, Dfl. 220 ($96.50) to Dfl. 250 ($110).

Moderate

Die Port van Cleve, Voorburgwail 178-180, 1012 SJ Amsterdam (tel. 020/24-48-60). In a great old building just off Dam Square, this hotel features guest rooms done up in modern furnishings, and a marvelously atmospheric Old Dutch Inn restaurant that's one of the oldest restaurants in Amsterdam and specializes in beefsteak. Great comfort here, and in spite of being in the middle of the busy city center, behind the hotel's façade all is quiet and peaceful. Rates are Dfl. 139 ($61) to Dfl. 160 ($70.25) single, Dfl. 218 ($95.50) to Dfl. 257 ($112.75) double. On weekends, rates include free lodging and breakfast for wife or husband.

Het Canal House, Keizersgracht 148, 1015 CX Amsterdam (tel. 020/22-51-82). With the acquisition of the building next door, there are now 27 guest rooms and an elevator in this canalside hostelry that has proved a favorite with our readers. Behind a 1630 façade, the salon is a cozy collection of Victoriana overlooking a small, charming back garden, which is softly illuminated at night. Rooms are furnished and decorated in antique style, with canopy beds and other period pieces. There's a Victorian bar and a lovely chandeliered breakfast room. Rates are Dfl. 95 ($41.75) to Dfl. 115 ($50.50) for singles, Dfl. 110 ($48.25) to Dfl. 165 ($72.25) for doubles.

Hotel Wiechmann, Prinsengracht 328-330, 1016 HX Amsterdam (tel. 020/26-33-21). This lovely old canal house has been furnished with antiques, yet maintains an air of friendly informality. Its location is superb—within walking distance of good shopping, restaurants, sightseeing, and nightlife. Rates for the 35 rooms with bath are Dfl. 75 ($33) to Dfl. 90 ($39.50) single, Dfl. 135 ($59.25) to Dfl. 160 ($70.25) double, breakfast included.

Hotel Asterisk, Den Texstraat 14-16, 1017 ZA Amsterdam (tel. 020/26-23-96). This small hotel across the canal from the Museumplein has surprisingly high standards for its price range. Guest rooms are nicely done up, and most have private baths. There's a pretty dining room and a lobby that is positively plush. Rates range from Dfl. 100 ($43.75) to Dfl. 200 ($87.75) for rooms with bath, less for those without. Closed January and February.

Hotel Apollofirst, Apollolaan 123-125, 1077 Amsterdam (tel. 020/73-03-33). Guest rooms here are roomy and nicely furnished, all with private baths. There are gardens out back, a summer terrace, and a small restaurant. Rates begin at Dfl. 145 ($63.50) for singles, Dfl. 160 ($70.25) for doubles.

Hotel Ambassade, Herengracht 341, 1016 AZ Amsterdam (tel. 020/26-23-33). There's a decidedly homey ambience to the Ambassade, which has been created from seven patrician canal houses. Access to guest rooms is by way of a narrow, curving staircase, but once on the upper floors you'll find very spacious rooms (some of those in front have two large windows overlooking the canal) with comfortable and attractive furnishings, private baths, telephones, TVs, hairdryers, and wall safes. The parlor is all Georgian elegance and the two-level breakfast room gives full canal view. Rates are Dfl. 180 ($79) for singles, Dfl. 200 ($87.75)

Hotel Agora, Singel 462, 1017 AW Amsterdam (tel. 020/27- small and comfortable hotel, another old canal house that has beer modernized inside, is right in the middle of things. Rooms are nicely fu each comes with a big easy chair in addition to standard fixtures. All have baths, direct-dial telephones, and color TVs. Rates for singles are Dfl. 89 ($39) to Dfl. 115 ($50.50); for doubles, Dfl. 110 ($48.25) to Dfl. 146 ($64).

AMS Hotel Beethoven, Beethovenstraat 42–51, 1077 HN Amsterdam (tel. 020/83-18-11 for reservations). Located on a beautiful shopping street, the Beethoven has a good restaurant with a cozy bar and a glassed-in sidewalk café that's heated in winter. Its guest rooms all have private bath or shower, TV, radio, telephone, mini-bar, hairdryer, and a personal safe. There's a good restaurant with a year-round sidewalk café. Rates (which drop considerably between mid-November and mid-March) are Dfl. 190 ($83.25) for singles, Dfl. 250 ($109.75) for doubles.

Museum Hotel, P. C. Hoofstraat 2, 1071 BX Amsterdam (tel. 020/62-14-02, 73-39-18 for reservations). In a corner location on a leading shopping street just steps away from the Rijksmuseum and its museum neighbors, this attractive hotel features rooms done in contemporary décor that come with bath or shower, radio, and telephone. Singles are Dfl. 150 ($65.75); doubles, Dfl. 210 ($92); lower off-season rates.

Hotel Trianon, J. W. Brouwersstraat 3-7, 1071 LH Amsterdam (tel. 020/73-39-18 for reservations). On a quiet street next to the Concertgebouw and near the museums, this sophisticated small hotel has a charming restaurant and nicely done-up rooms that come with private bath, radio, and telephone. Rates are Dfl. 150 ($65.75) for singles, Dfl. 210 ($92) for doubles during high season, lower from mid-November to mid-March.

AMS Hotel Terdam, Tesselschadestraat 23, 1054 ET Amsterdam (tel. 020/12-68-76 for reservations). All the entertainment and nightlife brashness of the Leidseplein is just around the corner from this quiet refuge on a tree-lined street, with its sophisticated bar for those times you don't want to leave the premises for a drink. The attractive rooms all have private baths and standard equipment, and there are also small apartments with kitchenettes. Singles are Dfl. 150 ($65.75) and doubles run Dfl. 210 ($92) with lower off-season rates.

AMS Hotel Holland, P. C. Hooftstraat 162, 1071 CH Amsterdam (tel. 020/73-42-53 for reservations). With all the Centrum attractions just an easy walk away, this nice modern hotel is on one of Amsterdam's better shopping streets. Its contemporary guest rooms all have private baths, and there's a nice bar and lounge Rates are Dfl. 150 ($65.75) for singles, Dfl. 210 ($92) for doubles, with lower rate in fall and winter.

Hotel Delphi, Apollolaan 101-105, 1077 AN Amsterdam (tel. 020/79-51-52). This homey little red-brick hotel shares its residential area location with the nearby posh Hilton and Apollo Hotels. Its guest rooms, all done in contemporary décor, have private baths and standard amenities, and some face a pretty garden out back. For singles, rates range from Dfl. 125 ($54.75) to Dfl. 140 ($61.50); for doubles, Dfl. 170 ($74.50) to Dfl. 200 ($87.75).

Inexpensive

Owl Hotel, Roemer Visscherstraat 1, 1054 EV Amsterdam (tel. 020/18-94-84). Originally a private residence in a peaceful neighborhood close to the museums, this family-run hotel now provides bright, average-size rooms with private baths, telephones, and radios. You can opt for breakfast in your room or in the small bar adjoining the garden. Rates for singles are Dfl. 110 ($48.25); for doubles, Dfl. 125 ($54.75) to Dfl. 155 ($68).

Hotel P. C. Hooft, P. C. Hooftstraat 63, 1071 CH Amsterdam (tel. 020/62-71-07). Rooms all come without private bath facilities in this attractive little budget hotel, but all are bright and comfortable, and at rates of Dfl. 55 ($24) to Dfl. 85 ($37.25) single, Dfl. 75 ($33) to Dfl. 110 ($48.25) double, you can save your dollars for shopping on the street where you live while in Amsterdam.

Quentin Hotel, Leidsekade 89, 1017 PN Amsterdam (tel. 020/26-21-87). canalside hotel is near the Leidseplein, and its proximity to a small theater seems appropriate, since many of its regular guests are theatrical people and artists. Rooms are rather plain, but comfortably furnished, and there's a garden. Singles start at Dfl. 60 ($26.25); doubles, at Dfl. 90 ($39.50).

The **Mikado Hotel,** Amstel 107-111, 1018 Amsterdam (tel. 020/23-70-68). The spacious guest rooms here have comfortable seating areas, as well as private baths; there's a sauna, and a restaurant on the premises. Rates range from Dfl. 60 ($26.25) to Dfl. 95 ($41.75) for singles or doubles.

Note: For a long list of quite nice budget hotels in virtually every area of Amsterdam, ask the VVV for their list of "Plain but Comfortable" hotels and hostel accommodations. In connection with the latter, you should know that although the idea of staying in one of the houseboat hostels you'll see advertised may be very appealing, there are safety factors involved in some—best consult the VVV before checking in.

5. Where to Eat

It has been estimated that there are between 1,500 and 2,000 places to eat in Amsterdam, and I don't doubt those figures for one minute. What mere numbers don't tell, however, is the sheer *variety* of places to eat. Not only are there all those different ethnic cuisines mentioned in Chapter XIII, but there are even more settings in which to eat them. From elegant 17th-century dining rooms to sophisticated rooms lit by candlelight to cozy canalside bistros to exuberant taverns with equally exuberant Greek waiters, to exotic Indonesian rooms attended by turbaned waiters, to the *bruine kroegjes* (brown cafés) with their smoke-stained walls and friendly table conversations, the eateries of Amsterdam confront the tourist with the exquisite agony of being able to choose only one or two from their vast numbers each day.

Needless to say, the listings below don't come close to covering Amsterdam's restaurant scene in detail: they simply point out those places that have captured my own heart because of the fare, the ambience, the good-value prices, convenience, or —in more cases than any other one place in my travel experience—a delicious combination of all or most of those factors. You can supplement these recommendations by referring to the VVV's handy restaurant guide with its map reference for instant location of each and a breakdown by type of cuisine. Be sure to pick one up on your first visit to that office.

SEASONAL SPECIALTIES

See Chapter XIII for a discussion of Dutch specialties, but there are a few distinctively Dutch foods whose availability is determined by when you visit. Among them: asparagus, beautifully white and tender, in May; "new" herring, fresh from the North Sea and eaten raw, in May or early June (great excitement surrounds the first catch of the season, part of which goes to the Queen and the rest to restaurateurs amid spirited competition); Zeeland oysters and mussels *(Zeeuwsoesters* and *Zeeuwesmoselen)*, from September to March.

ABOUT HOURS

Unless otherwise stated, lunch hours for the restaurants listed are noon to 2:30 p.m., and dinner hours are 6 to 10 or 10:30 p.m. The Dutch dine early, and with few exceptions last orders are taken no later than 10 p.m.

In the top restaurants, *it is absolutely necessary to reserve,* and for others it's a good idea to phone ahead to avoid disappointment, especially if you have your heart set on dining in a small restaurant. Casual cafés, coffeeshops, sandwich shops, etc., are of course exceptions to that rule.

ABOUT PRICES

Those shown below, unless noted to the contrary, are average prices for a three-course meal *without wine or other beverages,* but including service charge and VAT. Wine by the bottle will add anywhere from Dfl. 19 ($8.25) to Dfl. 27 ($11.75) to your bill; by the glass, about Dfl. 4 ($1.75) per glass.

In the city's best restaurants you can expect à la carte prices for three courses to total about Dfl. 80 ($35), with prix-fixe menus in the Dfl. 60 ($26.25) to Dfl. 80 ($35) range.

In the moderately priced restaurants (the majority of those listed here), three courses average Dfl. 30 ($13.25) to Dfl. 50 ($22).

Budget prices (listed under "inexpensive") for simple, but tasty and filling, meals will run anywhere from Dfl. 8 ($3.50) to Dfl. 30 ($13.25).

For the absolute best value for the dollar, look for the blue-and-white "Tourist Menu" sign that pictures a fork-turned-tourist (complete with hat and camera) displayed on restaurant doors or windows. Wherever you see it, you'll pay only Dfl. 19.50 ($8.50) for three courses *if you order the set Tourist Menu*—no substitutions from the regular menu, but the day's specialties are usually included in the set menu. Dutch specialties offered by restaurants displaying the "Nederlands Dis" soup-tureen sign will average about Dfl. 30 ($13.25) for three courses, although in some cases they fall into the moderate price range.

The recommendations that follow are grouped by these price categories for your guidance.

EXPENSIVE RESTAURANTS

Expensive these most assuredly are, but you'll get your money's worth in every one. Prices average Dfl. 80 ($35) and up for three courses, except for lower prix-fixe menus.

D'Vijff Vlieghan (The Five Flies), Spuistraat 294-302 (tel. 24-52-14 or 24-83-69). There are seven interesting dining rooms (each of which is a miniature museum) in the five slightly tilting canal houses that date from 1627 and make up this quintessential Amsterdam restaurant—and its popularity is such that all seven are always filled. The magic of the place, however, is that each room takes on a cozy, intimate air that banishes any feeling of being in a big, busy restaurant. The menu and specialties are as inherently Dutch as the setting, and prix-fixe selections are available at Dfl. 60 ($26.25) for three courses, Dfl. 80 ($35) for five. Open for dinner only, starting at 5 p.m. Book ahead.

Dikker & Thijs, Prinsengracht 444 (tel. 26-77-21 or 25-88-76). Amsterdammers have been flocking here for the best in Dutch cuisine since 1915, and with good reason. The kitchen takes great pride in the freshness of every ingredient used, and even though the menu has been lightly touched by French importations, the basic offerings are traditional. The dining room overlooks the canal, and service is as top-quality as the food. Open for lunch on weekdays, and for dinner Monday through Saturday; closed Sunday and Christmas holidays.

Excelsior, Nieuwe Doelenstraat (tel. 23-48-36). One of the finest dining rooms in town, the Excelsior is in the Hôtel de l'Europe, and its wide windows overlook the Amstel River and the Mint Tower. Crystal chandeliers, fresh flowers, candlelight and soft piano music in the evening—all contribute to the classic elegance here, and though you can soar just about as high as you'd like in the price department, there are very good prix-fixe menus for Dfl. 65 ($28.50) and Dfl. 75 ($33). Open for lunch and dinner.

De Goudsbloem, Reestraat 8 (tel. 25-32-88). This delightful restaurant in the Hotel Pulitzer (see "Where to Stay") has the airy look of a summer garden, and it fairly blooms with gourmet dishes of the nouvelle cuisine variety, such as escalopes de turbot et saumon, cuit sous vide, purée de persil (steamed turbot and salmon with purée of parsley). There's an elegant "menu gourmand" that gives you six courses for Dfl. 110 ($48.25), or the four-course "menu gastronomique" for Dfl. 80 ($35). Open for lunch and dinner weekdays, dinner only on weekends.

La Rive, Professor Tulpplein 1 (tel. 22-60-60). In the lovely old Amstel Hotel (see "Where to Stay"), this beautiful wood-paneled dining room has the look and feel of the library in a private home. French doors open onto a riverside terrace, and both the menu (with emphasis on French cuisine) and the service are outstanding. As a budget measure, consider lunch instead of dinner and choose the "business lunch" menu. At dinner, look for the prix-fixe menu. Open for lunch and dinner.

Tout Court, Runstraat 13 (tel. 25-86-37). You'll find this unpretentious, but striking restaurant between Prinsengracht and Keizersgracht (look for the window with a lighted sculpture in the shape of a napkin). Inside, you'll find superb seafood dishes, the best in French haute cuisine, and a friendly ambience created by its many regular patrons, many from Amsterdam's entertainment community. One of the nicest things about the place is the fact that its doors are open until midnight, seven days a week (last orders at 11:30 p.m.)—a perfect setting for after-concert (after-*anything*, actually) dining. Expect your dinner check to run Dfl. 90 ($39.50) and up.

Dinner Afloat

During the summer months, a marvelous three-hour cruise through Amsterdam's canals is combined with a very good five-course dinner with before and after drinks and wine with dinner, via Holland International's **Amsterdam Dinner Cruise** (tel. 22-77-88). The cost, which includes pickup and delivery at most major hotels, is Dfl. 125 ($54.75).

MODERATELY PRICED CHOICES

Expect a three-course meal to average between Dfl. 30 ($13.75) and Dfl. 50 ($22).

Haesje Claes, Nieuwe Zijds Voorburgwal 320 (tel. 24-99-98). It's long and narrow, dark as a brown café, cozy, and named for a 16th-century nun who ran an orphanage across the street. This is also one of the most convivial and comfortable eateries in this part of town. A great neighborhood favorite, it features heaping portions of hearty traditional hot and cold dishes, as well as simpler fare (Dover sole, Dutch steaks, omelets, etc.) that falls into the inexpensive category, and the Tourist Menu. Highly recommended. Open from noon to 10 p.m. Monday through Saturday and 5 to 10 p.m. on Sunday.

Oesterbar, Leidseplein 10 (tel. 26-34-63). Dine casually at the tiled street level, or more formally upstairs in the pretty red-and-white dining room. This longtime favorite with locals and visitors alike boasts an extensive menu that includes just about any fish you can name. Open for lunch and dinner.

De Prinsenkelder, Prinsengracht 438 (tel. 26-77-21). The menu is a happy mix of Dutch and continental dishes in this inviting restaurant reminiscent of an oldtime tavern, beamed ceiling and all. This is one of the Dikker & Thijs (see above) group, with quality that meets its demanding standards. Open for lunch and dinner every day except Monday.

Die Port Van Cleve, Nieuwe Zijds Voorburgwal 178 (tel. 24-48-60). This highly regarded vaulted steakhouse is in the hotel by the same name (see "Where to Stay"), and every steak served since 1870 has been numbered—if your steak number should end in 000, it will be complimentary and accompanied by a free bottle of wine. In the smaller Old Dutch Bodega just off the lobby, Delft tiles and magnificent wood paneling create a cozier ambience for a more diversified menu. Open for lunch and dinner.

Sama Sebo, P. C. Hoofstraat 27 (tel. 662-81-46). Acknowledged by all and sundry as Amsterdam's leading Indonesian restaurant, this pretty establishment decorated with Indonesian artifacts is known for its rijsttafels and an impressive menu of more expensive dishes, although there are lunch selections that qualify for the "inexpensive" label. Open for lunch and dinner; closed Sunday.

Indonesia, Singel 550 (tel. 23-20-35 or 23-17-58). Upstairs in the Jolly Carlton Hotel building, this excellent Indonesian restaurant has decorative leftovers from the French restaurant that was its predecessor. Menu, ambience, and service are all good. Open daily from noon to 10 p.m., and they also offer a special children's menu.

Sherry Can Bodega, Spui 30 (tel. 23-22-73). A great favorite of students, business people, and tourists, this is another restaurant that has both moderate and inexpensive selections. The attractive sidewalk café (where you need order nothing more than a beer or glass of wine) serves light snacks and an inexpensive lunch menu, while in the cozy upstairs dining room traditional Dutch cuisine is featured, and the candlelight downstairs dining room has an extensive à la carte dinner menu of steaks, fish, chicken, and pork. Hours for the sidewalk café are 11 a.m. to 11 p.m.; dinner only in the two dining rooms; closed Monday.

Den Duvelshoeck, Vijzelstraat (tel. 24-76-15). Located on a busy street near the Mint Tower and the floating flower market, this is a bright, pleasant spot for lunch and a relaxing, candlelit setting for dinner. Fresh fish, steak, pork, lamb, and chicken are featured. It's upstairs from the bar, which also makes a pleasant stopoff during shopping or sightseeing. Open for lunch and dinner, except Sunday when it's dinner only.

De Kelderhof, Prinsengracht 494 (tel. 22-06-82). A Mediterranean courtyard has been created in the ground floor of this graceful old canal house, with lots of exposed brick, wicker furniture, and fairy lights in potted trees. Strolling musicians add to the ambience, and there are nine four-course set-menu offerings centered around fish, steak, and pork, as well as an extensive à la carte menu. If you come Monday through Thursday between 5 and 7:30 p.m. there's a "Red Menu" with three courses for under Dfl. 25 ($11). This is one of the few Amsterdam restaurants that serves until midnight, seven days a week.

Acropolis, Leidse Kruisstraat 4 (tel. 22-70-14). On a tiny street just off the Prinsengracht, this Greek taverna has live music every night but Monday. The mood is festive, the food is good, and hours are 4 p.m. to midnight daily.

d'Theeboom, Singel 210 (tel. 23-84-20). This lively café–wine bar has a devoted following among the younger Amsterdam set, and its menu is innovative, featuring dishes that combine ingredients in fresh, new ways, with very good results. Open for lunch (usually crowded) and dinner.

Coffee Shop Pulitzer, Keizersgracht 236 (tel. 22-83-33). More a full-fledged restaurant than a true coffeeshop, this cheerful place serves moderately priced meals from the same kitchen as the pricey De Goudsbloem. Open for all three meals, seven days a week.

Casa Tobio, Lindengracht (tel. 24-89-87). This atmospheric little bit of Spain in the Jordaan neighborhood features Spanish music and a very good paella. Open for dinner only, every day except Wednesday.

De Boerderij, Korte Leidsedwarsstraat 69 (tel. 23-69-29). This attractive rustic restaurant is next door to the KLM ticket office on Leidseplein and features meats and grills, with game on the menu in season. The décor, with its brick fireplace, is a tipoff that its name means "farmhouse." Something to treasure here is their insistence that every dish be cooked to order—not too many places left that do that! Open for lunch and dinner every day but Sunday.

De Keyzer Bodega, Van Baerlestraat (tel. 71-14-41). Partly because of its proximity to the Concertgebouw, but mostly because of its comfortable tavern-like interior, excellent menu, and good service, this is one of the most popular dining spots in the area. Serving fish and meat, with game dishes in season, it stays open after concerts (another reason for its popularity). There's a not-so-taverny French-oriented dining room in the back, and reservations—preferably a day or so in advance—are definitely in order. Open daily from 9 a.m. to midnight.

You'll wonder how **De Groene Lanteerne** (The Green Lantern), Haarlemmerstraat 43 (tel. 24-19-52), manages to squeeze a restaurant into such a narrow space. Yet its 17th-century interior is the setting for some very good Dutch and French dishes, and at prices around Dfl. 40 ($17.50) they're good value, indeed.

It's steak and seafood at **De Nachtwacht,** Theorbeckeplein 2 (tel. 22-47-94). It's a popular place with Amsterdammers, which just about says it all for the quality of its culinary offerings.

Bols Taverne, Rozengracht 106 (tel. 24-57-52). This old 17th-century place won its reputation as a tasting room for Dutch gin and liqueurs, but its nautical interior now houses a good seafood restaurant as well. Landlubbers will also find non-seafood dishes on the menu.

To find **Speciaal,** Nieuwe Leliestraat 142 (tel. 24-97-06), you'll have to venture out to the fringes of the central city. The trip, however, is well worth the effort, for this is one of Amsterdam's best rijsttafel restaurants. It's small, but cozy, with Javanese décor and a friendly staff.

Note: A stroll along the little **Reguliersdwarsstraat,** one block off and parallel to the floating flower market, will give you a choice of moderate meals of the Dutch, French, Mexican, and several other cultures persuasion. Many of the small restaurants also function as bars, so you can have a drink and "window-shop" before making a decision as to the cuisine of choice.

INEXPENSIVE DINING

Café-Restaurant De Passagebar, Nieuwendijk 224 (tel. 24-84-39). On one of Amsterdam's busiest pedestrian shopping streets near Dam Square, Sjusi and Ruud Wildbret have created a haven for weary feet and an attractive setting for budget eating. It's a pleasant place, the sidewalk café opening to a cozy interior with lots of dark wood and red plush upholstery. You can just stop in for a beer, indulge in their pancakes with a choice of a dozen or more fillings, order light meals of omelets and salad plates, or go for the excellent dinner menu that includes fish, steak, pork, shish kebab, wienerschnitzel, and several other selections. Open every day from 11 a.m. to 8 p.m., and until 10 p.m. on Thursday.

House of Cutty Sark, Spuistraat 304 (tel. 24-29-77). You'll rub elbows with journalists, students, artists, and art dealers in this popular place that serves good budget food in a pubby setting. Open for lunch and dinner every day except Sunday.

Café 'tZwaantje, Berenstraat 12 (tel. 23-23-73). Delicious spareribs with the chef's special sauce are the specialty at this pretty little neighborhood café between the Prinsengracht and Keizersgracht. The menu also includes hamburgers, salad plates, and omelets for light meals, and full dinners of fish or meat. Open every day from 4 to 11 p.m. for food service; the bar is open until 1 a.m.

Café 'tSmalle, Egelantiersgracht 12 (tel. 23-96-17). This small corner café near the Jordaan section, with its high, beamed ceiling, old genève pump on the bar, magazines and newspapers on a wall rack, and generous complement of neighborhood regulars, is a delightful place to stop for tostis, sandwiches, quiche, pastries, coffee, beer, and wine. Benches are just outside the door for canal- and people-watching in good weather (although the people-watching inside is terrific). The place dates back to 1780, and its walls are a mini-museum of old beer kegs, bottles, brass, and a tall grandfather clock.

De Stationsrestauratie, Central Station (tel. 27-33-06). One of the most overlooked by all but rail passengers is this large self-service restaurant upstairs at Central Station. It's a handsome room, with several divisions to dilute the "barn-y" feeling, and a huge selection of hot and cold plates for under Dfl. 13 ($5.75) and any number of snacks and pastries for much less.

Some of Amsterdam's best sandwich shops (broodjeswinkel) are the three branches of the **Broodje van Kootje** shops sporting bright yellow signs at Spui, the Rembrandtsplein, and the Leidseplein.

Pancakes are the specialty at both the **Bredero Pannekoekenhuysje,** Voorburgwal 244 (tel. 22-94-61), and **Pancake Bakery,** Prinsengracht 191 (tel. 25-13-33).

6. Things to See and Do

To be a tourist in Amsterdam is to be thrust into an instant quandary—it's not *what* to see and do that's the problem, it's *how much* of this intriguing city's fascinating sights and activities will you be able to work into the time you have!

There are miles and miles of canals to float, hundreds of narrow streets to wander, historic buildings to visit, over 40 museums holding collections of everything from artistic wonders to obscure curiosities, diamond cutters and craftspeople to watch as they practice generations-old skills, and . . . the list is as long as every tourist's individual interests. And these are just a few of Amsterdam's *daytime* things to see and do. When night falls, another bag of treasures opens for examination, and we'll get to that in this chapter's next section. Here I'll deal with some of those attractions to help you set your own priorities.

A SPECIAL NOTE FOR AMERICANS

There's a strong connection between Amsterdam and America, and you may want to seek out a few places where those links were forged. To begin at the beginning, go by the **Schreierstoren** tower on Prins Hendrikkade (the street directly across from the Central Station; the tower is a short walk away). Here you'll see a plaque marking the point where Henry Hudson embarked on a voyage in 1609 that would take him to the New World to discover a wide river that would bear his name and an island he would know as "Manhattes." At nearby Haarlemmerstraat, to the right of the Central Station, read the plaque at no. 75, where the 1623 Dutch West India Company directors planned a settlement to be called Nieuw Amsterdam on the tip of that island, a settlement we know as New York as a result of its seizure by the British in 1664. When you're wandering along the Singel canal, look for no. 460—in 1782 this building was the premises of the Van Staphorst banking house, where John Adams came to ask for, and received, the first of some $30 million in loans to launch a new and uncertain United States government.

HOW TO SEE AMSTERDAM

Your very first stop on any sightseeing excursion, of course, should be the **VVV office**—they have information on anything you might want to know and some things you might not have even known you wanted to know.

There are many ways to explore Amsterdam's riches, and you may wish to approach them by one or all of the following ways.

From the Water

A cruise through the city's canals should top every visitor's list—even if your time is unlimited, do this first. The fan-shaped canal system dates back to 1609; some 75,000 trees (mostly elms) shade its course, and it holds within its confines more than 7,000 buildings of centuries past. The water-level view of those gabled houses and hundreds of picturesque bridges will lend meaning and color to everything else you do during your stay. Amsterdam's 17th-century Golden Age becomes a vivid reality as you glide through the waterways that were largely responsible for those years of prosperity. On the one-hour trip aboard glass-topped launches, you'll learn more about the canals and those who have lived along their banks from the informative narrative (delivered in several languages) than you could absorb in hours and hours of study, and photo buffs will be kept busy snapping shots that can only be made from this vantage point.

Your itinerary will take you past such landmarks as the Schreierstoren, or "Weeping Tower," where sorrowful women bade farewell to their menfolk as they set off across the seas; the narrowest house in Amsterdam; the flood gates that nightly open to cleanse the canals; the official residence of the city's mayor (burgomaster); and before returning to the dock, the drydocks that are so vital to Amsterdam's harbor.

Canal cruises depart from rondvaart (canal circuit) docks every 30 minutes from 8:30 a.m. to 10 p.m. during summer months (see Section 7 for information on after-dark cruises), every 45 minutes from 10 a.m. to 4 p.m. in winter, with a fare of Dfl. 7.50 ($3.25).

Cruise operators and their departure points are: **Holland International** (tel. 22-77-88), at Central Station; **Smits Koffiehuis B. V.** (tel. 23-37-77), at Stationsplein 10; **Rederij Lovers B. V.** (tel. 22-21-81), from the Prins Hendrikkade dock opposite no. 25/27; **Rederij P. Kooy B. V.** (tel. 23-38-10), from the Rokin near Spui; **Meyers Rondvaarten** (tel. 23-42-08), from Damrak jetty 4-5; **Rederij Plas C. V.** (tel. 24-54-06), from Damrak jetty 1-3; and **Rederij Noord-Zuid** (tel. 79-13-70), from Stadhouderskade 25, opposite the Parkhotel.

If the launch cruise simply whets your appetite to ramble the canals on your own, there are sturdy **pedal boats** that seat two or four and come with a detailed map, route suggestions, and a bit about the places you'll pedal past. It's great fun in sunny weather, and a different experience (interesting?) when it rains and your bike is covered with a rain shield. You can also rent a "canal bike" for evening rambles, when the canals are illuminated and your bike comes with a Chinese lantern. You'll find moorings at the Leidseplein, between the Marriott and American Hotels; between the Rijksmuseum and the Heineken Brewery; Prinsengracht at the Westerkerk; and on the Keizersgracht near the Leidsestraat (a nice feature is that you can rent your bike at one of these and return it at another). For two people, the rental is Dfl. 16 ($7) per hour.

By Bus

For the quickest overview of the city, take one of several three-hour coach tours. It's a good orientation, and you'll drop in on the Rijksmuseum and visit a diamond factory, for a fare of Dfl. 32 ($14). A four-hour afternoon tour takes you to the Anne Frank House and the Holland Art and Craft Center before ending with a canal cruise, with a Dfl. 37 ($16.25) fare.

Major tour operators are **Key Tours,** Dam 19 (tel. 24-73-04); **Holland International Excursions,** Damrak 7 (tel. 22-25-50); **American Express,** Damrak 66 (tel. 26-20-42); and **Lindbergh,** Damrak 26 (tel. 22-27-66).

From the Air

A 30-minute bird's-eye view of Amsterdam, the tulip fields, the beaches, and nearby Volendam helps you fix the city firmly in its environs and presents quite graphically its all-important relation to the sea. During summer months, **NLM City Hopper,** KLM's domestic affiliate, flies Saturday- and Sunday-afternoon sightseeing flights from Schiphol Airport, with a fare of Dfl. 75 ($33) for adults, Dfl. 50 ($22) for children. For details and booking, telephone 49-32-52.

On Foot

One of the nicer things about this gracious city is that she has somehow managed to collect her most precious sightseeing jewels in an area compact enough for easy walking from one to the other. The Centrum, or center city, is the old medieval heart of Amsterdam, and all major sightseeing attractions are within the boundaries of its concentric canals, with the exception of the leading museums. And even those are close by—only if you opt for a tram instead of a longish walk to the Museumplein will you need transport other than shank's mare.

There is more to be seen, however, than just sightseeing highlights—every Amsterdam street holds architectural gems and a plethora of street scenes that are the makings of memorable strolls. The VVV has put together a series of walking-tour booklets to point you to such diverse points of interest as Jewish Amsterdam, the statues of Amsterdam, the Jordaan neighborhood, and a marvelous "Voyage of Discovery Through Amsterdam" orientation walk that even points out such things as interesting tea and coffeeshops.

THE MUSEUMS

While it's impossible to list here all of Amsterdam's museums, the following fall into the "you really shouldn't miss" category. The VVV can furnish a complete list, which could well reveal others with special appeal to you—they cover such diverse subjects as the press (Nederlands Persmuseum), geology (Gelogisches Museum Der Amsterdamer Universitaet), and even a money-box museum (Sparbuechsenmuseum), some of which perhaps you won't want to miss.

The first three museums listed here are clustered around the Museumplein, but be warned that although they are next-door neighbors, it would be a mistake to take them all in at one whack—these are not places to pass through quickly, and it's a good idea to devote at least half a day to each. If the very thought of museum-hopping makes your feet hurt, there are all those lovely brown cafés down adjacent streets to rest the weary body and quench a mighty thirst.

You should know that you can purchase a **Museum Pass** for Dfl. 25 ($11), or Dfl. 7.50 ($3.25) if you're under 25, that covers free admission to some 250 museums throughout the country. The pass can be bought from the VVV, as well as most museums, and if museums are high on your sightseeing agenda, it's a good investment even if Amsterdam is your only stop in Holland.

One thing to remember in planning museum visits: many are closed on Monday and have hours of 10 a.m. to 5 p.m. Tuesday through Saturday, 1 to 5 p.m. on Sunday and holidays.

The Rijksmuseum

This magnificent structure at Stadhouderskade 42 (tel. 73-21-21), on the Museumplein, is the crown jewel of Holland's art treasures and ranks among the greatest in all of Europe. It owes its beginnings to Louis Napoleon, who founded it in 1808 during his brief sojourn as King of Holland; the building itself is the work of Petrus J. Cuypers and was opened in 1885. Its pride and joy is the huge Rembrandt canvas miscalled *The Night Watch,* whose true name is *The Company of Captain Frans Banning Coq and Lieutenant Willem van Ruytenburg.* The misnomer came about because years of accumulated grime and dirt made it appear to be a night scene; it wasn't until a thorough cleaning revealed otherwise that authorities realized the group portrait actually depicted these Amsterdammers in broad daylight.

Rembrandt is only one of the Dutch masters represented in the Rijksmuseum. Works by virtually every Dutch artist of stature from the 16th through the 19th centuries hang in these galleries—Frans Hals, Jan Vermeer, Paulus Potter, Jacob van Ruisdael, Jan Steen, de Hooch, Gerard Dou, and Ter Borch among them. Painters from other countries whose masterpieces may be seen include Goya, Fra Angelico, van Dyck, and Rubens. The paintings, of course, are the museum's highlights, but there are also marvelous collections of prints (starting with the 15th century), beautiful tapestries from France and Belgium and Holland, Dutch and German sculpture, Dresden china and Delft porcelain, laces, ship models, glassware, room after room of furniture, and more.

Hours are 10 a.m. to 5 p.m. Tuesday through Saturday, 1 to 5 p.m. on Sunday and holidays. Admission is Dfl. 6.50 ($2.75) for adults, Dfl. 3.50 ($1.50) for ages 6 to 18, free for those 6 and under. Tram 16, 24, or 25.

Vincent van Gogh Museum

Anyone who has ever responded to van Gogh's vibrant colors and vivid landscapes will find it a moving experience to walk through the rooms of this rather stark contemporary building at Paulus Potterstraat 7-11 (tel. 76-48-81), at the Museumplein. Built in 1973 to house the more than 200 van Gogh paintings zealously guarded by his brother's wife and her son and presented to the nation with the proviso that they not leave his native land, it displays the artist's works in chronological order. There are no guided tours, and you are only required to stand one foot back from the paintings, allowing a closer inspection than is usually the case. As you move through the rooms, the canvases reflect his changing environment and much of his inner life, so that gradually the artist himself becomes almost a tangible presence standing at your elbow. Here is the early, brooding *The Potato Eaters, The Yellow House* from his sojourn in Arles, and the painting known around the world simply as *Sunflowers,* although he titled it *Still Life with Fourteen Sunflowers.* By the time you reach the vaguely threatening painting of a flock of black crows rising from a waving cornfield, you can feel as if it were your own, the artist's mounting inner pain that finally he was unable to bear. The enormity of his talent is overwhelming, and even more so in light of the short ten years in which he painted, selling only one canvas before his 1890 suicide when he was 37.

In addition to the paintings, there are nearly 600 drawings by van Gogh, and a series of paintings by his contemporaries. There's also a wonderful "self-expression" room, where you're invited to take up paintbrush, pencil, or clay, and pour out any pent-up artistic talent of your own. A very good self-service restaurant opens onto a pleasant terrace for sunny-day lunches.

Hours are 10 a.m. to 5 p.m. Tuesday through Saturday, 1 to 5 p.m. on Sunday and holidays; closed Monday and January 1. Admission is Dfl. 6.50 ($2.75) for adults, Dfl. 3.50 ($1.50) for children to age 18. Tram 2 or 5, or 16 to Museumplein-Concertgebouw.

Stedelijk Museum

Lovers of modern art will revel in this collection at Paulus Potterstraat 13, at the Museumplein, that features works by the likes of De Kooning, Mondrian, Appel, Picasso, Chagall, Cézanne, Monet, Manet, Renoir, Calder, Pollock, Dubuffet, Rodin, and even Andy Warhol. With more than 1,000 exhibits, it is for the modern schools of art what the Rijksmuseum is to the Dutch masters.

The museum is open every day from 11 a.m. to 5 p.m., with admission of Dfl. 7 ($3) for adults, Dfl. 3.50 ($1.50) for children ages 8 to 17, free for under-8s with adults. Tram 2 or 5, or 16 to Museumplein-Concertgebouw.

Rembrandt's House

Rembrandt was bankrupt when he left this house at Jodenbreestraat 4-6 (tel. 24-94-86), near Waterlooplein, in 1659 (purchased in 1639 when he was Amsterdam's most fashionable portrait painter), and it wasn't until 1906 that it was rescued from a succession of subsequent owners and restored as a museum. Because of his insolvency, the artist drew up an inventory for his creditors that proved invaluable in the restoration—could he return to the house today, he would find it very much as it was when he lived and worked here. The self-portraits that preoccupied him hang here, along with some 250 etchings. For the greatest of his masterpieces you must visit the Rijksmuseum, but it is in this house that you will find a sense of the artist himself, his daily life, and his work studios.

Open from 10 a.m. to 5 p.m. Monday through Saturday, from 1 to 5 p.m. on Sunday and holidays; closed New Year's Day. Admission is Dfl. 3.50 ($1.50) for adults, Dfl. 2 (90¢) for children (under 10, free). Nearest tram stop is Visserplein, tram 9.

Amsterdam Historical Museum

A tiny setback alleyway at Kalverstraat 92 (tel. 523-18-22) leads to a beautiful 1581 gate opening into the courtyard of a 300-year-old complex of classic buildings that served for many years as Amsterdam's orphanage, and before that as a monastery. The children to whom these buildings were home were identified by garb with one red and one black sleeve (the colors in the city's coat-of-arms), and in walls around the courtyard you can still see the set-in lockers that held these uniforms at night. The orphans are gone now, but the old buildings are home to a fascinating record of Amsterdam's history, with room after room of documents, maps, prints, works of art, and artifacts unearthed as recently as the subway excavations. In a unique street gallery, historical paintings from the 17th century are hung along the glass-covered passageway leading from the museum into the Begijnhof (see below). This is another loitering place, and the exposed brick walls and beams of the David and Goliath restaurant that opens into the courtyard (with service under the great linden tree outside) offer a pleasant respite for tired feet under the watchful eye of a huge wooden statue of the giant for whom the restaurant is named.

Open from 11 a.m. to 5 p.m. daily except New Year's Day, with admission of Dfl. 3.50 ($1.50) for adults and Dfl. 1.75 (75¢) for ages 16 and under.

The Begijnhof

Although not technically a museum, this serene 14th-century garden surrounded by small houses that date from the 16th and 17th centuries preserves as faithfully as any museum could an integral part of Amsterdam's past. It was here that the begijnes, a dedicated group of laywomen, devoted their lives to the city's poor and other good works. You can pay homage to these pious women by pausing for a moment at the small flower-planted mound that lies just at the center garden's edge across from the English Reformed church. A simple stone is inscribed "Hier Rust Cornelia Arens, Begijn, Overleden 2 Mei 1654." She is the only one of the begijnes who claimed the right to be buried near the church, a right granted them when it was handed over to the Protestant community; all others lie in city cemeteries. Just opposite the front of the church is a secret Catholic chapel built in 1671 and still in use. You can enter the Begijnhof from the Historical Museum (see above), or through the small alley-like Begijnensteeg off the Kalverstraat, and you're welcomed during daylight hours (the city's poor senior citizens now reside in the old homes, and their privacy is respected after sunset).

"Our Lord in the Attic" (Amstelkring Museum)

This museum, at Oude Zijds Voorburgwal 40 (tel. 24-66-04), is about a two-minute walk from Dam Square via Damstraat to Oude Zijds Voorburgwal. For some 200 years, beginning in 1578 when Holland fervently embraced Protestantism and forbade the practice of any other religion, Amsterdam's vaunted sense of tolerance had to go underground. With religious bigotry running rampant, Catholics were forced to hold clandestine services, and this moving museum is just one of the 62 hidden chapels that eventually existed in the city. So long as they remained out of public sight, municipal authorities turned a blind eye, and the chapel you climb well-worn steps to see today was used right up to 1887, when Catholics were once more allowed to worship in St. Nicholaaskerk. The chapel occupies the attic space of a canal house and two smaller ones just behind it that were built in 1661 by an Amsterdammer who gave his blessings to the illicit worship in 1663. The long, narrow space is quite plain except for its baroque alter and the swinging pulpit that could be stored out of sight. The 1794 organ is pumped by hand and sometimes comes into use today for special occasions. Like the Anne Frank House, "Our Lord in the Attic" is a monument to Amsterdam's typical reaction to oppression.

Hours are 10 a.m. to 5 p.m. Monday through Saturday and 1 to 5 p.m. on Sunday and holidays. Admission is Dfl. 3.50 ($1.50) for adults, Dfl. 2 (90¢) for children to age 14.

Anne Frank House

During World War II Amsterdammers went far beyond mere tolerance in finding ways of thwarting Nazi oppression of its Jewish population. As more and more Jews were deported to the infamous "death camps" (some 100,000 Amsterdam Jews never returned), Anne Frank's father hid his family and the family of one of his employees in the attic of an annex to this 1635 canal house at Prinsengracht 263 (tel. 26-45-33), which had been his place of business. For 25 months the young girl lived in these cramped quarters, passing long days in silence for fear of being overheard. Only 13 years old, she kept a daily record of her innermost thoughts as well as the life she and her family were living. In 1944 the family was betrayed, arrested, and sent to separate camps in Germany, where Anne perished at Bergen-Belsen in 1945. Of the family members, only her father, Otto Frank, survived. In 1947 her diary was published, and more than 13 million copies, in 50 languages, have been sold. The rooms you visit are much as they were during those long months of hiding, and downstairs is a small museum, which documents the terrible years of the Holocaust and monitors any current signs of fascism, racism, and anti-Semitism.

Hours are 9 a.m. to 5 p.m. Monday through Saturday, from 10 a.m. to 5 p.m. on Sunday and holidays; closed Christmas and New Year's Days, and Yom Kippur. Admission is Dfl. 5 ($2.25) for adults, Dfl. 3 ($1.25) for children up to 18. Tram 13, 14, or 17 to Westermarkt (the house is along the canal past the Westerkerk).

The Netherlands Maritime Museum

What a bonanza for anyone who loves the sea! Here, on Kattenburgerplein just off Prins Hendrikkade (tel. 26-22-55), in the ancient arsenal of the Amsterdam Admirality that dates from 1656, exhibits of ship models, charts, instruments, maps, prints, and paintings that chronicle Holland's abiding ties to the sea through commerce, fishing, yachting, navigational development, and even war at sea. There are brief texts explaining each exhibit, and for those loitering souls, desks with more extensive information in every room. Moored at the landing stage are a steam icebreaker, a motor lifeboat, and a sailing lugger, while the historic Royal Barge and two towing barges are lodged indoors.

Open from 10 a.m. to 5 p.m. Tuesday through Saturday, from 1 to 5 p.m. on Sunday; closed Monday and New Year's Day. Admission is Dfl. 5 ($2.25) for adults, Dfl. 3 ($1.25) for ages 17 and under. Bus 22 or 28 from Central Station, or take a 20-minute walk along the historical waterfront, the "Nautisch Kwartier."

Netherlands Theater Institute

Housed in five architectural gems on the canal at Herengracht 168-170 (tel. 23-51-04), the Theater Institute uses two to house—in galleries connected by marble hallways with lavishly decorated ceilings and wall paintings—a wonderfully eclectic collection of theater memorabilia. "Theater" in this case includes opera, cabaret, puppetry, and even the circus. Exhibitions change frequently and include both historical and contemporary items. There are puppets, costumes, masks, models, miniature stages, props, drawings, prints, paintings, and a wealth of other informative material. There is also a library of books, films, videos, and records, as well as a theater bookshop. There's a lovely garden out back in which you can enjoy drinks and snacks.

Open every day but Monday from 11 a.m. to 5 p.m., with admission of Dfl. 3.50 ($1.50) for adults, Dfl. 2 (90¢) for children under 10. Tram 13, 14, or 17.

THE OTHER SIGHTS OF AMSTERDAM

Many of your most treasured memories of Amsterdam will come from her streets—brightly painted barrel organs, the sound of carillons ringing out over the city every 15 minutes, flowers everywhere, herring stands, sidewalk cafés lining busy squares, crowds ambling leisurely down pedestrian shopping streets, and a multitude of other visual impressions.

Amsterdam's Churches

Religion has always played an important part in Amsterdam's history, and hundreds of churches are testimony to the great variety of religious beliefs still alive in the city. Most can be visited during regular services (the VVV can furnish a complete list by denomination and hours of service), some have open doors during weekdays so that *reverent* visitors may have a look around, and the Nieuwe Kerk has regular visiting hours. Those below are churches of special interest.

Nieuwe Kerk, Dam Square (across from the Royal Palace). This beautiful church was built in the last years of the 14th century, when the Oud Kerk (St. Nicolaaskerk) had become too small to accommodate its congregation. Many of its priceless treasures were removed and colorful frescos painted over in 1578 when it passed into the hands of Protestants, but since 1814 (when the king first took the oath of office and was inaugurated here—Dutch royalty are not *crowned),* much of its original grandeur has been restored. Aside from its stately arched nave, elaborately carved altar, great pipe organ that dates from 1645, and several noteworthy stained-glass windows, it holds sepulchral monuments for many of Holland's most revered poets and naval heroes. Admission is sometimes charged for special exhibits, and visiting hours vary, but are generally Monday through Saturday from 11 a.m. to 4 p.m., on Sunday from noon to 2 p.m.; closed January and February and for private events.

The **Oude Kerk** is at Oudekerksplein on Oude Zijds Voorburgwaal (tel. 24-91-83 for information about visits and periodic organ recitals) and dates from the 14th century.

On the corner of Westermarkt and Prinsengracht, the **Westerkerk** (tel. 24-77-66) holds the remains of Rembrandt and his son, Titus, and this is where Queen Beatrix said her marriage vows in 1966. It was built between 1620 and 1631, and its 275-foot tower, which you can climb during summer months, is the highest in Amsterdam. Open from 10 a.m. to 4 p.m. May through September; church services are at 10:30 a.m. on Sunday.

The 17th-century **Portuguese Synagogue,** Mr. Visserplein 3 (tel. 24-53-51), is open to visitors by appointment. The interesting neo-baroque **St. Nicolaas Church,** Prins Hendrikkade 73 (tel. 24-87-49), was built in the late 1800s; there are organ recitals during September, and a traditional crèche and special church tours during the Christmas holidays. And to round things off, there's the Islamic mosque **Moskee Thaiba,** Kraaiennest 125 (tel. 98-25-26).

World War II Memorial

From the beginning the spot now covered by Dam Square has been the very heart of Amsterdam. At one end, on the site of the ancient Vischmarkt, or fishmarket, where fishing boats came up the Amstel to sell the day's catch, a tall, simple spire commemorates Dutch victims of World War II. Holland suffered greatly during the Nazi occupation, and its Dutch East Indies holdings fared no better under Japanese domination. In remembrance of those who did not survive, the urns at the base of the spire hold soil from Holland's 11 provinces and its Indonesian colonies. Somehow it seems fitting that Holland should hold their memory to its heart in the heart of its principal city.

The Royal Palace (Koninklijk Paleis)

Built as a Town Hall to replace the one on this same spot that burned down in 1655, this massive, beautifully proportioned building on Dam Square required a total of 13,659 wooden pilings to support it in the marshy soil underneath. It was only in 1808, when Napoleon Bonaparte's brother, Louis, reigned as King of Holland, that it became a palace, quickly filled with Empire-style furniture courtesy of the French ruler. Today it's the official residence of the royal family (Amsterdam is, after all, capital of the country even though it is *not* the seat of government), but remains unoccupied since Queen Beatrix and her family prefer living at Huis ten Bosch in The Hague, using this palace only for the occasional state reception. During the summer months you can visit its impressive high-ceilinged Citizens' Hall, the Burgomasters' Chambers, and the Council Room, as well as the Vierschaar, the marble Tribunal in which death sentences were pronounced during the 17th century. Hours are 12:30 to 4 p.m. (last admission at 3:45 p.m.) daily, with an admission of Dfl. 1.50 (65¢) for adults, Dfl. .50 (20¢) for children up to the age of 16.

The Floating Flower Market

If there is one single image people around the world have of Amsterdam, it's of this stunning mass of flowers strung along the Singel canal at the Muntplein. From permanently moored barges, awnings stretch to cover stall after stall of brightly colored blossoms, bulbs, and potted plants. A stroll down that fragrant line is surely one of Amsterdam's most heart-lifting experiences, and more than one tourist yields to the temptation to buy an armful of color and scent to brighten a hotel room. Should you be invited to the home of an Amsterdammer, this is where you'll go for flowers to take along with you, a ritual the natives practice themselves. Prices are incredibly low—so go ahead, yield!

Holland Art and Craft Center

There are more than a dozen Dutch crafts represented at this interesting center, at Nieuwendijk 16 (tel. 24-65-01), among them the painting of Delft Blue, cheese making, and the chiseling of wooden shoes. It's an ideal place to pick up souvenirs you've actually seen in the making. Not far from the Central Station and the Dam, it's open every day from 10 a.m. to 5 p.m. (closed Wednesday from November to April), and there's an admission fee of Dfl. 5 ($2.25) for adults, Dfl. 4 ($1.75) for children.

The Jordaan

A hodgepodge of narrow streets and canals running from the Rosengracht to Haarlemmerdijk and from the Prinsengracht to the Lijnbaansgracht, this charming little neighborhood lies west of the Centrum and until recent years was strictly a working-class habitat. Nowadays it has become quite fashionable, with its old houses fast being renovated as chic (and high-priced) apartments. Lots of boutiques and restaurants are sprouting up among the long-established brown cafés, and a stroll through streets and along canals with names like Bloemgracht (Flower Canal) and Leiegracht (Lily Canal) makes for a delightful afternoon, especially on a Sunday when residents are at home, traffic is sparse, and its "neighborhood" character is in full bloom.

Vogel Park

The 120 acres that make up this oasis of greenery close to the Museumplein (with an entrance at Zandpad) are a tidy collection of willow-bordered ponds, flower beds, and a bandshell. Named for a famous Dutch poet, it's open until 8 p.m. Lovely place for a picnic.

Artis (Amsterdam Zoo)

At Plantage Kerklaan 38-40 and easily reached by tram (tram 9 from Central Station), this collection of animals will delight young and old and those in-between. There's an aquarium with rare fish and several animal species that are fast disappearing in the wild. Open daily from 9 a.m. to 5 p.m., with an admission of Dfl. 10 ($4.25) for adults, Dfl. 5 ($2.10) for children up to 9.

7. Amsterdam After Dark

When the sun goes down, the curtain goes up on a night scene in Amsterdam that can be as highbrow or as lowbrow or as in-between as you choose. In this cosmopolitan city, its citizens seem to take it for granted that there are times when nothing will suit as much as a performance of the classical arts, others when it's jazz or disco music the soul calls for, still others when good conversation in good company over good drinks is the perfect end of a day, and sometimes something a little less tame than any of those fills the bill (even if it's just to look, not touch!). And with typical Amsterdam respect for individual tastes, they provide it all so you can fit the evening to your mood.

WHAT'S ON AND HOW TO GET TICKETS

Before setting out for the evening, pick up a copy of the VVV publication ***This Week in Amsterdam*** (from the VVV office or your hotel), check its listings, and when you've made your selections, contact either individual box offices, nightclubs, etc., or head for the VVV office, where they'll book everything for you at a very small fee.

SOME AFTER-DARK TIPS

Because Amsterdammers do take evening "culture"—in whatever form—as just a part of everyday living, dress tends to be more casual than elsewhere, and prices are within an ordinary citizen's reach. That's not to say that nighttime entertainment is cheap or that it's acceptable to show up for a symphony concert in jeans and T-shirt, but neither do you have to get to the concert hall in a tuxedo and armed with a millionaire's bankroll. Many nightspots charge only for drinks, although others have a nominal cover charge; and there are summer outdoor concerts that are free, where jeans are expected.

Will you be safe moving around Amsterdam after dark? Well, as is true in any large city these days, you'll be safer in some ares than in others. And the cardinal rule of travel safety applies: don't flash your money around inviting some nefarious character to take it away from you. The places listed in this section are located in areas where you need exercise only normal caution, and if you're tempted to explore others on your own, just remember that taxis have to be called by phone and Amsterdam street corners don't have telephone booths. If you should find yourself in need of a taxi on the street at night, go into the nearest brown café to call.

Just one more thing: That famous Amsterdam red-light district, the Rosse Buurt, is in the Zeedijk, the so-called sailors' quarter east of the Dam—should you decide to take a look, leave your passport and other valuables in the hotel safe (purse-snatching is common in this area) and be prepared to feel a little sad at the spectacle of rather bored ladies in various states of undress draped over a chair or sofa prominantly displayed in picture windows.

Nightlife in Amsterdam is centered mainly around the **Leidseplein** and **Rembrandtplein,** where you'll find a concentration of nightclubs, discos, theaters, cinemas, and restaurants. Most do not require advance reservations, and part of the fun is strolling the streets and "window-shopping" for the night's entertainment. Best of all, there are all those brown cafés where a convivial evening slips by before you know it.

THE BROWN CAFÉS

You'll see them everywhere: on street corners, on corners where two canals intersect, down narrow little lanes. They look like they've been there forever, and they have (rumor has it there's one that hasn't closed its doors since 1574, but I never found it). These are the favorite local haunts and quite likely to become yours as well—they're positively addictive. Typically they will sport lace half-curtains at the front window, and ancient Oriental rugs on the table tops (to sop up any spills from your beer). Wooden floors, overhead beams, and plastered walls blend into a murky brown background painted by smoke from centuries of Dutch pipes. Frequently there's a wall rack with newspapers and magazines, but they get little attention in the evening when conversations flow as readily as *pils* (beer). If you really want an imported beer, it's usually available at prices considerably higher than the excellent

Dutch brews. Jenever, the lovely (and potent!) Dutch gin, is on hand in several different flavors, all served ice cold—but never on the rocks.

Your hotel neighborhood is sure to have at least one brown café close at hand, and far be it from me to set any sort of brown café *kroegentocht* (pub crawl), but you just might want to look into the following.

Hoppe, on the corner of Spui and Spuistraat, has been a student and journalist hangout since 1670 and is always packed to the gills, but loads of fun. **Kalkhoven,** at Prinsengracht and Westermarkt, dates back to 1670; **Schiller,** Rembrandtsplein 26, has an art deco décor; and **Gambit,** Bloemgracht 20, if you're a chess buff. **Papeneiland,** Prinsengracht 2, carries its 300 years lightly and still has a secret tunnel leading under the canal that was used by Catholics in the 17th century. **De Eland,** Prinsengracht 296, and **De Pieper,** Prinsengracht 424, on the corner of Leidsegracht, are longtime favorites of Amsterdammers. And in the Jordaan section, look for **Café Chris,** Bloemstraat 42, and **No. 1,** on Westerstraat.

TASTING HOUSES

As atmospheric and as much fun as the brown cafés are the *proeflokaal,* centuries-old drinking establishments where the favored drink is jenever or liquor instead of beer. Do not, however, simply pick up your first drink and swill it down—it's an absolute ritual that you must approach that first drink with your hands behind your back and bend over the bar to take the first drink from a *borreltje* (small drinking glass) that will be filled to the brim.

Three to look for, all in the Dam area, are **Bols House of Liqueurs,** Damstraat 36; **De Drie Fleschjes,** Gravenstraat 18 (behind the Nieuwe Kerk); and **Wynand Fockink,** Pijlsteeg 31 (that's the tiny street alongside the Grand Hotel Krasnapolsky).

CANDLELIGHT CANAL CRUISE

No one should leave Amsterdam without memories of a leisurely two-hour cruise through the illuminated canals in a glass-roofed launch. It's one of the city's special treats, with wine and cheese served to make it even better, and there's a stop at one of the canalside brown cafés for a typical Dutch drink. This is an enchanting look at Amsterdam in her sparkling evening attire. **Holland International** (tel. 22-77-88), opposite the Central Station (you can book by phone), operates the cruises at a fare of Dfl. 38 ($16.75), and they run a coach pickup service to most major hotel areas. For details of the three-hour dinner cruises, see "Where to Eat."

THE HOLLAND FESTIVAL

Culture buffs will do well to plan their visit during the first three weeks in June. That's when Amsterdam presents the Holland Festival, with music, opera, dance, theater, and film performances that range from the classics to works commissioned especially for the festival, to the obscure, to some that are decidedly avant garde. Most are in Amsterdam, but a few are in The Hague. It's an event of international fame, and you should write ahead—way ahead—for tickets and a full program of each year's performances. Contact Holland Festival, Klein-Gartmanplantsoen 21, 1017 RP Amsterdam, Netherlands.

CLASSICAL MUSIC

One of the world's greatest symphonic orchestras, the Amsterdam Concertgebouw Orchestra draws audiences from all over Holland and other European countries. So popular are its performances in the graceful **Concertgebouw,** 98 Van Baerlestraat (tel. 71-83-45; box office hours, 10 a.m. to 3 p.m. Monday through Saturday), that seats are often placed right on the stage at the sides and rear of the orchestra. The Great Hall in which the orchestra plays is so well planned that every seat has a clear view of the stage, and acoustics are perfect no matter where you sit. Recitals are given in the Little Hall, and the Amsterdam Philharmonic Orchestra also performs at the Concertgebouw. The concert season is September to mid-June, but periodic concerts are given during summer months, so check when you're there.

Amsterdam also has many excellent chamber music ensembles that give concerts at various museums and churches in the city, as well as in the Concertgebouw's Little Hall.

OPERA

Opera is performed from September through March by the Netherlands Opera Society at the **Muziektheater** (opera house) at Waterlooplein 22 (tel. 25-54-55).

DANCE

Check to see if either of Holland's two important dance companies, the **Netherlands National Ballet** and the **Netherlands Dance Theater,** is performing during your visit. Both are excellent and may be seen at the Muziektheater, Waterlooplein 22.

THEATER

Home-grown theater productions are almost always in Dutch, but because English is so widely spoken in Amsterdam it's a favorite venue for road shows from the U.S. and England. Check *This Week* to see what's doing when you're there. Also, there is now a resident English-language theater company, **English Speaking Theatre Amsterdam** (tel. 24-72-48).

JAZZ

Amsterdammers love jazz and jazz musicians love Amsterdam. They come from America and all over Europe to play in the city's clubs. When the North Sea Jazz Festival is held each July in The Hague, the best of the entire jazz world shows up to put on over 100 concerts in three days.

In Amsterdam, look for good jazz at the following: **Cab Kaye's Jazz Piano Bar,** Beulingstraat 9 (tel. 23-35-94); **Alto,** Korte Leidsedwarsstraat 115 (tel. 26-32-49); and **Joseph Lam Jazzclub,** Diemenstraat 8 (tel. 22-80-86).

DISCOS

Amsterdam's disco scene embraces every type of ambience and clientele, from the more sophisticated rooms in large hotels to those that cater to the punk crowd to those favored by the gay community. Most operate on a "members only" basis (except for those in large hotels), but will usually admit tourists if you fit in with the crowd. As in most places, Amsterdam's discos come and go with startling rapidity, so best check the listings in *This Week in Amsterdam* for current addresses when you're there.

CASINOS

The first casino in the country was in Zandvoort (near Haarlem), which can be reached by train in a half hour. You'll need your passport, appropriate dress (jacket and tie for men, dress for women), and to be over 18. Hours are 2 p.m. to 2 a.m. every day, and there's an admission charge of Dfl. 7.50 ($3.25).

8. Shopping in Amsterdam

Amsterdam is a city built on trading, and its modern-day shops uphold the long tradition behind them very well. In flea markets, boutiques, standard shops, large department stores, and diamond centers the trading goes on, offering shoppers goods from around the world as well as the best of Dutch products. Outward-bound airline passengers are treated to an incredible array of duty-free goods that range from luxury extravagances to utilitarian items, at savings of 20% to 40% or more over prices elsewhere.

ABOUT PRICES

What a relief—no haggling over prices! For the most part we Americans seem to be fundamentally disinclined to bargain, and when Dutch practicality sets a reasonable price to begin with, then makes it uniform in all shops, it simplifies things all around. Another relief: The prices you see displayed are the prices you'll pay—all taxes are included. So when you see what you want, buy it then and there, secure in the knowledge that you won't find it cheaper elsewhere. Of course there are periodic sales, but no discount stores as we know them.

SHOPPING HOURS

Amsterdam shops are generally open from 1 to 6 p.m. on Monday; from 9 a.m. to 6 p.m. on Tuesday, Wednesday, and Friday; to 9 p.m. on Thursday; and to 5 p.m. on Saturday.

SHOPPING STREETS

Major shopping streets in Amsterdam, many of which are shut off for vehicular traffic, are: **Kalverstraat,** from Dam Square to the Muntplein (inexpensive and moderately priced shops); **Rokin,** parallel to the Kalverstraat (quality fashions, art galleries, antique shops); **Leidsestraat** (up-market shops for clothing, china, gifts); **P.C. Hooftstraat** and **Van Baerlestraat,** near the Museumplein (posh fashion, accessories, china, gifts); and **Spiegelstraat,** near the Rijksmuseum (antiques).

STREET MARKETS

Nothing is quite as much fun as browsing through the open-air stalls of a European street market, and in Europe, nothing beats the street markets of Amsterdam. There's the famous **Waterlooplein flea market** from 9 a.m. to 4 p.m. every day but Sunday; the marvelous **Oudemanhuispoort bookstalls** between Oude Zijds Achterburgwal and Kloveniersburgwal canals near the Muntplein from 10 a.m. to 4 p.m.; several antique markets, a stamp market, bird market, and others that defy description. The VVV can give you a complete list, along with addresses and times of operation.

DEPARTMENT STORES

Bijenkorf, Damrak at Dam Square, is Amsterdam's largest department store, with a vast array of goods in all price ranges and a very good restaurant. Others are **Vroom & Dreesmann,** Kalverstraat near the Muntplein; **Peek and Cloppenburg,** Dam Square (mainly clothing); and **C&A,** between Damrak and Nieuwendijk (mostly clothing).

WHAT TO SHOP FOR

The things that are uniquely Dutch should top your shopping list. True, shops in Amsterdam are filled to bursting with items from around the globe, and you may well run across some especially coveted, hard-to-find bauble. But much of what you see will also be available at home with prices too similar to justify the luggage space. Dutch-made products, on the other hand, will cost far less here and, aside from their practical or esthetic value, are lasting souvenirs of your visit.

Antiques

Amsterdam's antique shops rank among the best in Europe, and you'll find the best of them around Nieuwe Spiegelstraat and in the Jordaan section. The VVV can also furnish a list of antique street markets, which can offer a glorious mix of junk and treasure or some very good selective arrays.

Art

Paintings large and small, originals and reproductions, peer out of every other shop window. You may not pick up the work of a budding Rembrandt for a song, but there's a whole bevy of talented young Dutch artists working away these days, painting the same low landscape under scudding clouds, the same cityscapes, and the same ruddy Dutch faces that their forebears found so fascinating. Exquisite small paintings come with moderate prices, and unless you're a serious art collector, they'll bring you as much pleasure as one of the Dutch masters' paintings. Shop owners are very good about packing paintings for travel, and if the canvas is a large one, they'll take care of shipping it home for you. And who knows, maybe you *will* pick up a budding Rembrandt!

Browse through the large gallery at **Hassel Art** in the shopping arcade of the Grand Hotel Krasnapolsky, Dam 9, or the small **Art Gallery Amsterdam,** Westermarkt 3 (tel. 22-41-71), run by Mr. and Mrs. Krüzmann (open from 10 a.m. to 5:30 p.m.). For good-quality reproductions of the masters, museum shops are your best bet.

Clocks

Dutch clockmakers turn out timepieces in exquisite Old Dutch–style handcrafted cases covered with tiny figures and mottos, insets of hand-painted porcelain, hand-painted Dutch scenes, and soft-toned chimes. They're hard to resist, and a small shop (also with a good stock of delftware, chocolates, and quality gifts) across from the Central Station near the Victoria Hotel, **B. V. Victoria,** Prins Hendrikkade 47 (open from 10 a.m. to 6 p.m. daily), has a particularly good selection, with reasonable prices and friendly, personal service from Theo, one of the owners and his staff. You can pay in U.S. dollars if you wish.

Delft

By far the most ubiquitous items you'll see will be those in the familiar blue-and-white "Delft" colors that have almost become synonymous with the world's conception of Holland itself. Souvenir shops, specialty shops, and department stores feature "delftware" earthenware products in the widest variety of forms imaginable. If one has particular appeal, by all means buy it—but be aware that unless it meets certain specifications you are *not* carting home a piece of the hand-painted earthenware pottery that has made the Delft name famous.

First of all, "delftware" is the accurate name for much of what you see displayed, and it can also be red and white or multicolored. If, however, a piece carries the hallmark "Delftware" or "Delft Blue" (with a *capital* "D"), you may be certain it came from one factory only, in the city of Delft (see Chapter XVI). Of equal quality and value are those hallmarked "Makkumware" (again with a capital "M"), fine hand-painted earthenware made only by one firm in the Friesian town of Makkum and often multicolored (see Chapter XIX). Technically, *copies* of each should be called "delftware" and "makkumware" (small "d" and small "m"), and in most cases you will immediately see the difference. You should learn to recognize the hallmarks of each, however, if you're doing serious shopping. A wide selection of Delftware can be found at **De Porceleyne Fles,** Muntplein 12.

Diamonds

Amsterdam diamond cutters have an international reputation for high standards, and when you buy from them you'll be given a certificate as to the weight, color, cut, and identifying marks of the gem you purchase. Many open their cutting room (or "factory") to visitors and are happy to give you a quick course in how to recognize the varying types and quality of diamonds. And, happily, there is no pressure to buy, so you can come along for the education and the inevitable test of your willpower. Among those you may visit are: **Amsterdam Diamond Center B.V.,**

Rokin 1; **A. Van Moppes & Zoon B.V.,** Albert Cuypstraat 2-6; and **Coster Diamonds,** Paulus Potterstraat 2-4. Hours are 9 a.m. to 5 p.m.

Flower Bulbs

Gardeners will find it well-nigh impossible to leave Amsterdam without at least one purchase from the **Floating Flower Market** on the Singel canal at Muntplein. Just be certain that the bulbs you buy carry with them the obligatory certificate for entry into the United States.

Pipes, Cigars, and Tobacco

Amsterdammers treasure **P. G. C. Hajenius,** Rokin 92-96 (tel. 23-74-94), almost as much as they treasure their pipes. Indeed, the elegant and gracious tobacco and pipe shop is the sort I, for one, thought had long vanished from the face of the earth. Run by the same family since 1826, the warm, wood-paneled store is virtually a museum of antique tobacco humidors (not for sale), and has a beautiful selection of distinctively Dutch styles for sale. Pipes of all description are displayed for your selection, and fine Sumatra and Havana cigars are kept in a room-size glass humidor. Best of all, however, is the courteous interest bestowed on everyone who comes through the door, whether it be for cigarettes, pipe tobacco, or one of their most expensive pipes.

9. Day Trips from Amsterdam

The Holland of your fondest fancies lies just outside Amsterdam—the dikes that have brought into being this improbable country, windmills, wooden shoes, tidy farms, tiny harbors filled with sails, flower fields reaching to the horizon, and sandy beaches looking out to the North Sea.

All are easy day trips from an Amsterdam base, but don't try to see them all in one day—you'll need at least two days, and preferably three, to get to all the places listed in this section. If you're driving, there are suggested day-long itineraries, with a couple of overnight possibilities in case you should decide to move out of the city and combine any or all of these junkets. One note of caution: You *must* keep headlights on when driving on polder dikes—"polder blindness" can result from a combination of water glare and the unbending, straight-as-an-arrow roads that sometimes bring on a case of semihypnosis for drivers.

If, on the other hand, you take the easy way out and make use of the excellent bus tours available from Amsterdam, may I suggest that you alternate a day of forays into the countryside with one in the city—morning and afternoon schedules make it possible to get in a full day of touring, returning to the city for dinner and an evening out.

It's also possible to reach virtually every town listed in this section by train, with frequent schedules daily, and with pretty good public transportation once you get there. Your best bet if you plan to visit only one destination is to buy a special one-day round-trip excursion ticket at a discount of about 15%; for more than one destination, the one-day unlimited ticket is better value at Dfl. 52 ($22.75) second class and Dfl. 78 ($34.25) first class.

Missing from this discussion are the South Holland province cities of The Hague, Delft, and Rotterdam, which will be discussed in more detail in later chapters. All three, however, are well suited for day excursions from Amsterdam.

BUS TOURS

No matter what time of year you come, there's an 8½-hour Grand Holland Tour available that will take you to The Hague, Delft, and Rotterdam, for Dfl. 47.50 ($20.75) to Dfl. 57.50 ($25.25); half-day tours to Volendam and Marken, Edam and its windmills, and an afternoon tour of The Hague and Delft cost Dfl. 22 ($9.75) to Dfl. 36 ($15.75).

During the summer months even more destinations are available, including an 8-hour excursion to the Enclosing Dike and a circle around the Ijsselmeer (formerly the Zuiderzee), for Dfl. 57.50 ($25.25); the bulb fields and Keukenhof Gardens (March to May only), for Dfl. 42 ($18.50); and a Friday-morning visit to Alkmaar and its famed cheese market, for Dfl. 42 ($18.50).

These major coach-tour companies offer much the same tours at the same prices: **Key Tours,** Dam 19 (tel. 24-73-04); **Holland International,** Damrak 7 (tel. 22-25-50); **American Express,** Damrak 66 (tel. 26-20-42); and **Lindbergh,** Damrak 26 (tel. 22-27-66).

Note: There are also coach tours that go as far afield as Antwerp and Brussels, one way to work in a bit of Belgium if your time is limited.

SUGGESTED ONE-DAY ITINERARIES

Full descriptions of each destination follow to help you choose the route with the most appeal.

Day Tour 1: Amsterdam to Zaanse Schans, Edam, Volendam, Marken, Monnickendam, Broek in Waterland (to visit cheese factory), Amsterdam.

Day Tour 2: Amsterdam to Hoorn, Enkhuizen, Enclosing Dike (drive to monument at midpoint), Den Helder, Alkmaar, Zaanse Schans, Amsterdam.

Day Tour 3: Amsterdam to Lelystad, Enkhuizen (via dike road), Hoorn, Zaanse Schans, Amsterdam.

Day Tour 4: Amsterdam to Aalsmeer, through bulb fields to Lisse (Keukenhof Gardens), Zandvoort (beach, racetrack, casino), Spaarndam, Amsterdam.

These routes are easily juggled to cover those points you'd most like to see, and an overnight in Volendam or Den Helder will eliminate the return to Amsterdam. Also, if you will be driving on to Friesland, you can go by way of the Enclosing Dike and do this touring en route.

ONE-DAY DESTINATIONS

The descriptions below, though brief, will give you an idea of where to find what.

Zaanse Schans

This charming little artificial village sits right in the middle of an industrial area just 10½ miles northwest of Amsterdam, not far from Zaandam. These delightful houses painted the traditional green and white might have disappeared forever in the wake of industrialization had they not been moved to this location to re-create the "dike villages" that once dotted the Zaan region. All but one or two (which have been converted to museums open to the public) are still private residences, set along typical village streets and along a pretty canal. Stop in at the bakery and the old-fashioned grocery store, then stop in at the clog shop to see how the wooden shoes are made. You may be interested to know that they are still a staple in many farming areas, where they are much more effective against wetness and cold than leather shoes or boots. They are also, of course, a tourist staple, and if you plan to buy a pair, this is a good place to do it. Traditionally, those with pointed toes are for women and rounded toes are for men. All must be worn with heavy socks, so when buying, allow the width of one finger when measuring for size. Don't leave without walking over to the four windmills that line the dike. A short tour of one shows you just how these wind machines worked. Open for visitors at varying hours (check with the VVV in Amsterdam) from late March to October.

At nearby **Koog aan de Zaan** there's a 1751 windmill museum, Het Pink; **Zaandijk** offers the tourist an 18th-century merchant's home furnished in Zaanse style; and at **Zaandam,** a 17th-century shipbuilding center for all of Europe, visit the Het-Peterhuisje, the residence of Peter the Great, Czar of Russia, when he worked in the shipyards here under an assumed name in order to learn skills that would be helpful to his country. You'll see his statue in the marketplace, a gift from Czar Nicholas II.

Broek in Waterland

This small village seven miles from Amsterdam is worth a stop during the summer months to visit the Jakob Wiedermeier & Son farmhouse, where you can see Edam cheeses being made.

Monnickendam

Visit the Town Hall, at Noordeinde 5, that began life as a private residence in 1746, and step inside to admire the elaborately decorated ceiling. Then take a walk through streets lined with gabled houses, with a stop to admire the 15th-century late-Gothic Sint Nicolaaskerk, at Zarken 2.

Marken

This tiny fishing village was once an island, but is now reached by a two-mile-long causeway from Monnickendam. You must leave your car in the parking lot outside before entering the narrow streets lined with green-and-white houses. Occupants of those houses wear traditional dress, although these days it's as much to preserve the custom as for the tourists who pour in daily. There's a typical house open as a sort of museum, a clog maker, and a tiny harbor. You'll be happy to know that photosnapping is not frowned upon here, as it is in some other villages that still adhere to the old customs.

Now in case you feel a bit uncomfortable (as I confess I many times do) at seeming to gawk at "the picturesque locals" as they go about their daily routine of hanging out laundry, washing windows, shopping for groceries, etc., it's a comfort to know that in the case of Marken your visit is not crass exploitation. This is a village that lost its livelihood when access to the Zuiderzee was cut off (some of their fishing boats that now sail the Ijsselmeer hoist dark-brown sails as a sign of mourning for their lost sea fishing), and tourism has become an alternative industry, with a tax that goes directly into the village coffers levied on every tour. Gawking has quite literally saved Marken's life!

Volendam

Larger than Marken, the town of Volendam is quite obviously geared for tourism in a big way, with lots of souvenir shops, boutiques, gift shops, and restaurants in full swing during summer months. Still, its boat-filled harbor, tiny streets, and traditional houses have an undeniable charm. Its inhabitants, like those in Marken, wear traditional Dutch costumes, although you may see young people of the town clad in the dress of today. If your camera finger develops an itch to preserve all this quaintness on film, feel free—Volendammers will gladly pose.

Volendam is, in fact, a nice base for exploring this area, and the old-fashioned **Hotel Spaander** (tel. 02993/63-595) with its Old Dutch interior, offers comfortable and attractive rooms, all with private facilities, in a waterfront location for rates of Dfl. 120 ($52.75) double with private bath.

If you're here at lunchtime, the two dining rooms and outside terrace café of the Hotel Spaander are excellent restaurant choices, with moderate prices: dinner averages Dfl. 25 ($11), without wine!

Edam

About three miles north of Volendam, Edam is the town that has given its name to one of Holland's most famous cheeses. Don't expect to find it in the familiar red skin, however—that's for export, and in Holland the skin is yellow. This pretty little town is centered around canals you cross by way of drawbridges, with views on either side of lovely canal houses, complete with beautiful gardens and canalside tea houses.

This was once a port of some prominence, and a visit to the **Captain's House,** just opposite the Town Hall, not only gives you a peek at its history, but also at some of its most illustrious citizens of past centuries (look for the portrait of one Pieter Dirksz, one-time mayor and proud possessor of what is probably the longest beard on record anywhere). Take a look at the lovely "wedding room" in the **Town Hall,** and if you visit during summer months, don't miss the cheese-making display at the **Kaaswaag** (Weigh House). The **Speeltoren** (carillon tower) tilts a bit, and it was very nearly lost when the church to which it belonged was destroyed—no danger now, though, as it is securely shored up. Its carillon dates back to 1561.

Alkmaar

Do try to get to Alkmaar on a summer Friday morning to see the fascinating **cheese market** held in the square adjoining its ancient Weigh House. It's a fascinating spectacle, as teams of cheese carriers dressed in white, with straw hats of red, blue, yellow, or green, trot from the auction ring to the Weigh House pulling sleds piled high with cheeses to be weighed. A handclasp seals bids in the ring before the sleds are loaded, and the bill is tallied by each guild's scales. Carriers, members of four sections of their guild (identified by the color of their hats), are so proud of their standards that every week they post on a "shame board" the name of any carrier who has indulged in profanity or been late arriving at the auction. The square is thronged with sightseers, barrel organs, souvenir stalls, and an excitement that is almost tangible.

If you can't make it for the cheese market, Alkmaar is worth a visit for a ramble through its historic 12th-century streets. There's also an excellent porcelain collection in the 1520 Town Hall.

Hoorn

Hoorn is the home of Willem Cornelis Schouten, who rounded the southernmost tip of South America in 1616 and promptly dubbed it Cape Horn. The **VVV office,** at Statenpoort, Nieuwstraat 23 (tel. 02290/1-83-42), can furnish information on Hoorn's many historic buildings and interesting houses.

Visit the **Westfries Museum,** Rode Steen. The beautiful 1632 building holds 17th-century artifacts brought from Indonesia by the East India Company, armor, weapons, porcelain, and a second-floor exhibit that details the town's maritime history. A collection of Bronze Age relics is exhibited in basement rooms.

During July there's an interesting **craft market** in the marketplace every Wednesday, with demonstrations as well as items for sale, and during most summer months an antique steam train takes tourists from Hoorn to Medemblik.

Enkhuizen

A great herring fleet of some 400 boats once sailed out of the Enkhuizen harbor, and then came the Enclosing Dike, closing off the North Sea. Now Enkhuizen looks to tourism and pleasure boating for its livelihood, and its population has declined from 30,000 in its 17th-century glory days to a mere 13,000 today.

For the story of this entire region—its lifestyle, furniture, customs, etc.—head for the waterfront **Zuiderzeemuseum.** It's in a three-centuries-old warehouse once used by the East India Company, and there are amazingly accurate period rooms complete with costumed dummies. Its most fascinating collections, however, are those of the boats from all periods tied up at the pier and those in the huge covered hall that hold relics recovered from the depths of the Ijsselmeer, some dating back to Roman times.

From the Enkhuizen/Lelystad dike car park you can take a ferry over to an **open-air Zuiderzeemuseum,** where old farmhouses, public buildings, shops, and a church from around the Zuiderzee have been brought together to form a cobblestone-street village.

Not far away, near the little town of Medemblik, the 8th-century **Radboud Castle,** which was fortified in 1288 against possible rebellion from those troublesome Frisians, has been restored to its original state and is well worth a visit. It's open every day from June to August, on Sunday afternoon other months.

Enclosing Dike

Its official name is the Afsluitdijk, and it is simply impossible to grasp just what a monumental work this is until you've driven its 18-mile length. Dr. Cornelis Lely came up with the plans in 1891, but work was delayed for 25 years as he labored to convince the government to allocate funds for its construction.

The imagination boggles at the thought of what massive effort and back-breaking labor went into this 300-foot-wide dike that stands a full 21 feet above mean water level, keeps back the sea, and through ingenuous engineering has converted the salty Zuiderzee into the freshwater Ijsselmeer and transformed large areas of its muddy bottom into productive (and dry!) land. It is a heroic achievement.

Midway along its length—at the point where the dike was closed in 1932—there's a beautiful monument to the men who put their backs to the task and a memorial to Dr. Lely. Stop for a light lunch at the café in the monument's base and pick up an illustrated booklet that explains the dike's construction. Nondrivers will find both a biking and a pedestrian path crossing the dike.

When you approach the dike from the town of Wieringerwerf, keep an eye out for the marker about 3½ miles to the east that tells of a Nazi last-ditch tactic in 1945 when the dike was breached only 18 days before their surrender. The indomitable Dutch repaired the dike, pumped the polder dry, and were growing crops in polder fields again by the very next spring!

Den Helder

Den Helder is Holland's most important naval base, the site of its **Royal Naval College.** It also has the dubious distinction of being possibly the only port in the world that ever lost a fleet to a company of horsemen! That unique event took place back in January 1794, when the Dutch fleet found itself stuck fast in the frozen waters between Den Helder and Texel Island—French cavalry simply rode out to the ships and captured them all. That was quite a fall from the heights of glory it had known a century earlier when Admirals de Ruyter and Tromp led Dutch ships to victory over a combined English and French fleet just off this very coast in 1673.

Today you can visit the **Helders Marinemuseum (Maritime Museum),** which holds exhibits illustrating the Dutch Royal Navy's history, and take a look at the state shipyards.

If you plan to travel on to Friesland via the Enclosing Dike, Den Helder makes a good overnight stop, with good accommodations at the **Hotel Beatrix** Badhuisstraat 2, 1783 AK Den Helder (tel. 02230/1-48-00), at rates of Dfl. 130 ($57) to Dfl. 200 ($87.75) double. During the summer months an even more pleasant idea is to take the 25-minute ferry ride to Texel Island for the night. It's a quiet, family-oriented island resort, with double rooms at the **Hotel Opduin,** Ruyslaan 22, 1796 De Koog, Texel Island (tel. 02228/445), in the same rate range.

Lelystad

This is the new city in Holland's newest polder (see Chapter XIX for more detailed information on Flevoland), and is worth a visit—either as a day trip from Amsterdam or an enroute stop as you drive to Friesland—to see the **New Land Information Center,** or **Informatiecentrum Nieuw Land** (tel. 03200/6-07-99), off the Markerwaard Dike approach road. Its three buildings hold fascinating exhibits explaining in detail the whole Zuiderzee Project, from the construction of the dikes to the pumping operation to the drying-up process. You'll also see shipwrecks recovered from the bottom of the Zuiderzee when this land was drained. Hours are 10 a.m. to 5 p.m. daily during the summer, weekdays only in winter, with shorter Sunday hours.

Should you come on a Saturday, be sure to go by this still-wet-behind-the-ears town square to see vendors clad in traditional dress hawking everything from smoked eels to crafts to cheese—a delightful example of a people holding onto tradition in the middle of modern-day progress!

If you have time for the 20-mile drive south to Harderwijk, there's a fascinating **Dolpinarium,** with both a dolphin research station and an entertaining performance by the resident dolphins. Not far away is the **Flevohof Park,** with entertainment and water sports for children and a marvelous working exhibition of a typical farm.

Aalsmeer

About three miles from Schiphol Airport, Aalsmeer is famed for its year-round **flower auction,** the world's largest. From 7:30 to 11:30 a.m., buyers bid with electric buttons on flowers by the lot. The huge clock-like device that keeps track of all the bids is a marvel of efficiency, and it's great fun to watch as about 600 lots change hands every hour.

Bulb Fields

The largest bulb growers are in the northern corner of the South Holland province and the southern part of North Holland, with the heaviest concentration along the 25-mile Haarlem–Leiden drive. Those organized Dutch make it easy with a signposted "Bulb Route" that covers about 38½ miles, and they suggest that you plan to drive it during weekdays, when stalls along the roads sell flower garlands (do as the natives do and buy one for yourself, another for the car).

Lisse

The 70-acre **Keukenhof Gardens** here once belonged to one Jacoba van Beieren, who kept a hunting lodge on these grounds in the 15th century. Today they hold breathtakingly beautiful exhibitions of floral beauty, with nearly eight million bulbs in bloom from the end of March right through May. Winding streams pass beneath ancient shade trees, and there's a sculpture garden, as well as a windmill. Hours are 8 a.m. to 8 p.m., and you can reach the famous gardens from Amsterdam by taking a train to Haarlem and a connecting bus to Lisse.

Zandvoort

This popular North Sea resort was completely demolished by Nazi forces in World War II as they built their Atlantic Wall. Completely rebuilt, it is now the site of international motorcycle and auto races in June and July, and a casino, with the Bloemendaal amphitheater nearby that presents Shakespearean plays during the summer.

Haarlem

Haarlem is a marvelous mix of medieval buildings, museums, and churches. The buildings around its market square date from the 15th through the 19th centuries and are a visual mini-course in the development of Dutch architecture. Visit the 14th-century **Town Hall** and 17th-century **Meat Market,** a veritable Renaissance palace. At Groot Heiligland 62, in what was an almshouse back in 1608, you'll find the **Frans Hals Museum,** a wondrous collection of works by this great Dutch master as well as other artists from the 16th and 17th centuries. Stop by the magnificent **Church of St. Bavo,** and if you're lucky you'll arrive during one of the periodic concerts on its famous 1738 organ whose keyboard has known the touch of such musical greats as Handel and Mozart.

While you're in the Haarlem area, you might want to visit **Beeckestijn,** a lovely old manor house that dates from the 18th century, at Velsen-Zuid. At **Ijmuiden,** take a close look at three great locks of the North Sea Canal, and early risers can go along to the fish auctions at Halkade 4 (from 7 to 11 a.m. Monday through Friday).

Spaarndam

This little village north of Haarlem is picturesque enough to warrant a visit just for the scenery, but its main claim to fame is a monument to a fictional character who has become an everlasting symbol of Holland and the Dutch people. You remember, of course, Young Pieter (of *Hans Brinker or the Silver Skates*), who saved Haarlem from disaster when he plugged a hole in the dike with his finger and steadfastly refused to leave until help came at the end of a long night. His vigil cost him his life, and because that heroic act of this fictional boy so caught the imagination of people around the world, the Dutch government erected a memorial in 1950, dedicating it to the courage of Dutch youth in general.

XV

THE HAGUE, SCHEVENINGEN, AND ROTTERDAM

The Hague and Rotterdam are about as different as any two cities could be, yet The Hague—stately, dignified, dinner-jacket elegant—is quite at ease with its brash, modern-as-tomorrow, mod-clad neighbor.

History, of course, accounts for much of the difference. **The Hague,** with close ties to nobility since the 13th century, has seen the centuries come and go with scarcely a rumble in the foundations of its lofty perch. Technically it's not even a true "city," never having been granted a charter or city rights, but never has a "village" maintained such an imperial disdain for such a triviality. Secure in its regal position, The Hague goes serenely on its way as the seat of Holland's government, even if not its capital, content to be what is undoubtedly the largest "village" in Europe.

Rotterdam, on the other hand, sits on delta land at the junction of the Rhine and Maas Rivers and has been commercial to the core from the very beginning. The legacy of its centuries has always been somewhat less than elegant, related more to bustling port activity than to nobility, and even its historically significant landmarks literally "bit the dust" when World War II bombings left little but rubble in their wake. Rebuilding has been in a determinedly modern vein, raising a monument to the technology that is responsible for the development of a staggering annual shipping tonnage and the influx of more and more new residents.

1. The Hague

In the beginning, a small village named Haag ("hedge") was chosen by the counts of Holland as the setting for their hunting lodge, earning the future town its official name of 's Gravenhage ("the Count's hedge"). By the time the then count, Willem II, was named King of the Romans in 1247, his father, Floris IV, had already begun construction of the Binnenhof, and Willem quickly appointed it the official royal residence. Willem's son, Floris V, added the massive Hall of Knights

(Ridderaal), expanding a complex that today is the heart of the country's administrative government.

As the center of government, The Hague ("Den Haag" in Dutch) has grown into a cosmopolitan city that is now the site of no fewer than three royal palaces, some 64 foreign embassies, and European headquarters for innumerable international engineering, oil, and chemical concerns. The lush greenery that brought those long-ago counts here to hunt has never been allowed to disappear as The Hague grew in size, and large areas of parks, gardens, and woods continue to thrive within the city limits. The ancient seaside fishing village of Scheveningen has blossomed into a popular resort, so close by that a short tram ride connects it to the city center.

This is above all a city of style and culture, and many tourists choose a touring base in this oasis of elegance in preference to Amsterdam or Rotterdam.

HOW TO GET THERE

The Hague is within easy reach of all major Dutch airports and harbors. A "Schiphol Line" offers fast rail service (30 minutes) to Amsterdam's airport; the Hook of Holland sea ferries are only 12½ miles away (35 minutes by car, 45 by train); and Rotterdam's Europoort is about an hour's drive away, with good bus and train connections.

WHERE TO STAY

Hospitality has been a tradition in The Hague since the counts of Holland welcomed visiting royalty, and you will find hotel accommodations of high standards in every price range. If you prefer seaside accommodations, see Section 2 of this chapter.

Out of Town

Auberge de Kieviet, Stoeplaan 27, 2243 CX Wassenaar (tel. 01751/192-32). Only ten minutes' drive from The Hague, and about 1½ miles from the sea, this luxurious small hotel is well worth the drive. All 25 attractive guest rooms have direct-dial telephone, private bath, TV, etc., and there's 24-hour room service, something not always available in the smaller hostelries. There's a bar and a brasserie, and the excellence of its gourmet restaurant is attested to by the prestigious (and demanding) Alliance Gastronomique Néerlandaise, of which it is a member. Rates range from Dfl. 175 ($76.75) to Dfl. 350 ($153.50).

In-Town Choices

The following selections are given roughly in order of price, from most to least expensive.

Hotel des Indes, Lange Voorhout 54-56 (P.O. Box 30514), 2500 GM The Hague (tel. 070/46-95-53). This elegant Old-World hotel began life as the residence of the Baron van Brienen (its luxurious, open lobby with a graceful staircase opposite the entrance was in fact the entrance to his *stable*—very hard to believe when you see it now), but began its hotel career in 1881. Since then it has welcomed royalty, diplomats, celebrities, and just plain tourists, as well as held a prominent place in the social life of The Hague. The 77 guest rooms are done up in classic décor and furnishings, and are the very ultimate in comfort. All have private bath, TV with remote control, telephones (in both bedroom and bath), radio, and such extras as bathrobes and hairdryers. Some baths even contain a Jacuzzi whirlpool. Public rooms are breathtakingly beautiful, with lots of marble, polished wood, chandeliers, and velvet upholstery. The gracious lobby lounge is a favorite place with Hagenaars to meet for tea or other refreshments, and there's a clubby elegance to "Le Bar," another popular meeting place. Its fine restaurant is a favorite with locals. Rates for such luxury are Dfl. 342 ($150) single, Dfl. 444 ($194.75) double. *Note:* This hotel's location, right in the center of the oldest part of the city, more than justifies its top rates. Highly recommended.

Hotel Promenade, Van Stolkweg 1,2585 JL The Hague (tel. 070/52-51-61). This 100-bed high-rise a bit out of the city center features luxury guest rooms with balconies, mini-bars, wakeup alarms, and the other amenities you'd expect, all with modern and comfortable furnishings and private baths. There's a good terrace café and a gourmet restaurant. Rates are Dfl. 250 ($109.75) to Dfl. 300 ($131.50).

Hotel Corona, Buitenhof 39-42, 2513 AH The Hague (tel. 070/36-79-30). This charming small hotel (26 rooms) with a large terrace café, is centrally located between the Binnenhof and the Passage. Public rooms are quite nicely done up, while guest rooms are very comfortable, all with private bath. Rates are Dfl. 195 ($85.50) to Dfl. 225 ($98.75) single, Dfl. 220 ($96.50) to Dfl. 275 ($120.50) double.

Parkhotel De Zalm, Molenstraat 53, 2513 BJ The Hague (tel. 070/62-43-71). Close to good shopping streets, this pleasant hotel is on a quiet street, and its breakfast room overlooks the gardens of a former royal palace. Comfortable and attractive guest rooms with private baths range from Dfl. 200 ($87.75) to Dfl. 275 ($120.50).

Paleishotel, Molenstraat 26, 2513 BL The Hague (tel. 070/62-46-21). This centrally located hotel is convenient for shopping as well as sightseeing, and guest rooms are both attractive and of a very high standard, with all the standard amenities you'd expect in a hotel of this standing. Rates run Dfl. 150 ($65.75) to Dfl. 200 ($87.75).

Hotel Petit, Groot Hertoginnelaan 42, 2517 EH The Hague (tel. 070/46-55-00). Situated not far from the Peace Palace, this attractive hotel offers rooms with and without private facilities, at prices of Dfl. 55 ($24) to Dfl. 130 ($57).

If you're looking for clean, comfortable, no-frills accommodations, both the **Du Commerce,** Stationsplein 64, 2515 BW The Hague (tel. 070/80-85-11), and the **Neuf,** Rijswijkseweg 119, 2516 HA The Hague (tel. 070/90-07-48), can provide the same (almost all without private baths) for rates in the Dfl.-70 ($30.75) to Dfl.-90 ($39.50) price range.

WHERE TO EAT

In both ambience and cuisine, The Hague offers a wide range of places to eat, thanks primarily to its wealth of international visitors. The following selections appear roughly in order of price, from most to least expensive.

Restaurant Saur, Lange Voorhout 47-53 (tel. 46-33-44). Overlooking a beautiful square, the Saur has been a favorite of Hagenaars for generations. Both the downstairs and upstairs rooms are lovely, with much more formality above stairs. Its traditional French cuisine is superb, and service is impeccable. Prices are in the Dfl. 55 ($24) and up neighborhood for lunch without wine, Dfl. 90 ($39.50) to Dfl. 175 ($76.75) for dinner, also without wine. Reservations are a must.

't Goude Hooft, Groenmarkt 13 (tel. 46-97-13). There's a definite Old Dutch flavor to this large, happy restaurant, yet its 1600s exterior cloaks a 1938 interior installed after a disastrous fire. The wooden beams, brass chandeliers, rustic chairs and tables blend harmoniously with stained-glass windows and here and there a touch of whimsy. There's a large terrace café overlooking the "Green Market" square, pleasant on sunny days, and the long menu covers everything from snacks to light lunches to full dinners, as well as the budget-priced Tourist Menu for Dfl. 19.50 ($8.50) and a child's plate for just Dfl. 7.25 ($3.25). It's also a good place to drop by for nothing more than a beer or coffee. Continuous service from noon to 9:30 p.m. daily. Highly recommended (I love this place!).

Restaurant Garoeda, Kneuterdijk 18a (tel. 46-53-19). If it's rijsttafel you're hankering for, you couldn't find it any better than at this pleasant and very popular Indonesian restaurant. The rice table starts at Dfl. 35 ($15.25), and other dishes are priced from Dfl. 30 ($13.25) up (but not very far up). Crowded at lunch, so reserve

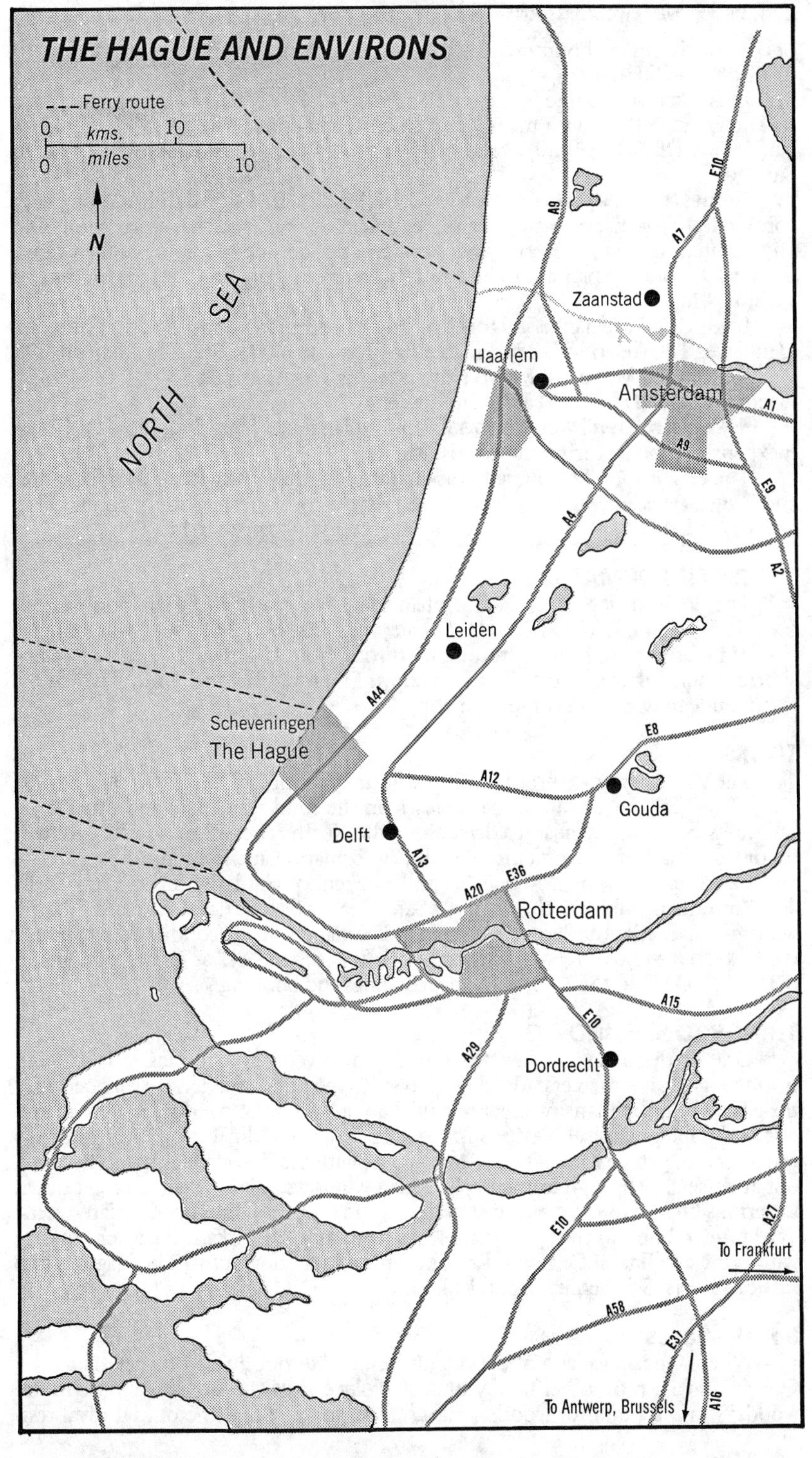
THE HAGUE AND ENVIRONS
Ferry route
0 kms. 10
0 miles 10
N
NORTH SEA
Zaanstad
Haarlem
Amsterdam
A1
A9
A9
A7
E10
E9
A4
A2
Leiden
A44
Scheveningen
The Hague
E8
A12
Gouda
Delft
A13
A20
E36
Rotterdam
A15
E10
A29
Dordrecht
E10
A27
To Frankfurt
A58
E37
A16
To Antwerp, Brussels

or come early or late; hours are 11 a.m. to 11 p.m. Monday through Saturday and 4 to 11 p.m. on Sunday.

Le Bistroquet, Lange Voorhout 98 (tel. 60-11-70). This small restaurant is one of The Hague's best, with mostly French cuisine. Dinner without wine will likely run around Dfl. 90 ($39.50) or more. It's very popular, so be sure to reserve. Closed Sunday.

Gemeste Schaap, Raamstraat 9 (tel. 63-95-72). Traditional dishes, along with continental choices, are featured in this excellent eatery, which has a marvelous Old Dutch interior. Best to reserve, and when you do, be sure to ask for explicit directions, as this one is a bit hard to find. You'll pay around Dfl. 95 ($41.75) for dinner, without wine.

If you develop a hankering for charcoal-grilled steaks, chops, etc., try **Charcoal,** Denneweg 130 (tel. 65-97-88). Prices range from Dfl. 30 ($13.25) to Dfl. 50 ($22).

Vegetarians will be drawn to **Hortus,** Prins Hendrikstraat 53 (tel. 45-67-36), where prices are Dfl. 30 ($13.25) and under.

Restaurant Den Haag Centraal, Kon. Julianaplein 10 (tel. 47-06-41). Good, inexpensive food featuring the Tourist Menu.

The Hague is broken out with casual outdoor cafés, sandwich and coffee shops, and brown cafés, any one of which will serve you good, fresh food for about Dfl. 5 ($2.25) to Dfl. 10 ($4.50). Just drop in wherever you happen to be.

TOURIST INFORMATION

The **VVV office** is at Kon. Julianaplein, in the Central Station (Groot Hertoginnelaan 41, 2517 EC The Hague; tel. 070/54-62-00), open in summer from 9 a.m. to 9 p.m. Monday through Saturday, from 10 a.m. to 5 p.m. on Sunday; shorter hours other months. Pick up a copy of their publication "Info," which is a good guide to what's on at the moment.

TOURS

The **VVV** operates a three-hour Royal Tour by coach for Dfl. 25 ($11) for adults, Dfl. 17 ($7.50) for children, that focuses on the royal residences and other royal buildings, Scheveningen, and a drive along the North Sea coast, with a stop for coffee or tea. Call the VVV office for schedule information and booking.

Coach tours to the flower fields and Keukenhof Gardens, Amsterdam, Delft and Rotterdam, Alkmaar cheese market and Zaanse Schans (see Chapter XIV), the windmill district of Kinderdijk, and a Grand Holland tour are conducted by **Speedwell Reisbureaux B.V.,** Valeriusstraat 65 (tel. 65-48-48), at prices of Dfl. 35 ($15.25) to Dfl. 40 ($17.50). Call for schedules and booking.

THINGS TO SEE AND DO

One of the great pleasures of one day or several in The Hague is walking through its pleasant streets. Match your pace to the unhurried leisure that pervades the city. Stroll past mansions that line the Lange Voorhout, overlooking broad avenues of popular and elm trees, and notice how they differ from Amsterdam's ornamented, gabled canal houses—spacious, with unadorned elegance, they look out at passersby through immense Georgian windows. Window-shop or get down to serious buying in the covered shopping arcades or shop-lined pedestrian streets. Take time to loiter in the more than 430 square miles of parks and gardens that lie within the city limits. Or hop on a tram for the short ride out to The Hague's two seaside resorts, Scheveningen and Kijkduin.

Royal Palaces

When Queen Juliana abdicated the Dutch throne in 1980, her daughter, Queen Beatrix, moved her family into the **Palace Huis ten Bosch** ("house in the woods") in the beautiful wooded Haagse Bos, making that the official royal residence. Built in 1645, it was for many years a summer residence for the royal families. Originally it was a small, rather plain palace consisting of several rooms opening from a domed central hall, and it was Prince Willem IV who added the two large side wings in the 1700s.

The **Palace Noordeinde,** on the elegant shopping street Noordeinde, dates back to 1553 and is the "working palace" for Queen Beatrix and her staff. The splendid neoclassical town palace was quite elegantly furnished when Willem of Orange's widow was in residence, but had become almost derelict by the beginning of the 19th century. In 1815 restoration brought it back to a state suitable for the residence of Willem I. In 1948 fire damage necessitated extensive renovation, and in the early 1980s further restoration was begun. It is from this palace that Queen Beatrix and Prince Claus, on the third Tuesday of September each year, depart in a golden coach drawn by eight horses, escorted by military corps, bands, local authorities, and a blaze of street pageantry, to proceed to the Binnenhof, where the Queen officially opens Parliament with an address to the States General and parliamentary members in the Ridderzaal.

The small, imposing **Palace Lange Voorhout,** overlooking the Lange Voorhout, is now used only for receptions and other official functions, but during renovations on the Palace Noordeinde, the Queen and her staff had offices here.

The Binnenhof

This magnificent "Inner Court," the 13th-century courtyard of the counts of Holland, Binnenhof 8A (tel. 64-61-44), is the center of Holland's political life and the official seat of government. In the center of the Binnenhof, the beautiful **Ridderzaal** (Hall of Knights), measuring 126 by 59 feet and soaring 85 feet to its oak roof, has witnessed great feasts and receptions, a ragtag collection of early-19th-century shops built around it, lottery draws, and a messy lot of bits and pieces piled high for storage. Since 1904 its immense interior—adorned with provincial flags and leaded-glass windows depicting the coats-of-arms of Dutch cities—has been given its dignified due during the Queen's annual address (the third Tuesday in September) to the Parliament, official receptions, and interparliamentary conferences.

There are three entrances and four gates to the Binnenhof. The buildings on the left and right of the Ridderzaal are the former Stadtholders Quarters, which now house the First and Second Chamber of the States General.

Open year round from 10 a.m. to 4 p.m. Monday through Saturday; closed Sunday and public holidays. Admission, depending on the length of the tour, is Dfl. 1 (44¢) to Dfl. 4.50 ($2).

The Peace Palace

This imposing building, whose construction between 1907 and 1913 was largely due to donations of Andrew Carnegie, houses the Permanent Court of Arbitration, the International Court of Justice, the International Law Academy, and an extensive library. Its furnishings have been donated by countries around the world.

Open Monday through Friday from 10 a.m. to noon and 2 to 4 p.m., with guided tours on the hour; closed Saturday and Sunday. Admission is Dfl. 2.50 ($1.10) for adults, Dfl. 1.50 (65¢) for children.

Haags Gemeentemuseum (Municipal Museum)

Located at Stadhouderslaan 41 (tel. 51-41-81), this fine museum has three separate departments. The modern art section focuses on early-19th-century Dutch romantic paintings, the impressionist Hague School, an internationally famous collection of works by Piet Mondrian (Dutch pioneer of abstract art), and 20th-century art, including a fine collection of prints and drawings by K. Appel, M. C. Escher, O. Redon, De Stijl, and Toulouse Lautrec. The Department of Decorative Arts shows ceramics from China, Islam, and Delft; Venetian and Dutch glass; and

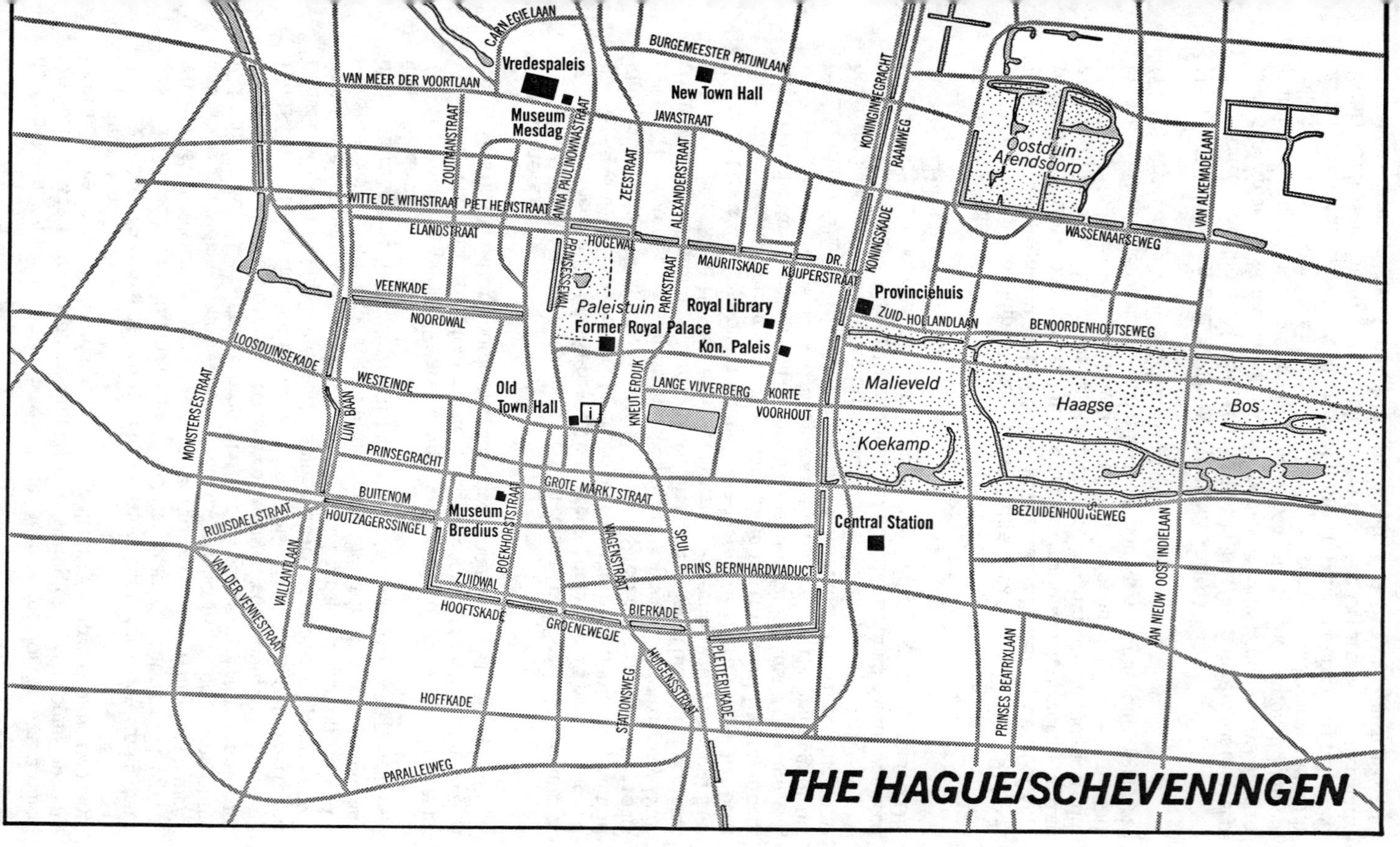
THE HAGUE/SCHEVENINGEN
CARNEGIELAAN
Vredespaleis
VAN MEER DER VOORTLAAN
Museum Mesdag
BURGEMEESTER PATIJNLAAN
New Town Hall
JAVASTRAAT
ZOUTMANSTRAAT
ANNA PAULINOWNASTRAAT
ZEESTRAAT
ALEXANDERSTRAAT
KONINGINNEGRACHT
RAAMWEG
Oostduin Arendsdorp
VAN ALKEMADELAAN
WITTE DE WITHSTRAAT
PIET HEINSTRAAT
ELANDSTRAAT
HOGEWAL
PRINSESSEWAL
MAURITSKADE
DR. KUIJPERSTRAAT
KONINGSKADE
WASSENAARSEWEG
VEENKADE
NOORDWAL
Paleistuin
PARKSTRAAT
Royal Library
Former Royal Palace
Kon. Paleis
Provinciehuis
ZUID-HOLLANDLAAN
BENOORDENHOUTSEWEG
LOOSDUINSEKADE
WESTEINDE
Old Town Hall
KNEUT ERDIJK
LANGE VIJVERBERG
KORTE VOORHOUT
Malieveld
Haagse Bos
Koekamp
MONSTERSESTRAAT
LIJN BAAN
PRINSEGRACHT
GROTE MARKTSTRAAT
BUITENOM
HOUTZAGERSSINGEL
RUIJSDAELSTRAAT
Museum Bredius
BOEKHORSTSTRAAT
WAGENSTRAAT
SPUI
Central Station
BEZUIDENHOUTSEWEG
VAN DER VENNESTRAAT
VAILLANTLAAN
ZUIDWAL
PRINS BERNHARDVIADUCT
HOOFTSKADE
GROENEWEGJE
BIERKADE
HUIGENSSTRAAT
PLETTERIJKADE
VAN NIEUW OOST INDIELAAN
HOFFKADE
STATIONSWEG
PRINSES BEATRIXLAAN
PARALLELWEG

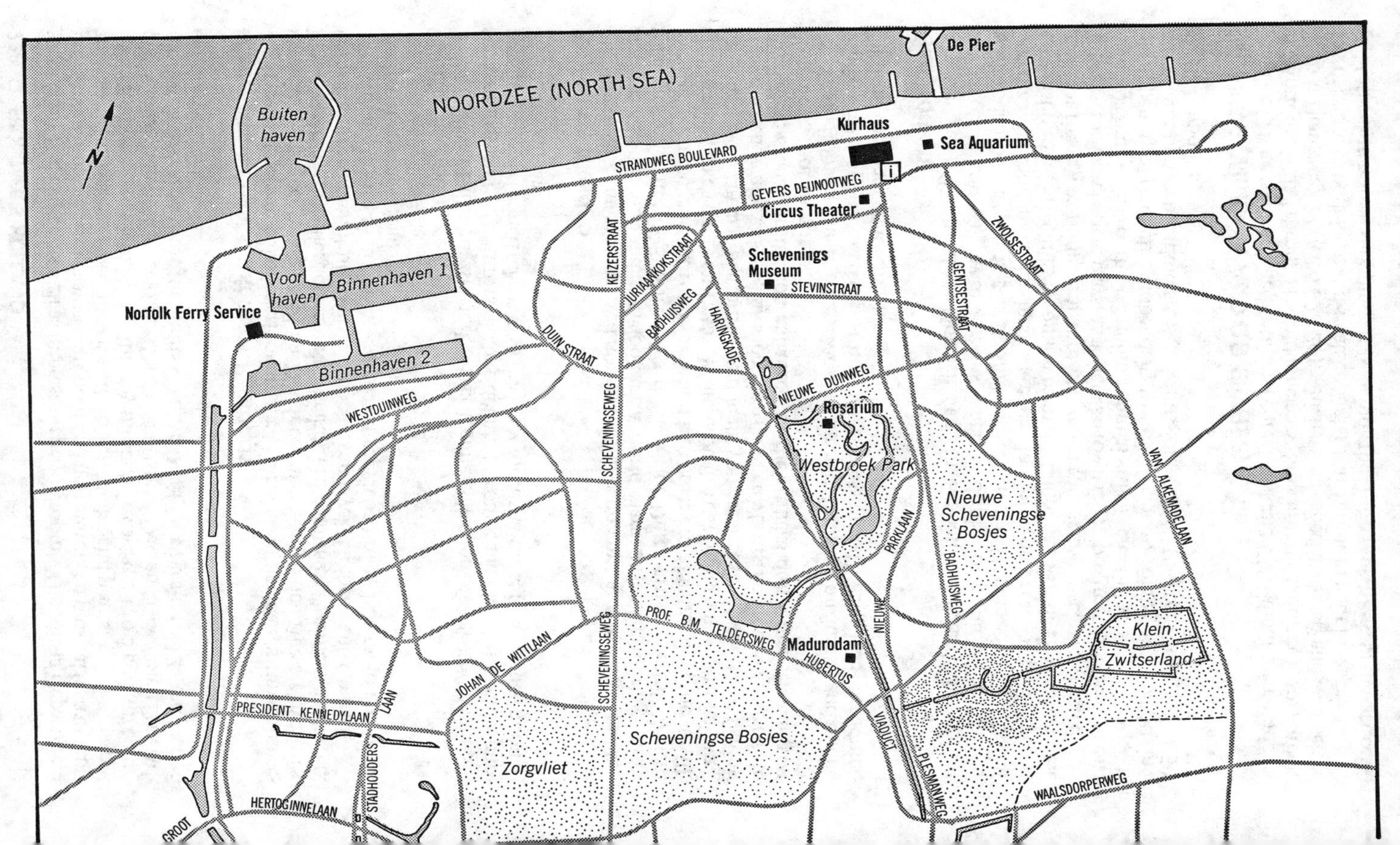

N
NOORDZEE (NORTH SEA)
Buiten haven
De Pier
Kurhaus
Sea Aquarium
STRANDWEG BOULEVARD
GEVERS DEIJNOOTWEG
i
Circus Theater
Schevenings Museum
STEVINSTRAAT
Voor haven
Binnenhaven 1
Binnenhaven 2
Norfolk Ferry Service
WESTDUINWEG
DUIN STRAAT
KEIZERSTRAAT
JURIAANKOKSTRAAT
BADHUISWEG
HARINGKADE
ZWOLSESTRAAT
GENTSESTRAAT
NIEUWE DUINWEG
Rosarium
Westbroek Park
Nieuwe Scheveningse Bosjes
PARKLAAN
NIEUWE
BADHUISWEG
VAN ALKEMADELAAN
SCHEVENINGSEWEG
PROF. B.M. TELDERSWEG
Madurodam
HUBERTUS
VIADUCT
PLESMANWEG
Klein Zwitserland
WAALSDORPERWEG
JOHAN DE WITTLAAN
PRESIDENT KENNEDYLAAN
LAAN
STADHOUDERS
Zorgvliet
Scheveningse Bosjes
HERTOGINNELAAN
GROOT

silver from The Hague, as well as interesting period rooms. The Music Department presents an interesting display of European and non-European musical instruments and has an impressive music library, with scores, books, and prints.

Hours are 10 a.m. to 5 p.m. Tuesday through Friday, and 1 to 5 p.m. on Saturday, Sunday, and holidays; closed Monday, Christmas Day, and New Year's Day. Admission is Dfl. 3 ($1.25) for adults, Dfl. 2.50 ($1) for ages 5 to 12, and free to children under 5.

Mauritshuis Royal Cabinet of Paintings

Next to the Binnenhof overlooking the Court Lake, this small, intimate museum in the 17th-century palace of a Dutch count holds Golden Age art treasures. Represented in the collections are Rembrandt (16 paintings), Vermeer, Jan Steen, Frans Hals, Ruysdael, Paulus Potter, Rubens, van Dyck, Holbein, and Cranach.

Hours are 10 a.m. to 5 p.m. Tuesday through Saturday, 11 a.m. to 5 p.m. on Sunday and public holidays.

Puppet Museum

At Nassau Dillenburgstraat 8, this charming collection of over 1,000 puppets, some more than two centuries old, is a delight to young and old. Periodically, puppet shows are performed (check with the VVV for current schedules). Open noon to 2 p.m. on Sunday.

Panorama Mesdag

If you have any preconceived notion that all panoramas are alike, forget it! Go along to Zeestraat 65b and take a look at the world's largest circular painting, with a total circumference of 395 feet. It's the work of Dutch artist Hendrik Willem Mesdag, with the assistance of his wife and two other prominent artists, and it will, quite simply, take your breath away. Walk through a dark passageway, up a stairway, and out onto a circular platform—suddenly you are actually in the 1880 fishing village of Scheveningen! Its dunes, beach, fishermen's boats, and the village itself are three dimensional, an illusion enhanced by the artificial dunes that separate you from the realistic paintings.

Open from 10 a.m. to 5 p.m. Monday through Saturday, on Sunday and public holidays from noon; closed Christmas Day. Admission is Dfl. 3 ($1.25) for adults, Dfl. 1.50 (65¢) for children.

Madurodam

They call it "Holland in a Nutshell," and that's about as accurate a description as you could come up with for this fantastic display of a miniature "city of Madurodam" that sprawls over 28,000 square yards at Haringkade 175. Typical Dutch towns and famous landmarks are here in replica on a scale of 1:25—you'll leave feeling a bit like Gulliver coming from the Lilliputian world. The wonder of it all is that this is a working miniature city: trains run, ships move, planes taxi down runways, the barrel organ plays, and there's a town fair in progress. Children love it, but surprisingly, 75% of the 1.2 million annual visitors are adults!

Open April through October daily from 9:30 a.m. to 10:30 p.m. (50,000 tiny lamps light up when darkness falls). Admission is Dfl. 9 ($4) for adults, Dfl. 4.50 ($2) for children.

SHOPPING (WINDOW AND OTHERWISE)

The Hague is a renowned antiques center—ask the VVV about their guide to an "Antiques Walk" through the old inner city. Stop in at the exquisite **Floor Antick Shop** at Denneweg 33 (tel. 64-23-26), which has an especially lovely and wide selection of antiques both large and small enough to take home in your luggage.

Other interesting shopping areas include the **Oude Molstraat,** in the city center, where you'll find a concentration of authentic Dutch shops. Connected to the Central Station, **Babylon shopping complex** has two floors of over 60 shops, restaurants, and a luxury hotel. Several streets running off the **Groenmarkt** are pedestrian shopping streets.

ENTERTAINMENT

There's nearly always something going on culturally in The Hague, and nearby Scheveningen has a casino and nightspots. Check "Info" and local newspapers for concerts, theater, etc., as well as names and addresses of after-dark entertainment spots.

2. Scheveningen

First of all, there's its name—just *try* to pronounce it! It's so difficult to do that correctly, in fact, that during World War II the Dutch underground used it as a code name for identification—not even the Germans, whose language is similar—could get it right!

Until about 1813 Scheveningen was a sleepy little fishing village. It wasn't until its beaches began to attract holiday crowds that it began to evolve as an internationally known seaside resort. The magnificent Kurhaus Hotel draws Europe's crowned heads and celebrities from around the globe, and gamblers flock to the casino nightly. Businessmen and diplomats stay here, making the ten-minute drive into The Hague to conduct their affairs. Accommodations in all price ranges, restaurants with international cuisines, shops that run the gamut from exclusive to budget, and nighttime entertainment that never stops have changed the fishing village into one of the North Sea's most popular vacation havens, although the little harbor is still crowded with fishing boats and lined with restaurants that feature fish right off the boats. This is where the Dutch herring fleet is launched each year in May with a colorful Flag Day celebration and returns with the first herring catch amid just as much whoop-de-doo, sending the first batch off to the Queen and conducting a lively auction with leading restaurateurs for the rest.

Because so many of its attractions are now enclosed against the elements, Scheveningen has become a year-round resort.

WHERE TO STAY

Budget bed-and-breakfast hotels, family hotels with kitchenettes, modern high-rise hotels with moderate rates, and the incomparable Kurhaus that provides ultimate luxury, all make up the accommodation scene in Scheveningen.

Expensive

The fanciful **Kurhaus,** Gevers Deynootplein 30, 2586 CK Den Haag/Scheveningen (tel. 070/52-00-52), undisputed grande dame of the North Sea coast, is rooted in the humble beginnings of a four-room wooden pavilion in which bathtubs were filled daily with warm or cold sea water and guests were transported to the sea in enclosed "bathing coaches" so they would not shock the public by their daring! That was in 1818, and in the years since it has survived fires, several rebuildings, two World Wars, depression that left it bankrupt, plans to demolish it and build apartments (which set the Dutch up in arms to prevent such a fate), designation as a national monument, and in the late 1970s, a 110-million-guilder renovation. Its Kurzaal concert hall has seen performances by leading musical artists as disparate as violinist Yehudi Menuhin and the Rolling Stones, and its casino rivals any in the world. Its leather-bound guest register, which opens with the signature of 13-year-old Queen Wilhelmina, is filled with names of the world's great and illustrated by leading artists who embellished their signatures with original drawings.

Actually, all that just sort of hints at the rich history of this lovely place that, in the words of one writer, goes beyond fantasy.

As for the 250 luxury guest rooms and suites, many of those facing the sea have balconies, and all have private baths, hairdryers, radios, TVs, mini-bars, electronic safes, trouser presses, and direct-dial telephones. They are spacious, with décor as luxurious as their fittings. There are two restaurants (see below), and to accommodate the business people who make up a large percentage of its clientele, the hotel has installed 14 conference and banqueting rooms with a capacity of 450 people. Rates, which include breakfast, service, and **VAT,** also cover free admission to the casino and enclosed wave pool: Dfl. 250 ($109.75) to Dfl. 310 ($136) single, Dfl. 295 ($129.50) to Dfl. 375 ($164.50) double, depending on location (sea or town view) and season. Highly recommended—one of the great hotel experiences.

Moderately Priced

Flora Beach Hotel, Gevers Deynootweg 63, 2586 BJ Scheveningen (tel. 070/54-33-00). This bright, attractive hotel sits just one block from the sea and offers apartments as well as moderately priced accommodations in standard single and double rooms. Double rooms are spacious, and have mini-bars in addition to private baths, telephones, radios, and TVs; most have balconies, and many have sea views. The hotel's amenities include a good, moderately priced à la carte restaurant (see below), a sunny Coffee Corner, lounge and bar, sauna, and solarium. Rates, which include a full breakfast, service, and **VAT,** are Dfl. 95 ($41.75) for singles, Dfl. 200 ($87.75) for doubles, and children in the same room with their parents stay free. Apartment rates, exclusive of breakfast, are Dfl. 125 ($56) for one bedroom, Dfl. 195 ($87) for two, with a Dfl.-30 ($13.35) one-time cleaning cost for kitchen facilities.

Carlton Beach Hotel, Gevers Deynootweg 201, 2586 HZ Scheveningen (tel. 070/54-14-14). This large modern hotel, with restaurant and bar/lounge on the premises, has attractive guest rooms with private baths, mini-bars, radios, TVs, and telephones, at rates of Dfl. 147.50 ($64.75) single, Dfl. 195 ($85.50) double.

Inexpensive

Hotel Bali, Badhuisweg 1, 2587 CA Scheveningen (tel. 070/50-24-34). This comfortable budget hotel offers rooms without private facilities for Dfl. 40 ($17.50), and a few with bath at Dfl. 50 ($22) single; doubles are Dfl. 70 ($30.75) without private bath, Dfl. 95 ($41.75) with. It has a very good Indonesian restaurant.

The **Seinduin,** Seinpostduin 15, Scheveningen (tel. 070/55-19-71). All rooms, though budget priced, come with showers, and this location is very near the beach. Rates run Dfl. 70 ($30.75) to Dfl. 90 ($39.50).

The **City Hotel,** Renbaanstraat 1, Scheveningen (tel. 070/55-79-66). About half of the pleasant, comfortable rooms here have private baths, and rates are in the Dfl. 70 ($30.75) to Dfl. 90 ($39.50) range.

WHERE TO EAT

Save your most special Scheveningen meal for the beautiful **Kandinsky Restaurant** (tel. 52-00-52) in the Kurhaus Hotel (see above). Officially opened by Mme Claude Pompidou, widow of the former French president. The dining room overlooks the sea and its décor features signed lithographs by the abstract artist Wassily Kandinsky. Cuisine here is classic French, and a five-course dinner will run between Dfl. 90 ($39.50) and Dfl. 150 ($65.75), without wine, but thanks to new technical facilities you can order vintage wines by the glass, without the expense of a full bottle. Needless to say, reservations are required in this small, exquisite restaurant.

The **Kurhaus** also serves a lavish buffet daily at Dfl. 40 ($17.75) for lunch, Dfl. 43 ($18.75) for dinner, both spread in the gorgeous Kurzaal area, where dancing is added to dinner on Friday and Saturday nights at only slightly elevated prices.

For moderately priced meals in pleasant surroundings, there's the **Flora Beach Hotel,** Gevers Deynootweg 63, with a good à la carte selection and several set three-course menus and the Indonesian restaurant at the **Hotel Bali,** Badhuisweg 1.

Scheveningen is filled with restaurants of all price ranges, cuisines, and ambience. The square in front of the Kurhaus (the Gevers Deynootplein) holds a nest of international restaurants: **La Galleria** (tel. 55-50-06) serves good Italian fare, everything from pizza to full dinners, at moderate prices. The wharf is lined with good seafood eateries on a street called Dr. Lelykade—try **Ducdalf,** at no. 5 (tel. 55-76-92), or **De Lobsterpot,** at no. 23 (tel. 50-10-39), both with moderate prices. The Promenade and Strandweg have a variety of eating places; **De Bomschuit,** Strandweg 15 (tel. 55-02-80), is a good year-round seaside place for both the Neerlands Dis and Tourist Menus, features vegetarian dishes, stays open till midnight, and has live music on summer weekends.

TOURIST INFORMATION

The Scheveningen VVV office is at the corner of Scheveningseslag and Gevers Deyjnootweg (tel. 070/54-62-00).

THINGS TO SEE AND DO

In addition to the beach, Scheveningen has the Kurhaus casino (open 2 p.m. to 2 a.m. daily); the 400-yard Pier with four entertainment "islands," one of which holds a replica of Jules Verne's submarine *Nautilus* of *20,000 Leagues Under the Sea* fame; a glassed-in Wave Pool and sports hall with saunas and solariums; and the seashore Promenade and the Palace Promenade, both with scores of interesting year-round shops that are open seven days a week.

After dark, look for nightclubs in the Gevers Deynootplein in front of the Kurhaus and theater productions at the Circustheatre, which may include opera and ballet as well as musical theater.

Scheveningen's neighbor, Kijkduin, is a quieter, family-oriented beach resort, where the main attractions are the sea and dunes. There's a covered shopping complex with 50 interesting shops open seven days a week, year round.

NORTH SEA JAZZ FESTIVAL

Each year, usually in late June or early July, jazz greats from around the world gather in Scheveningen for three days of non-stop music. It's an exciting, energizing experience, and a delight to meet some of those "greats" mingling with audiences to hear some of *their* favorites.

3. Rotterdam

Rotterdam is only a half hour away from The Hague, an hour from Amsterdam, but it's centuries away from both in appearance and personality.

Although it, too, is of great age (it was founded in 1228), was a small fishing village much like Amsterdam's beginnings, and developed as a major port, again like Amsterdam, there is an all-important difference between modern-day Rotterdam and the other two—in only one tiny section will you see any trace of its ancient history. World War II took care of that. The city center was totally burned out by incendiary bombs in 1940, and in 1944 Nazi occupation forces sent demolition squads to finish off the entire harbor, including every one of its ancillary installations. When the war ended Rotterdam lay utterly devastated, scarcely one brick left standing on another.

With incredible efficiency and fortitude, Rotterdam's city fathers *within four days* had set in motion plans to rebuild their city, and they were determined that it should adhere to *modern* standards, with no attempt to raise ancient styles from the still-smouldering ashes. Although the task was to consume several years, the wonder is that it did not require decades.

Today Rotterdam stands as a bustling metropolis with the world's largest port, created when its several harbors were opened directly to the sea (some 20 miles away) by the dredging of a deep-water channel that will accommodate even the largest oil tankers, as well as cargo vessels representing over 400 international concerns. Its population numbers over one million, and more arrive annually. Indeed it's expanding at such a rate that many Dutch believe a few more decades will see it reach the outskirts of The Hague, swallowing up Delft on its way—what a megalopolis *that* would be!

WHERE TO EAT

As a city long accustomed to feeding the hearty appetites of seafarers and international business people, Rotterdam provides restaurants to suit them all, from a posh member of the distinguished Alliance Gastronomique Néerlandaise to humble brown cafés. My selections are listed in order of price, beginning with the top range.

'La Vilette, Westblaak 160 (tel. 010/414-86-92). Without doubt the most elegant restaurant in town, 'La Vilette is a plant- and flower-filled oasis in the city center, with restful soft rose-colored walls and starched white table linen. Cuisine is classic French (awarded one star by Michelin), service is both polished and friendly, and prices run Dfl. 100 ($43.75) and up. Open for lunch from noon to 2 p.m., for dinner from 6 to 10 p.m. Reservations recommended.

The Old Dutch, Rochussenstraat (tel. 36-02-42). A leading Rotterdam restaurant that is (as its name implies) traditional Dutch in décor and cuisine. Prices range from Dfl. 80 ($36) to Dfl. 130 ($58).

Le Coq d'Or, Van Vollenhovenstraat 25 (tel. 436-64-05 or 436-59-06). Close to the harbor by the river, this fine restaurant has a spacious secluded garden for outdoor dining in the summer months. Indoors it's a classic rustic décor with open hearth and exposed beams, and paintings by van Meegeren and other artists hung about. Cuisine is French, and specialties change with the seasons. Prices run Dfl. 80 ($35) to Dfl. 135 ($59.25), without wine (the wine cellar here is excellent). Open for lunch and dinner Monday through Saturday, and book ahead if you can.

Restaurant Engels, Stationsplein 45 (tel. 010/11-95-50 or 11-95-51). Located next to the Central Station in the huge Engels Groothandelsgebouw (Business Center), this marvelous restaurant is actually a complex of seven dining rooms, each dedicated to a different international cuisine: Viking (Scandinavian); Don Quijote (Spanish); Tokaj (Hungarian); Bistro Chez François (French); Beefeater and Pub Old John (British); New Yorker (American); and 't Oude Engels (Old Dutch). There's live music in Tokaj and Don Quijote. Three-course meals from the set ethnic menu run about Dfl. 25 ($11), and the Beefeater and Tokaj each have a dinner buffet at Dfl. 35 ($15.25). In addition there's an à la carte menu (full dinners, light meals, sandwiches, omelets, snacks, etc.), the Tourist Menu, and a Vegetarian Menu. In short, Engels will feed you well whether you're looking for nothing more than a snack or are ravenous. No need to reserve unless you have your heart set on a particular room.

De Pijp, Gaffelstraat 90 (tel. 436-62-96). Steaks and a number of international dishes are prepared right in the middle of this delightful restaurant that attracts a mixed bag of regulars—students, bankers, business executives, blue-collar workers—a real "Rotterdam" ambience. Prices range from Dfl. 25 ($11) to Dfl. 50 ($22).

For good meals that cost between Dfl. 15 ($6.50) and Dfl. 30 ($13.25), look for the following: **Bongers,** Meent 20 (tel. 12-86-68), where pancakes are a specialty; **Koditorei,** Coolsingel 105, in the Bijenkorf department store; and **La Boca,** at several locations around town.

TOURIST INFORMATION

The **VVV Office** is at Coolsingel 67, on the corner of Stadhuisplein, 3012 AR Rotterdam (tel. 010/413-60-00). Hours are 9 a.m. to 6 p.m. Monday through Saturday (to 9 p.m. on Friday), 10 a.m. to 6 p.m. on Sunday (closed on Sunday from October to March). Pick up a copy of their publication "Deze Maand" (This Month) for listings of current happenings. They can also furnish a city map that shows major attractions.

TOURS

A one-hour city sightseeing tour that includes a short **boat ride in the harbor** is organized by the VVV during the summer months. Consult the VVV for full information (tel. 413-60-00). A tour of the harbor by boat is practically obligatory for every visitor, and it certainly gives the most graphic insight as to how and why Rotterdam has developed into the world's leading port. For full details, contact **Spido Harbour Tours,** Willemsplein (tel. 413-54-00).

During the summer months full-day coach tours are available to the Kinderdijk windmills, the Delta Project, and Europoont. For information and booking, contact the VVV (tel. 413-60-00).

THINGS TO SEE AND DO

To see the only corner of Old Rotterdam that's left, take tram 6 or 9 to **Delfshaven,** what many years ago was the harbor of Delft. Of special interest to Americans is the old church in which the Pilgrims said their last prayers before boarding the *Speedwell* for the New World in 1620. They are remembered each Thanksgiving Day by special services. Look also for the two quayside warehouses that have been restored as the city of Rotterdam's official **historical museum,** de Dubbelde Palmboom (treat yourself to a stop in the atmospheric coffeeshop upstairs). Craftspeople are at work in the old **Grain Sack Carriers Guild House** (zakkendragershuisje), and many of their products are ideal gift items.

At **Boymans Van-Beuningen Museum,** Mathenesserlaan 20, art lovers will find a collection of works by Dutch and Flemish artists of the 16th and 17th centuries, among them masterpieces by Rubens, Hals, Rembrandt, and Steen. Other galleries hold international modern art, applied arts, ceramics, sculpture, prints, and drawings. Open Tuesday through Saturday from 10 a.m. to 5 p.m., on Sunday from 11 a.m. to 5 p.m., with a Dfl. 3.50 ($1.50) admission.

Located near the water (on the Leuvehaven in the center of the city), Rotterdam's **Maritime Museum** holds a marvelous collection of nautical lore and technical references. Marine archeology is a prime subject, and now under construction is the replica of a ship from some 2,000 years ago. Constantly changing exhibits keep this place lively, and a visit will give you new insight into the close relationship between the Dutch and the sea. In the museum harbor basin, some 20 vessels dating from 1850 to 1950 are moored, including the beautifully restored *Buffel,* an 1868 warship. Hours are 10 a.m. to 5 p.m. Tuesday through Saturday, 11 a.m. to 5 p.m. on Sunday. Admission on every day except Wednesday (when it's free) is Dfl. 3.50 ($1.50).

Belastingmuseum Professor Van Der Poel, Parklaan 14. You may well want to skip this one, but I thought you should know it's there—it's a *tax museum,* with collections having to do with taxation down through the centuries. Open from 9 a.m. to 5 p.m. Monday through Friday.

XVI

SOUTH HOLLAND'S HISTORIC TOWNS

The triangle formed by historic Gouda, Delft, and Leiden makes for leisurely sightseeing, with distances short enough to allow you to visit all three while rambling instead of rushing. The roads you travel will take you through a landscape straight out of a Dutch masters painting, with flat, green fields ribboned by canals, distant church spires piercing a wide sky—and, it must be said, from time to time a clump of industrial smokestacks that brings a 20th-century intrusion. For the most part, however, this is the Holland of your imagination, the Holland you came to see.

1. Gouda

Well, you know about its cheeses, but do you know that in Holland its name is pronounced "How-dah"? Try to come on a Thursday morning during June, July, and August—that's when the lively cheese market brings farmers in their everyday work clothes to town driving farm wagons painted with bright designs and piled high with round cheeses in their orange skins. It's an altogether different scene from the market in Alkmaar, and probably as old as Gouda itself, which received its charter in 1272.

WHERE TO EAT

Gouda's excellent traditional restaurant, **Mallemolen,** Oosthaven 72 (tel. 15-430), is located on what is known as Rembrandt's corner, and there's even an ancient windmill in the street. The setting sets the tone of the restaurant, which is Old Dutch, although the cuisine is chiefly French. For the set menu, you'll pay about Dfl. 70 ($30.75); à la carte will run a bit more. Open for dinner only, beginning at 5 p.m.; closed Thursday.

More moderately priced Dutch cuisine may be found at **Old Dutch,** Markt 25 (tel. 21-347), and **Centraal,** Markt 23 (tel. 12-576).

TOURIST INFORMATION

You'll find the **VVV office** at Markt 27 (tel. 01820/13-666).

THINGS TO SEE

If you arrive on **cheese market** day (Thursday from 9:30 a.m. to noon), walk to the back of the Town Hall, where you'll be given a sample of the famous cheese and treated to a video explaining how it's made. The gray stone **Town Hall** with its stepped gables and red shutters is reputed to be the oldest in Holland, and parts of its Gothic façade go back to 1449.

The majestic 15th-century **Sint Janskerk (Cathedral of St. John)** is Holland's largest, and it holds some of Europe's most beautiful stained-glass windows—64 in all, with a total of 2,412 panels. Some date back to the mid-1500s, and they represent a craft that in the 16th century had been elevated to an art. To see the contrast between that long-vanished art and the work being done today, take a look at the most recent window, no. 28a, commemorating the World War II years in Holland. Open weekdays from 10 a.m. to 5 p.m.

The 1665 mansion at Oosthaven 10 houses the **Stedelijk Museum Het Catharina Gasthuis** (tel. 13-800), Gouda's municipal museum. The jewel of its collections is a beautiful gold chalice that Countess Jacqueline of Bavaria presented to the Society of Archers in 1465. Its whereabouts were unknown for over a century before it was recovered and brought here. There's also a terracotta plaque whose Latin inscription proclaims that the great humanist Erasmus may have been born in Rotterdam, but he was *conceived* in Gouda. Take a look at the colorful guild relics and furniture from a long-ago age. Open Monday through Saturday from 10 a.m. to 5 p.m., on Sunday from noon to 5 p.m. Admission is Dfl. 3 ($1.25), and there's limited access for wheelchairs.

Besides cheese, Gouda is famous for its clay pipes made in the **Goedewaagen Pipe Factory.** Stop by to see their fascinating collection, including one style that has a pattern on the bowl that is invisible when the pipe is new and only appears as the pipe is smoked and darkens—it's called a "mystery pipe" because the designs vary and the buyer never knows what it will be until he smokes the pipe. Open from 10 a.m. to 5 p.m. on Thursday and Saturday in July and August, daily by appointment in other months.

For pottery as well as pipes, go by the **Adrie Moerings factory,** Peperstraat 76 (tel. 12-842), open on Thursday from 8 a.m. to 5 p.m. and every other weekday from noon to 5 p.m.

Then, there's the **Stedelijk Museum De Moriaan,** Westhaven 29 (tel. 13-800). During the 17th century this was the home of a Gouda merchant. Today it holds a large and interesting pipe collection, as well as many beautiful ceramics. Open from 10 a.m. to 5 p.m. Monday through Friday, 10 a.m. to 12:30 p.m. and 1:30 to 5 p.m. on Saturday, and noon to 5 p.m. on Sunday and holidays.

The 1727 **windmill,** known as "The Red Lion," is at Vest 65 and has been completely renovated and put in good working order. It's open from 9 a.m. to 5 p.m. Monday through Friday.

There are two interesting Gouda churches well worth a visit. **St. John's Church,** Achter de Kerk (tel. 12-684), is the longest church in Holland and has no fewer than 70 brightly colored 16th-century stained-glass windows depicting biblical and Dutch historical scenes. There's wheelchair access, and guided tours can be arranged by appointment. Hours are 9 a.m. to 5 p.m. Monday through Saturday, March through October; 10 a.m. to 4 p.m. Monday through Saturday in other months. **Gouwe Church,** Hoge Gouwe 39-41 (tel. 11-808), is an interesting three-naved, neo-Gothic cross-basilica that dates from 1904. Wheelchair access, free admission, with summer hours of 10 a.m. to noon on Thursday and 10 a.m. to 4 p.m. on Saturday.

IN THE AREA

There are several places of interest within easy driving distance of Gouda that can be worked into a day's excursion.

Kinderdijk

If you're into windmills, this is where you'll find the largest concentration in Holland today. Most are in full operation on summer Saturday afternoons, and there's a mill open to the public Monday through Saturday in summer. To see the 19 mills, their sails whirling away in the summer breeze, is to know that the Holland of your fantasies is real!

Oudewater

Only about eight miles from Gouda is a charming little village that looks anything but sinister. Yet back in the 1500s this was the scene of some of Europe's most horrifying witch trials. The situation got so bad that the town's reputation of having the most honest merchants with the most accurate scales on the continent was in danger of being ruined forever. To remedy that bad press, the town fathers devised a system of judging accused witches by having them stand on scales clad in nothing but a paper costume and paper broom. Present for this "trial" were the mayor, the alderman, the weighmaster, and the local midwife. When the weighmaster had finished juggling his weights and balancing the scales, he then could honestly proclaim that the accused witch weighed far too much to fly through the air supported only by a broomstick, thus could not possibly be a witch, and a certificate was issued stating just that. You can believe that Europe's accused witches flocked here in droves! Now, if you have some doubt about anyone in your party (or yourself!), between May and September you can step on the Oudewater Weigh House scales and—provided you're not too skinny—walk away with your very own certificate.

As you walk through the quaint streets of this village, take a look at the storks' nests on the Town Hall roof—the big birds have been nesting here for over three centuries.

Schoonhoven

This quaint little town is where they make much of the silver filigree jewelry and souvenirs you see around the country. The small workshops welcome visitors, and it's fascinating to see the skill required to produce the delicate work. The place to see it demonstrated is the **Edelambachtshis,** on the main canal. When you're walking past the lovely old Town Hall (1452), give a thought to the poor "witch" who never made it to those scales in Oudewater and was burned to death at the spot marked now by a circle of stones.

The **Nederlands Goud, Zilver en Klokkenmuseum,** Kazerneplein 4, holds a wonderful collection of old clocks, as well as gold and silver objects of great beauty. Open from noon to 5 p.m. Tuesday through Sunday; closed Monday.

2. Delft

Delft is sheer delight! Perhaps the prettiest little town in all of Holland, it presents without pretentiousness streets lined with houses whose Renaissance and Gothic façades reflect age-old beauty and tree-bordered canals which enhance the sense of tranquility that pervades the very air. Around every corner and down every street you'll walk into a scene that might have been composed solely for the canvas of a great artist. Indeed, it's easy to understand why Vermeer chose to spend most of his life surrounded by Delft's soft beauty.

Royalty lies buried in Delft—Willem the Silent met his death by assassination in the Prinsenhof and now rests in a magnificent tomb in the Nieuw Kerk. Every member of the House of Orange-Nassau since King Willem I has been brought to Delft for burial, and it is the final resting place of someone named as Karl Naundorf, but who is suspected of being Louis XVII, Dauphin of France. Two of Holland's greatest naval figures, Admirals Tromp and Heyn, are entombed in the Oude Kerk. A good part of Holland's history, it would seem, is preserved in the tombs of Delft.

Of course, to many tourists Delft means just one thing—the distinctive blue-and-white earthenware still produced by the tedious methods of old and every piece still painted by hand.

WHERE TO EAT

For classic French cuisine in a setting of soft pinks and candlelight, book at **Le Chevalier,** Oude Delft 125 (tel. 12-46-21). It's on Delft's oldest canal, right in the center of town. Expect to pay between Dfl. 90 ($39.50) and Dfl. 125 ($54.75), without wine.

Moderately priced Dutch dishes are served at **De Dis,** Beestenmarkt 36 (tel. 13-17-82); food comes in the medieval manner at **Stadsherberg De Mol,** Molslaan 48a (tel. 12-13-43), along with live music; and the Tourist Menu is featured at **Het Wapen van Delft,** Markt 34 (tel. 12-31-68).

TOURIST INFORMATION

You'll find the VVV office at Markt 85 (tel. 015/12-61-00).

THINGS TO SEE AND DO

The first thing to do is park the car and walk! Although the town's layout allows easy driving, it's by strolling its streets that you absorb its special ambience. Walking can be supplemented, of course, by a leisurely tour of its canals via the numerous **water taxis** that ply their waters during summer months.

Nieuw Kerk, at the market square, is a 14th-century splendor well worth a visit on its own, but you won't want to miss the magnificent tomb of Willem the Silent, surrounded by 22 columns and embellished with figures representing Liberty, Justice, Valor, and Religion. The royal dead of the House of Orange-Nassau lie in a crypt beneath the remains of the founder of their line.

On the banks of Delft's oldest canal, the **Prinsenhof,** at Oude Delft 185 (entrance at St. Agathaplein 1), dates from the late 1400s and was originally a convent. This is where Willem the Silent elected to stay when in Delft, and where an assassin's bullets ended his life in 1584 (you can still see the bullet holes near the bottom of a staircase). Its restoration has re-created the interior Willem would have known, and within its walls a museum preserves the record of Dutch struggles to throw off the yoke of Spanish occupation between 1568 and 1648. There are impressive tapestries and paintings, and every autumn the Delft Antiques Fair held here attracts dealers from all over the world. Hours are 10 a.m. to 5 p.m. Tuesday through Saturday, from 1 to 5 p.m. on Sunday, and on Monday from 1 to 5 p.m. in June, July, and August. Admission is Dfl. 3.50 ($1.55).

At what is now the **Museum Paul Tetar Van Elven,** Koornmarkt 67, the 19th-century artist Van Elven lived and worked, and his furnishings are just as he left them. The 17th-century-style studio stands ready for the artist to enter and pick up his brushes. Open from 11 a.m. to 5 p.m. Tuesday through Saturday, summer months only. Admission is Dfl. 2 (85¢).

If you came to Delft to see its famous earthenware, you'll find the most fascinating collection in the 19th-century mansion at Oude Delft 199, now the **Museum Huis Lambert Van Meerten.** Hours are 10 a.m. to 5 p.m. Tuesday through Saturday, from 1 to 5 p.m. on Sunday, with an admission of Dfl. 3.50 ($1.50).

The Delft Blue you came to town to find is made by a traditional painstaking method at **De Porceleyne Fles,** Rotterdamseweg 196, where you can watch the hand-painting of each item and see an audio-slide show that explains the entire process. Delft potters have been at it since they met the competition of Chinese porcelain imported by the East India Company. And if you thought the trademark blue-and-white colors were the only Delft, here is where you will see exquisite multicolored patterns that also carry the name proudly. Your purchases can be packed carefully and shipped home directly from this factory.

3. Leiden

A visit to Leiden is in the nature of a pilgrimage (you should pardon the pun) for Americans, for it was here that the Pilgrim Fathers found refuge during the long years they waited to sail to a fresh beginning in the New World. Their sojourn was, however, but one small incident in Leiden's long history.

The high point in that history is surely the heroism with which it met a five-month siege by the Spanish in 1574. Thousands of its residents perished, and the food situation became so intolerable that the mayor offered his own body to be used as nourishment for the starving population—talk about heroism! His offer was not accepted, but his memory is honored by a town park in which his statue stands.

The Dutch fleet finally rescued Leiden on October 3 after a dramatic advance over fields flooded as dikes were broken to open up a watery route to the beleaguered citizens. From that terrible siege came one of Holland's most beloved national dishes, hutspot ("hot pot"), so named for the bubbling kettle of stew left behind by fleeing Spaniards—a kettle now ensconced in the Lakenhal Museum (see below). If you should be in Leiden on any October 3, you'll see that anniversary observed as haren en witte brood (herring and loaves of white bread) are distributed just as they were in 1574.

Willem the Silent, in recognition of Leiden's courage, rewarded the city with a choice between freedom from taxation and the founding of a university in the town. Perhaps to the consternation of present-day residents, but with remarkable long-range vision, those 16th-century residents chose the university. It was Holland's first, and is a leader today in the fields of medicine and law.

Leiden is also known in artistic circles as the birthplace of Rembrandt, Jan Steen, and Lucas van Leyden.

WHERE TO EAT

The traditional décor and cuisine at **Rotisserie Oudt Leyden,** Steenstraat 51 (tel. 13-31-44), will sustain Leiden's historical atmosphere. Near the Lakenhal, its prices are high for the area—around Dfl. 60 ($26.25) to Dfl. 90 ($39.50)—but you'll count it money well spent.

Traditional Neerlands Dis dishes at moderate prices are featured at **De Doelen,** Rapenburg 2 (tel. 12-05-27), and you'll find the inexpensive Tourist Menu at both the **Restaurant Bernsen,** Breestraat 157 (tel. 12-45-63), and the Indonesian restaurant **Surakarta,** Steenstraat 51 (tel. 12-35-24).

TOURIST INFORMATION

The **VVV office** is at Stationsplein 210 (tel. 071/14-68-46). Ask about their guided tours during the summer months, as well as their self-guided walking-tour brochure.

THINGS TO SEE AND DO

To touch base with the courageous spirit of those humble Pilgrim Fathers, stop by the tiny **Documentatie Centrum,** Boisotkade 2, near the Vliet River, and walk past the house on Herensteeg (marked by a plaque) where William Brewster's Pilgrim Press published the religious views that so angered the Church of England.

Plaques at **Sint Pieterskerk** also remember the Pilgrim Fathers, especially the Rev. Jon Robinson, who was forced to stay behind because of illness and is buried in this church (an almshouse, the Jean Pesijnhofje, now occupies the house in which he died). Special Thanksgiving Day services are held each year in honor of the little band of refugees who worshipped here. There is also an exhibit of Pilgrim documents in the Lakenhal (see below).

The **University of Leiden** is located near the Rapenburg Canal, and the small street on which Rembrandt was born is the Weddesteeg, on the north side of Noordeinde.

Stedelijk Museum De Lakenhal, at Oude Singel 28, a 17th-century guild hall, is Leiden's municipal museum. Its fine collections of paintings by Dutch artists of the 16th and 17th centuries include works by Lucas van Leyden, Rembrandt, Steen, and Dou. The cloth merchants guild (original occupants of the building) is represented in historical exhibits, and there are maps and other documents relating to this town of the Pilgrim Fathers.

Among the fascinating scientific exhibits housed in the **Museum Boerhaave (National Science Museum),** at Lange Sint Agnietenstraat 10 (tel. 21-42-29), are thermometers made by Farenheit, globes that once belonged to the cartographer Blaeu, and microscopes made by Van Leeuwenhoek. Astronomy, chemistry, biology, and other scientific subjects are also represented. The museum will be closed during most of 1989, but will reopen in 1990. Telephone for hours.

The small **Molenmuseum de Valk,** is located in a monumental windmill at Tweede Binnenvestgracht 1, with exhibits dedicated to various types of windmills. Open Tuesday through Saturday from 10 a.m. to 5 p.m., on Sunday from 1 to 5 p.m. Admission is Dfl. 2.50 ($1).

HOLLAND'S NORTHERN PROVINCES

1. FRIESLAND
2. GRONINGEN
3. DRENTHE

Home to Holland's earliest settlers, Holland's northern provinces compress an astounding geographic and historical encyclopedia into an amazingly compact area. Friesland, so ancient as to be almost another world, complete with customs and a language all its own, is a landscape of charming little villages and 11 cities surrounded by miles of flat farmlands. It is dotted by huge earthen mounds (terps) that were the forerunners of Holland's dikes, has some 30 lakes scattered about, and two large islands off its coast. From its farms have come the world-renowned Frisian cattle and the lovely black Frisian horses which so respond to music that they are favorites with circuses around the globe.

Groningen's capital city is the north's most important commercial and industrial center and university city, in striking contrast to the medieval monastery in the southeastern corner of the province.

Drenthe, as old as Friesland, hides the 20th-century intrusion of oil wells behind stands of trees to lessen their impact on its natural scenic beauty of lakes and forests and moors, with here and there a picturesque village.

1. Friesland

One of the first things you will notice as you drive along Frisian roads is road signs in two languages, one of which you have not seen elsewhere. Nor will you, for this is the ancient Frisian language that broke off from the Germanic tongue long before the Dutch language followed suit. That it is spoken daily by some 70% of the Frisian population today is only one of the ways in which these fiercely independent people demonstrate their deep sense of place—they also have their own flag, their own coat-of-arms, and their own national anthem! Which is not to say they're not Dutch: they are, but *first* they are Frisian.

That independent spirit has stood the United States in good stead, for it was here, in the capital city of Leeuwarden, that documents were signed making Holland the first nation officially to recognize the new nation.

HOW TO SEE FRIESLAND

You can tour the Friesland province by car, bicycle, boat, and during the winter on skates. Its 11 cities are arranged in such a way that you can make the circuit with ease, stopping overnight in good, moderately priced hotels or selecting as a home base the beautiful château that is now a luxury inn in centrally located Beetsterzwaag. You can, of course, plot your own way from a map, but a much better idea is to go directly to the VVV office in Leeuwarden and pick up one of their carefully routed tour guides. They can even arrange do-it-yourself auto or bicycle tours with prebooked accommodations each night.

WHERE TO STAY

Move each night or settle down in a home base? The choice is yours—distances in this province are so short that you'll never be far from that home base, yet there are small hotels (although they're a bit sparse) all along your way.

A Luxury Château

Hotel Lauswolt, Van Harinxmaweg 10, 9244 CJ Beetsterzwaag (tel. 05126/12-45). About 28 miles from Leeuwarden, the typical Frisian village of Beetsterzwaag is set in an enormous woodland, on the edge of which you'll find this gracious three-story château surrounded by green lawns and huge shade trees. There's a nine-hole golf course on the grounds, tennis courts, and any number of beautiful forest walks. The restaurant enjoys a top reputation throughout this part of Holland and is a member of the prestigious Alliance Gastronomique Néerlandaise. The décor throughout the château, in both public rooms and guest rooms, is one of quiet elegance, and all 32 spacious guest rooms are luxuriously furnished, with private baths as well as the usual amenities. Rates are Dfl. 95 ($41.75) single, Dfl. 133 ($58.25) double, with special weekday and weekend packages available. Highly recommended.

In Leeuwarden

Oranje Hotel, Stationsweg 4, 8901 BL Leeuwarden (tel. 058/12-62-41). You'd never suspect that this beautiful hotel is actually over a century old, so successful has its modernization been. The nice thing is that the management failed to modernize its old-fashioned hospitality liberally laced with genuine friendliness. The staff goes out of its way to make you feel at home, and you'll find yourself among lots of local residents in the bright, moderately priced restaurant and cozy bar. There's also a formal gourmet restaurant (see below) where I had perhaps my best meal in Holland. Guest rooms are luxuriously done up, with a table-and-armchairs grouping in one corner, private baths, telephones, radios, and TVs. Its location is convenient to the railway station, yet within an easy walk of everything you'll want to see in Leeuwarden. Rates, which include breakfast, service, and VAT, are Dfl. 140 ($61.50) to Dfl. 180 ($79) single, Dfl. 180 ($79) to Dfl. 220 ($96.50) double. Recommended.

Hotel De Pauw, Stationsweg 10, 8911 AH Leeuwarden (tel. 058/12-36-51). This old-fashioned budget hotel, with its Old Dutch lobby furnishings and wood-paneled bar, has rooms with and without private shower (all toilets are down the hall). Guest rooms are all quite adequate, but of varying standards. There's a good restaurant on the premises that serves lunch and dinner at moderate prices. Rates for rooms with shower run Dfl. 40 ($17.50) to Dfl. 55 ($24) single, and Dfl. 78 ($34.25) to Dfl. 98 ($43) double.

In Drachten

Cresthotel Drachten, Zonnedauw 1, 9202 PE Drachten (tel. 05120/2-07-05). This modern motel sits at the junction of two major motorways (the A-1 and the N-7), and has attractive, well-furnished guest rooms, a restaurant, coffeeshop, and bar. Rates are Dfl. 145 ($63.50) single, Dfl. 150 ($65.75) to Dfl. 185 ($81.25) double.

In Harlingen

Hotel Anna Casparii, Noorderhaven 67-71, 8861 AL Harlingen (tel. 05178/120-65). This charming little canal-house hotel has just 11 rooms with private bath, all comfortable and newly decorated, and all with mini-bars. Rates are Dfl. 75 ($33) single, Dfl. 105 ($46) double.

In Bolsward

Hotel De Wijnberg, Marktplein 5, 8701 KG Bolsward (tel. 051572/2-20). Located on the town square, this is a modern hotel with comfortable double rooms and private baths at Dfl. 75 ($33) and up.

Bed and Breakfast

The VVV, Stationsplein 1, Leeuwarden (tel. 058/13-22-24), can furnish names of town and country homes that welcome guests.

WHERE TO EAT

Leeuwarden has several very good restaurants, and you'll find outdoor cafés and small local eateries serving good food at low prices in almost every village.

In Leeuwarden

Restaurant L'Orangerie, Stationsweg 4 (tel. 12-62-41). This is the gourmet restaurant of the Oranje Hotel, surprisingly sophisticated in both ambience and service. The menu is mostly French, and dishes are beautifully prepared with fresh, fresh ingredients. There's an à la carte menu with main courses ranging from Dfl. 33 ($14.50) to Dfl. 45 ($19.75), and a three-course set menu at Dfl. 45 ($19.75) without wine, a four-course menu at Dfl. 55 ($24), as well as five courses at Dfl. 83 ($36.50). As I said above in the hotel description, the dinner I had here ranked with the best I experienced in Holland. Reservations required.

The **Oranje Tavern,** Stationsweg 4 (tel. 12-62-41). This is the pleasant informal restaurant of the Oranje Hotel, with moderate prices and typical Dutch dishes available, as well as a wide range of other selections, sandwiches, and salads.

't Pannekoekschip, Willemkade 22 (tel. 12-09-03). Two brothers, who told me that this boat moored alongside the canal was "two generations" old, have left its interior's nautical décor intact and lined its sides with wide wooden booths. Umpteen varieties of pancakes are served, and you can leave stuffed for as little as Dfl. 7.50 ($3.25) or go all out for Dfl. 20 ($8.75).

Café Wouters, Sophialaan 5 (tel. 13-36-68). This pleasant café near the railway station has a glassed-in terrace room and a rustic interior with a long bar. Light meals and pastries are moderately priced.

You might also wander along the Nieuwestad canal, where there are several interesting choices.

In Beetsterzwaag

Hotel Lauswolt, van Harinxmaweg 10 (tel. 05126/12-45). Dine by candlelight in the gracious paneled dining room overlooking the garden in this lovely château. The kitchen prides itself on the freshness of ingredients that go into the classic French dishes that star on the menu, and there's an exceptionally good wine cellar.

Expect to pay Dfl. 100 ($43.75) to Dfl. 150 ($65.75) without wine, and be sure to reserve ahead.

In Harlingen

Hotel Anna Casparii, Noorderhaven 67-71 (tel. 05178/120-65). Seafood fresh from the boats that come into this fishing village is served here at very modest prices.

TOURIST INFORMATION

The **VVV office** for both the city of Leeuwarden and the province of Friesland is next door to the railway station at Stationsplein 1, Leeuwarden (tel. 058/13-22-24), with hours of 9 a.m. to 6 p.m. Monday through Friday, from 9 a.m. to 2 p.m. Saturday. The staff is exceptionally helpful, and they can provide directions for several interesting tours of Friesland, among them the *terpen* tour to see the earthen mounds built to escape flood waters, the *wouden* tour through Friesland's beautiful woodlands, the lakes tour, and the "Forefathers Heritage Route."

THINGS TO SEE AND DO

Before setting off to explore the rest of Friesland, take time to look around its capital city. Like most Dutch cities, Leeuwarden is best seen afoot. The VVV has an excellent walking-tour guide, "A Walk Through the Town of Leeuwarden," that will take you to major points of interest.

In Leeuwarden

At **Provincial House,** Tweebaksmarkt 52, there's a bit of New York State here in the form of a bronze plaque that the DeWitt Historical Society of Tompkins County in Ithaca presented to the people of Leeuwarden in 1909 in gratitude for their having been the first to vote for Holland's recognition of the infant United States in 1782. There's also a much earlier letter, written by John Adams in 1783, expressing that same gratitude. Another document of interest to Americans is that relating to one Petrus Stuiffsandt, the same Peter Stuyvesant who played such an important part in America's beginnings and who was born in Scherpenzeel, a Friesland town.

Your journey through the province will be much more meaningful after you've visited the fine **Fries Museum,** at Turfmarkt 24. Here are artifacts of pre-history dating back to the Ice Age that will spur your imagination, and treasures from medieval and Renaissance times, and colorful painted furniture from Hindeloopen, and Rembrandt's painting of his Frisian wife, Saskia (they were married in the village of St. Anna Parochie in 1634), and a replica of a tobacco shop, and costumes, and . . . well a multitude of items that will give you a better understanding of these hardy, resourceful people and their past. Hours are 10 a.m. to 5 p.m. Tuesday through Saturday, from 1 to 5 p.m. on Sunday.

The **Frisian Resistance Museum,** Zuiderplein 9-13 (tel. 058/13-33-35), documents the heroism of the Frisian people during Nazi occupation in World War II with photos, personal mementos, and a taped radio message that actually went out over Radio Oranje played as you view a very moving diorama depicting a Frisian farmer listening intently. There's detailed information available in English to explain the exhibits and tell the story of the Dutch resistance movement. It's a certainty that you will look at the Frisian farmer in his fields through different eyes after a visit to this museum. Hours are 10 a.m. to 5 p.m. Tuesday through Saturday, from 1 to 5 p.m. on Sunday, and there's a small charge for admission.

In the beautiful building at Grote Kerkstraat 9-15, the **Het Princessehof Museum** holds a large collection of porcelain and ceramics, some from China, others made in Holland. Open from 10 a.m. to 5 p.m. Monday through Saturday, from 2 to 5 p.m. on Sunday.

In Franeker

In this enchanting little town 10½ miles west of Leeuwarden, stop to visit the **Planetarium of Eise Eisinga,** Eise Eisingastraat 3. This simple house was the home of a woolcomber who in the late 1700s spent seven years building a replica of the planetary system in his evening leisure hours. It is amazingly accurate even today, and the story of how he came to build it is an interesting one. Guides are on hand to explain the works, which are in an attic room. Hours are 9 a.m. to 12:30 p.m. and 1:30 to 5 p.m. Monday through Saturday, May through September; closed Monday other months.

In Harlingen

This picture-postcard-pretty little harbor town sits by the Wadden Sea that separates the mainland from the offshore sandbar islands of Terschelling and Vlieland, whose wide strands draw vacationers every summer and whose bird sanctuaries attract a host of feathered visitors. Harlingen itself is a maze of tiny canals filled with fishing boats and lined with gabled canal houses. Take time to go by the **Hannemahuis Museum,** Voorstraat 56 (open from 2 to 5 p.m. Tuesday through Saturday, April to July; from 10 a.m. July through mid-August, when it also opens Monday afternoon from 2 to 5 p.m.), to see its seafaring exhibits, and stop in to see the tile-painting workshop **Harlinger Tegelfabriek** at Voorstraat 75.

If you have the time and can't resist the temptation, you can take a 1½-hour ferry ride out to **Terschelling or Vlieland** islands for about Dfl. 35 ($15.25) plus another Dfl. 18 ($8) for your car (round-trip fares). A hovercraft crossing (subject to the weather) costs an additional Dfl. 15 ($6.50).

In Makkum

There have been tile makers and ceramics craftsmen in Makkum since the 1500s, and the craft is carried on today at the **Tichelaar** workshop, where you are taken through the entire process and see the exquisite designs being painted by hand. This interesting firm has been in operation for over 300 years, and in 1960 the "royal" designation was conferred on their work. This is the only Dutch ornamental earthenware made from Dutch clay, and the factory has used the same procedures without a break since the 17th century. The salesroom is a bonanza for buying anything from a simple tile to a larger piece with an elaborate design as a lasting souvenir of your visit.

In the old **Weigh House** there's a fascinating museum of five rooms filled with examples of Makkum earthenware from the 17th through the 19th centuries. The building itself is worth the stop.

In Hindeloopen

In this tiny little town on the shores of the Ijsselmeer, talented craftspeople have for centuries adorned their homes, their furniture, their built-in cupboard beds, and even their wooden coathangers with the vivid colors and intricately entwined vines and flowers that we associate with the Pennsylvania Dutch in America. It is thought that originally the designs were brought from Scandinavia by Hindeloopen sailors who sailed the North Sea in the days when the Ijsselmeer was the Zuiderzee. Wherever it originated, this colorful decoration has reached its highest development in this little village, and a good place to view it is at **Roosje's,** Nieuwstad 19 (tel. 05142/12-51 or 14-11). Every wooden surface in the house, which dates from 1650, is covered with delightful designs.

The Aldfaers Erf Route

Not one town, but an entire small area of restored buildings grouped into three country villages, the Aldfaers Erf (Forefathers' Heritage) leads you to **Exmorra,** with its 19th-century grocer's and schoolhouse; to **Allingawier,** where a bakery serves Frisian pastries and snacks and a slide presentation is given in an old church; and to **Piaam,** with its bird museum. The buildings are open every day from 9 a.m. to 6 p.m. during the summer months.

2. Groningen

The province of Groningen is one of Holland's most commercial and industrial, and at the same time one of its most historic. The busy capital city is an important port, with ocean-going vessels sailing up the 15-mile-long Eems Canal from Delfzijl, the province's largest port. Its long history, stretching back beyond the 12th century, is reflected in the architecture of many buildings in the capital city, in numerous *terp* (mound) villages, in a 15th-century castle, in a 14th-century monastery, and in any number of picturesque villages that almost beg for the camera. Among historical figures it can claim as its own is Abel Tasman, one of the greatest of Dutch navigators, who sailed the South Seas and discovered New Zealand, the Tonga Island, Fiji Islands, and Tasmania—he was born in 1603 in the town of Lutjegast.

WHERE TO STAY

Most visitors base themselves in the city of Groningen, but there are one or two optional choices worthy of note.

In Groningen

Altea Hotel Groningen, Expositielaan 7, 9727 AK Groningen (tel. 050/25-84-00), is a modern motel convenient to downtown, the city park, and the university. There's a good restaurant featuring French and Dutch cuisine, a cocktail bar, indoor swimming pool, solarium, and sauna. Among the extras in its well-appointed guest rooms, all with private bath, are satellite TVs, videos, mini-bars, and trouser presses. Rates start at Dfl. 125 ($54.75).

De Doelen, Grote Markt 36, 9711 VL Groningen (tel. 050/12-70-41). This is about as centrally located as you can get. No restaurant, but nice guest rooms at moderate rates beginning at Dfl. 90 ($39.50).

In Delfzijl

Du Bastion, Waterstraat 78, 9934AX Delfzijl (tel. 05960/1-87-71). This small hotel has comfortable rooms at moderate rates that range from Dfl. 90 ($39.50) to about Dfl. 150 ($65.75). There's a good moderately priced restaurant.

In Haren

Postiljon Hotel, Emmalaan 33, 9752KS Haren (tel. 050/34-70-41). Rates are in the moderate range of Dfl. 50 ($22) to Dfl. 130 ($57) in this comfortable motor hotel. There are three restaurants.

WHERE TO EAT

In Groningen, hotel restaurants offer the best top-level dining. There are, however, small local restaurants throughout the province that serve very good food at moderate prices.

In Groningen

Altea Restaurant, in the Altea Hotel Groningen, Expositielaan 7 (tel. 25-84-00). French and Dutch cuisine at moderate-to-expensive prices are featured in this modern motor hotel.

You'll find moderately priced Neerlands Dis (traditional Dutch) dishes at both **Naberhof,** Naberpassage 8 (tel. 13-55-22), and **Restaria Zuid,** Verlengde Heerweg

81 (tel. 26-25-82); and the Tourist Menu at **Eet-café De Stadlander,** Poelestraat 35 (tel. 12-71-91).

In Delfzijl

The Tourist Menu is served in the restaurant of the **Hotel Du Bastion,** Waterstraat 74-78 (tel. 1-87-71), as well as traditional Dutch cuisine.

In Haren

The restaurant of the **Postiljon Hotel,** Emmalaan 33 (tel. 34-70-41), serves the inexpensive Tourist Menu, as well as other moderately priced meals.

In Stadskanaal

If you plan to visit the monastery near the village of Ter Apel, stop for meals in this nearest town of any size, where the **Hotel-Restaurant Dopper,** Hoofdstraat 33 (tel. 1-20-08), serves a traditional Neerlands Dis menu, as well as an inexpensive menu.

TOURIST INFORMATION

The **VVV office** is in Groningen, at Naberpassage 3 (tel. 050/13-97-00).

THINGS TO SEE AND DO

You'll want to spend some time in the city of Groningen, with its *two* beautifully designed **central squares,** 15th-century **St. Martinkerk** (St. Martin is Groningen's patron saint and deserves a passing tip of the hat from travelers, since he is also the patron saint of tourists!), and the Renaissance **Goudkantoor** (gold office) near the Town Hall.

Other Sights in Groningen

The **Groninger Museum Voor Stad En Lande,** Praediniussingel 59 (open Tuesday through Saturday from 10 a.m. to 5 p.m. and on Sunday from 1 to 5 p.m.), is devoted to antiquities relating to the history of the city and the province, with a collection of Eastern ceramics and paintings, and prints, and sculpture from the 16th century to present-day modern art.

The interesting **Nordelijk Scheepvaart en Tabacologisch Museum,** Brugstraat 24-26, traces the history of shipping in the northern provinces and the history of Holland's long involvement with the tobacco trade. Hours are 10 a.m. to 5 p.m. Tuesday through Saturday, from 1 to 5 p.m. on Sunday.

More than 250 years of topiary gardening have produced the breathtaking **Prinsenhof Gardens** in the Prinsenhof, which has been the seat of the bishops of Groningen since 1568.

In Uithuizen

Some 20 miles north of Groningen, the **Castle of Menkemaborg,** a double-moated fortified manor house, dates from the 14th century, with 17th- and 18th-century wings. It's beautifully furnished in the style of its past and is noted for its 18th-century formal gardens. There's a restaurant in the old stables. Open Tuesday through Saturday from 10 a.m. to 5 p.m., on Sunday from 1 to 5 p.m. in summer; shorter hours in winter.

In Haren

Exotic flowers and plants of all climates, from alpine to tropical, are collected in the **Botanical Garden and Tropical Paradise,** located in Haren, but an adjunct to Groningen University.

In Leek

The **Rijtuigmuseum (National Carriage Museum)** here has a wonderful collection of antique horse-drawn carriages, sleighs, and the uniforms and accessories of their drivers. Open daily from 9 a.m. to 5 p.m. (on Sunday from 1 to 5 p.m.), Easter through September.

A Terp Village

Warffum is typical of the "mound villages" built above flood level in past centuries, and **Het Hogeland (Highland Museum)** holds fascinating relics from the mounds, as well as medieval costumes and other artifacts. Open daily during the summer months.

A Medieval Monastery

Hidden away in a peaceful forest of beech trees near the little village of **Ter Apel** (not far from Stadskanaal) is a tranquil monastery whose cloister dates from the 1300s. Plan time for walking into the surrounding woods.

Picturesque Villages

Your camera will work overtime in Vlagtwedde, Onstwedde, Sellingen, and Wallinghuizen.

Industrial Towns

The port city of **Delfzijl** is also a shipbuilding city; **Slochteren** is the source of the world's largest-known natural-gas deposit (discovered in 1959) and supplies over one-third of Holland's power and heat requirements, and also has some very attractive old buildings; **Heiligerlee** is an agricultural industry center, and has as well famous bell factories that produce bells from the smallest dinner-bell size right up to massive carillons.

---

3. Drenthe

Mooi Drenthe, the Dutch call it—"beautiful Drenthe." And with good reason, for this is a land of deep forests, broad moors and peat bogs, small lakes, and picturesque villages. Its beauty and the traditional life of its peasant farmers and peatcutters drew Vincent van Gogh for a three-month sojourn when he first began painting, and his moody, moving canvases *The Potato Eaters* and *Weavers* came out of those short months.

Drenthe is also a land of prehistoric mysteries in the form of *hunebedden* ("giants' beds"), huge boulders that must have served as burial mounds. It is believed that these gigantic smooth stones were transported here from Scandinavia by Ice Age glaciers, and legend has it that they were the home of a race of giants. Be that as it may, Holland's earliest inhabitants obviously used them to mark tombs since they have yielded stone axes, wooden vessels, and other relics of an era shrouded in the mists of centuries. As if all that weren't enough treasure, Drenthe has also been the recipient—fortunate or unfortunate, depending on your point of view—of large deposits of oil, providing roughly one-third of the country's total production from wells that are carefully landscaped to prevent their marring the lovely countryside.

Easily toured from an Amsterdam, Leeuwarden, or Groningen base, Drenthe provides scanty accommodations. Small local restaurants are the best source of meals, with reference to the VVV Tourist Menu and Neersland Dis booklets.

TOURIST INFORMATION

The **VVV office** may be found in Drenthe's capital city of Assen, at Brink 42 (tel. 05920/1-43-24).

THINGS TO SEE AND DO

There are more than 50 hunebedden in the province, found primarily around Borger, Rolde, Anlo, Emmen, Sleen, Vries, and Havelte. In Havelte, residents have had to restore their treasured "giants' beds" to where they lay for centuries, since during World War II Nazi occupying troops dislodged the huge boulders to clear an airstrip and dumped them all into a large hole. Had it not been for a scale model of their original locations made by a local archeologist, they might have lain forever in that ignominious grave.

In Assen

Situated in the former Provinciehuis (Provincial Hall), the fascinating **Provinciaal Museum van Drenthe,** Brink 5, exhibits the Stone Age artifacts that have come from Drenthe's hunebedden, as well as weapons, pottery, and jewelry of Celtic and Merovingian origin. There are also Roman sarcophagi and other well-preserved items that have turned up in the peat bogs of Drenthe. These silent relics of the past are captivating to anyone with the tiniest interest in history. Hours are 9:30 a.m. to 5 p.m. Tuesday through Friday, from 1 to 5 p.m. on Saturday and Sunday.

In Barger-Compascuum

Set squarely in the peat moors southeast of Emmen, the open-air museum called **'t Aole Compas,** at Berkenrode 4, is actually a reconstructed peatcutters' village, where you can see demonstrations of peatcutting, as well as butter churning, weaving, and clog making. Open every day from 9 a.m. to 6 p.m. from mid-March through October.

In Schoonoord

Included in the grounds at the **De Zeven Marken Open-Air Museum,** Tramstraat 73, are sod huts, a smithy, saw mill, bee farm, and geological exhibits. It's open from March through October, 9 a.m. to 5 p.m. seven days a week. Admission is Dfl. 2.50 ($1.10) for adults.

The Oil Fields

The oil field near Coevorden and Schoonebeek is one of Europe's largest, and while it has indisputably brought change to this part of sleepy Drenthe, beauty-conscious natives hurry to surround each pumping installation with a grove of fast-growing trees to cloak these industrial pockmarks in nature's green drapery. Schoonebeek has, in fact, been called "the best-dressed oil field in the world."

The Lakes

While there are scores of lovely small lakes within Drenthe's borders, it shares its two largest with neighboring Groningen province. **Lake Paterswolde,** some 12 miles northeast of Assen on the Groningen border, is a sailing and water sports center, with a holiday village on its shores. To the southeast, **Lake Zuidlaren** also has a village by the same name and also attracts water sports enthusiasts. It is also the setting, in October, for one of Holland's largest horse fairs.

XVIII

CENTRAL HOLLAND

1. THE POLDERS
2. OVERIJSSEL
3. GELDERLAND
4. UTRECHT

From the new to the very old, Holland's central provinces spread before you its unique history, incomparable scenic beauties, and incredible engineering feats. The Ijsselmeer polders are the country's newest land, reclaimed from the former Zuiderzee. Utrecht is nearly 2,000 years old. Overijssel and Gelderland share a park-like landscape punctuated by historic towns, castles, industrial towns, and villages that can only be described as "quaint."

1. The Polders

For centuries the Dutch have been protecting themselves from an ever-encroaching sea. One of its most formidable opponents has always been the Zuiderzee, a salty incursion of the North Sea that began about A.D. 200 to 300, when it washed over Frisian dunes to flood vast inland areas, and culminated in the 1200s, when a series of storms drove it all the way to the inland lake known as Flevo. Around its shores the sleepy, picturesque villages we visit today presented quite a different picture when their harbors were alive with great ships that sailed for the Dutch West and East Indian Companies, and carried Dutch navigators on explorations to the far reaches of the South Pacific and around Cape Horn, North Sea fishermen returned to Zuiderzee home ports, and Amsterdam flourished as ships from around the world sailed to its front door.

Still, Holland needed to control the waterway, which had earned a reputation as a "graveyard of ships," and as early as the 1600s there was talk of driving back the sea and reclaiming the land it then covered. Parliament—in the manner of governments since time began—finally got around to authorizing such a project in 1918, and in the 1920s work was begun. By 1930 some 50,000 acres had been dried out in the Wieringermeer Polder and four more polders were on the drawing board. In 1932, in an unparalleled feat of engineering, the North Sea was sealed off when the 19-mile Enclosing Dike was closed, and since then the Dutch have been busily pumping dry thousands of acres, in the process converting fishing villages into farming villages, joining island villages to the mainland, and transforming North Sea fishermen into Ijsselmeer freshwater fishermen.

Periodic storms and floods hindered the on-going work, but the most devastating blow came in April 1945 during the final days of World War II. Nazi troops, in a desperate effort to hold back Allied forces, bombed the Enclosing Dike and sent the sea flooding over the entire polder, leaving a seascape 12 to 14 feet in depth, dotted with church spires. The Nazis surrendered just 18 days later, and the Dutch lost no time in setting things right again—they pumped the polder dry in an incredible four months, and in the space of 12 months homes were once more occupied and crops were being sown in the fields. As they have done over the ages, Hollanders had accomplished the impossible!

Today the ten villages surrounding Emmerloord township occupy the 119,000 acres in the second of the projected polders; the third (East Flevoland Polder) came dry in 1957, adding some 133,000 acres of usable land; the South Flevoland Polder (142,000 acres) fell dry in 1968; and the Markerwaard dike that will make possible completion of the five-polder plan has been completed.

From time to time in the polders you'll come across groups of men working alongside the road. These are the *polderjongens* ("polder men"), who travel from place to place, wherever there is a need for their special training. The polder settlers, incidentally, only *rent* their land from the government, which retains title, and obtaining a lease entails work on the polders for extended periods before an application can even be filed.

Riding along broad, straight roads between flat fields laced with equally straight canals, even the most world-weary traveler must thrill to this awesome accomplishment in facing down the forces of the sea!

THINGS TO SEE AND DO

The polders can easily be visited from a base in Amsterdam or The Hague, as a natural incorporation of one route to the northern provinces, or as part of a one- or two-day circle of the Ijsselmeer (see Chapter XIV).

In Lelystad

Take time to walk around this newest of the polder towns, with a population of some 50,000. On Saturday mornings the town square is filled with vendors, many in traditional dress, carrying on the old market-day traditions.

Look for the **Informatiecentrum Nieuw Land** (tel. 03200/6-07-99) just off the Markerwaard Dike approach road and allow plenty of time to ponder the exhibits that explain the Zuiderzee Project in great detail. You'll learn how the dikes were built, all about the pumping process, and the final drying-up operation. There are also relics of ships that went to a watery grave in the Zuiderzee, possibly at the very spot on which you stand. It's a fascinating place that will send you off with a much deeper understanding of what you'll be seeing. It's open from 10 a.m. to 5 p.m. daily during the summer; closed on Saturday in winter.

In Ketelhaven

In this little town on the shores of the Ketelmeer (between Lelystad and Urk), the **Museum voor Sheepsarcheologie** exhibits ships wrecked in the Zuiderzee as far back as Roman times, all revealed as waters were pumped out to make the polder. It's open seven days a week from 10 a.m. to 5 p.m., and admission is Dfl. 1.50 (65¢).

In Urk

This quaint little fishing village was for more than 700 years a Zuiderzee island, its isolation undisturbed until the reclamation project joined it to the mainland in 1942. In 1948 a roadway was constructed to facilitate an overland route to the village, a roadway so unwelcome to residents that they promptly banned all automobiles, requiring them to park on the outskirts. In the end, practicalities (and the Dutch are nothing if not *practical)* such as getting to market the eels for which their fishing fleet is famous, forced them to reconsider and lift the restriction. So while you will certainly encounter automobiles in the narrow, brick-paved streets of Urk, it's *still* a good idea to park outside and take to your feet.

As you walk past picturesque brick homes lining those tiny streets, notice the decorated wooden doors and elaborate wrought ironwork. At long piers in the harbor, you'll see the sturdy fishing boats that sail in search of eels. A word of caution: Smoked eel is sold everywhere in Urk, and you'll show yourself an expert if you select only the skinny ones (fat ones aren't nearly so nice).

Many of the women of Urk still wear traditional long dresses, light-blue corsets with protective patches of chamois leather for longer wear, and a hand-embroidered *kraplap,* or bodice cover, as well as garnet necklaces and bonnets with ear flaps. Men sport baggy felt pants held up with silver buttons adorned with scenes from the Bible and blue knit stockings with their hand-stitched shoes. Many do not speak English, and while they are quite cordial to outsiders like you and me (and provide plenty of souvenirs for sale), they still insist—actually, *require*—that we respect their Sunday customs, when it is forbidden to drive an automobile, sail a boat, or ride a bicycle. If you can walk into town on a Sunday morning just after church services end, you'll see most of Urk's citizens making a ritual walk through the town and down to the harbor.

In Schokland

Schokland is not much more than a wide spot in the road nowadays. Located on the road from Nagele to Ens (east of Urk), it now consists of a church, a cannon from the 1500s that once was fired to warn of rising waters, and a few old anchors left from the days when there was an island fishing village here. Unlike Urk, which was left with an Ijsselmeer harbor, the polder completely surrounded Schokland and the village faded away. Keep a sharp eye out for this place, however, for the museum in that church is not to be missed. Called the **Ijsselmeer Poldersmuseum (Seafloor Museum),** it holds Bronze Age tools, mammoth bones, and other prehistoric relics, as well as stone coffins from the 1100s and pottery dating as far back as 900. All were discovered on the sea bottom when the polder was drained. It's open from 10 a.m. to 5 p.m. every day but Sunday, when hours are 1 to 5 p.m.

2. Overijssel

The province of Overijssel is all too often a pass-through part of Holland for tourists. And that's really a shame, because within its boundaries lie beautiful forests, lakes, and parks, steep-roofed, half-timbered farmhouses, the medieval town of Ootmarsum, the Venicelike village of Giethoorn where everyone gets around on canals instead of streets, picturesque castles and villages where your camera will be welcomed, and the strict Calvinist village of Staphorst where it won't. Its capital is Zwolle, where the fortified walls have been demolished and replaced by the greenery of parks and landscaped lawns, the moat transformed into a tree-lined canal.

WHERE TO STAY

Because Overijssel is so easily reached from major centers like Amsterdam, few tourists seek accommodations within the province itself. There is, however, one very special inn that will tempt you to move in for a few days as you explore the contrasting face of Overijssel.

In Ootmarsum

Hotel de Wiemsel, Winhofflaan 2, 7631 HX Ootmarsum (tel. 054/19-21-55). This country inn has the look of a traditional farmhouse, with timber-and-brick construction topped by a steeply sloping roof. Inside, all is graciousness, from the antique-filled lobby and lounges to the attractive dining room. Each of the 49 guest rooms has a terrace and is exceptionally spacious, with dividers separating a living room area from sleeping quarters. In each, there is a private bath with heated towel racks, refrigerator, TV, radio, and telephone.

The setting, in a scenically beautiful area not far from the German border, lends itself to peaceful days of outdoor rambling, and the hotel can send you off via bicycle or on horseback (from its own stables). They'll even pack a picnic lunch for you to carry along. On the grounds there are lighted tennis courts and an indoor swimming pool, as well as a solarium and sauna. Aside from nature's beauties, there is the lovely village of Ootmarsum and other nearby sights to fill your days.

Rates are Dfl. 150 ($65.75) to Dfl. 268 ($117.50), including service charge and VAT, but exclusive of breakfast, for which there is a small additional charge.

WHERE TO EAT

Meals in the **Hotel de Wiemsel** (see above) are in the gourmet class and run Dfl. 70 ($30.75) to Dfl. 120 ($52.75), without wine.

In Blokzijl

Kaatje bij de Sluis, Brouwerstraat 20, Blokzijl (tel. 05272/033). Its name means "Kate's by the Sluice," appropriate enough in this former fortified Zuiderzee port that has become forever landlocked. The kitchen here has earned a fine reputation that lures Amsterdammers to make the 60-mile drive across the polder just to have dinner. It's almost a cliché to say that only the freshest ingredients are used, but that phrase takes on new meaning when you learn that the menu changes daily—and sometimes *twice* in the course of a day—according to what's available. Seafood, as you might expect, is high on the list of specialties, along with beef and wild duck. Prices range from Dfl. 55 ($24) to Dfl. 135 ($59.25), without wine. Lunch is served only Wednesday through Friday and Sunday, and it's closed on Monday and Tuesday. Reservations are recommended. There are also eight comfortable double rooms if you decide to stop overnight.

TOURIST INFORMATION

You'll find the regional **VVV office** at Grote Kerkplein 14, Zwolle (tel. 038/21-39-00).

THINGS TO SEE AND DO

This province extends from the young Noordoostpolder in the northwest to Twente in the east with its history rooted in antiquity to the Salland district bordered by the Vecht and Ijssel Rivers where historic towns have found prosperity through 20th-century industry.

In Zwolle

The city of Zwolle is ringed by canals and fortified gates that remind us of its long history. Look for the **Sassenpoort** gateway that dates from 1408 and sports four octagonal towers.

The **Provincial Overijssels Museum (Provinciaal Overijssel Museum),** in the Melkmarkt, in addition to exhibits relating to Zwolle's history contains an authentically restored 16th-century kitchen and an interesting collection of French furniture. Open Tuesday through Saturday from 10 a.m. to 5 p.m., on Sunday from 1 to 5 p.m.

St. Michaelskerk dates from the early 1400s and is interesting for its triangular hall, its famous 4,000-pipe Schnitger organ, and as the burial place of the renowned religious writer Thomas à Kempis, who spent over 70 years here.

In Deventer

This town had its beginnings in the 11th century, but has kept pace with the march of time in its economic life. Among the products manufactured here are

Smyrna carpets and metal goods, and its own Deventer Koek (a delicious spicy gingerbread) has outgrown the cottage-industry stage. With all that, you'll see some fine medieval houses along its streets.

The **Municipal Museum** holds artifacts relating to the area and a marvelous collection of costumes.

The large library of medieval books and manuscripts in the **Town Hall** is well worth a look.

In Kampen

Ocean-going vessels tie up at Kampen wharves on the River Ijssel, continuing a tradition of trade that goes back to the Middle Ages.

Stop in at the **Town Hall (Oude Raadhuis)** for a look at the Aldermen's Room (Schepenzaal), with its rich paneling and great carved fireplace that date from the 1540s.

In Biddinghuizen

In the Overijssel polder country, not far from Kampen, the marvelous recreation center of **Flevohof,** at Spijkweg 30 in Biddinghuizen/Dronten (tel. 03211/15-14), centers on the activities of farms that cover some 350 acres. On the livestock farm you can actually spend a day engaged in such rural chores as milking a cow or churning butter, pitching hay, and any of a number of other things. It's great for children, but even better for adults who long for a hands-on reunion with this sort of basic lifestyle. There are also modern demonstration and exhibition centers, where you can see the *Holland Happening* audio-visual presentation, the beautiful Gardens of the World, and a great fun park with horse-drawn trains, a Children's Village, and a Red Indian village. Several restaurants take care of any hunger pangs. Open daily from 10 a.m. to 6 p.m. April through October. Admission is Dfl. 17.50 ($7.75) for adults, Dfl. 15 ($6.50) for children.

Picturesque Villages

You wouldn't want to miss **Giethoorn**—it's the town with no streets, only canals. Leave the car and follow a path to the main canal, where motorboats and punts wait to take you past enchanting canalside cottages.

Staphorst (north of Zwolle on the Meppel road) is the Dutch village of your imagination, with colorfully dressed residents living as their ancestors did. This is no tourist act, and you'll seldom get an enthusiastic welcome from these devout Calvinists. That especially applies on Sunday, when the entire population observes a regimen that dates back centuries: with downcast eyes, separate lines of men and women form a silent procession to the churches. No automobiles are allowed into the village on the Sabbath, nor is there anything so frivolous as bicycle riding. Whenever you come to Staphorst—on Sunday or a weekday—be sure to respect their conservative ways and keep the cameras out of sight.

Blokzijl and **Vollenhove** are small fishing villages that lost their ports to the Zuiderzee Project.

Other charming villages to seek out are **Ommen** (look for the Eerde castle), **Dalfsen, Rijssen,** and **Holten,** whose grateful residents tenderly care for the graves in a Canadian war cemetery.

3. Gelderland

Gelderland is the province of the Rhine, and its large parks, nature reserves, and recreation centers are favorite holiday venues of Dutch from all over the country. North of the Rhine, stretching to sandy beaches along the Veluwemeer that separate it from the Flevoland polder, the region known as "The Veluwe" is the largest nature reserve in Holland, and offers all kinds of camping facilities as well as bungalow and other holiday accommodations.

The Veluwe, however, is just one face of this large province. Its cities beckon with attractions like the royal palace museum in Apeldoorn and Arnhem's National Open-Air Museum. For centuries an independent duchy ruled by the Dukes of Gelderland, the province has castles all over the place, some to be visited, others only seen in passing.

Gelderland is, of course, easily toured by car, but it's also perfect cycling country, and a dense network of bus and train connections makes it easily accessible to those without a car.

WHERE TO STAY

Although most tourists prefer to visit Gelderland from an Amsterdam base, you may want to move to a central location in Apeldoorn—and if you succumb to all that scenic beauty and decide to follow the Dutch example of making this your holiday home, the listing below gives you several options for accommodations, and the VVV in Amsterdam or the Netherlands Tourist Office in New York can provide a list of many more similar facilities.

In Apeldoorn

Hotel Golden Tulip de Keizerskroon, Koingstraat 7, 7315 HR Apeldoorn (tel. 055/21-77-44). In a setting on the edge of town, not far from the **Het Loo,** this attractive hotel has spacious rooms whose furnishings include a writing desk in each room. Each also has a private bath, radio, TV, and telephone. Some have balconies overlooking the landscaped grounds. There is one restaurant with moderate prices and a gourmet dining room that's more expensive. The cozy pub serves drinks around an open fire. Amenities include a sauna, solarium, and indoor pool; there's bowling just across the street. Rates are Dfl. 195 ($85.50) to Dfl. 230 ($101).

Hotel Bloemink, Loolaan 56, Apeldoorn (tel. 055/21-41-41). In the Het Loo palace vicinity, this hostelry offers spacious rooms, nicely furnished, with baths, TVs, and telephones (some with terraces). Suites come with kitchenettes. Rates range from Dfl. 57 ($25) to Dfl. 150 ($65.75) single, Dfl. 85 ($37.25) to Dfl. 160 ($70.25) double.

The **Motel Apeldoorn,** J. C. Wilslaan 200, Apeldoorn (tel. 055/08-55). This is a modern motel cast in the American mold, with all the amenities you'd expect from the nicer motel chains in the States. Rooms all have patios, there's good parking, and there's a restaurant. Singles run Dfl. 82.50 ($36.25); doubles, Dfl. 110 ($48.25).

Hotel-Pension Berg en Bos, Aquamarijnstraat 58, 7314 HZ Apeldoorn (tel. 055/55-23-52). This inexpensive little hotel (only 17 rooms) has a quiet, peaceful setting and provides comfortable rooms with private bath for rates of Dfl. 44 ($19.25) for bed-and-breakfast, Dfl. 62 ($27.25) for half board (breakfast and dinner). There's a bar and lounge.

In Harderwijk

Vakantiecentrum Dennenhoek, Parallelweg 25, 3849 ML Harderwijk/Hierden (tel. 03413/14-15). This holiday camp offers you a choice of bungalows, camping huts, and campsites for caravans, at varying rates, all moderate. In a beautiful location, its facilities include a restaurant, bar, pools, tennis court, supermarket, and a laundrette.

WHERE TO EAT

In addition to the Apeldoorn hotel dining rooms listed above, there is a very special, widely acclaimed restaurant about ten miles west of Apeldoorn you should know about.

Restaurant de Echoput, Amersfoortseweg 86, Apeldoorn (tel. 05769/2-48). This lovely place on the edge of the Royal Wood is named for the old well at which travelers once watered their horses (its name means "echoing well"). From the outside it has the look of a luxury hunting lodge, and the surprise comes when you enter an ultra-sophisticated lounge and dining room done up in shades of chocolate and pewter. Window walls look out to pools and fountains and forest greenery. The specialty here is game in season (fall and winter), and summer specialties include lamb, beef, pork, and poultry. No matter what the season, you may be sure your meal will be both superb and memorable. Expect prices from Dfl. 90 ($39.50) and up, and be sure to reserve ahead. It's closed on Monday and for lunch on Sunday.

TOURIST INFORMATION

You will find VVV offices at: Stationsplein 28, **Apeldoorn** (tel. 033/63-51-51); Stationsplein 45, **Arnhem** (tel. 085/42-03-30); and St. Jorisstraat 72, **Nijmegen** (tel. 080/22-54-40).

THINGS TO SEE AND DO

Gelderland is a tourist's bonanza, with attractions of every description.

In Arnhem

Arnhem is Gelderland's capital city. Its name became a household word during World War II when it sustained massive Allied air attacks against its Nazi occupiers, and today thousands make pilgrimages to its battlefields each year. On a less grim note, however, Arnhem is a city of parks, a marvelous open-air museum, two zoos, and the departure point for boat trips on the Rhine.

Right in the heart of the city, the 100 acres of the **Netherlands Open-Air Museum,** Schelmseweg 89 (tel. 57-61-11), hold a delightful mini-course in Dutch history, customs, dress, and architecture. Gathered from all around the country, farmhouses, step-gabled town houses, windmills, colorful costumes of the past, and even ancient means of transport bring together in one place much of the Holland of years gone by. If you see nothing else in Arnhem, don't miss this. Open from 9 a.m. to 5 p.m. daily. Admission is Dfl. 7 ($3). The nearby De Oude Bijenkorf restaurant makes a good lunch stop.

In the **Arnhem Municipal Museum,** Utrechtseweg 87, are archeological relics found in the province, an interesting topographical map of Holland, and artworks that range from the contemporary to the classic, with an emphasis on contemporary Dutch painting and sculpture. There's also a sculpture garden. A coffee room and open-air café provide refreshment and rest for weary feet. Hours are 10 a.m. to 5 p.m. Tuesday through Saturday, from 11 a.m. to 5 p.m. on Sunday and holidays.

Located in the former Hotel Hartenstein (British Command Center during World War II) in Oosterbeek, which adjoins Arnhem, the **Airborne Museum,** Utrechtseweg 232 (tel. 33-77-10), has exhibits detailing the 1944 Battle of Arnhem. Open Monday through Saturday from 11 a.m. to 5 p.m., on Sunday and holidays from noon to 5 p.m. Admission is Dfl. 2.50 ($1). *Note:* There's an excellent café-restaurant, the **Klein Hartenstein,** Utrechtseweg 226 (tel. 34-21-21), next to the museum, with a cozy bar, fireplace, and terrace.

Also, while in Oosterbeek (which traces its history back to the Roman era), stop in its old Catholic church to see Jan Toorop's famous *Fourteen Stations of the Cross.*

In Doorwerth (just beyond Oosterbeek), the former residence of a Rhine baron was rebuilt after heavy damage in World War II in its original architectural style. Today, as the **Hunting Museum,** Doorwerth Castle, Fonteinalee, Doorwerth (tel. 33-53-75), it holds interesting exhibits on game animals and antique weapons. Open weekdays except Tuesday from 10 a.m. to 5 p.m., on Saturday and Sunday and holidays from 1 to 5 p.m.

The beautiful **De Hoge Veluwe National Park,** Apeldoornseweg 250, covering some 22 square miles in a setting flanked by Arnhem, Apeldoorn, and Ede, shelters a wealth of nature's treasures, and also has a statue park within its boundaries as well as the art museum listed below. Open daily from 8 a.m. to sunset.

Located in De Hoge Veluwe National Park, the **National Museum Kröller-Müller,** Houtkampweg 6 (tel. 08382/12-41), is where you'll find most of the Vincent van Gogh paintings, not in the Amsterdam museum. Also included in this major art collection are paintings by Mondrian, Braque, and Picasso. A sculpture park holds works by Rodin, Moore, and Lipchitz, among others, and there are exhibitions of Chinese porcelain, and Delft. Open from 10 a.m. to 5 p.m. Tuesday through Saturday, from 1 to 5 p.m. on Sunday and holidays.

The 90-acre **Burgers' Zoo and Safaripark,** Schelmseweg 85 (tel. 42-45-34), allows you to drive slowly through its grounds as more than 300 animals roam freely behind protective fencing. Its chimpanzee and gorilla enclosures are internationally acclaimed, and there's a new three-acre tropical rain forest. Hours are 9 a.m. to 8 p.m. daily in summer, until 6 p.m. in winter.

Rhenen is a short distance out from Arnhem (past Oosterbeek, Doorwerth, and Renkum), and **Ouwehand's Zoo,** Grebbeweg 109, Rhenen (tel. 08376/91-10), makes the trip well worthwhile. In addition to royal Bengal tigers, lions, elephants, reindeer, polar bears, and a host of other animals and birds, there's an aquarium and a dolphinarium with daily performances. There's also a playground for children, a swimming pool, and a terrace café. Open daily from 9 a.m. to 6 p.m.

For **boat rides on the Rhine,** from April to August there are ten cruises each day from Arnhem into the Rhine region, which include a short incursion into Germany. For schedules, fares, and booking, contact the VVV or Rederij Heymen (tel. 51-51-81).

In Nijmegen

One of Holland's two oldest cities (Maastricht is the other), Nijmegen dates back to A.D. 105. Its strategic position is clearly visible from the **Valkhof,** where there are magnificent views of the surrounding region. Here you will also find the ruins of 12th-century **St. Martin's Chapel** and another little 1030 chapel that has been called the **Carolingian Chapel** because of the long-held belief that it was built by Charlemagne (Nijmegen was a favorite residence for the emperor), although it was actually built by Conraad II. More excellent views are visible at the 15th-century **Belvedere** watchtower. Around the picturesque **Grote Markt,** look for the 1612 **Weigh House** (Waag), and the **Kerkboog** vaulted passageway that dates from 1545.

The **Stedelijk Museum (Municipal Museum),** Franse Plaats 3, is open Monday through Saturday from 10 a.m. to 5 p.m., on Sunday from 1 to 5 p.m. This interesting reconstruction of a 1600 Knights of St. John hospital holds contemporary exhibits, as well as artifacts tracing regional history.

At the **Provincial Museum G. M. KAM,** Museum Kamstraat 45, relics of the prehistoric, Roman, and Frankish eras in this region form the bulk of the exhibitions. Hours are Tuesday through Saturday from 10 a.m. to 5 p.m., on Sunday from 1 to 5 p.m.

In nearby Groesbeek, through the use of a model of the area as it was in the war, photographs, films, and a slide show, the **Liberation Museum 1944,** Wylerbaan 4, Groesbeek (tel. 08891/744-04), tells the story of the airborne operation that liberated Nijmegen from Nazi forces in 1944. It was the largest airborne operation in history, and the museum has been maintained as a token of local gratitude. Hours are 10 a.m. to 5 p.m. Monday through Saturday, from noon to 5 p.m. on Sunday and holidays. There's a small admission charge.

A little to the southeast of town on the road to Groesbeek, the 120-acre **Holy Land Open-Air Museum** holds life-size replicas of biblical scenes, its main purpose to present the life of Christ in terms of his human environment. Open daily, Easter through October, from 9 a.m. to 5 p.m. weekdays. Admission is Dfl. 7.50 ($3.25).

In Apeldoorn

"Royal Apeldoorn" is a title often bestowed on this city, as well it might be, since it has played host to the likes of Willem III in 1685, Louis Napoleon in 1809, Queen Wilhelmina from 1948 until her death in 1962, and Princess Margriet from 1962 to 1975. From all that evidence, the title is well deserved! It's also a city of many parks and gardens.

It is a 1685 palace that has sheltered all that royalty, and since 1984 it has served as the magnificent home for the **Het Loo Palace National Museum,** Koninklijk Park 1 (tel. 21-22-44), celebrating the history of the House of Orange. The splendid palace is an ideal setting for paintings, furniture, silver, glassware, and ceramics, as well as memorabilia of the royal family. The vintage cars and carriage collection is also fascinating, and the formal gardens are truly worthy of royalty. Hours are 10 a.m. to 5 p.m. Tuesday through Sunday. Admission is Dfl. 7 ($3) for adults, Dfl. 5 ($2.25) for children.

In Wageningen

This ancient town about 10½ miles west of Arnhem holds the famous agricultural university, where experiments vital to Holland's agro-economy are carried out. It was also the scene (in the De Wereld restaurant) of the German surrender in May of 1945. Models of new ship designs are tested in ship basins in Wageningen, where they are put through simulated weather conditions that their full-scale counterparts will have to face on the open seas.

In Zutphen

On the banks of the Ijssel River in the old town of Zutphen and in a magnificent structure that also houses important works of art, the **Walburgiskerk Library** of medieval books and manuscripts is still in use, its rare publications all chained to reading desks. Hours are 10 a.m. to 5 p.m. Tuesday through Friday.

The **Eight Castles Tour** actually begins in Vorden, some six miles southeast of Zutphen, and you can pick up a booklet detailing the route from the Zutphen VVV office at Wijnhuis/Markt (tel. 05750/1-93-55). Not all the castles are open to the public, but the scenery is terrific and even from the outside the castles are worth seeing.

4. Utrecht

The smallest of Holland's provinces, Utrecht would come in a very close second to Gelderland if there were ever a contest for the *official* title of "royal." This is where Queen Juliana chose to live when she abdicated in favor of her daughter, Beatrix, and castles of one sort or another literally dot the landscape. The provincial capital, also named Utrecht, is at least 2,000 years old, yet is one of Holland's most progressive industrial centers. New Yorkers will want to look up the tiny village of Breukelen (it's on the River Vecht) and drive across the *original* Brooklyn Bridge—exactly 20 feet long and one car wide (and I'm sure it's not for sale!). Medieval centuries are recalled in Amersfoort and Oudewater, and Doorn was the home in exile of Kaiser Wilhelm, of World War I fame.

WHERE TO STAY

Like most of central Holland, Utrecht is usually toured from a base in Amsterdam or The Hague. The listing below is simply to let you know of special lodgings you may want to consider.

In Heusden

Hotel In den Verdwaalde Koogel, Vismarkt 1, 5256 BC Heusden (tel. 041/62-19-33). The tiny village of Heusden has a tiny harbor, a tiny white balance bridge, and two not-so-tiny windmills atop earthen ramparts. It's almost due south of the city of Utrecht, and "charm" is the first word that comes to mind. That overworked word also applies to this 17th-century town house, now converted into a 12-room inn whose name means "The Stray Bullet." Rooms here are small and furnishings are not luxurious, although those on the upper floors qualify as quite charming, with exposed beams or rafters. All have private, modern bathrooms, color TVs, and mini-bars. The largest room is the honeymoon suite, which is furnished with antiques and has nice views (only slightly more expensive than other rooms). The café-restaurant is quite good (see below), and the village is a sightseeing destination in itself. Rates are a moderate Dfl. 85 ($37.25) single, Dfl. 110 ($48.25) double.

WHERE TO EAT

Again, these are special places where a meal is also a memorable experience.

In Bosch en Duin

Restaurant de Hoefslag, Vossenlaan 28, Bosch en Duin (tel. 030/78-43-95). Considered by many to be Holland's top restaurant, this beautiful dining spot sits in wooded grounds just a little northeast of the city of Utrecht. There's a sort of Victorian-garden feel to the lounge, while the dining room is reminiscent of a rather upscale hunting lodge, with lots of dark wood, an open hearth, and ceiling-to-floor doors opening to the terrace. Originally a coaching inn, the de Hoefslag changes its menu daily, setting specialties *after* the chef has done the marketing. Seafoods are superb, as are pork, lamb, and other meats, and venison and other game dishes are served in season. Prices range from Dfl. 90 ($39.50) up, and best book ahead—Amsterdammers think nothing of driving the 30 miles down here for dinner. Closed Sunday and Monday.

In Heusden

Hotel In den Verdwaalde Koogel, Vismarkt 1 (tel. 041/62-19-33). See above for a description of this small hotel. Its restaurant, decorated in Vermeer colors, with antique-gray beams overhead and antique clocks among its decorations, is a cozy setting for superior meals such as Texel Island lamb or salmon smoked over oak by the chef. Prices are moderate, the service is friendly, and the restaurant alone is sufficient reason for a detour through this picturesque little village.

TOURIST INFORMATION

VVV offices are located at Vredenburg 90, in the Music Centre, in **Utrecht** (tel. 030/31-41-32), and at Stationsplein 28, in **Amersfoort** (tel. 033/6-51-51).

THINGS TO SEE AND DO

The capital city is a good starting point for exploring the province. The interesting "witch city" of Oudewater, which lies in the province of Utrecht, has been described in Section 9 of Chapter XIV.

In Utrecht

From June to August, the VVV office sponsors a **walking tour** of the city that leaves about 10:30 a.m. daily. Check for exact time and booking.

Sightseeing **coach tours** are conducted during the summer months by the VVV at a cost of about Dfl. 10 ($4.50) for adults, less for children under 12. Check at the VVV office for schedules and booking.

One-hour **boat tours** through the Utrecht canals are also available in the summer for about Dfl. 8 ($3.50) for adults, half that for children under 14. There are trips by boat on the River Vecht to Loenen, with a stop to visit the Terra Nova estate, and a boat trip on the Kromme Rijn to the Rhijnauwen estate. Check with the VVV for schedules and booking.

The **Domkerk (cathedral)** was built between 1254 and 1517, with a 365-foot tower that until recently dominated Utrecht's skyline (modern buildings now surpass its height, though they don't come close to its beauty). That tower now stands across a square from its mother building, a circumstance that came about in rebuilding after the church collapsed during a storm, leaving the tower unharmed. One of the best views of Utrecht is from the top of the **Domkerk tower,** a climb of some 465 steps (don't faint—about halfway up there's the 14th-century St. Michael's Chapel where you can stop and ease the panting!). The climb goes past the 50 massive church bells you'll hear all through your stay in Utrecht. The cathedral cloisters are connected to the former Hall of the Chapter, where the signing of the 1579 Union of Utrecht took place. It is open to tourists from May through September, Monday to Saturday, 10 a.m. to 5 p.m. and Sundays from 2 to 4 p.m. In October through April weekday opening time is 11 a.m.

In the **Rijks Museum Het Catharijneconvent (St. Catherine's Convent),** Nieuwe Gracht 63, the extensive collections of paintings, religious relics, carvings, and church robes trace the development of Christian religions in Holland from the 8th through the 20th centuries. Open from 10 a.m. to 5 p.m. Tuesday through Friday, from 11 a.m. to 5 p.m. on Saturday and Sunday.

The **Nationaal Museum van Speelklok tot Pierement** (from Musical Box to Barrel Organ), Achter de Dom 12, is a delightful display of mechanical music makers of all descriptions, including those street organs you see on Dutch streets. Open Tuesday through Saturday from 11 a.m. to 5 p.m., on Sunday from 1 to 5 p.m.

At the **Nederlands Spoorwegmuseum (Dutch Rail Museum),** Johan van Oldenbarneveltlaan 6, rail buffs will find it difficult to tear themselves away from this former railway station and its marvelous collection of steam engines and a lot of other things connected with rail travel. Hours are 10 a.m. to 5 p.m. Tuesday through Saturday and 1 to 5 p.m. on Sunday; closed Monday.

The vast covered shopping mall of **Hoog Catherine,** Central Station, is a six-block, multitiered shopper's paradise, and is so large it encompasses a 40-room exhibition hall.

In Amersfoort

This lovely old medieval city has held onto its ancient character despite its development as an industrial city. Indeed, its medieval heart is guarded by a double ring of canals—the only city in Europe to have this feature. Look for the tall 15th-century Gothic **Tower of Our Lady,** and if you're here on a Friday, listen for its carillon concert between 10 and 11 a.m. If you should be here on a summer Saturday, you may be lucky enough to encounter the colorful trumpeters who show up from time to time in the city center.

At the **Museum Flehite,** Westingel 50, the history of Amersfoort is the subject of the large collection of artifacts.

In Soestduk

The beautiful **Palace of the Queen Mother** (sometimes called the "white palace") is located in this town near Baarn.

Castles in Utrecht

As I said before, Utrecht is a treasure trove of castles. Some of those you may visit are: **Zuylen and Haarzuilens,** near Utrecht; **Guntherstein,** near Breukelen; and **Zuilenstein,** near Amerongen.

If you only have time for one castle jaunt, make it to **De Haar** at Kasteellaan 1,

Haarzuilens (tel. 03407/12-75). The imposing 15th-century castle suffered a disastrous fire in the 1800s, but it has now been restored to its former glory and its owners use it as their primary residence. You can, however, take a look at the gorgeous furnishings and priceless paintings between March and mid-August and from mid-October to mid-November. Go to see the formal gardens, if nothing else—they're magnificent. Hours are 11 a.m. to 4 p.m. Monday through Friday, and 1 to 4 p.m. on Saturday and Sunday. There's a small admission fee.

Slot Zuylen, on Zuilenselaan, in Maarsen, is one of Holland's best examples of medieval castles. It was built in the 1200s and was lived in until the early part of this century. Since 1952 it has been a museum, with rooms left just as they were when the family was in residence. Open during the summer from 10 a.m. to 4 p.m. Tuesday through Saturday, from 2 to 4 p.m. on Sunday, for a small admission charge.

Kasteel Sypesteyn, Nieuw Loosdrechtsedijk 150, Nieu Loosdrecht (tel. 02158/32-08), is a castle turned art gallery and museum. Rebuilt in the early 1900s on the foundations of a late-medieval manor house that was destroyed about 1580, it now holds some 80 paintings from the 16th, 17th, and 18th centuries, with artists such as Moreelse, Maes, and Mierevelt represented. There are also collections of old weapons, glassware, silverware, pottery, porcelain, and furnishings. The park-like grounds hold a lovely rose garden. From May 1 to September 15, there are tours Tuesday through Friday at 10:15 and 11:15 a.m., and 2 and 3 p.m.

XIX

HOLLAND'S SOUTHERNMOST PROVINCES

1. ZEELAND
2. NOORD BRABANT
3. LIMBURG

All too often, the southernmost provinces of Holland are merely entrance or exit routes for tourists who rush through on their way to or from Belgium, Luxembourg, and other European destinations. Yet from the watery islands of Zeeland to the forests and moors of Noord Brabant to Limburg's wooded hill country, there is a rich vein of tourist experience waiting to be mined, and no visit to Holland is complete without a foray into these interesting provinces. History, recreational activities, and some of Holland's most beautiful scenery are in this southern region.

1. Zeeland

This "Sea Land" on Holland's western coast has often been likened to three fingers of land pointing out into the North Sea, and Napoleon declared in 1810 that it was little more than "the silt thrown up by French rivers" (and in truth, much of the province is formed by alluvial deposits at the mouth of the Sheldt, the river that controls access to Antwerp). Zeelanders, however, cling to the firm Dutch belief that "who cannot master the sea is not worthy of the land," and century after century they have cherished their precious group of islands and former islands, rescuing them each time the sea has roared in to claim them as its own.

In 1421 the St. Elizabeth Flood came close to tipping the balance in favor of the North Sea; in 1944 it was bombs from Allied planes that loosed flood waters to flush out Nazi troops entrenched in bunkers along the coast; and in 1953 a fierce hurricane sent sea water crashing through the province and as far inland as Rotterdam. In between those disasters were numerous "little floods" that swamped only a few islands. Always, Zeelanders have pushed back the angry sea and reinforced protective measures in this on-going, uncompromising battle. Today, with the completion of an ingenious system of dikes, storm-surge barriers, and sluice gates known as the

Delta Project, it's more likely the North Sea that will finally have to concede defeat, acknowledging for all time Zeeland's firm grasp on its cluster of islands.

At the center of Zeeland, Walcheren (still called Walcheren Island even though polders have long connected it to South Beveland and the mainland) holds the provincial capital of Middelburg, a medieval city that has resolutely rebuilt its historic landmarks, so steadfastly holding to their original designs that, seeing them today, it's difficult to believe they have not stood undisturbed through the centuries. To the north lie North Beveland and the islands of Schouwen-Duiveland, St. Philipsland (now a peninsula), and Tholen. To the south of Walcheren and separated from it by the River Shelde, Zeeuwsch-Vlaanderen (Zeeland Flanders) reaches to the Belgian border.

WHERE TO STAY

Take your pick: a base in charming, historic Middelburg, the little harbor town of Veere that's virtually an open-air museum, the bustling port of Vlissingen (Flushing), the medieval village of Zierikzee, or holiday digs at small beach villages such as Westkapelle, Oostkapelle, and Domburg. In this small province, you're never far from any of its attractions.

In Middelburg

Best Western Hotel du Commerce, Loskade 1, 4331 HV Middelburg (tel. 01180/3-60-51). This small canalside hotel is just opposite the railway and bus terminal and an easy walk from the town center, in one of the most convenient locations in town. Its rooms all have private bath, TV, telephone, and mini-bar. There is also a good restaurant with moderate prices. Rates range from Dfl. 57.50 ($25.25) to Dfl. 95 ($41.75) per person, depending on size and location, including breakfast.

Hotel De Nieuwe Doelen, Loskade 3-7, 4331 HV Middelburg (tel. 01180/1-21-21). Conveniently located, this small hotel facing a canal has comfortable rooms both with and without private facilities. The rate per person for those without is Dfl. 52 ($22.75); for those with, Dfl. 70 ($30.75).

Hotel De Huifkar, Markt 19, 4331 LJ Middelburg (tel. 01180/1-29-98). There are only four rooms in this pleasant little hotel overlooking the Market Square, but all have private baths, and it's really in the heart of the city. The rate is Dfl. 52 ($22.75) per person.

Hotel-Pension Court Oxhooft, Singelstraat 14, 4331 SV Middelburg (tel. 01180/2-68-23). The 15 rooms here all come without private facilities at a rate of Dfl. 35 ($15.25) per person.

In Veere

De Campveerse Toren, Kade 2, 4351 AA Veere (tel. 01181/2-91). This delightful hotel (with the same ownership as the adjoining restaurant, one of the best in Zeeland) consists of only seven rather plain, but comfortable, rooms with private baths. You couldn't ask for a more romantic location than the 16th-century waterfront fortress of which it is a part. Just steps away are the equally ancient and historic buildings that make of Veere a charming open-air museum. Rates are Dfl. 52 ($22.75) to Dfl. 95 ($41.75) per person.

In Vlissingen

Hotel Britannia-Watentoren, boulevard Evertsen 244, 4382 AG Vlissingen (tel. 01184/1-32-55). All 35 of the attractive rooms in this waterfront hotel face the sea, and all have private baths. Its restaurant serves excellent meals at moderate prices. Rates run Dfl. 105 ($46) to Dfl. 148 ($65).

Golden Tulip Strandhotel, boulevard Evertsen 4, 4382 AD Vlissingen (tel. 01184/1-22-97). Located among a string of hostelries facing the beach drive, this attractive hotel features waterfront rooms with balconies and private facilities, and town-view rooms without balconies but with private baths and lower rates. Its dining room is also a very good restaurant with moderate prices, and also looks out to the water. Rates here are Dfl. 80 ($35) to Dfl. 160 ($70), and they have attractive weekend package rates that include some meals. It also offers laundry and dry-cleaning services, but be sure to check if return is in one, or in two, days.

Best Western Hotel Piccard, Badhuisstraat 178, 4382 AR Vlissingen (tel. 01184/1-35-51). There are studios and full apartments available in addition to rooms with private bath at this modern hostelry. Its amenities include an indoor saltwater pool and a health club. Room rates range from Dfl. 70 ($30.75) to Dfl. 130 ($57), and apartments from Dfl. 225 ($98.75) to Dfl. 275 ($120.50).

In Renesse

Hotel De Zeeuwse Stromen, Duinwekken 5, 4325 ZG Renesse (tel. 01116/20-40). With the sea just over the dunes, this modern hotel is one of the best in the area. Its attractive guest rooms are spacious and comfortable, with private baths, radios, TVs, and telephones, and its public rooms vary from cozy (the lounge) to elegant (the dining room) to garden-like (a glassed-in terrace where light meals, snacks, and drinks are available). Other amenities include a swimming pool and tennis courts. Rates range from Dfl. 70 ($30.75) to Dfl. 130 ($57), and there are several attractive package rates available. Highly recommended.

In Westkapelle

Golden Tulip Hotel Zuiderduin, De Bucksweg 2, 4361 SM Westkapelle (tel. 01186/18-10). A variety of accommodations are offered at this modern hotel set just behind the dunes. There are spacious rooms with private baths and kitchenettes, each with either a private balcony or a terrace, as well as complete apartments that can sleep up to five persons. On the premises are tennis courts and a heated swimming pool, and the restaurant attracts natives as well as tourists. Rates for rooms range from Dfl. 100 ($43.75) to Dfl. 200 ($87.75); for apartments, from Dfl. 210 ($92) to Dfl. 300 ($131.50).

In Oostkapelle

Hotel Zeelandia, Dorpsstraat 39-41, 4356 AH Oostkapelle (tel. 01188/13-66). In this small hotel the attractive rooms feature picture windows, and they come both with and without private facilities, at rates of Dfl. 40 ($17.50) to Dfl. 52 ($22.75).

In Domburg

Hotel De Burg, Ooststraat 5, 4357 BE Domburg (tel. 01188/13-37). The eight guest rooms in this hotel set on Domburg's main street have private baths and are modern and comfortable, with rates of Dfl. 50 ($22) to Dfl. 65 ($28.50).

Ruimzicht Appartementen, Schelpweg 24, 4357 BR Domburg (tel. 01188/14-09). Only apartments (which will sleep four or five persons) are offered in this attractive hotel. All have large glass sliding doors opening to private balconies, and among the on-premises conveniences are a washerette and garage parking. Rates range from Dfl. 285 ($125) to Dfl. 760 ($333) per week.

In Zierikzee

Hotel Garni Mondragon, Havenpark 21, 4301 JG Zierikzee (tel. 01110/30-51). All nine rooms in this canalside hotel have private facilities, and the rate is Dfl. 90 ($39.50) per person.

WHERE TO EAT

Your best meals in Zeeland will be in hotel dining rooms, but inquiry of the locals or in local VVV offices will often unearth good small restaurants that are beginning to open with more frequency than in past years. Needless to say, any seafood you order in this watery province will be fresher than fresh—right off local boats.

Special sweet-tooth note: A Zeeland specialty is called "bolus," and when I asked my Zeelander friends to define it exactly for me, the only explanation they could come up with was "they're these round things with sugar and. . . ." Well, actually, I think its base is bread, but no matter what the ingredients, do stop by a pastry shop or bakery and try them.

My top recommendation in the area is located in Yerseke (see below), but let's begin in the capital.

In Middelburg

Visrestaurant Bij Het Stadhuis, Lange Noordstraat 8 (tel. 2-70-58). Almost every variety of fish and shellfish you can name is offered on the extensive and moderately priced menu at this restaurant across from the Town Hall.

Den Gespleten Arent, Vlasmarkt 25 (tel. 3-61-22). Priced a bit above most local restaurants, meals in this patrician house setting are exceptionally good, and run about Dfl. 30 ($13.25) to Dfl. 70 ($30.75), without wine.

Old Dutch specialties at reasonable prices are offered at **De Blauwe Haan,** Markt 53a (tel. 1-37-39), and **De Huifkar,** Markt 19 (tel. 1-29-98).

Dutch pancakes are the specialty at **De Kabouterhut,** Oostkerkplein 8 (tel. 1-22-76), which also serves the Tourist Menu.

Note: Don't overlook the excellent restaurant just inside the abbey walls that serves everything from snacks to complete three-course menus for Dfl. 25 ($11). It's a good idea to plan your sightseeing (see "Things to See and Do," below) so as to lunch here.

In Veere

If you don't bust the budget anywhere else in Zeeland, do it here in the wonderfully atmospheric **De Campveerse Toren,** Kade 2 (tel. 01181/2-91). It perches in a 16th-century tower room overlooking the Veersemeer, a lake busy with the comings and goings of sailboats, yachts, and swans. The tower has an interesting history and is filled with brass and copper antiques; the restaurant was a great favorite of Grace Kelly's when she was a special guest here (ask about the "parfait d'amour" created just for her). The menu is extensive, seafood dishes are specialties, and the atmosphere is not only gracious but also a lot of fun. Prices will run about Dfl. 50 ($22) to Dfl. 95 ($41.75), without wine.

In Vlissingen

De Gevangentoren, boulevard de Ruyter (tel. 01184/1-70-76). Open for dinner only, this interesting restaurant is set in a 1491 tower, and despite its grim history of serving as a military prison, it's surprisingly cozy. Expect prices ranging from Dfl. 60 ($26.25) to Dfl. 90 ($39.50), without wine. Closed Monday; reservations recommended.

Dining rooms of the hotels listed above are all excellent, and prices are in the moderate range. The **Hotel Britannia-Watertoren** serves Neersland Dis Old Dutch specialties and the budget Tourist Menu, which you will also find at the **Strandhotel Vlissingen** and the **Visrestaurant Station Vlissingen,** Stationsplein 5.

In Renesse

The lovely dining room at the **Hotel de Zeeuwse Stromen,** Dunwekken 5 (tel. 01116/20-40), offers excellent meals (especially seafood dishes) at moderate prices ranging from Dfl. 30 ($13.25) to Dfl. 55 ($24). Food service is also available in the lounge and on the glassed-in terrace.

In Tholen

You'll find the reasonably priced Neerlands Dis Old Dutch specialties at **Hof van Holland,** Kaai 1 (tel. 01660/25-90).

In Yerseke

Restaurant Nolet Het Reymerswale, Jachthaven 5 (tel. 01131/16-42). About a 25-mile drive from Middelburg, this very special fish restaurant is worth the trip to a busy little port town you might otherwise overlook. This cozy upstairs room is right at the waterfront and, under the watchful eye of owner Theo Nolet and his wife, Gerda, has become one of the country's best seafood restaurants. Theo is also the chef, with extensive training and experience behind him, and you may be sure that whatever lands on your plate has just come from fishing boats in the harbor below. Expect a price range of Dfl. 75 ($33) to Dfl. 95 ($41.75), without wine, and be assured you'll feel those are bargain prices for the meals! Closed Tuesday and Wednesday, and best reserve ahead.

In Zierikzee

Arberge Maritime, Nieuwe Haven 21 (tel. 01110/21-56). This informal bar-café-restaurant makes a pleasant stop for just a drink, snacks, or full meals (especially their seafood specialties) at moderate prices.

Concordia Restaurant, Appelmarkt 29 (tel. 01110/51-22). The Neerlands Dis menu of Old Dutch specialties is featured here at moderate prices.

TOURIST INFORMATION

The **Provincial VVV Office** is at Markt 65A, Middelburg (tel. 01180/1-68-51). They can help you with bike rentals (Zeeland is wonderful biking country—park the car and hit the pedals if the spirit moves you!), special events during your visit, market days in the various villages, where to find 17th- and 18th-century windmills, accommodations as you travel, and a host of other matters.

Scattered about the province are some 40 local VVV offices, so keep a lookout for the blue-and-white triangular sign that identifies them.

THINGS TO SEE AND DO

As you explore Zeeland, keep an eye out for the **national costume,** still worn here in Walcheren and South Beveland (in the latter, the women wearing bonnets shaped like conch shells are Protestant, those whose bonnets form a trapezium with a light-blue underbonnet showing through are Catholic). Incidentally, the gold and silver ornaments you see worn by both men and women with the national costume can be bought as souvenirs. Also, if you're lucky you'll happen on the traditional game of tilting at the ring from bare horseback—it's called **krulbollen,** and the VVV can tell you if, when, and where you can see it during your visit.

Because it's so vital to the future of Zeeland, and because it's one of the most exciting engineering feats of the modern world, your first sightseeing priority should be the Delta Expo.

The Delta Expo

The whole of Holland is, of course, awe-inspiring because of the way in which land has been snatched from the very bottom of the sea, but nothing within Holland is quite so breathtakingly impressive as the massive system of dikes, sluice gates, and storm-surge barriers known collectively as the Delta Project. It was begun as a protective measure for Zeeland, but in the course of its development revolutionary ideas about sea management have surfaced and been implemented. As a result, rather than simply a system of dams to hold the sea *back,* there is in place a gigantic network of barriers that can be opened and closed as storms and tidal variations demand.

It took a good 15 years of, as the Delta people told me, "dredging, dumping, towing, and building" to create the component parts of this network, and when I remarked on the dedication of the hardworking men who never flagged during all those years of dredging, dumping, etc., the reply was simply, "The water is in these men—they know it well and what it can do and they know it must be managed."

To give visitors an overall view of the undertaking and an easily understood explanation of how everything works, the Delta people have built a huge scale model of the complex, as well as a map of the entire country on which tiny lights switch on and off to show how the Delta Project also plays a vital role in freshwater management of virtually the whole of Holland. At the end of a slide show and the map demonstration you can descend into the very innards of one of the 36 sluice-gate engine rooms. Allow yourself no less than an hour at this intriguing place, even if you don't think you have any interest in dams and engine rooms, etc. At the end of your tour there's a cozy coffeeshop whose terrace affords panoramic views that would be worth the trip on their own.

The Delta Expo is located at Stellendam (tel. 01879/16-00) and is open from April 1 through mid-November daily, including Sunday, from 10 a.m. to 5 p.m., with an admission fee of Dfl. 3.25 ($1.50) per person (children under 6 admitted free).

In Middelburg

Make your first stop the **VVV Office,** Markt 65A (tel. 1-68-51). Among the mass of informative and helpful literature they furnish is an excellent walking-tour brochure. They also conduct guided walking tours.

Middelburg began as a 9th-century fortress, erected as a defense against Norman attacks. The fortifications expanded into a real settlement about A.D. 1150, when the abbey was established (see below). Today the abbey is just one of the city's more than 1,000 historic buildings. Middelburg's colorful market day is Thursday, when you can mingle in the Markt Square with Zeelanders, many of whom are in native dress.

The **Town Hall,** another of Middelburg's miraculous reconstructions, consists of two distinct sections. The side facing the Markt is Gothic and dates from the 15th century, while the Noordstraat side, from the 17th and 18th centuries, is classic in style. Inside are such treasures as Belgian tapestries from the 1600s, a brass model of de Ruyter's flagship, 17th-century Makkum tiles, and the Middelburg coat-of-arms, originally located on the eastern façade of the building. The old tribunal hall is now known as the "wedding hall," and several ceremonies are held there each week. The banquet hall, originally the first cloth market in the Netherlands, is now used for official receptions, "welcome" evenings for new residents of Middelburg, and periodic concerts. From April through October, conducted tours take you through this interesting building every day except Sunday from 1:30 to 3 p.m. Admission is Dfl. 5 ($2.25) for adults, Dfl. 3.50 ($1.50) for children.

The sprawling 13th-century **Middelburg Abbey,** Abdijplein at Onder de Toren, had a life of traumatic ups and downs over the centuries, as it went from Catholic to Protestant to secular headquarters for governmental agencies and suffered the devastation of fires and careless alterations at the hands of whoever happened to be in charge. When 1940 bombings left it virtually leveled, it would doubtless have passed into history as nothing but a dim memory had it not been for the dedication of Middelburg authorities and Zeeland citizens. At the close of World War II they set about a restoration that amounted to a complete rebuilding—each brick had to be individually scraped and chipped smooth by human hands before it could be put into place. It was an enormous task, and the abbey you see today, a replica of its original glory, is an astonishing monument to all that work and dedication. As in medieval days, the abbey, its magnificent courtyard, and its tall Lange Jan Tower serve as the very heart of Middelburg. During the months of July and August the courtyard is the setting on Wednesday, Thursday, and Friday nights for a sound-and-light pageant that portrays its history in drama and music. The courtyard is a shady rest stop during sightseeing, and there's an excellent restaurant, with

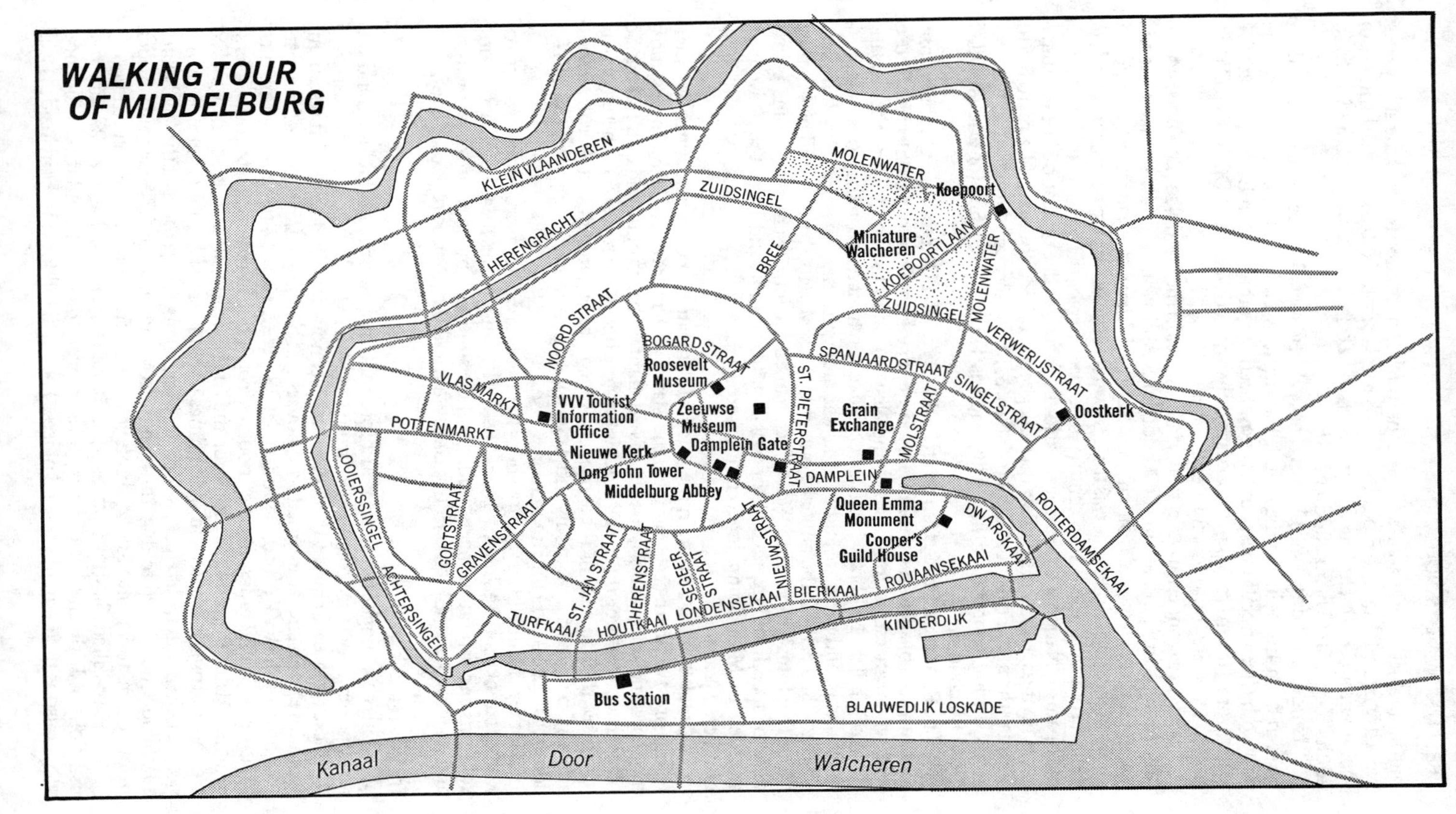
WALKING TOUR
OF MIDDELBURG
KLEIN VLAANDEREN
MOLENWATER
Koepoort
ZUIDSINGEL
HERENGRACHT
Miniature
Walcheren
KOEPOORTLAAN
BREE
MOLENWATER
ZUIDSINGEL
VERWERIJSTRAAT
NOORD STRAAT
BOGARDSTRAAT
Roosevelt
Museum
SPANJAARDSTRAAT
ST. PIETERSTRAAT
SINGELSTRAAT
Oostkerk
VLASMARKT
VVV Tourist
Information
Office
Zeeuwse
Museum
Grain
Exchange
MOLSTRAAT
POTTENMARKT
Nieuwe Kerk
Damplein Gate
Long John Tower
Middelburg Abbey
DAMPLEIN
Queen Emma
Monument
DWARSKAAI
Cooper's
Guild House
ROTTERDAMSEKAAI
LOOIERSSINGEL
GORTSTRAAT
GRAVENSTRAAT
ST. JAN STRAAT
HERENSTRAAT
SEGEER
STRAAT
NIEUWSTRAAT
ROUAANSEKAAI
ACHTERSINGEL
TURFKAAI
HOUTKAAI
LONDENSEKAAI
BIERKAAI
KINDERDIJK
Bus Station
BLAUWEDIJK LOSKADE
Kanaal
Door
Walcheren

outdoor tables during good weather, for lunch. The guided tours of the abbey every weekday from 10 a.m. to 5 p.m. and on Saturday from 1:30 to 3 p.m. during summer months cost (including admission to the Zeeland Museum) Dfl. 5 ($2.25) for adults, Dfl. 2.50 ($1) for children.

Lange Jan (Long John) Tower, at the abbey, soars 289 feet into the air and can be seen from any point on the island. Dating from the early 14th century it was destroyed by fire several times, but has now been rebuilt. It's open Easter through October from 10 a.m. to 5 p.m. weekdays only, with admission of Dfl. 1.35 (60¢) for adults, Dfl. 0.90 (40¢) for children.

There's a wonderful collection of antiquities in the **Zeeuwse (Zeeland) Museum,** Abdijplein 3, located in the Middelburg Abbey, including a Roman altar to a pagan goddess recovered from the beach after a 17th-century storm and a stone coffin from medieval times that was used to water cattle before its true purpose and age were recognized. Also, 16th-century tapestries depict the victory of Zeeland over the Spanish. National costumes are also displayed, with explanations of the differences in dress from one island or one village to another. Hours are 11 a.m. to 5 p.m. Tuesday through Friday and 1:30 to 5 p.m. Saturday through Monday (no weekend hours during winter months). Admission is Dfl. 3.50 ($1.50) for adults, Dfl. 2 (90¢) for children.

The **Roosevelt Study Center** (tel. 01180/3-10-11), located in the abbey complex, was established in honor of Theodore, Franklin Delano, and Eleanor Roosevelt, whose ancestors emigrated to the New World in the 1640s from the Zeeland town of Tholen. Its library holds extensive research material on the Roosevelt presidential eras, and there are audio-visual and slide presentations for use by European scholars. Since 1982 the annual Four Freedoms Medals (based on FDR's famous "four freedoms" speech in 1941, which named the four essential freedoms as freedom of speech and expression, of worship, from want, and from fear) have been awarded in Middelburg in even-numbered years, in Hyde Park, N.Y., in odd-numbered years.

Miniature Walcheren, in the small Molenwater park near the abbey, is a marvelous one-twentieth-scale model of the island, with more than 200 buildings, moving trains and ships, and windmills. It's a delight for both young and old, and a good place to visit before you leave Middelburg to explore the rest of Walcheren, where you'll see the originals of these models. Open Easter through October from 9:30 a.m. to 5 p.m. (to 6 p.m. in July and August), with an admission of Dfl. 5 ($2.25) for adults, Dfl. 2.50 ($1) for children.

Other Middelburg sights not to miss are the picturesque streets of **Kuiperspoort** and **Bellinkstraat;** the **Vismarkt,** which dates from 1559, with Doric columns and little auctioneers' houses, where summer Thursdays are days for an art and craft market; the **Blauw (Blue) Gateway;** and the **Koepoort** (Cow Gate).

In Veere

This charming little village is just four miles northeast of Middelburg, and was an important port for Scottish wool from the 14th to the 18th century. The original fortifications are still intact, their ancient tower now housing an excellent restaurant (see above), and streets are lined with houses and buildings straight out of the past.

Stop by the **VVV office,** at Oudestraat 28 (tel. 01181/13-65), and pick up their "Historical Walk Through Veere" booklet. You shouldn't miss the **Stadhuis,** Markt 5, which dates from 1474—look for the *kaak* outside, an iron brace that locked around a wrongdoer's neck in olden times to hold him or her in disgrace as townspeople pelted him with refuse and spittal; over it hangs the "stones of the law" which an offender was forced to drag through the town in penance. The Stadhuis is open from 10 a.m. to 5 p.m. Monday through Saturday from June to mid-September.

The so-called **Scotch Houses (De Schotse Huizen),** Kade 25-27, are two mansions of 16th- and 17th-century Scottish wool merchants, and these residences served also as their warehouses and offices. The small folklore museum inside is well worth a visit; it's open Tuesday through Saturday from 10 a.m. to noon and 1:30 to 5 p.m. during the summer.

Other Veere "don't miss" sights include the **Campveerse Toren** (Tower of Campveer), which sits at the entrance to the harbor and dates from 1500; and the **Grote Kerk,** whose construction took more than a century (1405–1560), and which Napoleon turned into a stable, barracks, and hospital.

In Vlissingen

The port city of Vlissingen (with ferry service to England and river pilots who guide Antwerp-bound ships down the River Schelde) is also a popular seaside resort. Go by the **VVV office** at Nieuwendijk 15 (tel. 01184/1-23-45) for information on the town's long and interesting history, and visit the **Stedelijk Museum,** the **Grote Kerk** (dating from the 14th century), and **St. Jacobskerk.** Don't leave the city without at least one stroll down the seafront promenade that is named variously De Ruyter, Bankert, and Evertsen in honor of those Dutch naval heros.

The Zeeland Riviera

The western part of Walcheren, from Westkapelle to Dishoek, is a string of delightful small seaside villages, with all sorts of recreational facilities. About the only somber note along the coast at this point is struck by bunkers and other mementoes of World War II.

In Zierikzee

This 11-centuries-old little town on the Oosterschelde lives within its medieval town walls, still guarded by fortifications built during the Middle Ages. Go by the **VVV office** at Havenpark 29 (tel. 01110/124-50) for walking-tour information, as well as details and booking on cruises on the Oosterschelde during summer months.

2. Noord Brabant

Brabant is one of Holland's most scenically beautiful provinces, forestland alternating with neat farmsteads and parkland edging its moors. The people who live in this part of the country, "below" the Rivers Rhine and Meuse, sometimes seem as much Belgian as Dutch, with a more relaxed view of the world and great emphasis on the joys of eating well and life's other pleasures—a bit different from the Dutch who live "above" the rivers. Brabant is a province of blurred cultural distinctions, and one town where even the national border itself becomes more than a little blurred, with homes on one side of a street inside Holland, those across the street in Belgium!

For the visitor, this is a restful, interesting area filled with historic towns, castles, and important centers of industry dotted about the lovely countryside.

WHERE TO STAY

Standards are quite high and hotels numerous in Brabant, yet during July and August they tend to be especially tightly booked, making it highly advisable to make your reservations in advance if you plan to stay the night in any of the province's excellent accommodations.

In Oisterwijk

Hotel-Restaurant de Swaen, De Lind 47, 5061 HT Oisterwijk (tel. 04242/1-90-06). Here in this quiet little village just 9½ miles from Eindhoven, de Swaen follows a three-centuries-old tradition of innkeeping. Indeed, the exterior of the neat white two-story hotel on the market square, with its long veranda across the front and neat, blue-trimmed windows, calls to mind the coaching inn that preceded it in this same location. Since its complete renovation to top 20th-century standards, however, its guest rooms and fine restaurant have transformed it into one of Holland's best-loved hostelries, and its dining room has earned international renown (see below). The 19 plush guest rooms all have private baths done up in Italian marble, with such luxurious touches as gold-plated faucets. Tiny chocolates decorated with white swans appear on your pillow each evening, just one more example of the qualities that make this place so special. Rates begin at Dfl. 250 ($109.75), and the hotel closes for two weeks in July. Highly recommended—well worth seeking out this off-the-beaten-track village.

In Eindhoven

Hotel Cocagne, Vestdijk 47, 5611 CA Eindhoven (tel. 040/44-47-55). This modern hotel is located in the city center, not far from the central railway station. Guest rooms, which underwent extensive renovation in 1987, are spacious, with bright, attractive décor, private bath, telephone, TV, and radio. There's indoor Par-T-Golf, garage parking, and a good restaurant. Rates range from Dfl. 225 ($98.75) to Dfl. 225 ($120.50).

Golden Tulip Geldrop, Bogardeind 219, 5664 EG Geldrop (tel. 040/86-75-10). At the outskirts of Eindhoven (on Hwy. A3), this modern hotel sits at the edge of the Strabrechtse heath, a restful retreat away from the bustle of city streets. Its large guest rooms have private baths, hairdryers, mini-bars, in-house movies, radios, TVs, and telephones, and amenities include a good restaurant, indoor swimming pool, tennis courts, solarium, keep-fit track, and sauna. Rates run Dfl. 175 ($76.75) to Dfl. 225 ($98.75).

Motel Eindhoven, Aalsterweg 322, 5644 RL Eindhoven (tel. 040/11-60-33). Guest rooms are comfortable and nicely furnished at this moderately priced motel, where there's ample parking and a restaurant. Rates begin at Dfl. 75 ($33).

In Heeze

Hostellerie du Château, Kapelstraat 48, 5591 HE Heeze (tel. 04907/35-15). Situated in this little village about a 20-minute drive from Eindhoven and directly across from a 17th-century château, this old 18th-century coaching inn has been redone in a fashion that disavows its somewhat rustic heritage. Its 14 guest rooms welcome you with opulent furnishings and tasteful décor, as well as private baths. Its restaurant is considered one of Holland's best (see below). Rates range from Dfl. 125 ($54.75) to Dfl. 190 ($83.25).

In's Hertogenbosch

Golden Tulip Central, Mr. Loeffplein 98, 5211 RX's Hertogenbosch (tel. 073/12-51-51). You couldn't ask for a more romantic location than at this large hotel on the city's medieval market square. The Central somehow manages to be both modern and cozy, and its guest rooms have private baths, telephones, radios, and TVs. There's a coffeeshop, a bar, an à la carte restaurant, a 14th-century cellar eatery ("de Hoofdwacht"), and the pricier De Raadskelder restaurant, also in a Gothic setting in the cellar of the Town Hall. Rates run Dfl. 150 ($65.75) to Dfl. 200 ($87.75).

Eurohotel, Hinthamerstraat 63, 5211 MG's Hertogenbosch (tel. 073/13-77-77). This small (46 rooms) hotel offers comfortable guest rooms at Dfl. 80 ($35) to Dfl. 110 ($48.25), and a restaurant with moderate prices.

In Breda

Hotel Mastbosch, Burg. Kerstenslaan 20, 4837 BM Breda (tel. 076/65-00-50). In a wooded site near the Mastbosch woods, this 50-room, first-class hotel offers a relaxing atmosphere, modern, comfortable rooms with private bath, a sun terrace, and a good restaurant. Rates run Dfl. 80 ($35) to Dfl. 190 ($83.25).

Hotel Breda, Roskam 20, 4813 GZ Breda (tel. 076/22-21-77). This large modern hotel just southwest of Breda (Exit Rijsbergen from Hwy. E19) has well-equipped guest rooms with private baths, radios, TVs, and telephones. Its cozy bar and lounge features an open fireplace, and there's an excellent à la carte restaurant. Other amenities include an indoor pool, sauna, and solarium. Good parking. Rates are Dfl. 100 ($43.75) to Dfl. 130 ($57).

WHERE TO EAT

The most widely recognized restaurant in Noord Brabant is **De Swaen,** De Lind 47, Oisterwijk (tel. 04242/1-90-06). Its chef, Cas Spijkers, was born in this region and trained in leading kitchens throughout Europe before coming back to lead De Swaen to its prestigious position. A firm believer in freshness, he believes "the choice of your products determines the quality of your kitchen," and he takes great pains to select nothing less than the best of local products, as well as traveling to Brussels twice a month to the excellent markets there. He smokes his own fish, meat, and game and bakes all breads and pastries right on the premises. The result is meals that have earned De Swaen a Michelin star and a devoted following. In the elegant cream-and-gilt dining room you'll be thrown into an agony of indecision as you read through the tantalizing menu, but let me suggest that you simply order his five-course menu of the day—rest assured it will be the best of the day's ingredients and prepared to perfection. Expect to pay between Dfl. 90 ($39.50) and Dfl. 150 ($65.75), without wine. Reservations are recommended, and the restaurant is closed on Monday and for two weeks in July.

In Eindhoven

De Karpendonkse Hoeve, Sumatralaan 3 (tel. 040/81-36-63). This first-class restaurant, a member of the prestigious Alliance Gastronomique Néerlandaise, specializes in game in season and always the best of local products in a pretty setting with terrace dining in good weather. Prices range from Dfl. 90 ($39.50) and up. Closed Sunday and at lunch on Saturday.

Restaurant Étoile, in the Hotel Cocagne, Vestdijk 47 (tel. 040/44-47-55). In addition to this excellent restaurant, with continental specialties in the moderate to expensive price range, the hotel has a very good café, the Bruegel (which serves the Neerlands Dis Old Dutch menu), and a terrace café—a good, centrally located stopping place for almost any kind of meal you're in the mood for.

Mei Ling, Geldropseweg 17 (tel. 040/12-50-55). This leading Chinese-Indonesian restaurant offers more than 300 choices. All are excellent, and prices are moderate.

The Neerlands Dis traditional Dutch menu is served, along with other moderately priced meals, at the **Restaurant Trocadero,** Stationsplein 15 (tel. 040/44-90-16).

In Heeze

Hostellerie du Château, Kapelstraat 48 (tel. 04907/35-15). Even if you're staying in Eindhoven, it's worth the 20-minute drive to Heeze for a meal under the watchful eye of owner/chef Hans Huisman. The cuisine is basically classic French, and gourmet regulars often come from Belgium and Germany when the season is right for asparagus from his own fields. The wine cellar is one of the best in Holland. Expect dinner to run about Dfl. 90 ($39.50) without wine. Closed for lunch on Saturday.

In's Hertogenbosch

De Pettelaar, Pettelaarseschans 1 (tel. 073/13-73-52). This pretty restaurant in a scenic location specializes in classic continental dishes and nouvelle cuisine. Open continuously from noon to midnight, with prices of Dfl. 55 ($24) and up. Saturday and Sunday opening is 3 p.m.

De Raadskelder, in the Golden Tulip Central Hotel, Mr. Loeffplein 98 (tel. 073/12-51-51). This atmospheric cellar restaurant in the Gothic Town Hall serves excellent meals at moderate prices. The hotel also has a good à la carte restaurant and an inexpensive coffeeshop.

In Breda

Restaurant Mastbosch, in the Hotel Mastbosch, Burg. Kerstenslaan 20 (tel. 076/65-00-50), offers traditional Dutch food at moderate prices.

TOURIST INFORMATION

In the provincial capital, **'s Hertogenbosch,** the VVV office is at Markt 77 (tel. 073/12-30-71); in **Breda,** its address is Willemstraat 17 (tel. 076/22-24-44); and in **Eindhoven,** Stationsplein 17 (tel. 040/44-92-31).

THINGS TO SEE AND DO

While there is sightseeing aplenty in the province of Noord Brabant, it's the scenery that will enthrall you most of all. There are the waterways and polders in the north and west; the sand drifts, fir and deciduous woods in the south and east; and everywhere picturesque villages and ancient towns.

In's Hertogenbosch (Den Bosch)

The capital city, 's Hertogenbosch, is affectionately known simply as Den Bosch (the Woods)—maybe they, too, have given up on the pronunciation of the longer version! Over 800 years old, it's a cathedral town and seat of a bishop, and was once a heavily fortified city. **Sint Janskathedraal** is a magnificent Gothic cathedral whose origins date back to the 1100s, although the present church was rebuilt over the course of a century when the earlier structure burned in 1240. Notice the little stone mannikins on the flying buttresses and up the copings—miniature copies of these delightful figures are on sale in local gift shops and make marvelous souvenirs to take home.

Het Zwanenbroedershuis Lieve Vrouwebroederschap (Illustrious Brotherhood of Our Lady), Hinthamerstraat 94, is an interesting small museum depicting monastic life during the Middle Ages, and the **Noordbrabants Museum,** Bethaniestraat 4, holds manuscripts, maps, weapons, coins, and archeological finds from this region.

In Overloon

In and around this little village some 35 miles southeast of Den Bosch, tank corps of opposing forces met in fierce and sustained combat during September and October of 1944, toward the end of World War II. It was a battle that left some 300 tanks wrecked in the area. Today the 35-acre **Oorlogsmuseum (War Museum)** commemorates that awful battle in this park holding a vast collection of mechanized war vehicles, as well as an incredible display of antitank devices. There are also moving exhibits documenting the Nazi occupation of Holland during World War II. Open daily from 9 a.m. to 6 p.m. during the summer months, 9:30 a.m. to 5 p.m. during the winter.

In Tilburg

Some 14 miles southwest of Den Bosch, Tilburg is interesting for its Town Hall, which is a palace that once housed Willem II. At nearby Hilvarenbeek there's the **Beekse Bergen Safari Park,** where some 40 different species live together freely.

In Oisterwijk

It is in Oisterwijk, sometimes called the "Pearl of Brabant," that you'll find the unique **Eurobird Park,** with a large collection of tropical and other foreign birds, as well as European species.

In Kaatsheuvel

De Efteling Family Leisure Park (tel. 01031/416/780-505), just outside town, is a 700-acre recreational park with all sorts of amusements, restaurants, and facilities for swimming and boating. Its most outstanding feature, however, is the remarkable miniature city, with towers and castles that serve as the setting for just about every fairytale character who ever stirred childhood's imagination. A good day's outing for all ages. It's open from 10 a.m. to 6 p.m. daily, April through October, with an admission of Dfl. 19 ($8.25), free for children up to age 3.

In Breda

Check with the VVV office for details on their conducted "Historical Kilometer" walking tour that takes you to the **Castle of Breda** (from 1536, now a military academy), the **Great Church of Our Lady** (with its striking tomb of Count Engelbert II and his wife), and other historical points of the town.

Breda is surrounded by beautiful **rural estates,** many of which open their grounds to the public, and great **public forests** such as the Mastbos and Liesbosch, whose ancient trees form peaceful retreats.

Art lovers will want to stop by the village of **Zundert,** just south of Breda—this is the birthplace of Vincent van Gogh, and there's a touching statue of the painter and his devoted brother, Theo, commissioned by the townspeople and sculpted by Zadkine.

In Baarle-Nassau / Baarle Hertog

This is the town that *literally* can't make up its mind whether to be in Belgium or in Holland, so exists in both. The line wavers so that houses use colored number plates to identify their citizenship—if the figures are blue, the occupants are Dutch; if they're black on a white plate with a black, yellow, and red vertical stripe, the occupants are Belgian. Must get confusing!

In Eindhoven

Its core dates from 1232, yet today it has grown into Holland's fifth-largest town with the appearance of a modern industrial city. The Philips electronics company has headquartered here for over 80 years, galloping out to encircle more and more neighboring villages and make them a part of Eindhoven. Not only is this a manufacturing center, but much important research is conducted by the company, research that has had far-reaching applications in the modern world of electronics.

3. Limburg

Of all Holland's provinces, Limburg is the least likely to fit any "Dutch" image you bring with you. Missing are the flat fields interlaced with canals, the windmills (although there are a few), and most of the other traditions we associate with Holland. It is, however, one of the most beautiful of the provinces, and it's such marvelous holiday country that the Dutch themselves flock there in droves.

Limburg is surrounded on three sides by Germany and Belgium, and since Roman times it has been a well-trod pathway for invaders, defenders, refugees, and just plain travelers. Its own cities draw liberally from the richness of other European cultures and cities that are close at hand. For those of a gambling nature, it provides the casino at Valkenburg, near Maastricht.

Northern Limburg shelters holiday parks and villages in a landscape of wooded hills and broad heaths that extend across central Limburg; southern Limburg occupies the highest ground in Holland, with its capital city, Maastricht, an exuberant, joyful center of history, higher education, and inborn hospitality extended at the drop of a smile.

There's a wealth of sightseeing—numerous castles and mansions, historic churches, picturesque villages, and mysterious caverns that tunnel into the heart of high cliffs. To all that, add the attractions of cities like Liège, Antwerp, Brussels, Cologne, Aachen, Düsseldorf, Bonn, and Luxembourg, all just a hop, skip, and a jump away. By no means, however, would I want to imply that Limburg is simply a province to pass through on your way elsewhere in Europe—this is a province so rich in holiday attractions that I urge you to make your base here and let day trips take care of all those adjacent destinations.

WHERE TO STAY

Accommodations come in all shapes, sizes, locations, and price ranges in Limburg. There are castle hotels, posh luxury establishments, homey small hotels with moderate rates, and bed-and-breakfast accommodations in private homes.

In the Castles

Kasteel Wittem, Wittemerallee 3, 6286 AA Wittem (tel. 04450/12-08). If you're lucky, you'll draw one of the two tower rooms (one even has panoramic windows in the bathroom!) in this romantic 12th-century castle some 12½ miles from Maastricht where stately swans adorn an ancient moat. Its guests over the centuries have included the Knights of Julémont, Willem the Silent, Charles V, other noblemen, and humble folk such as traveling monks. That impressive company would no doubt be astonished to see the cozy charm that now distinguishes the 12 guest rooms, each with country-style décor, beautiful furnishings, and a private bath. The dining room boasts a Michelin star (see below), and in good weather you can enjoy drinks on the garden terrace. The rate of Dfl. 165 ($72.25) for double occupancy includes breakfast.

Kasteel Erenstein, Oud Erensteinerweg 6, 6468 PC Kerkrade (tel. 045/46-13-33). Located in a small town on the old Roman route between Holland and Aachen (which is only about a 20-minute drive away), this splendid Renaissance castle is actually used now only for its renowned restaurant (see below). Accommodations are just across the road in a beautifully remodeled 270-year-old *boerderij* (a two-story, fortified farmhouse built around a central courtyard). The farmhouse, a national monument, is a surprisingly warm setting for the contemporary décor and furnishings. Glass has been used imaginatively in doors and to enclose walkways and the winter garden (open terrace in summer) that now occupies the courtyard. All 45 guest rooms are beautifully furnished, with modern bathrooms, color TVs, radios, and telephones, and the ten suites, some with private terraces, are spacious. There's also a health club, where you can luxuriate in the whirlpool, sauna, steambath, or hot tub for a very small fee. Breakfast is not included in the rates of Dfl. 85 ($37.25) single, Dfl. 100 ($43.75) to Dfl. 170 ($74.50) double, but the additional charge is minimal and a real bargain when you consider that your morning repast can be served in your room, in the winter garden/terrace, or in the castle's grand hall.

In Maastricht

Although accommodations are plentiful in Maastricht, they can also be booked up in peak summer months, so reserve ahead if possible and turn to the VVV office for help if you arrive without a place to rest your head. Also, if you'd like to stay in a private home, the VVV can arrange that for you.

Golden Tulip Hotel Derlon, Onze Lieve Vrouweplein 6, 6211 HD Maastricht (tel. 043/21-67-70). This jewel of a deluxe, five-star hotel sits on one of the loveliest of the city's small squares, and in summer operates a terrace café out under the trees. The hotel is built over ancient Roman ruins, and in its basement you can view excavated Roman foundations and many of the artifacts uncovered during excavation.

Upstairs in public rooms and the 42 guest rooms there is a beautiful blending of classic and modern décor. Each guest room has a bright, airy décor, with a private bath, mini-bar, hairdryer, TV, radio, and telephone. Rates, which do not include breakfast, range seasonally from Dfl. 206 ($90.25) to Dfl. 226 ($99) single, Dfl. 262 ($115) to Dfl. 322 ($141.25) double. Highest recommendation.

Golden Tulip Hotel Maastricht, De Ruiterij 1, 6221 EW Maastricht (tel. 043/25-41-71). Stretched along the riverfront, this modern deluxe (five-star) hotel is elegant from top to bottom. Some of the spacious guest rooms come with balconies or terraces, and all have private baths, mini-bars, TVs, radios, and telephones. There's a lively bar and lounge overlooking the river, a coffeeshop, and a good restaurant. Rates range from Dfl. 206 ($90.25) to Dfl. 226 ($99) for singles, Dfl. 262 ($115) to Dfl. 322 ($141.25) for doubles.

For those who don't mind being a bit farther from the city center, there's the luxurious new **Golden Tulip Barbizon Maastricht,** Forum 110, 6229 GV Maastricht (tel. 043/83-82-81), at the Maastricht Exposition and Congress Center. Its deluxe rooms all have private baths, TVs, in-house movies, mini-bars, hairdryers, and telephones. On the premises, there's a gourmet restaurant specializing in French cuisine, bar, and a sauna/fitness center. Singles begin at Dfl. 170 ($74.50); doubles, at Dfl. 225 ($98.75).

Hotel Pauw, Plankstraat 6, 6211 GA Maastricht (tel. 043/21-84-56 or 21-22-22). Right in the heart of the city center, overlooking the old inner harbor called Bassin, the Hotel Pauw couldn't be more convenient for sightseeing, shopping, dining, and just plain people-watching. Its 70 rooms all come with private baths, TVs, and telephones. No restaurant on the premises, but plenty nearby. There's a nice bar and lounge, and garage parking nearby. Rates range from Dfl. 90 ($39.50) to Dfl. 150 ($65.75).

Hotel Du Casque, Vrijthof 52, 6211 TA Maastricht (tel. 043/21-43-43). There's been an inn at this location since the 15th century, and the present family-run hotel carries on the tradition in good style. There are some 40 modern rooms, with private baths, TVs, telephones, and mini-bars. Located on the Vrijthof Square, across from an enclosed shopping mall and the Bonnefanten Museum, the hotel has a gourmet restaurant, bar, and a very good restaurant. An added bonus is garage parking. Rates begin at Dfl. 66 ($29) for singles, Dfl. 155 ($68) for doubles.

Hotel Beaumont, Stationstraat, 6221 Maastricht (tel. 043/25-44-33). This well-established hotel is located between the railway station and the river, just a short walk from the town center. Rooms are comfortable and attractive, and all have private bath, TV, and telephone. There's a cozy, semi-elegant restaurant serving very good, moderately priced meals. Rates for singles are Dfl. 65 ($28.50) and up; for doubles, Dfl. 125 ($54.75) and up.

Grand Hotel de L'Empereur, Stationstraat 2, 6221 BP Maastricht (tel. 043/21-38-38). Set on a corner across from the railway station, this lovely old turreted hotel has comfortable, attractive guest rooms with private baths, as well as apartments that can sleep up to four persons. All rooms have mini-bars, safes, radios, TVs, and telephones, and some also come with a trouser press. There's a cozy lounge bar that draws a local clientele and a restaurant. Other amenities include a sauna and whirlpool. Rates for rooms are Dfl. 187 ($82) and up single, Dfl. 262 ($115) and up double. Garage parking is available for a small additional charge.

Hotel-Café De Poshoorn, Stationstraat 47, 6221 BN Maastricht (tel. 043/21-73-34). This small corner hotel has rooms above a ground-floor café, where you register with the friendly owner. Its 12 comfortable rooms cost Dfl. 70 ($30) and up single, Dfl. 150 ($65.75) and up double.

In Valkenburg

Prinses Juliana, Broekhem 11, 6301 HD Valkenburg (tel. 04406/1-22-44). Only about a ten-minute drive from Maastricht, this pleasant small hotel houses one of Holland's most respected restaurants. There are 17 luxury guest rooms, all tastefully decorated and with private baths or showers, at rates of Dfl. 180 ($79) to Dfl. 210 ($92), single or double.

In Heerlen

Hotel Heerlen, Wilhelminaplein 17, 6411 KW Heerlen (tel. 045/71-33-33). Not far from the Aambos park and in the center of town, this member of the Golden Tulip hotel chain has deluxe rooms and suites, all with private bath, TV, radio, and telephone. It has a very good, attractive restaurant, a coffeeshop, and a nice bar/lounge with an open fire. Rates for singles begin at Dfl. 90 ($39.50); for doubles, Dfl. 150 ($65.75).

In Thorn

Hotel Golden Tulip Thorn, Hoogstraat 2, 6017 AR Thorn (tel. 04756/23-41). Right in the center of this lovely medieval townlet (often called the "White Village" because all the houses are painted white), this small hotel offers 19 nicely done-up guest rooms with private baths, TVs, radios, and telephones. Amenities include the Cellar Bar and the attractive La Ville Blanche restaurant. Singles range from Dfl. 125 ($54.75) up; doubles, from Dfl. 160 ($70.25) up.

In Venlo

Novotel Venlo, Nijmeegseweg 90, 5916 Venlo (tel. 077/54-41-41). Rooms (132, all with private bath and standard fittings) are modern, attractive, and well furnished in this large motel, which also has a very good restaurant. Single rates begin at Dfl. 120 ($52.75); doubles, at Dfl. 130 ($57).

In Landgraff

Hotel Winselerhof, Tunnelweg 99, 6372 XH Landgraff (tel. 045/46-43-43). Not far from the Belgian border, this lovely deluxe hotel occupies what was once a gentleman farmer's estate, built in 1500. Guest rooms are in two wings surrounding a large cobbled courtyard, and on the third side, there's a spectacular ballroom in what used to be a lowly barn. The remaining side of the square holds a candlelit cocktail lounge, with a gourmet Italian restaurant upstairs. While the 49 guest rooms are equipped with the very latest comforts, there are such historical touches as exposed brick walls and original ceiling beams. Rates begin at about Dfl. 171 ($75); suites, at Dfl. 194 ($85).

In Epen

The **Golden Tulip Zuid Limburg,** Julianastraat 23a, 6285 AH Epen (tel. 04455/18-18). Set among beautiful wooded hills in the Geul river valley, this comfortable first-class hotel offers easy access to the main roads to Maastricht, Belgium, and Germany. Accommodations consist of nicely furnished and appointed apartments for two to four people, all with kitchenette, mini-bar, private bath, TV, telephone, and a terrace. There's an indoor swimming pool, a sauna/fitness center, a bar, and a lovely restaurant with valley views. Rates range from Dfl. 190 ($83.25) up.

WHERE TO EAT

Maastricht, the capital of Limburg, is filled with good places to eat—it's not uncommon for people to drive from nearby Liège or Aachen just to have dinner there. Spotted around the province are several outstanding restaurants, and many others that serve excellent meals at moderate prices. And, of course, there are those castles.

In the Castles

Château Neercanne, Cannerweg 800, Maastricht (tel. 043/25-13-59). Set into a high hill about two miles south of Maastricht above the River Jeker and the Belgian border, this gracious château was built in 1698 for a Dutch nobleman, who once entertained Czar Peter the Great within its walls. Less welcome guests were the Nazi occupiers of World War II, but Allied troops who came later were greeted warmly. From its wide stone terrace, where you can dine or have drinks in fine weather, views of the beautiful Jeker valley form a pleasing backdrop. Inside, tasteful renovations have created a classic, romantic ambience with baroque wallpaper, shades of beige and burgundy, and Venetian glass chandeliers. Marlstone caves extending back into the hillside serve as wine cellars, with an arched-roof, candlelit room just made for cozy before- or after-dinner drinks. A member of Alliance Gastronomique Néerlandaise, the restaurant specializes in fine French dishes, with fresh herbs and vegetables straight from its own gardens and the best of local ingredients assuring top quality. The menu changes almost daily, depending on what's available, and prices run about Dfl. 75 ($33) and up, without wine. Closed Monday and Saturday for lunch. Reservations recommended.

Kasteel Erenstein, Oud Erensteinerweg 6, Kerkrade (tel. 045/46-13-33). In a beautiful natural park and surrounded by a moat, this marvelous 14th-century Renaissance castle serves meals in its grand hall, an elegant setting entirely suitable for the gourmet dishes that come to table. Hotel accommodations are offered just across the road in a 17th-century farmhouse (see above). Cuisine is mainly French, and specialties change daily according to what's available locally to ensure freshness of every ingredient. Set menu prices run about Dfl. 75 ($33), with à la carte meals that can go as high as Dfl. 125 ($54.75). Closed Saturday for lunch. Reservations recommended.

Kasteel Wittem, Wittemerallée 3, Wittem (tel. 044/50-12-08). See above for accommodations. The beautiful dining room in this lovely castle is paneled in French oak and has a warm, clubby atmosphere. Its French cuisine is of such high quality that it has long boasted a coveted Michelin star, and prices are in the Dfl. 75 ($33) to Dfl. 125 ($54.75) range, without wine. Reservations recommended.

In Maastricht

In Mestreechter Geis, Hoenderstraat 16 (tel. 25-09-23). This lovely little restaurant, located in a former mussels shop, is now an intimate oasis of white walls, dark exposed beams, and open fireplace. It's a warm, friendly, family-owned-and-operated place specializing in excellent fish dishes, with a talented chef (son of the owners) using fresh, seasonal catches to create real taste treats. Dinner prices run Dfl. 38 ($16.75) to Dfl. 65 ($28.50) without wine, and reservations are recommended for both lunch and dinner, since they can only serve 35 diners. Closed Monday. Highly recommended.

Au Coin des Bons Enfants, Ezelmarkt 4 (tel. 21-23-59). Beauty and sophistication plus an open log fire create an elegant ambience in which French and Belgian cuisine star. In fine weather there's outdoor dining in a rustic courtyard. Prices run about Dfl. 65 ($28.50) to Dfl. 100 ($43.75) for three to six courses without wine (there's an exceptionally good wine cellar here). Closed Saturday for lunch and all day Sunday. Reservations recommended.

Grand-Mère, Vrijthof/Helmstraat 16 (tel. 25-23-25). Named for the large bell in St. Servatius Cathedral, this beautiful little restaurant on one of Maastricht's historic squares serves excellent meals for moderate to slightly higher prices. Open for lunch and dinner, seven days a week.

In the moderate-to-expensive range, **'t Plenkske,** Plankstraat 6 (tel. 21-84-56), located in the beautifully renovated Stokstraat quarter, features regional specialties from Maastricht and Liège, with a goodly share of French classics thrown in for good measure. This lovely restaurant, with its light, airy décor and outdoor patio overlooking the Thermen (site of ancient Roman baths), is a great local favorite, and advance reservations are advised.

Also in the moderate-to-expensive range, **Au Premier,** Brusselsestraat 15 (tel. 21-97-61), is a stylish, intimate restaurant whose menus lean toward local and French specialties. In summer, you can dine on the pretty garden patio.

Restaurant Jean-Pierre, Platielstraat 9 (tel. 21-26-51). With white stucco walls and dark overhead beams, this is a cozy spot for dinner. Prices are in the moderate range. Dinner service begins at 5 p.m.; closed Monday.

Sirtaki, Kesselskade 2 (tel. 21-20-30). From its décor and the delicious aromas that fill the air, you'll know immediately that this cozy restaurant specializes in Greek dishes. The extensive à la carte menu also offers lighter selections of salads, omelets, and such, but if you take my advice, you'll skip right to the lamb, fish, and other Greek goodies. There's a good wine list, and several nice wines (including the Greek retsina) are available by the carafe. Open for dinner only, from 5 to 10 p.m., seven days a week.

De Trepkes, Stationstraat (tel. 21-69-58). Not far from the railway station, De Trepkes (it takes its name from the hardstone steps at the entrance) is a warm, homey place that serves excellent selections of meat and fish dishes at reasonable prices. In good weather there's outdoor dining. Set menus are available for Dfl. 50 ($22) and up, and à la carte options are in similarly moderate ranges. There's also a good wine list. Closed Monday and Sunday for lunch. Reservations recommended.

Sagittarius, Bredestraat 7 (tel. 21-14-92). This light, airy, two-level restaurant is on one of Maastricht's prettiest streets, across from the Stadsschouwburg theater. Chef Jan van Werven prepares modern and classic variations of local and French cuisine as you watch in his open kitchen. In summer there's garden dining. Prices are moderate, and it's open from 6 p.m. every day but Sunday.

In den Ouden Vogelstruys, Vrijthof 15 (tel. 21-48-88). This traditional café-bar is wonderfully atmospheric (there's a cannonball in its wall that lodged there in 1653—ask about the story), and it sits diagonally across from a white house that over the centuries has guested both Charlemagne and Napoleon. The bar's rustic interior and faithful local clientele make it a great place to stop for a light lunch or just for a drink (it's on the VVV's pub-crawl list mentioned below). Lunches of traditional Dutch specialties run Dfl. 25 ($11) and below.

Stap In, Kesselskade 61 (tel. 21-97-10). The extensive menu at this bright, popular spot features Dutch traditional specialties, hamburgers, omelets, spaghetti, sandwiches, and who knows what else, all at budget prices. Tables are set outside in fine weather, and you can eat well for Dfl. 12 ($5.25) to Dfl. 20 ($8.75).

In Thorn

La Ville Blanche, Hoogstraat 2 (tel. 04756/23-41). This excellent restaurant is in the Hotel Golden Tulip Thorn (see above) and its French cuisine menu is moderate to expensive in price.

In Venlo

De Watermeule, Molenkampweg 3 (tel. 077/2-52-14). Game, in season, is the specialty here, but meat and fish dishes are always excellent. Prices are in the fairly expensive range, but good value.

TOURIST INFORMATION

You'll find the **Maastricht VVV tourist office** at Het Dinghuis, Kleinstraat 1, 6211 ED Maastricht (tel. 043/25-21-21). One of the best equipped, most helpful, and friendliest in Holland, its hours are 9 a.m. to 6 p.m. Monday through Saturday, and in July and August also from 11 a.m. to 3 p.m. on Sunday.

The **Limburg provincial VVV office** is at Den Halder Castle, Valkenburg (tel. 04406/1-39-93).

THINGS TO SEE AND DO

The province of Limburg is easily toured by car, of course, but nondrivers will also find it easy to get around by either train or bus. The scenic countryside also lends itself to hiking or cycling.

In Maastricht

Maastricht is Holland's oldest fortified city, tracing its roots back to a Roman settlement in 50 B.C. here on the Rivers Meuse and Jeker at the foot of Mount St. Peter. From Mount St. Peter, the Romans and all those who came after them took great chunks of marlstone, a type of limestone that is as soft to carve and chisel as soap until it hits the air, when it quickly becomes as hard as any stone. Many of Maastricht's buildings are constructed of marlstone, and as more and more was extracted, Mount St. Peter became honeycombed with great caverns, some 20,000 passages boring into the cliff.

The Romans stayed four centuries, and with their departure, Maastricht was, for nearly another 400 years, the seat of bishops (Saint Servatius was the first, about 380, and Saint Hubert was the last, in 722), and from the early 1200s until the late 1700s it was under the feudal rule of the Dukes of Brabant. The city was also the last earthly sight for the hero of Alexandre Dumas's *The Three Musketeers:* it was here that D'Artagnan lost his life during King Louis XIV's seige of Maastricht in 1673. It was French forces who, in 1795, occupied the city and declared it capital of a French province.

That changed with Napoleon's defeat at Waterloo, and when Belgium gained its separation from Holland in 1839, this little province stayed Dutch, with Maastricht its capital. During the course of all that history Maastricht has sustained 21 sieges as one ruler after another sought to control its strategic position. Today the city is a charming mixture of historic buildings and monuments (more than 1,450), university students, cultural activities, a lighthearted carnival famous throughout Europe, and some of the finest restaurants to be found in any Dutch city its size.

TOURING THE TOWN To begin your tour of this lovely and lively city, go by the VVV office and pick up their "Historic Walk Tour of Maastricht" brochure. It guides you from their office, located in the busy shopping district, through city streets to a fair few of all those historic buildings and monuments. If you fall under Maastricht's spell as completely as I have done, you'll keep the brochure with you and ramble, finally completing the entire 1½-hour route in two or three days! Keep your eye out for the little square called Op de Thermen, where you can still see the outline in its cobblestones of a Roman bath; the Markt square, where vendors gather on Wednesday and Friday mornings to open colorful stalls (some from as far away as Belgium and Germany); the statue of the cheerful little *'t Mooswief* (Vegetable Woman) in the Markt square; the small, impish *Mestreechter Geis* statue in a tiny square at Klein Stokstraat (he embodies the joie de vivre of Maastrichters, and his name means "Spirit of Maastrichters"); and the Vrijthof square at the heart of the old city. The St. Servatius Bridge dates from 1280 and is one of the oldest in Holland. And as you walk around the city, look for the 250 or so 17th- and 18th-century houses with sculpted gable stones showing the name of the house and the year it was built. Some of the prettiest are on Hoogbrugstraat, Rechtstraat, Markt Square, Boschstraat, Stokstraat Quartier, Platielstraat, and Achter het Vleeshuis.

The VVV also conducts **guided walking tours** from late June through August that cost Dfl. 3.75 ($1.75) for adults, Dfl. 2.25 ($1) for children.

One of the nicest ways of all to get an overall look at the oldest part of the city is to take a 45-minute tour in an old-fashioned horse-drawn hunting coach. There are daily morning and afternoon tours from May to September, with fares of Dfl. 12 ($5.25) for adults, Dfl. 5 ($2.25) for children, and there's a minimum fare of Dfl. 24

($10.50). For exact schedules and booking, call **Coach-Hire G. Costongs,** Koestraat 14-16 (tel. 21-48-12).

SEEING THE SIGHTS The **Caves of St. Pietersberg**—if you do no other sightseeing during your Maastricht visit, you should not miss these unique underground chambers. From the days of the Romans to the long days of several sieges to the months and years of enemy occupation during two World Wars, these 20,000 passages have served as a place of refuge to people who have left behind interesting drawings and signatures on the marlstone walls. During World War II they also served as a refuge for such Dutch masterpieces as Rembrandt's *Night Watch* and other treasures that were hidden away from the avaricious Nazi grasp. You'll follow your guide's lantern through about two miles of what some say are the nearly 200 miles (others will downgrade that figure to *6* miles) of 20- to 40-foot high tunnels. Do stay close to that lantern—there are tales told in Maastricht of those who entered here and were never seen again (ask about the four monks). Look closely at the signatures you pass and you'll see many names straight from the history books. The caves are open daily from Easter to September and on weekends in other months. Admission is Dfl. 3.75 ($1.75) for adults, Dfl. 2.25 ($1) for children. Check with the VVV office for exact tour hours and directions to reach the caves by city bus (tours leave from two entrances at different hours).

The majestic medieval cruciform **St. Servaasbasiliek (Basilica of Saint Servatius),** Vrijthof Square, dates its oldest parts back to the year 1,000, and it was considerably enlarged in the 14th and 15th centuries. Saint Servatius, Maastricht's first bishop, is buried in its crypt, and its treasury holds a large reliquary of the saint and several of his religious items (staff, pectoral cross, drinking beaker, etc.), as well as a rich collection of religious vestments and other objects. The southern tower of the cathedral's west wall holds Grameer (Grandmother), the largest clock in Holland and a beloved symbol of the city. You can tour the treasury from 10 a.m. to 5 p.m. daily; admission is Dfl. 3.50 ($1.50) for adults, Dfl. 1 (44¢) for children.

At the **Basilica of Our Beloved Lady,** in Vrouweplein, the west wing and crypts of this medieval Romanesque cruciform structure date from the 12th century, and there is evidence of an even earlier Christian church, as well as a pagan place of worship, on this same site. But it is the side chapel sheltering the pilgrim's statue of Our Beloved Lady *Stella Mare* (dating from 1500) that most people come to see. The richly robed statue dates from the 14th century and is credited with many miracles, even during long years when it had to be hidden away because of religious persecution. It is said that in the early 1600s, when the Catholic religion was once more recognized, as many as 20,000 pilgrims came to worship at her shrine every Easter Monday. When the Calvinists came into power in 1632 the statue once more went into hiding, and in 1699 legend says Our Lady herself established the "prayer route" by which she was returned to her proper place by stepping down from her pedestal and leading a devout parishioner through the muddy streets. In support of the legend, it is recorded that the morning after the miraculous walk there was indeed mud on the hem of Our Lady's robe! Legend or no, those with strong religious beliefs and those with none will be equally touched by the beauty of the statue and her shrine. The church treasury, a rich collection of tapestries, reliquaries, church silver, etc., may be visited daily from 11 a.m. to 5 p.m., from 1 to 5 p.m. on Sunday. There's a small admission charge.

Near Vrijthof Square, the **Bonnefanten Museum** (Provincial Museum of Art and Archeology), Dominikanerplein, holds an intriguing collection of art and artifacts. Glass from the Roman era, medieval altarpieces, sculpture, silverwork, and paintings that trace the work of artists from Limburg through the centuries—its an impressive record of Limburg's multifaceted history. Hours are 10 a.m. to 5 p.m. Monday through Friday, 2 to 5 p.m. on Saturday and Sunday. Small admission fee.

You really should visit the marvelous **Natuur Historisch Museum,** Bosquetplein 6-7, *after* you've seen the Caves of St. Pietersberg, for then you can

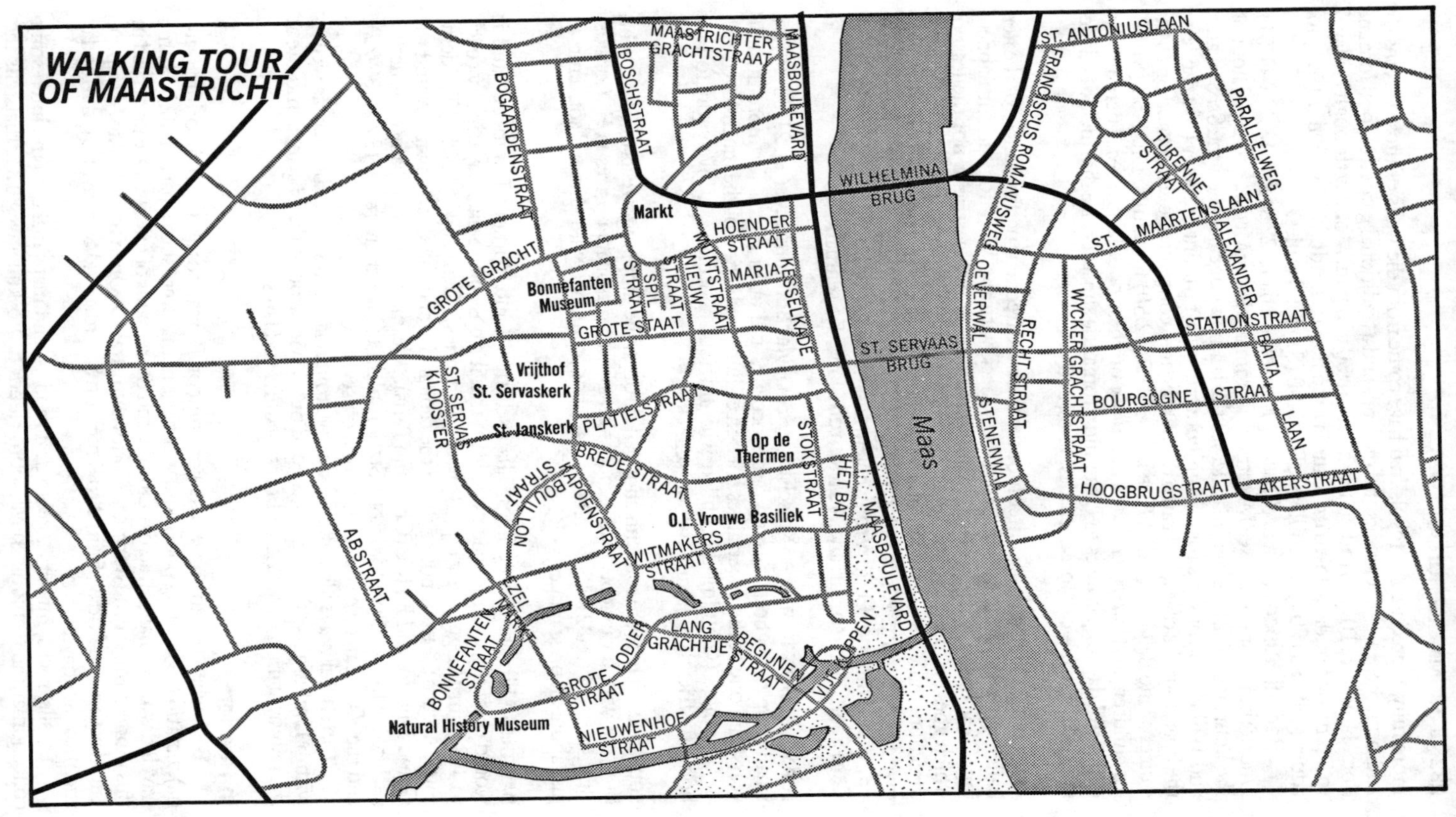
WALKING TOUR OF MAASTRICHT
MAASTRICHTER GRACHTSTRAAT
BOSCHSTRAAT
MAASBOULEVARD
BOGAARDENSTRAAT
Markt
HOENDER STRAAT
MUNTSTRAAT
NIEUW STRAAT
SPIL STRAAT
MARIA
KESSELKADE
GROTE GRACHT
Bonnefanten Museum
GROTE STAAT
Vrijthof
St. Servaskerk
ST. SERVAS KLOOSTER
St. Janskerk
PLATIELSTRAAT
BREDE STRAAT
BOUILLON STRAAT
KAPOENSTRAAT
Op de Thermen
STOKSTRAAT
HET BAT
O.L. Vrouwe Basiliek
WITMAKERS STRAAT
ABSTRAAT
EZEL MARKT
BONNEFANTEN STRAAT
LANG GRACHTJE
LODIER
GROTE STRAAT
BEGIJNEN STRAAT
VIJF KOPPEN
NIEUWENHOF STRAAT
Natural History Museum
Maas
WILHELMINA BRUG
ST. SERVAAS BRUG
ST. ANTONIUSLAAN
FRANCISCUS ROMANUSWEG
OEVERWAL
STENENWAL
RECHT STRAAT
WYCKER GRACHTSTRAAT
TURENNE STRAAT
PARALLELWEG
ST. MAARTENSLAAN
ALEXANDER
STATIONSTRAAT
BATTA LAAN
BOURGOGNE STRAAT
HOOGBRUGSTRAAT
AKERSTRAAT

more fully appreciate the fossils that have come from the walls of those caverns. In addition, there are other rocks and minerals and a traditional garden of local lore and flora. Hours are 10 a.m. to 12:30 p.m. and 1:30 to 5 p.m. Monday through Friday, 2 to 5 p.m. on Sunday; closed on Saturday and holidays. Admission is Dfl. 1 (44¢) for adults, Dfl. .50 (20¢) for children, Dfl. 2.50 ($1) for families.

Rederij Stiphout River Cruises, Maaspromenade 27 (tel. 043/25-41-51). One of the nicest ways to see Maastricht is from the River Meuse, and every hour on the hour one of these river boats leaves the landing stage between the St. Servatius and Wilhelmina bridges for a 55-minute cruise past Mount St. Peter (you can leave the boat, tour the caves, and catch the next boat to continue the cruise) and on to the sluices at the Belgian border. Fare is Dfl. 5.75 ($2.50) for adults, Dfl. 3.50 ($1.50) for children, and *you should book a day ahead* on these popular cruises. There are also delightful day-long cruises to Liège and a romantic sunset cruise that includes dancing and dinner—call for schedules, fares, and booking.

AFTER DARK During the winter months there are frequent performances of theater, ballet, operettas, musicals, cabaret, etc. Check with the VVV for current happenings. Year round, there's plenty going on after dark in Maastricht, not the least of which goes on in more than 500 cozy bars and cafés. To get you started in the right direction, the VVV issues a "Pub Crawl" booklet, but you'll undoubtedly find your own favorite route. A few outstanding places are **In 't Knijpke,** St. Bernardusstraat 13; **Charlemagne,** O. L. Vrouweplein 24; **In de Oude Vogelstruys,** Vrijthof 15; **Café Sjiek,** Pietersstraat; and **Au Mouton Blanc,** Kersenmarkt 10.

FOR YOUR SWEET TOOTH At Kesselskade 55, **Olivier Bonbons b.v.** (tel. 21-55-26) is a small shop that's been turning out chocolates and other sweets for more than 30 years, and one of their specialties is a porcelain reproduction of the much-loved Bell of Granmère (Grandmother) filled with luscious chocolates, a lovely gift to take home for friends or family (or yourself?).

SOUVENIRS There are souvenir shops all through the shopping streets of Maastricht, but one with an exceptionally good selection at reasonable prices is **H. Corsius,** Brugstraat 34 (tel. 21-42-26). It's a small shop, crammed with gifts and souvenirs in just about all price ranges.

DAY TRIPS Limburg sometimes calls itself the "Land Without Frontiers," and it would certainly seem so when you learn that it's possible to plan day trips by coach to Belgium (Liège, Antwerp, Brussels, Ardennes), Germany (Moselle, Tuddern, Eifel, Aachen), Luxembourg (both the capital city and the small towns around the Grand Duchy), and France (Givet and Paris). A leading coach company conducting such coach tours is **Splendid Cars,** Stationsplein 1, Maastricht (tel. 043/21-39-72), and the VVV can give you information on several other options.

Dutch Railways also offers attractive routes and rates across borders as well as within Limburg itself, and there is good bus service around the province. Inquire at the railway station in Maastricht for schedules and fares.

In Heerlen

Back when this town was a major point on Roman roads, the sudatorium (sauna), natatio (swimming pool), and gymnasium that were such a part of life in Rome traveled with Romans all across Europe, and the remains of one such are preserved in this modern **Museum Thermen,** Coriovalumstraat 9. Open from 10 a.m. to 5 p.m. Tuesday through Friday, from 2 to 5 p.m. on Saturday and Sunday; closed Monday and most holidays.

Fossils, rocks, minerals, geological models, and maps make up the interesting collection at the **Geologisch Museum Heerlen,** Voskuilenweg 131, that tells the story of Limburg's landscape history. Hours are 9 a.m. to noon and 2 to 5 p.m. Monday through Friday; closed weekends and holidays.

In Valkenburg

In an art deco setting, the **Casion (Casino) Valkenburg,** Odapark, Valkenburg (tel. 04406/1-55-50), operates French and American roulette and blackjack, and there's a restaurant, bar, and lounge. A dress code is observed (jacket and tie—or turtleneck—for men, dress or dressy pants suit for the ladies), and you'll need your passport to show you're over 18 years of age.

About three miles south of Valkenburg, the **Margraten Military Cemetery,** on the Maastricht–Aachen highway, the final resting place for all American troops who died in Holland in World War II, is a place much revered by the Dutch, who tend the graves and many times leave wreaths and flowers behind as symbols of gratitude for the sacrifices that liberated them from Nazi oppressors.

In Venlo

The beautiful period rooms in the **Goltzius Museum,** Goltziusstraat 21, bring to life the history of Venlo and North Limburg, and there are also interesting coin and medal collections. Hours are 10 a.m. to noon and 2 to 5 p.m. Monday through Friday, from 2 to 5 p.m. on Saturday, Sunday, and holidays.

The fortified town of Venlo received its city rights as far back as 1343, and although it is now a thriving industrial and commercial center, its history is apparent in the Renaissance 16th-century **Town Hall,** where the walls in its council room are covered with Cordova leather.

In Thorn

In this lovely little townlet, many of the buildings are painted white, and its huge **Abdijkerk stone church** has a stunning baroque interior and high altar, as well as a small museum well worth a visit.

PART THREE

LUXEMBOURG

INTRODUCING LUXEMBOURG

The Grand Duchy of Luxembourg is such a tiny little country (only 999 square miles) it hardly seems possible that its borders could embrace a treasure trove of travel delights worthy of a nation many times its size. Yet within those borders are the remnants of a rich history and a landscape whose scenic beauties vary from wild highlands to peaceful river valleys to southern plains dotted with picturesque villages and farmlands. Its people have emerged from a turbulent past to forge a prosperous present and build the framework for an optimistic future not only for their own country, but for the entire European community.

This is a land that captures the imagination and begs the traveler to tarry—a unique, colorful bazaar of travel memories.

1. A Brief History

Long before recorded history, the Grand Duchy was home to Magdalenian, Neolithic, and Celtic tribes. It was the Celts, those fiercely loyal people who resisted invaders to the death, whose Treviri tribe finally fell to Roman legions intent on bringing all of Europe under Caesar's rule. Their defeat came in the 1st century A.D., and for almost 500 years afterward one Roman emperor after another put down one uprising after another as their independent-minded subjects stubbornly refused to replace their strong Druidism worship with the paganism of Rome.

Christianity succeeded where paganism failed, however, and by the 5th century about all that was left of the Romans in Luxembourg were the bits and pieces of their urban civilization, a network of bridges that marked their progress across the land, and place names such as Ettelbruck (Attila's Bridge). Luxembourg was by then quite firmly in the Frankish camp.

Along with the monasteries that sprang up and flourished (with the support of the people) came educational and cultural influences that helped form the foundation of today's Luxembourg. The great Frankish leader Charlemagne brought in

Saxons to settle in the Ardennes and added another ethnic imprint to the face of the region.

It was the youngest of the counts of Ardennes, Sigefroi, who obtained a large land grant from the Abbey of Saint Maximin (the deed, dated April 12, 963, is still kept in the Municipal Library in Trier). He built his castle on the ruins of Castellum Lucilinburhuc, an ancient Roman fort that had guarded the crossing of the Paris–Trier road with that connecting Metz with Aix-la-Chapelle. From that strategic spot there grew a town and eventually a country that went by the name of Lützelburg.

By the 12th century the counts of Luxembourg were at the helm, and they enlarged their ship of state by wars with other noblemen, fortunate marriages, and all sorts of diplomatic shennanigans until they took to absenting themselves for long periods, joining the forces of Godfrey of Bouillon to travel to the Holy City during the Crusades. Some never returned, having fallen in battle, and those who did found their land in disarray, much of it confiscated by other overlords during their absence.

When Henry IV the Blind's daughter, the Countess Ermesinde, came along in the early 1200s, things were in a right mess. Through a couple of marriages Ermesinde was able to restore some of Luxembourg's lost territory, and when her last husband died in 1225 she boldly took charge of things. By bringing together in a central governing body noblemen who had always been at each other's throats, she pushed through such revolutionary reforms as a court of justice and extended limited rights of justice to citizens. A host of individual rights were granted to lessen the tight rein of feudal lords over their burghers, and this forward-looking lady set about establishing convents and monasteries to bring education and culture to her people. When she died at the age of 51, her legacy was a united nation with enduring social standards.

In 1308 Henry VII of the House of Luxembourg became emperor of the Holy Roman Empire and spent the rest of his life trying to unite all of Europe under his rule. His son, John the Blind, was a valiant warrior who perished at Crécy fighting the forces of Edward III of England, after ordering his men to lead him into the thickest battle. Today he is revered as Luxembourg's national hero. His son, Charles IV, favored the gentler means of treaty and marriage to extend his domain, and by the time *his* son, Wenceslas, gained the throne, the House of Luxembourg ruled a territory some 500 times the size of the Luxembourg of today's Europe.

The glory days were not to last long, however. King Wenceslas' son, Sigismund, proved to be far less able than his ancestors, and by the mid-1400s Luxembourg was reduced to the status of a province ruled over by the dukes of Burgundy. The next 400 years or so saw that rule shuttled between Spain, France, Austria, and Burgundy. For Luxembourgers, it was enough to crush forever the strong spirit of independence that started with their Celtic forebears and had grown stronger than ever from the time the Countess Ermesinde started handing out all those individual rights!

Yet that stubborn sense of individual worth refused to be crushed, no matter who sat on the throne, and in self-protection, each successive ruler found it necessary to strengthen even more a capital city that was already one of Europe's strongest. Luxembourg, then, became rather a problem to the rest of Europe: its position was too strategic and its fortifications too strong to allow it to be self-governing, or even to be controlled by any one nation. The answer seemed to be to divide the country among several nations, so the Congress of Vienna handed over the eastern part to Prussia and the rest to William of Orange-Nassau, in Holland. Then, in 1839, more than half of Holland's Luxembourg went to Belgium!

The boundaries were growing smaller and smaller, and what was now the Grand Duchy of Luxembourg posed no real threat to anyone. Still, there were all those fortifications. So in 1867 the decision was made by European powers convened in London that freedom would be granted the Grand Duchy on the condition that its fortifications be dismantled. Luxembourgers were overjoyed, and in October 1868 they affirmed a constitution that boldly proclaimed "The Grand Duchy of Luxembourg forms a free state, independent and indivisible." Today there are green parks all through their capital city to mark the sites of those mighty fortifications, and tiny Luxembourg has led the way toward peaceful economic unification of Europe's separate nations.

Since that momentous announcement of independence, Luxembourg has seen periods of prosperity (largely due to an important steel industry) and periods of decline that sent thousands emigrating in search of a living wage (it is said there are more Luxembourgers in the United States than there are in the Grand Duchy!). Twice—in World Wars I and II—it has suffered the agonies of military occupation. Some 3,000 Luxembourgers perished fighting with the Allies between 1914 and 1918, and the heroism of the Luxembourg underground resistance movement in the 1940s is legendary. Many of the younger men made their way to Allied countries to fight in their ranks, while those at home actually *went out on strike* when a Nazi ruling imposed compulsory service in the Wehrmacht, a move that brought swift retributions that only added to their suffering, already severe. By the time the country was liberated in 1945, more than 60,000 homes and 160 bridges and tunnels had been destroyed. Once more the determined Luxembourgers set to with a will, and within a remarkably short time, fields were once more under the plow, highways and railways were restored, and homes were made habitable.

Since 1934 Luxembourg has been active in the Benelux Economic Union, and since 1957 it has been in the forefront of European Economic Community development. For three months of each year, the EEC Council of Ministers meets in the impressive European Center in the capital city, which is also the home of the Secretariat of the European Parliament. This is also where the Court of Justice of the EEC holds its meetings.

2. Luxembourg Today

Today the Grand Duchy of Luxembourg is a constitutional monarchy with a population of about 364,000. Its government is headed by Grand Duke Jean, of the house of Nassau-Weilburg, whose position is hereditary and who shares executive power with a 12-minister cabinet. An elected Chamber of Deputies holds legislative power.

Economically, the Grand Duchy has a strong iron-and-steel industry and a growing number of light-industry firms. Its banking climate has attracted over 100 foreign banks (which employ one out of every 40 Luxembourgers) and it has been selected as headquarters of the European Investment Bank. Agriculture, once its primary industry, is still important, as are the vineyards of the Moselle Valley. The enchanting Luxembourg countryside has become a favorite holiday location for many Europeans, adding a tourist industry to the mix.

3. The Lay of the Land

Geographically, the Grand Duchy consists of two very distinct regions. The Ardennes hills, richly forested, lie in the northern half, while to the south are rolling farmlands, woods, and the valley of the Moselle with its famous vineyards. The mining district is tucked away in the extreme south.

Luxembourg City sits in the center of the southern region and is a marvelously contrasting mix of the old and the new. The older city runs along a deep valley beneath the brooding casements that have lent themselves so readily to defense in times of war, while the more modern part of town crowns steep cliffs overlooking the old.

In the northern Ardennes region handsome castles are found around virtually every bend, with especially interesting ones at Clervaux and Esch-sur-Sûre. Medieval Vianden, surrounded by beautiful forests and proud site of a huge restored fortress, is a pretty Ardennes holiday town.

For Americans the Ardennes hold another fascination, for it was here, in places like Berdorf and Clervaux and Ettelbruck, that U.S. forces engaged Nazi troops in the fierce Battle of the Bulge. Memorials to those who fell during those closing days of World War II mark the route that finally led to Luxembourg's total liberation on February 12, 1945.

Along the valley of the Moselle, vacationers camp and hike and fish, and tourists come by the busload to visit world-famous wineries.

4. The People

"We are very much a combination of what surrounds us," Prince Jean de Luxembourg (second son of Grand Duke Jean) is quoted as saying. That is undeniably true—in such a small country it could hardly be otherwise. But it's a strange sort of combination. Take their language, for example. Letzebuergesch has a vague Germanic base with overtones of French, yet is as distinctly different from either language as Luxembourgers are different from either nationality. They learn and use their native tongue from earliest childhood, study German in their first school years, and add French to their curriculum early on. English is also widely spoken. As for anyone who isn't native born *learning* Letzebuergesch, forget it—it's a tongue twister, and as any Luxembourger will tell you, one must be born to it.

A combination they and their language may be, but that combination has produced a people who are very much their own, with a personality and inborn traits that are hard to pin down in mere words. And while those unique traits may elude description, Luxembourgers seem content to leave it simply at *"Mir woelle bleiwe wat mir sin"* ("We want to remain what we are") with no need to spell out "what we are" in detail. You will see that national motto inscribed in Letzebuergesch over old doorframes, hear it echoed in songs, and recognize its essence in everyone you meet in the Grand Duchy.

Among the things they are is hard working. Foreign firms that open branches in Luxembourg will tell you that productivity is far higher than in other locations. One look at well-tended farms or shops will reveal the industry of their owners. Go into a Luxembourg home and the cleanliness and order will speak more loudly than words of the homemaker's pride in her work. And of course the swiftness with which Luxembourgers repaired World War II devastation in their country is ample testimony to their collective abilities.

Another thing they are is fond of eating. Cafés are everywhere, and if there's an important matter to discuss, decision to be taken, or social crisis to resolve, Luxembourgers repair to the nearest café or pastry shop. It goes without saying, then, that they are also fond of cooking—don't go away without indulging in their luscious pastries, and let the calories go hang!

In the cultural sphere, Luxembourg has produced the contemporary expressionist painter Joseph Kutter, the internationally acclaimed photographer Edward Steichen, and many lesser-known artists whose works are displayed in galleries throughout the Grand Duchy. As for music, it's the first love of most Luxembourgers, and wherever you travel you'll encounter local bands, choral groups, and musical theater groups—in the capital city hardly a summer evening passes without open-air concerts in the Place d'Armes.

The people of Luxembourg are also quite cosmopolitan. From their cuisine (also a combination of the best from those who surround them) to their culture to their dress, they are at home in the world, eager to travel and secure enough in their own uniqueness to appreciate the special qualities of others.

Above all else Luxembourgers are patriotic. Despite centuries of domination by first one ruler then another, there is a collective memory of independence and individual liberties they have always claimed as their own even as they endured those who would deny them.

Spend a little time in Luxembourg with these proud and charming people and you may well find yourself silently echoing their motto, with the slight addition, "We want you to remain what you are!"

LUXEMBOURG PRACTICALITIES

As is true of the other two Benelux countries, Belgium and Holland, Luxembourg is an easy country in which to travel, and whether you plan to go top-drawer or pinch pennies all the way, you'll find that the Grand Duchy has smoothed the way.

1. Getting to Luxembourg

How you reach the Grand Duchy will depend on whether it's your primary destination, a stop on your tour of the continent, or a few days' detour while visiting Holland or Belgium.

BY AIR

For years, **Icelandair** has led all other airlines in providing the most direct and inexpensive way to reach Luxembourg from the United States. With departures from New York, Orlando, Baltimore-Washington, Chicago, and Boston, and only one stop in Iceland, schedules from U.S. gateways are for various days of the week, daily from New York only in summer. Stopovers in Iceland of up to 21 days are allowed for no additional air fare.

In 1988 round-trip fares between New York and Luxembourg were in the following ranges, depending on season: regular coach fare, $449 to $699; APEX (two weeks' advance booking), $358 to $599. Three-day package rates, including accommodations at top hotels, all transfers, and breakfasts, were available for $49 per person per day, double occupancy. Car rentals can be arranged through Icelandair for rates (in 1988) of $79 to $185 per week, depending on the make and model.

Icelandair also has excellent connecting service from Luxembourg with **Luxair** to London, Munich, Geneva, Amsterdam, Frankfurt, Nice, Paris, Rome, Zurich, Cyprus, and Copenhagen, as well as to other important European and Middle Eastern destinations by major carriers.

Luxembourg's modern airport is 3½ miles outside Luxembourg City, with a Luxair bus service into the central station for LF 150 ($4.75). City bus service from the city center, the youth hostel, and the central station costs LF 25 (80¢) plus LF 25 (80¢) per piece of luggage, but you should know that this service can be refused during peak hours (around noon) to those carrying a mountain of luggage. Taxi fare from the airport into the city is LF 400 ($13).

BY TRAIN

The **Luxembourg National Railways** network has excellent connections with most major European destination cities, and if you're coming from either Holland or Belgium, the **Benelux Tourrail Ticket,** good for unlimited travel in all three countries on any 5 days in a 17-day period, is a good buy at BF4,150 ($133.75) first class, BF2,800 ($90.25) second class.

If Luxembourg is only one destination in your travels around the whole of Europe, the **Eurailpass** is your best buy. It permits unlimited travel on the rail systems of 15 countries at a cost of $298 for 15 days, $370 for 21 days, $470 for one month, $650 for two months, and $798 for three months. It must be purchased before leaving the U.S., and is available from travel agents. The **Eurail-Youth Pass** is available to those under 26 years of age at a cost of $320 for one month, $420 for two months. For full details and a helpful guide to the use of Eurailpasses, contact Eurailpass, P.O. Box 325, Old Greenwich, CT 06870.

For advance information and a current timetable, contact: **C.F.L.,** 9 place de la Gare (B.P. 1803), 1018 Luxembourg; or the Office National du Tourisme, B.P. 1001, 1010 Luxembourg.

BY BUS

There's very good motorcoach transportation between Luxembourg City and most major European cities.

BY CAR

Luxembourg City is connected by first-class highways to such European cities as Brussels (119 miles), Amsterdam (187 miles), Paris (181 miles), Aachen (53 miles), and Frankfurt (139 miles).

2. Getting Around Luxembourg

BY TRAIN AND BUS

Luxembourg National Railways (Chemins de Fer Luxembourgeois) operates fast and frequent schedules throughout the Grand Duchy, with good connecting bus service to those points it doesn't reach. Travelers over the age of 65 are eligible for a 50% reduction in both first and second class *except to or from a frontier point.* In addition, special half-fare weekend and holiday round-trip tickets are offered throughout the system *except from frontier points.* A one-day **network ticket,** good for unlimited travel by rail and bus, costs LF 217 ($7); for five days, the cost is LF 658 ($21.25), and travel may be for any five days within a one-month period; for one month (from the first to last day of a specific month), it's LF 1,748 ($56.50).

Porters (available only at Luxembourg City station) charge a flat fee of LF 25 (80¢) per bag. For rail and bus information, telephone 49-24-24 any day from 7 a.m. to 8 p.m.

In addition to frequent bus service to all points in the Grand Duchy, there are

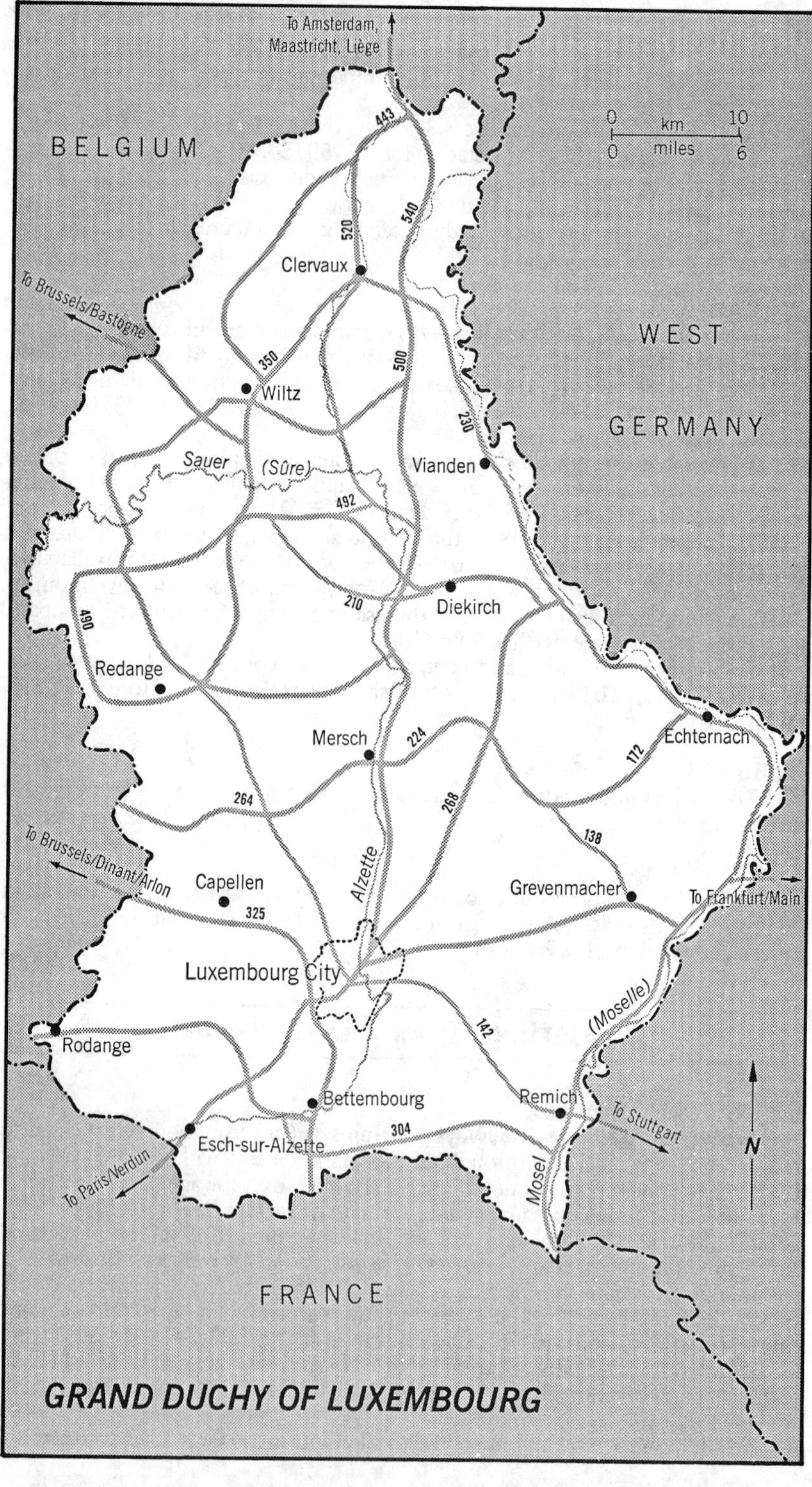

GRAND DUCHY OF LUXEMBOURG

several well-planned motorcoach tours from Luxembourg City that cover the most scenic countryside locations (see Chapter XXII).

BY AUTO

Roads within the Grand Duchy are kept in very good repair and well signposted, although some roadways are narrow, with many curves, especially in the Ardennes region. Speed limits are set at 60 km/h (37 mph) in built-up areas, 90 km/h (57 mph) on rural roadways, and 120 km/h (75 mph) on motorways. The accompanying chart shows distances between key points around the Grand Duchy.

Parking discs (available in stores and banks at no charge) are required in "blue zones" in Luxembourg City, Esch-sur Alzette, Dudelange, Remich, and Wiltz, and in many other places there are parking meters or half-hour parking-ticket dispensers. The use of seatbelts is compulsory, and horn blowing is permitted *only in case of imminent danger.*

If you plan to rent a car after your arrival in the Grand Duchy, you'll need a driver's license valid in your own country, and you'll be required to purchase insurance when you book the car. Car-rental rates begin at about LF 715 ($23) a day, and leading car-rental firms in Luxembourg City are: **Europcar,** boulevard Prince Henri 33 (tel. 352/2-11-81); **Budget Rent a Car,** Luxembourg airport (tel. 352/43-34-12); **Avis,** rue Duchscher 13, place de Paris (tel. 352/48-95-95); and **Hertz,** avenue de la Liberté 25 (tel. 352/48-54-85).

The **Automobile Club du Grand Duché de Luxembourg** is at route de Longway 13, Luxembourg-Helfenterbruck (tel. 352/45-00-45).

BY BICYCLE

The Luxembourg countryside lends itself to cycling, and while you're free to ramble down any road that strikes your fancy, there are several cycling tracks leading through some of the most scenic regions. Local VVV offices can furnish suggestions for cycling tours on these tracks or less-traveled roadways. Also, VVV offices in Luxembourg, Diekirch, Echternach, Mondorf-les-Bains, Reisdorf, and Vianden can arrange bike rentals. Bicycles are transported by train for a very small set fee, regardless of distance traveled, but this is *subject to space availability* (not usually a problem).

BY FOOT

If ever the Almighty planned a country especially for the walkers of the world, it must have been the Grand Duchy of Luxembourg! Shank's mare, in fact, is perhaps the best way of all to travel through this beautiful land. Great walkers themselves, Luxembourgers have set out some 20 walking paths (one of the densest networks of any country in the world!), most of them signposted. All youth hostels are linked by walking paths designated by white triangular signs, and bookshops carry maps of some 142 walking routes. Many local VVV offices have brochures of walking tours, and the Luxembourg Youth Hostels Association, place d'Armes, Luxembourg (tel. 352/2-55-88), issues ordinance survey maps on which walking paths are marked in red.

3. The ABCs of Luxembourg

These practical details will be helpful as you move around the city.

AMERICAN EMBASSY The American Embassy is located at boulevard Emmanuel Servais 22, Luxembourg (tel. 352/4-01-23).

AMERICAN EXPRESS American Express International, Inc., is located at rue Origer 6-8, Luxembourg (tel. 352/48-99-66).

DISTANCE BETWEEN LUXEMBOURG'S MAJOR CITIES

(Distance in Kilometers)

	Berdorf	Clervaux	Diekirch	Echternach	Esch-Alzette	Esch-Sûre	Ettelbruck	Grevenmacher	LUXEMBOURG	Mersch	Mondorf	Remich	Saeul	Troisvierges	Vianden	Wiltz
Berdorf	—	55	23	6	55	47	28	28	32	27	56	57	37	69	30	54
Clervaux	55	—	32	59	84	37	36	70	66	49	86	89	60	13	29	17
Diekirch	23	32	—	27	54	24	5	38	35	19	56	59	30	46	11	31
Echternach	6	59	27	—	52	51	32	24	34	30	54	45	41	73	34	58
Esch-Alzette	55	84	54	52	—	68	49	46	18	35	28	35	40	101	64	74
Esch-Sûre	47	37	24	51	68	—	19	70	45	33	70	73	30	37	34	11
Ettelbruck	28	36	5	32	49	19	—	41	30	14	51	54	25	49	16	26
Grevenmacher	28	70	38	24	46	70	41	—	28	37	31	22	48	84	48	67
LUXEMBOURG	32	66	35	34	18	45	30	28	—	17	20	23	22	84	46	58
Mersch	27	49	19	30	35	33	14	37	17	—	37	40	11	65	28	38
Mondorf	56	86	56	54	28	70	51	31	20	37	—	9	42	103	66	78
Remich	57	89	59	45	35	73	54	22	23	40	9	—	45	106	69	81
Saeul	37	60	30	41	40	30	25	48	22	11	42	45	—	76	39	36
Troisvierges	69	13	46	73	101	37	49	84	84	65	103	106	76	—	42	25
Vianden	30	29	11	34	64	34	16	48	46	28	66	69	39	42	—	37
Wiltz	54	17	31	58	74	11	26	67	58	38	78	81	36	25	37	—

BANKING HOURS Banks are open Monday through Friday from 9:15 a.m. to noon and 1 to 3:30 p.m. Currency-exchange offices are open daily at the airport and the central station in Luxembourg City.

CLIMATE The Grand Duchy is blessed with a moderate climate, with less annual rainfall than either Belgium or Holland, since North Sea winds have usually wept their tears before they get this far inland. May to about mid-October are the most agreeable months to visit, with highest temperatures—around 60°F (16°C)—in July and August and winter temperatures averaging about 37°F (3°C).

CRIME Whenever you're traveling in an unfamiliar city or country, stay alert. Be aware of your immediate surroundings. Wear a moneybelt and don't sling your camera or purse over your shoulder; wear the strap diagonally across your body. This will minimize the possibility of your becoming a victim of crime. Every society has its criminals. It's your responsibility to be aware and be alert even in the most heavily touristed areas.

CURRENCY Luxembourg's currency is tied to the Belgian franc, and Belgian currency is freely accepted throughout the Grand Duchy. The **Luxembourg franc** is made up of 100 centimes, and notes are issued in 50-, 100-, 500-, 1,000-, and 5,000-franc denominations. Coins come in 1, 5, 10, and 20 francs, and it's a good idea to keep a small supply of these on hand for small tips, telephone calls, and the like. As we go to press, the exchange rate is hovering around $1 U.S.= LF 31, which is the figure used in the table below, but in light of currency fluctuations in past months, you should *be sure to check the current rate when you travel.*

LF	U.S. $
1	.03
5	.16
10	.32
20	.64
50	1.61
75	2.42
100	3.23
500	16.13
1,000	32.26
5,000	161.29

CUSTOMS Before leaving home, be sure to register with Customs (at the airport) any camera, typewriter, etc., you plan to carry with you that could have been purchased abroad; otherwise you may very well have to pay duty on these items when you return home if you cannot prove they were not bought on your trip.

When reentering the U.S., citizens (regardless of age) are allowed up to $400 exemption for goods bought overseas if they have been away for more than two days and have not had the same duty exemption within one month. Those over 21 are allowed, within that amount, one liter of alcohol, 100 cigars (no Cuban cigars, however), 200 cigarettes, and one bottle of perfume with a U.S. trademark. Works of art and antiques more than 100 years old may be brought in duty free (be sure to have verification of age to present to Customs). No agricultural products or meats from overseas may be brought into the U.S., and will be confiscated if they're in your luggage. With the exception of alcohol, tobacco, and perfumes valued at more than $5, gifts worth up to $50 may be mailed to the U.S. as gifts, but only one per day to the same addressee.

ELECTRIC CURRENT If you plan to bring a hairdryer, radio (other than battery-operated), travel iron, or any other small appliance with you, pack a European-style transformer, adapter, and several different style plugs, since the electric current in Luxembourg is almost always 220 or 130 volts AC, 50 cycles, and outlets come in various sizes and shapes.

EMERGENCIES In case of accident, dial 012.

HOLIDAYS Public holidays in Luxembourg are: January 1, New Year's Day; Shrove Monday; Easter Monday; May 1, Labor Day; Ascension Day; Whit Monday; June 23, Luxembourg National Holiday (the grand duke's birthday); Assumption Day; November 1, All Saints' Day; December 25, Christmas Day; December 26, Boxing Day.

INFORMATION In the United States, the **Luxembourg National Tourist Office** is at 801 Second Ave., New York, NY 10017 (tel. 212/370-9850). In Luxembourg, the **Grand Duchy of Luxembourg Office du Tourisme** is in the place de la Gare (tel. 352/48-11-99) by the Central Station, with hours of 9 a.m. to noon and 2 to 6:30 p.m. (9 a.m. to 7:30 p.m. from July 1 to mid-September), with another office at the airport (tel. 352/40-08-08), open from 10 a.m. to 6:30 p.m.

The local **Tourist Information Office** for Luxembourg City is in the place d'Armes (tel. 2-28-09 or 2-75-65), open on weekdays from 9 a.m. to 1 p.m. and 2 to 6 p.m. (hours are extended to 7 p.m. and on Sunday from 10 a.m. to noon and 2 to 6 p.m. during the summer months).

Throughout the Grand Duchy there are some 15 local Tourist Information Services in small villages and towns.

PASSPORTS AND VISAS U.S. and Canadian citizens who plan to be in the country 90 days or less need bring only a valid passport—no visa is required. Citizens of other countries should consult the nearest Belgian consulate.

POSTAL SERVICES The post office at place de la Gare 1 in Luxembourg City is open daily from 6 a.m. to 10 p.m., but packages are not accepted for mailing after 5 p.m. At the airport post office, hours are 7 a.m. to 10 p.m. daily.

SHOPPING HOURS Shops generally stay open from 10 a.m. to 6 p.m. Monday through Saturday, and many also open on Sunday for shorter hours.

TAXIS During the day taxis charge LF 25 (80¢) per kilometer, with a 10% surcharge at night. Waiting time is charged at the rate of LF 8 (25¢) per minute.

TELEPHONE Luxembourg's national area code (applicable to all parts of the country) is 352; to dial to Luxembourg from within Europe, you must dial 09-352. Direct dialing to other European countries as well as overseas (including the U.S. and Canada) is available in most hotels. You'll save money on calls to the U.S. if you request AT&T's USADirect Service, but you must call collect or use an AT&T credit card. Coin telephone boxes that display stickers showing flags of different countries also accept international calls with operator assistance. Coin telephones accept LF 5 (15¢) and LF 20 (65¢), and it's advisable to have a good supply of these coins when you place a call.

TIME Luxembourg is six hours ahead of Eastern Standard Time in the U.S. (9 a.m. in New York = 3 p.m. in Luxembourg).

TIPPING Restaurants and hotels will almost always include a 16% service charge and the 19% Value Added Tax (VAT). If you've had really exceptional service you may want to add a little more, but it isn't necessary. Porters at Luxembourg's Central Station charge a fixed LF 30 (95¢) per bag.

4. Where to Stay

The Grand Duchy has good accommodations in almost every category, with most of its luxury hotels located in the capital city and small, comfortable hotels in villages spotted around the countryside. Hostels are within a day's walk of each other, and camping facilities are both plentiful and popular. You can obtain at no charge a complete listing of all hotels, inns, and restaurants in the Grand Duchy from the addresses listed under "Information" in the foregoing section of this chapter. Also free of charge are separate listings for holiday apartments and chalets, camping facilities, and hostels.

The 5% visitor's tax levied on all accommodations in the Grand Duchy is included in all rates quoted.

HOTELS

You can expect to pay between LF 2,600 ($83.75) and LF 3,500 ($113) single, LF 3,100 ($100) and LF 4,000 ($129) double for luxury hotel accommodations in Luxembourg City; city hotels in the moderate range charge about LF 1,600 ($51.50) to LF 2,000 ($64.50) single, LF 2,200 ($71) to LF 2,500 ($80.75) double. In the provinces, small hotels and inns run about LF 900 ($29) single, LF 1,500 ($48.50) double.

HOSTELS

Hostels are located in Beaufort, Bourglinster, Echternach, Ettelbruck, Grevenmacher, Hollenfels, Lultzhausen, Luxembourg, Troisvierges, Vianden, and Wiltz. Standards are exceptionally high in all, and rates range from LF 150 ($4.75) for a bed only to LF 225 ($7.25) for bed-and-breakfast to LF 330 ($10.75) for bed and one meal, to LF 405 ($13) for bed, breakfast, and one meal, to LF 610 ($19.75) for bed and all three meals. All prices are increased by LF 20 (65¢) for the Luxembourg City hostel. There is a LF-70 ($2.25) additional charge for bed sheets.

For complete details, including extra services available, write for the Youth Hostels Guide from the **Luxembourg Youth Hostels Association,** place d'Armes 18, Luxembourg (tel. 352/2-55-88).

5. Where and What to Eat

Luxembourg City, because of its large number of international diplomatic and business visitors, has many fine restaurants with international cuisine. There are, however, just as many small cafés and bistros featuring traditional dishes. In towns and villages around the Grand Duchy, hotel restaurants are often quite good, and there's excellent eating in small local cafés.

Note: Most restaurants are open for lunch from noon to 2:30 p.m. and for dinner from 7 to 10 p.m. The hours, however, may be flexible. Some are closed one day a week.

Among the national favorites are some of the best pastries you're ever likely to eat; Luxembourg cheese (delicious); trout, crayfish, and pike from local rivers; hare (during the hunting season); and in September, lovely small plum tarts called *quetsch.*

In the beverage department, while you'll be able to order almost any of the fine beers you've come to appreciate in Belgium and Holland, Luxembourg has its own that take a backseat to none—look for brand names such as Mousel (pronounced "mouse-ell"), Bofferding, and Henri Funck. And of course the Moselle wines will top any list—look for the National Mark, which certifies that they are true Luxembourg wines.

6. Where to Go and What to Do

Forget that this is a small country—in the realm of things to see and do, it becomes *very* large!

SIGHTSEEING

Luxembourg City will fill several days with sights such as the Bock casements, the State Museum, the Grand Ducal Palace, ruins of several castles, etc. Outside its confines, there are castles to be seen, ancient monasteries, picturesque villages, wineries, and museums such as the one in Echternach devoted to prehistory.

SPORTS

Golfers will want to try their luck on the course maintained by the Grand-Ducal Golf Club in Luxembourg City, a course known throughout Europe for its difficult, narrow fairways. Arrangements can be made for visitors to play by contacting **Golf Club Grand-Ducal,** Senningerberg/Luxembourg (tel. 352/3-40-90).

Walkers will find marked **walking paths** throughout the Grand Duchy (see Section 2, above), and during the summer, organized walking tours of 6 to 25 miles are run from Luxembourg City. Contact the **Fédération Luxembourgeoise des Marches Populaires,** rue de Rollingergrund 176, Luxembourg (tel. 352/44-93-02).

Many of the resort areas offer **tennis** facilities, and there are **squash** courts in Luxembourg. Contact the Institute National des Sports (tel. 352/43-10-14) for details on where to find them and how to arrange to play.

Horseback riding is a favorite sport in Luxembourg, with several very good stables offering mounts at about LF 300 ($9.75) per hour. For a full list of stables and riding schools, contact Sports et Loisirs de la Fédération Luxembourgeoise des Sports Equestres, rue du Fort Elisabeth 9, Luxembourg. The organization also puts together horseback tours of Luxembourg City and of the Valley of the Seven Castles.

The rivers of the Grand Duchy are a fisherperson's paradise, and licenses are issued by the district commissioners in Luxembourg, Diekirch, and Grevenmacher and by a few communal administrations like those in Ettelbruck, Vianden, and Wiltz. If you're suddenly bitten by the **fishing** bug, just ask locally where you may obtain a license—there's sure to be a source close by. A license to fish from the banks of eastern-border rivers and lakes costs LF 200 ($6.50) for a week, LF 400 ($13) for a month. Fishing from boats requires a special license for LF 400 ($13) per week, LF 1,000 ($32.25) per month. There are several rather complex and often-changing regulations governing fishing in frontier waters. For complete details on all types of fishing, contact the Administration des Eaux et Forêts, B.P. 411, Luxembourg.

AFTER DARK

Luxembourg City offers several nightspots, including an excellent Jazz Club and a few discos. Outside the city a few hotels offer after-dark entertainment, but most activity when the sun goes down is centered in local cafés.

The country's only casino is at Mondorf-les-Bains, where there's also an excellent spa and a host of concerts and sporting activities.

7. The Language

Luxembourgish is the national language and is widely used among Luxembourgers, although French is most often used in official and cultural activities. German, too, is heard frequently, and *everyone* speaks English. In other words, you'll encounter few, if any, language difficulties in the Grand Duchy.

THE CITY OF LUXEMBOURG

Often called the "Gibraltar of the North," Luxembourg City is an attractive mixture of the remnants of Europe's unceasing battles for power in the past, Luxembourgers' equally unceasing determination to create a comfortable lifestyle, and modern Europe's search for peaceful cooperation between nations.

1. By Way of Background

The city of Luxembourg grew up around Count Siegfroi's fortifications on the Bock promentory. It was an astute choice of location for the count, since the 52-yard-high cliffs overlooking the Pétrusse and Alzette Valleys were natural obstacles to invading forces. In time there came to be three rings of battlements around the city, including the cliff bastions, some 15 forts surrounding them, and an exterior wall around those that was interspersed with nine more forts, three of them cut right into the rocks. Even more impressive than those above-ground fortifications were the more than 15½ miles of underground tunnels that sheltered troops by the thousands, their equipment, horses, workshops, artillery, arms, kitchens, bakeries, and even slaughterhouses!

Now, listen to what *else* legend says that tremendous rocky fortress holds. If the tale is true, within its stony walls a beautiful maiden named Mélusine sits knitting, but she manages only one stitch each year—and that's a very good thing. You see, should she finish her knitting before she is released from the rock, all of Luxembourg and its people will vanish into the rock with her! How did she come to be there, and how can her release be won? Well, she got there when Siegfroi married her in ignorance that she was really a mermaid, a secret she managed to keep by reverting to her natural state only on Saturday, on which day of every week she had pledged her husband to observe her personal privacy. When his curiosity got the better of him and he peeked, she vanished into the rock. Once every seven years Mélusine returns, either as a serpent with a golden key in its mouth or as a beautiful woman.

All it will take to win her freedom is for some brave soul to kiss the womanly vision or take the key from the serpent's mouth. That brave soul has yet to appear, and in the meantime all of Luxembourg (or at least that part of Luxembourg that credits the legend) prays she will drop a stitch or two or else that whatever it is she's knitting will take a *very* long time to complete!

Over the centuries, Burgundians, French, Spanish, Austrian, and Germanic Confederation forces managed to take control of the strategic Luxembourg fortifications, each in turn adding to its already-formidable defenses. Eventually its strength so frightened the rest of Europe that those fears stood in the way of Luxembourg's very freedom and independence. Finally in 1867 the Treaty of London mandated the dismantling of all those battlements, and what you see today represents only about 10% of the original fortifications. Beautiful parks, that so distinguish the face of today's city of Luxembourg, now cover ground once occupied by strong forts.

Today it seems fitting indeed that the EEC Council of Ministers meets here, since it was Luxembourg City that gave Europe Robert Schuman, often called the "Father of Europe" because of his important role in bringing together the European Economic Community.

2. Where to Stay

Luxembourg's top hotels are designed to answer the needs of some of Europe's most discriminating diplomats and business people, and they rank with the best luxury hostelries anywhere in the world. The city provides many small hotels in the more moderate price ranges, some with rooms above excellent ground-floor restaurants, with comfortable and attractive accommodations. Unless otherwise stated, breakfast, service, and tax are all included.

EXPENSIVE

The **Grand Hotel Cravat,** boulevard Roosevelt 29, 2450 Luxembourg (tel. 352/2-62-11). For nigh onto a full century there's been a Hotel Grand Cravat at this location in the very heart of the city overlooking place de la Constitution. Under third-generation management of the same family, the luxury hotel retains much of its Old-World charm and maintains the family tradition of high standards and friendly hospitality. Guest rooms are beautifully furnished and have private baths, mini-bars, hairdryers, courtesy terry bathrobes, TVs, radios, and telephones. Some come with balconies. Its Restaurant Le Normandy is noted for fine French and seafood cuisine served in elegant surroundings—the average dinner price without wine is LF 1,500 ($48.50) and there's a set menu for LF 700 ($22.50). Just off the lobby is the gracious Le Trianon Bar, where you'll often see Luxembourg's leading businessmen gathered at the end of the day. Inexpensive meals are served in the traditional restaurant La Taverne. Rates at this highly recommended hotel, including a buffet breakfast, are LF 3,000 ($96.75) to LF 3,200 ($103.25) single, LF 3,600 ($116.25) to LF 4,300 ($138.75) double.

Hotel Inter-Continental, rue Jean-Engling 12, 1466 Luxembourg-Dommeldange (tel. 352/4-37-81). A little out from the city center, the Inter-Continental is the epitome of luxury in its guest rooms and its public facilities. Catering to a business and EEC clientele, it upholds the highest standards, and each guest room has a private bath, TV, radio, and telephone. Other amenities include an indoor swimming pool and health club. Rates range from LF 4,700 ($151.50) to LF 6,700 ($216.25) single, LF 5,700 ($183.75) to LF 7,700 ($248.50) double.

Hotel Le Royal, boulevard Royal 12, 2449 Luxembourg (tel. 352/4-16-16).

LUXEMBOURG CITY

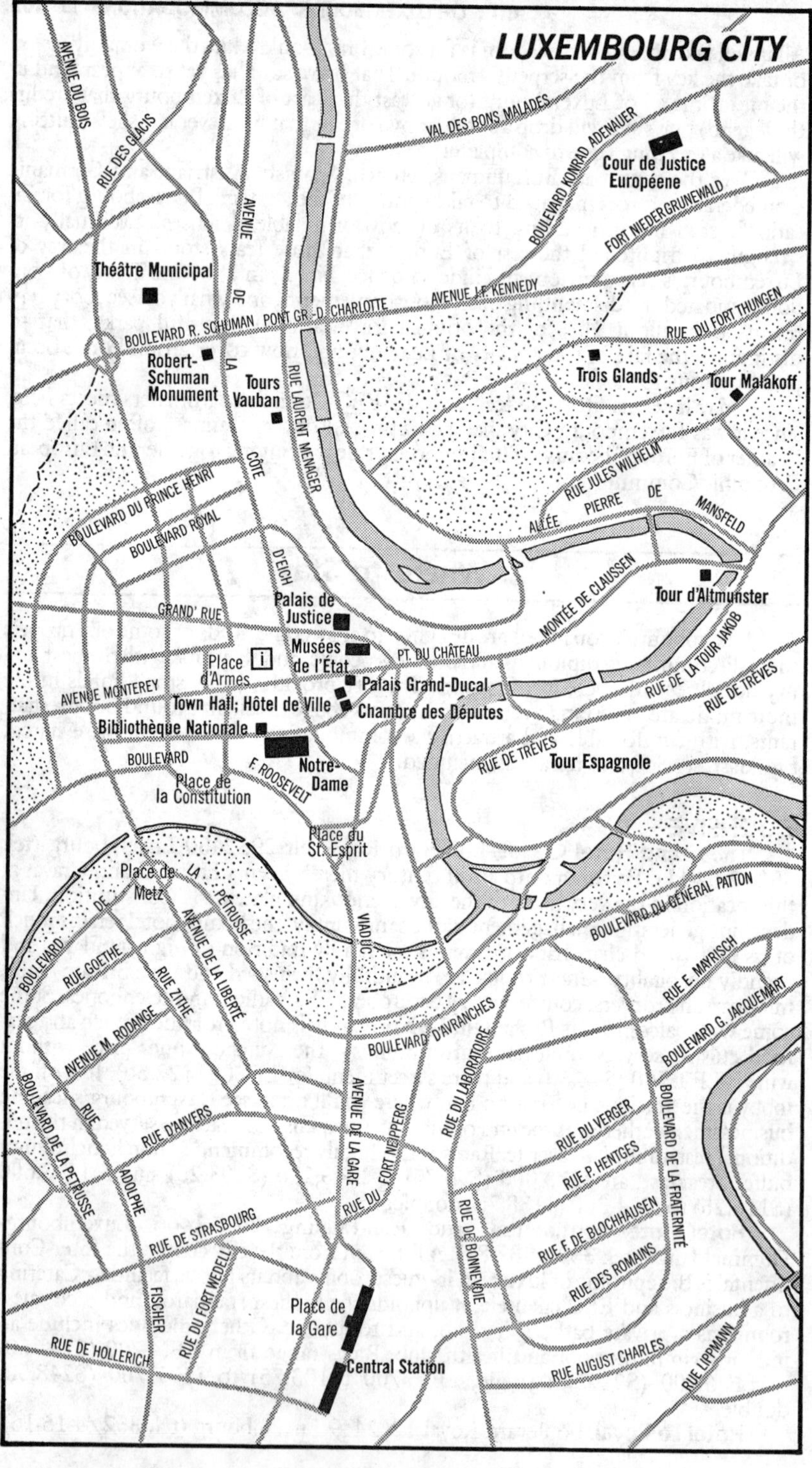

This pretty luxury hotel is located across from a park. Guest rooms are beautifully decorated, with private baths, TVs, videos, radios, and telephones. There are two good restaurants, the gourmet Le Relais Royal and Le Jardin, with terrace dining in summer. Its piano bar features live music after 6 p.m., and other amenities include a hairdresser, boutiques, sauna, solarium, massage, bodybuilding, and a swimming pool as well as 24-hour TV news from the U.S. and 24-hour Reuters information service. There's also a free shuttle service to and from the airport. Rates run LF 5,600 ($180.75) to LF 9,700 ($313) single, LF 6,750 ($217.75) to LF 9,700 ($313) double.

MODERATE

The **Auberge du Coin,** boulevard de la Pétrusse 2, 2320 Luxembourg (tel. 352/48-88-47 or 48-94-10). This small hotel, owned and operated by the friendly and gracious Mr. and Mrs. Ferd Lorang-Rieck, is a longtime favorite of visiting academics and business people. Its 23 rooms are divided between two lovely old Luxembourg homes, and all have modern, comfortable, and attractive furnishings. The rustic restaurant serves traditional Luxembourg specialties as well as a nice variety of fish and meat dishes at very moderate prices, and is a local favorite. Rates for rooms with private bath run LF 1,550 ($50) to LF 1,700 ($54.75) single, LF 1,750 ($56.50) to LF 2,200 ($71) double.

Hotel-Restaurant Italia, rue d'Anvers 15-17, 1130 Luxembourg (tel. 352/48-66-26 or 48-66-27). Not far from the central railway station in a quiet location, this lovely small hotel has guest rooms upstairs from one of the city's best Italian restaurants. The attractive guest rooms all have private baths, TVs, and telephones. Rates are LF 1,700 ($54.75) to LF 2,200 ($71) for one or two people.

Hôtel Français, place d'Armes 14, 2014 Luxembourg (tel. 352/47-45-34). Guest rooms in the small hotel are above a popular restaurant. Some are rather small, but all have modern, comfortable furnishings, private baths, and TVs. Rates run LF 2,100 ($67.75) to LF 2,200 ($71) single, LF 2,500 ($80.75) to LF 2,800 ($90.25) double.

Hotel Central Molitor, avenue de la Liberté 28, 1930 Luxembourg (tel. 352/48-99-11). This traditional hotel is located in a handsome corner building not far from the central railway station and is very handy to good shopping, restaurants, and nightspots. Its guest rooms come with private baths, TVs, radios, private wall safes, and telephones, and all are nicely furnished. There's a good restaurant and underground parking. Rates, which include breakfast, are LF 2,300 ($74.25) single, LF 3,000 ($96.75) double.

Hotel Bristol, rue de Strasbourg 11, 2561 Luxembourg (tel. 352/48-58-29 or 48-58-30). Guest rooms in this conveniently located hotel (near financial and shopping centers) are attractive and comfortable, with private bath, TV, and telephone. There's garage parking. Rates run LF 2,000 ($64.50) single, LF 2,400 ($77.50) double.

Cheminée de Paris, rue d'Anvers 10, 1130 Luxembourg (tel. 352/49-29-31). A small hotel on a quiet street, the Cheminée de Paris features comfortable guest rooms with private baths, TVs, and telephones. It has a reasonably priced restaurant (see below) that specializes in regional favorites. Rates range from LF 2,000 ($64.50) to LF 2,200 ($71) single, LF 2,200 ($71) to LF 2,500 ($80.75) double.

INEXPENSIVE

Hôtel Du Théâtre, rue Beaumont 3, 1219 Luxembourg (tel. 352/2-53-37). Comfortable guest rooms with private baths run LF 1,150 ($37) single, LF 1,600 ($51.50) double. Without private bath, rates are LF 950 ($30.75) single and LF 1,300 ($42) double.

3. Where to Eat

Some of my greatest dining pleasures in Luxembourg have come on balmy summer evenings as I've enjoyed a meal in almost any of the sidewalk cafés under the trees in the place d'Armes while listening to a band concert in the square. Reflected in every face around me has been an obvious appreciation for the food and the ambience, and if there's a more relaxing pastime, I have yet to find it. There are, however, many very fine restaurants down quiet little streets, in old and elegant buildings, just waiting for those times when my mood calls for something a little less informal.

EXPENSIVE

Saint Michel, rue de l'Eau 32 (tel. 2-32-15). Elegance in setting, service, and classic French cuisine make this one of Luxembourg's most highly esteemed restaurants. Situated in the old part of the city, down a narrow little street, the restaurant more than justifies its high price range of LF 1,500 ($48.50) to LF 2,500 ($80.75), without wine (there's an excellent wine list). Closed Saturday and Sunday, and advance reservations are recommended (at least a day in advance if possible).

Au Gourmet, rue Chimay 8 (tel. 2-55-61). Set in an atmospheric old town house, this fine restaurant serves traditional Luxembourg favorites, as well as superb fish dishes (try the turbotin with hollandaise sauce). Desserts are excellent, and there's a good wine list. Dinner will run between LF 1,400 ($45.25) and LF 1,750 ($56.50), without wine. Closed Sunday for dinner and all day Monday. Best reserve ahead.

La Marée, avenue de la Liberté 37 (tel. 49-08-99). This excellent fish house looks just as a fish house should look—unpretentious and friendly. Fish is as fresh as at any seaside restaurant, and the variety of dishes is astonishing. The à la carte menu is long, with prices that range as high as LF 2,000 ($64.50), although it's possible to eat well for considerably less.

La Lorraine, place d'Armes 6 (tel. 47-46-20). On a prominent corner of the place d'Armes, with both outdoor and indoor dining, this popular fish restaurant excels in preparation of its many specialties of the sea as well as the friendly efficiency of its staff. Dinner will run anywhere from LF 1,700 ($54.75) to LF 2,500 ($80.75).

MODERATE

Scandia Um Bock, rue de la Loge 4-8 (tel. 2-22-36 or 2-20-55). Steak is the star of the menu in this rather plain restaurant, but the duck is very good, and there's a limited selection of fish dishes. Dinner prices can range up to the LF-2,000 ($64.50) neighborhood, but most main courses run around LF 650 ($21) to LF 750 ($24.25).

Le Poseidon, rue de la Loge 8B (tel. 2-39-90). To reach this lively Greek restaurant, turn off rue de l'Eau through a stone-arched passageway and walk down a short flight of stone steps. The long menu lists every Greek specialty you can imagine, with à la carte prices of LF 300 ($9.75) to LF 700 ($22.50) for main courses. Closed Monday and Tuesday at lunch.

La Taverne, in the Grand Hotel Cravat, boulevard Roosevelt 29 (tel. 2-19-75). This casual ground-floor restaurant serves marvelous traditional dishes, as well as a wide range of fish, meat, and chicken selections, as well as light salads and snacks such as herring, smoked salad, shrimp cocktail, and escargots at à la carte prices that range from LF 120 ($3.75) for soups to LF 750 ($24.25) for tournedos Rossini. There are also set menus of LF 700 ($22.50) for three courses, LF 1,000 ($32.25) for five courses. It's a great lunchtime favorite with local business people, but reservations are not usually necessary.

Auberge du Coin, boulevard de la Pétrusse 2 (tel. 48-88-47 or 48-94-10). This friendly little neighborhood restaurant (some 80% of the daily clientele are people who live nearby) serves an excellent lunch menu for LF 400 ($13), with main courses featuring steak, pork chops, ham, fish, and smoked fish. Evening meals (such as entrecôte, french fries, and salad) run about LF 600 ($19.25).

Ming Dynasty, Grand Rue 6 (tel. 2-61-97). Walk through an old carriage drive to reach a charming courtyard and you'll find this large Chinese restaurant, new in 1986. In good weather there's terrace dining; the ground-floor dining room is done up in creams and pinks, with small crystal chandeliers and Oriental touches scattered about. Downstairs, there's a cozy cellar room. Chinese dishes are superb, and the long menu lists main courses for LF 360 ($11.50) to LF 900 ($29), with a set menu at LF 750 ($24.25).

Pechvillchen, rue de l'Eau 26. This tiny, rustic eatery specializes in Luxembourg traditional dishes (try the veal à la moularde) for prices in the LF-450 ($14.50) to LF-600 ($19.25) range.

Don Quijote, rue de l'Eau 32 (tel. 2-95-38). Steak and other beef specialties have star billing at this colorful Spanish restaurant, where prices for main courses run LF 400 ($13) to LF 750 ($24.25).

Du Commerce, place d'Armes 13 (tel. 2-69-30). This pleasant restaurant, with both indoor and outdoor dining, features traditional Luxembourg fare at reasonable prices. Set menus run LF 500 ($16.25) to LF 900 ($29).

Hotel-Restaurant Français, place d'Armes 14 (tel. 47-45-34). French and Italian specialties are featured in both outdoor and indoor dining, with set-menu prices of LF 590 ($19) to LF 900 ($29) and an extensive à la carte menu.

Cheminée de Paris, rue d'Anvers 10 (tel. 49-29-31 or 49-29-32). This attractive restaurant on the ground floor of the small hotel upstairs (see above) presents excellent traditional dishes, grills, and pizzas—you can eat well for almost any price range, with the assurance that quality will be high even when the price is low. Top dinner prices are not likely to exceed LF 900 ($29).

Italia, rue d'Anvers 15-17 (tel. 48-66-26 or 48-66-27). Italian and other continental dishes are featured at this pretty restaurant in the small hotel by the same name (see above). Set menus run LF 500 ($16.25) to LF 900 ($29), and there's a long à la carte menu.

INEXPENSIVE

Roma, rue Louvigny 5 (tel. 1-36-92). In the center of the old city, this is a cheerful, attractive restaurant specializing (as if you couldn't guess) in Italian dishes. The menu is extensive (there are seven kinds of spaghetti!), and à la carte prices range from LF 450 ($14.50) up.

All the terrace cafés around the place d'Armes serve excellent meals for budget prices. I'm especially fond of the **Café de Paris,** where tomato with crevettes (tiny North Sea shrimp) and salads run as low as LF 275 ($8.75); meat and fish dishes are a little higher.

For pastries, snacks (ham with melon, etc.), and coffee, stop in at the **Brasserie Chimay,** rue Chimay 15.

4. Things to See and Do

Luxembourg City is a delight for the sightseer. Most of its attractions are in a compact, easily walked area and there are inexpensive coach tours to take you to those farther afield. My best advice, in fact, is to stash the car in a garage and take it out only when you head out to see the rest of the Grand Duchy.

TOURIST INFORMATION

Your very first stop should be at the place d'Armes **Tourist Information Office** (tel. 2-28-09 or 2-75-65). It's open on weekdays from 9 a.m. to 1 p.m. and 2 to 6 p.m.; during the summer months those hours are extended to 7 p.m., and from 10 a.m. to noon and 2 to 6 p.m. on Sunday.

TOURS

The Tourist Information Office has an excellent brochure titled **"A Walk Through the Green Heart of Europe"** to guide you through the heart of Luxembourg City. It's designed to be covered in one segment of an hour and another of 1½ hours, or in 2½ hours for the energetic.

One of the nicest tours is the brightly painted **miniature train** on tires that leaves twice each hour between 9:30 a.m. and sundown from the Grand Duke Adolphe Bridge to travel paved pathways through the Pétrusse and Alzette Valleys, and on through some of the oldest sections of town to one of the original city gates. You can simply sit back and enjoy the passing scenery, or you can don earphones and listen to a commentary (given in English, French, German, Dutch, and Luxembourgish) that fills you in on all the history that transpired on the very ground you're covering. The 45-minute ride costs LF 200 ($6.50) for adults, half that for children (under 4, free).

There are **coach tours** of the city every morning during the summer months that run from 9:30 to 11:30 a.m. and visit the cathedral, the Grand Duke's Palace, the remains of the fortress, the European Center, the U.S. and German cemeteries, Radio Television Luxembourg, and some of the most important of Luxembourg's avenues. Adults pay LF 240 ($7.75); children, LF 140 ($4.50). Book at the Tourist Office or through **Henri Sales,** rue du Curé 26 (tel. 46-18-18), the day before. There are several pickup points, and the Tourist Office can tell you which is closest to your hotel.

A three-hour afternoon tour covers much of the same territory as the city tour above, and adds a foray to several outlying destinations, including a restored castle, the Gréngewald Forest, and the airport. Cost is LF 260 ($8.50) for adults, LF 150 ($4.75) for children. Book at the Tourist Office.

THE SIGHTS

The **place de la Constitution,** across from rue Chimay on boulevard Roosevelt, affords a marvelous view of the Pétrusse Valley and the impressive Adolphe Bridge that spans it. This is also where you enter the Pétrusse casemates during summer months to explore a small sample of those miles of tunnels.

The **Luxembourg casemates** may be entered from two points: the place de la Constitution entrance is to the Pétrusse casemates, and the Montée de Clausen entry leads to the Bock casemates. These vast, hand-hewn fortifications are extremely moving when you realize the numbers they sheltered over the centuries. They're open from 10 a.m. to 5 p.m. daily during the summer months only, and there's an admission charge of LF 35 ($1.25).

The tall **Monument du Souvenir** in the center of the square is in memory of those who have perished in Luxembourg's wars—take time to read the bronze plaque at its base that declares in four languages: "This is to remind us of the brutal act of the Nazi occupant who, in destroying this monument on October 21, 1940, turned it into a symbol of our freedom, thus sparking off the desperate resistance of a deeply humiliated nation whose only weapon was its bravery." Luxembourgers who remember those bitter years give an involuntary shudder when they pass the villa at 57 boulevard de la Pétrusse; it now houses the Ministry of Public Health, but was the dreaded Gestapo headquarters from 1940 to 1944. The monument, known affectionately as "Gelle Fra," was erected in 1923. In 1958 it was partly rebuilt, but it wasn't until 1985 that it was finally restored to its original form, with funds raised by national subscription.

The **Cathedral of Our Lady of Luxembourg,** with an entrance on boulevard Roosevelt, is a magnificent structure built between 1613 and 1621. Gothic in design, it has a Renaissance entrance on rue Notre-Dame. It holds the royal family vault and the huge sarcophagus of John the Blind, as well as a remarkable treasury (seen only on request, made to the sacristan, whose office is on the right as you enter). It's also the scene of a lovely ceremony every year on the fifth Sunday following Easter, when thousands of pilgrims arrive to pray for protection by the miraculous statue of the Holy Virgin before forming a procession to carry the statue from the cathedral through the streets to altars covered with flowers. There is no charge to visit the cathedral.

Located in the oldest part of the city, the **State Museum,** Marché-aux-Poissons (Fish Market), holds fascinating archeological, geological, and historical exhibits, as well as some exquisite works of art. There's no charge to visit, and hours are 10 a.m. to noon and 1 to 5 p.m. Tuesday through Friday, and 10 a.m. to noon and 2 to 6 p.m. on Saturday and Sunday.

At the **Grand Ducal Palace,** rue de la Reine, the oldest part of this interesting building dates back to 1572 (its "new" right wing was built in 1741 and renovated in the 1890s). Next door is the Chamber of Deputies. The palace is open every day except Wednesday and Sunday during the summer months at varying hours (ask for a current schedule at the Tourist Information Office), with an admission fee of LF 80 ($2.50) for adults, LF 40 ($1.25) for children.

The ruin of the **Castle of Sigefroi,** Montée de Clausen, is all that's left of the original fortification built in 963 by the city's founder. It is always open, and there's no charge.

The suburbs of **Clausen** and **Pfaffenthal** are two of the oldest, most picturesque sections of Luxembourg, and both merit an hour's stroll, although you should be warned that you'll probably want to loiter at least half a day.

The **United States Military Cemetery** is three miles east of Luxembourg, where some 5,076 of the 10,000 American troops who fell in Luxembourg during World War II lie in a peaceful setting surrounded by pine woods. There are 101 graves of unknown soldiers and airmen, and 22 sets of brothers buried side by side. The graves are arranged with no distinction by rank, religion, race, or state of origin, the only exception being the grave of Gen. George Patton because of the many visitors to his final resting place. Over the doorway of the nondenominational chapel is the moving inscription "Here is enshrined the memory of valor and sacrifice." About a mile away is the German Military Cemetery, which holds 11,000 graves.

Saturday is market day in Luxembourg City, when the **place Guillaume** is awash with the color and exuberance of country folk manning stalls filled with brilliant blooms, fresh vegetables, and a vast assortment of other goods and the townspeople who have come to buy.

Luxembourg City is filled with **souvenir shops** selling attractive handcrafted items, clocks, pottery, and miscellaneous objects. One that has an exceptionally good stock, good values, and a courteous, efficient staff is the small shop (larger than it looks from outside) at rue Chimay 23, owned and managed by Mr. A. Rottigni. For upmarket shops, head for the rue de la Poste.

5. After Dark

Luxembourg City stays up late, and there are numerous nightspots, jazz clubs, theater performances, concerts, etc., all during the summer months. It's as true here as in any other city, however, that clubs come and go rather frequently, so your best bet is to stop by the Tourist Information Office on the place d'Armes and pick up a copy of "La Semaine à Luxembourg" ("The Week in Luxembourg") to see what's doing during your visit. Also, pick up a copy of the *Luxembourg News Digest,* Luxembourg's only English-language newspaper (published every Friday), which carries several listings of current happenings.

A particularly attractive, casually sophisticated club in one of the city's oldest streets is **Le Bistro d'Artscene,** rue Sigefroi 6 (tel. 47-00-36), where jazz can usually be heard on Friday and Saturday nights, but there's live music every night.

Also, deluxe hotels such as the Royal and Inter-Continental offer nighttime entertainment.

XXIII

AROUND THE GRAND DUCHY

Once outside Luxembourg City you find yourself in a magical, fairyland countryside. It's as though Mother Nature drew together her most sparkling scenic beauties of high hills, rushing rivers, and broad plains and plunked them down in this tiny corner of Europe. Mankind then came along and sprinkled her stunning landscape liberally with lovely little medieval villages, picture-book castles, wineries, and idyllic holiday retreats.

If it's *romantic* Europe you're looking for, you'll find it right here inside the borders of the Grand Duchy.

HOW TO SEE THE GRAND DUCHY

Good train and bus connections, as well as a wealth of walking and cycling paths, make it easy for the nondriver to ramble around all parts of the Grand Duchy. Drivers will find good roads and more than adequate signposting.

If time is limited, however, or your own interests dictate more time in Luxembourg City itself, there are excellent motorcoach day and half-day trips to provide tantalizing glimpses of the Grand Duchy. For example, one 9:30 a.m. to 5 p.m. tour takes you to the Valley of the Seven Castles, the Ardennes, Vianden, and a good part of the Moselle Valley; another visits the Ardennes, the Upper Sûre Valley, Clervaux, and Vianden; and still another covers Little Switzerland, Echternach, and the Moselle Valley. Full details and booking are available at the Tourist Information Office in the place d'Armes, most hotels, and **Voyages Henri Sales,** rue du Curé 26 (tel. 46-18-18).

1. The Ardennes Region

Spilling over from the Belgian Ardennes, this region is a treat for the nature lover and a haven for those in search of a quiet holiday. It also bears more visible scars of World War II than other regions because of the fierce fighting that took place here as Allied troops valiantly pushed back von Rundstedt's forces during the Battle of the Bulge.

While it is easily explored from a Luxembourg City base, it begs more time of travelers and provides country inns and small hotels to accommodate their needs.

WHERE TO STAY

The Luxembourg Ardennes have become such a popular European holiday spot that accommodations of all price ranges and amenities abound. Summer months can bring an influx of visitors who rapidly settle in, and there can sometimes be a problem booking into your choice of accommodations—the moral, of course, is to reserve as far in advance as possible.

In Echternach

Hotel Bel-Air, route de Berdorf 1, 6409 Echternach (tel. 352/72-93-83). Friends in other European countries have extolled the excellence of this luxury hotel, and personal inspection bore out all their raves. About half a mile out from Echternach, the hotel sits in its own park overlooking the Sûre Valley, with lovely terraces, glass-walled gourmet restaurants, attractive lounges, tennis, and serene wooded walks just outside the door. Guest rooms have private baths, TVs and telephones, and rates range from LF 2,200 ($71) to LF 3,500 ($113) single, LF 3,000 ($96.75) to LF 5,000 ($161.25) double.

À La Petite Marquise, place du Marché 18, 6460 Echternach (tel. 352/7-23-82). This small, homey hotel has a very good restaurant, as well as comfortable rooms with private baths at rates of LF 1,000 ($32.25) and up single, LF 1,750 ($56.50) to LF 2,000 ($64.50) double (the higher rate is for rooms with a view of the square). Without private facilities, rates are LF 850 ($27.50) single and LF 1,750 ($56.50) double.

Le Petit Poète, place du Marché 13, 6460 Echternach (tel. 352/7-20-72). This is a sister hotel to À La Petite Marquise, with the same owner management and a slightly different view of the square. It also has a very good restaurant, and its attractive rooms with private facilities have rates of LF 900 ($29) single, LF 1,500 ($48.50) double. Those without private bath are LF 750 ($24.25) single and LF 1,150 ($37) double.

In Clervaux

Grand Hôtel du Parc, 9708 Clervaux (tel. 352/9-10-68 or 9-26-50). Surrounded by a beautiful wooded park, this lovely old manor house has been completely modernized inside to offer ten attractive and comfortable guest rooms, each with a private bath, radio, and telephone. Public rooms have an Old-World charm, and outside terraces overlook the picturesque little township of Clervaux. There's an excellent chef in the kitchen here, as well as a good wine list, and other amenities include a sauna and solarium. Rates are LF 1,200 ($38.75) to LF 2,000 ($64.50), single or double.

Hotel Koener, Grand-Rue 14, 9701 Clervaux (tel. 352/9-10-02). This century-old hotel right in the center of Clervaux faces on the town square and has 42 comfortable guest rooms with private baths, telephones, radios, and TVs. There's also a good restaurant on the ground floor. Rates run LF 1,300 ($42) to LF 1,400 ($45.25) single, LF 1,600 ($51.50) to LF 1,900 ($61.25) double.

Hôtel du Commerce, rue de Marnach 2, 9709 Clervaux (tel. 352/9-10-32). This attractive hotel sits at the foot of the castle, and its public facilities include two good restaurants, a warm, friendly bar, and a television room. Some of the 54 guest rooms have balconies, and each has a private bath. Rates are LF 1,300 ($42) for singles, LF 1,500 ($48.50) to LF 1,900 ($61.25) for doubles.

In Asselborn

Vieux Moulin d'Asselborn, 9940 Asselborn (tel. 352/9-86-16 or 9-86-17). For a complete change of pace, take yourself off to this country inn nestled in the Ardennes a little north of Clervaux, only four miles from the Belgian border. The 15 guest rooms all have private toilet and shower, and are done up in an attractive rustic décor. After a day of sightseeing or fishing in the hotel's own stretch of river you can relax around a roaring log fire in the lounge. The owner is also the chef, and if your luck was running at the river, he'll gladly cook up your catch for your evening meal (otherwise, you can be sure his own creations will be delicious). Rates are LF 1,350 ($43.50) single and LF 2,200 ($71) double.

In Vianden

Hotel Heintz, Grand-Rue 55, 9410 Vianden (tel. 352/8-41-55 or 8-45-59). Set in a former monastery, one of the Grand Duchy's oldest buildings, this lovely hotel has thoroughly modernized guest rooms with private baths and telephones (you can request a TV in your room; otherwise there's a TV lounge). Rooms facing south have large balconies, and there's a cozy bar and a good restaurant. Rates are LF 1,050 ($33.75) to LF 1,400 ($45.25) single, LF 1,600 ($51.50) to LF 2,400 ($77.50) double.

WHERE TO EAT

Restaurants in the hotels listed above (indeed, in most hotels in the Ardennes) reach high standards in the preparation of meals, and you will find prices a bit lower than in Luxembourg City.

In Echternach

Quatre Saisons, rue du Haut-Ruisseau 2 (tel. 72-80-39). To reach this highly regarded restaurant, walk through the tunnel (next to Optique Gangolf) at the Market Square. Expect your meal to run anywhere from LF 300 ($9.75) to LF 1,100 ($35.50), without wine. Closed Wednesday.

Melickshaff (tel. 1-22-05). About half a mile outside town on the Luxembourg road, this farmhouse restaurant offers good value in a nice setting. Prices range from LF 300 ($9.75) to LF 800 ($25.75).

In Diekirch

Two good restaurants with moderate-to-inexpensive prices are **Giorgio,** Grand-Rue 15 (tel. 80-89-17), and **Le Tivoli,** avenue de la Gare 53 (tel. 80-88-51).

TOURIST INFORMATION

In **Vianden,** the Tourist Information Office is in Victor Hugo House, rue de la Gare 37 (tel. 8-42-57), with hours of 9:30 a.m. to noon and 2 to 6 p.m. daily during the summer months. In **Clervaux,** the Tourist Information Office is in the castle (tel. 9-20-72), open from 10 a.m. to noon and 2 to 6 p.m. weekdays during the summer months.

THINGS TO SEE AND DO

First and foremost, of course, there's that gorgeous scenery. You'll be astounded at how it can change in the space of a few miles, and if you're a dedicated shutterbug, you'll click away to your heart's content as you pass through wooded hills that dip down to flat pastures that curve into village streets right out of the Middle Ages. To help you plan an itinerary that suits your personal interests, the principal villages and their attractions are listed below.

In Echternach

This little town is a living open-air museum. From its picturesque market square to its medieval walls and towers to its beautiful Town Hall (1444) to its 18th-century abbey and basilica to its patrician houses, it is the repository of the ages since St. Willibrord arrived from Northumberland as a missionary in 658 and established the abbey to make this one of the continent's earliest centers of Christianity. If you arrive on Whit Tuesday, there's religious solemnity mixed with a liberal dose of native gaiety in the world-famous dancing parade of pilgrims from all over Europe who march and chant, sing and dance to an ancient tune performed by bands, violinists, and other musicians in the procession. Allow yourself enough time in this enchanting town to soak up the medieval atmosphere that permeates the very air you breathe.

In Vianden

In 1871 an exiled writer-resident of Vianden—Victor Hugo by name—wrote of the town as a "jewel set in its splendid scenery, characterized by two, both comforting and magnificent elements: the sinister ruins of its fortress and its cheerful breed of men." The **Tourist Information Office** is located in the house at rue de la Gare 37 in which he lived, and you can tour the rooms from 9:30 a.m. to noon and 2 to 6 p.m. daily during the summer for a small admission fee.

It is the mighty 9th-century **Château de Vianden,** a fortress castle perched on a hill above the town, however, that draws most visitors to Vianden. Restored to its original plans, you can now see the 11th-, 12th-, and 15th-century additions that are even more impressive than the earlier sections. The castle is open during the summer months from 9 a.m. to 7 p.m., with shorter hours other times of the year, and an admission fee of LF 80 ($2.50).

For the best view of Vianden's narrow, winding streets, the castle, and the river valley, take the **chair lift** that operates daily from 11 a.m. to 6 p.m. for an LF-110 ($3.50) charge.

Vianden also has a charming folklore museum, the **Musée d'Art Rustique,** Grand-Rue 98, open daily from 9 a.m. to noon and 2 to 6 p.m., with a small admission fee.

In Diekirch

Be sure to see the ancient **church** here—it dates back to the 7th and 9th centuries and is open at no charge from 10 a.m. to noon and 3 to 5 p.m. daily. There are Roman mosaics from as far back as the 4th century in the **Roman Museum,** open from 9 a.m. to noon and 2 to 6 p.m., with an LF-15 (50¢) admission. This was a Celtic stronghold in the days before recorded history, and a relic from those long-ago ages is the dolmen called "Devil's Altar."

Don't miss the **Diekirch Historical Museum,** commonly known as the **Museum of the Battle of the Bulge,** Bamertal 10 (tel. 80-89-08 or 80-87-80). Situated in an old brewery that's part of a 130-year-old complex, the museum presents a series of life-size dioramas depicting American and German military forces, as well as civilians in the area. There's also a diorama of the crossing of the Sauer River near Diekirch in January 1945, an event that marked the turning point in the Battle of the Bulge. All in all it's an incredibly realistic and moving display, augmented by artifacts such as military equipment, uniforms, weapons, maps, and several large items such as a tank, artillery guns, tracked vehicles, etc. The week preceding and following Easter, and from May through October, the museum is open daily from 10 a.m. to noon and 2 to 6 p.m., with an admission of LF 80 ($2.50).

In Ettlebruck

The most interesting thing to Americans about this crossroads of tourist routes is **Patton Square,** on the edge of town in Patton Park. The park holds a nine-foot statue of the general, and close by is a Sherman M4-A1 tank similar to the ones that arrived to liberate Ettlebruck in 1944. The **Patton Museum** in town is open daily during the summer from 10 a.m. to noon and 2 to 4:45 p.m.

In Clervaux

The 12th-century **castle** at Clervaux dominates this little town, and although it was heavily damaged during World War II fighting, it has now been restored. It houses scale models of several other medieval fortresses, uniforms and arms from

World War II, and Edward Steichen's moving *Family of Man* photographic essay. You can visit any day during the summer months from 10 a.m. to 5 p.m., and there's an admission fee of LF 25 (80¢).

In Wiltz

You might call Wiltz schizophrenic! It's split right down the middle, with a 500-foot difference in height between "uptown" and "downtown." Almost as wide a chasm in time separates the 1502 stone cross at whose feet the powerful Lords of Wiltz once meted out justice and the 1944 armored tank that sits at the bend of the approach road. The 12th-century **castle** ("modernized" in the 1600s) perhaps best telescopes the town's history, since its ancient left wing houses a museum commemorating the 1944–1945 fighting. There is also in the town a memorial to those who died following a general strike protesting military conscription during German occupation. The **Niederwiltz Church,** a Romanesque and Renaissance marvel, holds richly ornamented tombs of the counts of Wiltz, and there's a beautiful 1743 Renaissance altar made by a local artist in the Oberwiltz church.

Wiltz is also a popular holiday town, with beautiful walks in its heavily wooded setting and many sports facilities.

In Esch-sur-Sûre

This popular angling center on the River Sûre has a picturesque ruined medieval castle, floodlit on summer evenings. But it's fishing, boating, hiking, and other outdoor sports, however, that bring tourists in such hordes.

2. The Moselle Valley

This vineyard and winery region of Luxembourg is set in a landscape quite different from that of the Ardennes. Your drive will take you along the flat banks of the broad Moselle River, with the gentle slope of low hills rising on both sides of the river. For miles those slopes are covered with vineyards and the riverbanks are alive with campers, boaters, and fisherpeople. Several wineries open their doors to visitors, and for a fee of LF 35 ($1) to LF 50 ($1.50) they'll take you on a guided tour, explain just how still wine or the sparkling varieties are made, and top off your visit with a glass of what comes out of their vats.

At the southern end of the wine district, Luxembourg's only casino and a widely recognized health spa are located at Mondorf-les-Bains, and almost on the French border are the mining towns of Dudelange and Kayl.

WHERE TO STAY

Most tourists make the Moselle Valley tour a day trip from Luxembourg City. If you're beguiled by this peaceful part of the country, however, there are accommodations aplenty.

In Grevenmacher

Le Roi Dagobert, rue de Trèves, 6793 Grevenmacher (tel. 352/7-57-17 or 7-57-18). This picturesque old-style hotel (a turn-of-the-century manor house) is located in a wine center close to several leading wineries and is ideal as a touring base. Guest rooms are nicely done up and all have private baths. Rates range from LF 1,400 ($45.25) to LF 2,000 ($64.50) single, LF 1,900 ($61.25) to LF 2,400 ($77.50) double.

In Ehnen

Bamberg's Hotel-Restaurant, route du Vin 131, 5416 Ehnen (tel. 352/7-60-22 or 7-67-17). This lovely small traditional hotel is also known for its very good restaurant. Guest rooms have private baths, TVs, and telephones, and rates are LF 850 ($27.50) to LF 1,600 ($51.50) single, LF 1,600 ($51.50) to LF 2,100 ($67.75) double.

In Remich

Hôtel Saint-Nicolas, esplanade 31, 5533 Remich (tel. 352/69-83-33 or 69-88-88). Overlooking the Moselle, on a broad promenade along the river, this large hotel has 50 attractive, comfortable guest rooms, all with private bath, TV, and telephone. There's a good restaurant, nice bar and lounge, and a solarium. Rates are LF 1,000 ($32.25) to LF 1,800 ($58) single, LF 1,500 ($48.50) to LF 2,300 ($74.25) double.

In Mondorf-les-Bains

Casino de Jeux, rue Th-Flammang, 5618 Mondorf-les-Baines (tel. 59/66-10-10-1). If gambling's your main interest in this little town, you just couldn't be closer to the action than this four-star, first-class hotel. It has 34 elegantly furnished guest rooms and three lovely suites; there's a gourmet French restaurant, and of course, the casino itself. Rates are LF 2,400 ($77.50) and up single, LF 3,300 ($106.50) and up double.

Hôtel du Grand Chef, avenue des Bains 36, 5601 Mondorf-les-Bains (tel. 352/6-81-22 or 6-80-12). Set in its own private park within walking distance of the casino, this gracious hotel occupies the 1852 home of a French nobleman. Although completely modernized, it has lost none of the charm and elegance of its beginnings. If it's peace and quiet you're after, take note that this hotel is a member of the Relais du Silence. Guest rooms have private baths, TVs, and telephones. There are heated terraces, and there's a good restaurant and attractive bar. Rates run LF 1,750 ($56.50) to LF 2,200 ($71) for singles, LF 2,100 ($67.75) to LF 2,800 ($90.25) for doubles.

WHERE TO EAT

As elsewhere in the Grand Duchy, your best meals will probably be in hotels, although small local restaurants almost always take pride in the excellence of their kitchens.

In Machtum

Chalet de la Moselle, route du Vin 35 (tel. 7-50-46). Conveniently located in this town between Grevenmacher and Ahn on the Moselle "wine route," this charming chalet restaurant specializes in fish and seafood dishes—and of course it prides itself on its wine list! Prices range from LF 700 ($22.50) to LF 2,000 ($64.50), and it's closed Tuesday for dinner and all day Wednesday.

In Mondorf-les-Bains

Sulky, in the Hôtel du Casino de Jeux de Mondorf, rue Th-Flammang (tel. 66-10-10). This large gourmet restaurant serves classic French dishes in an elegant setting. Service by formally attired waiters is polished, yet friendly, and it's open until 3 a.m. Prices are in the LF 700 ($22.50) to LF 2,000 ($64.50) range.

TOURIST INFORMATION

You will find Tourist Information Offices at the following locations: Esplanade (in the bus station), **Remich** (tel. 352/69-84-88), with hours of 10:30 a.m. to noon and 3 to 7 p.m., daily in summer; and avenue Fr-Clement 31, **Mondorf-les-Bains** (tel. 352/6-75-75), open from 9 a.m. to noon and 2 to 6 p.m. weekdays and 2 to 6 p.m. on Saturday and Sunday during the summer months.

THINGS TO SEE AND DO

The Moselle Valley is definitely "leisure country." Take time to amble along the river route, maybe stop for a little fishing (or watch others as they fish), spend an hour or two at a winery and perhaps take home a bottle or two, or plan an elegant casino night out.

Points of Interest

For the small charge of LF 35 ($1) to LF 50 ($1.50), you can visit renowned **wineries** along the Moselle. You'll find cooperative wine cellars open to the public at Grevenmacher and Wellenstein, with daily hours of 9 to 11 a.m. and 1 to 4 p.m. Those at Wormeldange are open from 9:30 to 11:30 a.m. and 1:30 to 5 p.m.

Interesting tours of the sparkling wine cellars of Bernard-Massard are at Grevenmacher, with hours of 9 to 11:30 a.m. and 2 to 5:30 p.m.; the St-Martin cellars are at Remich, with the same hours.

There's a delightful **aquarium** at Wasserbillig, open daily from 10 to 11:30 a.m. and 2:30 to 6 p.m. during the summer months (weekends and holidays only other months), with an admission charge of LF 40 ($1.25).

At Ehnen, visit the **wine museum** (tel. 75-82-05), open every day except Monday from 9:30 to 11:30 a.m. and 2 to 5 p.m., with an LF-60 ($2) admission charge.

The **Casino de Jeux** at Mondorf-les-Bains is open year round from 4 p.m. until the wee hours (they simply put it, "from 4 p.m. on . . ."—which usually means 3 a.m.). A dress code requires jacket and tie (or turtleneck) for men and suitable dress for the ladies, and you must have your passport to prove you're over 18. Admission is LF 100 ($3.25), which you stand to win back if you stay at the tables long enough. There's the lively Vis-à-Vis bar, and the gourmet Sulky restaurant (which stays open until 3 a.m.).

Children young and old will enjoy a day or half day at the **Parc Merveilleux** in Bettembourg, a wonderfully fanciful entertainment park alive with fairytale characters, games, a mini-train, pony rides, miniature golf, mini-boats, a luna park, and outdoor concerts. Its hours are 9:30 a.m. to 7 p.m. every day from April 1 to October 15, and admission is LF 70 ($2.25) for adults, LF 50 ($1.50) for children.

If mining interests you, the **Mining Museum** at Rumelange gives you a chance to experience exactly what the miners feel as they head underground, for this unusual museum is located right inside a mine—you get to ride the mine cars and see the works firsthand. Hours are 2 to 5 p.m. every day during the summer, with an LF-60 ($2) admission fee. Open during summer months only.

3. Valley of the Seven Castles

It's really the Valley of the Eisch River, but somehow that just doesn't have the same panache as "Valley of the Seven Castles"! And if any country in the world deserves a region designated by castles, the Grand Duchy has to be it—since this little triangular area holds one of the country's most spectacular concentrations of those grand edifices, the name is well taken.

To explore the valley, one of the most scenically beautiful in the country, leave Luxembourg City on Hwy. E9 west to Steinfort, the location of the first castle.

WHERE TO STAY AND WHERE TO EAT

There are three outstanding hotels, both with special character, in this area. Two are known for their restaurants, and if possible you should try to have lunch at one or the other, even if you plan to return to a Luxembourg base. Failing that, if it's fine weather, take along a picnic (or stop and buy the makings in one of the villages you pass through) at Hunnebour, a beautiful picnic spot between Hollenfels and

Mersch (its name means "Huns' Spring," and the story is that Attila's army pitched camp here).

In Gaichel/Eischen

Hôtel de la Gaichel, 8469 Gaichel/Eischen (tel. 352/3-91-29). This small hotel (only 15 rooms) is a gracious old home surrounded by green lawns and luxurious shade trees. There's a terrace for outdoor dining in good weather, and the guest rooms, all with private bath, are attractively done up, some with good views of the surrounding countryside. The restaurant specializes in seafood, as well as expert use of meats, such as veal with rhubarb. The room rate is LF 3,200 ($103.25), single or double, and you can expect dinner without wine to be about LF 2,000 ($64.50).

Hostellerie La Bonne Auberge, 8469 Gaichel/Eischen (tel. 352/3-91-40 or 39-84-08). This is a delightful small hotel (17 rooms) with attractive and comfortable guest rooms, most with good views and all with private baths. In the excellent restaurant, wild boar in wine sauce is a specialty in season, while fish and local meats star other times. Rates for guest rooms range from LF 2,200 ($71) up, single or double, and menu prices run LF 1,000 ($32.25) and up.

In Finsterthal

Hôtel Du Finsterthal, 7425 Finsterthal (tel. 352/6-31-92). This unpretentious country inn situated in central Luxembourg is an ideal touring base. Its rustic charm extends throughout, from the lounge bar and dining room to its attractive guest rooms, each of which has a private bath and telephone. Rates range from LF 1,200 ($38.75) to LF 1,600 ($51.50) single or double.

TOURIST INFORMATION

There's a Tourist Information Office in the Town Hall at Mersch (tel. 352/3-25-23).

THINGS TO SEE AND DO

The landscape and numerous small, picturesque villages will keep you enthralled as you ramble through the valley from castle to castle.

Most of the castles you see along this route are in ruins and not open to the public. Nevertheless, perched on rocky hilltops or nestled in foothills, they are an impressive sight and by the end of the day you're sure to feel something of what life was like when those majestic piles housed powerful men and their families.

The **route** to follow is: Steinfort through Koerich to Septfontaines to Ansembourg (with a castle high on a hill and another in the valley) to Marienthal to Hollenfels (stop at this castle, now a youth hostel, to see the beautiful carving in the Knights' Hall) to Mersch, the geographical center of the Grand Duchy, with a feudal castle and an interesting Roman Museum on rue des Romains that exhibits mosaics, sculpture, and wall paintings. To return to Luxembourg City, take Hwy. 7.

A BENELUX VOCABULARY

While it's true that you will get along famously in the Low Countries with no knowledge of French, Flemish, or Dutch, the following words and expressions might be useful to know.

GENERAL

English	French	Dutch/Flemish
Please	**S'il vous plaît**	**Alstublieft**
Thank you very much	**Merci beaucoup**	**Dank U zeer**
Good morning	**Bonjour**	**Dag**
Good evening	**Bonsoir**	**Goeden**
Good night	**Bonne nuit**	**Goede nacht**
Good-bye	**Au revoir**	**Tot ziens**
Sir (or Mr.)	**Monsieur**	**Mijnheer**
Miss	**Mademoiselle**	**Juffrouw**
Mrs.	**Madame**	**Mevrouw**
Gentlemen	**Messieurs**	**Heren**
Ladies	**Dames**	**Dames**
Excuse me	**Excusez-moi**	**Pardon**
I understand	**Je comprends**	**Dat begrijp ik**
I don't understand	**Je ne comprends pas**	**Dat begrijp ik niet**
I would like a single room	**Je voudrais avoir un chambre à un lit**	**Ik zou willen een eenpersoonskamer**
I would like a double room with twin beds	**Je voudrais avoir un chambre à deux lits**	**Ik zou willen een kamer met twee bedden**
. . . with bath	**. . . avec salle de bain**	**. . . met bad**
round-trip ticket	**billet aller-retour**	**retour**
one-way ticket	**billet aller**	**enkele reis**
fare	**prix du billet**	**prijs van het reiskaartje**
No smoking	**Défense de fumer**	**Verboden te roken**
All aboard!	**En voiture!**	**Instappen!**
How much?	**Combien?**	**Hoeveel?**
expensive	**cher**	**duur**
cheap	**bon marché**	**goedkoop**
Where is. . . ?	**Où est. . . ?**	**Waar is. . . ?**

English	French	Dutch/Flemish
Is this the right way to. . . ?	Est-ce bien la route de . . . ?	Is dit de goed weg naar. . . ?
Town Hall	Hôtel de Ville	Raadhuis (*or Stadhuis*)
art gallery	musée d'art	schilderijenmuseum
airmail	par avion	Luchtpost
ordinary mail	comme lettre ordinaire	Gewone post
special delivery	comme exprès	Express
stamp	timbre	Postzegel
Monday	Lundi	Maandag
Tuesday	Mardi	Dinsdag
Wednesday	Mercredi	Woensdag
Thursday	Jeudi	Donderdag
Friday	Vendredi	Vrijdag
Saturday	Samedi	Zaterdag
Sunday	Dimanche	Zondag
one (1)	un, une	een
two (2)	deux	twee
three (3)	trois	drie
four (4)	quatre	vier
five (5)	cinq	vifj
six (6)	six	zes
seven (7)	sept	zeven
eight (8)	huit	acht
nine (9)	neuf	negen
ten (10)	dix	tien
fifty (50)	cinquante	vijftig
one hundred (100)	cent	honderd
two hundred (200)	deux cent	tweehonderd
one thousand (1,000)	mille	duizend

DINING

English	French	Dutch/Flemish
Waiter!	Garçon!	Garcon!
Waitress!	Mam'selle!	Juffrouw!
Please give us the menu	Donnez-nous la carte s'il vous plaît	Mag ik het menu zien?
Please give me the check	L'addition, s'il vous plaît	Ober, mag ik afrekenen
Have you included the tip?	Est-ce que le service est compris?	Service inclusief?
Please give us some . . .	Servez-nous, s'il vous plaît . . .	Geeft U ons wat . . .
fried	frit	gebakken
roasted	rôti	gebraden
smoked	fumé	gerookt
stewed	en ragoût (*or* étuvé)	gestoofd
rare	saignant	bleu
medium	a point	half gaar
well done	bien cuit	goed gaar

English	French	Dutch/Flemish
pork chop	côtelette de porc	varkenskotelet
roast beef	rosbif	rosbief
chicken	poulet	kip
duck	canard	eend
goose	oie	gans
rabbit	lapin	konijn
flounder	limande	bot
herring	hareng	haring
salmon	saumon	zalm
trout	truite	forel
lobster	homard	kreeft
oysters	huîtres	oesters
shrimp	crevettes	garnalen
asparagus	asperges	asperges
beans	fèves	bonen
cabbage	chou	kool
carrots	carottes	wortelen
mushrooms	champignons	champignons
onions	oignons	uien
peas	petit pois	erwten
potatoes	pommes de terre	aardapplen
tomatoes	tomates	tomate
water	eau	water
milk	lait	melk
coffee	café	koffie
tea	thé	thee
beer	bière	bier
wine	vin	wijn
red	rouge	rode
white	blanc	witte

INDEX

GENERAL

BELGIUM

HOLLAND

LUXEMBOURG

NOW!

ARTHUR FROMMER LAUNCHES HIS SECOND TRAVEL REVOLUTION with

The New World of Travel

The hottest news and latest trends in travel today—heretofore the closely guarded secrets of the travel trade—are revealed in this new sourcebook by the dean of American travel. Here, collected in one book that is updated every year, are the most exciting, challenging, and money-saving ideas in travel today.

You'll find out about hundreds of alternative new modes of travel—and the many organizations that sponsor them—that will lead you to vacations that cater to your mind, your spirit, and your sense of thrift.

Learn how to fly for free as an air courier; travel for free as a tour escort; live for free on a hospitality exchange; add earnings as a part-time travel agent; pay less for air tickets, cruises, and hotels; enhance your life through cooperative camping, political tours, and adventure trips; change your life at utopian communities, low-cost spas, and yoga retreats; pursue low-cost studies and language training; travel comfortably while single or over 60; sail on passenger freighters; and vacation in the cheapest places on earth.

And in every yearly edition, Arthur Frommer spotlights the 10 GREATEST TRAVEL VALUES for the coming year. 400 pages, large-format with many, many illustrations. All for $14.95!

ORDER NOW

TURN TO THE LAST PAGE OF THIS BOOK FOR ORDER FORM.

NOW, SAVE MONEY ON ALL YOUR TRAVELS!
Join Frommer's™ Dollarwise® Travel Club

Saving money while traveling is never a simple matter, which is why, over 28 years ago, the **Dollarwise Travel Club** was formed. Actually, the idea came from readers of the Frommer publications who felt that such an organization could bring financial benefits, continuing travel information, and a sense of community to economy-minded travelers all over the world.

In keeping with the money-saving concept, the annual membership fee is low—$18 (U.S. residents) or $20 U.S. (Canadian, Mexican, and foreign residents)—and is immediately exceeded by the value of your benefits which include:

1. The latest edition of any TWO of the books listed on the following pages.

2. A copy of any Frommer City Guide.

3. An annual subscription to an 8-page quarterly newspaper *The Dollarwise Traveler* which keeps you up-to-date on fastbreaking developments in good-value travel in all parts of the world—bringing you the kind of information you'd have to pay over $35 a year to obtain elsewhere. This consumer-conscious publication also includes the following columns:

Hospitality Exchange—members all over the world who are willing to provide hospitality to other members as they pass through their home cities.

Share-a-Trip—requests from members for travel companions who can share costs and help avoid the burdensome single supplement.

Readers Ask . . . Readers Reply—travel questions from members to which other members reply with authentic firsthand information.

4. Your personal membership card which entitles you to purchase through the club all Frommer publications for a third to a half off their regular retail prices during the term of your membership.

So why not join this hardy band of international Dollarwise travelers now and participate in its exchange of information and hospitality? Simply send $18 (U.S. residents) or $20 U.S. (Canadian, Mexican, and other foreign residents) along with your name and address to: Frommer's Dollarwise Travel Club, Inc., 15 Columbus Circle, New York, NY 10023. Remember to specify which *two* of the books in section (1) and which *one* in section (2) above you wish to receive in your initial package of member's benefits. Or tear out the next page, check off your choices, and send the page to us with your membership fee.

FROMMER BOOKS
PRENTICE HALL TRAVEL
15 COLUMBUS CIRCLE
NEW YORK, NY 10023

Date____________________

Friends:
Please send me the books checked below:

FROMMER™ GUIDES

(Guides to sightseeing and tourist accommodations and facilities from budget to deluxe, with emphasis on the medium-priced.)

- ☐ Alaska $13.95
- ☐ Australia $14.95
- ☐ Austria & Hungary $14.95
- ☐ Belgium, Holland & Luxembourg $13.95
- ☐ Bermuda & The Bahamas $14.95
- ☐ Brazil $14.95
- ☐ Canada $14.95
- ☐ Caribbean $14.95
- ☐ Cruises (incl. Alask, Carib, Mex, Hawaii, Panama, Canada & US) $14.95
- ☐ California & Las Vegas $14.95
- ☐ England & Scotland $14.95
- ☐ Egypt $13.95
- ☐ Florida $14.95
- ☐ France $14.95
- ☐ Germany $14.95
- ☐ Italy $14.95
- ☐ Japan & Hong Kong $13.95
- ☐ Mid-Atlantic States $13.95
- ☐ New England $14.95
- ☐ New York State $13.95
- ☐ Northwest $14.95
- ☐ Portugal, Madeira & the Azores $13.95
- ☐ Skiing Europe $14.95
- ☐ Skiing USA—East $13.95
- ☐ Skiing USA—West $13.95
- ☐ South Pacific $13.95
- ☐ Southeast & New Orleans $14.95
- ☐ Southeast Asia $14.95
- ☐ Southwest $14.95
- ☐ Switzerland & Liechtenstein $13.95
- ☐ Texas $13.95
- ☐ USA $15.95

FROMMER $-A-DAY® GUIDES

(In-depth guides to sightseeing and low-cost tourist accommodations and facilities.)

- ☐ Europe on $40 a Day $15.95
- ☐ Australia on $30 a Day $12.95
- ☐ Eastern Europe on $25 a Day $13.95
- ☐ England on $50 a Day $13.95
- ☐ Greece on $30 a Day $12.95
- ☐ Hawaii on $60 a Day $13.95
- ☐ India on $25 a Day $12.95
- ☐ Ireland on $35 a Day $13.95
- ☐ Israel on $35 a Day $13.95
- ☐ Mexico on $25 a Day $13.95
- ☐ New Zealand on $40 a Day $12.95
- ☐ New York on $50 a Day $13.95
- ☐ Scandinavia on $60 a Day $13.95
- ☐ Scotland & Wales on $40 a Day $12.95
- ☐ South America on $35 a Day $13.95
- ☐ Spain & Morocco on $40 a Day $13.95
- ☐ Turkey on $30 a Day $12.95
- ☐ Washington, D.C., & Historic Va. on $40 a Day $13.95

FROMMER TOURING GUIDES

(Color illustrated guides that include walking tours, cultural & historic sites, and other vital travel information.)

- ☐ Australia $9.95
- ☐ Egypt $8.95
- ☐ Florence $8.95
- ☐ London $8.95
- ☐ Paris $8.95
- ☐ Scotland $9.95
- ☐ Thailand $9.95
- ☐ Venice $8.95

TURN PAGE FOR ADDITONAL BOOKS AND ORDER FORM.